The University of Chicago

The University of Chicago

✳

A HISTORY

John W. Boyer

The University of Chicago Press   CHICAGO AND LONDON

JOHN W. BOYER is the Martin A. Ryerson Distinguished Service
Professor in History at the University of Chicago. In 2012 he was
appointed to a fifth term as Dean of the College. A specialist in the
history of the Habsburg Empire, he has written three books on
Austrian history, including, most recently, *Karl Lueger (1844–1910):
Christlichsoziale Politik als Beruf.*

The University of Chicago Press, Chicago 60637
The University of Chicago Press, Ltd., London
© 2015 by The University of Chicago
All rights reserved. Published 2015.
Printed in the United States of America

24 23 22 21 20 19 18 17 16 15   1 2 3 4 5

ISBN-13: 978-0-226-38120-6 (cloth: limited edition)
ISBN-13: 978-0-226-24251-4 (cloth)
ISBN-13: 978-0-226-24265-1 (e-book)
DOI: 10.7208/chicago/9780226242651.001.0001

Library of Congress Control Number: 2015021573

♾ This paper meets the requirements of ANSI/NISO Z39.48-1992
(Permanence of Paper).

THIS BOOK IS FOR
Olivia, Amelia, Sebastian, Lucy, Brijzha,
Charlotte, Josephine, and Jocelyn

Contents

Introduction

This book is based in part on the seventeen historical monographs that I wrote about various aspects of the history of the University of Chicago between 1996 and 2013.[1] The monographs have an interconnected logic, and they reflect the political, cultural, and intellectual challenges I have faced as dean of the College during the radical transformation of the College and the University over the past two decades. The University of Chicago's recent history has seen an acceleration of changes, accompanied by both conflicting memories and, for some, no memory at all of the deeper past that has defined and constituted the work and identity of the University and its several communities. There are dangers in a-historicism or even anti-historicism,[2] and it is hazardous for an institution to live simply in the present, with no sense of its past. Lacking a past, we have no plausible ways to understand the choices that previous leaders made about their (and our) future, much less to embrace and intelligently shape the futures that the present faculty wish to create. This book is an attempt to delineate the past of the University of Chicago, in hopes that readers will better grasp the deep complexity of its origins and development.

I began to write the monographs in the mid-1990s at a critical point, when institutional changes led by then president Hugo F. Sonnenschein and other academic leaders ran up against often clamorous opposition from faculty, alumni, and students. These expressions of *ressentiment* were often based on forcefully articulated conceptions of what the University should "stand for," and many invoked an imagined noble past to justify a pleasing status quo. I was both fascinated and frustrated by the ways in which random (and often misunderstood) tidbits of Chicago's history shaped these conversations, even when most observers acknowledged that they lacked knowledge of the institutional history. I could not help recalling Thucydides's sense that traditions are received as they are delivered, "without applying any critical test whatever."[3] Out of vexation but also curiosity, I decided to find out for myself what had "really happened." This book is the product of extensive archival research, and the topics that I have selected reflect certain basic themes. The University's archives are unusually rich and varied, and they offer a vast array of fascinating information about many known and unknown events and larger cultural trends in Chicago's history. Of course, an archive itself is not a history, and as Arlette Farge has noted, if archives have the ability to "reattach the past to the present," the meaning of their story "takes shape only when you ask a specific question of them, not when you first discover them, no matter how happy the discovery might have been."[4]

The University has an unusually complicated and often controversial history, which is shrouded at many points in layers of myth and hearsay. It is an institution that loves to generate and then to repeat myths about itself. Like all great universities, its history also encompasses a vast sea of private memories, friendships and enmities, personal conversations, individual stories, and fascinating rumors. A university's history can be most accurately and fairly discovered by addressing questions to sources that can be authenticated and compared to other, similar sources. This is why a thick, archival source base is crucial to the logic and identity of this book.

This is not a history of every department and every school at the University, nor is it a running biography of the renowned researchers who have populated our campus. It is the story of the emergence and growth of a complex and diverse academic community, particularly the College, focusing on the nature of its academic culture and its curricula, on the experience of its students, on its engagement with Chicago's civic community, and on the financial resources and developmental conditions that have enabled the University to sustain itself. This means that many noteworthy and even fascinating subjects are not included in this book. Edward Levi once observed that no single person could ever "own" the University of Chicago, and this is true of the history of the University and its historians as well.

This is also a history written by someone who has played a modest role in many of the events of the past twenty years, so the book consciously walks a delicate line between the principle of scholarly objectivity and access to sensitive and sometimes confidential knowledge. This position affords advantages but also hazards, and the reader should be aware of both. In writing about the contemporary University, I faced the special difficulty that many of the dynamics narrated in the final chapter are still unfolding, and cannot be consigned to a settled past. As the narrative moves toward the present, some elements are necessarily presented in broad strokes. At the same time, I have tried to account for the ways in which the University's long-running themes have intertwined and re-solved themselves in the recent past, in the process bearing upon issues that have aroused strong reactions. In general, I have striven to follow the red thread of the narrative while trying to respect the sensitive blend of issues and personalities implicated in certain episodes.

The history of the University of Chicago has been marked by extraor-dinary continuities of normative values and educational practices, de-spite stormy ruptures and discontinuities. Both continuity and change are inevitable features of the lives of individuals and of institutions. These patterns of change and continuity are not simply heuristic devices that a historian imposes on the messy details of the past.[5] Rather, they involve fundamental approaches to educational policy, administrative structures, and normative rhetorical traditions that have endured over many gener-ations, in the midst of often disruptive changes, to define the workings of the University. Institutions like universities have an embedded, historical reality and a baseline organizational logic, which makes histories of them different from those of cultural phenomena like national identity, taste, and religious prejudice. This book discusses various facets of the Univer-sity's commitment to educational innovation and its capacity to sustain its core values while sponsoring (or enduring) significant change. As Robert Maynard Hutchins once observed about the long-term welfare of univer-sities, "The real question is how do you get a place to be continuously vitalized and re-vitalized."[6]

This book also focuses on two issues particular to undergraduate lib-eral arts colleges that are set within larger research universities. First, the University's engagement with the College and undergraduate education has varied and often been unpredictable, but that relationship has had enormous influence on the intellectual identity and fiscal health of the larger institution. When the College has been neglected, underresourced, or treated as of a lesser priority, the result has meant "a near-death expe-rience for the entire University, at least as an institution of the first rank."[7] Second, Chicago's history reveals a different chronological flow in that its "Golden Age," a term most often deployed to describe the fiscal bounty and rising ambitions of American higher education in two decades after 1945, came earlier than that of most of its peers. Indeed, the tendency to elevate the 1920s, 1930s, and early 1940s is very clear in President Edward Levi's speeches in the late 1960s and early 1970s. This reflected genuine pride that Chicago had achieved suddenly and with great intellectual style what few other universities could possibly have accomplished be-fore World War II. And yet, as we will see, these successes proved fragile and were subject to great stresses after 1945 precisely because Chicago ended up on a different (and disastrous) demographic trajectory apart from almost all of its peers, with an unintended and unplanned collapse of its undergraduate enrollments in the 1950s that, in turn, profoundly disadvantaged the longer-term welfare of the University over the next forty years.

The claim of this book that the University's ambitious present and future are anchored in the decisions of its past is captured by a phrase that President Ernest DeWitt Burton used in 1924 in his eulogy in honor of Charles L. Hutchinson, an early trustee and leader of the University. Hutchinson was deeply involved in the design of the neo-Gothic buildings that still form the aesthetic nucleus of the early University's built environment. Burton argued that Hutchinson "had a keen sense of the influence of architecture on the formation of taste, and a strong desire, happily shared by many of his associates, that what the University built should be so built that it would stand and be worthy to last. He built for a long future."[8] Today's University lives in its own time, but that present is an intricate cultural and intellectual ensemble shaped by the continuities and changes wrought by previous times. Chicago lives in the long future that scholars and trustees like Burton and Hutchinson created, but it is also obliged to re-create that future for its successors.

* 1 *

Two Universities of Chicago, 1857–1892

The anniversary of the University of Chicago's refounding 125 years ago, in 1890, invites us to consider how the University has sustained itself over the decades and how it has acquired its identity as a great research university. Founded with revolutionary ambitions in the late nineteenth century, Chicago aimed to become a model university for the city, the region, and the nation. Now, when the public understanding of universities' core mission is less clear than ever before and when universities and their faculties face competing challenges on many fronts, it is useful to recount the odyssey of one institution from its inception, focusing not only on its academic values and practices but also on the efforts to sustain its welfare, intellectual and otherwise. Such an understanding is needed to answer the critics, some friendly, others not so, who challenge the operational assumptions of American research universities like Chicago.

Fifty years ago, Christopher Jencks offered a pessimistic and perhaps familiar evaluation of the future of American undergraduate education. For Jencks, the problem was twofold: at the elite colleges and universities, most faculty cared only about teaching specialized knowledge, in the hope that they would persuade their students to embark on academic careers and become professors like themselves. Jencks argued that Harvard had essentially become a "cram school for graduate study" and that the Hutchins College experiment at the University of Chicago had been savaged by graduate departments that wanted to cannibalize its faculty. At major public colleges, in contrast, most students cared little for ideas or learning, which made their faculty despair of doing a responsible job in trying to educate them. For Jencks, students at these institutions did not take ideas seriously, and faculty had no way to force them to do so. What was missing, in Jencks's account, was general intellectual education, which would develop critical analytic skills and present students with a broad perspective without trying to make undergraduate students into mini doctoral candidates.[1]

The past fifty years have seen a continuation of the concerns that Jencks articulated, with many new ones added.[2] Even if many critics came to see the period from 1945 to 1975 as the golden age of American higher education, this era of optimism was soon fractured by uncertainty in many domains of intellectual and pedagogical practice.[3] But Jencks's pessimism did not hold true at the University of Chicago, for the Chicago faculty never lost sight of the fact that students who are generally and broadly educated usually make the best young academics, just as they make the most effective young lawyers, doctors, and businesspeople. Both long before and long after 1960 the University of Chicago tried to sustain a system that had general education at its core and, equally important, to create a campus culture of learning, egalitarian merit, and academic rigor that challenged all highly motivated and talented students, whatever their ultimate professional career goals.

From the University's inception in the 1890s, its conception of higher education as a public and private good was unusual in the marketplace of American higher education. If anything, Chicago's golden age came before 1945, when the University marshaled enormous and sudden wealth and managed to combine it with extraordinary levels of intellectual seriousness and academic achievement. In this sense Chicago anticipated many features of the "academic revolution" that underwrote a profound shift in the self-understanding of the top American research universities after 1945.[4]

But the University of Chicago did find its academic culture at risk in the decades after World War II as it struggled to sort out the social, cultural, and intellectual tensions generated by Hutchins's revolution in the College, among other crises, and to maintain financial solvency for the university at large. The fiscal and developmental underpinnings proved inadequate by the 1940s and 1950s in view of the University's outsize ambitions, and the inadequacies led to ongoing frustration in explaining itself to its own alumni and other potential supporters. As a consequence, the history of Chicago became a fascinating exercise in principled intellectual ambition constantly butting up against stubborn and unpleasant social and economic realities.

How and why was Chicago able to sustain its educational success amid such pendulating fiscal fortunes? How did it maintain its unique campus culture in the face of often self-destructive policy decisions about its future? This culture and the (often competing) curricular practices that have both informed and divided it have, in turn, depended on the dedication of generations of faculty to excellence in teaching. But those same faculty also aspired, indeed felt compelled, to be outstanding scholars for whom teaching might easily have been a useless distraction. Chicago's prolonged success in promoting teaching and research was never easy to attain, and it was subject to severe internal tangles, controversies, and debates. The stories underlying these struggles are complex and knotty.

For most who arrived after 1892, the new University of Chicago was *the* University of Chicago. Robert Herrick, an early recruit from Harvard, wrote a remarkable appreciation of the newness of the University in 1895, as if it had been created de novo out of ambition, openness, a penchant for risk taking, and seriousness, with Herrick taking particular pride in the "phenomenal birth and growth and the material side of the new institution."[5] For Herrick, the new University was an almost providential act that was bound to be hugely successful, set in the dynamic West and in a burgeoning city whose hardworking people were eager for a rich intellectual and cultural life. This image of a new, hyperinnovative creation, brilliantly launched by William Rainey Harper in 1892, dominates most historical accounts of the origins of the modern American university, alongside the opening of Johns Hopkins University in 1876. Images of instantaneous creation also dominate much of the fund-raising literature that the University produced in the twentieth century. *The Responsibility of Greatness*, the lead publication for the capital campaign of 1955–58, proudly recounted, "No other university ever began like Chicago. Its founders quite literally knew what *they* were doing. Other universities grew from small colleges, but Chicago started as a *university*. It was founded for leadership sixty-five years ago, and in ten short years it had become a leader." Similarly, in the lavish campaign book of 1925, the authors noted, "In 1892, Mr. John D. Rockefeller, inspired by a deep impulse to advance civilization and to meet more specifically the needs for intellectual leadership of a population exceeding 50,000,000 people, founded a great university in the center of the Middle West.... [He] called it The University of Chicago."[6]

Neither of these statements is inaccurate. Yet there was a titular predecessor, the first University of Chicago, which had been founded in 1857 and collapsed in 1886, and the historical threads connecting the two institutions were complex. The image of newness was not an accident. The men most closely associated with the reestablishment of the University in Chicago in 1888 and 1889, Frederick Gates and Thomas Goodspeed, were acutely aware of the misery and public humiliation that had accompanied the collapse of the first institution, having had considerable difficulty raising the $400,000 needed to match John D. Rockefeller's historic offer of $600,000 to re-create a first-rate Baptist college in Chicago. Much of the rhetoric they deployed was designed to negate the long, dark shadow cast by the old University. But the new University of Chicago was also deeply indebted to a group of leaders who were profoundly influenced by the old University and *its* educational goals and pedagogical ideals.

The Founding of the First University

The first institution to bear the name of the University of Chicago began as a modest denominational college founded by Senator Stephen A. Douglas in 1856–57. The Baptist denomination in Chicago was small—with about 5,500 members in 1872—and the Baptist communities in the western states had long wanted an institution of higher education to educate ministers for their region.[7] Between 1849 and 1851, Stephen Douglas purchased seventy-five acres of lakeside land between Thirty-First and Thirty-Third Streets on the South Side of the city. Douglas sold part of the land to the Illinois Central Railroad and planned to build a large mansion on the rest.[8] Douglas's tomb at Thirty-Fifth Street and the lake is the last vestige of this estate, which Douglas called Oakenwald. Douglas was a strong advocate of the commercial and cultural development of Chicago, particularly federal investments in infrastructure. He was also a strong believer in "practical science" and was one of the prime supporters of the creation of the Smithsonian Institution in 1846, as well as of the transcontinental telegraph system. His enthusiasm for the development of Chicago led Douglas to proselytize younger men, and he helped persuade a young lawyer from frontier Illinois, Paul Cornell, to purchase three hundred acres in 1853 in what would become the core district of the township of Hyde Park. Ironically, Cornell sought to lure an institution of higher learning to his investment area, offering Presbyterians free land to build a seminary, though this gambit failed.

Douglas's awareness of "the importance of higher education in the rapidly growing west" led him to want to found a college in Chicago.[9] Douglas's recently deceased wife, Martha Douglas, was a Baptist, and his willingness to give land to the Baptists was said to reflect his desire to honor her affiliation. But the real motivation to found a college may have come from a trip that Douglas took in 1853 to Europe, where he visited several leading universities; according to John C. Burroughs, the pastor of the First Baptist Church in Chicago, who knew Douglas's motives well, "while [Douglas's] main errand abroad was political, his quick insight had not failed to discover the bearing of its universities on the social and political development of Europe, and he had returned, full of the idea of a university at Chicago, which should be for the Northwest what he had seen those of England, and Germany, and France, and Russia to be to their States. This was the real main-spring of his project."[10]

Douglas was grateful for the support that Burroughs had given him in the mid-1850s during the heated controversy surrounding the Kansas-Nebraska Act, of which Douglas had been the principal architect.[11] Yet when Douglas decided to create a college in Chicago, he first opened negotiations with local Presbyterians in the spring of 1855, offering them ten acres of his South Side land if they could raise $100,000 by December 1 (which Douglas later extended to March 1, 1856). At the urging of prominent Baptists in Chicago, including Charles Walker and Daniel Cameron, Burroughs visited Douglas in November 1855 in Terre Haute, Indiana, where Douglas was staying at the time, and proposed that Douglas give his land to the Baptists if the Presbyterians were unable to meet his stipulations. When the Presbyterians decided not to exercise the option, most likely because of opposition to Douglas's unresponsiveness on the slavery issue, Douglas informed Burroughs in April 1856 that he was willing to offer the Baptists a site on Thirty-Fourth Street between Cottage Grove and Rhodes Avenues.[12] Working with Mrs. Douglas's former pastor, Dr. G. W. Samson, Burroughs fashioned a proposal that was acceptable to Douglas, including a commitment to construct a building on the land within one year at a cost of not less than $100,000. Douglas's motives in making this gift have been variously interpreted, but it seems clear that he viewed the addition of a college not only as an asset to the fledgling city, but also as a way to enhance the value of the land that he intended to develop on the South Side.[13]

Burroughs also agreed to organize a fund-raising campaign for the construction of the new building. He was able to secure oral endorsements from many Baptist leaders and collected pledges well beyond $100,000, but when the time came to persuade donors to honor their commitments he ran into difficulties. Douglas's name and his close association with the project were controversial among antislavery factions within the Baptist denomination, especially in eastern states and in Chicago. All told, Douglas proved to be more of a hindrance than a help to the Baptists, and he certainly provided no support to the fledgling University beyond his original donation of land. In August 1857 Douglas sent a public letter to Burroughs, offering to withdraw his grant of land and instead give the University a gift of $50,000.[14] Burroughs and his fellow trustees unanimously rejected Douglas's offer, also in a public letter, which presented an idealistic statement of the goals of the founders and argued that since the University was a nonpolitical institution, it would never engage in partisan political activity, whatever Douglas's views on any given issue:

> The establishment of the University of Chicago was looked upon by the Board as a matter above and beyond all political considerations, not as a thing for the moment, but for all time, not as a thing which concerns

you immediately, or any other persons, but of the youth of Chicago and of the Northwest generally, not only of the Chicago of today but of that Chicago which in the fullness of time, will become a city of which the sanguine can hardly tend for an adequate conception, to enable them to accomplish that high and literal purpose they have steadily sought and obtained subscriptions and donations from the men of all parties and of all denominations.... It would moreover be a little less than a betrayal of the sacred trust committed to their hands, accompanied by a loss of all self-respect on the part of the Board of Trustees, to yield their unanimous judgment to mere temporary, personal or political considerations.[15]

In its charter, the new institution was not defined as exclusively Baptist, and Burroughs later insisted that Douglas had deeded the land to an individual (himself) in trust who happened to be a Baptist, but not to the denomination as a corporation, in order to avoid the appearance that the new University was overtly sectarian.[16] But the popular press and public sentiment in Chicago viewed it as such (the *Christian Times* proudly announced in October 1856, "The subscription of $100,000 for the building of a Baptist university in the city has now been completed").[17] Although a majority of the board and the president were mandated to be Baptist, the charter opened the school to students and faculty of all faiths, setting up a tension in institutional identity and pragmatic policy that would plague the new school.

The institution was incorporated in the state of Illinois on January 30, 1857, as "The University of Chicago," and the board of trustees had its first meetings on May 21–22 of that year. The first board had thirty-six members, including little-known local Baptist ministers and also prominent business and political leaders like William B. Ogden and John H. Kinzie. Douglas agreed to serve as chairman of the board. Other prominent Chicagoans on the early board included William Jones, a hardware merchant and real estate investor; James H. Woodworth, a dry goods merchant and former mayor; Thomas Hoyne, US attorney and politician; Charles Walker, a major real estate and lumber developer; and J. Young Scammon, a prominent banker and newspaper publisher. Few on the board, however, viewed the University as their primary philanthropy. With the exception of Jones and Scammon, none gave the new University a major gift during their tenure.[18] Upon his death in June 1861, Stephen Douglas was overwhelmed with debts, having long since disposed of most of the property he owned in Chicago, and was unable to leave the University any legacy.[19]

After some hesitation, John Burroughs agreed to become the first president of the new University in July 1859.[20] He served for more than sixteen years, and he left behind many staunch friends and advocates. The editor of the *Standard*, Justin A. Smith, later insisted, "Dr. Burroughs had proved himself an instructor, a leader, and an administrator of marked ability, of course, patience, and resource. The affection and honor in which his memory has been cherished by those who were his pupils, and by those who knew him in such relations as to reveal the man as he truly was, are personal attributes whose emphasis is not to be doubted."[21] That said, if leaders are judged on the long-term institutional consequences of their decisions, Burroughs's legacy is an ambiguous one.

The University's first building was a capacious structure designed by a prominent local architect, William W. Boyington, in a "castellated Gothic" style. The first section built was the south wing, named Jones Hall in honor of William Jones, whose support had helped to finance the laying of the foundation. The construction of the remainder of the hall required additional cash, and this was slow in coming. By mid-1858 Burroughs had secured pledges of more than $200,000 for the University, but in the aftermath of the panic of 1857 most of the pledges proved worthless. In July 1858, for example, he reported to the board that he had accumulated $112,600 in local subscription pledges but was able to translate that figure into only $20,000 of actual cash.[22] Thomas Goodspeed later estimated that more than 75 percent of the early pledges were uncollectable and thus worthless.[23] It was only by persuading Stephen Douglas to transfer title of the land to the trustees in late August 1858 that Burroughs issued bonds for $25,000 with the property as security in order to start construction on the walls of the building. This act launched a debt-based financial strategy that, while typical in the West, soon proved disastrous. Then, three years later—in 1861—the board negotiated a loan of $25,000 from the Union Life Insurance Company of Maine to cover this debt, with the insurance company issuing a first mortgage on the property. In a stunning conflict of interest, the agent for the insurance company in Chicago was Levi D. Boone, a University trustee, medical doctor, and former mayor of Chicago, who happily negotiated a five-year-term loan at 10 percent per annum. The most elementary challenge faced by the trustees was to generate basic operational revenues while gaining support from the larger metropolitan community, and on both counts they proved inept and unlucky. Most colleges in mid-nineteenth-century America hovered between genial penury and unmitigated fiscal disaster, having to rely on ad hoc charitable contributions and often uncollectable subscriptions, as well as meager tuition revenues, and the new University of Chicago was typical in this regard.[24] What set the University apart was the disjunction between its inflated ambitions—represented by its expensive building program—and the realistic capacity of its leaders to sustain an institution worthy of such dreams.

At the ceremony for the laying of the cornerstone of Jones Hall on July 4, 1857, a crowd of several thousand heard a clutter of longish speeches, ranging from covert political critiques of Douglas's ambivalence on slavery to pleas that education serve the cause of public morality. But Rev. Adoniram J. Joslyn of Elgin, Illinois, captured the moment best when he pronounced the new University's devotion to the indissoluble trinity of "religion, science, and liberty."[25] Douglas's University had as its mission to be a "decidedly Christian but not sectarian" institution under the stewardship of the Baptist church. On the day-to-day level, this ideal translated into a university devoted to the customary fields: classics and grammar foremost, a more modern course of science for some, and scientific agriculture. The fact that the University offered a separate track in science reflected currents of reform that had begun in the 1840s that suggested the need to be both more professionally relevant and more reflective of modern needs, and thus move away from classical studies.[26] In many respects, the curriculum at Chicago reflected many of the concerns articulated by Brown University president Francis Wayland in his classic critiques of antebellum American colleges.[27] John Burroughs had visited with Wayland on his way to meet with Stephen Douglas in Washington, DC, in the spring of 1856, and Burroughs later recalled that "for most of two days he continued the discussion of the merits and demerits of our project, examining statistics of population of the states and territories of the Northwest, the number and condition of the colleges, and especially the condition and prospects of Chicago, then rapidly rising into notice; and also the whole question of the work and influence of the colleges, particularly as a means of religious advancement." Burroughs acknowledged the force of Wayland's ideas about "the breaking up of the old conventionalism, and the widening scope of the college to meet the practical wants of the people."[28] The college founded by Douglas and Burroughs represented an unsteady compromise between traditional nineteenth-century educational values and calls for greater vocational pragmatism.[29]

ACADEMIC PROGRAMS, FACULTY, AND STUDENTS

The site on which the University was built was largely uninhabited in 1858. Thomas Goodspeed, a student at the early University, later remembered the site as an isolated, semirural place on the deserted outskirts of the town:

> The street cars, then horse cars, ran on Cottage Grove Avenue only as far south as Thirty-first street, nearly half a mile north of the University. On Thirty-fifth street, just west of the Avenue, was a small, dingy saloon,

appropriately named "The Shades." There was but one building, a small one-story cottage, on Thirty-fifth Street between "The Shades" and State Street, nearly a mile west. There were a few houses to the southeast—Cleaverville—but none to the south or southwest, and only two or three between the University and Thirty-first Street. Across the Avenue from the University was "Oakenwald", the Chicago home of Senator Douglas. A fine oak grove covered the ground for several hundred feet on both sides of the Avenue and the whole country south of the University was a region of oak openings, every slight ridge being covered with trees.[30]

The University of Chicago opened its doors for the fall term of 1859. There were twenty students, twelve freshmen and eight sophomores, though the University also ran a preparatory academy, first housed in the basement of St. Paul's Universalist Church at the corner of Wabash and Van Buren. The academic year was divided into three terms, a fall term of fifteen weeks, followed by winter and spring terms of thirteen and twelve weeks, respectively—a structural innovation that offered a strong precedent for Harper's decision to create a quarter system in 1892. Students had to be at least fifteen years old and demonstrate prior knowledge of Latin, Greek, mathematics, geography, US history, and English grammar. The curriculum was divided into two tracks, a classical one that was heavy on ancient languages, and a scientific course that stressed modern languages and the natural sciences (chemistry, zoology, physiology, meteorology, civil engineering, etc.) and had a reduced classical component. By 1870, candidates for the science track were excused from any prior knowledge of Greek, and they were held to a less rigorous Latin requirement. Both tracks resulted in a bachelor's degree, of arts or of science.

The University's two-year course of study in scientific agriculture, begun in 1859, was "adequate of itself to meet that claim for liberal culture which the sons of farmers, not less than other young men are asserting for themselves."[31] Its two-year curriculum encompassed mathematics, the natural sciences, and some history and philosophy, as well as bookkeeping and surveying. This program never took root, however, and catalogues from the 1870s and 1880s made no mention of it. Instead, the University tried programs in astronomy and "practical chemistry," but these too failed to gain matriculants. The University also announced that it would award master's degrees to students who had successfully passed its baccalaureate program in the arts and who had over the course of (at least) three additional years pursued either a literary or a scientific calling.

Burroughs added a law department, which was located in a downtown commercial building adjacent to the federal courthouse. The department offered a two-year curriculum over six quarters in which students studied common law, constitutional law, equity, commercial law, international and admiralty law, and the history of jurisprudence of the United States. Upon passing an examination at the end of three full terms, students received a bachelor of law degree. Unlike students in the undergraduate program, law students did not have to meet age or knowledge requirements, being expected only to demonstrate a "good, common English education." The law department lasted until 1873, when it was merged into the Union College of Law, which was also supported by Northwestern University. That experiment lasted until 1886, when upon Chicago's collapse the law department became part of Northwestern. It was immediately successful there—in the 1859–60 academic year, 48 students matriculated in law, and by 1884 it had graduated 745 students, compared to 290 in the collegiate programs.

On the whole, the University of Chicago's curricular structures were progressive for their time. They offered students various options toward the baccalaureate degree, while also sustaining the charges to civilize the young by building moral character, to educate gentlemen as future leaders of a frontier society, and to offer substantial opportunities for social mobility.[32] The academic quality of these programs varied. Instruction in the arts and humanities enjoyed a certain traditional esteem and rigor, whereas instruction in the natural sciences was perceived by many students as less impressive. In 1873 the student newspaper slammed the science programs as being "loose and jointless" and "a fraud on the student and a disgrace to the University," insisting that teaching was poor, the students were unmotivated, and a shorter and more effective "practical" science curriculum should be developed.[33] But such comments may have reflected the cultural bias that still hindered nineteenth-century colleges from developing creditable programs in the natural sciences, as well as a chronic lack of resources (one faculty member at the University of Chicago was responsible for teaching chemistry, geology, mineralogy, and agriculture).[34] Given that the advancement of scientific knowledge was not part of the mission of midcentury colleges and in some quarters was even looked upon with suspicion, it was natural that experimental science felt itself an orphan.[35]

For its first two decades, the University admitted only male students, but in 1873–74 women students were admitted on equal terms. The first woman to graduate was Alice Boise, the daughter of Professor James R. Boise. Ms. Boise was referred to as "the Entering Wedge" for her revolutionary achievement in securing a BA.[36] Coeducation was a national and regional trend after 1860—women were first admitted to the University of Wisconsin in 1867, to the University of Michigan in 1871, and to Cornell

University in 1872 — and demonstrated a capacity at Chicago for modest innovation, even in the face of opposition from the male students.[37]

For an urban university Chicago's enrollments were quite small, with typical graduating classes of 10 to 20. By 1884 the University had approximately 1,035 living alumni, more than 700 of whom had attended the Union College of Law. Of the 200 plus arts and sciences graduates, 74 chose careers as ministers, 72 went on to law schools, 55 became businessmen, 35 became schoolteachers and professors, 15 were physicians, 13 were journalists, and 6 were farmers. Geographically, the alumni were distributed across the United States, but 90 remained in Chicago.[38]

Between 1870 and 1880 the undergraduate school averaged 102 students per year. While the average size of a US college in 1870 was only 112 students, the University's student population did not grow as the population of the city of Chicago mushroomed between 1870 and 1880, increasing from 298,977 to 503,185 — a sign that the University had failed to take advantage of the metropolis.[39] During the next decade, in which the city's population more than doubled, annual enrollments at the University declined steeply, from 107 in 1880 to 67 in 1883 and 73 in 1885.

The cost of tuition for a full academic year in 1860 was $50. Many students lived at home or in boardinghouses, but the University did provide rooms for those who wished to live on campus. Room charges were $15 a year, with $2 a week required to eat in the dining hall. Students also had to provide wood for heating and oil for their lamps. The total cost of residential attendance at the University was estimated at approximately $150 a year. Attendance was possible for only a very small minority of young people at this time (in 1869–70 only 1.3 percent of the US population between the ages of eighteen and twenty-four was enrolled in one of the 563 existing institutions of higher education).[40] Most of the very wealthy families in Chicago sent their children to the East for college, so the University did not have a deep reservoir of patronage from alumni with ample family resources. In 1869, the only year in which the occupations of the parents of University students are known, 25 percent of those who sent their children to the University were farmers, 25 percent were merchants or other businessmen like bankers, and 21 percent were ministers. Physicians and lawyers made up another 20 percent, with a few teachers, real estate developers, and artists thrown in. A small minority of students came from wealthy social backgrounds, but the great majority seem to have been children from enterprising middle-class and lower-middle-class families whose parents were willing to allow their children to leave the labor market for an extended period of time, and some of whom were also able to offer partial support to their children while they were in college. Still, many students had to work to meet their expenses, which made it possible (in theory) for a student of modest means to attend the University.

A student culture began to cohere, and a student association was created to give voice to student concerns and interests, along with several honor societies (including the Tri Kappa and the Athenaeum) and four Greek letter fraternities (Delta Kappa Epsilon, Phi Kappa Psi, Psi Upsilon, and Zeta Psi). By the early 1870s a student newspaper, the *Volante*, was being regularly published, its editors elected by the senior class. Beyond ritualistic expressions of school pride and confidence in the liberal arts, the newspaper offered valuable insights into student views about the institution and its financial peril, including analyses of students' religious beliefs, curricular improvements, and the school's enrollment problems. Other ad hoc groupings of students also came together—during the Civil War, students helped prisoners at nearby Camp Douglas and also created a student militia group. What was most curious about the early student culture was what it lacked—there were no recorded conflicts between the fraternities and the university administration, no formal athletic leagues (a student baseball club—the "College Nine"—played an annual series with Northwestern University, and the students also had an amateur boating club), and few reports of the petty violence, alcoholism, hooliganism, and social hedonism that marked much of undergraduate life at nineteenth-century American colleges.[41] A later memoir on student life suggested that competitive oratorical contests between Chicago and neighboring colleges served the role of football games as occasions for student entertainment and sociability.[42] The majority of students had to find part-time and even full-time jobs to cover their expenses, reducing the temptation and the opportunity for socially aberrant behavior.[43] Describing the cultural differences between leading eastern colleges and the University of Chicago, one student wrote in 1873, "In boating, at the bat, and in other sports we may not be able to compare with the Eastern clubs; but while these are of benefit in themselves, they are, or should be of second rate importance to the student. To drill and strengthen the *mental* faculties is the prime area of college life; and the school that does this the most thoroughly is the most successful."[44] In all, the academic culture of the old University was serious, engaged, and (literally) sober, worthy of its Baptist origins, although the trustees' minutes do record one incident in 1883 in which a student threatened the president with a pistol over the award of a prize for an oratorical contest, with the student being summarily expelled.[45]

In a typical year the arts and sciences faculty numbered about a dozen (including the president, who regularly taught classes), with four to five additional faculty in the Law School. Some were regionally prominent, like James R. Boise in Greek literature and John C. Freeman in Latin, and a few former faculty ended up in prominent professorships elsewhere. When faculty published books, these were usually grammars or other pedagogical texts, including selections from ancient authors and from the Bible.[46] Occasionally a faculty member might gain wider recognition, as did William Mathews, a former lawyer turned publicist, financial writer, and rhetoric professor, who published a remarkable success manual in 1872 called *Getting On in the World, or Hints on Success in Life* that sold 70,000 copies.[47] For the most part, the majority were competent instructors with no significant professional reputations as scholars. Their academic backgrounds reflected the intellectual attainments expected of faculty: they were intelligent and dedicated pedagogues, fiercely loyal to the idea of the liberal arts, not original thinkers, writers, or scientists. In 1875 none of the faculty had an earned doctoral degree.

The University had difficulty retaining faculty, and the records of the board are filled with notations of departures for better-paying jobs elsewhere. Far too often the trustees struggled to meet the regular payroll, with the result that faculty were often forced to appeal to the board to honor their contracts—though many nineteenth-century colleges had feeble records of compensating their faculty, sometimes not meeting salary payrolls at all and assuming that faculty would either work for free or have family members who would otherwise support them.[48] In his comprehensive survey of the state of Baptist colleges in 1888, Frederick Gates discovered that faculty at most western Baptist colleges were paid salaries about half the value of those earned by teachers at more prominent eastern colleges.[49] Haphazard payrolls also meant that faculty had to take on part-time jobs outside of the University to make ends meet. In 1878 a young instructor of botany, Edson S. Bastin, explained to his sister that he was "still living on the hope that the University will be able to throw off the incubus of debt & that better times will come to us when salaries will be paid promptly & fully; still hoping that I shall not always be required to teach so many different things, & do such a variety of work that I may have the chance to do some one thing well."[50] By the mid-1880s the University was able to pay its teachers only 59 percent of the nominal value of their annual salaries ($885, as opposed to their official pay of $1,500).

The surviving records of the University's fund-raising efforts reveal a constant effort to seek small contributions from local and regional Baptist congregations, many of which made subscription pledges that they were in no position to honor. The financial files are full of accounts such as those of Lincoln Patterson, who was found to be "dead and family destitute; worthless," while I. R. Gale was "old & sick & will not pay as he has no property," and S. S. Davis was reported as having "gone to California[,] has no means, probably worthless."[51] In spite of efforts to persuade "wealthy men" of Chicago to give contributions, the University was bereft of any significant capitalist support in the 1870s and 1880s. The alternative was to rely heavily on Baptist clergy to undertake fund-raising, but this was a mixed blessing, given that the ministers were complex personalities with budgetary claims from their own congregations who required a great deal of hand-holding and who could easily lose focus and undermine broader institutional priorities.[52] This was the case with William W. Everts, who claimed to have raised $150,000 for the new college and who was touted in an early biographical sketch as someone who used "his marvelous faculty for 'raising money' with great effect," but who spent years feuding with many of his fellow trustees.[53]

FINANCIAL CRISES IN THE 1860S AND THE 1870S

The University was severely caught up in the strains and dislocations of the Civil War. The northern boundary of the campus was across the road from Camp Douglas, which housed thousands of Confederate prisoners of war. But the war's most serious effect on the University was a severe loss of financial resources. As in the aftermath of the panic of 1857, many donors found themselves unable to honor their pledges, creating a balance sheet overwhelmed with red ink. Enrollments in the undergraduate and law programs remained steady, but dipped in the preparatory school.

Ignoring the financial gloom, however, the board of trustees started construction on the main section of the University building in 1864, which was designated as Douglas Hall, at a cost of $120,000. A subscription campaign was mounted to cover these costs, but it fell short. Rather than delay construction, the trustees proceeded with the venture, since the hall was needed for an astronomical observatory that was urgently wanted.[54] In order to complete the building—the roof was missing—the trustees voted to deploy $14,000 from an endowment of $23,000 that had recently been given to establish a professorship of Greek.[55] This professorship had been raised by William W. Everts, the outspoken pastor of the First Baptist Church of Chicago, from Baptists in New York City, and Everts happened to be out of town when the board voted to appropriate the funds.[56]

As the institution's financial plight worsened in the 1860s, some trustees faulted Burroughs's financial assistant, James B. Olcott, for financial ineptitude and poor decision making. Olcott resigned in disgust in July 1862, resentful that Burroughs had not only failed to defend his reputation but had sought to take credit for successful pledges that Olcott himself had engineered.[57] Burroughs's most significant critic on the board was Everts, who was convinced that Burroughs was a weak leader engaging in financially irresponsible activities, such as booking pledges from potential donors who had neither the capacity nor real intent to pay, and then using the existence of such pledges as a kind of moral collateral to justify the University's increasing accumulation of debt. Without consulting his fellow trustees Everts invited Burroughs to his home in the summer of 1863, urging him to resign and promising (as a not-so-subtle bribe) to send Burroughs to Europe, free of charge.[58] Burroughs refused, and thus began a nasty and increasingly public feud between the two men that festered and worsened over the years.

That same year, the Committee on Finances was asked to report on the University's finances, yet it had little understanding of the real state of budgetary affairs. The trustees, in another risky act, took out a second loan of $15,000 in October 1864 from the Union Mutual Life Insurance Company, adding a second mortgage to the University's physical property.[59] The trustees hoped to complete the main building by adding a north wing. In 1864 they had obtained a pledge from board chairman William B. Ogden to cover the $50,000 cost of that wing, but only if sufficient funds—$100,000—were raised to eliminate the debt and to provide for the permanent operating costs of the University. Failing to meet Ogden's stipulation because of more feuding (including the sudden dismissal of the two men who were charged with leading a canvass for the building), the board was unable to get the north wing built.[60]

After the cessation of military hostilities in 1865, financial distress continued to plague the University. At a meeting on June 30, 1865, Thomas Hoyne offered a resolution to the effect that "this Board deemed it essential to a clearer apprehension and understanding of the present condition of the Institution, pecuniary and otherwise, that there should be some clearer and well digested report of all its affairs, embraced in a single Report to this Board."[61] When a summary of the University's finances was produced a few weeks later, it revealed that the institution had vastly overreached its available resources.[62] In August 1866 the trustees again appealed to the Union Mutual Life Insurance Company, this time requesting $25,000 to cover (among other things) unpaid bills and assessments that the city had levied against the University for street and lighting improvements. By 1866 the University owed the insurance company $75,000 in principal and interest.[63]

In 1869 the board hit upon the idea of asking other Christian denominations to fund individual faculty positions. When the incumbent chair in mathematics, Alonzo J. Sawyer, was asked to solicit the Presbyterians for the costs of his salary, he refused and threatened to resign. Sawyer complained that "if the Trustees will also keep in mind the great aversion which every literary man must have to begging for a matter in which he is personally interested and which he cannot do without sacrifice of his finer feelings, they will perceive the exceedingly unpleasant nature of the task they wish me to perform."[64] The board, "while regretting to part with so old and faithful a professor," felt "compelled under the present pecuniary necessities of the institution to accept the tendered resignation."[65] Most fascinating about this incident was the board's strange conviction that selling off professorships to other denominations would "plac[e] this institution among the most useful and commanding Universities in the country." Yet the resignation of Sawyer in fact showed how marginal the faculty were in the life of the institution. Rather than viewing the faculty as key human capital resources to be protected, and as agents who would give a lustrous identity to the University, the trustees viewed them as (at best) genial teachers, respected by their students but eminently replaceable or exchangeable if there were some financial necessity.

In the face of such problems, President Burroughs was tempted to sanction extreme and unorthodox measures, such as the so-called land scheme of early 1871. Two laymen from the First Baptist Church obtained a guarantee of $50,000 from Burroughs to purchase 160 acres of land near the stockyards, which they then proposed to sell at a high profit, sharing the difference with the University. Burroughs acted without the board's official approval and in fact had no money available to join in the plan. The scheme soon collapsed, with the University gaining nothing except another blemish on its name.[66] Once again, the trustees returned to the Union Mutual Life Insurance Company in July 1869 for an additional $25,000 loan, making the total indebtedness now $100,000.[67] Squabbling on the board over how to deal with the debt continued, and then the University was hit with the dual blows of the fire of 1871 and the depression of 1873. The board noted in October 1872 that "a large part of the subscriptions for the University obtained in Chicago, within the last three years, have been rendered uncollectible by the fire of last October."[68] Even the usually optimistic student newspaper was forced to admit that the losses in the wake of the fire were "incalculable; many men of wealth in the city had declared grand intentions, and some had made generous provisions for large things for the college, whose fulfillment is now hopeless and impossible. The institution was seriously crippled — [it] labors now under great embarrassment, and therefore needs the support of all its friends at home and abroad."[69]

William Everts continued his campaign to force Burroughs's dismissal, even ghostwriting attacks on Burroughs that were published in the *Chicago Tribune*.[70] Everts was forced to resign from the board in October 1872, having been accused of "impudence, dishonesty or infidelity" in leaking damaging material concerning University finances to the press, although he denied wrongdoing.[71] Burroughs finally agreed (in principle) to step down from the presidency as soon as a suitable successor could be identified. But in fact he refused to abandon his position, and by the time a new president was elected in July 1874—Dr. Lemuel Moss, a respected professor of theology at Crozer Seminary near Philadelphia—Burroughs had engineered his own appointment to a newly created office of chancellor of the University, with specific responsibility to supervise the finances of the institution.[72]

The problem with this arrangement was that no one had consulted Moss about it, and he had assumed that his appointment as president involved "the whole of it," with "all of its duties and prerogatives."[73] Within a few months Moss was at daggers drawn with Burroughs over the authority vested in the presidency—Burroughs insisted that Moss could not make any decisions involving money without his prior consent, while Moss sought to persuade the board to eliminate Burroughs's position. The board then became badly polarized. Among Moss's supporters were Francis E. Hinckley, George Walker, and E. Nelson Blake, donors who were to play a major role in the development of the Morgan Park Seminary and, eventually, the new University of Chicago. The anti-Burroughs faction proposed that Burroughs's office be vacated and that he be retired "with every expression of honor and respect on the part of the Board and all interested in the University."[74] This motion was met with one that proposed firing Moss. The consequence was that Moss was fired by a 16–8 vote on July 13, 1875, for spreading "dissatisfactions" and undermining a "harmony of interests" in the administration, and Burroughs was put back in charge of the University until an interim president could be identified.[75]

The Moss scandal proved to be a turning point in the history of the institution's governance. First, it generated a huge cloud of negative publicity about the University, with the majority of the board being accused of undignified, petty, and irresponsible behavior. The *Standard*, the main newspaper of the Baptist communities in Chicago, reported, "The action of the Trustees of this institution, at their last meeting, has called forth an indignant and almost unanimous protest on the part of the general public and the denominational press. We have met, personally, no man during this week of anxiety and agitation who has not declared the act alike unjust and suicidal; while the utterances of the press, both denominational and secular ... is to the effect that the course of the Board is wholly without justification."[76] Second, it became clear that the motives behind this putsch had everything to do with Burroughs's unwillingness to surrender his status and nothing to do with the welfare of the University. Levi D. Boone emerged as the public spokesperson for the anti-Moss faction and published several explanatory letters in the press, insisting that the issue was one of formal honor—Moss had agreed originally to live with the dual system of governance (which Moss denied) and he now found it unworkable. This made the situation worse, since Boone offered no substantive reason why Moss had been terminated, and, as trustee J. A. Smith observed, "throughout the letter [from Boone] ... scarcely one word of allusion appears to the University considered as an institution of learning, representing the great interest of higher education. It is nowhere implied that any other point is at issue save the one personal to Dr. Burroughs."[77] Smith, who tried to mediate between warring factions on the board, publicly characterized Moss's dismissal as a "signal injustice" and rightly predicted that "it probably puts an end to all hope that the University will become, at least in this present generation, what so many have hoped to see it, and labored to make it."[78] Moss landed on his feet, for he was immediately hired as president of Indiana University, where he served with distinction from 1875 to 1884.

The public scandal frightened the board. A Moss supporter and former senator from Wisconsin, James R. Doolittle, was persuaded to serve as acting president while the board searched for a replacement. In mid-1876 Alonzo Abernethy, a University alumnus who was the superintendent of public instruction in Iowa, was chosen to become the permanent president, but Abernethy himself doubted that he was up to the rigors of the job and served for only two lackluster years.[79]

Reports of dissension among members of the board made fund-raising appeals virtually impossible.[80] In December 1875, the *Chicago Tribune* wrote in an editorial, "The University is probably now in a worse condition, pecuniarily speaking, than at any time during its history.... It has been difficult to get money from the members of the Board of Trustees, and from friends of the University in the city, for the reason that they have been paying steadily for years to support what seems to be a failing institution, and they are at last getting weary in good-doing," seeming to imply that the financial misery was owing to poor administrative control by university leaders and not errors by the board.[81] Yet substantial responsibility for the University's dismal performance has to lie with the board's erratic behavior. Even though the trustees had pledged in October 1872 that "no liability shall be contracted by the trustees above the cash resources for the fiscal year in which the same matures," in February 1876 they took out an additional loan of $13,200 from the Union Mutual Life Insurance Company to cover unpaid faculty salaries. The company used this opportunity to consolidate past debts and unpaid interest into a new mortgage note for $150,000, at 8 percent interest, but with the stipulation that if the interest were unpaid, the rate would increase to 10 percent.[82] An attempt to gain support from the educational fund associated with the

Baptist Centennial Movement of 1876 failed when Burroughs refused to allow agents of the American Baptist Educational Commission to inspect the University's financial records.[83]

Between 1862 and 1878, the University graduated several hundred students, yet it remained underfunded, paralyzed by tensions on its board of trustees, and increasingly isolated from the burgeoning metropolis growing up around it. In February 1873, a planning committee appointed by the board presented a critical discussion of the profile of the University, admitting that there was a serious disconnect between the University's educational programs and Chicago's changing economy and demography: "[In] such a city as ours, with its extended commerce, its vast industries, its energetic and enterprising people," the University ought to appeal to those seeking the application "of theoretical learning in practical affairs." The committee recommended that "wealthy and generous citizens" be approached to endow "a school of this kind, under some appropriate designation, as an organic part of the University ... [to] help greatly in rallying to the institution public interest and enthusiasm." The committee also urged that more attention be devoted to stabilizing the University's finances, and toward that end suggested expanding the student body.[84]

While perceptive, this diagnosis was short on specific ideas that might lead to such a shift in direction, and the subsequent track record of the board suggested that these proposals too were another exercise in wishful thinking. By 1877, citing the fact that "many citizens of Chicago from whom the University had realized liberal support and encouragement of future aid had been unable to continue their donations and will probably never be able to fulfill what they had proposed," the board considered selling "one hundred perpetual scholarships at one thousand dollars each" as a way of raising immediate cash for operations, but this too proved to be a chimera.[85]

The disjunction between the University and the city was further aggravated by new kinds of elites who came to prominence after 1870. Displacing an older generation of "Christian gentlemen" civic leaders like William Ogden, J. Young Scammon, and John Woodworth (all trustees), the new industrial and commercial leaders were much more focused on managerial discipline, financial efficiency, and wealth generation as a sign of conspicuous social consumption. The Great Chicago Fire, in 1871, further empowered this new "plutocratic" elite to gain social and cultural hegemony in the city.[86] These men were, according to Kathleen McCarthy, "richer, younger, and more ambitious than [their] antebellum predecessors. While the prewar generation had built a city from a prairie swamp, this group would fashion Chicago into the second largest city in the nation, the hub of a network of national and international business concerns."[87] These elites—men like Marshall Field, Philip D. Armour, George Pullman, Richard T. Crane, Charles L. Hutchinson, and N. K. Fairbank—were more assertive in viewing investment in cultural institutions as a way to enhance the luster and reputation of the city, and they tended to direct their philanthropy toward organizations that were well run with sound business practices, that had a broad self-help mission to improve the lives of the ambitious poor, and that would enhance Chicago's status. As Helen Horowitz has argued, men like Hutchinson "not only wanted their city to be a good place to live and work; they wanted it to be thought of as the very best. As their horizons had expanded, they increasingly compared their city to other great cities of the world. It was no longer enough for Chicago to be economically powerful or even moral: the test it was forced to meet was the level of culture."[88] To men of such mind-sets, the forlorn image of the University as both debt ridden and badly managed would not attract the kind of investments required to make the institution worthy of the newly emerging industrial metropolis. For them, a different kind of university, one focused on the conspicuous production and consumption of research, might better demonstrate both the moral authority and public prestige of new investments in science and higher education.[89] Sadly, the faculty of the first University were in no position to play that transformational role.

THE SECESSION OF THE SEMINARY

Another unhappy outcome of the hard times between 1872 and 1878 was the decision of the leaders of the Chicago Baptist Union Theological Seminary to break their ties with the University and to move their campus to a distant part of the metropolitan area. When the University was founded, many in the denomination expected that it would eventually house a seminary for Baptist ministers. Yet while almost 30 percent of the three hundred-odd alumni of the University's collegiate programs by the mid-1880s had entered the ministry as their professional vocation, the initial financial and planning difficulties encountered by the University had made it impossible to develop a seminary there.

In August 1863 a group of Baptist leaders met in Chicago and created the Baptist Theological Union, located in Chicago, which would serve as the parent organizing group for a seminary.[90] Several of the men who attended the meeting were University trustees (including Nathaniel Culver and William Everts), but the question at hand was whether the seminary would coordinate its fund-raising energies with those of the University. Everts, for example, approached several potential donors to the University who indicated that they would prefer to give to the seminary. This inevitably led to unpleasant tensions between the boards of the University and of the seminary.

The seminary was launched in September 1866, with the understanding that it would exist "by the side of the University of Chicago, yet without organic connection."[91] The trustees of the seminary authorized the construction of a building directly across the street from the University, which opened in July 1869. The land on which the building stood was not part of the Douglas gift, but was purchased separately and remained in the possession of the Baptist church well into the twentieth century.[92] The first president of the seminary was George W. Northrup, who held a chair in church history at the Rochester Theological Seminary in New York and who was to play a minor but critical role in the founding of the new University in 1890–91.

For nearly a decade, the seminary seemed to prosper, attracting a small but dedicated group of students (enrollments grew from twenty in 1867 to sixty students by 1875).[93] The seminary attracted students from across the nation, including from Brown, Yale, Harvard, Princeton, Amherst, and Rochester.[94] But it depended both on small-scale voluntary contributions from all over the western states as well as from generous donors in the East, and the late 1860s and early 1870s proved to be as challenging for it as for the University. By 1876, with the second Chicago fire of 1874 having "affected our interests even more severely than the first," the chairman of the board of the seminary, D. B. Cheney, complained that it could not raise cash from its own assets or look to friends (or approach strangers) for support: "We have been unable to dispose of the large amount of real estate held by us, many of our notes have yielded no income, the warmest friends of the enterprise have been forced by the exigencies of the time to deny themselves the pleasure of carrying out their cherished plans of liberality towards it. To secure help from strangers or new friends was well nigh impossible."[95]

Facing this crisis in funding, the seminary leaders came to believe that their best hope was to divorce themselves from the Oakenwald site, sell or lease their land and the existing building to help finance a move, and start anew, with a new location distant from the grimness and noise of the city. The aesthetic difference between the old site and the new one in Morgan Park was stunning:

> The new site is on an elevated plateau, nearly one hundred feet above the level of the lake, less exposed to the damp, cold winds from the lake, commanding an extensive and beautiful view of the surrounding country, and susceptible of most perfect drainage. It is attractive and healthful.... The Seminary now stands immediately in [the] rear of the University, which

dwarfs and overshadows it, on less than [an] acre of ground, closely shut in by other buildings, which obscure the view, increase the noise, and multiply the risk of fire. The residences built for the professors in connection with the Seminary are larger and more expensive than they can afford to live in, besides being too public for that retirement which every studious teacher so greatly desires. . . . The site chosen contains more than five acres, ample for all time to come, with streets on three sides, which prevent the possibility of encroachment, ensuring sunlight, air, freedom from noise and fire.

Finally, the move would be a financial boon in that "the new building affords commodious and pleasant accommodations for all purposes for the present. . . . The removal [from the Thirty-Fourth Street site] . . . enables us to dispose of the present site and buildings, and to devote the proceeds to the liquidation of our indebtedness. It gives us a new site, and building complete. It secures us a large quantity of land, which when sold, will add very considerably to our means."[96]

The leaders of the seminary were also motivated by the largesse of George C. Walker, a financier who, with other real estate investors, controlled a huge tract of land in Morgan Park.[97] Walker led a group of investors who offered the Baptists a large tract of land, as well as plots for homes for the seminary's leaders and additional land that could be sold for profit. In addition, Walker's consortium provided the first building for the seminary, Morgan Hall.[98] Thomas Goodspeed himself was given a half acre of land on which to build a home at One Hundred Twelfth Street and Oakley Avenue, a structure that still exists today. Walker's father, Charles, was a personal friend of Stephen Douglas and was present at the dinner in 1856 where Douglas announced his intention to give land to the Baptists for a college. The elder Walker became a trustee and was succeeded by his son, who later became a trustee of the second University. In 1892 he donated $100,000 to the new University to create a museum building for the natural sciences, which he insisted not be used for classroom instruction.[99]

An alumnus of the old University, who also studied theology at the University of Rochester, Thomas Goodspeed became the secretary and financial agent of the new Morgan Park Seminary in 1876. In January 1876 Goodspeed led a fund-raising campaign for the seminary and raised a respectable $50,000. Five years later he launched a second, more ambitious appeal in the Chicago area for $100,000, for which he was able to secure a $30,000 matching gift from an unusually generous Baptist businessman, E. Nelson Blake. Another, far wealthier Baptist, John D. Rockefeller, then matched Blake's gift.[100] These gifts enabled Goodspeed to raise an additional $200,000 for an endowment for the seminary, a record that stood in stark contrast to the miserable record of the University. Goodspeed then launched a third campaign in the autumn of 1885 to raise $50,000 to build a library, a new dormitory, and a fund for operating expenses, and he again persuaded Rockefeller to provide a matching gift, this one for $20,000.[101] Goodspeed publicly acknowledged, "We need large contributions, and hope it may be laid on the hearts of some who have already done much for the Seminary to crown their benefactions with large gifts at this critical juncture. They are necessary. *We cannot succeed without them.*"[102] These efforts gave Goodspeed a wide network of acquaintances among the national Baptist community, including Rockefeller, and a rich abundance of fund-raising experience that would serve him well in the critical years between 1887 and 1891. Characterized by his colleague C. E. Hewitt as "a conquering general in the financial field," over time Goodspeed developed an uncanny ability to solicit large gifts from wealthy donors, a skill and facility that seemed to escape those who sought to raise money for the old University.[103]

The decision to relocate to Morgan Park was the most negative turn of events endured by the University in this tumultuous decade. Henceforth, Baptists in Chicago had to raise funds for two independent institutions in direct competition, and the University was the big loser, for the seminary represented a pragmatic vocational program with a clear educational mission that Baptists—most of whom had no university training—could more easily understand. Had the seminary stayed in Oakenwald, the University's chances for survival might have been greater. By 1892 the seminary had built an endowment of nearly $250,000, with a student body that had steadily increased to over a hundred and a respectable library of almost 30,000 volumes, including the famous Hengstenberg Library of biblical literature, a collection of 12,000 volumes that Northrup and Everts purchased in 1869.[104] The seminary not only survived but modestly prospered, and in the course of its new existence attracted loyal support from the denomination and a respectable teaching faculty, including an unusually promising young professor of Semitic languages, William Rainey Harper, who joined the faculty in the winter term of 1880. Harper would first begin to make a name for himself with his Hebrew Correspondence School and the summer school sessions for the intensive study of Hebrew that he organized at Morgan Park in the early 1880s.[105] The seminary also enjoyed a board of trustees that was generally harmonious. Financial problems always remained, but by the early 1880s, compared to the University, the seminary seemed like a model of wise governance. Goodspeed later remembered, "The Theological Seminary always had loyal and generous friends. It always had an able, conservative, interested and faithful Board of Trustees. The Board always conducted its work with the utmost harmony.... They won and retained the confidence of the people. A united Board had behind it a united denomination."[106]

Seminary leaders were confident that theirs could become the leading seminary west of the Allegheny Mountains. As one eastern colleague, J. Warren Merrill of Cambridge, Massachusetts, wrote enviously to Goodspeed in 1886, "The Star of Empire has gone West. You must increase, *we* must decrease. You will have a constantly increasing number of students. You must have accommodations for them. You must have the Professors chairs filled with the best talent, [and] you must increase your salaries.... Chicago, if Rome, Communism, Socialism and Infidelity do not run riot, is to be the largest city in the country, it will reach out to you and you must do a large share towards saving it from the fate of Sodom."[107] Frederick Gates and William Rainey Harper would later seize upon such rhetoric of a surging, gilded age Chicago, filled with both apocalyptic promise and fearsome evil and having a special destiny in the West, to affirm the special opportunity that awaited new forms of higher education in the burgeoning metropolis.

The University faced still other problems in this period. Just as it sought to deepen its connections to other Protestant denominations, the city saw an explosion of new forms of nondenominational evangelism, like the YMCA movement and the "big tent" Moody movement, as well as a mushrooming interest in large-scale charitable activities on behalf of the newly arrived poor.[108] These causes claimed substantial financial backing from wealthy Chicagoans, eager to provide ways to civilize rough-hewn immigrants arriving in Chicago, and the humble South Side college was easily lost in the shuffle. And given their deep ambivalence about immigrants, early Baptist leaders in Chicago were badly positioned to seek philanthropic assistance for social projects that would broaden their denomination's altruistic social profile with the new wealthy of Chicago.[109]

Equally challenging was the success of Northwestern University. Northwestern was founded by Methodists in 1851, and it endured the same financial environment and same demographic challenges as the University of Chicago. But Northwestern had key advantages, which proved crucial to its relative success.[110] It had a group of early donors who committed relatively large gifts to help launch its building and construction programs; it enjoyed an amicable and profitable relationship with its sister seminary, the Garrett Biblical Institute; it enjoyed strong and stable leadership from its first presidents and steady and generous support from its trustees; and it had the support of key capitalists, like John Evans and Orrington Lunt, who stood by Northwestern when it encountered difficulties.

In 1884 a prominent Baptist educator in Chicago complained that "the Northwestern University at Evanston, under the control of the Methodists, has already virtually paid its debts, and has, in its real estate, a very large endowment." After noting similar positive stories about Beloit College and Knox College, this writer observed, "What can be said truthfully of these, can be said of many others, while our own university goes begging from church to church and door to door. Its President carries his hat in his hand outstretched to every passerby, until, at this state of things, his cheek mantles with shame."[111] The writer who invoked this unhappy comparison with Northwestern was Galusha Anderson, the last president of the first University of Chicago.

Galusha Anderson and the Collapse of the First University of Chicago

By 1880 the city in which the University was located was profoundly different from the 1855 frontier town in which it was initially founded. The population of Chicago had increased to more than 500,000 (ten years later it would top 1 million), the economic structures of the city were much more varied and complex, and the social problems raised by the legions of new immigrants were ever more acute. Chicago was already home to a new generation of immensely wealthy entrepreneurs, businessmen, and speculators, who were generating new networks of philanthropic resources. The University had no plausible or evident way to appeal to these new elites, and its institutional modesty made it almost impossible for serious connections to be made. Nor was there huge wealth among the Baptists, for, as Frederick Gates later noted, "The fact is, there is not much more money among them. The fire [of 1871] swept away what little money there used to be and most of the brethren have been doing business on small capital, with heavy debts, ever since."[112]

Anderson, the last president of the first University of Chicago, would experience colossal frustrations over the gap between the good intentions of the University and its lack of legitimacy. In so doing Anderson became the most visible victim of the last stage of the University's history. A graduate of the University of Rochester and the Rochester Theological Seminary, Anderson had led Baptist congregations in the East and Midwest before succeeding Thomas Goodspeed as pastor of the Second Baptist Church in Chicago in 1876, where he made an excellent impression. He seemed the ideal choice to step into the leadership vacuum and administrative chaos created by Alonzo Abernethy's sudden departure in early 1878. As a sign of the desperation of the trustees, John Burroughs was finally pressured to resign as chancellor.[113]

Anderson was elected president in March 1878. He lived in North Kenwood, where he was a respected leader in local cultural life. Ander-

son involved himself extensively in local Republican politics, seeking to
displace the hold of the Democratic Party on municipal politics. He was
a popular civic speaker on current public policy topics, and he became
a close acquaintance of Paul Cornell, the founder of Hyde Park. From
appearances it seemed the University had chosen well. Anderson was
honest, forthright, and a man of integrity, and his view of the University
was primarily as a teaching institution, as a site of higher culture where
the sons and daughters of the Baptist community might gain exposure to
the knowledge and skills of general education that would prepare them
effectively for any career. He sought to counter the idea that the University
existed mainly to train men for the ministry. Rather, its real goal was "to
make educated men, educated merchants, educated mechanics, educated
people in all walks of life."[114] Yet the task before him was daunting, made
all the more so when he discovered that many of the alleged assets of the
University were worthless, that the salaries of the faculty had gone unpaid
for several months, and that Burroughs and his cronies had run up large
unpaid debts in the operational side of the budget that impeded such basic
things as obtaining coal for heating the University building.[115]

In June 1881 Anderson reported to the board, "We have only $600 of
endowment and the few dollars of income from that are applied to the
extinguishment of an old debt. Our reliance is on our tuitions." Although
the Law School just managed to cover its costs with tuition, the undergraduate college and the preparatory school were unable to meet their expenses, in part because "the endowment [for] scholarships was consumed
as it was gathered" and because "children of ministers of all denominations
are required to pay half the ordinary rates." In 1882 Anderson again complained to the trustees to the effect that "the able professors ought to be
more liberally compensated. Their salaries are less than the salaries of
some of our teachers in the public schools of the city.... As to the college
building, taste and convenience suggest many improvements. Some of the
floors and ceilings are so defective that they ought to be replaced; the roof
leaks so that several rooms are wetted whenever it storms, and the library
has been injured by rains."[116] Equally critical, Anderson discovered that
Burroughs had spent endowment money for current expenses, which reduced substantially the number of tuition-paying students the University
could recruit each year.

Anderson was offended by the debt to the Union Mutual Life Insurance
Company and tried to find ways to resolve it.[117] In 1878, the company
proposed waiving the full amount of the debt if the University could pay
$100,000 in cash within one calendar year. Anderson agreed to try to
meet this goal, but found that raising such a sum was beyond his capabilities, and the company withdrew its offer. In 1881 the trustees approached

the company with a similar proposal, but this time the company insisted on repayment of the total debt.

Anderson worked assiduously to raise money for the University, spending endless hours in appeals to downtown businessmen and to Baptist communities across the region. Yet he failed miserably. Even direct appeals to John D. Rockefeller led to sour results, with Rockefeller candidly informing Anderson that he regretted "not to be able to give you any encouragement. I have promised to do something for the [Morgan Park] Seminary.... This with my other engagements, is all that I can take now, but I sincerely hope that you will work it through all right."[118] So troubled were the finances of the University by 1884 that Anderson wrote to a friend, "I have had no pay for services for months, except as I have received a few dollars for the preaching of a Sunday now and then; am deeply in debt and don't know just now which way to turn. People are apparently more willing to help anything rather than this University."[119] In a memoir of his father's experiences in Chicago, Frederick L. Anderson observed:

> He left the largest, pleasantest, and most fruitful of his pastorates and a salary of $5,000 to embark upon a sea of troubles at $3,000 a year. This was guaranteed him by three or four of the Trustees, but they paid it in full only for the first quarter and none at all after the first year of the seven years' war. For the last six years, as he himself expressed it, "The President of the University had no stated salary; he skirmished for it." ... He taught Psychology, Ethics, Logic and International Law, and often a term of English history. Every morning he walked or rode two miles with me to the University, taught and attended to his administrative duties there and disappeared about ten for his downtown office and his begging. Free evenings and often midnight hours, as well as the time on trains and horse cars, he devoted to the subjects he taught. But it was a good school and he did high-grade teaching. As he said in leaving it, "the University has done more on less money in the last seven years than any institution in the United States."[120]

The months between November 1884 and February 1885 saw the final public humiliation of the University, as the Union Mutual Life Insurance Company sued to foreclose on the University's property. Stories first appeared in 1877 to the effect that the University was near bankruptcy, with the *Chicago Tribune* reporting that the insurance company was threatening foreclosure over nonpayment of the interest on the loan on the property.[121] In response, some board members argued that the trustees who had voted to approve the original loan in the 1860s had not understood that a not-for-profit organization could not alienate its own property, as provided by the original charter of gift of Senator Douglas from April 1856, and that the University's land holdings were protected against any foreclosure action. This position was widely viewed as the University's attempt to repudiate its debt. A clash in court was avoided in 1877 when the company agreed to renegotiate the loan, but by the early 1880s it was clear that the company would never be repaid, given the financial trajectory of the University.[122] Upon assuming the presidency, Galusha Anderson supported a lawsuit filed in the state courts in March 1881 by friends of the University to clarify the question of whether the original trustees had the right to encumber the University's property with a mortgage. That suit led Union Mutual to file a foreclosure suit in federal district court to recover the $320,000 in principal and interest that the company claimed was owed to it. In late November 1884 the attorney for the company, Leonard Swett, excoriated the trustees for financial mismanagement and unethical behavior:

> This institution professes to stand for the great Baptist Church of America! An ordinary uncircumcised sinner who expects, in the next world, the *quantum meruit* of his deserts, would not dare to do such a thing. It is reserved for the elect, the predestinate, the foreordained, to borrow other people's money, to build the walls of their building, to roof it in from the storms of winter, to pay bills long past due for its construction, to insure that building from year to year, to erect lamp-posts to light them at night, to build pavements and walks to walk over, and even, lastly, to borrow $13,000 to pay their own salaries, and repudiate the debt, and still to believe that such election will not be contested. It is to be hoped when this President and these Professors teach moral philosophy and the evidences and principles of Christianity to the youth of our land, that they teach solely the principles laid down in the text-books, keeping far in the background, and if possible wholly out of sight, their own personal example.[123]

Galusha Anderson's defenders insisted that he was willing to negotiate a reasonable settlement with the insurance company, but it was too late. Whether the insurance company actually wanted to foreclose or was merely using this legal weapon to pressure Anderson and the trustees to come up with a plausible counteroffer is not clear, but the final result was the same—namely, another public relations disaster for the University, even worse than the Moss affair. A final judgment by Judge Henry W. Blodgett in early January 1885 rejected the inalienability argument on the grounds that when Douglas deeded the land to the Baptists in September

1858 he did so unconditionally in fee simple and with "no restriction or limitation upon the title with which it clothed the University." Since the University had been legally entitled to secure loans using its property as security, Judge Blodgett concluded that the insurance company was legally entitled to foreclose.[124]

The financial mess took a toll on Anderson's professional reputation. In July 1885 he came close to being elected president of Vassar College, but was ultimately turned down because of the adverse publicity surrounding the bankruptcy of the University of Chicago. Feeling overwhelmed by his burdens, Anderson resigned from the presidency that same month and was replaced by George C. Lorimer, the pastor of the Immanuel Baptist Church, on an interim basis. Anderson soon rebounded, however, becoming president of Denison University and later returning to Chicago to teach homiletics, first at Morgan Park and then at the University of Chicago Divinity School, from which he retired as a full professor in 1904.[125]

In January 1886, when Union Mutual rejected a last-ditch offer by Lorimer to settle the debt with a one-time payment of $100,000, the game was over. The Baptist ministers of Chicago met on February 8 to discuss whether to abandon the old institution to the insurance company and to reestablish it in a different location with new leadership and new sources of support—a move tantamount to "the founding of a new University." George Northrup urged the Baptists to rent rooms in the city and retain the current faculty, immediately raising $10,000 to keep a bare-bones operation going, and then try to raise a permanent endowment of $250,000. Thomas Goodspeed, in contrast, argued that it made most sense to kill off the old University legally, secure a new charter and appoint a new board of trustees, and move south to Morgan Park, where the new University would be linked to the seminary. The ministers voted to endorse the idea of founding a new University.[126] On February 12 George Lorimer informed the board of trustees of the ministers' views, which he endorsed.

As the end neared, accusations and ruminations abounded as to why the University was on the verge of financial collapse. One easy answer was its denominational character, which a *Chicago Tribune* editorial had strongly criticized back in 1874, arguing, "that the University is not a financial success, and, as a consequence, not an educational success, is due to a radical defect which requires a radical remedy. It is a sectarian institution. This may be denied, but the fact remains unchanged, and, wherever it is known at all, it is known as a Baptist university. The day of denominational schools and colleges has gone by. They are a relic of the past, as is attested by the scores of starveling colleges of that kind scattered all over the country."[127] Twelve years later, the *Hyde Park Herald* took up the same refrain when it asserted that "the one great draw-back with the Chicago University is that it is in the hands of a denomination—and a denomination too, in regard to which there is a strong feeling among western people, that it is illiberal with respect to other Christian denominations."[128] In contrast, George Northrup argued that the old University collapsed both because of miserable leadership *and* because it was insufficiently Baptist, and thus lost support within the denomination (in contrast to his seminary):

> The ruin of that educational undertaking, of such magnificent promise in its beginning, was due, mainly, if not exclusively, to the mismanagement of its Board, a close corporation, sustaining no direct relation to our churches, and having among its most influential members Jews, Swedenborgians, Unitarians, and men of no religious belief. It was this body, whose history was marked by bitter personal conflicts, perversion of trust funds, and violation of sacred pledges, that utterly destroyed, in the course of twenty-five years, the confidence, interest, and hopes of our people.[129]

Part of this rhetoric was sour grapes, with men like Northrup feeling that the old board was to blame for having allowed uncommitted and irresponsible non-Baptists to join its ranks. The question remains: Was the first University doomed to fail from the beginning because of its Baptist identity, or was its ultimate failure the result of unwise and unfavorable decisions by the board and its various presidents, taken in the midst of a series of catastrophic economic crises?

Edson Bastin again wrote to his sister in April 1882 describing the demoralized state of the faculty and assigning much of the responsibility to the Baptist community: "I used to have some respect for the Baptist denomination, but I fear I am fast losing it all. I once supposed they took an intelligent interest in higher education, but I now see they do not. We are not supported by the Baptists, and the fact that we bear the unfortunate name of Baptist prevents people who do appreciate the needs of a University from giving us their support."[130]

The old University had two rival identities, which had come more and more into conflict—one as a Baptist denominational school, the other as a general agent of civic progress for the city, aiding Chicago in its general cultural development. As a missionary church, the Baptists in Chicago were most at home on the margins, where conversion was crucial, not in an increasingly wealthy metropolis where new cultural structures and new understandings of American identity were quickly built and deposited. Yet a committee of three alumni leaders had argued in 1878 that the denominational issue was a red herring: "While the university is under the charge of the Baptist churches it is not used as an apparatus for the propagation of Baptist tenets, nor even for the propagation of general Christian doctrine.... There is no effort made to influence students in favor of or against any one church or denomination, or to indoctrinate students one way or another. The University of Chicago is Baptist only as Yale College is Congregational, or Harvard, Unitarian."[131] Aside from the unrealistic comparison with Harvard and Yale, this was a reasonable statement and accurate on its own terms. But the denominational issue was cited on numerous occasions to explain why wealthy Chicagoans refused to give. Hard-line Baptists like Northrup might argue that the University was not Baptist enough, but such assertions simply confirmed the fact that, for better or worse, denominational identity was a powerful signaling device in a multireligious, multiethnic city like Chicago, and it created a claustro-phobic image for the University. And it is undeniable that the University presented an ambivalent object to most Chicago Baptists who were, as Frederick Gates argued, poor and middling folk and not inclined to support higher education beyond the work of their local seminary. E. Nelson Blake, the chairman of the board of the seminary, captured this paradox when he insisted to Thomas Goodspeed, "I should be more ready to favor an un-denominational school that could appeal to the neutral wealth of the city. The denomination is *not wealthy*, and the givers are hard pressed now. The membership have not been educated to give by their spiritual fathers."[132] Baptists were a poor denomination, with unsteady membership levels and with no formal ecclesiastical structure, no synod, no bishops, and no national system of governance. They were not really a "church" in the European sense of the word, and their early colleges like Shurtleff, Franklin, and Granville were often poor creatures, badly financed, and underendowed. Earlier in the nineteenth century some Baptists had even been hostile to the idea that their ministers should be well educated.[133] Moreover, whatever chance the University might have had to appeal to Blake's "neutral wealthy" became less plausible as its internal disorganiza-tion and public feuding became objects of public derision. Wealthy donors viewed colleges and universities as businesses, like railroads or steel mills, and successful businesses did not take on excessive debt or tolerate weak, incompetent leadership.

Finally, the University failed to project a compelling model of educa-tional or research professionalism that would have made investments in faculty and their research socially gratifying. The University's educational programs provided ample evidence of useful service, and the fact that it educated a number of successful lawyers and businessmen might have been touted more than it was. Moreover, most extant reports on the qual-ity of teaching at the University suggest that it was reasonably high and that most alumni remembered their studies as having been valuable and informative. Even during the chaotic final year of 1885–86, the dean reported that "the work of the class-rooms has been carried on with a vigor and enthusiasm which are remarkable when we consider the uncertainties that have been before us."[134] But this was not enough. Not until a much wealthier Baptist, John D. Rockefeller, was persuaded to invest in higher education in Chicago did a radically different platform of Baptist philanthropy become imaginable, one that could attract the social emulation of wealthy Chicagoans.

The Transition from the Old to the New University

The story of the founding of the second University of Chicago is filled with many twists and turns, and not a few heroes. William Rainey Harper was one of these heroes, but not the only one. In fact, the founding of the new University was a drama starring several different actors. It began with Thomas W. Goodspeed, the financial secretary of the Morgan Park Seminary and a local Baptist loyalist. Goodspeed was a gentle, earnest man—not a natural leader of charismatic ability, but a talented agent and an eloquent spokesperson for those who could provide visionary leadership. Although a perennial worrier, Goodspeed had great civic courage and an almost unshakable conviction that he was doing the work of the Lord by trying to revive a Christian university in Chicago. All of these traits, together with a friendly demeanor and the remarkable trust that he engendered in even casual acquaintances, made him an ideal local representative for the new enterprise.

The collapse of the old University generated immense shame among local Baptist leaders, and Goodspeed sought to capitalize on their humiliation by organizing a provisional committee to seek outside funding to relaunch the University. Goodspeed had already been involved in a last-ditch effort to save the old University when he engineered the offer of its presidency to William Rainey Harper in April 1886 at a salary of $2,000. Goodspeed had even appealed to John D. Rockefeller, who was willing to support Harper but wanted nothing to do with the University at this time.[135] Harper was already seen as a rising star among local Chicago Baptists, but he dismissed the offer as lacking either political sense or financial substance. Instead, Harper headed off to Yale University, where he became a full professor of Semitic languages at an annual salary of $4,000 in the fall of 1886.[136]

Had Harper accepted the presidency of the University of Chicago in the spring of 1886, he would have ruined his career. The Harper presidential episode, however, fueled Goodspeed's determination. In June 1886 he declined an offer to become president of Kalamazoo College, telling John D.

Rockefeller, "I have felt that I could not leave the Seminary until I had carried to success the undertaking your kindness has made possible.... I could not get the consent of my conscience to go." He again insisted, "We need here a college. The seminary needs it. Our cause needs it, and I cannot but believe that it is certain to come.... I hope you will not be unwilling to permit me to say a word from time to time of the hopes of those who cannot willingly let our University die without making an effort to rebuild it under better auspices."[137] When the old University officially collapsed in the summer of 1886, Goodspeed led an effort to organize a temporary academy in rooms in the old seminary building on Thirty-Fourth Street, with three former faculty members.[138] Goodspeed then organized an appeal to George Walker and the Blue Island Land and Building Company in October 1886, asking that they support the re-creation of the University in Morgan Park and soliciting the gift of a partial share of the rental or sales value of one hundred acres of land, the income from which would cover the operating costs of the new University, plus land for the college itself and a gift of $25,000 for a new building. Goodspeed pleaded, "We must avoid the mistakes that led to the destruction of that institution. We cannot go before our people with any new enterprise, the success of which is not completely assured from the outset. If you can do what we suggest, we believe it will be assured. We can build in Morgan Park a great institution that will be the glory of the place, in which our denomination will feel a universal interest, and that will attract scores of families to the neighborhood and hundreds of students to its halls."[139] Walker balked at Goodspeed's request, and subsequent negotiations resulted in a more modest proposition; namely, the company agreed to give the Baptists twenty acres of land in Morgan Park, an existing building currently occupied by an academy for girls, and $5,000 to help pay for a new building, on the condition that they raise $100,000 in operating costs within one year and commit to build the new building for no less than $20,000. This offer was finalized in late November 1886.[140]

Now Goodspeed and his colleagues simply needed to find a donor with $100,000. For Goodspeed the answer lay in the East, in the person of John D. Rockefeller. Rockefeller was the wealthiest Baptist in the United States and a loyal member of the denomination. Over the course of his life, he gave many millions of dollars to sundry charities and religious institutions.[141] Goodspeed had corresponded with Rockefeller since the early 1880s when Goodspeed had first asked for money for the Morgan Park Seminary. Rockefeller trusted Goodspeed, and he gave the seminary small, intermittent but generous gifts, in four- and five-figure amounts, most recently a pledge of $20,000 in October 1885.[142] Their mutual confidence was crucial to the events of the next four years, for Rockefeller was exceptionally careful in his judgment of potential gift beneficiaries.[143] Rockefeller often deferred a decision until he was persuaded of the virtue and the reliability of the recipient. Rockefeller's equivocations were always offered in the most cordial and polite terms, and this quality of tactical inscrutability—the result of what Frederick Gates later called "the extraordinary alertness of his mind and his skill in balanced phrasing"— sometimes led eager petitioners to misread Rockefeller's intentions.[144]

Goodspeed patiently pursued Rockefeller throughout 1887, and by October Goodspeed wrote with growing urgency and impatience, reporting that one way or another his "brethren" intended to revive the University: "There is a general and profound interest being manifested and a harmony of views that surprises and cheers me. We shall go slow and launch no new enterprise prematurely.... If we had $50,000 we could speedily add $50,000 to it and thus make a good and safe beginning, for there is a living interest in the matter among all our people. The trouble is they are discouraged over the former disasters and afraid to begin."[145] Over this time, Goodspeed had realized that the disastrous image of the old University, which he himself called an "unmixed calamity," hung over his project like a curse.[146] He reported despondently to Harper in October 1888, "Our ablest men ... look with distrust on the launching of a feeble and struggling enterprise and are not disposed to go into it."[147] As another Baptist minister, Poindexter S. Henson, put it in describing the disorder of the Chicago Baptists in June 1888, "It has been next to impossible to rouse them to effort on account of the discouragement arising from past disaster and disgrace."[148]

Rockefeller may have respected Goodspeed, but he remained studiously noncommittal and left little doubt that he had no interest in pouring money into the same swamp twice.[149] Other Baptists with Chicago connections also appealed to him, but he remained unmoved. To George C. Lorimer, Rockefeller wrote in February 1888 that as to "the effort to establish a university in Chicago,... I am so heavily weighted with other undertakings I cannot give any encouragement in this direction."[150] He was more blunt to Henson a few months later, telling him that local self-help was the only relief on the horizon: "As you deem it so important, I assume you will persevere in other directions to secure necessary funds."[151]

While Goodspeed struggled with his local canvass among the much-chastened Chicago Baptists, another player joined the drama: Augustus H. Strong, the president of the Rochester Theological Seminary and the father-in-law of one of John D. Rockefeller's daughters. Strong was a patriarchal figure among nineteenth-century Baptist theologians, an influential and respected church leader whose lifework was his three-volume *Systematic Theology*. In Grant Wacker's estimation, Strong was in

1900 "one of the most visible churchmen in the United States."[152] Over the course of the 1880s Strong had formulated a grand and highly expensive plan to create a new research university in New York City, which he hoped Rockefeller would bankroll. Throughout 1887 and 1888 Strong inundated Rockefeller with appeals, urging his vision of a graduate theological faculty—to be expanded eventually to include arts and sciences graduate departments and professional schools of medicine and law—which would serve as the premier place of advanced education for Baptists in the United States. The price tag was steep, for Strong believed that such an institution would require at least $20 million in endowment. Strong wanted Rockefeller to launch the scheme with an immediate gift of $3 million in cash. Strong deliberately excluded undergraduate work from his model, arguing, "We need an institution which shall be truly a University, where, as at Johns Hopkins, there shall be a large number of fellowships, where research shall be endowed, where the brightest men shall be attracted and helped through their studies, where the institution shall furnish a real society of people distinguished in science and art."[153] Strong's plans owed much to his admiration of the imperial German universities. He claimed to Rockefeller that "the true Universities are found only in Europe," with the University of Berlin at the pinnacle of distinction.[154]

In the autumn of 1887 Augustus Strong persuaded William Rainey Harper to join his venture, inviting him to review and comment on Strong's plans and offering him a senior faculty position and the vice presidency.[155] Harper was flattered, and Strong immediately reported to Rockefeller that Harper "thinks it in the whole and in its several parts not only a practicable plan, but a plan the carrying out of which would transform our whole denomination in ten years, both in New York and in the country. He says he would give his whole life to such an enterprise if he could further it."[156] Strong assured Rockefeller that Harper "is willing to give up at New Haven and throw his whole soul into our new enterprise, if only it can be begun without delay."[157] A few days later, Strong claimed, "Professor Harper … jumps at the chance of carrying out my plan."[158] The surviving correspondence between the two men from late 1887 and early 1888 suggests that a robust collaboration and planning process did take place, with detailed discussions about budget arrangements and with Harper pushing for the creation of a "complete university" all at once.[159]

Rockefeller decided to consult with Harper in late October 1887 about the rival plans of Goodspeed and Strong, and predictably both men urged Harper to support their competing ventures.[160] Strong caustically dismissed the Chicago scheme as little more than a "great High School" next to a seminary that was "planted in the mud. The surroundings are forlorn. The place is still like the backwoods."[161] Harper seems to have enthusiastically lobbied for the Strong plan, which in early 1888 would become a point of intense controversy, for Strong soon came to feel that Harper had betrayed him.[162]

The year 1887 thus ended with two plans on Rockefeller's table. Strong had the more plausible and ambitious plan, but unlike Goodspeed he was brash and sought to take advantage of his familial relationship with Rockefeller, which Rockefeller roundly resented. In Strong's own words, "[Rockefeller] turned red, and he looked very angry."[163] Whether because of Strong's abrasive personality or because of his strident demands, Rockefeller felt little enthusiasm.[164] Yet Strong's contempt for the Chicago scheme also had its impact on Rockefeller. Nevertheless, Goodspeed's humble pleas soon gained a considerable tactical advantage when the National Educational Convention of Baptists in May 1888 voted to create the American Baptist Education Society to investigate options for strengthening higher education in the Midwest. The principal proponent of the society, Pastor Henry Morehouse of New York City, was a leader of the American Baptist Home Mission Society. Morehouse's plan met with hard-hitting opposition from eastern Baptist leaders (including, not surprisingly, Augustus Strong), who feared a shift in denominational resources westward.[165] Morehouse's motivations reflected both the embarrassment that Baptists across the United States felt about the collapse of the old University in Chicago and his own fervent view that a new institution of higher learning should be built in the West. A former member of the Board of Trustees of the Morgan Park Seminary in Chicago and of the board of Kalamazoo College in Michigan, Morehouse was closely familiar with the feuding personalities and financial dilemmas that had impeded the chances of effective higher education in the Midwest and Chicago. In a survey of the activity of Baptist missions between 1880 and 1886, Morehouse was particularly concerned with the fate of Christianity in the western states, and in near-apocalyptic terms he asked, "Who shall have that mighty West—Satan or the Lord Jesus Christ? What is our duty to these swarming millions of immigrants, among whom are communists, socialists, nihilists, anarchists, haters of government and of God?"[166] Morehouse defined the mission of his new society to "gather on a common platform, untainted by past bitterness, our leading educators from every section, whose hands and hearts shall be united in high endeavor, and whose faces shall glow with the dawning day of a brighter future." Morehouse certainly had Rockefeller in mind when he hoped that "it would not be surprising to hear almost any day that some broad-minded, large-hearted man among us had given a million or two for the upbuilding of a great institution or for the establishment of a dozen struggling institutions in the South and West."[167]

The Baptist leaders at the May 1888 meeting knew exactly what was at stake—namely, whether and where to build a single great Baptist institution of higher education.[168] Had Morehouse not created the American Baptist Education Society and then appointed Frederick Gates as its strategic leader, a new University of Chicago would never have been created. As much as Rockefeller respected Goodspeed and his ministerial colleagues, he felt profoundly uneasy about their amateurish pleas, especially since he was also being bombarded by rival petitioners asking for support for universities in New York City and Washington, DC. The new society quickly became a rational platform from which to organize and screen the many pleas for help that were ending up on Rockefeller's doorstep, for which Rockefeller was extremely grateful.

While Morehouse sought to give structure and direction to a new national strategy, self-help initiatives in Chicago continued to percolate. In early May 1888, the Chicago Baptists Pastors' Conference tried to reclaim the initiative by voting to proceed with a modified version of the offer that they had received in late 1886 from George Walker to donate land in Morgan Park for a university campus (Walker had agreed to extend the offer until November 1889). Led by Henson and Lorimer, the ministers polled 150 prominent Baptist laymen in Chicago about the feasibility of this plan, under which Walker offered "in substance (33) thirty-three acres of land, valued by them at $66,000, a building which cost $24,000, and $5,000 in cash toward another building—on condition that within one year a [second] building worth from $25,000 to $30,000 shall be erected and an endowment of $100,000 be secured." The ministers asked their lay colleagues if they should call a conference of the "principal brethren" to discuss the idea, inquiring further, "Are you willing to cooperate as far as in you lies, for the accomplishment of such a purpose?"[169] Unfortunately, most who responded were not wealthy, and the few who were gave openly negative responses. E. Nelson Blake refused to join the push, arguing, "I do not believe that the denomination is ready or able to properly carry on the two enterprises.... Let us have no more failures [to] shame us." John M. Van Asdel warned, "I would deprecate another University fiasco"; and given the difficulty of raising an endowment, he observed, "I would not be in favor of the institute starting off in a crippled condition."[170]

The only hope now lay with Morehouse. To launch the work of his new society Morehouse appointed a gifted young minister from Minnesota, Frederick Taylor Gates, as its secretary. So committed was Morehouse to Gates that he wrote in his private diary, "I fully decided that if he (Mr. Gates) did not accept, I would resign, giving at length my reason for doing so, and ... dedicate myself to this work rather than to have a halt or failure, even though it should reduce me to poverty."[171] Happily, Gates accepted the offer. Gates was a smart, quick-witted organizer who became the most forceful advocate of a strategic plan to broaden and deepen higher education among western Baptists. Gates favored the creation of a central university that would draw on a network of Baptist secondary schools and smaller colleges.[172] Trained at the University of Rochester and the Rochester Theological Seminary, Gates served for eight years as a pastor of the Central Baptist Church in Minneapolis, but resigned in March 1888 to work as a fund-raiser for the Pillsbury Academy, a Baptist secondary school in Owatonna, Minnesota, for which he was able to raise $50,000. He proved to be fearless and unflappable in the often-contentious world of Baptist denominational politics, and he was a shrewd and relentless fund-raiser.[173] He had a strong pragmatic streak and little patience with theological squabbling, which gave him the agility to outwit intractable personalities and dodge vexing issues. Gates was also a tough-minded rationalist with little patience for soft-hearted social causes.[174] He was to play a critical role in advocating Goodspeed's cause, but with some major modifications.

Gates played a particularly crucial role in organizing a lobbying network within the Baptist denomination, which gave Rockefeller the public cover and denominational legitimacy that he both needed and expected.[175] During the summer and early autumn of 1888, Gates conducted confidential meetings with Chicago Baptists to gauge their support for the Morgan Park option. He was stunned by the lack of solidity and knowledge he encountered: "There is not among the Chicago brethren that perfect freedom and outspoken frankness born of mutual love and confidence that I have been accustomed to see in our Minnesota counsels, and which we ought to expect among Baptist brethren. While brethren spoke freely, there was a certain lack of seriousness, a certain lightness of tone, on the part of most of the brethren that disappointed me." Gates deliberately exempted Goodspeed and Northrup, both of whom he admired for their energy and consistency, but he concluded that the others "did not exhibit that sort of feeling out of which great things are carried to successful issue amid difficulty. Besides this, I felt constantly that there was a lack of perfect frankness.... The men of means among Baptists in and around Chicago are little interested in the question at best, and besides are exceedingly distrustful of any attempt to found a college. Some of them say that if it could start with a million or so they would give large sums, but to start with no more than is involved in the Morgan Park proposition does not appeal to their pride, and does not furnish them with the security they demand."[176] Gates also began to negotiate with the local Baptists for the new society to take over the sponsorship of their university project and quietly imagined a national communications strategy that would be "a lifting of the veil from many eyes."[177]

The timid reaction of the Chicago lay community had not dissuaded the irrepressible pastors in early July from officially endorsing Walker's offer, but they also agreed to invite Gates and the society to take over the planning and fund-raising process for the new institution in Morgan Park.[178] Gates agreed to do so, arguing, "We should take hold of it, provided we can, by a quiet and underground canvass, assure ourselves of success before we become publicly involved in it. ... The case is the biggest and resistless in appeal and furnishing a wider constituency than anything in sight or that has been in sight for many years in our denomination." But Gates made it clear that he was dissatisfied with the rhetorical arguments and political savvy of the pastors: "I have never yet heard the case stated for a tithe [tenth] of what in my opinion there is in it. ... These brethren have never had the leisure or the data for studying the question on its merits. It has been chiefly a matter of denominational and local pride. ... Their failure with Rockefeller and others, and among them some of the wealthiest brethren in Chicago, does not necessarily close the case. Still we ought to be exceedingly cautious. To succeed is to open a path for measureless good, but to fail is to close that path completely for our generation at least."[179]

During these months Gates launched a survey of all Baptist institutions of higher learning in the Midwest and on the Great Plains, trying to gauge what they were doing compared to other denominations. In the context of this survey, Gates informed Morehouse in late June 1888, "My present opinion is that there is a greater case, better prospects, more need, and, for the Society better outcome here [in Chicago] than anywhere else. If we can take hold of the matter, raise half a million, ... and set an institution on its feet, we shall have done more for education and made the Society a more powerful machine than in any other way." Gates also cautioned, "We can not afford now to make any false moves, and can touch nothing that has not substance in it and sure success. We must have a big case, an overwhelming case."[180] But Gates soon came to the conclusion that relaunching the University in Morgan Park would be a huge mistake: it was too isolated from the city; it was surrounded by unattractive settlements; students who needed part-time work to pay their tuition would be unable to obtain employment; if the new University decided to have professional schools they would have to be located in Chicago in any event; and, finally, the city gave the Baptists access to potential wealthy donors.

On October 15, 1888, Gates presented a detailed report about the need for higher educational resources in the West to a conference of ministers in Chicago. This report constituted a vital step in mobilizing public opinion in order to persuade Rockefeller that the denomination as a whole—and not merely a small band of poor, if sincere, true believers led by Goodspeed—wanted a university in Chicago. Gates argued that national demographic trends favored Baptists in the Midwest and West against those living in the East, and that these growing numbers of faithful needed an infusion of new academic resources, for the current state of Baptist educational institutions was one of "destitution," marked by poorly endowed colleges often located in "small obscure towns." Gates then made an even greater claim: what was needed was a systematic, national approach in which Baptist academies would feed Baptist colleges, which in turn would draw encouragement and support from a larger Baptist university: "Such an institution would immediately give stimulus and inspiration to all our preparatory schools, and we have no schools that are not chiefly such. Before its walls were reared, before its foundations could be laid, the mere assurance of such an enterprise made certain by means provided would lift up the heads of our colleges and clothe them with renewed vigor and larger influence." Gates was certain that the only logical place for such a central Baptist university was Chicago, the "centre and heart" of the West. For Gates, only large cities had wealth, and the Baptists needed to unlock that wealth. He insisted:

> [Chicago] is the most commanding social, financial, literary, and religious eminence in the west. It will lift so far aloft a Baptist college as an intellectual and religious luminary, that its light would illumine every state and penetrate every home from Lake Erie to the Rocky Mountains. The Old University in '82–83 when moribund and ready to drop into its grave attracted students from sixteen states. Chicago is the heart of the west, the foundation of western life.... Chicago is quickly and cheaply accessible from every part of the west. All roads lead to Chicago, all cities, all rural homes face Chicago. Already the chief seat of western learning, the educational supremacy of Chicago is becoming every year more marked.

Thousands of young Baptists would come to Chicago who would otherwise be lost to the denomination. What would attract them would be a major institution of learning with an "endowment of several millions, with buildings, library, and other appliances equal to any on the continent, an institution commanding the services of the ablest specialists in every department, giving the highest classical as well scientific culture and aiming to counteract the western tendency to a merely superficial and utilitarian education, an institution wholly under the Baptist control as a chartered right, loyal to Christ and his church, employing none but Christians in any department of instruction, a school not only evangelical but evangelistic, seeking to bring every student into surrender to Jesus Christ as Lord."[181]

Gates described his ultimate goal as "a complete educational system … graduated from the home upward, symmetrical in its extension and broad enough to cover the whole land, the parts being related logically if not indeed organically to the whole."[182] Western Baptists would be encouraged to convert many struggling colleges into academies, and move their regional colleges to larger cities. At the center of this system would stand a "great and overshadowing" college "planted in Chicago."[183] Leaving aside the narrow denominational impulse, which Gates was soon forced to modify to elicit financial participation by Chicago business elites, his bold systematic planning laid a sturdy foundation for Harper's later vision of a new University of Chicago.

Gates reported to Henry Morehouse that he received a wildly enthusiastic reaction from the Chicago ministers: "The room was full with several standing. To say that such a paper or rather the facts presented produced a sensation would be mild language. The Brethren were 'all torn up' over it. They were astonished, astounded, confounded, dumfounded, amazed, bewildered, overwhelmed." The ministers were particularly startled by Gates's "terrible truths" pertaining to the weakness of existing Baptist colleges: "The truth has never before been told, but I told it for once without reproach of course and mingled with praise for the heroism and self abnegation of our western educators. I am greatly encouraged, believing that a great victory has been won in Chicago from which we shall reap substantial and lasting fruits."[184] In formulating his intrepid plan Gates came to a second critical decision: the new institution had to be located in or near the central business district of Chicago and had to be completely divorced from any emotional or structural connections with the old University. He wrote to Morehouse several days later, arguing that a city location would attract far more capital for the University than one in Morgan Park—"We can get ultimately hundreds of thousands of dollars from moneyed men [who are] not Baptists for the ONLY institution in the city where we would get tens of thousands with the location at Morgan Park, a suburb seldom or never visited by wealthy men"—and confiding that a copy of his report had been given privately to Rockefeller's education adviser.[185] Morehouse concurred: "I fully believe that he [Rockefeller] will yet see that the establishment of a strong institution at Chicago will do more for the denomination in the west than possibly could be done by the establishment of a great university leaving the west unprovided for…. The institution must be located in the city. Scores of students living at home will attend such an institution, who would not attend it if located at Morgan Park."[186]

Thomas Goodspeed was present at the October 15 meeting and immediately asked Gates for a copy of his report, adding, "I do not wish to steal your thunder for any public use whatever, but ... the paper stirred my heart. I want it to stir another's heart."[187] Goodspeed sent it on to Harper, noting that what made Gates's report "extraordinarily impressive" was that it was "not the view of a Chicago man, or of a man who has any interest in Chicago, but in the first place, of a stranger to this city and in the second place, of the Secretary of the American Baptist Education Society," who reached his conclusions "after profound study of the entire educational situation."[188]

The executive board of the American Baptist Education Society adopted Frederick Gates's plan on December 4, 1888, which effectively killed off the Morgan Park option. The next six months were filled with anxious skirmishing, weaving, and counterweaving, as Goodspeed and Gates sought to persuade Rockefeller to commit himself. In the meantime, Harper was waiting patiently in New Haven. Perhaps because he sensed that Augustus Strong had alienated Rockefeller, Harper quietly abandoned his efforts on behalf of Strong's plan during the summer of 1888; he instead became a strong advocate of the idea of a new university in Chicago, but on a more ambitious scale.[189] He secured interviews with Rockefeller in October and November 1888 at which he carefully rehearsed the arguments that Goodspeed had formulated, but expanded the vision to include the establishment of a research university and not merely a college.[190] Harper's interviews gave him hope that Rockefeller might be persuaded to act, and he relayed his optimism in confidence to Gates in mid-November 1888: "Quite a movement has been made toward the university in Chicago by Mr. Rockefeller.... He is coming to see the necessity of the thing and will be ready within a short time to make a definite proposition to the denomination as a whole."[191] Harper also secured a personal interview for Goodspeed with Rockefeller in early November, and the combination of Gates's vision and Harper's enthusiasm led Goodspeed to vastly expand his goal. Goodspeed now proposed that Rockefeller give $1.5 million to create a real university, and that he further agree to give an additional $200,000 for every $100,000 that could be raised locally, up to a total of $4 million within ten years. Goodspeed dreamed of a university of "the first order" and the enlistment of the denomination "on a large scale."[192]

These developments led Augustus Strong to write a blistering denunciation to Harper in November 1888. Strong insisted that the Chicago scheme would lead to a "mongrel institution ... which is neither fish nor fowl," combining undergraduate and graduate work that would be bound to fail.[193] Late in his life, Strong accused Harper of stealing his plans for a new research university: "Harper … promised to cooperate with me in the effort to induce Mr. Rockefeller to found a university in New York City.… Here I must accuse Dr. Harper of unfaithlessness to his agreement. He no longer cooperated with me, but, without giving me notice and without explaining his action, he threw his influence with Mr. Rockefeller in favor of the Chicago project.… After all I had done for fifteen years, my New York University was gobbled up and transferred to Chicago."[194]

In the face of Strong's démarche to Harper, Goodspeed backtracked and urged Harper to put as much rhetorical distance as they could between Strong's $20 million university project and their plans for Chicago by dialing their rhetoric back down toward a four-year college. Goodspeed urged Harper to "disarm" Strong by stressing that the institution in Chicago would only gradually grow into a full university.[195] A week later he wrote to Harper, "We want a first-class College with certain graduate departments, a western Yale. A University in the American sense, but not according to Strong's understanding of the word." Innocently, Goodspeed then confessed, "To tell him [Strong] that the University he has in mind is to be transferred to Chicago would be to deceive him and gratuitously engage him in active hostility. I may myself be altogether deceived, but I do not understand that Mr. R. has it in mind to build here that New York University."[196]

Harper would have none of this. He responded aggressively to Goodspeed's cautions by indicating that he had no interest in mollifying Strong, and he challenged Goodspeed with the observation that "if the thing you are wanting in Chicago is only a college, I have been working upon a wrong track." If all they asked Rockefeller for were a college, "the result will be that a college is all that we shall get. This would be very sad, indeed, for it is not a college, but a university that is wanted. I can hardly think that anything but a straightforward, definite line of action will be successful."[197] Harper believed that Strong was "desperate. Gates will probably visit him and try to mollify him, but it is really impossible."[198] Harper was correct about Strong's state of mind. When the board of the American Baptist Education Society agreed in December 1888 to take over Goodspeed's campaign to create a new institution of higher education in Chicago, it pushed Strong over the edge into irrational behavior.[199] Strong now tried to stop the Chicago project by launching a direct, ad hominem attack on Harper's orthodoxy as a scholar of the Bible. In a letter to Rockefeller on Christmas Day 1888, Strong reported that his daughter had attended a series of Bible lectures given by Harper that suggested that Harper "has departed from the sound faith as to inspiration and prophecy, and is no longer to be trusted in his teachings."[200] Harper met with Rockefeller several days after Strong's letter, and found him "a little less ready now than before."[201] Harper frequently exaggerated or misread Rockefeller's willingness to accede to requests, and it seems improbable that Rockefeller was worried about Strong's accusations. Rockefeller was deeply concerned that whatever he did in Chicago have the strong backing of the denomination, though, and Strong's attack certainly had the potential to muddy the denominational waters.[202] Goodspeed mobilized prominent Baptists, notably George Northrup of the Morgan Park Seminary, to proclaim their enthusiastic confidence in Harper's theological respectability.[203] Gates worried less about Strong's allegations—they were the work of a "melancholy, a profoundly unhappy and disappointed man, I fear almost desperate"—and more about Harper's state of mind. To Morehouse he confided, "I hope the result of this latest attack will be to fix Rockefeller more firmly to Harper. But I fear its effects on Harper himself. He is timid and in doubt about his position with the denomination at large."[204] As rumors abounded, the negotiations stalled for the first three months of 1889, with Rockefeller still undecided. Harper feared more than once that Goodspeed and he might have overplayed their hand.

Finally, it was Gates the pragmatist who got things back on track with two key interventions. First, he bluntly told Morehouse and Harper that if they had any hope of getting funding from Rockefeller in the near future, the Chicago lobby would have to return to the idea of creating a "very high grade college" and drop the idea of a university, at least for the foreseeable future.[205] Gates later reflected that "Harper was too ambitious and exacting in his ideas. It was not until less ambitious counsels prevailed that Mr. R was again brought to the point of action."[206] Second, Gates proposed in late February 1889 to Rockefeller that he, Gates, create a high-level committee of distinguished Baptists to evaluate the necessity and plausibility of a college in Chicago.[207] Rockefeller quickly assented.[208] This nine-man group, to which Harper was appointed, met in mid-April and approved Gates's revised plan for a "well-equipped college, leaving any desirable further development to the natural growth of time," to be located "within the city limits of Chicago."[209] This report gave Rockefeller the public justification he needed to make a credible decision in favor of Chicago.[210] Gates's unflappability, together with Morehouse's political wiliness and Goodspeed's keenness for the central city, finally persuaded Rockefeller to support Gates's plan.

Frederick Gates visited Rockefeller at his home in New York City on the morning of May 15, 1889, to make his final plea. Gates later remembered in his autobiography:

It was agreed between us that the least possible sum for a mere start, that would give confidence of perpetuity, would be One Million Dollars. He confided to me that he thought he might give as much as Four Hundred Thousand Dollars.... Mr. Rockefeller's present proposal was entirely consistent with every word he had said up to that time. But I was obliged to reply with sincerity to Mr. Rockefeller that with Four Hundred Thousand Dollars we could not raise the balance of the Million. He then offered Five Hundred Thousand. I told him also regretfully that we could not possibly wing the other half. I then called his attention to the advantage of going before the denomination with *more than half already pledged*. Such a leverage we would be obliged to have. Such a gift would win. The denomination could not and would not let it fail. He would have to start the movement with nothing less than Six Hundred Thousand Dollars toward the Million. Otherwise the attempt would be hopeless. At last he yielded the point, promised the Six Hundred Thousand, and we went down to his office to write out the pledge.[211]

Accordingly, John D. Rockefeller offered an endowment gift of $600,000 to establish a college in Chicago, on the condition that the Chicago organizers obtain a matching fund of $400,000 to achieve a foundational gift of $1 million within one year. The decision reflected Rockefeller's deeply personal Christian piety, for, as Barry Karl and Stanley Katz have noted, Rockefeller saw his endowment of Chicago as an exercise in religious obligation, even if that dutifulness would in no way compromise the scientific progressiveness of the institution itself.[212]

Coming at the end of a long chain of contingent shifts, in which pressures, pleas, and hopes from the local Baptist community in Chicago melded together with Gates's and Morehouse's brilliant outsider strategies, the re-creation of the University in Chicago as a college was as much an indigenous and organic Chicago event as it was a national and regional event. Yet if Gates forced Goodspeed to give up Morgan Park, it would fall to Harper to compel Gates, as well as Goodspeed, Morehouse, and eventually Rockefeller, to accept a broader and less denominationally fixed understanding of the new University. Gates had secured Rockefeller's support, but only for a big college, and a Baptist college at that. In December 1888 Goodspeed was convinced that "the plan" that was shaping up did not involve "a great Baptist national university" but rather a "university for the West."[213] The only world of higher learning that Goodspeed understood was a universe of *teaching*—he was profoundly grateful for the excellent teaching that he had received as a student at the old University, and his focus on a collegiate education made perfect sense.[214] Gates, too, had insisted on a more modest agenda, largely because this could be sold to Rockefeller. To Rockefeller, Gates posed the query, "May not the question whether the institution contemplated in Chicago shall be a college or a university be held in abeyance for a few days [years?] without imperiling any valuable interest? Even if a university were more designed the college would naturally be the first work, and to thoroughly equip a college in the wisest way will almost of necessity be the exclusive work of the earlier years and would probably require all the funds we reasonably anticipate in that time."[215]

Two issues were in play—size and mission on the one hand, and cultural identity on the other. Goodspeed and Gates wanted a first-class Baptist college, but Harper had a radically dissimilar agenda: a nondenominational "university of the highest character, having also a college," equipped with an endowment that within ten years "will place it in the rank with the first six universities in the land."[216] The difference was notable, on the level of both resources and ideology, and the essential cultural character of the University was at stake. Harper's combination of patient diplomacy and gentle threats over the course of 1889 and 1890 gradually brought Gates and Goodspeed to understand that the only plausible guarantee for the success of a new "University of the West" in Chicago was for it to become a great national university.

The eventual settlement of June 18, 1890, designed by Goodspeed and Gates as a letter to the secretary of state of Illinois requesting the incorporation of the new institution, resolved the issue of cultural identity by providing that two-thirds of the board of trustees and the president of the university had to be Baptists, but that "no other test or particular religious profession shall ever be held as a requisite" for students, faculty, or any other aspect of the institution. Essentially, the University as Baptist and evangelical gave way to the University as Christian and agnostically religious. Gates later wrote that "the college ..., being of a purely literary and scientific character, is not designed to be sectarian."[217] The only tangible authority that the Baptists would have was of a general foundational nature, having nothing to do with instructional or research content; the University would function as a nondenominational institution.

The fundamental scope and mission of the new institution remained unresolved, however, and even though the logic of Gates's own rhetoric about the need of the Baptists to gain the support of the "moneyed men" meant that the new University would profit most from adopting a radically different self-understanding from that which Gates outlined to the ministers in October 1888, Gates was content to leave the structural conundrum in an indeterminate state while launching the fund-raising campaign to match Rockefeller's gift. Following Rockefeller's pledge, Goodspeed and Gates devoted the next twelve months to campaigning for $400,000. This canvass was surely one of the most remarkable fund-raising ventures ever undertaken in the history of American higher education. Together Goodspeed and Gates trooped the streets of Chicago in search of subscriptions, knocking on doors and "working together first rate without friction and best of all successfully."[218] Goodspeed was at first hopeful that the target could be met within a few months, but it soon became apparent that local Baptists had neither the capacity nor the enthusiasm to generate $400,000 from their own ranks. By February 1890 Gates was gloomily reporting to Henry Morehouse, "Dr. Goodspeed and I work very hard and sometimes get into the depression of overwork. With few exceptions we have spent the whole day of every day in Chicago and returning at night, we spend the evenings and often far into the night in correspondence. We walk many miles every day in the streets of the city. Our delays and difficulties are astonishing. We find not over 2/5ths of the men we seek to see when we call.... Man after man delays or evades in other ways our pressing appeals." Still, Gates was confident of ultimate success: "We shall push it through *somehow* and make a big rumpus."[219] This diligence led Gates to move beyond the local Baptists, a strategy made both urgent and difficult because of Protestant interdenominational rivalries. Gates reported to Harper:

> The fact is that the other denominations have waked up and passed the word around that we must not be encouraged. At least it begins to appear that way. Sectarian!! Sectarian!! Baptist!! Baptist!! That is the eternal cry in nearly every office and our utmost endeavors on the street and in the papers are powerless to arrest the note of alarm. I do privately believe that Lake Forest and Evanston are quaking, and that the whole Pres[byterian] and Meth[odist] denominations since the [Marshall] Field gift [of land in Hyde Park], have come to fear Baptist supremacy in this city and the west educationally, and have rallied their friends against us. The tremendous lever this institution will give the Baptists is now clearly seen and dreaded.[220]

Gates and Goodspeed worked especially hard to dispel the bogeyman of sectarianism, which meant decoupling themselves from the old University that the local Baptists had run into the ground. Gates reported candidly to Harper:

> We have been importuned by our largest givers and ablest men not to commit ourselves in any way to any part of the old affair. We have been obliged frequently to disconnect this movement bag and baggage from the old in order to get a respectful hearing. Only today Drs. Goodspeed and Lorimer [were] in conversation with C. L. Hutchinson, President of the Commercial Club (who promises our cause a hearing before the club

next month), [who] inquired anxiously if this had anything to do with the old institution in any way. Their assurance that it had *not* unlocked him and the Commercial Club.[221]

Slowly, Gates and Goodspeed built up trust among wealthy non-Baptists. Gates reported enthusiastically to Harper in November 1889, "Our largest hope is from the rich outside men.... We have secured the names of a hundred or more men and firms each worth from $500,000 up to many millions, whom we are going to see. With one or two exceptions *every one* of the big men has received us with marked courtesy and encouragement, several saying that this must not by any means be allowed to fail and promising not only to do their full share, but to work for us."[222] Charles Hutchinson's help was particularly critical, since it set off a dynamic chain reaction that led not only to more gifts but also to the involvement of Martin A. Ryerson and other key civic leaders in the cause. The spring of 1890 netted many successes, including a $35,000 subscription by local Jewish businessmen offered in April. All of these gifts affirmed that the new institution would avoid a narrow denominational identity.[223]

Finally, having exceeded the target by slightly more than $2,000, Gates was able to telegraph Rockefeller on May 23, 1890, that the $400,000 had been raised. Rockefeller accepted the pledges the next day, and the new University of Chicago was about to become a reality. Gates initiated the process by which the American Baptist Education Society transferred fiduciary control of the new institution and all of the assets assembled to a newly constituted board of trustees, consisting of twenty-one men, fourteen of whom were Baptists. This board held its first official meeting on July 9, 1890, to organize itself and elect officers. The University was then officially chartered as a not-for-profit corporation under state law on September 10, 1890.

The issue of the leadership of the new institution assumed the highest urgency in June 1890. William Rainey Harper had made no overt or covert commitment to serve as president, and in early 1889 Yale offered him a generous financial package—including a salary increase, time off with salary to travel in Europe, money to cover the debts generated by his publications, new facilities for his department, and a personal research assistant—in return for a commitment to remain in New Haven for an extended period of time.[224] Harper insisted to Rockefeller, "I have refused absolutely to consider the question of going myself to Chicago."[225] So consistent was this rhetoric that Gates and Goodspeed had for some months of 1889 tried to put together leadership strategies under which Harper would remain in New Haven for a number of years, one of which had Goodspeed serving as a kind of acting president.[226]

In early June 1890, Goodspeed and Gates formally appealed to Harper to acknowledge his interest in and willingness to accept the presidency.[227] The new board of trustees genuinely wanted Harper, and, equally important, they had no plausible alternative. This gave Harper a huge advantage in negotiations, which focused substantially on the issue of the scope and mission of the new institution. Harper's shrewdness and his genuinely conflicted motives converged to give him the upper hand. His opening bid was to ask why he should forgo being a full-time scholar at Yale. We have several commentaries on his frame of mind in these months. George S. Goodspeed of Yale recorded in late May 1890, "I found to my great surprise that he was quite favorably inclined to Chicago. Six months ago when we talked about it he was entirely opposed to the whole thing.... But some experiences which he has had in entering the academical faculty here and observing the working of things has seemed to entirely alter the state of his mind."[228] But when Frederick Gates saw him two months later, Harper seemed more uncertain than ever. Gates remarked, "I pity Dr. Harper. He seems in real and deep distress of mind.... The prestige of his position at Yale he values much, his associations there are inspiring as well as congenial, his life work he has regarded as Biblical Study, he is in love with his classes, they are large and eager, his evangelistic work there appeals to the highest motives."[229]

John D. Rockefeller wrote to Harper in early August 1890, urging him to accept the job: "I agree with the Board of Trustees of the Chicago University that you are the man for president and if you will take it I shall expect great results. I cannot conceive of a position where you can do the world more good; and I confidently expect that we will add funds, from time to time, to those already pledged, to place it upon the most favored basis financially."[230] Harper was touched by this assurance, but found Rockefeller's vague formulation about future support unacceptable.[231] In response, Harper made it clear that he would not leave a university for a liberal arts college: "The denomination and indeed the whole country are expecting the University of Chicago to be from the very beginning an institution of the highest rank and character.... It seems a great pity to wait for growth when we might be born full-fledged."[232]

More resources would have to be added to expand the new institution into something that more closely resembled the ambitions that Augustus Strong had put in play, a vision that Harper had found compelling. Earlier in 1889 Thomas Goodspeed had complained, "We should have no use for a purely post-graduate and professional University for many years to come." Yet, when Harper showed Strong his plan for the new University in late 1890, Strong responded, "To carry it out fully would require no less money than I wished for a University in the City of New York."[233]

Finally, Gates met with Harper in Morgan Park in mid-August 1890 for a long negotiating session. Gates essentially acted as an agent of Rockefeller, exploring the terms that Harper would accept. Gates's subsequent account from 1915 is lucid and revealing:

> Dr. Harper … was in a tender, fruitful mood, making a momentous life decision. The fundamental question was how could he become President of a university in Chicago and at the same time not practically renounce his chosen life work of Old Testament research, criticism, and instruction. Gradually, the following plan unfolded itself. 1. The Theo. Seminary to be removed to the campus of the University. 2. The Seminary to become an organic part of the University (it subsequently became contractual only). 3. The present Seminary buildings at Morgan Park to be used for a University academy. 4. Equivalent or better buildings for the Seminary to be erected on University [of Chicago] campus. 5. Instruction in Hebrew and Old Testament criticism to be transferred to University chairs. 6. Dr. Harper to be head Professor with salary and full authority over department. 7. Mr. Rockefeller to give $1,000,000 as a new unconditional gift, a part of which would go for aid to the Seminary in carrying out the programme. 8. Dr. Harper to visit Mr. Rockefeller and to agree to accept the Presidency on this programme.[234]

Harper insisted that the University must aspire to professional and graduate education. As Karl and Katz observed some years ago, Rockefeller viewed himself as a manager of men, not money, and he put great stock in managers whose character and professional expertise he could trust.[235] Because Harper's leadership of the new institution was critical for Rockefeller, Harper held the trump card.

The seminary had done well in Morgan Park, but its leaders realized that if the school were to continue to grow and flourish it should affiliate with the larger and more financially advantaged educational institution that Gates had created in the city with Rockefeller's largesse. Hence, Gates, Harper, and seminary president George Northrup skillfully merged the new college and the graduate seminary in order to persuade Rockefeller of the logic of a full research university. (Over Harper's objections, the Baptist Theological Union would continue to have a role in the management of the new Divinity School.)[236] The seminary thus became the tactical fulcrum for the founding of the larger graduate school. Harper gambled that the deeply pious Rockefeller would be sympathetic to a first-class graduate school of religious practice and studies. By framing the transfer of the seminary to the new University as the first step in creating graduate programs in theology, biblical studies, and other disciplines in the arts and sciences in his negotiations with Gates, Harper had opened a politically feasible and religiously compelling way for Rockefeller to give the University another $1 million to endow graduate and professional instruction.

Gates reported Harper's proposals to Rockefeller on August 25. Conferring with Harper on September 5 in Cleveland, Rockefeller agreed to Harper's terms (but not until after he had spent the better part of a day trying to get Harper to agree to payment via installments), including the additional $1 million, $200,000 of which was to be devoted to the new Divinity School.[237] As Harper informed Henry Morehouse, "Mr. Rockefeller has just given his pledge for a million dollars to the new university without any condition; it being understood, however, that the seminary at Morgan Park shall be united organically with the institution and moved to the city and that the million dollars shall be used for post-graduate instruction. The next step is the securing of a million dollars in Chicago for building. I think this can be done without much trouble. Keep the matter close. It is not yet time for the announcement."[238]

At its first official meeting on September 18, 1890, the board of trustees officially offered William Rainey Harper the presidency, giving him six months to accept. Harper used those months to articulate his plan of organization for the University, acting publicly as if he had already accepted the offer. Yet, he held off issuing a final acceptance; and in early 1891 he stunned Gates and Goodspeed by hesitating once more over the issue of his relationship with the conservative Baptists. Harper wrote to Rockefeller that the issue remained a deeply troubling one. Letters of congratulations like the one in which John Broadus insisted, "I hope you will see fit to prefer in all cases men who incline to conservative views about biblical inquiries and about the relations between Christianity and critical science.... I trust also that the theological seminary connected with the University will always be distinctly and decidedly Baptist," must have given Harper pause.[239] Uneasiness among conservative eastern Baptist leaders like Edward Bright about Harper's plans remained acute.[240] Augustus Strong's bitter personal animosity continued to trouble Harper, and he reminded Rockefeller that his views of the Bible "differ considerably" from those of Strong and other leaders of the denomination. Harper confessed to Rockefeller:

> When in Morgan Park Christmas week, I had three hours conversation with Dr. Northrup.... I indicated to him my opinions, my thorough belief in their correctness, and my conviction that it was my duty to promulgate these opinions. I also indicated to him my fear that the promulgation of such opinions, though absolutely true, would bring down upon my head and upon the University the indignation of some of the Baptist denom-

inational papers. I further indicated to him my reluctance to accept a position in which I should feel that my mouth was closed. I cannot but believe from the results connected with my teaching of the Bible, that it is the will of God that I should teach it in the way in which I have been teaching it. I cannot, therefore, consent to accept a position in which that privilege will be denied me. On the other hand, I do not wish to enter into the position and thereby bring upon the institution the distrust of the denomination. The views which I hold can be taught here at Yale not only without condemnation but with constant and hearty encouragement on the part of the President and the theological faculty.

It has been suggested to me that, under all these circumstances, I ought carefully to lay before you and any friends whom you would like to have consider it the exact situation, before any further steps are taken.[241]

This episode might be discounted simply as yet another sign of Harper's scrupulosity. Gates thought so, suggesting that the letter was the result of Harper's "morbid brooding on his heresies real or supposed" and of Harper being "overworked, worn out, and physically sensitive and weak in proportion." Gates was both shocked and outraged, not in the least because he was convinced that Harper handled his modernist theological positions diplomatically: "Having heard Harper and knowing his worst I must say that as for me I am rather pleased than otherwise with his teaching. I should not be surprised if God knows that Harper is right and useful and tradition both erroneous and harmful. He created a fine impression here on professors students and preachers, as being a needed mediator between the Higher Criticism and Orthodoxy."[242] Goodspeed was also frightened by Harper's maneuver, insisting that "the points in which you differ from others are not worth a theological war" and that the only result of Harper's belligerence would be that "the world will stand around and say 'See these Baptists fighting again over the University.'"[243]

But Harper feared that he had not heard the last of Strong's venomous attacks, and his failure to eliminate the Baptist Theological Union from governance of the Divinity School had given hostages to an uncertain future in which conservatives might try to blackmail the University (which in fact was precisely what happened in 1904 in the case of George Burman Foster). It is also possible that Harper had in mind the growing controversy surrounding the publications and speeches of the liberal theologian Charles A. Briggs that was being fought out among American Presbyterians, a battle that reached its first climax in 1891. Harper had published several articles by Briggs in his journals, and as a liberal biblical scholar and an ex-Presbyterian who knew the folkways of his former denomination, Harper would certainly have been sensitive to Briggs's predicament.

As Mark Massa has recently noted, Harper was among the "brightest lights in the liberal firmament" who rushed to congratulate Briggs when the New York Presbytery dismissed charges of heresy brought against him in early November 1891.[244]

Harper was saying that if he accepted the new position, he could not allow the constraints of the presidency to suppress or distort his own scholarly ideals and values. After he took the presidency, the burdens of the office naturally forced him into a more guarded mode. But the re-statement of the basic principle itself was important, and Harper was transparent about what was at stake. He wrote to Henry Morehouse, "My conscience, however, is free. I have told 'the whole truth and nothing but the truth'. I am ready to go to Chicago; in fact my resignation is now in the hands of Pres. Dwight and at such time as it may seem best I shall place my acceptance in the hands of the Chicago Board. I do so, however, with the understanding that the platform is broad and free; that everybody has known beforehand my position and my situation, and that I am free do in the way of teaching what, under all circumstances, seems to me wise."[245]

Rockefeller refused to take the bait. Henry Morehouse was authorized to respond to Harper that

> Mr. Rockefeller has neither the time nor the inclination to decide mooted theological questions and to assume the responsibility of saying what you teach.... It certainly would be unwise, after all that has been done, after all the expectations that have been raised, after the great momen-tum that has been obtained, to plunge the enterprise into confusion, to arrest progress, to destroy the bright hopes of the hour, by declining to give in your formal acceptance.... The wisdom of introducing new complications at this critical stage in the enterprise will be questioned by your best friends.[246]

This was checkmate. Morehouse essentially told Harper that, having led the board of trustees, John D. Rockefeller, and the Baptist denom-ination as a whole for six months to believe that he would accept the presidency, he had no wiggle room left. Having put a stake in the ground in defense of his own academic freedom, Harper notified the board on February 16, 1891, that he accepted the presidency of the new University of Chicago, effective July 1, 1891. Harper later reflected on how difficult the decision had proven for him: "There are many hours during which I look back to the days at New Haven, and sometimes I wonder whether I ought not to have remained. But in general I suppose that I did the right thing, and although it was done with much sacrifice, nevertheless I feel that it was duty."[247]

Memories of the Old University

The fanfare with which the new University was launched by William Rainey Harper, always a preeminent showman with a "magnetic personality," obscured significant institutional continuities between the old and new.[248] Several of the largest early gifts to the new University came from donors who were either associated with the old University or acting on behalf of those who did have durable ties. The gift of $1,000,000 to build several modern biological research laboratories largely came about because Helen Culver wished to honor the desire of her deceased cousin Charles J. Hull, who had been a trustee of the first University and whose son had attended the school, to make an estate gift to Chicago. When Culver announced her gift in 1895, George Walker congratulated her, "It is with peculiar satisfaction that I learned of your very generous gift to the University of Chicago. It brought up many recollections of former days, when my father was a Trustee of the old University, and in close touch with Mr. Hull on the Board; also later when I was elected to the same position.... You could not have done a wiser thing for his memory, and we honor you for the act."[249] And the executors of the estate of William Ogden provided a donation of over $560,000—basically the major gift that Ogden had refused to give to the old University because of his disgust with feuding on the old board of trustees.[250] Gifts from the Rosenberger and Culver estates also came from alumni of the first University who wished to bestow confidence on the second; and the gift by George Walker of $100,000 in 1892 came from a trustee of the old institution, now translated into the same role for the new. The first endowed professorship created at the new University was funded by contributions from alumni of the old, in honor of Edward Olson, an alumnus and former professor of Greek at Chicago. Finally, the peculiar strain of intellectual seriousness and dedication to liberal culture that defined the student *and* faculty ethos of the old University was a fitting prologue to the values with which the founders endowed the new University. An alumnus of the old institution like Professor Charles R. Henderson, whose commitment to social reform had the goal (as Andrew Abbott has argued) of "creating a world in which spiritual interests ultimately predominate," drew on notions of moral character development as a godly necessity and godly warrant from his earlier training and made them key assumptions for the mission of new University.[251] Hence, when Henderson described the alumni of the old University in 1907, he insisted that the "men who have gone out from it have had impulses to do the work of men and to make the world better than they found it. They have brought into the world of business, commerce, and law high and noble impulses."[252]

Five of the original twenty-one trustees of the new University had
served as trustees of the old University: E. Nelson Blake, Francis E.
Hinckley, Henry R. Rust, Charles W. Needham, and George C. Walker.
Other trustees, like Ferdinand W. Peck, Eli B. Felsenthal, and Frederick A.
Smith, were alumni of the old University. Still others had been supporters
of the first University, like Alonzo K. Parker, who was the pastor of the
Centennial Baptist Church, or active members of the Baptist community
in Chicago who had regularly interacted with the leaders of the University,
like Edward Goodman, the owner of the *Standard* who had also served
as the treasurer of the Morgan Park Seminary. All told, almost half of the
new board of trustees had some significant personal connection to the old
enterprise. Several of the leading donors to the new University, including
Silas Cobb and Sidney Kent, had had philanthropic conversations with
former president Galusha Anderson, and it is perhaps with some justice
that Anderson's son later claimed that his father had helped to pave the
way for Harper's successes in obtaining major gifts.[253]

The old University gave its successor institution both its name and its
people. In order to enable the new institution to use the name "The University of Chicago," the trustees of the old University met at the Grand
Pacific Hotel in Chicago on June 14, 1890, to acknowledge that their corporation "for want of financial aid has discontinued the work of maintaining a university" and that "it is requested by alumni of the old university
that the new institution shall bear the same name as the old." They then
voted to give permission "to the new corporation about to be organized as
aforesaid to take and use the name 'The University of Chicago.'" In February 1891 the board of the new University subsequently agreed to recognize
the alumni of the old university as alumni of the new, confirming and
reenacting the BA and BS degrees of the old institution as part of the new.
Thus did the new University gain, from an alumni relations perspective, a
plausible genealogy as a pre–Civil War institution.

But in spite of all such nominal (and sympathetic) efforts to make connections, a powerful ambivalence about the links between the old and
new remained, as revealed by the choice of a new campus. Ever the outspoken partisan of the old University William Everts urged the revival of
the site of Thirty-Fourth Street, issuing a public statement on October 15,
1889: "Would not the rehabilitation [of the Thirty-Fourth Street site] wipe
away the reproach of failure in a great public trust, and turn a painfully
conspicuous memorial of disaster into a glorious arch of triumph? May
we not best restore our credit where we lost it, and recover and wave
in triumph our banner over the field from which we were disgracefully
driven?"[254]

According to Henry C. Mabie, an alumnus of the old University and a local alumni leader, most of his fellow alumni agreed with Everts. Mabie was "much inclined to think the very reasons—petty in my judgment— which some Chicago men urge for abandoning the old site, form just the reason why all traces of former dishonor should now be wiped out, and chiefly by Chicago people."[255] Gates and Morehouse, in contrast, were profoundly noncommittal about the issue, which they rightly suspected of carrying immense emotional baggage, and they resented Everts's meddling in the affair.[256]

Morehouse thought they should try to avoid the question of the site as long as possible, until the fund-raising campaign was successfully concluded.[257] Similarly, Harper refused to be drawn out prematurely. Harper had no sympathy for Everts's plan, but he urged Gates to placate him by appointing a commission to study the dispute, which Harper deemed to be extremely divisive. The American Baptist Education Society would not have to follow the commission's report, but, Harper noted, "unless something like this is done, there will undoubtedly be estrangement on the part of a large number. Can it not be worked quietly, and carefully and harmoniously?"[258]

Gates was relieved when the Union Mutual Life Insurance Company overplayed its hand and demanded too much money for the old site, perhaps seeking to (finally) make a profit on their bad loans to the fallen school. With considerable delight Gates informed Harper in November 1889, "The insurance people ... will not take a cent less than $400,000 and agree with us and everybody else that this is beyond our means.... The old site is so completely out of the question that no one thinks for a moment of our buying it. So that question may be regarded as finally disposed of. Everything is bright, and barring our personal embarrassment for lack of funds, we are perfectly happy and confident."[259]

In early December 1889, Goodspeed and Gates approached the Chicago department store magnate Marshall Field; and after much back-and-forth they secured in mid-January 1890 a commitment for ten acres of land in the village of Hyde Park, which had just been incorporated into the city.[260] Field also gave the society the option to buy an additional ten acres at a discounted price of $132,500. The chance to secure property from a prominent Chicago business leader that was worth over $200,000 and that would greatly impress Rockefeller, and to gain a large piece of property in a more attractive, upper-class residential area of the city, was alluring. Gates alerted Morehouse in early January that "the Field site, if we get say 15 or 20 acres, would be a better one in some respects than the old one."[261] Two weeks later Gates happily informed Morehouse that the gift had been secured and that the University now had a perfect new site with which to work:

Mr. Field's gift ... is located twenty-one blocks south and four blocks east of [the] old site. The land is sufficiently elevated and drained—an important item here [—] is one block from the Cottage Grove Ave. Grip line running down this Ave and Wabash to the heart of the city, the loop turning on Lake Street. From the river dividing the north and south sides it is a 45-minutes ride in "Grip" to the site. The Ill. Cent. line with its city and suburban trains runs about 8 or 10 minutes walk from campus.... The territory of the south side and especially that for several miles in every direction from the site is residence property and forms the location of the higher middle and aristocratic classes. No manufacturing will ever be possible in the neighborhood. The land lies about 1200 feet East of Washington Park and about 2000 feet west of Jackson Park. These are the two great parks of the South Side. And are being developed with vast expense into great beauty. Each contains several hundred acres. The "Plaisance" which connects these two parks with a waterway Boulevard and pleasure grounds runs two blocks south of the site.[262]

Writing in the *Standard*, Justin A. Smith applauded Field's gift and predicted that the new site "is almost ideally perfect.... The locality for some miles in every direction forms the best residence portion of this city, while the immediate vicinity of the campus is not now so thickly peopled as to prevent the institution from surrounding itself with its own peculiar and stimulative social and intellectual atmosphere."[263]

Marshall Field's gift of land in Hyde Park, a Shangri-La of the "higher middle and aristocratic classes," was not only crucial in enabling Gates and Goodspeed to put five miles of city streets between themselves and the institutional memories cherished by Baptist pastors like William Everts, but also signified the galvanizing effect that the larger-than-life gift from the eastern Baptist had on the wealthy elites of Chicago. When Field wrote to Gates confirming his gift, he deliberately connected Rockefeller to all of Chicago, not just to the Baptists, and he invoked the impact the new institution would have on the whole metropolis: "In common with all citizens of this city, I appreciate the splendid benefaction of Mr. Rockefeller to Chicago. I congratulate the people of this city and the entire West on the success achieved, and with all friends of culture I rejoice that another noble institution of higher learning is to be founded, and founded in the heart of the continent."[264] In making itself worthy in the eyes of men like Marshall Field, the new University had now connected to those sectors of "the neutral wealth of the city" that Nelson Blake so avidly admired.

The decision to locate the new University in Hyde Park meant that memories of the now-defunct institution would inevitably slip into the deep freeze of history. And so, too, has the very existence of the early University been elided out of the University of Chicago's standard narratives of what it is and whence it came.[265] Other disjunctions soon followed, pushed by the revolution in faculty identity and institutional purpose that was at the heart of Harper's plans. In ruthless contrast to the old University, Harper treated his faculty as agents of professional prestige, whose individual and collective attainments, sanctioned by the competitive and meritocratic standards of a new national scholarly community filled with learned journals, international conferences, and professional organizations, would define the very essence of what the University was. Harper believed in relentless competition based on merit, even if weaker souls found this discomforting. Research was salutary not only as a way of advancing new knowledge, but as a way of demonstrating the imagination, the creativity, and the professionalism of the new faculty, and of mobilizing and legitimating the expertise of the new University to improve and enrich the civic world of the metropolis. This image of research as a social and professional prophylactic matched well the rising confidence and prestige of the university-based professoriate in the United States that had coalesced since the 1880s as a new professional community with enhanced scholarly standards and rising levels of compensation, and protected by the growing power and authority of the academic disciplines.[266] Harper well understood that he had the rare chance to launch his project at a time when a new national system of higher education in the United States was being born, which explains his frenzy in spending huge sums of money, even money that he did not have, as quickly as possible to push his schemes forward.

Harper also draped his new institution in a more capacious understanding of its responsibilities to the central city. Erudition and social improvement would combine to enhance the impact of science but also to elevate the quality of Chicago's public culture well beyond the local Baptist community. Hence Harper's frenzied efforts to take the University everywhere via an extension division—not only would Harper's University be public in a radically new way, but it would create its own grateful publics in the wider city and the region. Hence also Harper's conviction that the new University was not the closed keeper of a denominational creed, but instead an open defender of democracy and liberal values in its capacity to touch "life, every phase of life, at every point. It enters into every field of thought to which the human mind addresses itself. It has no fixed abode far away from man; for it goes to those who cannot come to it. It is shut in behind no lofty battlement, for it has no enemy which it would ward off. Strangely enough, it vanquishes its enemies by inviting them into close association with itself. The university is of the people, and for the people, whether considered individually or collectively."[267]

Tendencies to make the early institution disappear by declaring its historical irrelevance were evident in Frederick Gates's own later appreciations and reflections. Thinking about how the second University was born and came to flourish, Gates minimized the role of the Baptists in a letter to Thomas Goodspeed in 1914: "The marvelous development into a great university in rapidity unapproached in human annals—all that was, if dreamed by anyone, the stuff of dreams only. The denomination did not foresee it, least of all accomplish it. All the wondrous growth has resulted from the large views of its two great Presidents, the limitless contributions of its founder, the wisdom and fidelity of the Trustees, the generosity of citizens of Chicago, the needs of a vast field and a rapidly increasing student body."[268] In this reading, the University of Chicago simply appeared out of the ethereal air of Harper's genius. Similarly, when Thomas Goodspeed was completing his history of the first quarter century of the University and sent draft chapters to Gates for his comments and review, Gates reacted with little enthusiasm to Goodspeed's detailed chronicle of the early University and the seminary. Gates thought that the old University and the seminary taken together were a "sad and disheartening story, notwithstanding your praiseworthy and successful efforts to qualify, excuse, [and] wherever possible to commend and praise." Gates wrote with some impatience, "Your paper would carry more weight and, in my opinion, suffer no loss of dignity, if the bouquets which you throw to a good many of the old seminary teachers, etc., were reserved for a history of the seminary to be distributed among its alumni[.] Your kind heart, your grateful memory, have betrayed you, as it seems to me, into a work of supererogation here, quite manifest to all your readers, which detracts from the unity, cogency, and disinterestedness of your presentation."[269]

Goodspeed persisted, however, and rightly so, because he understood that the very narrative of failure embedded within the history of the first University made denominational leaders so determined in the later 1880s to reclaim their reputations and their honor. It is telling, moreover, that in 1890 a much younger Frederick Gates, fresh from the political battles that led to the revival of the University, had seen things very differently. In addressing the newly constituted board of trustees of the University on July 9, 1890, Gates emphasized with great eloquence the moral and cultural links between the old and new universities:

The Trustees of the University of Chicago founded in 1857 ... have unanimously and heartily bequeathed to you the name [of] the University of Chicago, and with the name they bequeath also their alumni. The new University of Chicago rises out of the ruins of the old. The new University of Chicago, with a new site, a new management, new and greatly multi-

plied resources, and free from all embarrassing complications, nevertheless bears the name of the old, is located in the same community, under
the same general denominational auspices, is supported by the same class
of public spirited citizens, will enter on the same educational work, and
will aim to realize the highest hopes of those who were disappointed in
the old. A generation hence the break in legal life will have lapsed from
the memory of men. In the congeries of interests, affections, aspirations,
[and] endeavors which do in fact form the real life of an institution of
learning, in these there has been no break. The alumni of the institution
in its older form are the true sons of the new, and as such we bespeak for
them such appropriate and early recognition as your thoughtful courtesy
may suggest.[270]

There was indeed no break, if one saw the University through a Burkean
spectrum of transgenerational partnerships. As a self-governing *civitas*
of free scholars and students, defined by an intense love of learning and
suffused by resolute intergenerational loyalties over time, each generation
of the University has profited from the good works of those who came
before, and each generation has also added something of its own to the
collective virtue and resources of the University. What began as a humble
and inchoate project for a frontier college in the 1850s evolved into a noble
and sustainable ideal, grounded in the firm support of social elites of Chicago who believed that higher education was both a public and social
good and an emblem of civic prestige. The moral urgency of Baptists like
Goodspeed and Morehouse, the intellectual imagination and daring of
Harper, the cunning and deep pragmatism of Gates, and the extraordinary generosity of Rockefeller and his fellow Chicago donors combined
to relaunch the university founded by John Burroughs and his colleagues.
Ironically, the one thing that Burroughs and Harper had in common was
their willingness to spend large sums of money that they did not have.
Harper had a plausible and patient benefactor, a distinguished faculty, and
an attractive educational plan, however, while Burroughs lacked all three.

Yet in creating a new University of Chicago, Harper also defended the
intrinsic value of teaching in ways that honored the humble but transformational instructional work that defined the old University and the
Morgan Park Seminary. After all, Harper too came from that world, even
though his institutional ambitions and intellectual aspirations carried him
beyond it. Albion Small later observed that one of Harper's most original
conceptions was the idea that teaching was yet another way of discovering
new knowledge.[271]

The story of the old University confirmed that universities and colleges
did have to pay attention to the wider world with which they sought to

coexist and that, for better or worse, they had to change as that world changed. An institution's ideals might be constant, but its people and their lived environments were ever changing, with different habits, tastes, and social meanings governing their lives. In their role as charities, universities had to acknowledge their debts to their civic environments. The rise, fall, and re-creation of the University of Chicago demonstrated the importance of philanthropy and of "fit" with the larger socioeconomic and urban environment. The first University of Chicago tried going it alone, without the support of major donors that Goodspeed and Gates so coveted, and the result was disaster. The story of the old University was one of hope and faith in the value of the liberal arts, but also one of frustration born of penury and shame born of defeat.

The early trustees of the first University aspired, as they stated in 1857, to a university "not as a thing for the moment, but for all time." They were too maladroit (and unlucky) to sustain such an institution, but the urgency felt by local Chicago Baptists in the 1880s to make good on their failed leadership of the first University led them to again take up that cause. In the end, the new University was born because the unfulfilled promise of the old University, with all its shortcomings, had raised a profound consciousness of the importance of a noteworthy institution of higher education in Chicago, dedicated not only to the authority of research but to the cultivation of professional expertise. Goodspeed, Northrup, Gates, and Morehouse wanted an institution that would connect, in Thomas Bender's words, "civic culture and academic life" in a synthesis that was both peculiarly Midwestern and anchored in the liberal Protestant religious culture of the early 1890s.[272] It is fair to say that the demise of the old gave birth to both the possibility and the necessity of the new.

* 2 *

William Rainey Harper and the Establishment of the New University, 1892–1906

The University is a complex enterprise. It is invisible insofar as it consists of the work of the intellect, whether in the scholarly pursuit of knowledge or in the experience of learning. It is also visible, composed of people and buildings, libraries and furniture. No one person can manage such an enterprise, and not even at its founding was the University simple enough for one person to direct it. But among the founders of the University of Chicago, William Rainey Harper stands out, both for his capacious vision and for his relentless engagement with all aspects of the University, visible and invisible. Harper was responsible for shaping the University's basic structure and culture, and his successes derived from a mixture of scholarly genius, civic courage, and obliviousness to risk. The range of his activities could not be duplicated now, given the dense managerial layers of today's universities. But Harper's principled leadership and willingness to invest enormous effort in the realization of his ideals are well worth remembering.

Harper's Early Career

William Rainey Harper was born on July 24, 1856, in New Concord, Ohio, a small town about seventy miles east of Columbus.[1] Harper's parents, owners of a general store, ran a strict United Presbyterian household. Reading newspapers and secular books on Sundays was forbidden, and Harper himself recounted to his students how his father, an elder in the local church, had made him read the Bible through "again and again."[2]

Harper was a precocious child, preferring indoor pursuits such as reading, studying, and practicing the cornet and piano to outdoor activities. He attended a town school and was tutored by his father. Harper's academic gifts became apparent early on, and by the age of eight he matriculated in the preparatory program of local Muskingum College. He began college work at the age of ten and graduated four years later, having propelled himself through the college's curriculum by doing extra work—a model he would valorize in the new University via its four-quarter system. Among his favorite subjects were languages, and at graduation he delivered a short address in Hebrew.

After college, Harper worked in his father's store to save money, taught a course in Hebrew on a part-time basis at the college, and continued to study ancient languages privately with a minister in Zanesville, Ohio. In September 1873, at age seventeen, Harper matriculated in the graduate program of Yale University. A fellow student later remembered him as a "somewhat unsophisticated country lad" who at first seemed "not very well prepared" for postgraduate studies at Yale. But Harper worked assiduously and soon earned his colleagues' admiration.[3]

The Yale program involved two years of course work, a final examination, and a thesis.[4] Harper's dissertation, "A Comparative Study of the Prepositions in Latin, Greek, Sanskrit, and Gothic," was plainly influenced by Professor William Dwight Whitney, a distinguished philologist of Sanskrit who had studied in Germany between 1850 and 1853. The modern scholarly field of linguistics originated in Germany, and German or German-trained scholars dominated the field in the nineteenth century.[5] Whitney assimilated German learning and methods and adapted them to American educational institutions and religious practices.[6]

Harper's love of grammatical structure, and the way his teaching focused on grammar at the expense of literary feeling, were partly a matter of temperament but also an inheritance from Whitney and the contemporary scholarly milieu. Harper's love of grammatical order easily spilled over into a love of organizational planning, with fateful consequences for the new University in Chicago.[7] Harper used his training as a philologist and professional linguist throughout his life to frame his encounters with several scholarly disciplines.

After completing his studies at Yale in 1875, Harper headed a small secondary school in Macon, Tennessee, for a year, then secured a teaching position closer to home, at Denison University's secondary-school program in Granville, Ohio, about forty miles west of his hometown. There he taught ancient languages, and his dynamism quickly propelled him to the position of principal. Harper's experience teaching and mentoring high school students would have long-term ramifications in the way he viewed the relationship between secondary and tertiary sectors of higher education.

Denison was a strict Baptist college, but President Benjamin Andrews aspired to a more open-minded intellectual atmosphere. He took a liking to Harper, who was one of the first non-Baptist instructors ever hired on the small faculty, and the two men formed a close friendship that would endure over the next quarter century. Harper joined the Baptist church in late 1876, but it is unknown whether a desire to conform to his new cultural milieu and win the support of Andrews and others in his new surroundings played a role in his decision.[8] Harper later told his students at Yale that his early familiarity with the Old Testament and with Hebrew had led him during his college years to doubt the accuracy of much of the Bible, and that he became skeptical and critical of his faith until his time at Denison. Harper used this story in 1891 to argue that it was possible to reconcile a commitment to modern scholarship and personal faith, since the former had helped to illuminate the true meaning of sacred scripture.[9] Harper became a committed and loyal Baptist, so much so that his later embrace of scientific rationalism and the higher criticism presented him, at least initially, with serious professional challenges.[10]

In January 1879, at age twenty-two, Harper was recruited to teach Semitic languages and Old Testament literature at Morgan Park Seminary, a small Baptist institution about twelve miles from central Chicago.[11] The seminary enrolled about one hundred students each year, and Harper was given responsibility for all instruction involving the Old Testament. Harper proved to be a charismatic teacher, receiving praise for his enthusiasm in basic language teaching and his advanced course in the Messianic prophecies. As noted in chapter 1, Harper refused the chance to become president of the old University of Chicago in 1886, and in May of that year he resigned from Morgan Park to take up a full professorship of Semitic languages at Yale University, where he taught until 1891.

Charles Chandler later recalled that Harper's early intellectual priorities focused first on philology and linguistics, not on the Bible's theological nexus. At Denison, "in literature *as such* in any language, Harper showed not the slightest interest," Chandler wrote. Harper was not a trained theologian, and his "work and interest, being then concerned with Hebrew grammar, and with the Hebrew text only as material for grammatical investigation and illustration, did not tend to spirituality."[12] Clarence Castle, who studied Xenophon's *Anabasis* with Harper at Denison and later served as a professor of Greek at Chicago, remembered him as a model teacher, sensitive to the learning accomplished by his students and able to generate both ardent enthusiasm and much hard work. Harper's "charming personality, strong character, power to inspire, and his success in those days of his first teaching were prophetic of greater things to come."[13]

Harper's enthusiasm for the Hebrew language led him to found a summer school at Morgan Park for the teaching of Hebrew in July 1881, and a

Hebrew correspondence school for ministers and students in December 1880.[14] Both activities expanded rapidly over the course of the decade, creating a small business empire that earned the loyalty of thousands of eager participants but put Harper on the edge of financial disaster. In April 1882, Harper launched a monthly journal, the *Hebrew Student* (which went through several names, becoming the *Biblical World* in 1893), confident that his readers could make intelligent decisions about the new methods of studying the Bible and that his journal would be a fair and open-minded vehicle of such evaluations.[15]

In 1883 Harper began teaching Hebrew in the Chautauqua summer programs, and by 1892 he became principal of the Chautauqua System of Education. In October 1889 Harper consolidated his schools and journals under the aegis of a new American Institute of Sacred Literature, which published and circulated hundreds of thousands of pages of materials annually on the study of the Bible and religion for adults.[16] Harper's various projects generated a wide network of participants, giving him a huge reservoir of ministerial support in and beyond the Baptist church by the early 1890s. Shailer Mathews, an early faculty member in the Divinity School, observed that Harper "was the spiritual father of an entire generation of biblical teachers who are now in the seminaries and colleges of the country."[17] With his commitment to the continuing education of ministers and interested laypeople, Harper also played a critical role in the extensive popularization of the Bible among American Protestants in the 1880s and 1890s.[18]

Harper's engagement with Hebrew led him to the Pentateuch and the Prophets and to the immensely controversial questions about the historical development of the Bible raised by European critics like Julius Wellhausen, Franz Delitzsch, W. Robertson Smith, and others. In March 1884, Harper began publishing a second, more scholarly journal, *Hebraica*.[19] Harper's main preoccupations in the early 1880s may have centered on his editorial projects, his schools, and his publication projects, but after his return to Yale in 1886 he came into his own as a nationally recognized scholar of the Bible. He wrote regular editorials in the *Old Testament Student* defending his claims that the Bible was a legitimate historical document and that it had an authorial history that could be uncovered by scientific analysis.[20] As he put it in October 1889, "All that is of real value to us, that may be obtained from Bible study, must be either the facts in its history and its contents, or else the inductions based upon these facts.... For all knowledge of facts, and for all use of facts, the scientific method is confessed by all students to be the best. It is the great triumph and the great glory of modern thought."[21]

Harper remained an active scholar of the Bible to the end of his life.

In addition to continuing to coedit his journals, he also wrote teaching guides for the study of the Bible and a magnificent commentary on Amos and Hosea published in 1905 just before his death. This book occupied Harper over many years, giving him "change, comfort, and courage" throughout the hard times of his presidency, and it confirmed his reputation as a scholar of national standing and reputation.[22] James H. Tufts, a student of Harper's at Yale and later a colleague at Chicago, recalled the excitement that Harper's scholarly forays into the Prophets generated in the late 1880s at Yale:

> The ferment of these new conceptions of Old Testament scriptures and religion, reinforced by the dawning sciences of anthropology and comparative religion, was just beginning to work on this side of the Atlantic.... Harper threw himself into the task of introducing the forward-looking among the younger generation to the challenging hypotheses.... [Harper] rejected the conclusion that the change in perspective of Hebrew history necessitated a loss of spiritually valuable truth. The moral earnestness of Amos and the lofty idealism of Isaiah, he insisted, gained in significance when placed in relation to their times.[23]

Harper's scholarly career unfolded at a time when powerful intellectual currents began to undermine Protestant assumptions about the Bible and about God's relationship to human nature. New views of the Old Testament and of the relationship of science to history confronted traditional ways of understanding the sacred and profane worlds of the Bible. One crucial issue that divided conservatives and liberals was whether the books of the Old Testament came directly from God to Moses or whether a set of divinely inspired human writers, with all their imperfections, compiled the sacred stories. The first position conveyed the Bible's absolute authority and even infallibility; the second allowed for margins of human error, misunderstanding, and subjectivity.[24] Harper became an articulate proponent of the scientific analysis of the historical origins of the Old Testament. Yet he remained a staunch defender of the idea that the Bible was divinely inspired, and was convinced that more scientific research would ultimately allow more people to understand and accept the spiritual value of the Bible. Harper also believed that his audiences needed to grow accustomed to the methods and conclusions of modern scholarship in a gradual, progressive way, giving them the chance to think through controversial issues inductively. This approach often caused him to frame his analytic positions in cautious, nonconfrontational language, and led some commentators to accuse him of obfuscations or trimming.[25]

Harper's differences with biblical traditionalists were publicly manifested in a debate on "the Pentateuchal question" that he conducted with W. Henry Green in the pages of *Hebraica*. A senior professor at the Princeton Theological Seminary, Green was the author of a venerable, if dated, grammar of elementary Hebrew, and a conservative stalwart on matters of dogma and biblical interpretation. Green was one of many conservative Presbyterian opponents of the liberal theologian and biblical critic Charles A. Briggs and played a central role in engineering Briggs's heresy trial in 1891–93.[26] Debating Green, however strict the ground rules, was fraught with denominational land mines, and Harper was criticized for engaging in the dispute.[27] The Green debate was but one of Harper's attempts to confront conservative orthodoxies. His regular editorials were equally insistent challenges, even if they generally adopted centrist positions, not seeking to inflame denominational opinion. Writing in July 1889, Harper argued that if newer methods of biblical study were not taught, the churches would face a time "when intelligent men of all classes will say, 'if this is your Bible we will have none of it.'"[28] The Harper-Green debates tell us much about Harper's character and intellectual personality, his courage to confront "the facts" wherever they took him, his dislike of gratuitous provocations and hard words, and his love of the scholarly life. Harper's University manifested the highest dedication to original scholarship because its first president lived and admired such a life.

Four years after accepting the presidency, Harper would still protest to a friend that his "special business in the world is stirring up people on the English Bible. The University of Chicago is entirely a second hand matter."[29] William Hutchison has rightly suggested that Harper's *Biblical World* was "the most important American vehicle of the Higher Criticism."[30] Harper's University was to be, in the broadest sense, an instrument for the perfection of human reason, searching for social and ethical truth in a society that would become ever more Christian, more providential. Yet when faced with the crushing reality of his own premature death in early 1906, a death that left so many plans unfulfilled, Harper had to work to find consolation in this faith. In conversations with Ernest D. Burton and Albion Small, Harper rehearsed again and again his understanding of faith and hope for a life of grace beyond the grave. Burton in particular tried to reassure him about the growing goodness and progress of the world, about the slow but progressive approach of human society ever closer to God, and about Harper's own important role in bettering that society.[31] Harper's inductive method would not so easily rest, and Harper kept searching for more urgent and compelling reasons and facts that would dispel his fears of having lived an inadequate life and, more wretchedly, an overly ambitious life. Burton eventually appealed to the forgiveness of God, much like Harper as an earthly father would forgive a wayward son, and eventually Harper accepted his fate with greater confidence. The scenes, as recorded by Burton immediately after Harper's death, read like a slow-motion graduate seminar in biblical criticism. Harper died as he lived, as a skeptic in search of the truth, but also urgently applying reason to struggle with uncertain realities, and as an irrepressible maker of plans.

Harper's Vision of the University

Harper found the decision to abandon Yale and launch the new University an anguished one, made all the more problematic by the urgings of close friends not to go to Chicago. Harper admired Yale, felt at home there, and was respected by influential senior faculty members. President Timothy Dwight so admired Harper that he raised $50,000 to permanently endow a named professorship—the Woolsey Professorship in Biblical Literature—to help finance Harper's various publication projects. When Harper was tempted to leave for Chicago in 1890, his Yale colleague Professor Thomas D. Seymour tried to dissuade him: "My view remains strong, and grows stronger, that you throw away a marvelous opportunity by taking *any* position at the head of a college. And I feel more and more strongly that the presidency of a college is an exceedingly objectionable position. Doubtless every man who takes such a place thinks that he can avoid the rocks on which others have split, or that such rocks don't lie in his course. But the position is irksome and thankless. I presume you would not fail, but I do not believe you would satisfy your higher aspirations and ambitions nearly so well in Chicago as in New Haven."[32]

William Rainey Harper was an inveterate planner who could not resist the chance to mobilize men and ideas. His decision to resist the appeals of his Yale counterparts was driven both by his fascination with program building and planning and by his ambition to reshape the national system of American higher education. During the early autumn of 1890, even before he officially accepted the presidency, Harper sketched out his educational plans for the new University. In his autobiography, Edgar Goodspeed recounted the story of Harper's composing key parts of the plan as the two journeyed by train from Chicago to New York in mid-September.[33] "I have a plan," Harper wrote to Rockefeller, "which is at the same time unique and comprehensive, which I am persuaded will revolutionize university study in this country; nor is this only *my* opinion. It is very simple, but thorough-going."[34]

Before making a formal presentation to the board of trustees in late

December 1890, Harper shared his ideas with a number of colleagues and received their strong approbation. Professor Lewis Stuart's reaction was typical:

> You have out-Harpered Harper. "Unique and revolutionary" by no means adequately represent the situation. You give a three years' course without lowering the standard and provide for those who cannot keep up average work. You solve the problem of non-resident work, and provide for that large class, especially in our great cities, who want a broader outlook or special training. In a word, you set forth the ideal "University" in the old and in the new meaning of that much abused word, "all knowledge for all men." ... I wish you most sincerely the glorious success you deserve and for myself to see arise out of the ashes of the old U. of C. the greatest university in the world.[35]

The first installment of the plan was issued as *Official Bulletin No. 1*, January 1891, even before Harper had officially accepted the presidency.[36] Harper conceived of a university encompassing undergraduate and graduate instruction, and supporting aggressive programs of original research. The "work of the University" would encompass the University proper, including academies; several undergraduate colleges (including one for business and practical affairs); affiliated colleges elsewhere in the city and the nation; and graduate schools (both arts and sciences and divinity), with the creation of a law school, a medical school, a school of engineering, and schools of pedagogy, fine art, and music to be organized as soon as reasonably possible. Undergraduate instruction would be evenly divided between the first two years, termed "Academic," and the second two years, designated "University." The Academic program for younger undergraduates was marked by prescribed curricular distribution requirements, whereas in the University years third- and fourth-year students would have more elective opportunities as well as chances to specialize in specific disciplinary research areas.[37]

In addition to the University proper, the University extension would offer evening courses for adults in various locations around Chicago; correspondence courses for students "residing in parts of the country whose circumstances do not permit them to reside at an institution of learning during all of the year"; a program of public lectures, also in Chicago; and special courses in the study of the Bible, to be organized by University instructors "at times which shall not conflict with University work." Finally, the University publication work would include the printing and publishing of books authored or edited by the faculty and of journals or reviews also edited by members of the university faculty.

Equally revolutionary were the general regulations that would manage the pace and flow of academic work. The University would be organized into four equal academic terms, or quarters, each lasting twelve weeks, and each quarter would be in turn divided into two six-week segments. This would permit the institution to operate year-round and also allow students to begin their degree programs at any time of year and graduate as quickly as they desired. Faculty gained in flexibility as well since they were granted one quarter off with pay as a research leave and could teach extra courses to gain additional credits for more sabbatical time. Courses were divided between majors (which met for ten to twelve hours a week) and minors (which met for four to six hours a week). Initially, Harper thought that each student might take one major and one minor each six-week segment, thus allowing for in-depth learning and avoiding the superficiality of coverage that Harper despised. Very soon, however, the system evolved into students taking three majors, over twelve weeks, as a normal quarter's work.

The rhetorical structure governing the whole arrangement was highly systemized. Each part was assumed to be an integral part of a larger whole, encompassing high schools, undergraduate colleges, professional and graduate schools, extension programs, and a publication system to disseminate the scholarly research of the faculty across the nation and around the world. The vision was breathtaking, especially since the new University was to be created all at once, in a fully unified format, with its parts reinforcing or at least relating to one another. The logic of Harper's plan operated on two distinctive, but convergent, levels. Each of the elements was intrinsically related to all of the other parts of the plan within the organizational machinery of the University. But each element also had far-reaching national policy implications for improving American higher education in more general terms. The University's unity of culture and action—what Edward H. Levi would later refer to as the University's oneness—was defined by the systematic self-understanding and the structural logic of the plan itself.[38]

At the end of *Official Bulletin No. 1*, Harper listed twenty-six advantages of his new scheme of organization. They ran the gamut from enhancing the concentration of students to giving more freedom and flexibility to students by allowing them to study during the summer quarter to preventing students from taking too many subjects at a time. Harper even argued that his system would "make it possible for students to take, besides the regular subjects of the college curriculum, such practical subjects as bookkeeping, stenography, etc."[39] Many of Harper's imagined advantages had to do with an almost fanatical desire to help students and faculty maximize time and to achieve efficiency, discipline, and economy. For Harper, in

the ideal world every minute was accounted for, and no day properly concluded without a bounty of productive work. His son, Samuel, recalled
Harper's conviction that "his work, the building of a new university, had
to be done rapidly in order to be well done. Dawdling along was contrary
to his temperament and, he believed, inimical to the success of any job."[40]
He was a figure straight out of Max Weber's *Protestant Ethic.*

The plan privileged flexibility for both students and faculty and a serious expansion of the range of instructional opportunities. Students could
enter and leave the University with more flexibility than under a standard
two-semester paradigm. Instead of long summer vacations, which Harper
thought a waste of time, students would be able to work part-time for
advanced academic degrees and to accelerate their academic programs.
The summer quarter would be especially attractive to high school teachers
who wished to obtain advanced instruction to boost their careers. The
quarter system had a powerful impact on the subsequent culture of the
University. Dean James R. Angell would later argue that these innovations
had "done more to capitalize at something like their full value the educational resources of the colleges and universities of the country than any
other one thing that has occurred in this period."[41] The major/minor system was also a component of efficiency, since Harper was convinced that
the intensive study of a few subjects, rather than loose engagement with
many, would eliminate what James Tufts called the "policy of 'scatter'
which had crept into university programs as a greater variety of subjects
had come forward to lure both teachers and students."[42]

All this was also set in a milieu that, in Harper's mind, would esteem
performance over rank and class background. Harper despised any kind
of snobbish or presumptuous behavior, even when he saw it among his
own faculty colleagues. When plans for a new faculty club were discussed,
Harper insisted that it be open to all faculty and not merely to those "who
were inclined to look on themselves as the chosen social leaders because
of their former relation to famous eastern schools."[43] Harper's aversion
to the social hierarchies of the eastern universities reflected his deep
midwestern roots and his pride in having surmounted a humble personal
background to gain success at Yale, but on his own terms.[44] The result was
a relatively integrated faculty culture, in which there were significant dis-
parities in compensation but ease of intellectual intercourse and personal
interactions across rank and titular boundaries.

Two other features of Harper's original plan deserve mention. Harper's long experience as a journal editor and textbook author served as
prelude to his support for a university press with its learned journals and
books. As an editor, Harper was in his element—playing mediator and
coach, enjoining and cajoling, and encouraging novelty and creativity,

but also insisting on firm deadlines and high-quality work. Harper viewed his journals as crucial agents in public education and professional scholarship that would, in Shailer Mathews's words, "get people to study the Bible by historical methods and to build up in their hearts a religious faith born of biblical study."[45] Professional, scientific knowledge would lead to social betterment and civic enlightenment, and both were acts of a just and divine virtue. Harper's general intellectual project for the new University was defined by these expectations, and the press thus became a core agent of the spread of enlightenment on and off campus. By 1902, the press had published nearly two hundred books and pamphlets and also issued ten journals, most of them scholarly but others more popular or for professional practitioners (e.g., the *Biblical World*, the *School Review*).

Harper viewed his extension programs as vehicles to infuse higher levels of quality in the nation's educational system. "The work of diffusing scientific knowledge and creating a desire for a higher and better intellectual and aesthetic life is no less important than the advance of scientific knowledge itself by original investigation and discovery," Harper wrote. "Indeed, one may say that the latter will not find the fullest support and the most satisfactory field of progress, except in a community in which interest in a higher education is widely spread."[46] Harper wanted to generate "in the community at large that demand for the best of everything in the intellectual, aesthetic, and moral world which is at once the evidence of, and the surest means towards, the higher civic life."[47] Just as his Hebrew correspondence courses in the 1880s helped local Protestant ministers improve their linguistic and historical skills, the new extension system of the University would be particularly useful to urban and rural teachers who could, in turn, better prepare more students to go on to college- and university-level study. "Our idea is that if you as teachers will undertake this kind of work for one another the young people who come to the university to us will be far better prepared to prosecute the work provided by the university curriculum," he explained. Harper was convinced that the city of Chicago did not send enough students to college, and he wished to change that. He stated, "This university is here to help the people of Chicago, and especially those in position to receive the more definite character of aid we are able to render. We are here to assist teachers, students, businessmen and women, and particularly those whom circumstances have deprived of educational opportunities once eagerly sought."[48]

What were the precedents for Harper's plan? Augustus Strong believed that Harper had stolen his ideas about a national research university and simply shifted the site from New York to Chicago. As noted, there is a remarkable convergence of some of Harper's and Strong's ideas, and Harper was clearly influenced by Strong's passions and general conceptions, if not by all of his organizational specifics. Frederick Gates's ideas about a national system of education linking secondary and tertiary levels also left an imprint on Harper's imagination. But Harper had other sources to draw on, several of which were frankly autobiographical. His University would be modeled after the late nineteenth-century German university, as experienced by his mentor W. D. Whitney, with elements of Oxford and Cambridge added for good measure (particularly English university models of adult extension programs). But it would also be a western revival of Yale, a latter-day Chautauqua, a Chicago version of the Denison preparatory college, and a transformed and enlarged version of Harper's Hebrew correspondence school and summer programs from Morgan Park, all thrown together.[49] In spite of its hybrid nature, Harper was deeply confident that his University, unlike many eastern institutions, would have "a life that forms a complete whole."[50] In its capacity for radical experimentation and innovation, in its reshuffling of traditional academic boundaries, in its melding together of collegiate and graduate education to the advantage of both, and in its appeals for support from the wider civil society, the new University was very much an American institution, notwithstanding the neo-Gothic historicism of its first buildings. The Harvard historian Albert Bushnell Hart once suggested that Chicago's success became the success of Northwestern and the large and distinguished public universities of the Midwest, as those institutions sought funds "to compete with Chicago. Every good neighbor has prospered because of the rise of the new University."[51] That it so easily became a competitive model and a standard setter for the other great midwestern universities demonstrated, more than anything else, that Harper's vision was a uniquely American venture.

The first and most urgent step was to recruit the faculty. Harper was frustrated in his early offers. He complained to Gates in late December 1891 that he was "completely discouraged": "We have not a head professor after nine months of constant work," he groused. "Everything is unfinished; nothing seems capable of being finished and this uncertainty is crushing."[52] But by offering magnificent salaries of up to $7,000, a year later Harper had an impressive group of senior recruits, including William Gardner Hale and J. Laurence Laughlin of Cornell; William I. Knapp of Yale; Hermann von Holst of Freiburg; Thomas C. Chamberlin and Rollin D. Salisbury of Wisconsin; Albert A. Michelson, Charles O. Whitman, and John U. Nef of Clark; Albion W. Small of Colby; Paul Shorey of Bryn Mawr; and Eliakim Hastings Moore of Northwestern. Other younger luminaries, like John Dewey, George Herbert Mead, and James R. Angell, soon followed in 1894 and 1895. Harper's pride in assembling a "stronger and nobler body of men" raised the bar of his own expectations about what the University might accomplish. Laughlin later recalled, "One of the things which affected my decision was the policy of President Harper in trying to call the strongest men he could find, whether in Europe or America. This policy undoubtedly affected the acceptance by [Hermann] von Holst, as it did that of many others, no doubt."[53] Many of these scholars came to Chicago to head their departments; Harper's system for departmental governance was a hazy adaption of the German custom of having "heads" of university institutes (*Institutsvorstände*). Given Harper's compulsion to have a centralized and efficient system of administrative governance (with himself at the pinnacle), it was perfectly logical to have one prominent full professor as head, with a significantly higher salary than his peers, who would exercise semisovereign administrative authority and who was solely responsible for negotiating with Harper on faculty appointments and financial allocations for his department. With scholars of this caliber, among them several former college presidents, it was not surprising that they soon chafed at Harper's autocratic governing methods, eventually pushing for strong representation to voice their concerns and influence university policies.[54] The years between 1902 and 1908 saw repeated attempts by various faculty groups to gain more authority at the expense of the president's office.[55]

The rush to hire senior faculty and to sustain the kind of distinguished departments and academic programs that those scholars expected quickly led Harper into chronic patterns of deficit spending and ongoing appeals to Rockefeller for short-term budget relief, which were met with increasing frustration and skepticism. By 1903, Rockefeller and the trustees decided to curb the deficits, and Harper was left out in the cold. Beset by illness and personal anxiety, Harper spent his last two years as president struggling to apply budgetary stringencies to a university unaccustomed to fiscal discipline.[56] Did Harper intentionally run deficits, believing that he could compel Rockefeller to provide more resources? Opinions have differed. Samuel Harper recalled his father telling him that in administering the University "much of what he had done he had accomplished on sheer bluff."[57] Late in his life, Frederick Gates looked back on Harper's financial practices and saw in them a deliberate cunning to manipulate Rockefeller: "I thought at the time that the policy of Dr. Harper looked like compulsion, but was not intended to be compulsion.... From what I *now* know, from what I have heard *since*, I could not say with the same assurance that on Dr. Harper's part compulsion was not intended. There is much since which has led me to think that it *was* intended and that the compulsion was deliberate."[58]

In contrast, Emery Filbey, a veteran administrator during the Hutchins era and a skilled budgeter in his own right, thought that Harper was a victim of his own lack of structure: "Harper was a genius who would not recognize obstacles, including money. He did not run deficits deliberately to put pressure on JDR [John D. Rockefeller], but [he] just let U[niversity] men do things and run bills on their own uncentralized ordering. Deficits were made up of unpaid bills, the extent of which no one had knowledge until the end of the year. This was not a planned budget deficit."[59] Filbey's insight about Harper's administrative style makes sense in light of Harper's earlier practices in operating his journals. They inevitably ran deficits, and he would scramble to cover his debts, sometimes even with his own meager resources.[60] Once Harper was convinced of the importance of an initiative, he virtually willed it into existence regardless of financial consequences. With sham astonishment Harper once quipped to Robert Lovett, "They expect me to run a university on a budget."[61] Thomas Goodspeed later criticized this fiscal hurly-burly, but Harper could operate no other way—either for the University or for his own family. Samuel Harper once recalled that his family's budget operated just like the University budget, "always with a deficit," with Harper borrowing against his life insurance policies and giving too generously to charities and the local Baptist church.[62] He was a man on a mission, and no new idea that would enhance or enrich his University would be denied a chance of success.

The Early Educational System

UNDERGRADUATES

Of the challenges raised by Harper's plans, the role of undergraduate education was the most fascinating. Harper told the first meeting of the arts and sciences faculty at Chicago on October 1, 1892, "The time will come when the Academy College work may be transferred to some other place, and the higher work be given all our strength on this campus."[63] Harper's rhetoric about the early University thus highlighted the putative prominence of graduate education and research. He raised the rhetorical stakes considerably in his annual report on the University in the fall of 1892: "It is now expected by all who are interested that the University idea is to be emphasized. It is proposed to establish not a College, but a University, and it was with this thought in mind that the selection of the Faculty has been made."[64] This report was never published, perhaps because its rhetoric would have been misunderstood by donors who thought they had been contributing to an undergraduate college. Goodspeed himself challenged Harper on this issue when he insisted, "I am sure you will make a magnificent undergraduate school. You can't help it." He urged Harper to state publicly that it was the intention of the University "to say that we are going to do as good work for undergraduates as they can get anywhere in the world."[65] Interestingly, Harper alluded to one salient reason for his privileging of graduate education when he mentioned that a "large number of the professors have been selected with the understanding that their work is to be exclusively in the Graduate School."[66] Harper was probably not the first or the last university leader to attempt to recruit senior faculty with overt or covert promises that they would not have to teach undergraduates, but his words are striking nonetheless.

Yet Harper was not consistent on the question of privileging graduates as opposed to undergraduates. In a convocation address in December 1893, for example, Harper publicly defended the existence of academic programs for young college students, arguing that they were essential to the mission of the University:

> It has been feared by some that in the large emphasis laid upon the University work, the interests of the younger students in the earlier college years might be overlooked. Indeed, many think that higher work and lower work may not be carried on at the same time to advantage. The specific charge, for it has assumed the definiteness of a charge, and the general principle are alike wrong.... It is of the greatest advantage to the younger student to move in an atmosphere the characteristics of which are determined by men who have reached a more serious age. A stimulus is furnished in this way for thorough work which nothing else can furnish. The friends of the University may rest secure in mind in reference to this matter.[67]

A recent essay by Willard Pugh on Harper's administration argues that while Harper may have intended to privilege graduate education, by the end of his career he had essentially created a large undergraduate college, much to the dismay of senior faculty colleagues who believed their jobs had evolved in ways different from what they had been promised.[68] This is clear from the student enrollment and graduation statistics of the University over its first ten years. Each year the number of undergraduate students increased more rapidly than that of their graduate counterparts. In the autumn quarter of the 1893–94 academic year, the University had 232 graduate students and 357 undergraduates enrolled in arts and sciences programs. By the autumn quarter of the 1901–2 academic year, the number of graduate students had increased modestly to 346, but the number of undergraduates had mushroomed to 1,522, with much of this growth deriving from strong annual increases in matriculants to the Junior College. In the enrollments in individual departments this trend was equally notable. In 1893–94, the Department of Political Economy had

149 graduate registrations as opposed to 123 collegiate registrations, but by 1914–15 the ratios had changed profoundly: 343 graduate registrations as opposed to 1,194 undergraduate registrations.[69] Clearly, a revolution was taking place, and in his decennial report in 1902 Harper himself openly predicted that "on any reasonable calculation it seems certain that the number of undergraduate students, and especially of Junior College students, coming to the University in the next ten years will be largely increased."[70] In addition, because of the flexibility provided by the division of the undergraduate program between junior and senior levels, the University began to attract a large number of transfer students from other colleges as more advanced matriculants, further driving total undergraduate enrollments upward. If Augustus Strong thought that William Rainey Harper had stolen his plans in 1892, the argument was no longer relevant by 1902. Undergraduates had no place in the original Strong scenario, but apparently there was a considerable role for them in the pragmatic evolution of Harper's plans.

Harper's rhetoric about the demographic identity of his new research university was shaped by his fascination with the classic dilemma of how to connect high school to college and college to university in the most efficient and effective ways possible. Harper's early designation of the first two years of undergraduate study as the "Academic College" was a direct bow to the tradition of secondary education undertaken in nineteenth-century academies. Students in these years would complete the preparatory work for higher learning begun in the high schools.[71] The second two years logically became the "University College," so named to signify that students had completed all preparatory learning and had gained the skills and maturity necessary to do university-level work—that is, work conducted on an advanced level and undertaken with the exercise of more pronounced scholarly standards. On paper this division seemed shrewd and sensible, but in practice the boundary line between the first two years and the second became more fluid as the years passed. Some undergraduate students arrived at Chicago with sufficient credits to begin higher-level work immediately, and others who transferred to Chicago still needed to undertake subjects taught only in the Junior College. As James H. Tufts subsequently noted, "In actual practice it was not possible to conduct work for the two colleges in separate buildings because there was but one building. And the general policy of flexibility tended to weaken the other barriers set between the two.... The distinction between the colleges tended to become what John Locke called a 'nominal essence.'"[72]

Harper saw the undergraduate programs in the new University as feeding well-trained students into his new graduate programs, and he insisted on high admissions requirements for freshmen, even if this ruffled the feathers of contributors who thought they had assured their sons or daughters a place in the class.[73] In his unpublished first annual report, Harper attributed this strategy partly to an instrumental desire to hold down college enrollments so that graduate work might be emphasized. But the "chief reason" was his hope that "we may better prepare students for the graduate work which we wish to emphasize here," underscoring the connection between advanced undergraduate and graduate work that, Harper hoped, would become a hallmark of the new institution and that would raise academic standards across the West.[74] To Frederick Gates and others, Harper argued that upholding high standards was also vital for the reputation of the University, and thus a good thing in itself. He wrote to Gates in September 1892:

> There has been a great temptation, of course, to admit students unprepared, according to our standards, but we have constantly held ourselves in restraint, and while many men doubtless have been disgruntled, because of our refusal to admit their sons, we have felt that it was the only wise thing to do. You have no idea of the pressure which has been brought to bear to admit the sons of certain men, but I have determined that we shall be as impartial or as heartless if you will, as Harvard or Yale. Most of the Board of Trustees uphold me in this policy. Some, I am inclined to think, would rather have seen the bars let down. The fruitage will appear another year.[75]

Students applying to the University's collegiate programs were required to take an entrance examination that would demonstrate the effectiveness of their high school studies in subjects such as English, mathematics, Latin, Greek, history, the natural sciences, and a modern language (either French or German). Harper and his colleagues constantly adjusted which and how many of these subjects had to be presented for admission, suggesting how seriously they took the process.[76] Essentially, as Richard Storr has argued, Harper wanted to accomplish two ideals simultaneously:

> [The University] had to serve the West, which meant that it had to receive students educated in the high schools of the West; and it had to raise the level of education, which it would fail to do if it lost touch with the men and women to be educated.... The University also of course had its self-interest to consider. It wanted large enrollments to support the budget and also to stand as evidence of its success ... but the University in the very name of its mission as a standard institution could not automatically concede to the wishes of all students and high school principals, whose self-interests it might be to beat down high admission requirements.[77]

Having divided the new undergraduate programs into Academic (Junior) and University (Senior) Colleges, Harper then created three broad faculty domains of the arts, literature, and sciences that traversed these jurisdictions, each of which had its own baccalaureate degree (BA for the arts, PhB for philosophy, and SB for the sciences). Students had to complete at least eighteen "majors" in the Junior College (of which at least fifteen were required and three were electives) before proceeding to the Senior College, a "major" being the term for a course that met four or five times weekly for one quarter. Students normally took three majors each quarter. In order to receive a baccalaureate degree, students then needed another eighteen majors in the Senior College. From 1892 to 1902, Senior College students were permitted considerable freedom in choosing their courses, with the stipulation that no more than nine courses be from any single department. Beginning in 1905 the faculty encouraged greater specialization, by first insisting that each student take a minimum of six courses in one department and by increasing the amount of work allowed from a single department from nine to fifteen courses. In 1912 the curriculum was further tightened by the requirement that each Junior College student had to take at least four departmental courses from four large subject areas—philosophy, history, and social science; modern languages other than English; mathematics; and natural science—and by the stipulation that Senior College students now had to take nine courses in one disciplinary area (which could be a single department or a set of related departments) and six courses in a second.

In all cases the courses taken by undergraduates were departmentally based and sanctioned. Who taught these courses? Many professors were hired to teach at the graduate level, but as often happened with Harper's plans, reality proved different. Early course catalogues indicate that many senior faculty, and often men of considerable research distinction, taught beginning and intermediate undergraduate courses. In fact, teaching in the Junior College was done by a mix of regular faculty and graduate students, whereas the great majority of Senior College classes were taught by the professorial faculty.[78] As Storr has noted, "The University was pulled two ways, first by its dedication to higher studies and second by a desire to supply the wants of Junior College students. As the University became deeply engaged in the education of underclassmen, it felt the stresses created by the characteristically American conjunction of collegiate and higher learning."[79] Nor was there a strict dividing line between the populations of graduate and undergraduate students, for in most departments some graduate courses were open to advanced college students. The boundary lines between all levels were fluid, and the decennial report of 1902 observed that "many Graduate courses are electives for Seniors who have had the proper preliminary work, and many graduates find it desirable to take courses normally listed for Seniors. The same considerations apply to some degree as between Senior and Junior courses."[80] As early as 1894, Harper confessed, "The work of the junior and senior years is, however, so closely connected with graduate work that the two are inseparable."[81] Harper never failed to emphasize that Chicago was a university, not a college, and that students should profit from an entirely different experience than if they attended a hermetic collegiate program.[82]

As the University took root and the basic features of his plan for undergraduates gained traction and credibility, Harper was eager to comment on their national policy implications. Two speeches that he delivered in 1895 illustrated these ambitions. In early January, Harper defended the practice of universities mandating entrance examinations for applicants from secondary schools. He argued that since American secondary schools were so variable in quality—with no uniform standards and often with poorly trained teachers and badly organized curricula that stressed too many subjects in too superficial a way—universities could not possibly precertify the credentials of their students. Given the uneven preparation available to many students in American high schools, Harper posed an intriguing question: "Why not regard the freshman and sophomore years as a great clearing house and make entrance to the junior year the real university entrance instead of entrance to the freshman class?"[83]

The implications of this speech were presented more fully in a speech Harper delivered in the same year at a meeting of the National Education Association in Atlanta. In "Ideals of Educational Work," Harper argued that education in America was in a woeful state and uncompetitive with the best European systems because of chronic disorganization and lack of coordination and association between different levels of institutions.[84] Rigid curricula that sought to cover everything and ended up providing little real training in anything only compounded the problem. Harper advocated a system in which university reform and school reform would dovetail. Critical to this reform would be the recognition that the needs of individual students should drive the system, and that students should be given as much flexibility and opportunity as their individual talents could profitably use. Real structural changes would come by more carefully delineating the relationship of the high schools to the colleges and of the colleges to the universities working with these individual students. Harper believed that many smaller colleges were little more than glorified academies and needed to be reassessed. Perhaps some could become more ambitious high schools. Others could profitably undertake the first two years of college instruction, serving as "colleges of lower rank," and leaving the final, higher work to the stronger colleges and to the universities. Harper was elusive on where the dividing line would come between the smaller colleges and the universities, but at a conference for affiliated institutions in November 1902 he proposed the idea of a six-year high school that would encompass the last two years of primary instruction, high school, and the first two years of college, all this in the name of reducing formal education by two years, thus (in the words of a reporter attending the conference) saving "time in a student's schooling without losing anything of value from the curriculum."[85] Harper repeated this argument in a broad-based essay in the same year on trends in educational reform, when he argued that "the high school is rapidly coming to be a rival of the smaller college itself.... The time is coming when, in every State, the leading high schools will carry the work to the end of the Sophomore year of college."[86] Clearly, in Harper's mind the future fate of many small colleges involved either becoming super high schools or ceding the last two years of their programs to the larger universities and becoming junior colleges. Harper's neo-Darwinian, survival-of-the-fittest rhetoric may have raised hackles among presidents of small colleges, but he was convinced that at least 25 percent of the institutions calling themselves colleges "are doing work of a character only little removed from that of an academy."[87]

Harper managed by 1902 to create a distinctive undergraduate program. Because it afforded such flexibility and possibilities for acceleration, the early University immediately attracted a large number of transfer students from other institutions, in addition to students who enrolled as freshmen in the junior colleges. Between 1898 and 1902, the number of students receiving baccalaureate degrees from Chicago who had taken at least some work at another institution of higher education grew from 56 to 72 percent.[88] In some respects, the problem that Harper had sought to address in his early pronouncements—displacing the work of the first two years off onto other institutions—became an operational feature of the University simply by virtue of the competitive structure of the admissions marketplace. The substantial share of transfer students among undergraduate baccalaureates remained a feature of Chicago's student demography well into the interwar period. By 1929, almost 60 percent of the baccalaureate degrees awarded by the University of Chicago were given to undergraduate students who had one or more quarters of transfer credit.[89]

In contrast to the graduate-student population, the early demography of the Colleges was very much Chicago- and Illinois-based. Seventy percent of all Junior College students in 1902 came from Chicago and the state of Illinois. In the Senior College almost 60 percent came from Chicago and Illinois, with another 23 percent from six midwestern states (Indiana, Michigan, Ohio, Kansas, Iowa, and Wisconsin). Of the 1,297 undergraduates who received baccalaureate degrees from Chicago between 1893 and

1902, 699 were men and 598 were women. In the Junior College, however, the gender ratio was closer to parity (in 1902, for example, there were 373 men and 399 women registered as full-time students).

In the first decade of the University, teaching was the most popular occupational choice for both men and women undergraduates, amounting to 36 percent for men and 44 percent for women—an understandable dominance given the teaching experience many students had before enrolling in the University.[90] Even in the earliest days, the Colleges attracted many students who desired careers in higher education, law, and medicine: for the cohorts who graduated between 1893 and 1900, 22 percent of the male graduates and 8 percent of the female graduates pursued such careers. By the 1920s the distribution of careers for men became more varied: 35 percent of the male graduates pursued careers in business, with law (10 percent), medicine (10 percent), and higher education (9 percent) also continuing as popular choices. Between 1920 and 1929, women continued overwhelmingly to choose education (62 percent), including higher education (5 percent), but 18 percent of women graduates also opted for business careers.[91]

The presence of a large number of transfer students among the undergraduate population meant that the University was recruiting older students who often had more focused career goals than their younger counterparts and who "are all of a serious sort, and are anxious to make the most of their opportunities for study."[92] One alumna of the Colleges before 1914 later remembered that "the first day she came to the University, she went home and cried, as she felt so out of place with all these older students. Later she 'learned to like them.' They forced the younger, less serious students to work harder, for if they didn't the older ones would 'take over' in class."[93] Yet the gender dimensions of this student's commentary should also be stressed, for the presence of so many talented, hardworking women students among the early student body created richer and more complex conditions of academic competition—what one advocate of women students called "the steadying influence of intellectual association in the classroom"—that further accentuated norms of merit and individual achievement.[94] The University recruited particularly strong leadership on the part of Alice Freeman Palmer and Marion Talbot as early advocates for women's educational and social interests. Lynn Gordon has argued that "in its first decade the university was a particularly progressive place for female students," and that their successful academic records demonstrated considerable academic acumen.[95] The high percentage of undergraduates (close to 50 percent) who had to work part-time or full-time to finance their educations between 1893 and 1930 was yet another indicator of the urgency with which students viewed their educational investments.

As the years passed and the number of undergraduate students (and alumni) continued to grow, Harper became more sensitive to the needs of the undergraduate educational programs at Chicago and began issuing public statements on teaching as a fundamental part of the mission of the University.[96] When E. H. Moore of the mathematics department tried in March 1899 to privilege the value of graduate teaching, Harper firmly rejected any attempt by senior faculty to prioritize graduate over undergraduate teaching: "I would not say that the undergraduate work is primary and the graduate work is secondary, nor, on the other hand, would I say that the graduate work is primary and the undergraduate work secondary. They are of equal importance."[97]

Nor could Harper resist further tinkering and restructuring. On the eve of his death he presented a proposal to divide the students in the first two years at Chicago into eight administrative and curricular groups to be called "colleges" (within the larger framework of the Junior College), each of which would be no larger than 175 students. Students would thereby gain more of the advantages of attending a small college that was set within the wider framework of the University. Men and women in the first year of undergraduate work were to be enrolled in separate groups, reflecting Harper's ambivalent Victorian sensibilities about coeducation, which had led him in 1902 to propose segregating male and female students in introductory Junior College classes.[98] The "colleges" were to be "distinctive in their character, each representing a thematic stream of college work, for example, one laying stress on the classical curriculum, another upon the scientific curriculum, another upon that of commercial and industrial life, still another upon modern literature." Students would take approximately half of their course work in the first two years with their college group and the other half in the University at large.[99] Harper believed that this structure would afford younger students "some of these benefits which are found in a small college with the resources and cosmopolitanism of a great institution."[100]

Harper was personally supportive of all students, undergraduate and graduate. He was known to lend money to impoverished students, write reassuring letters to parents of sick students, and invite graduating students to visit him so that he could get to know them. When faced with the occasional undergraduate rowdy, Harper reacted sternly, but he also claimed that he was sensitive to the "old college spirit."[101] One undergraduate alumnus later remembered Harper summoning him to his office and asking him how he "was getting along." After reminding the student about the importance of physical exercise, Harper jumped up and demonstrated the calisthenics that he wanted the student to undertake on a daily basis.[102] By July 1896 Harper would be satisfied that "the more important traditions of student life may be regarded as established."[103] He quickly became an ardent enthusiast of nonprofessional collegiate athletics run, in the person of Amos Alonzo Stagg, by a professional coach. Working with Stagg, Harper imposed faculty control over the athletic program, which in many institutions had been left in the hands of students and alumni.[104] Harper's personal engagement as a leading booster of Chicago intercollegiate football, which developed intensively over the 1890s, was a sign of a broader rapprochement with the popular culture of undergraduate student and alumni life.[105] Harper became, in Robin Lester's words, an "evangelist of the gridiron gospel" and an "athletic entrepreneur," exploiting the University's newfound athletic prowess to cultivate wider civic and alumni support. Harper's admiration for his "boys" and his deep loyalty to Stagg led him to defend Stagg's practices against a significant group of faculty who believed by 1900 that "the present increasing interest in athletics in the University is undesirable."[106]

Like other senior faculty members, Harper had ambivalent feelings about allowing fraternities on campus but eventually concluded that "the facts show that their presence in the University has been a source of great advantage rather than of disadvantage. In almost every case the Fraternities have contributed each its share, not only to the social life of the institution, but to its general welfare."[107] When it came to the choice of his son, Samuel, Harper and his brother Robert debated vigorously whether Samuel should join the Psi U or the Alpha Delts, the latter of which was Harper's own preference, since "it would be better for the family to be represented in two societies than to have the whole representation in one."[108]

The growth of his children may have also played a role in Harper's thinking about undergraduate education. The presence of his daughter, Helen Davida, and his son, Samuel, in the undergraduate Colleges—the one matriculating in the winter quarter of 1896, the other in the autumn quarter of 1896—gave Harper a more vivid personal insight into the impact of the University on youthful minds. Davida's and Samuel's programs of studies ran the gamut of many departments, and in both cases even included early examples of study abroad, since both students managed to transfer credits (nine for Davida, seven for Samuel) from time spent studying in Paris toward their Chicago BA degrees.[109] Samuel, in turn, brought his creative powers to bear in celebrating his father within the specific milieu of undergraduate social life. At a concert of the Glee and Mandolin Clubs at the Studebaker Theater in March 1902, attended by many members of the fraternities and women's clubs, Samuel led his fellow students in genially roasting his father and other faculty members. The most popular song of the evening had the following refrain about Harper's fund-raising:

A million more. He's after a million more, more, more. He thinks he needs
it for U. of C. If he misses it how he will roar. A million more. He's after
a million more, more, more. His purpose is plain, just as plain as can be.
He's after a million more.[110]

Harper was sufficiently shrewd not to stress his graduate-school-
primacy rhetoric when it came to cultivating the loyalties of the alumni
and the wider public. He dutifully spoke at undergraduate alumni gatherings, using these occasions to stress the University's high standards for
undergraduate admissions and to nurture pride in the new University and
its students as part of that great experiment.[111] In the end, the University
offered a rigorous liberal education to all undergraduate students willing
to engage in the process, and the flexible curricular structures that Harper
created seemed to attract students who had the intellectual capacity and
stamina to take advantage of them. Harper was particularly proud of the
strong sense of individuality and the capacity for hard and disciplined
work of the Chicago students. In 1902, he confidently asserted:

> It has been a subject of general comment that the chief characteristics
> of the student body have been steadiness, sturdiness, strength, strong
> individuality, high ideals, and clear purpose. Members of the Faculties
> of eastern institutions have been struck with the individual strength and
> character of the student body. The student constituency does not perhaps
> equal in outward polish that of one of the larger institutions of the East,
> but in ability to organize work, in skill of adaptation of means to end,
> in determination of purpose to win, in readiness to make sacrifice for
> the sake of intellectual advancement, no body of students ever gathered
> together in this country, or in any other country, has shown itself superior
> to the student body of the University of Chicago.[112]

But there were also costs to Harper's revolution of flexibility and efficiency. For one thing, the organization of the quarter system, the ability
of students to matriculate and graduate whenever they wished, the fluidity
of boundaries between the Junior and Senior Colleges, and the large number of transfer students meant a loss of class identity among graduating
seniors and, thereafter, among the alumni of the University. This, in turn,
created serious problems for Chicago's future success in development and
fund-raising. That so many students who received baccalaureate degrees
were transfer students from other undergraduate institutions led Dean
of the Senior Colleges James H. Tufts to insist in 1902 that "it is certainly
desirable, in the interest of the cultivation and education which come
from intimate association, through a long period of undergraduate life,

that the proportion of students who do all, or nearly all, of their work at the University should be larger than it is."[113] In his unpublished memoirs, Tufts subsequently observed, "Efforts to cultivate class acquaintance and class spirit under such conditions were not fruitful. To some members of the faculty, this loss of class unity and class spirit seemed of negligible importance.... Others thought that there was a genuine loss in throwing out the baby with the bath. For one thing, Amherst College was finding in class organization the agency for raising annually an alumni fund of no mean total."[114]

Dean of the Faculties James R. Angell (who later became president of Yale University) would admit that by 1913 the University's preoccupation with research had sometimes gone too far at the expense of teaching, and "many an instructor has looked forward to the time when he might be freed from the labor of instruction to give his entire time and energy to research." Others saw things differently—namely, that Harper had allowed the University to become a big undergraduate college. In any event, the University of Chicago was not alien to the civic world in which it lived, and most people in that world inevitably saw the University through the prism of its undergraduate students and their activities and programs, and through the professional success of those students after they left the University. Angell saw this clearly when he observed that "no institution can be wholly free, either morally or practically, from the obligations entailed by its immediate surroundings."[115]

GRADUATE STUDENTS

Early accounts of the University offer a plentitude of stories about the faculty and their distinguished research activities, including the support the University gave to research, the freedom to teach, and the early sabbatical system that was part of the logic of the quarter system. Harper's dynamic personality and his sterling credentials as a biblical scholar made him a perfect spokesperson for the ideals of the new, research-based graduate education. However, Harper proved to be more interested in touting the research accomplishments of his faculty than he was in analyzing the particular professional accomplishments of his graduate students. "Graduate education" became, rhetorically speaking, defined more through the activities and interests of the early faculty than by accounts of the actual, pragmatic experiences of their graduate students.[116] Hence, less is actually known about the operations of the graduate programs themselves, about the students who enrolled in these programs, and about how effectively or ineffectively the graduate students were taught.

The first years of the University's educational programs were start-up in nature, but by the late 1890s, most departments were awarding both MA and PhD degrees.[117] The dividing line between MA work and doctoral work was fluid. MA degrees were often viewed as a kind of junior PhD, and most had a thesis requirement attached to them. For many students, the MA was thus a legitimate terminal degree that would prove valuable in their professional aspirations. The majority of students who came for what amounted to terminal MA degrees were interested in teaching careers, and some faculty regretted the lack of coordination between their students' substantive training and their career goals. The chair of the Department of History, Andrew McLaughlin, complained to Dean Albion Small in 1917, "I have long been convinced that the Master's degree is practically altogether a teachers' degree, and I think that the departments of the Graduate School ought to cooperate with the faculty of the School of Education in every possible way."[118]

Some PhD students entered the University with MA degrees from other institutions, and some had previous teaching experience as regular faculty at various colleges and even universities. Advanced graduate students were sometimes selected to serve as assistants in their departments and given responsibility for helping the regular faculty teach elementary undergraduate courses, usually meriting a tuition waiver and an annual stipend. The University quickly developed a system of one-year fellowships to support the most promising advanced graduate students, but the recipients of such grants (which varied from $320 to $520) were always a minority of the total population and were required to undertake university service such as elementary instruction or work in a library as part of their grant. As late as 1930, of the graduate students who applied for fellowships, only about 15 percent received them. Over time graduate education became a crucial element of the cultural self-understanding of the departments as small, autonomous professional worlds, and it is not surprising that the denser the practice of graduate training became, the less tenable was Harper's scheme of German-style headships, with other tenured faculty who supervised doctoral students demanding equal responsibility in the governance and curricular organization of their small collegial worlds, as well as more meritocratic financial compensation. In October 1910, following a complex set of debates, the senior faculty voted to replace the departmental headship system with elected chairs appointed to three-year terms who were (at least in formal terms) primus inter pares with their other full and associate professorial colleagues, and to stipulate that all senior faculty were eligible for compensation levels based on merit and not on administrative function, thus ending the regime under which the heads received substantially higher salaries.[119]

Two broad strata of graduate students came to Chicago. The first were graduate students who matriculated in one of the regular academic terms, especially the autumn quarter, and who intended to study for an MA degree or, less frequently, a PhD degree. The great majority of graduate students who achieved a doctorate at Chicago came from midwestern, western, or southern baccalaureate institutions, not from the prestigious private universities in the East. A survey of institutions that sent 5 or more successful doctoral candidates to Chicago between 1920 and 1930 (for a total of 801 students) found that 227 students came from the undergraduate programs of the University of Chicago itself, while Toronto sent 33, Missouri 21, Kansas 20, Texas 19, Indiana 19, Wisconsin 19, Illinois 18, Northwestern 16, McMaster 15, Nebraska 13, Ohio State 11, California 11, Ohio Wesleyan 10, Manitoba 10, Michigan 10, Minnesota 10, and Queens University 10 (to cite only institutions that sent 10 or more). In contrast, Harvard University sent only 11 students, Brown 8, Cornell 7, Yale 7, Columbia 6, and Dartmouth 6.[120] Chicago's doctoral market was, thus, very much midwestern.

The second stratum of graduate students attending the University of Chicago comprised part-time, transient students who journeyed to Chicago for the summer quarter only. MA students were particularly prevalent during the summer. In fact, before and just after World War I the summer quarter had the largest graduate enrollments at the University, bringing older (and often less prepared) graduate students to campus, many of them schoolteachers hoping to obtain an MA degree. Edwin E. Slosson reported that in the West "it is not uncommon to find colleges in which half or two-thirds of the faculty have studied at Chicago [during the summer]. The state of Texas alone sends 150 students. Every year the Texas students charter a special train for the University of Chicago. I should explain for the benefit of Eastern readers that this is the same geographically as if 150 Italian students came every year to Oxford."[121]

By 1910 Chicago had produced more doctorates than most universities in the United States: 573 PhDs were granted between 1892 and 1910, with an average of 30 annually.[122] The number of doctorates at Chicago grew substantially after World War I, with the average of doctorates between 1918 and 1931 increasing to 113. Departments in the physical sciences accounted for 30 percent of all doctorates granted between 1918 and 1931, with 25 percent in the biological sciences, 20 percent in the social sciences, and 16 percent in the humanities (the fledgling professional schools accounted for the remaining 9 percent). The largest single doctoral program was chemistry with 183 doctorates, followed by botany and mathematics with 112 and 104, respectively. Together these three doctoral programs encompassed almost 30 percent of the total doctorates awarded between 1918 and 1931, and they were among the most distinguished departments, as measured by faculty publications.[123] The largest MA program was in the Department of Education (905 graduates, as opposed to 454 for history, 391 for English, and 217 for chemistry), which gave the social sciences the largest total share of MA degrees (36 percent).

The model of the German *Seminar* as a vehicle in which current scholarship would be discussed and ongoing work debated, which was seen to be the pinnacle of the German doctoral system and which faculty at Johns Hopkins had made famous in the 1880s, was also adopted in many departments at the young University of Chicago, especially in the humanities and social sciences, with some departments developing departmental libraries in which their research classes might be held.[124] Among the science departments, the most advanced courses tended be research-driven colloquia that required considerable hands-on laboratory work with group discussions of current literature.

Harper claimed that his primary goal for the new graduate school was to train researchers:

The chief purpose of graduate work is not to stock the student's mind with knowledge of what has already been accomplished in a given field, but rather so to train him that he himself may be able to push out along new lines of investigation. Such work is of course of the most expensive character. Laboratories and libraries and apparatus must be lavishly provided in order to offer the necessary opportunities.... Here also is to be found the question of the effort to secure the best available men in the country as the head and director of each department. It is only the man who has made investigation who may teach others to investigate. Without this spirit in the instructor and without his example, students will never be led to undertake the work.[125]

Harper also wanted each department to establish a scholarly journal to report its work. The quarter system provided for sabbaticals from lectures to allow faculty "to give their entire time to the work of investigation."[126] Yet in contrast to its rigorous admissions process for undergraduates the early University had a virtually open admissions policy for graduate applicants,[127] which helps explain how Harper was able to drive up graduate enrollments so quickly. Applicants need only have graduated from a four-year institution that was recognized or approved as legitimate by the University.[128] Given the uncertain academic training that many of these early graduate students had had at their undergraduate colleges and the fact that many aspired only to MA degrees to enable them to teach in high schools and smaller colleges, it was understandable that the early departments created a host of lecture or lecture-and-discussion courses that they stipulated as fixed requirements. The graduate model at Chicago was similar to that of other early research universities in America—namely, a fusion of hands-on training in the techniques of original research, usually undertaken with the advice of a faculty sponsor or mentor, together with a large number of introductory courses in a wide variety of scholarly subfields. Instead of being centers of research, as Harper had hoped, the American graduate schools of the 1890s and early 1900s were becoming "schools for professional training," based on an elaborate credit system of formal course work.[129] Well into the 1930s, graduate students arrived at Chicago with uneven academic training and abilities and divergent career goals.[130] As late as 1928, a prominent dean would grumble that far too many graduate courses at Chicago still had an "apparently collegiate character," insisting that "many of these so-called '300' courses are excellent of their kind, but they lack the amount of constructive work that must be required from graduate students."[131] Two years later the same dean again complained that most graduate students were spending their time "not on the kind of work that would make them interested in research problems and skillful in the presentation of results, but in making up undergraduate deficiencies (for which they get graduate credit)."[132] When a proposal was raised in the mid-1920s that graduate programs emphasize the ability to conduct independent research, Carl F. Huth replied on behalf of the Department of History that this approach would not suit the students— even if they were grounded in the basics sufficiently—for their goal was to become teachers, not researchers.[133]

Not surprisingly, the turnover rates among early graduate students were high. Of the 3,969 graduate students registered at the University between 1892 and 1902, only 1,659 (42 percent) had been registered for three quarters or more. Floyd Reeves estimated in 1932 that of those graduate students who matriculated in the autumn quarters of 1920 and 1925, less than 30 percent completed more than six quarters of residence and only 15 percent completed nine or more quarters of residence, the usual standard for doctoral degrees.[134] Some doctoral students studied year-round, but others could study only during the summer quarter, piecing together course work over a series of years to attain a degree. Some students were tempted to leave after a year, given that many college teaching jobs were readily available for those with even modest training. James R. Angell, the dean of faculties, noted in 1913 that "in some instances the demand is so great for even imperfectly trained men that a department finds great difficulty in retaining its abler students long enough to win a doctorate. This is said to be true with some of our own departments, e.g., geology and economics."[135]

Harper set the standard teaching load for a regular faculty member at the relatively light level of (approximately) six quarter courses a year, two per quarter for three quarters.[136] Classes on both undergraduate and graduate levels were initially limited to thirty students, and most classes were significantly smaller. As late as 1927, one-third of all classes taught at the University had fewer than ten students enrolled.[137] Within those parameters, faculty, even younger ones, seem to have had considerable freedom to decide what courses they wished to teach. As Robert Herrick reported in 1895, "Each instructor has a wide liberty in conducting his courses, and I believe that no other college in America leaves her instructors so free to grow in the prosecution of their special studies."[138]

Given that the University was admitting accomplished undergraduates and graduate students with (often) patchy training and then mixing them in shared courses, styles of teaching necessarily blended formats. Lecturing was a standard format in both undergraduate and graduate courses, but the early faculty were willing to deploy other methods, especially those that involved original documents and other empirical materials. Describing the early operations of the Department of English in 1894, Albert Tolman insisted, "It seems desirable that the pupil be introduced promptly to the treasures of his own literature; it is well that he should learn early that the condensed milk of text-books cannot suffice for his mental nutriment."[139] In explaining the teaching practices at Chicago to a prospective faculty member in 1918, Andrew C. McLaughlin, the chair of the Department of History, observed that graduate courses "should be made up, I think, of lectures and reports in the classroom.... Discussions on subjects of all kinds are not only entirely appropriate but are desirable." But he then added about undergraduate teaching, "Even in the undergraduate course it is desirable to have a certain amount of give and take in the lecture room.... The formal lecture is much less in vogue here than at Ann Arbor or I think than in most universities."[140]

The early doctoral dissertations that resulted from this system were often modest affairs. As Professor Percy Gardner of Oxford University pointed out in 1899, however, "Their great value is to those who produce them. Until a man has grappled individually with some serious scientific or historic problem, he can have no experience in the use of authorities, in the weighing of evidence, or in the methods of research."[141] Still, although Chicago generated some distinctive work, much of it maintained a steady level of mediocrity. This experience paralleled that of other leading US institutions, giving rise to complaints like that of A. Lawrence Lowell at Harvard in 1909 that educators were "in danger of making the graduate school the easiest path for the good but docile scholar with little energy, independence, or ambition."[142]

Outside of academics, Harper's ideas on how graduate students should best prepare themselves for university careers were typical of his time. In a lecture before a group of graduate students in 1904, Harper advised them to marry and have three to four children: "A married instructor with three or four children is worth three times as much as an unmarried one, and he is a stronger man and a better teacher." In addition, the PhD degree was essential, as was a commitment to work in the summer months on research. Finally, graduate students should also be publicly identified with a religious denomination: "I don't see how a college education can be separated from Christian work.... I know of six or eight capable men who cannot secure positions in colleges because their attitude toward religion is—not hostile—but merely indifferent."[143]

Issues of academic supply and demand also worried the early faculty in thinking about the proper size of their doctoral programs. Writing to William Dodd in October 1913 about the size of his department's graduate program and the employment prospects for its students, Professor Andrew C. McLaughlin commented, "Why departments in graduate work should increase when one considers the small number of places open for graduate students, I am sure I don't know; and especially when one takes into consideration the number of colleges that are doing or trying to do advanced work." Dodd responded with the casual observation, "You feel the burden of finding places for each graduate student. I do not.... Though I try to do what I can to help students to jobs, ... my feeling is that our students must love history and find their rewards in broader knowledge. Whether they even become college professors depends on a number of contingencies."[144] Dodd's indifference notwithstanding, most faculty likely believed that they had a responsibility to help their doctoral students find suitable jobs. And those kinds of positions varied widely. A minority of Chicago PhDs ended up at leading private and public universities, but most populated the faculties of small colleges and regional universities.[145]

By the second decade of the University's existence, the fact that it had a reasonably large clutch of graduate students was seen as a competitive advantage in responding to outside offers. When Frank Abbott was offered a professorship in classics at Princeton, Harry Pratt Judson observed to Martin A. Ryerson that while Abbott might find the East Coast more attractive in residential and cultural terms, it would cost him the chance to do serious graduate teaching. "Graduate work at Princeton is as yet rather humorous," he observed.[146] Coming from Harvard, Robert Herrick was impressed with the graduate program that Harper had managed to set in place so quickly, and he rightly viewed that progress as a function of ground-up local management on the part of the individual departments. Herrick reported that the entire independence of separate departments, each like a small college in itself, the emphasis placed upon the doctor's degree, investigation, research, etc. and the activity of the graduate schools—all point to the German university influence.... The most distinctive move in American college life in the last decade has been in the sudden interest in post-graduate study. But hitherto no Western institution, whether college or so-called university, has had the means to provide liberally for advanced studies. This open field, therefore, it has been the ambition of the University of Chicago, situated in the centre of a vast inland constituency of small colleges, to develop.[147]

As late as 1923, Dean of the Graduate School Albion Small would complain of his powerlessness over departmental graduate programs, which he viewed as being run by "amorphous groups of autonomous Departments." Their independence was such that any inquiries from a graduate dean might well be viewed as coming from "an intruder and an interloper," Small lamented.[148] From the very first, graduate education at Chicago was a departmental enterprise organized with little quality control from the central administration. Such cultural norms privileging local autonomy would define the limits of coordination and reform in Chicago's doctoral programs that would-be revolutionaries like Robert Maynard Hutchins would confront throughout the twentieth century.

OUTCOMES

Teaching was a fundamental activity of the University from the beginning, but Harper vacillated between public statements about the superiority of research and the necessity of good teaching. In 1892, for example, he said, "It is expected that professors and other instructors will, at intervals, be excused entirely for a period from lecture work, in order that they may thus be able to give their entire time to the work of investigation.... In other words, it is proposed in this institution to make the work of investigation primary, the work of giving instruction secondary."[149] Another time Harper contradicted himself by urging that teaching was not only a moral responsibility but a way to make sure that faculty remained fresh and current in their own work. In April 1897, Harper asked rhetorically if "it be wise to establish chairs simply for investigation and research, without requirement in the way of instruction," to which he answered, "In general that investigator will accomplish most who is closely associated with a group of students.... It is best to include at least a minimum of instruction with every chair of investigation."[150] A year later he was even more forceful about teaching as a professional obligation, insisting that his deans also teach: "I cannot conceive that a man worthy to hold the place of Dean would accept the position without the privilege of giving instruction. A man who was a Dean and who gave no instruction would be merely a clerk, and would be so regarded by the students. So strongly do I feel this principle myself that I do the work of a professor, and shall continue to do so as long as I am President."[151]

The quality of teaching on the graduate and undergraduate levels seems to have been generally high, and many former students looked back on their association with senior faculty with pleasure and nostalgia. Writing to Oskar Bolza, one of the founders of the Department of Mathematics, a former MA student, Clara Latimer Bacon, recalled, "Your zest for the subject and your careful preparation for each class and the clearness and elegance of your lectures as well as your personal interest in your students have been an inspiration to me as a teacher ever since. Among the pleasantest memories of my life at the University of Chicago are the Sunday evenings in your home where you and Mrs. Bolza made your students so welcome."[152] Similar tributes could easily be identified for many of the other early faculty at the University.[153] As time passed, some early senior faculty accumulated lists of successful PhD students who were proud of their mentorship.[154]

Efforts soon emerged to coordinate and enrich undergraduate and graduate teaching across interdisciplinary departmental lines. Between 1895 and 1902, students were allowed to complete medical and law degrees within six years of matriculation in the Junior College, by double counting the senior year and using it as a site of the introductory professional school instruction.[155] In 1898 faculty from the various social sciences departments led by J. Laurence Laughlin also collaborated in creating a separate undergraduate College of Commerce and Politics for students interested in careers in business, drawing largely from courses offered by the Departments of Economics, History, Political Science, and Sociology.[156] The collegiate program of the College of Commerce (under varying names) lasted until the early 1950s and proved quite popular with Chicago undergraduates.[157] By the autumn of 1916, 29 percent of all registered third- and fourth-year undergraduate students at the University of Chicago were enrolled in programs in law, medicine, and business. Richard Storr has aptly described this trend as an early form of enlightened vocationalism: "The University was indeed working to soften or even to abolish the distinction—by making the professions truly liberal and the content of liberal education in part frankly professional."[158] The creation of the College of Commerce spurred further thinking about other forms of coordination within the social sciences, a process encouraged by Dean Small, who worried that "our programs in the social sciences involve wasteful failures of co-ordination and disproportionate degrees of attention to less and more important aspects of social relations," and who praised the "movement in the Departments of the social science group toward correlation of elementary instruction that will afford a much more definite and secure basis for graduate work than has heretofore been secured."[159] Speaking for the faculty in 1913, Dean of the Faculties James Angell applauded these trends toward greater specialization and high-level vocational preparation, arguing that they would encourage an attitude of mind marked by "the spirit of serious earnestness" in the student body and hoped that, in addition to the College of Commerce, "our other colleges may carry farther the same movement."[160]

The impact of the early University on all levels of students was remarkable, leading Edwin Slosson to observe that "no other university has exerted such an uplifting influence over so large a part of the country in so short a time."[161] Certainly Harper was deeply proud of the exemplary impact of his new programs. In February 1894 he wrote to trustee Charles Hutchinson about a recent visit to the University of Nebraska: "We found an intense interest in all that the University of Chicago is doing.... I think that they know more about our inside plans and experiments than some of our own gentlemen."[162] Class attendance for students was mandatory on all levels of instruction, and the student academic culture on both the graduate and the undergraduate levels was earnest and strongly goal oriented. Oskar Bolza remembered about his graduate students in mathematics, "Without exception they were hard working, which was related to the fact that most of them were not supported by their parents and had to support themselves either from savings—many of them were formerly teachers in high schools—or they earned money by picking up various forms of part-time work."[163] Slosson, who received his PhD from Chicago in 1902 and knew the undergraduate culture of the early campus, argued that college students worked harder at Chicago than at unnamed eastern universities and that the grading schemes were correspondingly more rigorous. He also insisted that "the University of Chicago was fortunate in starting unencumbered with the student customs of our boyish grandfathers. There has been practically no hazing, class-fighting, face painting, hair cutting, kidnapping, stealing of the chapel bell clapper, mobbing of professors, or similar student activities, and there are, I believe, no organized associations for the cultivation of hard drinking and the promotion of vice. Nevertheless the students seem to be as contented and happy as anywhere, so perhaps these things are not so essential to collegiate life as they are elsewhere supposed to be."[164] Similarly, in 1895 Robert Herrick recounted that each student "is unprejudiced in scholarship, accepting no traditions of what is really excellent to know.... He is untrained; even the ambitious candidate for a higher degree in the graduate schools is often lamentably unprejudiced about his foundation of knowledge, but he is eager, sensitive, industrious. College means for him work, and I am sure that the faculty rejoice in the fact that an industrious poverty will for a long time prevent any other conception from becoming universal."[165] Benjamin S. Terry, the dean of the Senior Colleges in 1898, took pride in the "uniformly serious character of our students": "Cases of rowdy outbreak are unknown. Flagrant breaches of discipline are also unknown. Cheating at examination, plagiarism, or other forms of dishonest practices are scarcely less rare. The sensitiveness of our students to a high code of honor is proverbial. The prevailing spirit of loyalty to the University and to its high ideals is also marked and is felt as a constant factor in the administration."[166]

In sum, the early decades of the University of Chicago established the durable authority of the departments over their individual graduate programs and manifested a serious student culture on the undergraduate level. Moreover, there were early attempts to insert undergraduate education all over the new University, including bridge programs in business, law, and medicine. As Chicago was a major research university serving the professional needs of a diversity of students, the majority of whom were commuters who lived at home or elsewhere in the city, and many of whom were also older transfer students who had clear professional and vocational objectives, a "collegiate" tradition of tightly circumscribed boundaries cordoning off undergraduates from and against the rest of the University never took hold. Indeed, Chicago's distinctiveness—already evident on the national scene by 1914—may have derived more from what Angell called the "serious earnestness" and intensity of the academic culture of its student body on all levels than from any single structural innovation of its faculty.[167] And this integrative tradition would prove sturdy enough to survive Robert Hutchins's attempts to wall off the undergraduate College from the rest of the University in the late 1940s and early 1950s.

The Board of Trustees and the Development of Harper's University

Harper's work in founding the University would have been impossible without the partnership of key members of the board of trustees. Given the feckless behavior of the board of the first University, Thomas Goodspeed realized that the new board had to play a more conscientious leadership role. He proudly predicted to Harper in June 1890 that the new board would constitute a "noble list," providing strong advisory leadership and considerable wealth.[168] The majority of the trustees did devote a substantial amount of their personal time to the work of the board, and several emerged as major benefactors in their own right. The two most active and influential trustees in the first two decades of the University's history were Martin A. Ryerson and Charles L. Hutchinson. Close friends, part of the same circle of social and business interests, they dominated the key deliberations of the board during both Harper's and Judson's presidencies.

Hutchinson once referred to Ryerson and himself as the "two bugbears of the Board"—and their interconnected lives demonstrated the qualities they valued in the University and in the city.[169] Ryerson and Hutchinson were members of a small group of progressive businessmen who sought to apply a veneer of gentility on the huge metropolis of Chicago, by 1890 the second largest city in America. Some scholars have seen these men as advocating an "urban imperialism" in Chicago to show to the outside world—particularly critics in New York—that Chicago was capable of generating cultural institutions on par with those of great European cities or the American East Coast.[170] Their willingness to help Harper and his compatriots might be seen as a convergent and timely meeting of virtue and necessity: they would help create a great and distinguished university, but it would be *their* university, not a modest Baptist institution. Harper's sweeping visions thus ran parallel to the ambitions of these representatives of the urban elite.

Yet, neither Ryerson nor Hutchinson typified the late nineteenth-century bourgeoisie. That Ryerson spent so much of his early life in Europe—he had lived in Paris and in Geneva for several years to attend private secondary schools—made his knowledge of European history and culture rich and textured. Like the senior professors at Chicago who had lived and studied in Germany and Austria, Ryerson had an intimate knowledge of the major cultural institutions of big European cities. Hutchinson too gradually gained a firsthand, if more self-guided, appreciation of the major institutional emblems of European art and architecture, exploring museums such as the South Kensington in London, the Prado in Madrid, and the Louvre in Paris.[171] Each man held considerable second-generation wealth, took great pride in his hometown, and linked the prosperity of the University and the greatness of Chicago. Both men were also young: in 1890 Hutchinson was thirty-six, and Ryerson was thirty-four, the same age as Harper. They were younger than many of the famous Chicago business leaders who wielded great power after 1870—leaders like George Pullman, Marshall Field, Richard T. Crane, Potter Palmer, and Philip Armour—whom James Gilbert and other scholars have characterized as constituting the founding generation of Chicago capitalists.[172] Their wealth allowed them to devote as much time as they wished to civic projects and cultural and educational causes. Equally important, Ryerson and Hutchinson had extensive social networks of friends and business partners, some of whom they inherited from their fathers. These elements of useful leisure, business acumen, large wealth, and a close personal understanding of the elite social networks of the burgeoning metropolis were critical in the work that both accomplished, not only at the University but also at other major civic institutions, such as the Art Institute of Chicago.

Both Ryerson and Hutchinson became involved with the University in 1890, during the early stages of the appeal by the American Baptist Education Society to obtain $400,000 to match Rockefeller's offer of $600,000. The men's association with the fledgling school was a turning point, on par with Harper's appointment as president, for their wealth as members of Chicago's "outside nobility" was critical to persuading a nervous Rockefeller that prominent citizens of Chicago would not leave him in the lurch in funding the new college.[173] A member of St. Paul's Universalist Church, Charles Hutchinson was the first non-Baptist civic leader approached by Thomas Goodspeed on behalf of the committee soliciting support from the Chicago business elite. Hutchinson agreed to support the cause with a modest subscription of $1,000 and the more valuable offer of his time and social connections. Thereafter, Gates and Goodspeed used Hutchinson's good offices in their interview with Marshall Field, which led to Field's donation of ten acres of land between Fifty-Seventh and Fifty-Ninth Streets to launch the new University.[174] Field, in turn, recommended that Hutchinson be named a trustee. Hutchinson assented but urged that his friend Martin Ryerson also be appointed to the board, perhaps because of Ryerson's greater financial capacity.[175] Ryerson then agreed to serve.

The new board held its first meeting in July 1890. Initially, the board selected a Baptist businessman and community leader, E. Nelson Blake, as its president. At the same meeting Ryerson was named vice president, with Hutchinson elected as treasurer. There is good reason to think that Ryerson's appointment was a deliberate move to place a non-Baptist within the University's leadership. So effective was Ryerson—his fellow board members passed a special resolution in June 1891 thanking him for his dedication—that Blake insisted in October 1890 on stepping aside to permit Ryerson to take charge.[176] Blake, in poor health and living out of state, was strongly seconded by Goodspeed, who realized both the material advantage and the symbolic significance of replacing Blake with Ryerson. "Mr. Ryerson charmed me," Goodspeed wrote to Harper.

> He is a quiet, but genial liberal, level headed and in every way fine man. He is without business practically, and worth $3,000,000 or $4,000,000.... There is no doubt but that our funds for [construction] must come from the businessmen of Chicago. Our own people [the Baptists] will not fur-

nish one dollar in five of it. Mr. Ryerson being the Vice President would naturally succeed Mr. Blake.... To name him as President will give us a President universally respected, with plenty of leisure, with great wealth, liberal, very close to the wealthiest and most liberal citizens.[177]

Although the University's charter of incorporation from July 1890 specified that two-thirds of the board—and the University president—be Baptist, it said nothing about the president of the board. For reasons that are unclear in the surviving correspondence, Ryerson did not formally succeed to the presidency until June 1892. The delay may have reflected tensions among the Baptists over the denominational identity of the new University, forcing Harper to move slowly in consolidating the leadership of the board.[178] Blake's own gracious letter after his resignation suggested as much when he observed that "it was only due to Mr. Ryerson from every point of view that he should be selected for the place, and I trust that the denominational friends will fully understand the case." Ryerson was not Baptist—his religious views were vaguely liberal Christian, bordering on agnostic—and making him the leader of the new board was a stunning demarche in favor of the idea of a secular university.[179]

Martin Ryerson was a calm, deliberate, thoughtful person who would be remembered for his discernment, aesthetic taste, and shrewd business sense. The son of a first-generation capitalist of the same name who made a fortune in timber and real estate, Ryerson was educated in Paris and Geneva and then attended Harvard Law School. Upon his father's death in 1887, he became one of the wealthiest men in the city, but chose to use his wealth to pursue cultural and artistic interests. His knowledge of art was on the level of a connoisseur. Stefan Germer has described Ryerson's home as a "scholarly treasure trove" that avoided any manifestation of conspicuous consumption.[180] His collection of art grew slowly and carefully, and upon his death in 1932 the Art Institute of Chicago, which he served for many years as vice president, received a breathtaking collection of French Impressionist and Postimpressionist works—including five superb paintings by Renoir and sixteen masterpieces by Monet—and an extraordinary group of paintings by early Flemish, Italian, and French masters.[181]

Ryerson quickly made his influence felt in several crucial policy issues, including the choice of an architect to plan the new campus and the size and domain of the territory on which the campus would be located. It was Ryerson who guided the deliberations of the Committee on Buildings and Grounds in its choice of Henry Ives Cobb and a neo-Gothic design of the first campus master plan, and perhaps equally important, it was Ryerson, working in tandem with Hutchinson, who urged that the original scope of the campus be expanded by acquiring additional territory owned by Marshall Field.[182] Ryerson even put up $25,000 in cash in 1891 as the major component of the down payment needed to acquire this additional property. Other trustees felt that this expansion was too ambitious and risky, but Ryerson and Hutchinson believed that a larger and more cohesive site would better serve the long-term interests of the University. Similarly, Ryerson was also the key figure in Harper's successful campaign to acquire the Berlin Collection, providing almost half of the funds raised to purchase the collection of books owned by S. Calvary and Company in Berlin in 1891. Overnight this collection transformed the University's fledgling library, and by 1896 the University of Chicago had the second largest university library collection in the country. But Ryerson's most significant donations lay ahead. As Harper and Goodspeed urgently sought gifts from local Chicagoans in the spring of 1892 to build the first set of buildings, Ryerson notified Harper in a cable from Paris that he would pledge $150,000 in memory of his father for the construction of the building that became the Ryerson Physical Laboratory.[183] A year later Ryerson intervened at an equally critical juncture, offering to provide $100,000 in cash if other Chicagoans would come up with another $400,000, a matching fund that, in turn, merited an additional $500,000 from John D. Rockefeller.[184]

Having funded the Physical Laboratory, Ryerson also became a patron of the work of its leading scientist and eventual Nobel Prize winner, Albert A. Michelson. In 1898 Ryerson invited Michelson to provide a list of the sums needed for research, and Ryerson then informed the board that he would personally cover these costs.[185] He later provided additional gifts to support Michelson's research in 1904, 1907, and 1924. Michelson's daughter later recalled that Ryerson took great personal pride in her father's research achievements.[186] Ryerson's subsequent investments after the First World War were equally significant: a gift of $250,000 in 1917–18 to help launch the Medical School; and, finally, an additional $200,000 to create the first endowed chair in the history of the new University, which, predictably, was awarded to Albert A. Michelson.[187]

Perhaps as important as Ryerson's financial largesse—his total gifts to the University exceeded $2 million, far surpassing Goodspeed's hoped-for $500,000—were his acute appreciation of Harper's educational vision, his respect for the faculty as scholars and not mere teachers, and his understanding of the special needs of a university that would devote huge resources to sponsoring original scientific research. These values were apparent in speeches that Ryerson gave on various public occasions in the 1890s. On the occasion of the dedication of the Yerkes Astronomical Observatory in October 1897, he argued that the new facility would not only serve powerful instrumental purposes but also enhance the analytic ideals of science. For Ryerson, the reconciliation of the practical and the ideal was a compelling challenge: "Let us by all means be practical if we can, at the same time [let us] broaden our conception of the meaning of the word, so that it may include that development of the intellectual side of life, without which any improvement of material conditions is absolutely vain."[188] Similarly, in June 1901, he insisted that the University's progress in the moral and intellectual domains characterized modern life in the United States as well, and he took pleasure in the fact that the world was "as ready to respond to earnest and devoted work in moral and intellectual fields" as it was "to efforts put forth for material gain."[189] At the same time, in defending the intrinsic value of research, Ryerson opposed a conception of the University as isolated from society. During a dinner meeting of alumni in February 1897, Ryerson spoke on behalf of the trustees, and the occasion called for what would now be called civic outreach. He insisted that the new "higher" education penetrate every stratum of society, shaping and preparing all for the "duties, the trials, and the pleasures of life." Ryerson then argued that the University community must continually engage the world. "While the problems of education must be solved by educators, those problems must be stated and the solutions verified by life itself, not alone the life of the scholar, nor that of any class of a community, but human life in its broadest sense," he said.[190] "The experiences and educational needs of all should be brought to the knowledge of educators, the practical as well as the intellectual and spiritual requirements of mankind should be made known by contact with the world which will test theories by practice and direct educational energies in useful channels." Ryerson also placed special emphasis on keeping the University open to evaluation from outsiders: "Management should be kept open to outside advice and criticism. We shall welcome through this body, which we hope will contain a constantly increasing circle of men and women who have gone forth from The University into the different walks of life, such advice and criticism." These were not profound intellectual formulations, but they revealed the mind of a subtle, articulate person who had immense respect for the integrity and power of the new research universities. If the faculty of the new research university wanted a Gilded Age capitalist in 1892 to lead their board of trustees, they were lucky to find a civic leader of Ryerson's stripe—the rare businessman who respected their scholarly work for its own sake as well as for its practical consequence.

Ryerson's values were shared by his regular dinner companion, close friend, and ally Charles Hutchinson, who was a perpetual-motion machine of civic leadership in Chicago. Like Ryerson, Hutchinson was the son of an early Chicago capitalist, Benjamin Hutchinson, who made a fortune in the stockyards and grain trade. The friendship of the two men, which began when they met at a dinner party in the late 1880s, was further strengthened by the parallel friendship of their wives and assumed remarkable forms of social and philanthropic tourism to Europe, India, Japan, and Egypt.[191] Yet, if Hutchinson's philanthropy paralleled Ryerson's, there were differences. Hutchinson was a joiner, an enthusiast, and an advocate, involved in a hundred different causes, although no closer than Ryerson to the "tycoon" mentality that Thorstein Veblen thought characteristic of the typical university board member. He was also self-educated—a recent biographer has described him in his youth as a "sensitive, intelligent, bookish, deeply religious boy who wanted to go to college but acceded to his father's wishes and went into the family business instead."[192] Hutchinson's social causes were as varied as his contacts in Chicago society: the Commercial Club, the World's Columbian Exposition, the Relief and Aid Society, Hull House, the Chicago Orphan Asylum, and the Chicago Public Library. He also supported Harriet Monroe's efforts to found *Poetry* magazine.

Hutchinson's greatest civic role was to serve as the president of the Art Institute of Chicago, of which Ryerson became a principal patron. Hutchinson was named president in April 1882, and his credentials as a civic booster of the arts were well established when the appeal for the new University started later in the decade. Hutchinson's theories about the importance of art in society paralleled Ryerson's views on the utility of science. An ardent social progressive, Hutchinson believed that the Art Institute had a responsibility to elevate the taste and sensibilities of the masses. Eager to spread the gospel of aesthetic rehabilitation, Hutchinson pushed the Art Institute to open its doors with free admission on Sundays and insisted that the museum building be located in the middle of the city, not in an isolated park. As Kathleen McCarthy has pointed out, it was also owing to Hutchinson that the Art Institute developed a socially inclusive, outward-looking notion of who should be its proper audience: "Artisans, blue- and white-collar workers, visitors from the country, and wealthy art patrons all appeared in the museum's halls, a fact which delighted Hutchinson, who made daily visits and constantly kept tabs on attendance records. With his usual ebullience, he declared that the Art Institute was overactive, overhospitable, overcrowded with passing exhibitions and students, but at least it was alive."[193] Hutchinson once quipped that "the state has a right to demand from a man not only part of his money, but also a tithe of his thought, his time, and his life. Everybody should put into the city in which he lives as much as he gets out of it."[194]

Commuting between the Art Institute and the University, Martin Ryerson and Charles Hutchinson exchanged roles, or, perhaps more accurately, adopted roles appropriate to their personalities. At the Art Institute, Hutchinson was president and Ryerson nominally the vice president, but, in fact, one of its chief artistic patrons. At the University, Ryerson was the board president, with Hutchinson serving as treasurer and as chair of the Committee on Buildings and Grounds, one of the board's most powerful standing committees. Hutchinson's enthusiastic jottings to Harper in April 1900 as he toured Oxford University looking for "great ideas" for the cluster of buildings that would be built at the corner of Fifty-Seventh and University (including the new Commons, which he financed and which is patterned on the great hall at Christ Church, Oxford), confirmed his early conviction that "this city of ours would be richer, filled with a higher intellectual life, had we more beautiful surroundings, monuments of art, buildings stored with books and paintings and sculpture. So that on every hand something should suggest high and noble thoughts."[195] Ernest Burton observed that "as each of the forty buildings of the University was planned, and finally built, Mr. Hutchinson gave prolonged and intelligent attention to the plans, considering carefully not only the larger matters of style and general structure, but even the minutest of details of arrangement, ornamentation, and furniture.... He had a keen sense of the influence of architecture on the formation of taste, and a strong desire, happily shared by many of his associates, that what the University built should be so built that it would stand and be worthy to last. He built for a long future."[196]

As the president of the fledging board, Martin Ryerson exercised three key roles. First, Ryerson's own substantial philanthropy, combined with his social prestige, set a powerful example for other influential Chicagoans to emulate. Second, his governance style was low key, conciliatory, and deeply respectful of Harper and the senior professoriate. Third, and perhaps most important, was Ryerson's help in sustaining successful financial lifelines to the powers that be in New York City. That Rockefeller trusted and respected Ryerson's steadiness and prudent judgment was a vital, if invisible, element in the success of the early University.

Ryerson reconciled Harper's craving for money and Rockefeller's endless worries about that craving. Ryerson never ceased to emphasize to Harper that the University had to live within its means, cautioning in February 1894 that fund-raising was "the most pressing matter which the Trustees have to consider at the present."[197] When Frederick Gates, whom Rockefeller hired in 1893 to help run his philanthropic ventures, expressed serious concerns about Harper's recurring deficits in early 1897, Ryerson carefully associated himself with Gates's position. "I think that we should ... at an early date trim our sails to meet the situation, unless we have very good assurances that Mr. Rockefeller intends to place us in a position to continue on the present scale," he wrote to Harper.[198] He also urged Harper to maintain simplicity in university organization. Ryerson was suspicious of too many specialized ruling bodies and administrative layers that might foster political strife in the University.[199] At the same time, the board under Ryerson was loath to force budgetary retrenchment strategies on Harper, and as Gates himself admitted in a confidential memo in 1897, there were good reasons for not engaging in capricious amputations:

> Most universities are the result of growth begun with a central germ or nucleus, they have developed year by year, gradually taking on new features as means have commanded and the times demanded. The history of the University of Chicago is altogether different.... What we have now may be fairly estimated to be the cost of a fairly complete University— excluding the applied sciences, law, medicine, and technology. When you come to the question, therefore, of retrenchment, you are confronted with the idea of tearing down your building, with reference to saving heat, light, and service, and after all comparatively minor expenditures.... The institution simply cannot retrench. It can close, it can go out of business but to retrench within the limits of this enormous deficit is simply to shut up shop. The fact is that the University is one whole. Every part is dependent on the other parts. It is like a living organism and any attempt at change of its present basis, involves all of the frightful wastes of amputation and disease.[200]

Ryerson's role as mediator between the "Founder" of the University, who was in New York, and the irrepressible president of the University, who was in Chicago, was all the more delicate because of Rockefeller's unwillingness to involve himself in the direct governance of the University. Rockefeller was adamant about not wanting a formal role on the board of trustees, preferring local officers to accept and maintain managerial responsibility. Gates reported to Harper that Rockefeller had no intention of controlling the board directly. He "would prefer in general not to take active part in the counsels of the management," Gates explained. "He prefers to rest the whole weight of the management on the shoulders of the proper officers.... The only way to assure a wise management ... is to continue the method employed hitherto, in the selection of members of the board, which is to make the most careful, the nicest possible choice of new men to fill necessary vacancies, as they shall from time to time occur, and so to keep the board at all times up to the highest point of skill and efficiency."[201]

Of course, in practice Rockefeller wielded enormous power over the development of the fledgling University. And after 1896 this power was formalized by the fact that both Frederick Gates and John D. Rockefeller Jr. joined the board of trustees as de facto agents, thus creating a strange dual governance system, lodged partly in Chicago and partly in New York City. Although proud of Harper's achievements, Rockefeller became increasingly apprehensive about Harper's propensity to run up huge deficits. Between 1894 and 1903, for example, annual deficits in the University's operating budget averaged $215,000.[202] This meant that 26–31 percent of each annual budget between 1894 and 1903 had to be covered by Rockefeller, but only by after-the-fact petitioning and occasional scheming on the part of Harper and Goodspeed that was tolerated, if not sanctioned, by the board in Chicago. These tensions were analyzed in two fascinating reports by Starr J. Murphy, a lawyer who worked for Rockefeller and who was sent to Chicago in late 1903 to undertake an "exhaustive inquiry" into the University's operations and especially its finances. As Gates discreetly informed Harper, Murphy was "to spend some time at the university, looking into all its various affairs with such eyes as Mr. Rockefeller and myself would hope to use were the time available."[203] Murphy's first attempt to assay the structure of the University resulted in a long, insightful report in early 1904 that was generally complimentary but also commented on the strange governance situation in which the board of trustees found itself: "The President is a man of great persuasiveness, and it is easy for him to present to his Trustees, in a very convincing way, the importance and necessity of the things which he desires to see accomplished.... The founder is well known to be a man of great resources and of great liberality, and ... year after year he has added princely sums to its endowment, and year after year as the annual budgets have been presented to him and his immediate representatives, the annual deficit has been provided for." But this situation, Murphy averred, must not be allowed to continue, and he left no doubt who was responsible:

> The existing financial situation, and the course of financial administration for the past few years is intolerable and must be altered. While it is desirable and necessary that the Trustees should be men of broad intellectual sympathy and of keen appreciation of educational needs and possibilities, it is also necessary that they should be men of iron resolution, capable, notwithstanding their full appreciation of these things, of appreciating, with equal force, the limitations imposed by financial considerations. This is where they have proved themselves lacking, and it is in this direction that a change must be sought.[204]

As the deficit continued to distress Rockefeller, Murphy submitted a second, blistering report in February 1905, laying the blame on the officers of the University, by whom he meant the local Chicago trustees as well as Harper and Goodspeed, for the "constant and alarming increase in the budget deficits." For Murphy the University's budget estimates were characterized by "utter worthlessness," offering Rockefeller "no protection whatever." Indeed, they were "purely a matter of form, as the University authorities do not consider themselves in any way bound by them."[205] The outraged reactions of Goodspeed and several trustees against Murphy's "offensive expressions" could not mask the fact that Murphy had not only called a fiscal spade a spade, but had also dared to say openly what others had been willing to ponder only silently.[206] In their own business careers the trustees were known as men of steadfast resolution. How could Ryerson and his colleagues explain the evident disjunction between their tough-minded worldliness in the affairs of their own businesses and their cavalier toleration of the free-spending ways of William Rainey Harper? Was their support for Harper an example of conflict avoidance, or was it a case of deliberate Machiavellianism, a charge that Murphy out of politeness dismissed in his first report, but which he came close to imputing in his second?[207] The trustees were certainly aware of what they had done (or not done).[208] During a crucial conference on the annual budget with Gates in February 1897, Thomas Goodspeed sought to deflect the trustees' and Harper's responsibility by arguing that the whole problem was one of good intentions coupled with faulty planning. In his unpublished memoirs, however, Goodspeed candidly confessed his ambivalence about his friend's tactics. "It sometimes seemed as though Dr. Harper was deliberately forcing the Founder's hand and had adapted this as a thoroughly considered and permanent policy," he wrote. "Was the method of extorting gifts from the Founder by what seemed like compulsion the best method? Was this the only way in which the great immediate success and growth of the University could have been attained?"[209]

Ryerson's and Hutchinson's own correspondence with Harper indicates that they were keenly aware of their leader's spending habits. In January 1896, Hutchinson cautioned Harper, "Don't let all this good fortune lead you astray. Go slow."[210] Similarly, in March 1900 Ryerson warned Harper against the temptation to construct new buildings on the basis of "inadequate gifts," urging instead patience and the construction of temporary facilities "outside of the Quadrangles" that might later be used for other purposes.[211] Ryerson was also aware of Rockefeller's and Gates's expectations that new gifts go toward eliminating the deficits rather than continued expansion. At a budget conference in New York in December 1898, Ryerson made a firm commitment to use new, locally generated funds to eliminate deficits, and not to expand programs: "So far as there is any opportunity of directing the application of the gifts to the University, the policy of the Board now is to provide for work already being done by the University rather than for any expansion of the work." But he also asserted that the journey to the promised land of budgetary equilibrium would not end in the near future: "I think the Board has in mind the importance of that fact and any delay in making efforts has been caused by the hopelessness of doing anything [on the fund-raising front] rather than through [the] forgetfulness of the Board. It is now planned to renew the efforts at an early date."[212] Ambition, not deception, was ultimately at work here.

Still, in spite of these well-meaning commitments, there is no evidence—pace Starr Murphy's suspicions—that Ryerson and his colleagues seriously sought to curb Harper's proclivity to spend money he did not have. Not until a summit meeting in late December 1903, where a decision was taken in Rockefeller's personal offices in New York that the deficit must be curbed, was Harper finally called up short.[213] Even then Ryerson defended Harper to Gates, suggesting that "it is difficult ... to keep Dr. Harper from interesting himself in all the details of affairs at the University and in cases where he thinks an emergency exists, from exceeding his authority in connection with them." Ryerson then added, in a cautionary observation, "It may not be expedient to run the risk of discrediting his proper authority by making it possible and even necessary for employees to question its extent."[214]

Perhaps Ryerson's willingness to play the middleman between Harper's buoyant ambition and Rockefeller's ongoing dismay reflected his pride in Harper's compelling, if expensive, educational vision. His and Hutchinson's extensive correspondence with Harper reveals an ongoing fascination with the unique qualities of the new University. In one of his earliest letters to Harper, Ryerson urged that "we cannot set our aims too high nor plan too broadly the future of the University."[215] Similarly, Hutchinson would write proudly to Harper in January 1892, congratulating him on having recruited both J. Laurence Laughlin and William G. Hale from Cornell: "Do not see how we could have done better. Indeed, we are to be congratulated in securing two such men as Hale and Laughlin. I have no fears of the future of the University. Listen to my 'fatherly' advice and go right on in the lines already adopted and success will attend your efforts."[216] Ryerson also understood that Rockefeller and Gates were bound up in the success of Harper's vision, all protests at annual budget meetings notwithstanding. For a patrician like Ryerson, the protestations of a legal hired gun like Starr Murphy were irrelevant unless they reflected a lasting alienation on the part of Rockefeller. Indeed, if anyone played the role of a Veblen-like "businessman" in these transactions, it was Murphy, not Harper and his capitalist friends on the board of trustees.[217] Given the fact that their own professional instincts were to follow the straight and narrow path of budgetary probity, it was extraordinary that Ryerson and Hutchinson were willing to accord to Harper an unusually broad range of flexibility and trust.

Ryerson, Hutchinson, and their fellow trustees served the University well by being discreetly and stubbornly caught in the middle. These were able, tough-minded businessmen and civic leaders, but either from personal commitment to Harper's vision of the wonder of a new, major university in the West or from a deep civic pride that wanted to get Chicago as much university as Rockefeller could be lobbied (tricked?) into paying for, they served the University by *not* doing what Murphy insisted that they should have done—namely, clamp down on their fast-talking president. According to Goodspeed, Gates believed that Rockefeller would have given as much, if not more, money and would have done so "not only more happily, but more freely, more rapidly, and more largely" if Harper (and the trustees) had only been forthright by consulting Rockefeller beforehand about their expansionist plans.[218] Harper clearly felt otherwise, and acted accordingly.

In the end, it was Rockefeller, after the fiscally conservative Harry Pratt Judson had succeeded the spendthrift Harper as president of the University, who solved the deficit problem with several massive additional gifts to the endowment between 1906 and 1910, concluding with Rockefeller's final donation of $10 million in December 1910. These gifts essentially capitalized the structural deficit and allowed the University to bring order to its financial affairs without immediate compromise to its scholarly reputation or educational quality.[219] Rockefeller's final gift was a logical, although certainly not inevitable, outcome of the board's strategy. Having launched the University with Rockefeller's money, having then contributed sizable sums of their own, and having prevailed on Rockefeller for still more massive contributions to cover the annual structural deficit, the Founder's final gift represented, from the perspective of the trustees, both a confession of the need for fiscal penitence and the reception of the good grace of a friendly providence.

It is difficult to imagine the success of Harper's daring without the patient leadership and careful mediation of the late nineteenth-century civic elite represented on the board of trustees. If that leadership appeared to outsiders like Murphy as too deferential toward Harper, perhaps that made it all the more effective, combining as it did an ardent civic boosterism, a belief in the pragmatic values of scientific research, great generosity with their own fortunes, and an unusual capacity to accept risk and, at the same time, exercise political common sense. Moreover, if Harper in 1902 could praise the trustees for having the wisdom to leave the academic affairs of the University to the exclusive control of the faculty, later generations of trustees continued to affirm that tradition. As we will see in chapter 4, severe tensions between some trustees and Robert Maynard Hutchins in the 1930s would test the "noninterventionist" traditions of the board, but in the end they were sustained throughout the twentieth century.

The Role of Religion in the New University

The role of religion in the University has been the subject of considerable debate over the decades. The University is a resolutely secular one, despite the presence of many religious groups on campus. Harper's conception of the role of religion deeply informed the value system of the University, the way it spoke about itself, and its cultural ambitions in the city and the world. For Harper and the late nineteenth-century corporate institutionalists of his generation, Christianity was an integral part of a system of norms that also defined community order and economic justice.[220] Harper's colleagues spoke of his nomination to the presidency and his plans for the new University as being directly given by God for him to carry out.[221] For Frederick Gates, the creation of the University was a work so remarkable, so progressive, and so efficacious that it must have been divinely inspired.[222]

Harper himself confirmed this legacy when he argued, "The name University will be a misnomer if any other spirit than a broad one is allowed to characterize it. There is but one thing in the Universe sacred aside from God; that thing is truth. Searching for truth is searching for God. Investigation must not be hampered. It should be honest and sincere, cautious and reverent, but it should also be broad; and the truth wherever and however found must be accepted at any cost." He further insisted that "if our work is not done for Christ, better it were left undone.... If we are to succeed, the spirit of the Christ must pervade and regulate and dominate it all.... The University of Chicago, whatever else it may be, by the grace of God shall be Christian in tone, in influence, and in work."[223] The University's Baptist identity was an appropriate entry point to undertaking this larger ecumenical and providential Christian work: "To be sure it will be a Baptist institution, under Baptist control, because we are Baptists. But we are also men, and men desirous of adding to the store of knowledge; and for this we shall make the University of Chicago broad and Christian in the fullest sense."[224]

How was this putative legacy to work its way in the world? Although the Baptists had founded the new institution, Gates's and Goodspeed's pragmatism had led them to seek vital outside support. Goodspeed became deeply sensitive about not damaging these external relationships.

In September 1890 when he learned that Harper was thinking of constructing a building for the Divinity School ahead of other buildings on campus, he worried that "if we begin with the Theological Seminary, erect its buildings first and open it first on our campus, we cannot but convey to the public the idea that we are sectarianizing the entire enterprise. They will say, this is Baptist and nothing but Baptist, sectarian all the way thro', and if we let this impression go abroad we destroy ourselves."[225] Goodspeed preferred that Harper talk about the University as having a broadly Christian identity:

> Tho' one denomination proposed the enterprise and has provided a very large part of the initial fund, the University is to be in no sense a sectarian institution, the charter being one of the broadest and most liberal in its spirit ever devised. The denominational character of the Divinity School will be preserved and abundantly protected under a separate Board of Trustees, but it is understood by all that the other departments of the University are to be unsectarian in their motives and methods, while they remain Christian in the highest and best sense of that word. You come to a university that is designed for no one section but for all the people and it will be your aim to so administer its affairs as to win for it the confidence of the public.[226]

Goodspeed's conception of the University as one that was "Christian in the highest and best sense of the word" allowed the institution to function in many and diverse roles under the direct and beneficent hand of God. Harper shared Goodspeed's newly acquired liberal sensibilities and found many opportunities to inscribe his own broad understanding of Christianity as an urgent aspiration of the University's mission.[227] When he spoke at the laying of the cornerstone of Haskell Oriental Museum in July 1895, Harper observed that "the thought that this building has been given by a generous Christian woman [Caroline Haskell] in order to make possible the broader and deeper study of the world's sacred scriptures, and especially those of Christianity, is still more significant and more inspiring. But most significant and most inspiring of all is the simple Christian faith and the generous Christian heart which prompted this magnificent gift for the cause of science and of truth."[228]

Religion also shaped Harper's public rhetoric about the larger work of the university. "The University and Democracy," a famous address that Harper delivered in March 1899 at the University of California at Berkeley, was a robust statement of Harper's political thought and revealed an overt linkage to religion and especially Christianity.[229] The speech came at the end of the Spanish-American War, and its patriotism was surely influenced by Harper's desire to set himself and his university on the upward tide of what he felt to be a positive democratic imperialism that would spread around the world. Harper began by drawing a portrait of the university that would have been reasonably familiar: the university as a historic corporation of near-equal (and thus democratic) members in search of truth. To exercise this mission the corporation upheld certain rules and values, above all freedom of thought and of expression, and an urgent willingness to spread new knowledge. In the past (and present), universities had been threatened by political and ecclesiastical control. But the modern university would tolerate neither, for it needed total freedom to undertake its search for truth. Truth might be messy and controversial, but it was better than ignorance. Man's highest nature demanded that he (or at least those capable of doing so at a university) move ever closer toward its comprehension and its distribution to a wider society.

Democracy was also a familiar term, although Harper loaded it with enormous ethical freight in that this modern and almost providential way of life was now fated to encompass more and more of the earth—if only society could generate proper leadership structures to guide the people in their achievement of effective self-governance, self-policing, and self-moralizing. Here then a specific and gratifying role for the university opened up. The democratic people, although virtuous in many ways, were not always capable of making wise choices in the process of self-rule. This meant that someone or something had to provide enlightened leadership. It fell to the university to do just this, for the university was "the agency established by heaven itself to proclaim the principles of democracy.... It is the university that, as a center of thought, is to maintain for democracy the unity so essential for its success." Harper did not stop with democracy as a gentle, elite-run institution of beneficent assistance in securing practical self-administration and self-rule in the Progressive Era. He insisted that democracy was the highest form of human organization and that it had all of the appurtenances of a religion, since it called its adherents forth to rise to ever more challenging levels of ethical and moral behavior.[230] As a system of strong ethical and moral affects, it needed democratic prophets who would proclaim its virtues and its righteousness, democratic priests who would ensure its cultic efficacy and collective mediation, and democratic philosophers who would help guide its theoretical self-understanding. The modern university, being well suited to play all three roles, was the priest, prophet, and philosopher of democracy.

This late nineteenth-century tract was in many respects pure midwestern progressivism. Educated, refined, and morally uplifted elites would lead the democratic masses, and their cultural values would shape mass society. But it was also a crucial statement of Harper's conviction that the core religious attribute of the university was its commitment to the pursuit of reason, knowledge, and truth. Harper thus made a fascinating attempt to move beyond a strict denominational identity as a marker for the institution's religious worthiness to search for a more ambitious way to link religion and the university by defining the latter as a corporate community of knowledge and reason, seeking the highest ethical good. Some conservative critics warned against such a path, fearing that it would lead to a kind of "solo Christianity" based on individualistic rationalism,[231] but Harper was convinced that the alternatives—censorship and a priori rules governing scholarship and teaching—were destructive of authentic and creative research.

In this scheme, the University would drive society not only forward but also upward. Grace flowed downward, but it also arose from the quotidian practices of the disciplined, enlightened Christian and Jewish scholars and students who dedicated themselves to a life of scientific knowledge in the name of fostering a more enlightened and better-managed society. Grant Wacker has argued that one common trait of all Protestant liberals was their belief that "God's self-revelation is mediated through the flow of history."[232] For Harper this godly flow of history would be shaped by the flow of knowledge and scientific truth, the agent of that process being the modern—and in his case Christian—university. The university that he created not only would be religious in a new way, but by enhancing the scientific study of religion would renew the credentials of professional theology to better meet the needs of an urban, mass society. As Clark Gilpin has rightly noted, the image that liberal Christian theologians imputed to the universities as powerful agents of the immanent work of the kingdom of God in the world also transformed and enhanced the roles of modern divinity schools embedded within such universities: "The rise of the modern university was, simultaneously, both the most visible symptom of America's cultural transition and the key to theology's successful adjustment to the emerging new society.... The university-related divinity school—Harvard, Yale, Chicago, or Union Theological Seminary—became the liberal paradigm for contemporary theological scholarship, and during the first three decades of the twentieth century they regarded it as a pivotal institution for religion's leverage on American society."[233]

This discourse played well with those who opposed a rigid denominational identity for the new University. The *Chicago Tribune* insisted that Harper disliked sectarianism, and that "it is an open secret ... to those who know Dr. Harper best that it is his desire to wholly divest the university of its threatened sectarian interference, and that he thoroughly believes denominationalism and a university of the cosmopolitan character he wishes it to acquire to be incompatible."[234] This interpretation of Harp-

er's motives was shared by many among Chicago's civic elites. Charles
Hutchinson, for example, was adamant to the young Baptist fund-raisers
that sectarianism had killed the first University of Chicago, and he and his
fellow capitalists had no desire to be tarred by a second debacle. When
negotiating for the gift from the William B. Ogden estate to create a graduate school of science, Harper was forced to assure Andrew H. Green, the
executor handling the negotiations, that "the denominational complexion
of the Board of Trustees will not affect in any way the broadest platform
of study and the freest admission to the proposed school of students and
professors alike of any shade of religious opinion or of none."[235]

The rapid evolution of the University into a community of scholars
and students, many of whom had no explicit affiliation with a Baptist
church, angered some of Harper's fellow denominationalists. As a parting
shot in his feud with Harper, Augustus Strong noted in December 1890
that there was "no provision for securing the theological orthodoxy or
religious character of the teachers" at the University. "This to me is the
most vital point of all," he wrote. "I do not know why Baptists should
concern themselves about education at all, unless they aim to establish
institutions which fill a totally different place from those founded on a
secular basis by individuals or the state.... What I desire is a University
on a different model from any existing one—a University in which Christ
is nominally and really the cornerstone, and rationalism, at least so far
as the teachers are concerned, is kept out."[236] Harper, of course, flatly
rejected this perspective, but it remained a thorny issue in Baptist circles.
Denominational consciousness died hard among local Baptist ministers.
When Charles Hutchinson expressed an interest in 1892 in raising money
for a university chapel, several trustees of the Baptist Theological Union
Trustees were outraged that a Universalist like Hutchinson might dare
to sponsor a sacred space.[237] In April 1896 one of the most charismatic
Baptist pastors in Chicago, P. S. Henson of the First Baptist Church at
Thirty-First Street and South Park Avenue, went public with a stunning
attack on Harper's putative evasiveness. Harper had treated Rockefeller
like a puppet on a string while subverting a genuine Baptist identity for
the University, according to Henson. In his eyes, Harper was a remarkable
"hypnotist" who had conned Rockefeller into supporting a university with
many senior professors who were agnostics and pantheists, and worst of
all "thorough-paced evolutionists."[238]

Henson's diatribe gained little traction, and Harper refused to be
dragged into a street fight. But tensions among Baptists over the theological direction of the Divinity School and the University in general continued while Harper lived, and grew worse after his death. Robert Carter has
argued that Harper became increasingly impatient and even strident with

conservative opponents of modern biblical criticism during the 1890s, abandoning his early editorial cautions and blaming ill-educated clerics for hindering effective Bible study by laypersons.[239] Harper's calls in 1898 and 1899 for a reform of Baptist seminary education to meet "the requirement of modern times" by integrating it more closely with the work of the universities followed directly from his concerns about the educational impoverishment of many ministers trained in small denominational seminaries.[240] The presence of the radical theologian and Nietzsche enthusiast George Burman Foster in the Department of Systematic Theology of the Divinity School led to further tensions with the Baptist Theological Union, which peaked in October 1904 when Harper found himself forced to broker a deal with moderate and conservative Baptists on the union's board of trustees under which Foster would be moved from the Divinity School to the Department of Comparative Religion in the arts and sciences.[241] Harper admitted to Andrew MacLeish six months later that rumors were circulating in Baptist circles to the effect that the University was having trouble raising the $250,000 needed to build a Divinity School building because of the liberal character of the faculty.[242] The unhappiness of more conservative and fundamentalist Chicago Baptists with the Divinity School grew so acute that a secessionist movement led to the founding of the Northern Baptist Theological Seminary in Chicago in 1913.[243] In the end, the Swift family, who were Methodists, gave the University over $300,000 for a new building for the Divinity School constructed in 1924–26.

For many liberal Baptists, this division came as a relief. In 1914 Frederick Gates, now with the experience of almost twenty-five years of philanthropic work with the Rockefellers under his belt and having experienced what Raymond Fosdick would later characterize as a "remarkable change in theological and philosophical thinking," wrote to John D. Rockefeller Jr., urging that the Baptists should face facts and relinquish all control over the University. "The Baptist denomination could now do in no way so great, so far reaching a service to mankind as publicly to emancipate the University from denominational control.... Nothing would so tend to exalt the true spirit of Christ among all Christian peoples as for the Baptist denomination, which has hitherto been one of the most narrowly sectarian of the Christian bodies, to unloose its hold upon an institution with forty millions of money and seventy-five hundred students, and with the supreme desire that truth and its ultimate triumph send forth this institution, free from every shackle on its great mission to humanity."[244]

Gates's invocation of "truth and its ultimate triumph" as the residual ethical character of the University had Harperian overtones. Although he loathed conflict with his fellow Baptists, Harper was convinced that the

University was most Christian—most religious—when it empowered the
freedom of individual students and faculty to seek truth. Harper's belief
in the liberal evangelical transformation of the world via the agency of
the new universities was a classic declaration of what David Hollinger
and others have characterized as the "essentialism" of the late nineteenth-
century liberal Protestant milieu, transposed to an academic setting.[245] At
the same time, conservative fears about the collapse of institutional religious practices at the University were exaggerated. Before World War I,
the University did not undertake a religious census of its students on the
grounds, as Dean James Angell put it, that the results would be "at best
an approximation of the facts," and perhaps also because Harper did not
want data circulating that might cause him trouble with his conservative
denominational brethren.[246] But there is no reason to believe that the
state of affairs that Charles R. Henderson described to Frederick Gates in
late 1892—"We have a body of students who are evidently in earnest....
A very large majority are from religious homes and are sincerely attached
to the Christian faith"—was not sustained during Harper's and Judson's
tenure.[247] In 1919–20, a survey of undergraduate-student behavior was
undertaken by Theodore G. Soares, a theology professor, and Harold D.
Lasswell, a precocious college student. As part of this larger survey on
student life, Lasswell and Soares examined the patterns of religious affiliation of undergraduate students.[248] They discovered widespread membership in a religious group or confession, and relatively widespread attendance patterns at church services. Of the 2,065 students, approximately
67 percent self-identified as belonging to a Protestant denomination,
12.5 percent declared themselves Jewish, 8.1 percent were Catholic, and
11.8 percent identified themselves as belonging to other groups, like the
Mormons, the Greek Orthodox, or the Confucians. Only one student
identified himself as an atheist, and only two declared themselves agnostic. Further, over 90 percent of these students reported that they regularly
attended a church service (exclusive of chapel) at least once a month,
and about 45 percent attended weekly services. Smaller proportions regularly participated in a class involving religious education at least once a
month, taught Sunday school, or served as officers or agents of a religious
organization.

Such survey data were (and still are) but a crude estimation of religios-
ity, and the authors were quick to point out that this data could at most be
taken as a "preliminary effort to get together certain isolated facts" about
student behavior. But it is instructive that a great majority of the student
body in the years between 1890 and 1920 had religious orientations of
some kind. If anything, the student body of the early Harper era would
have been even more Protestant, with connections to specific religious

groups in the neighborhood and in the city at large. Harper did not create a strictly Baptist university, but as late as the early 1920s, he had created a university in which involvement with religious institutions was still widespread among the student body, and most likely, among a majority of the faculty as well.[249]

Harper's Publics: Church, Neighborhood, and City

William Rainey Harper's scholarly work overflowed into the neighborhood and the city. His vocation as a public educator, a Christian missionary, and a social critic intermingled in these efforts. The neighbors within the community of Hyde Park with whom Harper most profitably and comfortably engaged were the evangelical Protestants who read the Bible and who felt a responsibility to understand it as a guide for moral living. Harper's closest outreach point in Hyde Park was thus the one that was most congenial to his temperament and religious convictions: his local Baptist church. The Hyde Park Baptist Church at Fifty-Sixth Street and Woodlawn Avenue became an outpost for Harper's vision of a saintly urban community. The congregation of Baptists in Hyde Park dated from 1874, but until the early 1890s it was a modest group, numbering less than 100 members and operating out of a small wooden church at Fifty-Fourth and Dorchester. The coming of the University led to a rapid, substantial increase in membership, and the congregation grew from 158 in 1890 to more than 600 members in 1900.[250] Harper and many of the University's top administrative leaders made their presence felt in this faith community. In March 1893 Harper was instrumental in persuading the congregation to build a more capacious church designed by James Gamble Rogers. Rogers's initial plans for a neo-Gothic edifice proved too costly, and a stately, but more economical Romanesque design was substituted. The new church was dedicated in January 1906, the month and year of Harper's death.[251] To aid in the financing of the new building, Harper and Goodspeed solicited a $15,000 gift from John D. Rockefeller in 1901. Until Rockefeller Chapel opened in 1928, the building at Fifty-Sixth and Woodlawn functioned as the University church.[252]

Harper's most decisive contribution to the Hyde Park Baptist Church came in April 1897, when he was elected superintendent of the church's Sunday school. Harper had long called for reforms to improve the effectiveness of the American Sunday school system, using the American Institute of Sacred Literature and his journal the *Biblical World* to advocate pedagogical approaches to the history of the Bible that were "comprehensive and connected."[253] In September 1895 he complained that "nine-tenths of the teaching in the Sunday school is, as teaching, a farce. The work of many of these so-called Sunday school teachers, if judged upon the standard of ordinary principles of pedagogy, is ludicrous and at the same time criminal."[254] Harper seized on the Hyde Park Baptist Church as a laboratory where he could test many of his reformist ideas, throwing himself into this task with the same ardor with which he had organized the University or spread the Bible study movement for adults. Harper restructured the school's curriculum, giving the students inductive, graded introductions to the developmental history of the Bible and requiring quarterly written examinations to ensure their mastery of the material presented.[255]

The Hyde Park Baptist Church became a kind of silent partner with the University in advancing practical religion in one neighborhood, as a potential model for other churches in other neighborhoods. Among its devoted supporters were many of the prominent administrative and academic leaders of the University, including Harry Pratt Judson, Thomas Goodspeed, and Albion Small. Many university faculty and senior staff taught Sunday school, served as deacons, were members of the church's building and finance committees, and participated in other functions. Together they and their fellow congregants at other local churches formed a web of neighborhood sociability that was distinct from, but overlapped with, the professional circles of the University—anchoring the University in the neighborhood through the routines of ecclesiastical, social, and charitable activities. This network of comfortable sociability and friendship among university leaders and others within neighborhood institutions in Hyde Park contributed to the dense fabric of cultural harmony enjoyed by the university faculty in its early decades.

If Harper's relations with his neighborhood and his local church were congenial, his relations to the city and the nation were more complicated. Harper's public image among the well-to-do elites and the educated classes in the city at large was, on balance, a positive asset to the early University. Press coverage often focused on the steady stream of gifts that he conjured up for the University, with the *Chicago Tribune* tagging him as a "Jupiter Pluvius who evokes the plenteous showers" of money.[256] But his immense energy, charisma, and constant proclivity to innovation and change also made for good copy. A long article in the *Tribune* in January 1896 described Harper as a mesmerist and magician, "perhaps the most striking figure today among contemporary Americans." He was a man of "enthusiasm, originality, and practical skill" who overflowed with new ideas and energy to implement them. He attended all baseball and football games, which gave him the image of the common man. Open and friendly to all, he never forgot names. No one was too high or low to gain Harper's interest and attention. He was a great fund-raiser because of "the fascination of his personal enthusiasm and the foresight and originality with which he projected the plans of the University." Even Harper's attire while riding a bicycle was closely observed; he was reported to have special riding clothes—"tight fitting black jersey suit, knee trousers, jockey cap, long stockings, and bicycle shoes." Another writer insisted that Harper was "the greatest pedagogue of his generation," using the inductive method, never presenting his own opinion, but instead presenting the facts and allowing students to reach their own opinions. With approval, Harper was compared to a modern railroad executive, and a yet another writer upped the ante by calling him "the Napoleon of higher education."[257]

This portrait of a modest, earnest, and friendly (but slightly self-conscious) man, who was deeply generous but also endlessly eager to secure funds, became part of the aura of the early University. Harper's love of pageantry, satisfied in quarterly convocations with processions of faculty with robes and brightly colored hoods and marching bands, drew more press attention to his personal idiosyncrasies.[258] Yet Harper disliked much of this public portrait. He took special offense at cartoons and essays that portrayed him as a craving petitioner of funds and as a sometime puppet and sometime manipulator of Rockefeller.[259] He went so far in 1900 as to deny that he had ever asked anyone for money for the University, a statement that must have astonished his audience.[260] At the end of his life, in January 1906, he complained that his scholarly reputation had been vastly and unfairly overshadowed by the public image of a fund-raising huckster:

> When I left my work in New Haven to come to Chicago, I was laying greatest emphasis on the scholarly side. Up to that time I had given myself largely to scholarly work. On coming to Chicago I had to turn aside for the next ten or twelve years to secure money for the University and in doing this, I was compelled to throw myself into that side of the work. The consequence is that Chicago and the Northwest think of me as a "money getter", and that is the reputation I have everywhere—[a] reputation which is hardly fair in view of my antipathy for this kind of work and my love for the other. I have had some measure of success also in the scholarly work. I am taking the liberty of sending you a copy of the commentary on Amos and Hosea.... This book represents more hours of work than I have spent altogether in the administrative work of the University of Chicago in fourteen years.... The thing that troubles me is that I seem to stand in the West for something that I do not really represent, and the thing which I represent is not appreciated or understood, or even known by the great majority of the people who are familiar with the working of the University.[261]

Harper also resented the intense press coverage of his personal life. In 1897, when ill over the Christmas season, Harper complained to a friend that "you must remember that when I have a bad cold the Chicago newspapers make it out [to be] something worse. I am to be pitied that I cannot even be sick without the matter being exploited in the newspapers."[262]

On the national political front, Harper was a liberal Republican from a small town in Ohio, who was presiding over a major urban university in a metropolis that was riven by ethnic, religious, class, and gender rivalries. This made opportunities where Harper could stand for national comity all the more welcome. During the Spanish-American War, for example, he easily slipped into the role of a public patriot—a defender of the nation in time of war, the giver of an honorary degree to President William McKinley in mid-October 1898, and an enthusiastic host to Colonel Theodore Roosevelt during the latter's visit to Chicago in April 1899 after his return from Cuba.[263] Harper also engineered an honorary degree for Roosevelt in April 1903, the ceremony filled with fulsome patriotic invocations and spectacle. Harper took special delight in Roosevelt's reelection in November 1904, indicating his strong allegiance to Roosevelt's ideals and to the Republican Party.[264]

Who ended up in the White House was not a matter of indifference to Harper. Harper wrote to his son, Samuel, after the 1900 presidential elections that "progress on the new buildings is being made.... McKinley's election means everything in financial circles. If Bryan had been elected we could not begin the buildings for five years."[265] Patriotism and institutional self-interest notwithstanding, Harper usually went to great pains to keep the University out of the crossfire of partisan politics, a stance that fit well with the ideal of many Progressives who advocated nonpartisanship in the governance of major civic institutions. When a few faculty members, led by historian Hermann von Holst, opposed American imperialism in 1898–99, Harper walked a careful line between defending academic freedom and asserting that the University stood on the side of McKinley and the nation at war.[266] Harper himself was convinced that war with Spain was justified, but he was forced to protect the faculty's right to dissent.[267] To C. F. Linzee he wrote in May 1899, "I agree with you in your position, and sincerely wish that all men might look at these matters as we do. As a matter of fact, there are many men who differ with us and we must give these men an opportunity to differ with us."[268]

Harper was a supporter of the reformist Municipal Voters League in Chicago, and he was so interested in urban reform movements that he ensured that the University's library included a comprehensive collection of administrative and political reference materials from large cities around the world.[269] Many of Harper's colleagues participated in various social reform schemes and institutions in Gilded Age Chicago—for example, Charles R. Henderson at Hull House, Albion Small in the new Civic Federation of Chicago, Sophonisba Breckinridge and Edith Abbott at the Chicago School of Civics and Philanthropy, and Charles E. Merriam with the Chicago Charter Convention, the City Club of Chicago, and (after 1909) as an alderman on the Chicago City Council—initiatives that also had rich research potential and later led to the academic urbanism that Chicago social scientists would make famous in the 1920s.[270] But Harper's own immersion in urban politics came via the public schools. His involvement with public education and the schools tested the limits of nonpartisan university reformers in a city known for its tangled politics, bringing him significant frustrations and eventually disconcerting failure. Early on in his presidency Harper showed a strong interest in improving public cultural resources. Harper believed that "it is our duty to come into contact with the people and we already feel the influence of our work among them. We know we have been helped quite as much as we have helped in the work of disseminating knowledge through University extension. I know of no better way to bring a college into larger sympathy with the people than by this work in whatever way it may be interpreted."[271]

Harper reached out to professional associations, teachers groups, and local educational and political leaders to encourage conversations about the state of the public schools and the University's possible role in effecting improvements.[272] Harper encouraged his faculty colleagues to bring teachers to campus for discussions about pedagogical methods and for regular professional meetings, as well as sponsoring public lectures by prominent educational leaders, and he spoke at many of these gatherings. Harper also created a Department of Pedagogy in alliance with the Department of Philosophy, and he lured the young John Dewey away from the University of Michigan in 1894 to run both. In response to a remark in 1896 by trustee Andrew MacLeish about why the University would publish a scholarly journal called the *School Review* that, MacLeish felt, was unworthy of the honor, Harper replied, "As a University we are interested above all things else in Pedagogy. Especially are we interested in the questions which deal with the preparation of students immediately for college."[273] In part this profile reflected Harper's genuine intellectual commitments—he believed strongly in the potential of teaching to improve urban society—but it also demonstrated once again the systematic quality of his larger educational ideals: upgrading Chicago high schools would be a small but significant step in advancing his larger plan of a general integration of secondary and tertiary education in the Midwest, under the leadership of the new research university. By 1896–97, Harper's goal of securing a network of affiliated or cooperating high schools was reached.

Fifty-four public high schools and a dozen private schools had formal relations with the University, with the University setting examination standards in many of these schools via a system of deputy examiners, as well as holding biennial teachers conferences on campus in November and March to discuss current issues of practical interest.[274]

Harper's challenges grew greater the more he became involved in the murky realities of late nineteenth-century Chicago school politics. The Republican civic elites called on him to serve as a spokesperson on urban educational issues, and in so doing Harper set himself at odds with labor and union movements in the city. In 1896, when Mayor George Swift, a Republican, nominated him for a two-year term on the Board of Education, several of Harper's trustee friends advised him against taking such a politically thorny assignment. Andrew MacLeish, for example, warned him that the job would be "an unwise and undesirable step" and would work against the interests of the University.[275]

Harper ignored such counsels and accepted the assignment, responding to MacLeish, "I am persuaded that I could perform a service for the cause of education in Chicago that would be of very great importance to the University."[276] Seats on the board were politically coveted jobs that controlled a considerable level of job patronage. Harper quickly found himself petitioned by various friends and acquaintances to intervene on their behalf. One acquaintance, the candidate for the principalship of a local school, wrote asking for positions for his sister and a male colleague, as well as an increase in his own salary.[277] Another supporter sought Harper's help in promoting his niece to a full-time permanent teaching job from a provisional assignment.[278] Harper himself nominated several candidates for teaching posts, despite his dislike for the system itself. Yet the visibility of the job also raised Harper's profile among potential enemies, who feared his connections with Rockefeller's oil wealth and resented the intrusion of the University into their customary worlds of school organization and labor politics. Harper's public pronouncements about the desirability of reconciling and coordinating the work of Chicago public high schools with University admissions standards soon gave rise to accusations that the University was trying to take over the public schools and to make appointment as a teacher contingent on a college degree.[279] Harper's allies in the school administration insisted that "no subversion, no radical changes of the High School curriculum are at all necessary," but critics like those of the local Socialist Alliance attacked Harper as being the "chief cook and bottle washer of the Standard Oil University."[280] When considering whether to reappoint Harper to a second term on the school board in July 1898, Mayor Carter H. Harrison sent Harper a candid letter reporting that he had encountered much opposition to Harper: "You know, of course, the old charges: that the public schools are being made a feeder of the Chicago University, that graduates of the University are given positions as teachers in preference to ordinary applicants, and that the schools are drifting away from the class of instruction for which they are intended. While the investigations I have made of these charges show them to be absolutely unfounded, the impression is abroad in the public mind and will not [go] down."[281]

Harper did have enough influence with Harrison, however, to lobby successfully for the appointment of E. Benjamin Andrews as the new reformist superintendent of city schools in July 1898.[282] Andrews was the president of Brown University and, equally significant, had been the sympathetic president of Denison when Harper was on the faculty in the 1870s. Further, Andrews had been a constructive member of the ad hoc committee of Baptist leaders whom Gates had summoned in April 1889 to persuade Rockefeller to bankroll a new institution of higher education in Chicago. Harper had tried to recruit Andrews to Chicago in the spring of 1893 for the position of chancellor and as a head professor of the philosophy department, essentially to serve as Harper's number-two administrative man who could spell him when he was on research leave.[283] The scheme collapsed when Andrews balked and senior Chicago faculty objected to the outrageous salary Harper had offered Andrews and to Harper's peremptory tactics in pushing the scheme, but Andrews's and Harper's similar views about the limitations of religious orthodoxy in a university context and the need for radical reform of the public schools kept Andrews in Harper's good graces.

Once in Chicago, Andrews had a difficult time making the transition from college president, where he held autarchic power, to city superintendent, which required endless political negotiations and compromises. Andrews styled himself as a tough, no-nonsense administrator, but this style of leadership led to charges of autocracy and pretentiousness. His enemies tagged him "Bulletin Ben" for his habit of issuing summary commands to his subordinates, including an order that teachers must live within the city limits and a warning to teachers against criticizing their superiors in the school system. His friendship with Harper was another source of discontent.[284]

Harper's greatest impact on the schools came not during his abbreviated term on the school board but in a related venue. In January 1898 Mayor Harrison, seeking to placate reformist Republicans in the business and professional community, appointed Harper to a special eleven-man commission charged with recommending reforms to improve the Chicago public school system; he selected Harper to be the chair of the commission.[285] Under Harper's intellectual leadership the commission worked assiduously for almost a year, issuing the *Report of the Educational Commission of the City of Chicago* in early 1899. Harper's final report was true to character and a logical extension of his previous thinking on educational reform in America. Harper confronted a politicized school system that suffered from a variety of ills, including overcrowding, lack of professional training, political patronage in the appointments process, inadequate physical facilities, an antiquated tax structure that could barely fund the status quo, and governance by committees of the board rather than by a strong executive leader. In the commission's report, Harper judged the administration of the school system "largely defective" and in need of "radical improvement."

Many of the report's recommendations were both uncontroversial and salutary—increasing the pace of new school construction, providing for more public kindergartens and for vacation programs, reducing student-teacher ratios in the classroom, creating more free evening lecture programs for adults, enforcing stricter attendance regulations to get more students in the schools, strengthening vocational training programs, and so forth—but several were politically explosive. First, Harper proposed radically reforming the governance structure of the schools, replacing the current twenty-one-member school board with an eleven-member board appointed by the mayor to four-year terms, and restructuring and strengthening the central administrative leadership of the system by creating two professional appointees: a school superintendent who would have vast power over the appointment, promotion, and dismissal of teachers, as well as over the structure and implementation of the curriculum; and a business manager who would be in charge of all financial affairs and who could hire and supervise all nonteaching personnel in the schools (e.g., janitors and engineers). Harper further proposed that both appointees be given six-year terms with high salaries (up to $10,000) comparable to those of executive positions in the business world, so as to recruit men of the highest administrative skill and eliminate political pressures. Finally, Harper proposed that the school board have exclusive power to acquire property and construct buildings without review by the city council.[286]

In a city in which political (as well as ethnic and religious) control of government jobs and contracts was already a tribal tradition, the creation of two nonpolitical administrative czars was bound to raise the hackles of those who profited from the current patronage system. Eliminating the authority of the city council over construction contracts was a stunning exercise in quixotic thinking. For the teachers, the report was a mixed blessing. Harper advocated further training for existing teachers and urged the hiring of more extensively trained new teachers. He also recommended that all applicants to the teacher's training academy have high school diplomas (or the equivalent), and he encouraged the hiring of more college-trained teachers for the high schools. Although such changes may have been desirable, they conveyed a negative assessment of the work of the current teachers, who were seen to be lacking an "incentive to good work."

The general structure of the report, replete as it was with expert testimonies from Harper's fellow presidential school-reformer Nicholas Murray Butler and other university-based authorities, conveyed a utopian optimism, as if Progressive rationality, scholarly knowledge, and administrative expertise could sweep away both human nature and Chicago-style patronage politics. When Harper argued that only the "best forces of the community" should be represented on the new school board, many cynics automatically associated "best" with "wealthiest," giving the report an elitist tinge despite Harper's intentions to the contrary.[287] The report also tended to privilege the city as a whole and worked against the autonomy of individual neighborhoods and ethnic groups.[288]

Once the report was finalized, Andrews and the Civic Federation lobbied the state legislature in Springfield to pass legislation to implement the plan. This set off a firestorm of protest from the Chicago Teachers Federation and the Chicago Federation of Labor. The latter denounced Andrews as a "creature of Rockefeller," whose purpose it was "to promote Rockefeller's ideas."[289] Harper was accused of trying to "take over" the public schools for the advantage of the University, with the idea of restructuring them so that a small, elite group of students would profit by gaining admission to the University.[290] Mayor Harrison, facing angry schoolteachers and other aggrieved interest groups, waffled in his support of Harper, and the Harper bill went down to defeat in the Illinois General Assembly in early March 1899. A year later, frustrated with a job that seemed little more than a "big clerkship," Benjamin Andrews resigned in April 1900 to return to university academic life as chancellor of the University of Nebraska.[291] Harper had tried to encourage his friend to stand firm in December 1898. "I appreciate the delicate position that you hold, and assure you that we are all standing off and watching the fight with intense interest," he wrote to Andrews. "If at any time I can serve you in a quiet way, please command me." Such words hardly reassured Andrews, however, who pointed out the albatross-like quality of Harper's support: "I know that you have the interests of the schools at heart, but it will be some time before people hereabouts will so believe. They think you want 'an educational trust', as I have heard it phrased, in which the public schools will be a tail to the university kite."[292]

Subsequent urban reformers tried to implement components of the Harper bill piecemeal via administrative decrees and state legislation. As the historian of the Chicago public school system, Mary Herrick, noted, "Its recommendations might have been ignored, but they could not be answered. Slowly, many of them actually went into effect. They are still worthy of thoughtful consideration by any student of the history of Chicago schools."[293] The bill was also one of decisive factors that pushed Chicago public school teachers, represented by the Chicago Teachers Federation, into formal affiliation with the Chicago Federation of Labor in 1902. Some of the tensions created by Harper's initiative were anchored in issues of culture and gender, in addition to class. Of the over five thousand teachers in Chicago in 1900, more than 80 percent were women. Most of these teachers, brilliantly led by Catherine Goggin and Margaret Haley, lacked university credentials and viewed the university-based rhetoric of expertise in Harper's report as an insult to their professional competence and self-esteem.[294] Harper's call for the hiring of more male teachers in the upper grades—and his further suggestion that higher salaries be paid to men on the grounds of their "superior physical endurance," which made them "more valuable in the school system"—generated bitter acrimony. Margaret Haley later commented acidly that "the teachers of Chicago did not believe that if he [Jesus] returned to earth that he would come to Chicago by way of the Midway Plaisance."[295]

This clash was emblematic of other disputes in Chicago involving business-dominated civic elites on the one side and labor and women's groups on the other.[296] Such conflicts played themselves out across the landscape of late nineteenth-century American cities, where elite-dominated Progressives sought to implement rationalization, administrative centralization, and professionalization by depoliticizing local institutions of municipal governance. Some tensions in the public schools were mitigated when a university-educated woman (and protégée of John Dewey), Ella Flagg Young, became school superintendent in 1909 and found ways to encourage administrative reform while also supporting the professional and financial interests of the teachers.[297] But the clash between the ideals of a university-influenced reform movement and the hard realities of pork barrel politics in a multiethnic, substantially Catholic Chicago was a perennial one. Even among those who were sympathetic with Harper's vision of stronger connections between the public schools and the University found the perceived arrogance of some senior faculty at the University to be frustrating.[298]

At the autumn quarter convocation of the University in October 1899, Harper engaged in a bold act of ecumenism by inviting the Roman Catholic bishop of Peoria, Illinois, Msgr. John L. Spalding, to speak. Arguing that good teaching was essential to the progress of mankind, Spalding insisted that "the whole question of educational reform and progress is simply a question of employing good and removing incompetent teachers. And they who have experience best know how extremely difficult this is. In a university, at least, it should be possible, for a university is a home of great teachers or it is not a university at all."[299] Coming on the heels of Harper's political fiasco involving teachers in Chicago, many of whom were Catholics, Spalding's speech was all the more ironic. Was good teaching only possible in a university? If so, what about the city and its publics?

At the same time, Harper's rocky experiences in the swamp of city hall politics hardly encouraged similar civic voluntarism by subsequent University presidents, and it is perhaps not accidental that Harper's immediate successor, Harry Pratt Judson, manifested a distaste for the kind of political outreach to the broader civic community that Harper had embraced. After Harper's death in 1906, the University as a total institution would slowly begin to turn inward, and with the brief exception of Ernest Burton's abortive civic campaign of 1924–25, a pattern set in that endured well into the 1950s.[300] Harper and Burton were exceptions to this tendency, but it proved powerful nonetheless.[301] As we will see in chapter 5, the University would pay a price for its disassociation from the civic and political elites of Chicago.

Chicago and the World: A "German" Research University?

In March 1904, on the occasion of its fiftieth quarterly convocation, the University of Chicago hosted a much-publicized visit by five distinguished German scholars who, with much fanfare, were awarded honorary degrees by William Rainey Harper. The head of the Department of Botany, John Merle Coulter, gave a celebratory lecture on the significance of German universities for the academic culture of the University of Chicago. Coulter argued that the nineteenth-century German research universities had offered their American cousins five exemplary norms: that the research university is a key asset to progress in modern life; that faculty must enjoy freedom to teach, unencumbered by external pressures; that students enjoy a similar privilege in determining the course of their studies; that scientific research in all fields should be pursued for its own sake; and that the instructor at a university (in contrast to a secondary school or other preparatory academy) must be both an active researcher and a teacher. Coulter was not indifferent to the cultural or social differences between Germany and America, and he acknowledged that the organizational ideals embodied in the German university would have to be "adapted to the peculiar genius of each people." The tradition of the college in American higher education was one substantive structural difference between the two systems, and Coulter admitted that the "imperceptible gradation from college to university that characterizes the American system of higher education is not a thing that can be abolished or that ought to be abolished." Still, the German university afforded a powerful valence in its dedication to academic freedom, its commitment to independent scientific research, and its belief in the value of enrichment of knowledge.[302]

The year 1904 proved to be auspicious for meetings of Central European scholars and Chicago faculty, moreover, for the five German scholars in March were followed six months later by another delegation of senior German scholars passing through Chicago in mid-September on the way to the International Exposition and Congress of Arts and Science in St. Louis, of which Professor Albion Small of the University of Chicago was one of the leading organizers.[303] Small hoped that bringing together European and American scholars at the Congress would not only give each side a better appreciation of the work of the other, but also that the distinguished Europeans would find in the new US community of professional scholars a worthy counterpoint to their own scientific endeavors. Tellingly, in assembling lists of possible invitees from Europe on the topics of international law, diplomacy, and national administration, Small reported to William Rainey Harper in April 1903, "The fact is that the prominent scholars are so overwhelmingly German that we have done our best to canvass the other [European] nations in order to make for them a respectable showing."[304]

If one took John Coulter's claims literally, the early University of Chicago seemed to owe an enormous debt to the paradigm of the German research university. Certainly many Chicago faculty interacted with English and French scholarly establishments in the 1890s, but university leaders honored neither British nor French scholars with the honorary degrees and the pompous rhetoric that were lavished on the Germans in March 1904. Why did the University feel so indebted to the model of the imperial German university? Equally important, did that model really have such a profound impact on the cultural and intellectual history of the University?

The question of the influence of German university ideals and norms on the late nineteenth-century American university has generated in recent decades a large and often controversial literature. Many scholars believe that there was no single causal process of influence between the German and American "models" of university education, and that if there was a strong German influence it was largely in the conception of professorial authority rather than in specific institutional innovations.[305] Jurgen Herbst has suggested that patterns of professionalism that emerged in Germany and the United States at the end of the nineteenth century were not strictly national and that both were part of "the now ubiquitous façade of academic professionalism, an 'ism' that is neither German nor American but, so to speak, purely and universally academic."[306] Moreover, German universities around 1900 were much more self-consciously Humboldtian than fifty years earlier, in the sense that their advocates more aggressively adopted the ideal of the unity of teaching and research.[307] But they were also deeply engaged in professional and even vocational education. Recently several scholars have illuminated how misleading the norm of the "German research university" was in reality, for most German universities by 1900 had become large certification machines for students pursuing careers in the civil service or in one of the learned professions, controlled by state education ministries that had enormous administrative authority over faculty appointments and financial resources for scholarly research. They were hardly idealized sites where liberal arts learning or even scientific research, much less pure academic freedom, could be cultivated. Further, given the strongly hierarchical structure of their faculties, with the domination of a small number of full professors over a large mass of underpaid assistants and associates who did not enjoy civil service protection, they were not ideal places for the intellectual or pedagogical development of young faculty. Finally, as Charles McClelland has recently reminded us, in contrast to their American cousins, German universities around 1910 did not profit from the huge increase in wealth generated among the *Besitzbürgertum*, meriting little philanthropic support from wealthy sectors of civil society.[308] Thus, scholars like Gabriele Lingelbach have argued that the impact of the German model has been exaggerated, and that many of the norms and behavioral models associated with academic life in Germany and in German conceptions of academic research were not viable in an American context. German models and practices were experienced by American faculty members in a "highly selective and in some cases clearly inaccurate" mode.[309]

Still, it is undeniable that the German universities offered a powerful allure to members of the first generation of Chicago's faculty. William Rainey Harper initially was quite enthusiastic about encouraging young American scholars to study in Europe, which essentially meant studying in Germany. Thomas Goodspeed later recalled that in the initial organizational period of the University Harper thought "it was a recommendation to have studied abroad and earned a higher degree."[310] According to Goodspeed, Harper even issued agreement forms to prospective younger scholars whom he thought would profit from an academic sojourn in Europe, promising to nominate them for jobs once they returned to Chicago: "In every case in which he made these contracts the prospective President was accustomed to require, or at least very strongly advise, the prospective instructor to go abroad for as long a stay as possible to better his preparation for his future work."[311]

Harper's putative search for men who had studied abroad made it into local newspapers, which accused the new president of traveling to Europe in the summer of 1891 with the intent of violating the Alien Contract Labor Law of 1885 (which prohibited the offering of broad categories of jobs to non-US citizens). Harper was portrayed as asking prospective nominees to travel to the city of Chicago without a legally binding job offer, where they would suddenly be discovered by the trustees and offered employment on the spot. As Goodspeed later remembered the alleged ploy, "What could be simpler than to advise a promising candidate to arrive in Chicago in the course of desultory world wanderings and there happily to fall in with the Trustees of the University? How gratifying to all parties concerned if it should be then and there discovered that this incidental tourist was precisely the man for whom they were looking?"[312]

In fact, Harper hired few senior foreign scholars directly from Europe. The most prominent was Hermann von Holst, a senior constitutional historian at the University of Freiburg, whose short tenure in Chicago nonetheless had a long-lasting impact on local faculty culture. But the presence of American-born scholars at Chicago who were trained at one or more German universities was extraordinary. Of the 189 members of the faculty of the University of Chicago in 1896–97, 76 had taken degrees or advanced training at a European university, and 65 of those had studied at one or more German universities. Thus, over one-third of the faculty members at the new University (and many of the most distinguished senior faculty) had a direct personal experience with the educational and research practices of the German university system.

Their experiences in Germany varied enormously. James Breasted spent three years in Berlin, assiduously mastering Hebrew, Arabic, and several other languages plus immersing himself in the arcane details of Near Eastern history and culture. Breasted had first come to know Harper at Yale, which he entered as a graduate student in the fall of 1890 in order to study divinity after graduating from North Central College in Naperville, Illinois. Breasted had wanted to devote himself full-time to the study of the Hebrew language, but his father insisted that he complete a course in divinity instead. Breasted cleverly managed to combine both interests, and he came to know Harper over the course of the 1890–91 academic year.[313] Encouraged by Harper to undertake a two-year course of doctoral study in Germany, Breasted left for Berlin in the fall of 1891. While in Berlin, Breasted served as an informal contact for Harper with German book dealers. He also helped Harper's wife and children during their residency there, and he tutored Harper's children in Latin. He initially devoted most of his efforts to learning Coptic, Arabic, and Hebrew, quickly establishing a warm relationship with the senior German Egyptologist Adolf Erman. Erman told Breasted that he must remain in Berlin for a three-year period if he hoped to achieve real mastery of his subjects: "He says that I must stay here *three years*, that one can get no more than a superficial knowledge of the subject in less time, and he is not one of the slow Germans either. The further I go in the subject the more thoroughly I agree with him. It is simply vast and broadens every day."[314] Breasted flourished in Berlin—taking courses in Egyptian grammar, doing archaeological exercises, and studying Plato and Aristotle—and found all of his work to be "intensely interesting." He soon received reassuring accolades from his German mentors that he proudly reported back to Harper.[315] Breasted came to master German and made many friends. He even met Frances Hart, the young American woman whom he would eventually marry. Like other young American academics on similar sojourns, Breasted encountered what Daniel Rodgers has characterized as "not simply the Germans' capacity for enjoyment but the publicness and sociality of their leisure."[316] Not only did he pursue intensive academic work, but he also vacationed with Erman and fellow German doctoral students, hiking through the Harz Mountains in the late summer of 1892 under conditions that he reported to Harper as idyllic.[317]

As his studies progressed, Breasted came to understand more broadly and fully the range of Egyptian history and culture. He proudly informed Harper that "the picture of Egyptian life, history and thought is gradually growing into completeness," a remarkable anticipation of the great works of synthesis (*Development of Religion and Thought in Ancient Egypt*; *History of Egypt*; *The Conquest of Civilization*; *The Dawn of Conscience*) that Breasted would produce later in his career.[318] When the big day came and Breasted passed his final oral examinations for the doctorate in July 1894, he was rewarded with high praise and the citation of *cum laude*, making him feel as if he was a natural son of German academic culture.[319] He proudly reported to Harper that the four German doctoral students who were also examined at the same session all received the grade of *sustinuit*, a "just passing" rank considerably below that which he had merited.[320]

Other young Chicagoans had different experiences from Breasted. James Tufts spent a year in Germany, but the experience did not transform his life or career. Yet Tufts afforded an example of Harper's perspicacity in identifying talented young American scholars, offering them a preliminary job contract, and then urging them to go to Europe for additional seasoning. Tufts, who eventually became a prominent American philosopher of pragmatism with a specialty in moral and social philosophy and in theories of social relations, taught at Chicago from 1892 to 1930. In 1889

Tufts had been appointed an instructor of philosophy at the University of Michigan. He was not unhappy with this job—he had a chance to work with John Dewey, who was already developing a reputation for analytic precociousness as a scholar and teacher, and he admired the less privileged and more open-minded atmosphere of the midwestern student body (Tufts called it a "stimulating and wholesome world").[321] But Tufts did have a long-standing wish to study for a doctorate in Germany, and it was impossible to combine this goal with his teaching responsibilities at Michigan. Tufts knew Harper from having taken his Hebrew language course while he was at the Yale Divinity School. When the president-elect contacted him in early November 1890 about a position at Chicago, the path to a German higher degree suddenly beckoned, because the new University would not open its doors until the fall of 1892. Tufts resigned his position at Ann Arbor in June 1891. In August Tufts married Cynthia Hobart Whitaker, a young schoolteacher from Massachusetts, and the newlyweds set off for a year in Germany. There followed a series of letters from Tufts to Harper from Berlin and then Freiburg, asking pertinent questions about how he could best use his time in Germany to prepare himself for the teaching assignments Harper had in mind.[322] Harper in fact had no fixed views about what Tufts should (or should not) study, and Tufts ended up writing a doctoral dissertation on Kant under the supervision of Alois Riehl at Freiburg.

In contrast to Breasted, Tufts experienced Germany as a leisurely expatriate, socializing with other Americans at the American Church in Berlin and enjoying many friendships in the expatriate community. Tufts disliked the militarism that suffused German public life but found the academic culture of the University of Berlin to be congenial and inspiring. Years later he still remembered "on the one side the spirit of inquiry and independent thinking embodied in a great university, and on the other, the experience of living among a people of different culture and in a land where music, the stage, and arts of form had a longer history and richer monuments to show.[323] Tufts moved to Freiburg midyear to work with Riehl, who was willing to count the two years Tufts had spent at Yale as fulfilling the degree requirements in Freiburg. After completing a hasty dissertation and passing his final examinations summa cum laude in July 1892, Tufts proudly returned to Chicago, where an assistant professorship awaited him at the new University. For Tufts the German academic world was admirable, except for the fact that it was surrounded by the "Germany of militaristic class and rule, of insolent officers and rigorously trained goose-step subordinates, of armed soldiery at street corners."[324]

If Tufts's experiences in Germany were pleasant and rewarding, those of Paul Shorey were strikingly different. A distinguished scholar of Greek literature and an early twentieth-century expert on Plato, Shorey spent three years at various German universities, and during his time abroad he regularly corresponded with William M. Payne, a close friend from high school days in Chicago. These letters and cards revealed a lonely, homesick young man who had great difficulties adjusting to his new surroundings and to German educational practices.[325] He found Cologne and other German cities he visited to be filled with "gloomy, dirty streets" and with "hideous shop windows and homely faces." In Leipzig his classmates were "all infected with Hegel to a greater or less extent," and "the ideas, methods, and illustrative quotations are all very stale to me." Ending up in Bonn at the university, he found the lectures "very dull" and German society "so unreal and vulgar that a true picture of it is not art—for the rest of the world." He had better luck in Munich, where he worked with Wilhelm von Christ on a dissertation on Plato's ideas about human nature. Christ was a supportive and sympathetic mentor, and Shorey completed his work in June 1884. But the more Shorey read German scholarship on Plato, the more he felt frustrated by its abstruse and highly technical nature.[326]

His unhappy memories of Germany persisted through his career. In 1911 Shorey authored a tough-minded critique of German educational practices in the *Nation*, warning that reliance on German training and values led to US educational institutions being badly integrated into the culture of their own nation. Americans should "emancipate" themselves from "slavish subservience to German influence without losing the lessons or forgetting the debt of gratitude" owed to Germany. American graduate students most needed general cultural training and erudition, and for this the German model was completely useless. What was wanted was a genuinely American tradition of higher education, closely integrated to English and French ideals of style, eloquence, and empirical restraint.[327]

Of the early senior faculty at Chicago who had studied in Germany, Albion Small, the founder and first head of the Department of Sociology, was among those whose scholarship was most directly influenced by contemporary German and Austrian academics in his field. Small studied in Berlin and Leipzig between 1879 and 1881. He never completed his doctorate, instead spending a year at Johns Hopkins in 1888–89 writing a dissertation under the direction of Herbert Baxter Adams. When Small returned to Germany in the summer of 1903, he found much that he disliked about the militarism that infused turn-of-the-century German political culture.[328] During World War I Small attacked Prussianism and the militaristic spirit that it embodied as a kind of "resuscitated paganism," and after the war he continued to reflect on his personal experiences in Germany with biting irony.[329] Still, Small devoted much of his career to interpreting the work of major German social scientists, and he urged his graduate students to spend time in Germany as well. Travel to Germany had also upended Small's familial milieu: late in his life Small recalled that the first time he had ever taken a walk with a girl on a Sunday afternoon was in Weimar in 1879. The young woman, the daughter of a German general, later became his wife. Growing up as the son of a Baptist minister in Maine in the 1860s and 1870s, where a strong residue of Puritan culture dominated public and private behavior, such "recreation" on the Sabbath—especially with a member of the opposite sex—would have been sternly forbidden. But in Germany, a new society in the Old World, it seemed plausible and natural for the young graduate student.[330]

Small's adult intellectual universe was Protestant American and urban, but many of his key ideas and concepts—involving social process and social planning and the linear movement of society toward greater progress and unity under the sponsorship of enlightened public authority—came from the Germans he studied.[331] Small's intense dislike of class conflict and his configuration of social conflict into patterns of competitive institutional interests also fit in well with this mental universe.[332] His book on the German and Austrian cameralists, published in 1909, was a searching effort to explain the origins of an elite-driven civic political system that was efficient, was goal oriented, and would and could restore itself to achieve a more coherent and integrated civil society. He insisted that "Americans have much to gain from better understanding of the Germans" and "the efficiency of the German civic system is beyond dispute. As an adaptation of means to ends, it operates with a remarkably low rate of waste."[333] He also believed that, in contrast to the financial and human wastage of the American system, "there is hardly room for debate upon the proposition that in sheer economy of social efficiency Germany has no near rival among the great nations."[334] Small was thus deeply indebted to the ideas of the German collectivists, a policy perspective that Small saw as an alternative to both capitalism and socialism. Moreover, the organizational example of the German *Verein für Sozialpolitik* provided a model of collaborative professionalism and research proclivity that Small and other early social scientists sought to transplant to America. Small's last book, *Origins of Sociology* (1924), self-consciously bypassed the recent jingoism of the war, regretting the militaristic behavior of many German scholars but also insisting on the theoretical import of their scholarship, and soberly acknowledged the huge intellectual debt that American scholars owed to their German counterparts.[335]

William Rainey Harper's own experience with German academic traditions was distant and secondhand. Harper read German, and he was conscious of the ways in which German biblical scholars shaped the fundamental paradigms of his scholarly field of Semitic studies, but Harper never studied in Germany. His most significant personal foray into German scholarly culture came in the late summer of 1891 when on a visit to Berlin he attempted to buy the so-called Berlin Collection from the antiquarian book dealer S. Calvary and Company. Purchased for $28,400, the Berlin Collection was touted as encompassing hundreds of thousands of volumes, but what actually arrived in Hyde Park in June 1892 was significantly smaller—about 58,000 books and 39,000 dissertations, according to later investigations. Harper's attempts to obtain reliable information about the discrepancy from his Berlin agents were frustrating, but even what was delivered from Germany immediately gave the fledgling University a splendid collection of books and learned journals relating to European history and culture from the Renaissance to the eighteenth century.[336]

In a few cases, a whole department at the new University was shaped by German paradigms. Harper appointed Eliakim Hastings Moore, who did lasting work in the classification of finite fields and in the foundations of general topology, as professor and acting head of the Department of Mathematics in February 1892. Moore had spent a postdoctoral year in Germany after completing a PhD at Yale in 1885, and his own work was indebted to his collaborations with Karl Theodor Weierstrass and Leopold Kronecker in Berlin.[337] Moore also received an honorary degree from the University of Göttingen in 1899. Moore was a brilliant and determined administrator who had an "uncanny hunter's instinct" for identifying new research problems and for discovering gifted students, and his early strategy for building his department focused on the recruitment of two talented German scholars.[338] Moore first hired Oskar Bolza of Clark University, an expert in the calculus of variations, who had studied at Berlin and Göttingen. Bolza in turn insisted that Moore hire Heinrich Maschke, an authority in group theory and group representations, who had studied at Göttingen as well as at Heidelberg and Berlin.[339] The three men worked together until Maschke's death in 1908. Together the three, in the words of R. C. Archibald, made the Chicago Department of Mathematics "unsurpassed in America as an institution for the study of higher mathematics."[340] In particular, Moore and Maschke launched a distinguished tradition in algebra at Chicago that endured for many decades. Moore and Bolza were also influential teachers who trained a number of promising doctoral students—among them Leonard E. Dickson, who was the first individual to receive a PhD in mathematics at Chicago, and Gilbert A. Bliss, who was chair of the department from 1927 to 1941. Both Dickson and Bliss later served as presidents of the American Mathematical Society.

Many other examples of German influences on the early faculty were evident. The first head of the Department of Chemistry was John U. Nef, an American chemist who spent three years in Munich working with the great German chemist and Nobel laureate Adolf von Baeyer. Nef received his PhD in 1889, summa cum laude, and Baeyer is reputed to have told his colleagues at the time that Nef was one of the best students he had ever had.[341] Nef's subsequent scholarly career was heavily indebted to the institutional matrix of the German academic world: of the forty scientific articles that he published over the course of his career between 1883 and 1917, twenty-seven were written in German and appeared in journals published in Germany, particularly *Liebigs Annalen der Chemie*. Nef left Germany with a robust sense of what it meant to belong to a scientific faculty, and he later opposed Harper's efforts to provide more resources for undergraduate teaching: "The development of the university in undergraduate numbers during the past 10 years has been made at the sacrifice of research and of the graduate schools.... In the end such a policy is bound to be ruinous, for time and experience have proved beyond doubt that the life and soul of a true University lies in those gifted men who are capable of extending the bounds of existing knowledge."[342] Nef's egregious dislike of undergraduates demonstrated that the German model, in its worst manifestations, could lead to a disregard for undergraduate teaching. This may explain Harper's eventual reluctance to hire Americans who were returning from long stays in Europe. By 1899 he insisted that prospective faculty returning from overseas spend at least two years elsewhere in America before he would consider them for a job at Chicago: "In my opinion it requires at least two or three years for a student who has studied five years abroad to become Americanized so as to take a satisfactory position in an American institution."[343]

Perhaps the most fascinating example of the early internationalism of the University was the case of Hermann von Holst, and Holst leads us back to the visit of the German professors in March 1904. Holst was the most distinguished European academic recruited by Harper for full-time service in the early faculty. A chaired professor at the University of Freiburg and the author of the monumental eight-volume *Constitutional and Political History of the United States* (published in translation between 1876 and 1892), Holst had already rejected offers of professorships at Johns Hopkins and Clark. Harper's vision of a great new university in the middle of the vast continent intrigued Holst, however, and he eventually succumbed to Harper's urgent appeals. When Holst arrived in Chicago in late 1892 he brought with him self-indulgent expectations about the life of a full professor, and Harper was forced to accommodate these demands.[344]

The prospect of hiring Hermann von Holst generated jealousy on the part of some. Harper's second-in-command at the early University, Harry Pratt Judson, considered Harper's estimation of the impact of German scholarship on the American universities to be inflated. He stubbornly opposed Harper's decision to appoint Holst, urging against the "slavish imitation of foreign ideas" and insisting that American scholarship be guided by ideals "materially different" from those of Germany: "The motives, methods, and spirit of an American department of history ... would in many essentials be radically antagonistic to those of a German university." Judson also resented having a German national lead a department that he, Judson, was a member of: "Departments involving American history, American literature, and American politics should be in charge of Americans, if possible. Personally, I must confess that I don't fancy having to work under a German. I doubt if many American professors would."[345] Unswayed, Harper recruited Holst. Given his age and troubled medical condition—he was on medical leave for serious gastrointestinal troubles for a significant part of his seven-year tenure—Holst did not nurture a school of doctoral disciples before he returned to Germany in 1900. He did have a powerful personal impact on the formation of the early faculty of the Department of History, in that both Benjamin Terry and Ferdinand Schevill had been his doctoral students at Freiburg, but his impact on the larger development of American historiography before 1914 was limited to the scholarship that he had produced at Freiburg.[346]

In his willingness to speak his mind on controversial public issues, such as denouncing American foreign policy in Latin America in 1895 and the American annexation of Hawaii in 1898 (much to Harper's chagrin), and in his staunch protection of his own *Lehrfreiheit*, Holst served as a powerful example of a senior German *Ordinarius*. The freedom that Holst claimed and regularly practiced must have offered an alluring model for other senior members of the faculty of the early University, who often felt slightly intimidated by their imperious president.[347] Yet even in the face of Harper's displeasure, Holst insisted that faculty were "not slaves but free men, everyone entitled to his own opinion and free to avow them."[348] Holst's status as a respected senior scholar ensured that he could defend his views with impunity, in stark contrast to Edward Bemis, a young economist hired by Harper to teach in the extension program, whose radical public policy views ran afoul of the powerful head of the Department of Political Economy, J. Laurence Laughlin, and who was eventually terminated in 1894.[349]

Holst was a tough advocate of academic quality control, and more than once he sent Harper comments to that effect.[350] At the same time, he defended the autonomy and freedom that he accorded to graduate students taking his seminar: "The work as conducted by myself does not admit of controlling the time spent by the students from day to day or even week to week. I necessarily must put the students upon their honor and try to make them realize that they do not work for my benefit, but for their own."[351]

This famous senior professor, steeped in the dignity and independence of the academic calling and defending uncompromising standards of rigor, offered his younger colleagues on the Chicago faculty a formidable model for their own professional self-development. After Holst's health forced him into early retirement in 1900, J. Laurence Laughlin, who admired Holst's courage in defending faculty rights, proposed that the University commission an oil portrait of Holst. The University Senate approved Laughlin's proposal, and within several months Karl Marr, a noted German American painter living in Munich, was busy at work on a full-length oil portrait. Marr completed his assignment within six months, shipping it to Chicago in early August 1903. Marr's portrait of Holst, which hangs in the Department of History's common room in the Social Science Research Building, portrays a stern, independent-minded *Ordinarius*, earnestly searching for truth while oblivious to local intramural university politics.

At the dedication ceremony for the portrait in October, Harper, J. Franklin Jameson, and Laughlin delivered stirring commendations of Holst as a scholar and an academic citizen. Although all praised his scholarly contributions, they gave even more emphasis to Holst's moral leadership and professional ethics. When Laughlin praised his friend's demeanor as that of a "whole mighty spirit—a great moral force—blazed and gathered in his commanding attack," he summed up beautifully the importance of the German *Ordinarius* for the early university faculty. For Laughlin "the one striking impression that he made, within the University and without, was that of a great moral force. With his students, as with the public, he not only set the chords of right and wrong to vibrating afresh, but he set every conscience on the right key."[352] Here was a living symbol of the Humboldtian ideal of the independent scientist, free from pestering publics or autocratic university administrations.

With the dedication of the portrait, the University Senate was free to pursue a second opportunity for value-laden rhetoric about the debt of the new University to German science. It was at this juncture that Walther Wever entered the picture. Wever was the incredibly energetic German consul in Chicago from 1900 to 1908, and he sought to cement good relations between America and Germany by bringing German and American universities closer together. During his eight years in Chicago, Wever undertook a number of ventures that included the creation of professorial exchange programs.[353] He also functioned as a de facto fund-raiser for the University, persuading Catherine Seipp, widow of wealthy German American businessman Conrad Seipp, to fund prizes for the best essays written on German literature and culture. Wever was well placed in German administrative politics, given that his older brother, Hermann, was a high-ranking civil servant in the Prussian Ministry of Culture in Berlin, where he quietly supported his brother's schemes.

With Walther Wever's support, invitations were sent to five leading German scholars, asking them to journey to Chicago for a special event to be held in March 1904 honoring the impact of German academic culture on the new University of Chicago. The visit was subsidized by the Imperial German Government and local German businessmen, through the mediation of Wever.[354] The honorees were Berthold Delbrück, professor of Sanskrit at Jena; Paul Ehrlich, professor of medicine at Berlin; Wilhelm Herrmann, professor of theology at Marburg; Josef Kohler, professor of law at Berlin; and Eduard Meyer, professor of ancient history at Berlin. All were eminent authorities, and as a group they represented such a high level of distinction that it was easy for the organizers to shape their visit into a public symbolic gesture. Arriving in Chicago in mid-March 1904, the German scholars were honored at various dinners and receptions, including a huge public reception at the Auditorium Hotel attended by no less than five thousand guests, with the scholars entering the room accompanied by a march from Wagner's *Tannhäuser*.[355] On March 22, 1904, John Coulter gave the speech at the convocation, proclaiming the University's allegiance to the values of *Lehrfreiheit* and *Lernfreiheit*.

The most remarkable speech of the day was Harper's. In introducing the ceremony Harper claimed that the University owed much to the "ideals of German scholarship" and was greatly indebted to German intellectual life. Ignoring Laughlin's initial subtext of the German *Ordinarius* as a defender of faculty rights against external authorities (including Harper himself as University president), Harper used the scene to paint a vast picture of the importance of international contacts and connections to the University as a whole. Reprising "The University and Democracy," his 1899 address, Harper insisted that universities were among the most powerful agents of international understanding and comity, and that their capacity to sponsor and encourage an "intermingling" of "widely diverging ideas" was bound to lead to closer connections between the nations of the world. The University of Chicago thus became a mediator not only of ideas but also of peoples, for its function was "to lead the souls of men and nations into close communion with the common soul of all humanity. This is a work which universities in the past have accomplished and which, perhaps, they are doing today more largely than ever before."[356] Although the March convocation originated as an act of reverence by local faculty for *their* locally distinguished German *Ordinarius*, Harper turned it into an opportunity to elevate his young University such that other senior

German *Ordinarien* would not only want to visit but also from which they would gladly receive honorary degrees.

In the end the heroic pageantry of Harper's fete burnished the luster of the University by using Chicago's appropriation of German research traditions to justify the almost instantaneous scholarly prestige claimed by the University in the Midwest. The many Chicago faculty who had studied at one or more German universities did not bring back an innocent or naive nostalgia, and certainly they had little admiration for the autocratic politics of the German government. Nor were they oblivious to the obvious structural differences that later scholars have insisted on between German and American research universities. The rebellion against Harper's headship system after 1907 demonstrated that more democratic and egalitarian forces were in play in the understanding of hierarchy and authority, reflecting the fact that the new American universities like Chicago were different *cultural* ensembles than their German cousins. What the Americans did acquire from the German model was a high valuation of the authority of scientific thinking, the weight of truth telling and scholarly discovery, the prestige of intellectual erudition, the need for institutional arrangements like large libraries and scientific laboratories to advance the discovery of new knowledge, and the controlling independence of the senior faculty as the preeminent corporate group in university life. Their idealization of German *Wissenschaft* was sober and selective, and they knew what they were borrowing and what they disdained to borrow. So capacious was this influence that even John Coulter, who had never studied in Germany, could easily cloak himself in the mantle of German scientific practices. To Charlemagne Tower, the American ambassador to Germany, Harper later effused that the convocation had been a "great success" and that in fact "it is the greatest event that has happened in the history of the University."[357]

Harper's Legacy

Charles Chandler once observed of his friend that no one could know the complete Harper, for "he was a many-sided personality, and *never* showed his whole self to any one person or group, not even to his wife or family. In my own limited contacts I have heard at least a dozen different Harpers described."[358] For some of his later critics, most notably Thorstein Veblen, Harper represented the commercialization and trivialization of higher education. Veblen thought of the true university in very austere terms—as a community of scholars pursuing knowledge with like-minded (and, for the most part, graduate) students. His portrayal of Harper (the "Great Pioneer") in *The Higher Learning in America* is of a man who began as a scholar but whose love of learning was overpowered by his passion for making a public mark as an institution builder, dedicated to public service at best and monetary gain at worst. For Veblen, Harper's entrepreneurial energy was further evidence of a boyish devotion to bustling efficiency and an indiscriminate pursuit of prestigious enterprises, no matter what their cost to the true scholarly purpose of the university.[359]

Harper was an easy target for such critiques, since he did believe that universities had a business and a service side and that university presidents had a fiduciary responsibility to care for their institutions' material as well as spiritual goals. In an essay entitled "The Business Side of a University," Harper wrote with evident relish about the multiple tasks and complex administrative structures characteristic of universities like Chicago. He also admitted that, for all of the noble ideals of service that circumscribed the office, a college president largely spent his time "in seeking ways and means to enable this or that professor to carry out some plan which he has deeply at heart—a plan, it may be, for research and investigation, or for improving the work of instruction."[360] Because the new University was founded by civic-minded, wealthy businessmen, along with earnest Baptist ministers, from the very beginning Chicago was a much more complex institution than the austere utopia that Veblen favored. It was designed to serve its communities in many ways, and its scale eventually matched and exceeded the ambitions of its founders. Size, then, and multiple purposes, forced Chicago like all modern universities to adopt the managerial structures of large commercial enterprises, and very soon the academic leader, no matter how strong his scholarly credentials, adopted the qualities and the purposes of a business manager. Even so, Harper was not a particularly successful business manager; as was evident from his collisions with Starr Murphy budget management was not his strong suit. He never ceased to be a scholar, and to fault him for his inveterate support of the popularization of scholarship is to misunderstand a crucial characteristic of his scholarly personality, for Harper believed that universities existed to spread knowledge to the literate masses.

Educational practitioners judged Harper with greater sympathy. One of the more fascinating tributes came from G. Stanley Hall, president of Clark University, an institution that had been ravaged by Harper's famous raid of the faculty in 1892. Hall wrote to John D. Rockefeller in late 1905 that Harper would be "shocked to know I thought of writing to you," since his own university had been seriously damaged by Harper's aggressive recruiting, but that

I think no one in the whole field of education has shown such genius for organization, has himself grown more rapidly in office, has given to college and university work so many new and good ideas, has been so unselfish, shown such powers of sustained and effective work, has so admirably combined the enthusiasm of a scholar and that of an administrator. Even his annual Register is full of stimulating new ideas. Eastern college presidents were a little disposed to look askance upon him at first, but their attitude has greatly changed, although even yet I do not think they appreciate him at his full worth. He will go down in the history of education as a man who marks a great and salutary epoch.[361]

This "sustained and effective work" came at a terrible physical and psychological cost. Harper was notorious for his capacity to work without sleep—Francis Parker Jr. recalled that his father often commented on Harper's ability to function with little rest, and that "many times he would telephone my father about something late at night or very early in the morning"—but the demands of building an academic empire slowly wore on him.[362] Harper would write in 1899 to an old friend from Denison days, "How often I long for the quiet pleasant days of old Granville!...I am living at a break-neck speed. Some morning you will read in the papers— Harper is gone. The pressure is tremendous. I cannot myself understand how I can stand it. My only consolation is that it will not last forever."[363] If Harper felt under tremendous stress throughout his presidency, it was because of his compulsion to function as a teacher, scholar, and editor in addition to fund-raiser, administrator, urban reformer, national patriot, and general visionary. His monomania to advance the (in his view) ineluctable destiny of the University was also infectious to those came in contact with him, even poorly paid assistant professors who craved more money. Paul Mandeville, an early alumnus and later a prominent library administrator, recalled that in meeting Harper his contemporaries were struck by the fact that "Harper lived and dreamed in terms of the University as predestined, and made his decisions on whether your destiny and that of the University were one. If so, you both felt it and the minor considerations fell into place around the work to be done, the opportunity and things like that, and many personal considerations were forgotten."[364] Harper presided over enormous wealth creation for the University, and he did so relying on his own judgment and that of a few trusted advisers. Some faculty viewed him as autocratic, but the autocracy arose from Harper's impatient sense of cultivating all parts of the University at all times even in the face of local self-interest. When Harper hoped that the University would become "one in spirit, not necessarily in opinion," this did not mean it would be one in governance. Rather, Harper established a tradition of the University as needing tough, self-willed presidents who, if necessary, would defy local faculty particularisms to advance the

larger progress of the institution as whole. In this mode Harper anticipated the development of strong, bureaucratically organized central
administrations—standing apart from the idiosyncrasies of the full professors of the *Ordinarienuniversität*—that marked the history of modern
research universities in both Europe and the United States in the twentieth century.[365] Moreover, Harper slowly built a firewall between external
money and the independence of the research faculty, bolstering the faculty's sense of scholarly authority by making them feel relatively immune
from the political whims of big business or frightened churchmen. This
autonomy gave the Chicago faculty a gently inflated (and pragmatically
protected) sense of their scholarly independence. Harper fashioned a visible academic aura for the University through the distinguished senior faculty scholars whom he recruited and through the university press and its
scholarly publications (the new academic journals, scholarly monographs,
the decennial reports, and even textbooks). This profile—together with
Harper's ideal of professional knowledge as a form of democratic service
and leadership infused with (sublimated) norms of Christian virtue, with
his eloquent defense of teaching and of the transformative power of liberal
education, and with his independence from the less seemly sides of high
capitalism and the other distractions of everyday life—led to a sense of
notability, institutional permanency, and self-regarding confidence that
had instant traction in the rapidly developing world of American higher
education. Harper was a successful president not only because his heroic
plans were right for his time but also because he had the scholarly legitimacy and personal authority to cajole his colleagues to embrace bold
innovations. Beardsley Ruml once observed that the pace of radical institutional change set by Harper served as an example for other senior faculty and helped to create the fearless, entrepreneurial faculty culture that
marked Chicago over the twentieth century: "The effect has been to make
some members of the faculty bold and adventurous, and to make others
timid and insecure. But the balance has been on the side of adventure."[366]

Edward Levi once argued that "no one owns this institution—not even
the students. In a more genuine way it possesses all of us."[367] But Harper's
case was instructive about the dependence that this particular university
has always had on strong, visionary presidents who were willing to take
enormous risks. Harper's greatness lay in his stunning combination of
intellectual vision, moral courage, confidence in the efficacy of knowledge, and impetuous institutional risk taking. Many of his schemes did
not work out, but this bothered him little. Colleagues at other universities
sometimes characterize the University of Chicago as a *real* university; in
doing so they are mirroring the self-representation of an institution whose
core vocation derived from the early faculty's certainty about the efficacy

of higher learning. Rockefeller, Ryerson, Field, and other capitalists endowed the University with bonds, real estate, and cash, but Harper gave Chicago clarity of mission. This mission had both secular and religious origins. Its genesis depended on enormous wealth, which gave the early University unimpeded scholarly freedom and individual autonomy, but it also depended on a robust belief in the moral virtue of learning and knowledge, which sanctioned the uncompromising quality of the University's educational and research programs. As Frederick Gates would later put it, the early University's growth was one that "for solidity, strength, rapidity, [and] wisdom has probably never been equaled in the history of learning."[368]

How effective were Harper's successors in sustaining and building on this complex blueprint? This will be the story of the next chapters.

* 3 *

Stabilization and Renewal, 1906–1929

The Era of Equilibrium and Retrenchment: Harry Pratt Judson, 1906–1922

Harry Pratt Judson is one of the University's forgotten presidents, yet his sixteen-year term was longer than that of any of Chicago's presidents except Robert Maynard Hutchins. Born in 1849, Judson attended Williams College, earning a BA in 1870 and an MA in 1883. He worked as a teacher and a high school principal for fifteen years in Troy, New York, before landing a teaching position in history at the University of Minnesota in 1885. Judson did not have a pronounced "scientific" background—he lacked a PhD—and he was always suspicious of the impact of German scholarly traditions and methods on the American academy.

Harper recruited Judson to join the original faculty of the University in 1892, as much as an administrator as a teacher or scholar. Judson became dean of the Faculties of Arts, Literature, and Science, as well as head of the Department of Political Science, and in most respects Harper's right-hand man. His temperament was the opposite of Harper's—Judson was cautious, laconic, phlegmatic. Richard Storr later characterized the social side of Judson's relationships with the faculty as "stiff and prig[g]ish." When Harper died in 1906, the trustees named Judson acting president, and then, in the face of opposition from faculty who wanted a more prominent researcher like Albion Small and a larger official role in the search process, in February 1907 they named him Harper's permanent successor.[1]

CHARACTERISTICS OF THE JUDSON ADMINISTRATION

Judson's main achievement as president was to wipe out the structural deficit that Harper had generated and thus to balance the University budget for most of his term in office. Judson's strategy of budgetary discipline and financial austerity renewed John D. Rockefeller's confidence in the future of the University and resulted in a series of large gifts between

1906 and 1909 that culminated in his final gift of $10 million on December 13, 1910. Rockefeller gave this gift in the expectation that in the future "the University [would] be supported and enlarged by the gifts of many [rather] than by those of a single donor," and enjoined the trustees that "this great institution, being the property of the people, should be controlled, conducted and supported by the people."[2] The same day that the gift was announced John D. Rockefeller Jr. and Frederick T. Gates resigned as trustees of the University, thus ending the strange governance configuration between New York City and Chicago that had challenged Harper. Even during the war, the University maintained a balanced budget. Judson was extremely proud of this record, and he took it for granted that the University should be run strictly as a business, with little or no input from faculty as to budgetary priorities.[3] Judson's other significant achievement was to encourage the trustees to create a faculty pension fund in February 1912, providing full, associate, and assistant professors with annual allowances ranging from (approximately) $1,000 up to $3,000 after their retirement at the age of sixty-five or seventy.[4]

In educational policy Judson's long presidency basically preserved the status quo of Harper's design for the University, neither adding new elements nor detracting substantially from what Harper had done. But the difference between the two men was immediately apparent. James H. Tufts recalled, "President Harper's characteristic attitude toward a new suggestion which appealed to him as a good one worth trying was, 'That's a good idea. We'll try it. I'll find the money for it somehow.' President Judson's reaction was likely to be 'If there are sufficient funds available, we'll consider it.'"[5] For many faculty this meant a president who was unresponsive to their research ambitions and who was so confident that the University was sufficiently well established that he did not have to fear threats of faculty defections.[6]

Faculty grumbling about inadequate research support percolated up to the board, leading a young trustee, Harold H. Swift, to draft a memorandum in 1915 arguing that Judson had gone too far in fiscal probity: "For the sake of saving $1,500 in the chemistry department, [administrators] were breaking the spirit of one the greatest scholars (along chemistry lines) on earth."[7] But for the time being, Swift was in the minority. In the wake of Harper's spending habits, most of the Chicago trustees, eager to please the Rockefeller staff in New York City, were content with and even grateful for Judson's parsimony. Judson shared Harper's inclinations toward autocracy and top-down administrative rule, but because he was both less generous and flexible than Harper and not a distinguished scholar in his own right, his credibility with the senior faculty was never high to begin with and lessened as austerity set in. New York may have been pleased, but Chicago grew restless.

Judson was a constitutional historian with an interest in national history and international law. His textbooks on modern European and American history were balanced and carefully executed, manifesting support for the nineteenth-century liberal tradition. Judson's sense of the world was cautiously optimistic. He viewed the nineteenth century as being "the most brilliant in the history of human achievement," a century that had equipped Europe with "the tools of civilization in rich abundance." But Judson also saw Europe as a continent riven by political distrust, beset by a dangerous arms race and "the dread of a gigantic war," and facing the danger of mass socialism. These phobias—militarism and socialism—were distinct clouds on liberal Europe's horizon.[8] As much as he admired the achievements of European civilization in the nineteenth century, Judson was convinced that America had become a "great power" and mature republic whose opinions in international affairs would have consequences.[9]

Although Judson demonstrated sympathy for Bismarck and presented a balanced view of the political structure of the German empire, in private he was uneasy about German influences on fledgling American universities. As early as 1891 Judson voiced what Daniel Meyer has termed "nativist" attitudes, demonstrating a special phobia for things German.[10] As noted in chapter 2, he stubbornly fought Harper's decision to appoint Hermann von Holst to be the first head professor of history. Judson also disagreed with Holst's opposition to American imperialism in the late 1890s, arguing that there was a proper role for American power in the world.[11] Ironically, Judson's own soft imperialism bore many similarities to the attitudes he would so openly criticize in his German opponents after 1916.

A staunch Republican, Judson voted for William Howard Taft and Charles Evans Hughes. He was a strong supporter of states' rights, opposing federal aid to education and opposing a national prohibition of alcohol.[12] Judson was opposed to labor unions, had mixed feelings about woman suffrage, and was a strict constructionist in relation to the role of the federal government.[13] His views of race relations were also benighted, almost the opposite of Holst's, although on this score Judson was probably no worse than Woodrow Wilson. In his private diary, historian William Dodd reported on a dinner party at Judson's house where "after dinner Judson once more made a point, he has made before with me, that slavery was the only proper way to manage and work the negroes in the Old South. This sounds like strange doctrine from one who served in the Union army at the end of the war to exterminate slavery! But that is the viewpoint of many people whom I meet in Chicago."[14] Judson was also intolerant of the foibles of faculty members whom he thought had embarrassed the University. He was responsible for the sudden dismissal of W. I. Thomas of the Department of Sociology in 1918 because of an extramarital affair, and he (along with other Chicago administrators) also had little good to say about Thorstein Veblen ("Mr. Veblen was once a member of our faculty, and we were quite willing to accept his resignation when he tendered it").[15]

Judson's friends and supporters viewed his phlegmatic personality in a more positive light. James Tufts remembered him as "reflective, cautious, taking few chances," while Theodore Soares called him a "genial, kindly man" with "sound practical judgment ... [whose] nature was most definitely conservative. He preferred assured ways to experiment."[16] Judson belonged to a generation of older American educational and cultural leaders who "were the beleaguered defenders of nineteenth-century tradition, and particularly the professional custodians of culture."[17]

THE CAMPUS AND THE GREAT WAR

With the declaration of war against Germany in early April 1917, universities across America mobilized to support the war. Accusations of deficient patriotism hit some universities, particularly the University of Wisconsin, and the stakes were high for Chicago not to appear lagging. The Columbia historian James Shotwell even urged universities to collect materials relating to their war contributions, with an eye on impressing public opinion and persuading Congress that donations to higher education should be made tax-exempt.[18]

Several weeks before Wilson's war message, in mid-March 1917, fifty members of the natural science departments at Chicago signed a petition recommending that the trustees "offer the scientific laboratories and equipment of the University to the federal government for use in case of war" and volunteering to assist the government in war-related activities.[19] Once hostilities commenced, Harry Pratt Judson became the moral and logistical leader of the University's war effort. Judson had a lifelong interest in military affairs. Too young to fight in the Civil War in 1861, Judson had later tried to enlist as a drummer boy in the Union Army. The Civil War was a living memory, horrible, fascinating, and persistently romantic, and it affected his thinking about World War I.[20] While teaching high school in upper New York State, Judson served in the Troy County Citizens Corps, a local militia company that was incorporated in the New York National Guard in 1877. He enjoyed drilling and marching with his comrades, and he took pleasure in the camaraderie afforded by volunteer military service. Just before moving to Minneapolis in 1885 to become a professor at the University of Minnesota, he wrote a eulogistic account of his New York militia, arguing: "Beneath the smooth surface of civilized society are always seething the savage elements of disorder. Behind the stately courtesies, which mark the intercourse of enlightened nations, are always lurking envy, jealousy, and cupidity, likely at any moment to bring opposing interests into hostile collision.... The experience even of our first century of national existence has taught us the absolute necessity of maintaining the military spirit, and of keeping alive a knowledge of the modes of military action."[21] Four years later, Judson published a study of Caesar's army during the Roman civil wars in which he acknowledged that "war is barbarism" but added that "the story of man has no epoch in which war has not existed. The history of war is the history of the development of the human mind."[22]

At first glance, Judson's energetic involvement in the war was surprising, given his reputation for caution and circumspection. Yet he was among the most partisan of those who before 1917 wished to pursue the war and the most eager after 1917 to engineer a total mobilization of campus resources. The Great War released Judson from Harper's long shadow, and he embraced it passionately. His early public statements about the war in 1914 were carefully neutral, but privately his sympathies were clearly pro-British and pro-rearmament. Judson joined the pro-preparedness National Security League in 1915 and became a member of the executive committee of its Chicago branch.[23] By the time of the American presidential elections in November 1916, Judson openly opposed Woodrow Wilson's attempts to maintain neutrality.[24] He had little sympathy with the plight of German Americans. When a local German American businessman wrote to him in March 1917 complaining about being "despised and rejected" because of his ethnic background, Judson assured him that "no one of our fellow citizens is 'despised and rejected' if in the last analysis he puts the United States of America before all other countries in the world."[25] Judson was also a robust advocate of peacetime universal military service. In late December 1916 Judson wrote to Harvard historian Albert Bushnell Hart, arguing that "the whole nation ought to be trained for national defense" and that "modern experience shows that the only adequate form of national defense is by the proper training of the entire nation to act quickly and efficiently in case of emergency."[26]

The war also offered Judson the opportunity to step out of his role as strict guardian of budgetary austerity, compensating for his unsteady relationship with the senior faculty.[27] What Robert Herrick would later characterize as "the contemptuous murmurs of the faculty about their

President" would now be repressed for the duration of the war.[28] Judson supported all possible measures to mobilize the campus, from encouraging students to volunteer for the new military science program that he had established in late 1916 to leading war bond solicitations. His secretary, David Robertson, proudly reported that Judson loved to drill: "From the beginning he has interested himself in the success of the Reserve Officers Training Corps, himself appearing on Stagg Field for drill; subsequently, after the recall of Major Bell ... he himself prepared to take charge of the drilling of the Corps."[29]

Judson's most notable war speech came in late April 1917 before a crowd in Mandel Hall. Later published by the University of Chicago Press as the first of the University of Chicago war papers, this document was an American equivalent of the prowar rhetoric that overtook German, French, and British academics in the autumn of 1914.[30] Judson's central premises—that Germany was evil; that its political system was dominated by undemocratic, Prussian elements; that it had deliberately started the war; that it was a danger to the international order; and that it must be severely punished—all bore a close resemblance to British war propaganda in the so-called war of the professors in 1914 and to similar pamphlets published by senior US historians in 1917–18.[31] The reception on campus was mixed. Even the deliberately neutral *Maroon* objected to the menacing tone of Judson's demand for a "complete victory over the Teutonic empires," arguing that it went beyond what Woodrow Wilson intended and failed to acknowledge Wilson's own expectations for the establishment of a democratic Germany.[32]

Most striking was Judson's claim to be speaking not as a private citizen but as the leader of an institution that could act as an official patriotic corporation. The University could send its boys to the army and its faculty to government agencies, but it could also act institutionally against Germany as a midwestern voice of patriotic propaganda. Indeed, the University mailed Judson's paper to 4,500 professionals and local notables in small towns all over the Midwest so as to "give the superior advantages of authoritative information to people who probably could not otherwise obtain them."[33]

As a public patriot, Judson engineered one of the most partisan actions ever taken by the University. In March 1918 the board of trustees voted to revoke the honorary degree awarded seven years earlier to the former German ambassador to the United States, Count Johann von Bernstorff. Judson had urged the board to do so, arguing that Bernstorff's actions were "contrary to peace and order of the Republic, and inimical to the rights of the United States as a neutral nation."[34] Judson was alluding to Bernstorff's role in the Zimmermann telegram affair of February and

March 1917. This episode involved a secret telegram from Arthur Zimmermann, the German foreign secretary, to the president of Mexico, Venustiano Carranza, on the eve of Germany's resumption of unrestricted submarine warfare, in which Berlin offered Mexico a chance to reclaim its former territories in Texas, Arizona, and New Mexico in return for siding with Germany against the United States. The Zimmermann affair has long been one of the great mysteries of modern intelligence history, but Bernstorff was in fact opposed both to his government's resumption of unrestricted submarine warfare and to the Zimmermann telegram itself.[35] On learning of the University's action, one of Judson's local ministerial friends congratulated him on a "fitting and patriotic" act, suggesting that the decision was indeed taken for political purposes.[36]

In addition to his advocacy of the war on campus, Judson was appointed to the Committee on Labor of the National Council on Defense and undertook other wartime roles, including service on the federal district board of the Selective Service system for Chicago, which was almost a full-time job.[37] Then in July 1918 he left for Europe, leading a fact-finding commission to survey social conditions in and around Persia as part of a larger strategy for war relief in the Middle East, and he was absent from campus for the summer and autumn quarters of 1918. Judson's example was emulated by many of Chicago's most distinguished faculty, who volunteered for or accepted special war jobs, and it was Judson's policy to guarantee the full salaries they would have earned on campus.[38] By January 1918 seventy faculty members were in war service, of whom twenty-seven were full professors.[39] Some applied for officer commissions, and others, failing to obtain assignment in the army, received work in government agencies. In addition to those faculty who entered government service and left Chicago, many others, especially in the sciences, undertook war work in the laboratories.[40]

The war left conflicting memories, some buoyant and enthusiastic, others mordant and depressing. Elizabeth Wallace, an associate professor of French and an ardent Francophile, remembered the enthusiasm of the majority of the faculty and trustees for the Allied cause. Wallace spent part of her war months in France, working as a translator for a mission sponsored by the Rockefeller Foundation; when she returned to campus, she chaired the Student War Activities Committee and helped to organize the Woman Students' Training Corps, a group that was dedicated in "organization, discipline, and devotion" to aiding the University "in every way possible to do its part to win the war."[41] If her war was a noble cause, another humanist, English professor Robert Lovett, held a radically different view. For Lovett the war was an episode of hysteria and hypernationalism; of chronic and shameful violations of the civil liberties of war protesters, conscientious objectors, and pacifists; a time in which his faculty colleagues embarrassed themselves by their egregious partisanship. When Lovett dared to speak at a peace rally in the Auditorium Theatre in late May 1917, urging that the United States make clear its war aims for a possible peace settlement, he was roundly denounced as a defeatist.[42]

Carol Gruber has argued that many American professors were uncertain about the civic value of their own professional roles before 1914 and that war helped to compensate for these feelings by providing them opportunities for a valuable public service role.[43] Robert Herrick, like his friend Lovett a professor of English, published an autobiographical novel, *Chimes*, in 1926, which has scenes of faculty preoccupied with the war and seeing it as an exciting escape from the monotony of their everyday lives.[44] Some faculty excelled in patriotic propaganda of an acutely vindictive sort. Albion Small harshly denounced Germany and its political culture in a published lecture entitled "Americans and the World Crisis."[45] Small believed that Germany was a nation and a civic culture gone mad in its obeisance to a militaristic caste and to the doctrine of might makes right in the service of state power. "Until the Germans repudiate this military caste and the creed it imposes," he argued, "to be at peace with Germany would make our nation a moral monstrosity." The war was a just crusade to protect the world against "the most hellish heresy that has ever menaced civilization: There is no God but power, and Prussia is its prophet." Classicist Paul Shorey joined the rhetorical fray in early May 1917 with an ominous warning to pacifists. "Germany is already planning the next war," he said. "A negotiated peace that on any pretext leaves her in control of Central Europe is merely a truce in which she may prepare to fight on more favorable conditions. That is the alternative which the pacifist dupes of German propaganda refuse to face."[46]

In contrast to such faculty hyperengagement, fewer changes were observable in the climate of student life at the University. Students were much less affected by the war than Judson would have wished. Enlistment information is scattered and imprecise, but enrollment data from the registrar's office suggested that while the number of undergraduate and graduate male students in the arts and sciences on campus between the spring of 1917 and the spring of 1918 declined significantly, a large number of male students were still enrolled in the University a year into the war, and female enrollments remained relatively stable.[47]

Student reaction to the war was mixed. By mid-May 1917, more than 100 fraternity men had entered the military training camp at Fort Sheridan or other service venues.[48] By October 1917, 225 fraternity men were in uniform, which amounted to 55 percent of the 409 men in campus fraternities during the previous year.[49] The majority of the student officers of the first ROTC unit organized on campus in May 1917 also came from the fraternities (of thirty-six student officers, twenty-five were members of the fraternities).[50] Still, most male students were unwilling to join the patriotic crusade, reflecting the fact that student attitudes about the war often seemed diametrically opposed to those of the faculty. When a student group—the Undergraduate Council—passed out cards asking students about their interest in participating in military drills and training, the *Maroon* noted that "many of the questions were left unanswered and some cards were never returned."[51] Moreover, the newspaper published ongoing litanies of complaints about the failure of male students to participate in voluntary after-school drills. In May 1917, of the 1,250 men eligible to participate in such drills, 700 had yet to show up.[52] Participation in the campus's ROTC program was similarly unimpressive. By October 1917, only 130 men had registered for ROTC, which led one student officer to complain that "the attendance is not as heavy as I would like to see, especially as we are at war."[53] Dean James Linn publicly reproached male students for avoiding military training in December 1917, observing that this was "a sign of a lack of appreciation on the part of the undergraduate male student body of the seriousness of the war situation."[54] The *Maroon* again complained in February 1918 about the "very small percentage of men students" who had enrolled in military science courses.[55] By April 1918 the situation had changed little—of the 1,500 male students eligible, only 187 had enrolled for such courses—and in early June the *Maroon* insisted that "the undergraduate body has not shown itself to be profoundly affected in any way by the war."[56] Later in 1918, after the armistice, James Angell, the University vice president, would admit to the board of trustees that the University's attempts to create voluntary military training programs for students had not been successful.[57]

Although the editors of the *Maroon* had been confident that war would transform the campus, making students more serious about their studies, social activities remained plentiful, and the schedule for seniors in 1918 was reported as being "the peppiest ever had."[58] In fact, the year was filled with false steps involving arbitrary assessments of student opinion. The organizers of the annual spring dance voted to call it off in 1918 in order to "awaken the student body to the fact that a great struggle is being carried on between the Allies and the Central Powers," even though the majority of students were opposed to canceling it. Then, members of the freshman class proceeded to organize a less formal dance in Bartlett Gymnasium open to all students that was essentially the spring dance under another name.[59] Blackfriars theatricals and interfraternity bowling, basketball, and tennis tournaments were canceled to save money, but the basic rhythms of life remained steady and uninterrupted for most students.[60]

Such evidence, while impressionistic, suggested that student opinion about the war was significantly less positive than the University's prowar faculty were willing to admit. A great majority of the University's undergraduates were from Chicago, a metropolis with large German, Austrian, Scandinavian, and Irish populations, so it seems hardly surprising that many of them felt deep ambivalence about the war.[61]

A few students openly rebelled. Ewald Pietsch, the son of Karl Pietsch, a professor of medieval Spanish literature at the University, was German by ethnicity and opposed the entry of the United States into the war. When Pietsch became involved in an angry altercation with two of his Beta Theta Pi fraternity brothers in late October 1917, he told them that "if I got the chance I'd stick a knife in the President's back." Pietsch was arrested and fined $500.[62] One brave soul wrote to the *Maroon* in mid-April 1917 denouncing the "mob tactics" of a "powerful and influential minority" who favored universal conscription, arguing that they "insisted that we dispense with all personal judgment and convictions and accept as law and gospel whatever their assumed superior insight and judgment deems necessary for what they consider the interest of the nation."[63] The student called this the "worst type of Prussianism."

The *Maroon* alluded to the existence of student pacifists in a December 1917 editorial, observing that some students "cannot reconcile their feeling of duty with their feeling that too much blood is being spilled, too much poverty is being caused, too much misery is being forced upon the peoples of the world."[64] Little is known about these pacifists, but one of their leaders was the young Louis Wirth, a student in the College from 1916 to 1919 who was later to become a key faculty member of the Department of Sociology and a distinguished expert in urban sociology.[65] A leader of the local chapter of the Cosmopolitan Club, a group of about thirty foreign students on campus founded in 1909, Wirth used one of the club's meetings in 1919 to denounce the Versailles peace treaty as "the most impudent document ever devised by the hands and brains of diplomats" and as a piece of "vengeance."[66] Fred Merrifield, an assistant professor of New Testament Studies and the faculty adviser to the club, denounced Wirth to Harry Pratt Judson, accusing him of being a "clever orator, cool, and daring," who opposed all established governments and of being "in favor of revolution."[67] Judson thereupon took the astonishing step of summoning an emergency meeting of the full professors of the arts and sciences to consider whether the University should withhold granting BA degrees to Wirth and Ephraim Gottlieb, another student radical, which would have been tantamount to expulsion.[68] Judson wanted Wirth expelled, but Ferdinand Schevill and Albion Small spoke out in Wirth's defense.[69] The assembled faculty rejected Judson's ploy. As Robert Lovett later recalled, "The President ... was unanimously told that if approval of the Treaty [of Versailles] was to be required for a degree, it should be so stated in the entrance requirements."[70]

A dramatic change was in the offing, however, that would have radically transformed Chicago's student culture had it been sustained. In late spring of 1918 the War Department announced the creation of a new campus-based military training program, the Student Army Training Corps. The SATC was to be a residential training program on college campuses sponsored by and paid for by the army, as part of a scheme to train 100,000 new officers by June 1919. SATC students were to be housed in university dormitories (Snell, Hitchcock, and Gates-Blake Halls) and in specially constructed barracks under the stands of Stagg Field. The University spent $50,000 on these conversions, with the goal of housing up to 1,500 student soldiers. At the same time, the University also announced that ten fraternity houses were to be requisitioned by the army.[71] The University was essentially to be converted into an encampment, run by seventeen army officers who would command and train the students. Students were to stand in line for "chow" and undertake guard duty, following a military training regimen modeled on that of the army's cantonments.[72] Given that SATC was a national training program, universities were forced to open admission to a wider pool of prospective students from their regions, in addition to regularly enrolled students. According to the registrar's statistics, 1,007 students joined the SATC program at the University of Chicago.[73] Of this number, several hundred were not regular students but had been recruited via public advertisements in Chicago newspapers inviting high school graduates eighteen years and older and others to enroll in late September.[74] The attrition rate for this group was high, and few of them returned in the winter quarter, since they lacked the academic qualifications to attend a normal undergraduate program.[75]

James Angell, vice president and dean of faculties, publicly welcomed the SATC program as one that would be remembered for "centuries to come" as having transformed "this peaceful University into an army camp."[76] Privately he acknowledged that the program would split the campus into two separate worlds—the men in service on the one side and the "girls and physically defective men, or men in the deferred classes of the draft" on the other, and would lead to "the most radical rearrangement of our instructional program, our methods, and distribution of our teaching force."[77] Faculty experience with the SATC was not encouraging. In briefing Samuel N. Harper on the kinds of lectures required for the SATC's historical "war aims" course in the fall of 1918, history department chair Andrew McLaughlin cautioned, "Please remember that these lectures must be very simple, given very slowly, and thoroughly outlined.... The lecturing is to be somewhat more simple than in an ordinary college course. You will have to remember that a lot of fellows do not know Peter the Great from Tamerlane the Great."[78] James Angell noted that the faculty tried to cooperate but in the end turned against the program: "The impossible character of the program, together with the wholly unsympathetic attitude of many of the younger officers—men in many cases of extreme youth, social callowness, and lack of education—made it increasingly difficult to preserve a satisfactory attitude on the part of the faculty."[79]

When the issue of renewing the wartime ROTC program on a postwar basis came before the board of trustees in late 1918, Judson was a steady enthusiast, while most faculty, even those who had been patriotic boosters in 1917, were "decidedly opposed" to renewing the program in peacetime.[80] Judson got his way, and an ROTC field artillery unit was created under the aegis of a Department of Military Science, which was (after 1930) attached to the Division of the Physical Sciences. The ROTC unit remained at the University of Chicago until the War Department transferred it to Michigan State University in 1936.[81] As early as 1924–25, the leaders of the ROTC program complained about "the apparent attitude of indecision as to whether the Military Department has a place at the University" and "the lack of active support by the faculty generally."[82] Judson's successor, Ernest DeWitt Burton, felt conflicted about a military science unit on campus, but did not force the issue. ROTC's final years on campus were marked by falling student enrollments and increasingly inadequate facilities, as well as the indifference of senior officials in the subsequent Hutchins administration, who refused to encourage students to take military science courses over any of the many other electives.[83]

THE AFTERMATH OF THE WAR

The sudden armistice and the SATC fiasco prevented the total militarization of the campus, and within six months life began to return to normal. But the war did have long-term consequences, both for the University and for Harry Pratt Judson. Former students clamored to return to the University's degree programs, and new students sought admission to colleges and graduate schools, increasing enrollments during and after the 1918–19 academic year. In 1913–14, the University had 1,766 undergraduate students in the arts and sciences, whereas by 1918–19 the number had increased to 1,996, and in 1919–20 to 2,382. By 1929–30, the undergraduate population stood at 2,970, an increase over prewar levels of almost 70 percent. Graduate enrollments followed the same pattern of robust growth, increasing from 500 students in 1913–14 to 696 in 1919–20 and

1,513 in 1929–30.[84] Many of these students were aided by grants from a new $1.5 million scholarship endowment established by LaVerne Noyes in 1918, with the express purpose of aiding veterans or family members of veterans who had fought in World War I. Once the trustees had officially accepted this gift, the University sent forms to all students in the service inviting them to apply for these scholarships. By 1921, 525 students were receiving Noyes scholarships, 316 undergraduates and 209 graduate and professional school students. Within three years of their creation, the University was also able to award scholarships to a number of women students whose fathers had served in the war.[85]

For some faculty the war had been the most exciting time of their personal lives, and when it ended they felt disappointed by the return to normalcy.[86] But others returned from war service with weightier ambitions and an urgent determination to make or remake their mark in their respective scholarly fields. The extraordinary national excellence that the University achieved in many scholarly fields in the 1920s and 1930s cannot be explained apart from the high expectations that the war unleashed. Barry Karl has cogently argued that Charles Merriam's scholarly and personal sensibilities were profoundly affected by his wartime experiences, and Merriam was not alone in this regard.[87] The creation of the National Research Council (NRC) in June 1916, led by former Chicago faculty member George E. Hale, was a visible symbol of the power of the collaboration between science and the national government, as well as a portent of the imposing achievements that were possible when universities, big foundations, and big business cooperated with one another.[88] Writing in the magazine *Science* in September 1919, Robert Millikan, who had served as a senior official on the NRC during the war, argued that "for the first time in history the world has been waked up by the war to an appreciation of what science can do." Millikan felt that American scientists now stood on the threshold of promising breakthroughs marked by enhanced scientific literacy in the schools, by fruitful cooperation of research scientists with industry, and by "the development of the possibilities of cooperative research among themselves." Millikan aspired to establish America as "a center of the world's scientific life and progress," which necessitated the creation of a series of great research institutes in the natural sciences, attached to universities but with key researchers released from mundane instructional responsibilities.[89]

Under pressure from Millikan and other top scientists like Julius Stieglitz, Albert Michelson, and E. H. Moore to create new organizations for scientific research within the University, Harry Pratt Judson announced in 1920 the creation of four new research institutes "devoted to conducting such research and such training in pure science as has an immediate bearing on the application of the sciences to the industries."[90] Having sanctioned the idea of these institutes, Judson did nothing to fund them, however, and a profound sense of inertia soon ensued that caused frustration among senior faculty members. When Robert Millikan resigned from Chicago in June 1921 to go to the new California Institute of Technology because of Judson's dithering and refusal to match the latter institution's offer of research support, the writing was on the wall.[91]

The frustrations of faculty researchers who demanded support for new research and pedagogical initiatives but who felt rebuffed by their timid, fiscalist chief executive came at the same moment that severe financial and demographic challenges appeared on the postwar horizon. The inflation wrought by the war led to a reduction of the real value of tuition income even as more students crowded the campus, and competition from other universities soon displaced the University's dominant prewar position on senior faculty salaries. By 1923 Chicago had fallen seriously behind Harvard and Columbia in the average value of full professorial salaries.[92] Swift complained to his fellow trustees in December 1922 that "the University of Chicago in the last ten years has gone down hill," citing especially the "false security" under Judson that had allowed faculty salaries to become uncompetitive: "We have failed to keep our eminent men. They have either died and have not been adequately replaced or they have been allowed to go to other institutions and then their places filled with cheaper men.... The University is woefully undercapitalized and we need considerable amounts of funds to put us in even a reasonably good position to carry on our present responsibilities."[93] The pressures caused by mushrooming enrollments, the rising professional expectations of the faculty for complex research, and faculty disgruntlement over the administration's penny-pinching ways required strong, imaginative presidential leadership, and it should have been apparent that Judson was not the man for the job. Judson's preoccupation with the draft board in 1917 led him to neglect university business for five months, and faculty grumbling about his inability to act decisively intensified.[94] By the time Judson returned in early 1919 from his trip to the Middle East on behalf of the American-Persian Relief Commission, he was exhausted, yet he refused to retire. University policy dictated retirement at the age of seventy, yet when Judson approached that age in 1919 he secured a waiver from the board of trustees to continue in office. Judson also found it difficult to carry out the University's remembrance of the Great War, hemming and hawing on plans to memorialize the students and alumni who had died in the war and unable to make up his mind what kind of memorial was suitable.[95] Not until November 1938, on the twentieth anniversary of the armistice, was an official memorial tablet in honor of the Chicago war dead dedicated in Rockefeller Chapel.[96]

By the time Judson left the presidency, he was an unwelcome guest. The war that he had championed created conditions that made his exit look like a slow political death. Many years later Harold Swift would reflect that "dry rot set in before the end of Judson's administration." Though "tired and old," Judson wished to stay on as president as long as his predecessor had stayed, and the board of trustees acquiesced, "grateful for the firm foundation Judson had put under Harper's brilliant superstructure." In contrast, Judson's successor, Ernest DeWitt Burton, seemed to have an "electric knowledge" of what needed to be done when he assumed the presidency: "Burton had been at the University since its beginning, as had Judson. He was a great scholar, had the scholar's point of view, and knew how the scholars of the University had suffered for five years [i.e., since 1918]. Therefore he was on fire to get the faculty back to real research and scholarship."[97]

Judson died in 1927. He was mourned by old friends, but on campus he was a forgotten figure.[98]

The Years of Renewal: Ernest De Witt Burton, 1922–1925

In early 1922 a faction of the board of trustees led by Swift insisted that Judson retire.[99] But having waited until then, the board had already lost the opportunity to secure James R. Angell as president. A distinguished functional psychologist and ambitious dean of the faculties who had served as acting president for several months during the war, Angell wanted the job and was highly popular with the senior faculty.[100] Judson saw Angell as a rival, however, and resented his energetic administrative practices as disturbing what Swift sarcastically called "the even tenor" of Judson's ways.[101] Faced with Judson's intransigence and the board's inaction on the succession issue, and the complicating factor that he was not a Baptist, Angell left Chicago in late 1920 for the presidency of the Carnegie Corporation (from which he quickly moved in 1921 to the presidency of Yale University).[102] Lacking a compelling candidate like Angell, the board was forced to cast a wider net, and in April 1922 the trustees asked Ernest DeWitt Burton, a close confidant of Harper and a senior scholar widely respected among his local peers, to explore possible successors. Burton conducted a confidential interview mission to New York City and New England to meet with possible candidates, but came back with less than enthusiastic reactions. Swift also took the innovative step of consulting faculty leaders, although this came late in the process and resulted in no real change in the outcome. The board briefly considered Raymond B. Fosdick, a trustee of the Rockefeller Foundation, and Ernest M. Hopkins, the president of Dartmouth College, but both men declined to be considered for the position, and by the end of 1922 Harold Swift and Martin Ryerson asked Burton to replace Judson, offering him the job in mid-January 1923.[103] Initially the trustees selected Burton to be acting president, but within six months they decided that he was a worthy permanent successor to Harper and dropped the modifier in Burton's title.

THE UNIVERSITY IN 1923: BURTON TAKES CONTROL

Ernest DeWitt Burton was sixty-six years old when he received the summons from Ryerson and Swift, and quite naturally felt himself to be near the end of his professional career. In private correspondence Burton acknowledged that, given his age, his tenure as president might be a brief one, but he accepted the new job with the same spirit of evangelical service as had defined his career since the 1880s.[104] Burton was a loyal product of Harper's vision of the early University, but he realized that the University after 1918 faced striking new social and political realities, not only increased student enrollment and a stronger sense of ambition and entitlement on the part of the faculty than Judson had been willing to countenance, but also the maturation of a system of meritocratic competition for talent and resources among leading American universities that made Judson's leisurely style of governance unsustainable.

Burton's fundamental contribution was to understand that the University needed new strategic leadership and new structural approaches to undergraduate education and to its research capacities and competencies, not simply more money. Abraham Flexner, who knew him well, later observed that with Burton at the helm, "the fur began to fly. Never in my experience have I encountered anyone who seized a point more rapidly or who proceeded more decisively to put his decisions into effect."[105] Well into the 1950s the memory of Burton's activism was vivid in the minds of faculty who had known him. As the distinguished political scientist Leonard White recalled, "No one who was here at the time can fail to have a vivid recollection of the energy and dynamic power which he imparted to every section of the University."[106] As late as 1968 Edward Levi would observe that "on the presidents, I suspect Burton was a great one."[107]

Burton was a distinguished New Testament scholar who was one of Harper's first appointees in 1892. The son of a Baptist preacher, Burton was born in Granville, Ohio, in 1856, the same year as Harper and just over fifty miles from Harper's birthplace.[108] Burton undertook his undergraduate studies at the local Baptist college in Granville—Denison University—

and then taught ancient Greek for several years at Kalamazoo College and the Norwood School in Ohio. In 1879, he moved to the Theological Seminary in Rochester for his graduate work. He taught New Testament Greek first at Rochester and then at the Newton Theological Institution, a Baptist seminary near Boston, between 1883 and 1892. In 1887, Burton was awarded a sabbatical year that he spent in Europe, visiting the University of Leipzig for advanced training in biblical research as part of the then-requisite German sojourn for young Americans seeking careers in modern *Wissenschaft*.

Burton was ordained as a Baptist minister in June 1883. So committed was he to a life of evangelical zeal, he considered serving as a missionary, even though he knew that he was not fit for such a physically strenuous life. Still, Burton's concern for missionary work remained a leitmotif of his career and led him to support a scheme proposed by William McKibben, an ex-Baptist missionary then living in Chicago, in 1904 to create a branch campus of the University of Chicago in China, under the supervision of the Divinity School. As a way of exploring such possibilities, Burton agreed to chair a commission in July 1908 sponsored by John D. Rockefeller to explore possible opportunities for establishing new Christian higher educational institutions in East Asia, and in August 1921 he led another commission to China.[109] Burton also chaired the board of the American Baptist Foreign Mission Society, and he was actively involved in supporting domestic and foreign missionary activity throughout his tenure at Chicago.

Harper first encountered Burton in 1882 when he invited him to join the Morgan Park Seminary's summer Hebrew program, but their relationship deepened after 1886, when Harper was teaching at Yale and Burton at Newton. Harper invited Burton to write a textbook in ancient Greek for his summer school programs, a task that Burton accepted but then was unable to complete because of ill health. Various conversations ensued between the two men on new research trends in New Testament studies, Burton's primary scholarly field and one of interest to Harper. So impressed was Harper by Burton's scholarly acumen and personal charisma that he sought to hire him in December 1891 to become the founding head of the new Department of New Testament and Early Christian Literature at his new university. Burton was initially unimpressed by Harper's offer, but acceded once Harper had given Burton pledges of substantial financial support.

Burton was a liberal Protestant with progressive ideas about the historicity of the New Testament, and he was even bolder and more decisive in embracing new trends in biblical scholarship than Harper.[110] His massive study from 1920 of the Epistle to the Galatians was a remarkable work, and demonstrated the refined craft of a senior scholar whose erudition afforded him professional legitimacy among senior faculty members at Chicago. The book also revealed Burton's profound admiration for Saint Paul, not only as remarkable missionary but also as a "commanding personality" who sought to make "religion personal rather than ecclesiastical, and morality a social relation grounded in religion."[111] At the same time, Burton had the interpersonal skills to get on well with conservative leaders in the Baptist establishment who differed with him theologically.

Burton was one of Harper's most successful appointments in his capacity for effective institutional leadership, and before long his talent for administrative management led him beyond the ken of the Divinity School. In June 1902 Harper asked Burton to assume the chair of the Joint Commission on Library Policy to plan the design and siting of a future university library and other new campus buildings that would be part of the library group on the south end of the central quadrangles. The assemblage of buildings constructed along Fifty-Ninth Street, from Social Sciences to Classics, essentially reflected Burton's scheme of August 1902. Burton also led the effort to plan the new William Rainey Harper Memorial Library between 1906 and 1910, built with contributions from faculty, alumni, civic donors, and a major grant from John D. Rockefeller (who ended up paying for two-thirds of the $1 million raised to cover the construction costs). So successful was Burton's diplomatic leadership of these complex political endeavors that he was asked in 1910 to take on the additional responsibility of director of the university libraries. Through judicious staff appointments and efficient departmental planning Burton became the founder of the University's modern library system. Equally important, Burton gained respect among often garrulous senior faculty as a patient but decisive leader who shared their intellectual values but who could maneuver in the realms of higher administrative management.

When Burton became president, he faced a disgruntled senior faculty, many of whom felt a loss of direction on the part of the University's leadership. Not only had Judson's austerity regime led to key faculty departures, but senior faculty experienced the final years of the Judson presidency as a period of intellectual stagnation at a time when the top Eastern universities were outspending Chicago for senior faculty. As a report by an outside consulting firm, the John Price Jones Corporation, observed in 1924, "Failure to raise faculty salaries, to meet increased living costs and competition with other universities, together with the failure to fill vacancies with new men of comparable attainments, has naturally had a detrimental effect on the morale and prestige of the teaching staff."[112] Burton sought to transform the University by appealing to an expanded donor base beyond the Rockefeller charities and by then using this appeal to energize the faculty to take up ambitious new scholarly projects. He aimed to create a campus environment that encouraged "thoroughness, accuracy, increase of knowledge and development of character" as opposed to work that led to "superficiality, stagnation, and low ideals of life." Burton realized that he had to act quickly to restore forward momentum, and the only way to do this was to raise substantial resources for new faculty appointments and enhanced salaries as well as for new research and teaching buildings.[113] As he put it to Martin Ryerson in 1924, Chicago needed "not slow increments of progress, but some mighty strides forward."[114]

Burton's appointment as president came less than nine months after another transition in power, when Harold H. Swift succeeded Martin A. Ryerson as president of the board of trustees in June 1922. Swift would serve until 1949. An alumnus of the College (class of 1907) and prominent young civic leader, Swift was elected to the board of trustees in 1914. He was resolute, well connected socially, and of a solidly pragmatic temper. As a senior member of the management of Swift and Company (he became a director and vice president in 1918, and vice chairman of the board in 1937), Swift enjoyed substantial personal wealth to pursue his philanthropic inclinations. He was a Methodist, so, like Ryerson, his divergence from the nominally Baptist character of the institution was another stake in the ground of nonsectarianism and academic secularism. Swift's admiration for the University dominated his professional and personal life. In contrast to his scarcely concealed doubts about Judson, he found Burton to be an engaging and engaged leader. Swift's tenure would be complicated by the fact that his generosity in supporting the University with major gifts was often not matched by many of his fellow trustees, a situation that would worsen during the 1930s as several key members of the board came to have an active dislike of Robert Hutchins.

BURTON'S "DREAM OF THE COLLEGES"

Ernest Burton devoted his presidency to three major strategic efforts, all of which marked his presidency as a decisive break with Harper and Judson: to fundamentally reimagine the role of undergraduate education at Chicago; to develop a more competitive and resilient research environment for top scientists and scholars; and to build out a more robust fund-raising and development capacity in the city and with the alumni, thus freeing the University from its dependency on the Rockefellers. The college issue was particularly appealing to Burton, for he was a late nineteenth-century liberal in his conviction that knowledge and culture were one and that a central responsibility of the universities was to empower young men and women to create a more progressive culture for all citizens to enjoy. Given the unity of knowledge and culture, the idea that the University would disavow or curtail undergraduate education was alien to Burton. As he insisted in June 1924, "To achieve its purpose the education of our youth must be vastly more than a process of impartation and acquisition of knowledge.... The college must concern itself with the development of personalities of men and women who to knowledge have added something worthy to be called culture, and to culture high ideals and strong character."[115]

Burton's views of undergraduate education led him into a battle with those who wished to marginalize Chicago's undergraduates. The primary advocate of this view was none other than Harry Pratt Judson, who in January 1923 in one of his final letters to Harold H. Swift had asserted, "As I look at it the University is at the parting of the ways. Either it is to be primarily a University in the highest sense, with distinct emphasis on its graduate work and its graduate professional work, or it is to be essentially a College with the higher work incidental." Judson left no doubts about which option he favored: "My own view is that the University idea ought to be made very prominent; that we should frankly recognize the College as of secondary importance." Judson concluded his swan song with the enjoinder that "the time should come also in the not distant future when the number of college students whom the University will receive should be limited."[116] Judson's ambivalence toward undergraduate education has to be set in the context of the strains produced by World War I. The crush of students who returned to the University after 1918, both undergraduate and graduate, put great pressure on instructional staff and on facilities and led to discontent among the senior faculty and a movement to limit or even abolish the first two years of the undergraduate program. In December 1922, just before Judson's departure, a report of the Committee on Research of the University Senate urged that Chicago should prioritize graduate education and research as the highest obligation of the University and impose limits on the numbers of undergraduates it would admit, since "the State Universities are able and obliged to provide for the great mass of college students."[117] These recommendations were duly passed by the full professors in the Senate on December 18, 1922, generating negative publicity for the University in the local press, which published alarming stories to the effect that the University intended to become a "high brow" graduate school and that it would abolish intercollegiate athletics.[118] Responding to an invitation of the curriculum committee for the arts and sciences in 1923 to comment on the future structure of undergraduate instruction, the faculty of the Department of History listed as their first choice "the elimination of the Junior College, either by a gradual process, beginning with the Freshman year and after a period, if the step seems to have justified itself, discarding the Sophomore year also, or by a direct striking of the whole Junior College."[119]

As Burton realized, such rhetoric was financially naive in its failure to recognize the significant support that undergraduate tuition provided for faculty salaries and faculty research. It also undercut future development support from the University's alumni, a subject in which Burton was keenly interested.[120] Upon assuming office in early 1923, Burton took an approach directly opposite to that of Judson, advocating new investments to support college teaching and residential life. Drawing on ideas for the built campus environment of the University that he had imagined decades earlier, in late January 1923 Burton proposed "transferring all undergraduate work to the south side of the Midway, building up here undergraduate colleges which would combine with the advantages of a Williams or a Balliol all the advantages also of connection with a great university carrying forward upon a high level research and professional study."[121] A year later, Burton insisted to Swift that the construction of a new College instructional building on the south campus be given very high priority, since it would "serve as a rallying point and unifying center for all Undergraduate life."[122] Burton juggled his priorities repeatedly over the next two years as he sought to fund a new medical center and to cover rising faculty salaries, but his commitment to a large-scale investment in the University's undergraduate program was consistent, and in one proposal submitted to the board of trustees he allocated almost $2 million, out of a total to be raised of $10.7 million, to improving undergraduate education and new residence halls.[123] Burton's support for student life was thus more focused than Harper's, and he went further than Hutchins in emphasizing sociability and community interaction as a defining feature of a student's education. Although most of Burton's ideas were in place long before he assumed the presidency, his pronounced concern for student welfare fit in well with the climate of opinion in the mid-1920s.[124]

Burton used his annual report to the University community in 1923 to launch these themes. He began with a bold reconceptualization of the University's early history: "The University of Chicago was thought of by its founders as a College. Before it opened its doors, however, their ideal had, under the influence of President Harper's dominant personality, been displaced by that of a University in which graduate work should hold the place of eminence, but in which undergraduates should also have place and consideration."[125] Burton then argued that this arrangement was inherently unsteady and structurally conflicted. The University's attempt to admit large numbers of undergraduates within an institutional culture that (on paper at least) so formally privileged graduate education was strategically unfortunate, he wrote, for it had led some to propose doing away with the undergraduate education altogether, if not to focus on graduate work to a degree "that would inevitably spell deterioration for the Colleges."

This last comment was both a statement of fact and a rebuke to Judson, who had favored marginalizing undergraduate teaching. "We have reached a stage in our development," Burton asserted, "when of the two great fields of the University's work, graduate and undergraduate, each must stand on its own merits, each must receive that discriminating attention which its own character demands, neither must be hindered or compromised by the other." He proposed a central College building for undergraduates that would include classrooms, labs, rooms for student organizations, a library, a theater, and an assembly room. This would "both relieve the pressure on some of our existing buildings and tend to create a College consciousness which so far from destroying would even tend to increase the consciousness of relationship to the University." Burton further envisioned a cluster of residential halls for men and women surrounding this College building, which would "greatly help in realizing our hope for a better type of undergraduate life."

Burton thus broke away from privileging graduate education and gave the College a prominent institutional identity by emphasizing both enhanced student welfare and innovative campus planning. At the early University, student housing was extremely meager: several residence halls were constructed in the 1890s (Kelly, Beecher, Green, and Foster Halls for women, Snell and Hitchcock Halls for men, and Gates and Blake Halls for Divinity School students), but together these on-campus halls, and several smaller off-campus buildings, housed only about six hundred students.[126] Too many other needs had loomed on the horizon, so the few residence halls that did exist had to be shared among the graduate, undergraduate, and professional school students. In 1910, the great majority of undergraduate students lived off campus, and more than half lived at home with their parents or other relatives. But after World War I demand for suitable campus housing outpaced resources, and complaints about unsatisfactory housing by students who often encountered high rent levels and poor living conditions became increasingly common.[127]

Burton had long been interested in the cultural valence of residential living. In 1902 he had visited Oxford University for a month, and over the next year he discussed the advantages of the Oxford model before several public audiences. Harper's death in early 1906 closed down any immediate action on Burton's schemes, but these ideas proved of great moment after 1923.[128] Burton's "dream of the Colleges" was brilliant in mobilizing space on behalf of institutional purpose. Given that instruction on the graduate and undergraduate levels had different agendas and purposes, Burton insisted that the two communities inhabit physically separate spaces but share the same faculty, with the undergraduate College of three thousand students divided into eight or ten distinct residential communities, each with its own cultural identity.[129] Unlike Harper, who esteemed such ideas in an indeterminate way, and Judson, for whom they were irrelevant, Burton considered life in a college residential community crucial to the full maturation of the cultivated and motivated personalities he sought to foster among his undergraduate students. Such halls would not be "mere dormitories, but places of humane educational residence. . . . All should be planned with a view to uniting, as far as possible, the two lines of influence which in our American colleges have been unfortunately separated in large measure as numbers have increased, namely, intellectual activity on the one hand and friendly contact with persons on the other."[130] Burton also stressed the University's role in the development of open-minded and morally responsible personalities. For Burton the "breadth of knowledge, power to think, are indispensable prerequisites to large participation in life or large contributions to life. But apart from high moral character they are not only inadequate but positively dangerous. And because this is so, no institution that undertakes to give these former things can escape the obligation to concern itself with the latter also."[131]

Burton's dedication to residentiality and to the cultivation of personality and character among his students reflected broader cultural trends in the history of private American universities after 1900 and especially after 1918. It was in these decades in American higher education that key leaders of the elite eastern universities began to fashion ambitious schemes of communitarian living for their students that eventually, in the case of Yale and Harvard, resulted in the great Harkness gifts of the later 1920s and 1930s.[132] These years were also filled with voices demanding that more attention be paid both to academic standards and to personality formation and the emotional welfare of undergraduate students, who, as future members of the American social elite, needed to be suitably socialized both by wealthier liberal arts colleges and by the new research universities.[133] Nor can the influence of John Dewey be discounted in Burton's rhetoric about the need to give relevance to liberal education by focusing on the real social needs of the time. But one also sees in Burton's writings his passions as a sometime missionary and as a student of late nineteenth-century liberal Christianity. In contrast to understandings of student "character" as an underpinning for the social elitism that often obtained in the eastern schools, Burton used the word in a more socially altruistic sense, viewing the students of his university as potential missionaries for the cause of cultural edification and moral uplift throughout the broader reaches of American civil society in the aftermath of World War I. Graduates of the

University carried an obligation "to make their contribution to the process of social evolution, the process, in other words, of making a better world for children to be born in and for men and women to live in by creating a better type of human society."[134] To the extent that a fundamental commitment to egalitarian merit as a public good came to define the student culture of the University over the course of the twentieth century, Ernest Burton was one of its most spirited sponsors. As such, Burton was also in decided opposition to popular trends in the 1920s that postulated social prestige and financial success as the only worthwhile goods that might be obtained via a college education.[135] His justification for college as a site of moral renewal and cultural enrichment was a forceful response to those who viewed higher education only as a means to financial advancement.

James H. Tufts, who served as a vice president and dean of faculties under Burton, later praised Burton's "magnificent vision and practical resourcefulness" in inspiring faculty and students alike, insisting that Burton's personality was a particularly strong asset: "Sincerity, modesty, clearness of thought and simplicity of statement characterized his addresses. And there was a certain fineness of spirit that shone in his face. He did not need to say much about the spiritual meanings and purposes of the education. He embodied them."[136] Nonetheless, Burton's scheme of a new residential campus for undergraduate learning and life encountered heated opposition from senior faculty members who despised undergraduates. Burton was a creature of the faculty, and he understood that, given the heightened research ambitions of the faculty after World War I, it would be difficult to push his program through without offering compensatory trade-offs (i.e., bribes) to gain at least their passive acceptance. In May 1924, when Burton officially informed the faculty of his plans for fundraising on behalf of the Colleges, the reaction of the full professors on the University Senate was strikingly cool toward the south Midway scheme, with the Senate passing a blunt resolution a month later—to which Burton was forced to agree—that "the Senate approves the erection of residence halls and of buildings for educational purposes south of the Midway to be devoted to the needs of the undergraduate colleges on the understanding that the educational buildings shall not be erected until the future educational policy of the university as regards undergraduate instruction and the relevant problems of graduate instruction shall have been considered and determined."[137] As if to stick their political finger in Burton's eye, they also passed a resolution to the effect that "the Senate believes that in the advertisement of the needs of the University the emphasis should be put on the intensive development of graduate work."

Essentially, if Burton wanted his college campus, the full professorial researchers demanded a whopping kickback in return. Harold Swift later remembered about Burton's support for undergraduate education in 1923–24 that Burton "practically had a mutiny on his hands" and that some senior faculty "reproached and reviled him for the emphasis upon the College. Mr. Burton won the battle but only after great difficulty."[138] And, in fact, the issue was not at all settled. Had Burton lived and pursued what Harold Swift called his "dream of the Colleges," he would most certainly have encountered the harsh opposition that Frederic Woodward and Harold Swift met in 1928–29 when they tried to move forward with Burton's ideas for a large residential complex on the south campus. Burton had taken the first public step in envisioning the role of undergraduate education to be of central importance to the University's basic institutional identity, but it would be decades before the legitimacy of Burton's ideals would be acknowledged in any permanent way.

BURTON'S PLAN FOR THE FUTURE: THE CAMPAIGN OF 1923–1925

Ernest Burton's second and third strategic contributions to the University were his leadership in organizing the first real fund-raising campaign and his plans to enliven and deepen the competitive research prowess of the faculty. Given that the success of the second objective was contingent on the achievement of the first, the two goals were interconnected. Harry Pratt Judson had been fortunate in the decisions of Julius Rosenwald, Hobart Williams, and LaVerne Noyes to give major gifts to the University between 1912 and 1918.[139] But these gifts came largely at the initiative of the donors; Judson himself did little active fund-raising, preferring to advocate the University's cause in a style of a "dignified silent appeal." Unfortunately this meant that the pace of gifts to the University slowed considerably from that of the Harper era.[140] Harold Swift ruminated in 1922 that "as a Board we have gotten out of the habit of collecting funds. We must get back into it, otherwise the University cannot hold her rank."[141] The early public enthusiasm among the civic elites of the Chicago for the young University gradually dissipated, and by 1924 the John Price Jones Corporation, a professional fund-raising firm hired by the University, reported of Judson's presidency, "The reason the University has not been receiving the support of Chicago people is not because people have lost interest, but because the University has failed to maintain contact"; and "The University has virtually neglected its Chicago contacts for many years, which will necessitate careful and intensive cultivation."[142]

Nor did the University do much to cultivate its alumni. Before the 1920s the University did not rely on alumni contributions for current expenses, nor did it actively solicit them for such purposes. What alumni gifts did come in were processed through Judson's assistant, David Robertson, since there was no professional development staff. An alumni fund was created in 1919, as the result of pressures from a key group of younger alumni leaders and some sympathetic faculty members, including Burton and Shailer Mathews, who felt that the alumni should be solicited regularly for a fund to support the University. The young Harold H. Swift urged Judson to arrange for the publication of a small booklet that would describe the current state of the University and its material needs. In a subsequent letter pushing the project, Swift insisted, "I earnestly believe that many of our alumni are thirsting for material from the University.... I think if the University will make the effort and show her real interest in her former students, the reward, both tangible and sentimental, will be very great."[143] Swift was convinced that it was essential to show to the alumni that Rockefeller's gifts were neither sufficient nor all-encompassing and that "actually we have departments that are almost suffering for the want of $50, which we can't fit into these great big schemes." Swift also insisted, "Let's stress the fact to the alumni that we need the alumni."[144]

Judson dithered about proceeding with Swift's proposal, but Swift's nudging finally led the administration to commission Thomas Goodspeed's son, Edgar, to draft such a pamphlet, *The University of Chicago in 1921*, in late 1920. Even then, Goodspeed could not resist proudly restating the status quo—namely, that "it is not the policy of the University to call upon its alumni to meet deficits or to help in carrying its current expenses."[145] The University sent the pamphlet to all subscribers to the University magazine and all subscribers to the Alumni Fund, as well as to other alumni for whom good addresses were available.

The attitude of the University toward fund-raising changed dramatically with Burton's assumption of power in 1923. Given Burton's sense that large new sums of money were needed to sustain the scholarly luster of the University after World War I, his decision to launch a major campaign was logical. It was also tactically urgent, in that Burton realized that continued support from the Rockefeller boards in New York City would be contingent upon the University finally doing what John D. Rockefeller had urged the institution's leaders to do in 1910—namely, cultivate widespread public support for the future financial welfare of the University.

Burton's energy and optimism were contagious, and other key opinion leaders soon acknowledged the need to raise new money. Albert Sherer, a recently appointed trustee, an alumnus of the Colleges (class of 1905), and a close friend of Harold Swift, wrote a memo in May 1923 urging that the University needed to increase the number of its donors and thus to enlarge its endowment. Sherer was especially interested in enhancing the University's support among the citizens of Chicago and the Midwest. He urged

Swift to appoint a committee of the board, to be known as the Committee on Public Relations, to study the problem of how to raise money and to appoint a person to work with the committee. Swift agreed to Sherer's scheme and appointed Sherer, Rosenwald, Burton, and himself to be an ad hoc "committee of four" that would have the authority to hire such a person.[146] But before hiring a fund-raising czar, Swift insisted that the University also come up with a systematic plan of what a fund-raising campaign might look like and how it might be executed. After consulting with Sherer and Rosenwald, Swift and Burton therefore asked the board to approve a campaign planning study in January 1924. Swift was convinced that the in-house methods of the past would not suffice. Hence, when Edgar Goodspeed argued against hiring external consultants to plan the campaign, Swift rejected the advice out of hand. Rather, Swift wanted a "comprehensive plan before going ahead to secure funds," and to start the planning process off, he hired the John Price Jones Corporation of New York City to undertake a preliminary report on the feasibility of raising funds.[147] While Swift took it upon himself to coordinate the structure of the campaign, he also tried to bolster Ernest Burton's resolve in the face of an impatient and ambitious senior faculty.

The report of the Jones Corporation was ready by March 1924.[148] It suggested that the University might successfully run a campaign that would invoke its past achievements and future promise, resonate with civic elites of Chicago by stressing the University as Chicago's university, highlight the tremendous prestige brought to the city by the University, and rely on alumni and trustee support: "The University has a strong appeal and a genuine need; it requires only the loyal effort of its Trustees, faculty, and alumni to bring the desired response." To coordinate and assist with the actual campaign the University hired the Jones Corporation, whose leaders had already staffed a number of other postwar college campaigns, beginning with the 1919–20 campaign at Harvard that had generated $14.2 million.[149] Jones assigned Robert F. Duncan to work on the Chicago campaign. A graduate of Harvard (class of 1912), Duncan was already a veteran of college fund-raising who had played an important role in the Harvard campaign. Duncan would stay with the University as an episodic adviser over the next three decades, and by the 1950s he had a unique historical perspective on the internal problems and potential of the institution. After leaving Chicago in 1956, he returned to his alma mater and helped launch the spectacularly successful Program for Harvard College campaign from 1957 to 1960, which netted nearly $83 million.[150] Inevitably, the advice (and subsequently, the criticisms) that Duncan provided to Chicago reflected the fund-raising experiences (and the successes) that he had had at Harvard.

Over the winter and spring of 1924 Duncan helped to engineer a highly sophisticated organization. Clerical and professional staff developed systems to research the giving capabilities of potential donors, organized donor assignment lists and prepared donor tracking and acknowledgments, launched a faculty speakers' bureau, and put in place many other operations that are still the core activities of a major fund-raising campaign. Duncan had a special flair for advertising, and, in addition to producing dozens of campaign publications, he rented four large billboards throughout the city displaying the slogan "The University of Chicago, It's Yours." In the planned public phase of the campaign Duncan also intended to put color posters about the University in all CTA transit stations. Trevor Arnett prepared a lucid explanation of the University's finances that demonstrated the need for new support.[151] The campaign was also noteworthy for giving birth to the word "development" as a key rhetorical symbol of the University's self-advancement.[152]

Swift and Burton wanted to launch the campaign in the fall of 1924.[153] To anchor it the University was able to parlay its contacts with the New York–based charities established by the Rockefeller family into a $2 million matching gift from the General Education Board at 61 Broadway (at two to one, with the University having to raise $4 million). Happily for the University, the officers and trustees of the Rockefeller boards included several men with strong Chicago connections (George E. Vincent, Trevor Arnett, James R. Angell, Beardsley Ruml, and later David H. Stevens and Max Mason). Vincent, who had served as both a professor of sociology and a dean under Harper and Judson before leaving to become president of the University of Minnesota in 1911, played a particularly influential role, as president of the Rockefeller Foundation from 1917 to 1929, in supporting Chicago's plans for a new medical school. Ruml, a brilliant if unconventional planner who had a PhD in psychology from Chicago and who became the director of the Laura Spelman Rockefeller Memorial in 1922, played a similar role for the social sciences.

The heart and soul of the campaign was Ernest D. Burton. The campaign gave Burton a chance to reinvigorate the University by inspiring new momentum among the faculty and setting new goals for the trustees, as well as rekindling enthusiasm among the public. Burton was shrewd enough to understand that a successful fund-raising campaign required a strategic vision for the University, and not simply a request for money. In a number of key speeches delivered in Chicago and in other cities around the country Burton sketched his plans for the future of the University. The basic theme of the speeches was the need to build on Harper's heritage by making the University not bigger but better, but the intellectual framework in which Burton articulated his goals was distinctly new.

Burton stressed the fundamental mission of research ("this mighty and fruitful thing, the quest for new truth"), but he was also able to translate "research" into a set of practices that involved undergraduate and professional education as well as doctoral training in the arts and sciences. He stated that a new ideal of college life was evolving in the United States, one that stressed the development of intellectual habits more than the "impartation of known facts," and that the University of Chicago would help to shape it: "The dominant element of that [college] life will be the recognition of the fact that life is more than lore, that character is more than facts; that college life is the period of the formation of habits, even more than of the acquisition of knowledge, and that the making of men and women with habits and character that will insure their being in after life men and women of power, achievement, and helpful influence in the world is the great task of the college." What better place to train young minds in the "capacity to think for themselves," he argued, than to place them under the influence of scholars "who are striking out new paths, fearlessly attacking the mysteries of truth.... It seems logical and right that the work of the colleges should be conducted in an atmosphere imparted by or akin to that of the great graduate schools, in places where freedom of the mind is encouraged."[154]

Consulting with various departmental leaders and other prominent faculty, Burton conducted a detailed survey of the University's future needs in February and March 1924, and by the summer he came up with the figure of $50–$60 million for current and long-range needs, $21 million of which should be raised in the next two years.[155] Burton essentially wanted to double the University's current endowment within fifteen years. Not all of this could be raised immediately, however, and in September 1924, after much negotiation among Burton, Duncan, Swift, and others, the final goal for the campaign was reduced to $17.5 million ($7.5 million for endowment, $10 million for new buildings).[156] The campaign centered on endowment support for the faculty and on the construction of new buildings, including a new undergraduate campus and a new administration building that would symbolize the growing research prowess and enhanced administrative burdens of the modern postwar University, which was now compared to a complex railway system in which "all parts of the machine" needed to be locked together.[157] Burton understood that ambitions to achieve ever-rising levels of research prestige had become the coin of the realm for American faculties after 1918, and that no plan would prove plausible with the University Senate that did not involve the extensive care and feeding of senior faculty ambitions. As a counterweight to investments in undergraduate education, Burton raised the stakes on the faculty front by foregrounding the need to raise a multimillion-dollar endowment to enhance faculty salaries. He wrote to the trustees that "Chicago must not only hold her great men but also draw others. At present her salary scale is below that of other leading universities.... This endowment is needed if Chicago is to meet the competition of other universities, not only of the great privately endowed Eastern Universities, but also of the state universities of the West."[158] Burton's privileging of senior faculty salary compensation became a cardinal strategy for most subsequent administrations at Chicago, the aim being to keep Chicago in the top three or four institutions in the United States even if this meant diverting money from other causes that sorely needed financing.

To further enhance the luster of the faculty, Burton created the first endowed professorships in the University's history, soliciting Martin A. Ryerson in April 1924 to endow ten Distinguished Service Professorships that would pay at least $10,000 annually, based on an endowment of $2 million.[159] His letter to Ryerson combined both gentle deference toward a venerable donor and iron logic about the need to bolster the University's prestige, insisting that "perhaps our greatest need is the establishment of outstanding professorships which on the one hand would pay the professor a conspicuously good stipend, and which on the other would be in themselves a recognition of ability, learning, and eminence." By creating these professorships, Burton hoped to attract academic luminaries and retain those already in the firmament. The new endowed chairs were characteristic of the competitive scientific ambitions of the 1920s, reflecting as they did "the extraordinary advance which the country is making in the field of education." Burton decided that the new chairs would be controlled by no single department in perpetuity, but would float at the discretion of future presidents to reward achievement and to incite competition among the departments. No longer would senior faculty receive feudal accolades via constitutional decrees of the president—Harper's headships. No longer would the University sit idly by and allow senior faculty to leave because they dared to "dicker" for better conditions—Judson's disregard for the national scientific markets. In the future a set of competitive, merit-driven honors would be bestowed based on the "distinguished" status of public scholarship that, in Burton's mind, was also one of the highest forms of "service" to the University. Not only would chair holders have to be at the top of their scholarly fields, but that level of achievement would be deliberately tested by a canvass of the "whole field" before the award of the chair. Hence the title that he created for his new chairs was conceived as a double-edged honorific, looking outward and inward. In the face of Burton's bold claim that "to hold a Martin A. Ryerson Professorship would be the highest honor we could bestow upon a man eminent in research and teaching," the elderly Ryerson agreed to give one such chair, and by 1930 the University had raised funding for an additional seven chairs.[160]

Burton used the public enthusiasm generated by the campaign to make significant progress on key construction and research projects that had either languished or not yet come to planning completion. Two huge buildings that came to fruition immediately after Burton's presidency still define the physical and cultural landscape of the campus and may properly be considered Burton's gifts to the built environment of the University. In 1924–25, architectural planning was finalized for the construction of Rockefeller Memorial Chapel, a majestic symbol of the optimism and buoyancy triggered by Burton's fund-raising efforts in the mid-1920s (the Joseph Regenstein Library would serve a similarly catalytic role for the campus in the mid-1960s). Before accepting the plans for the new chapel that had been proposed by architect Bertram Grosvenor Goodhue in June and July 1919, Burton toured twenty-two British cathedrals during the late summer of 1924 to reacquaint himself with the neo-medieval designs that had inspired early planning for the chapel.[161] As Burton reported to Goodspeed in September, "My experience in England has cleared my own mind entirely on the University Chapel. It remains to be seen whether the Board will agree with me, but I am fully persuaded that Mr. Goodhue's plan is fundamentally sound, and that we only need to restudy certain details."[162] After John D. Rockefeller Jr. approved the plans in October 1924, the board of trustees concurred with Burton's recommendation to proceed, approving the contract in February 1925. The cornerstone was laid in June 1926, and the Chapel dedicated in October 1928.

Burton played a critical leadership role in the final planning and financing of the University's Medical School and hospital, plans for which were approved by the board in April 1925. Constructed on the north side of the Midway west of Ellis Avenue, it officially opened its doors in November 1927—a second major institutional achievement of the 1920s.[163] Burton also led the negotiations to merge the faculty of Rush Medical College with that of the University, an agreement signed by both parties in May 1924. The massive investments undertaken to create the new Medical Center resulted in a powerful new locus of scientific authority and research investment in the biological sciences. This complemented earlier traditions in basic-science research in biology first launched by scholars such as Charles O. Whitman and John M. Coulter, and it was holistic and interdisciplinary by virtue of its combination of clinical-medical and basic-scientific teaching and research.[164] Because academic medicine came late to Chicago, senior biologists in the 1920s such as Frank R. Lillie, Charles M. Child, and Ezra J. Kraus were able to sustain vigorous, independent research traditions in the life sciences of the pre-1918 era, and their disciplines were not simply viewed as instrumental service tools for medical training and practice.[165] Over time, however, with the organization of the Division of Biological Sciences in 1931 and pressure from external funding authorities to organize research according to substantive function involving large scientific problems rather than conventional departmental lines, the intellectual boundaries between medical research and basic-science research in the biological sciences at Chicago became more porous.[166]

Other notable buildings that were planned and launched during or immediately after Burton's tenure included the Divinity School, Joseph Bond Chapel, the Field House, Wieboldt Hall, and Eckhart Hall. The last two buildings demonstrated the willingness of departmentally based faculties with broadly common professional interests to cohabit new spaces designated for interdisciplinary research and collaborative teaching in the 1920s. Wieboldt Hall was constructed for the modern language departments (including English), and Eckhart Hall was designed to serve physics, mathematics, and astronomy. Both were planned with the help of faculty committees whose members were drawn from several departments. Similar cohabitational tendencies were even more evident in the social sciences in the 1920s, where they found firm footing in the new interdisciplinary research projects sponsored by the Local Community Research Committee created in 1923.[167]

Burton's campaign consisted of appeals to the trustees, alumni, foundations, and the general public in Chicago. The trustee side of the campaign was moderately successful. Harold Swift contacted all of the other trustees via personal visit, phone, or letter, urging that they set a generous standard of participation.[168] In the end, the trustees committed to $1.68 million, or about 20 percent of the ultimate total. But it was telling, and not at all promising for the University's fate in the 1930s, that Swift had a hard time generating active participation and real enthusiasm from many of the trustees. Moreover, their gift patterns were uneven, with some trustees giving paltry amounts. Three trustees—Julius Rosenwald, Martin Ryerson, and Harold Swift himself—accounted for $1.5 million, with the remaining $168,000 coming in smaller gifts, some as small as $1,000.[169]

The campaign of 1924–25 was also the first time that the University systematically tried to mobilize its alumni. In contrast to its eastern peers, the University faced a special problem with its alumni in that Harper's quarter system made it virtually impossible to implant a sense of class identity and the value of reunion participation among graduating students.[170] The General Alumni Committee was organized in the autumn of 1924. By October it had 175 members and an executive committee of 18, and it developed a handbook to guide volunteers in their solicitations.

The committee in turn coordinated the work of a host of district and local alumni leaders around the country, who were poised to begin solicitations in March 1925 and whose task it was to obtain a pledge "from every Chicago man and woman in the locality over which he has jurisdiction, and as much more as is necessary to make up his quota."[171] The organization also included a detailed procedure for local leaders to rate the gift capacities of individual alumni in their area as to what they might be expected to give over a five-year period. Each district was also assigned a quota, and it was expected to fulfill that quota, come what may. The results were encouraging in Chicago and in other localities as well—by late 1925, out of approximately 20,000 alumni, more than 11,000 contributed, and a majority of these were College alumni. Total alumni giving was slightly over $2 million. Over 43 percent of the alumni in 1923 were employed in education—on the primary, secondary, and university levels—a characteristic that shaped the early alumni culture at the University, and often led to excuses that Chicago alumni were less well positioned to provide significant large gifts to the University than their counterparts at the eastern universities.[172] Even so, Burton sought to compensate by raising the total volume of individual participation, and his strategy succeeded. Alumni leaders would recall in 1926 that the "sudden and startling attention bestowed upon Alumni was unprecedented, and in marked contrast to any evident interest theretofore displayed by the University in its Alumni."[173] Given that a significant number of alumni had been transfer students who had not spent four years on campus, the results were all the more encouraging. Equally impressive was the fact that this was a relatively young or at least younger group of people—in 1923 the great majority of Chicago's alumni were under thirty-five years of age.

In the middle of the spring 1925 campaign activities, Ernest Burton died suddenly on May 26, of a recently diagnosed colon cancer. Burton's death was a terrible shock to the leaders of the campaign and to the faculty, and it created an immense leadership vacuum. Trustee Robert Lamont observed of Burton, "At 67 he undertook a work that would have daunted most men, and his last thought was that it should go forward. We must not fail him now."[174]

Burton's death cut short what would have been a transformational presidency, had Burton been able to complete the fund-raising campaign he had started and to launch the revolutions in faculty research and in undergraduate education to which he aspired. Harold Swift would later characterize Burton's two years as president as "the two most thrilling years in the University's history."[175] Burton's term in office was viewed as one of amazing energy and bold thinking, and the outpouring of sympathy at his death was remarkable. He was cast as a veritable saint who had brought grace and wisdom as well as new money to the University, a fully altruistic man who devoted his life to the service of the University. In retrospect, Burton's confident moral imperatives were well placed in the sanguine and booming 1920s. After the financial disaster of 1929 and the onset of the Great Depression, university leaders would face grueling choices among increasingly scarce resources that Burton and his generation had never been forced to contemplate.

Burton's successor was Max Mason, a distinguished mathematical physicist from the University of Wisconsin. Trained at Wisconsin and Göttingen in mathematics, Mason had taught at the Massachusetts Institute of Technology, Yale, and Wisconsin.[176] Although he began his career as a pure mathematician, his intellectual interests broadened to include the physical sciences, and his professorial appointment at Wisconsin from 1909 to 1925 was in the Department of Physics. During World War I Mason had worked on submarine warfare technology at the NRC and was one of the principal inventors of a hydrophonic detection system that later evolved into the sonar detectors used by the US Navy in World War II. Mason had no prior senior administrative experience when he accepted the presidency of Chicago. His selection came after a protracted national search by a joint trustee-faculty committee revealed no consensus on a local candidate and only lukewarm support for prominent outsiders like Ernest M. Hopkins, Ray L. Wilbur, and George E. Vincent. His name emerged late in the process, having been originally suggested by Henry Gale, the dean of the natural sciences. Mason's appointment was facilitated by the board's decision in May 1923 to change the university statutes and allow non-Baptists to be president.[177] Mason proved to be a charming and well-spoken colleague and an eloquent defender of the value of basic scientific research, but he was an ineffective and indecisive leader. Mason's performance as president was, in fact, profoundly disappointing. Mason also faced difficult personal issues, for his wife, Mary Freeman Mason, suffered from grave psychiatric problems, and her pronounced agoraphobia made it impossible for her to organize and host the many social and cultural events then expected of the spouse of a university president. For most of Mason's tenure she was either in seclusion in the President's House or in convalescent institutions. Harold Swift later fashioned a gentle public portrait by arguing "it was an unhappy period for him for he was beset with family problems.... He didn't really like administration. He said that he missed the smell of the laboratory,—he wanted to get back to scholarship."[178] In contrast to Swift's positive spin, Robert Kohler's harsh appraisal of Mason's tenure at the Rockefeller Foundation—"Mason was not a good administrator, simply leaving everyone to do as they pleased.... Charming and fascinating as a colleague, Mason never succeeded in any major undertaking"—suggests that Mason's difficulties as a president were part of a pattern of administrative ineptitude of which Swift, ever the activist, was certainly aware.[179]

After Burton's death, fund-raising activity slowed noticeably, largely owing to Mason's repudiation of Burton's campaign. Mason disliked the "go-get-em salesmanship" that Burton had put in place, believing (according to Swift) that this would "do so much harm as to make people sore and hurt us in the long run." Hence, according to Swift, "after Mr. Mason was elected, it was decided to call off the Campaign."[180] Mason's decision, which may have been influenced by his desire to avoid having to host large public gatherings, was supported by several key members of the board, led by Bernard Sunny, who lobbied Mason and Swift to substitute a campaign among local businessmen in place of the citywide effort advocated by Robert Duncan and John Price Jones. Sunny's motives are unknown, but Mason clearly welcomed Sunny's intervention. In mid-January 1926, the trustees' Committee on Development voted to close down the public campaign and recommended that the city campaign "take the form of a quiet canvass of the wealthier prospects under the leadership of and along the lines to be determined by Mr. Sunny and President Mason, it being understood that the former Campaign closing date of June 30, 1926, will be ignored, and, a vote having been taken the motion was declared adopted."[181] Robert Duncan's services were terminated, and the agreement with John Price Jones abrogated.

Mason's decision reflected his shy temperament and unsteady family situation, as well as his confidence that, in the booming economy of the later 1920s, personal fund-raising led by Sunny on a one-on-one basis might gain the University sufficiently large donations to finance necessary new buildings and create more professorships. During the remainder of Mason's short presidency, several wealthy citizens did in fact decide to fund new buildings, including Wieboldt Hall, Eckhart Hall, and Jones Hall. But these gifts came in because of idiosyncratic contacts with University officials, not because of Sunny's "quiet" campaign.[182] Moreover, the last years before the crash proved to be flush ones for the University largely because of the magnificent grants bestowed by the Rockefeller boards. Mason visited the headquarters of the General Education Board in January 1927 and came away confident that the GEB and its sister boards, like the Laura Spelman Rockefeller Memorial and the Rockefeller Foundation, would support most of the relevant research requests that the University might put forward. Mason reported happily, "I feel there is almost no limit to the support the Boards will give us provided we have important projects under the direction of able men."[183] In February, the GEB awarded $1.5 million to support research and facilities in chemistry, physics, mathematics, astronomy, and botany, followed by an additional $1.2 million for the physical sciences a year later. Equally impressive support, amounting to over $5 million, followed between 1926 and 1928 for the new Medical School and the hospitals. In 1927, the GEB gave the University $250,000 for support of research in the humanities, and the Laura Spelman Rockefeller Memorial awarded more than $2 million for the construction and operation of a new social sciences building as well as support for faculty research.[184] In 1928, the GEB and International Education Board then gave the University $6.2 million for the Oriental Institute, eventually providing more than $8 million in total support.[185] The year 1929 was also a fruitful one for Chicago, for the GEB voted in May to award the University $2 million in endowment support for the Medical School and $1 million to sustain its clinical operating expenses over ten years, and $1.5 million for the School of Education in November 1929, along with smaller grants in support of research in anthropology, comparative philology, and the biological sciences.[186]

In the 1920s, support from foundations for the research ambitions of top universities was impressive, and it came at a particularly fortuitous time for a university like Chicago, which had grown dependent on one donor's personal money but now quickly needed more diverse sources of support.[187] The largesse that Mason obtained from Rockefeller boards in New York City was astounding, and it seemed a much easier (and more dignified) way to raise money than running a municipal fund-raising campaign. But Mason's confidence that the University would have unlimited access to Rockefeller money in the future was a disastrous miscalculation, as Robert Hutchins would soon discover. Mason's decision to curtail the public appeal of the campaign was deeply unfortunate for three reasons. First, in relying on Bernard Sunny to carry on Burton's campaign in a more private way Mason had made a serious mistake, for it was soon clear that Sunny had no way to deliver such grandiose sums. Second, Mason's strategy deprived the University of the unique opportunity to make a systematic, citywide canvass for funds among prominent and not-so-prominent citizens in Chicago at a time when economic conditions were extremely favorable. Finally, Mason's decision resulted in a collapse of long-range development planning, halting the progress in donor cultivation made between 1924 and 1926 and returning the University to lethargic philanthropic practices involving its alumni and the general public reminiscent of the Judson days. By 1930, with final collections, the Development Fund started by Burton stood at $9.9 million, far short of the $17.5 million target set in 1924.[188]

In the end, Burton and his lieutenants failed to accomplish two of his three major aims—by 1929 the status of the undergraduate college was yet unresolved, and owing to Max Mason's disdain for fund-raising, the University failed to develop the kind of long-term presence among the civic and political elites of Chicago that Burton had thought critical for its viability. Burton's third goal—enhancing the University's research luster—was achieved, but ironically it came largely through the University's continued dependence on the largesse of the Rockefellers, via their boards, not from large new sources of financial self-sufficiency. Between 1911 and 1932 alone the Rockefeller boards gave the University $35.8 million, a sum slightly larger than the total personal benefactions of John D. Rockefeller. The extent of Chicago's continued dependence on Rockefeller generosity was demonstrated by the fact that of the $137 million that the University received in gifts between 1890 and 1939, Rockefeller contributions (personal or board-driven) amounted to more than $80 million, or almost 60 percent.[189] The University was financially very successful in the 1920s, but there were unresolved structural and programmatic challenges that might prove fateful to the University's future capacity to sustain itself as a leading destination of learning and teaching.

Academic and Social Life of the 1920s

The years following the conclusion of World War I were decisive for the educational programs of the University. During the decade that followed the war, many of the senior faculty leaders whom Harper had brought to the University in the 1890s began to retire or pass away. A new generation of senior faculty emerged who would define the University's prestige and mission up to 1945. The influx of undergraduates and graduate students seeking baccalaureate and MA degrees after 1918 stressed the system, particularly in the humanities, social sciences, and physical sciences. In the face of these demographic pressures, the 1920s would see searching and occasionally acrimonious debates about what the University was and in what educational and curricular directions it should move. And at the end of the decade, a series of interventions redefined the fundamental structures of teaching at the University, particularly on the undergraduate level.

GRADUATE EDUCATION

The debate in the 1920s about the future of the University was conducted on two broad levels—graduate and undergraduate—with intense discussions about the educational priorities stimulated by Burton's strategic goals for the University and in the context of the University's first capital campaign.

In January 1925 the University received extravagant praise for its graduate programs. One of the first modern attempts to evaluate and rank modern American research universities, developed by President Raymond M. Hughes of Miami University, gave positive and encouraging news about Chicago's relative prestige among peer research universities, lauding the graduate programs in the natural sciences and mathematics, but also ranking economics, history, sociology, political science, classics, English, and philosophy among the top five departments in their respective disciplines in the United States.[190] This report is now remembered as one of the first vehicles for assessing the prestige of American research universities, but it also offered a sharp critique of the way that graduate programs in the United States had prepared their doctoral students to be teachers. As John Brubaker and Willis Rudy would later observe, "Having failed to set up an acceptable M.A. as a standard for college teachers, American universities found themselves saddled, for better or worse, with a doctorate which had the weakness of trying to serve two ends, teaching and research, ends not always distinguished clearly by graduate schools."[191] Speaking from the perspective of a small college president, Hughes lamented the "highly specialized" nature of study that was prevalent in graduate schools. "We in the colleges are looking for men of broad, sound training in their fields, with enthusiasm for the general subject and a wide, generous interest in related subjects, rather than for men of a highly specialized training who express a lack of interest or even contempt for other phases of their own subject, to say nothing of the related fields of knowledge," he said. Hughes also decried the fact that "not a few [PhDs] are coming somewhat imbued with the idea that students are a nuisance and interfere with work, that teaching methods are unworthy of serious thought, that anybody who knows can teach, and a good many other ideas which are only half-truths or are wrong."[192]

All was not well with Chicago's graduate programs in the minds of key insiders either. After 1910 and especially after 1918, several prominent senior faculty members offered criticisms about weaknesses of doctoral programs at Chicago that paralleled similar apprehensions voiced at other leading doctoral institutions.[193] Frederick J. E. Woodbridge, the dean of the faculties at Columbia University from 1912 to 1929, complained in 1918 that "routine work in courses has been substituted for general examinations and for evidence of real mastery of fields of inquiry. The result has been that [graduate] students are kept largely in the state of tutelage and professors have been converted into schoolmasters."[194] At Chicago, Albion W. Small voiced even harsher criticisms. In addition to his activities as a scholar, editor, and teacher, Small was particularly knowledgeable about the University's early graduate programs, since he served as the dean of the Graduate School of Arts and Literature from 1905 to 1924.

Shortly before retiring from the deanship, Small composed a valedictory in late February 1923 arguing that much that passed for graduate education at Chicago was simple positivism, that students were being required to learn more about less, and that most disciplines had barricaded themselves against allied domains, so that graduate students in history knew nothing about political science or sociology and the reverse. Small had a long list of grievances, from the inadequate preparation of candidates admitted to graduate school to the narrow ways in which they were trained once they arrived. But Small was also concerned with larger structural and ideological issues. He was convinced that the departments had evolved into silos with no common understanding of the largest and most interesting intellectual issues that they needed to confront: "It is possible for a man to take his Doctor's degree in any one of our five departments without enough understanding of the technique of any other department in the group to inform him when and where his competence as a specialist ends and where flounderings as an amateur begins. To the extent that our students allow themselves to be misled by this possibility we are guilty of putting our stamp of approval upon men who are intellectual abortions from the standpoint of modern standards of methodology." Small also worried that the curriculum offered to graduate students was too heavy with regurgitated information in formal classroom settings and too little training in interdisciplinary research skills: "We waste a ruinous proportion of our time feeding graduate students with 'spoon-vittles.' We deal out predigested food of information which they might better go without till they have grown the guts to find out the facts for themselves."[195]

Small belonged to a generation of scholars who as young men had been trained in the classical canon of the nineteenth-century college but who had come to embrace modern scientific research and the professionalizing tendencies associated with the emergence of *Wissenschaft* based on powerful disciplinary units. But having accomplished this transformation, they were dissatisfied with the often lackluster scholarship they were sponsoring, and they were equally troubled by the failure of the new research universities to attract doctoral students of high talent and imagination to accomplish scholarly work worthy of the university's lofty aspirations.[196] William James's fears in 1903 about the mediocrity bred by "the PhD octopus" were still alive and well two decades later in the imagination of men like Albion Small.[197]

In 1923, Lawrence K. Frank conducted a study for the Rockefeller boards on the status of doctoral research in the social sciences in the United States. The findings confirmed many of Small's criticisms relating to graduate-student research training: most doctoral dissertations did not encompass original investigation and did not deploy modern scientific methods.[198] Frank also discovered that "only a few fellowships specifically provided for graduate students in the social sciences" and that universities had "little or no provision for training in scientific method." Frank called for "a new departure in social science, involving a break with the traditional scholastic efforts and the expenditure of funds for investigation and research."[199] Included centrally in Frank's desiderata were competitive programs of pre- and postdoctoral fellowships and the creation of bureaus or institutes within each university consisting of members from various disciplines that would fund and supervise research and encourage opportunities for cooperation and collaboration. Frank's investigation proved influential in charting the course that Beardsley Ruml would take with funding strategies for the Laura Spelman Rockefeller Memorial in the later 1920s.[200] Moreover, both Small's critique and Frank's intervention came at a time when ambitious Chicago social scientists such as Charles Merriam, Robert Park, and Leon C. Marshall were proposing more collaborative research structures and interdisciplinary approaches that would reshape the way in which doctoral education was both conducted and experienced and would, so they hoped, significantly improve the quality of the students attracted to Chicago's doctoral programs.[201]

Predictably, changes in graduate education would be encouraged or discouraged in the face of strong leadership on the part of the president and the various deans, and the different perspectives of Judson and Burton about undergraduate education were bound to have an impact on local campus thinking on graduate education, defining two poles around which much intense discussion was to play out. Among the faction of senior faculty who believed that Judson was right and Burton was wrong was Gordon J. Laing, an influential and vocal senior classicist who was originally hired as a junior professor of Latin in 1899 and was promoted to full professor in 1913. Laing also served as the general editor of the University of Chicago Press from 1908 to 1921 and 1923 to 1940. In mid-1923 Laing succeeded Small as dean of the Graduate School of Arts and Literature. Sensing Burton's inclinations to support substantial investments in undergraduate education, Laing lobbied for the formation of the Committee on Graduate Education in January 1924 with a mandate to survey the condition of graduate-student education and propose possible new investments.[202] Laing was worried that Chicago's research luster would dim as leading scholars of the first generation retired. Laing also wanted the committee to address the financing of graduate schools and the hiring of future faculty appointees. He hoped that his committee would propose the kinds of changes that would result in the development of graduate schools "more exclusively devoted to scholarship and research."[203]

The product of the committee's deliberations was a sprawling document lacking both the logic and the passion of Small's memorandum and including everything from subtle attacks on the current population of undergraduate students to pleas to build a special clubhouse for graduate students and to reduce faculty teaching obligations. Its principal recommendations involved both a proposed diminishment of undergraduate education at the University of Chicago and a recommitment by the faculty to a form of graduate education that was primarily, if not exclusively, to be directed by the ideal of training researchers (as opposed to teachers). Laing's committee also proposed restricting graduate training to one department and not allowing students to pursue secondary interests. The master's degree was to be maintained as a research degree, with a thesis, even though Laing admitted that the great majority of the students who took the degree would become secondary school teachers (to do otherwise would be "a frank admission that in the Graduate School of the University of Chicago vocational aims take precedence over training in the technique and ideals of scholarship"). In the future, graduate courses should use pass/fail evaluations rather than letter grades as a way of differentiating them from undergraduate courses. Graduate-student programs for doctoral students would be highly individualized, with no standard curriculum but focused on their specific research interests: "The curriculum for each student shall be arranged by the department with the approval of the Dean." In essence, a student's research topic would drive his or her selection of courses, not the reverse. Instruction and thus formal classroom teaching would be subordinated to the job of training students in research methods. Faculty too would profit in that the committee recommended that "accomplishment in research" become "the primary qualification for appointments and promotions" and that "productive [faculty] members" be relieved of "[teaching] duties which interfere with their research activities." Laing's report specifically recommended "an enlargement of the University's policy, so that research may in certain cases be officially recognized as the major duty and teaching as voluntary or subordinate."[204]

Laing's logic was not driven by any new substantive conception of interdisciplinary work such as Albion Small's and Charles Merriam's. It was an appeal for more resources and more time off for senior faculty to pursue research at the expense of teaching, however the word "research" might be defined.[205] Other than passing suggestions about restructuring PhD exams, the memo actually headed in a direction opposed to Small's concerns by playing down the value of courses that graduate students might take outside their research area and by urging that they should avoid courses not directly relevant to their dissertation project. Nor did Laing's ambivalence toward undergraduate education at Chicago change much over time. In his annual report on the Graduate School of Arts and Literature in 1930, Laing was intractable: "Perhaps the unsatisfactory condition of graduate schools in this country today is ultimately due to the fact that the original plan, which has been followed ever since, of attaching a German system of advanced work to the American college is fundamentally unsound and constitutes an educational hybrid that can never prosper."[206]

Laing's report proved to be a dud. But dramatic changes were afoot, driven by local faculty initiatives and outside money. The 1920s and 1930s saw not only the emergence of new forms of programmatic financial support for faculty and graduate students from the large private foundations in New York City, but also the rise of new intellectual traditions and cultural-pedagogical practices in graduate education generated locally by several prominent departments at Chicago that made it difficult for administrators to question either the effectiveness or autonomy of the individual graduate programs. This was particularly evident in the social science departments (economics, sociology, and political science), which became (in Thomas Bender's words) professionally preeminent in the nation. Ironically, as Bender notes, this success came because of their strictly academic-disciplinary focus, disjoined from any linkages to the city's literary or other cultural elites.[207] Chicago's foray into what Dorothy Ross has called the "cultural authority and social power of scientism" began in the 1920s with the convergence of massive new financial support from Beardsley Ruml at the Spelman Memorial and from other foundations, the creation of the Social Science Research Council (SSRC) in 1923, and the establishment of the Local Community Research Committee at Chicago, also in 1923.[208] With little exaggeration Lawrence Kimpton would later argue that Ruml was "the man perhaps more responsible than any other for the impetus which made the Social Sciences at the University of Chicago what they have become."[209] A number of advances during this time would lead to the emergence of the so-called Chicago Schools, at the heart of which lay not only the scholarly accomplishments of leading senior faculty but also the cultivation of what Melvin W. Reder has variously called (for economics) "a particular intellectual style among Chicago Ph.D.'s" and "the Chicago style of thought" among several generations of Chicago doctoral students. Among the innovations were the Field Studies seminar and the ethnographic training programs in the Department of Sociology, led by Robert E. Park and Ernest W. Burgess, as well as William Ogburn's work in quantitative sociology, both of which attracted a number of distinguished graduate students; the emergence of a disciplined program of graduate training in the Department of Economics, centered on Economics 301, taught by Jacob Viner and Frank Knight; and the imperialist strategy of Charles E. Merriam in the Department of

Political Science to expand doctoral production (between 1920 and 1940 the department awarded eighty doctorates, a vast increase over its record of thirteen doctorates between 1892 and 1920) under the aegis of a new behavioral science of urban politics.[210] Merriam was especially influential in brokering new interdisciplinary connections in and beyond the University that would generate more resources for graduate and postdoctoral students, including a long-standing collaboration with Ruml under SSRC sponsorship in summer workshops at Dartmouth College in Hanover, New Hampshire, between 1925 and 1930.[211] As Michael Heaney and John Hansen have argued, under Merriam's leadership "the department's curriculum was transformed over the decade of the 1920s from a focus on public law and historical institutionalism—the basis of the discipline at the time—to a focus on the scientific study of political behavior."[212]

The new "scientism" of the interwar period, underwritten with millions of the Laura Spelman Rockefeller Memorial's money and providing enhanced faculty support and fellowships and other research positions for doctoral students, revolutionized graduate education just as it elevated the professional prestige of key senior faculty in the social sciences.[213] It is no accident that Harper's earlier normative dictates about faculty teaching loads begin to break down in the 1920s, with individual departments being allowed to give various exemptions and reductions to individual (mainly senior) faculty in their formal teaching responsibilities, a practice that would accelerate rapidly after World War II.[214] Slowly, an autonomous graduate-student academic culture emerged in Chicago's social science departments, with doctoral students coming to interact with each other and rely on each other, often in the course of their academic training or in organizations such as the Society for Social Research in the Department of Sociology (founded in 1920 by Robert Park) and in shared residential experiences at the International House (which opened in September 1932).[215]

The dedication of the Social Science Research Building in December 1929, a building financed by the Spelman Memorial, was emblematic of the new authority, legitimacy, and prestige enjoyed by these reimagined graduate programs. In his remarks at the dedication ceremony Charles Merriam remarked, "We are left with the solemn responsibility of realizing the high purposes to which this edifice is dedicated.... We do not underestimate the task of advancing the social studies to a higher level of scientific attainment and human usefulness"; and deliberately combined the themes of theoretical prowess and practical utility that gave graduate programs in the social sciences at Chicago an ever-increasing legitimacy between 1918 and 1945.[216] As the scholarly impact of these doctoral programs at Chicago became recognized nationally during the 1930s and

1940s, and as the faculty came to have fewer doubts about the academic quality of the students who were admitted to these graduate programs, it would prove difficult for central administrators to force changes on faculty that they were unwilling to accept.[217]

The years after 1918 also brought greater self-confidence vis-à-vis older European models for research and graduate education. The scientific landscape in Germany after 1918 was no longer the mecca that young Americans had admired before 1914. Rather, in the aftermath of the war, German science and scholarship were marked (in Margit Szöllösi-Janze's words) by a desolate situation of isolation and austerity.[218] Part of this shift was also the result of the simple maturation of graduate study in the United States and the feeling of many graduate students that American doctoral programs were now rigorous enough to obviate the need for foreign study. Some of the young Americans who ventured to Europe did so with an air of skepticism, both about the state of the Old World and about the fustiness of its academic customs. After meeting a group of English academics in London, the young Harold Lasswell reported to Charles Merriam in 1923, "Curious atmosphere, this, near the decaying corpses of personalities and nations dead and dying.... The men who think in England are peering into a future for them very black."[219]

Americans may no longer have felt compelled to travel to Europe after 1918, or at least to evaluate their experiences in overly deferential, pietistic frames of mind, but the same could not be said for students coming in the other direction. After 1918 the University of Chicago became a destination for hundreds of students from abroad and replicated in mirror image the behavior of its own faculty in Europe before 1914. By 1923, 432 foreign-born students, representing 41 countries, were registered in various academic programs at Chicago across all departments and schools.[220] Several younger Europeans who came to Chicago in the 1920s to seek their professional and intellectual fortune ended up staying at the University. They included Otto Struve in astronomy and Thorkild Jacobsen in Assyrian and Sumerian studies, both of whom came in the 1920s as graduate students, received Chicago PhDs, and eventually were invited to join the faculty; and Wilhelm Pauck, who came to study at the Chicago Theological Seminary in 1925 but also ended up with a faculty appointment in the Divinity School.

In a few cases, brilliant young Europeans with European PhDs continued to find places on the Chicago faculty. On the eve of the Depression William H. Zachariasen, a young postdoctoral fellow from Norway, joined the Department of Physics. He spent the next forty-four years in a distinguished career at Chicago, including service as chair of the Department of Physics (1945–49 and 1956–59) and dean of the Division of the Physical

Sciences (1959–62). It was telling, moreover, that the most distinguished senior European to assume a full professorship at Chicago in the 1920s arrived not from Germany but from Great Britain. Sir William Craigie, who was the third editor of the *Oxford English Dictionary* and who abandoned an endowed chair at Oxford in 1925 to work on the *Dictionary of American English* project at Chicago, was viewed locally as a prestigious coup.[221]

Many younger scholars who had studied in Germany before the war now remembered their connections with German academic culture with more ambivalence. Barry Karl has shrewdly observed about Charles Merriam, who had studied with Otto Gierke and Hugo Preuss in Berlin in 1899–1900, that "after the war ... Merriam tended more to deny the relationship than affirm it, though his vacillation on the subject of his German intellectual forebears was characteristic of the problems his generation faced."[222] Meaningful scholarly connections between Europe and America continued in the 1920s, but they often came about via the initiatives of individual Chicago members reaching across the Atlantic with idealized American values in tow. Merriam's nine-volume *Studies in the Making of Citizens*, a series of books dealing with comparative civic training in various European nations and the United States and published by the University of Chicago Press between 1929 and 1933, was informed less by Merriam's appreciation for traditional European institutions and more by his belief that after the horrors of 1914–18 American political values of educating responsible citizens, and especially the American ideal of participatory democracy, were "a model for the rest of the world."[223] Similarly, the work of Merriam's colleague Quincy Wright on the causes and prevention of war enabled Wright to generate a large range of professional correspondents and other scholarly contacts in various European states, especially relating to the future of the League of Nations, but within a framework defined by Wright's conviction that America's involvement in European collective security was in the world's interest, not merely in America's self-interest.[224]

COLLEGIATE EDUCATION

On the undergraduate front serious changes were also afoot in the 1920s. Ernest Burton sought to improve the leadership of the Colleges by appointing Professor Ernest Wilkins, a distinguished scholar of early Italian Renaissance literature, as dean of the Colleges in the autumn of 1923. Wilkins sought to impose more coherence in the undergraduate curriculum by drafting a bold plan to create a distinctive program of liberal education for first- and second-year college students, articulated in a report on the future of the Colleges in the spring of 1924.[225] Wilkins was convinced that the current American college had "failed in the development of leaders for society," that it had also "failed to develop serious minded students," that it bred "social irresponsiveness," and that it "disregard[ed] a valid and significant cleavage in the educational process." His report consisted of specific recommendations for Chicago, accompanied several months later by a more general and speculative tract called "A Theory of Education." For Chicago, Wilkins proposed dividing undergraduate education into two parts, with the first two years organized in a college that had its own curriculum, its own teaching faculty, and its own administration; it would admit 1,500 students who would be taught by seventy-five specially selected teachers, none of whom would be expected to be members of departments or have research credentials (the instructors "should be free from any constraint to accomplish anything but success in teaching"). In his more theoretical statement Wilkins went even further, proposing to decouple the first two years of college and unite them with the last six years of primary and secondary education into an American version of the German gymnasium (Wilkins called it a "collegiate school") that would provide eight years of general education, a system that he believed would remedy the ills associated with the traditional four-year liberal-arts college.[226]

Advocating a "sharp cleavage" between the College and the rest of the University, the plan was fantastic, and it encountered immediate and strident opposition from senior faculty across the natural sciences led by Julius Stieglitz and Hermann Schlesinger of the chemistry department, W. C. Allee, H. C. Cowles, and A. J. Carlson of biology, E. S. Bastin of geology, and Harvey Lemon of physics, who were subsequently joined by faculty from the humanities and social sciences like T. V. Smith of philosophy and L. C. Marshall of economics. Stieglitz insisted that "the evils in the fields mentioned could not properly be laid at the door of the college, and that the charges against the American four-year college are just as applicable to the European systems similar to the ones outlined in the 'Theory of Education.'" Stieglitz was especially opposed to Wilkins's notions of allotting the first two years of undergraduate work to teachers who were not scholars, which would be destructive of the larger mission of the research university.[227] Wilkins's ideas went nowhere. Burton reported to Swift that Wilkins had "roused very vigorous opposition on the part of some of the most influential men in the faculty," and predicted that the report would be voted down "if there is a chance to do so."[228] After languishing for a decent time, it was officially buried at a joint meeting of the faculties of the Colleges and the Graduate Schools in early 1927.[229]

Having failed in his visionary scheme, Wilkins was forced to settle for more modest changes, such as the development of new introductory courses for younger undergraduate students based on interdisciplinary teaching practices. One such course, "The Nature of the World and of Man," was a two-quarter sequence launched in the autumn quarter of 1924 that proved quite popular with students, only some of whom were fortunate enough to take it (enrollment was by invitation only); it served as a prototype for the kinds of general-education courses that Chauncey S. Boucher later developed in the early 1930s. But one course did not make a revolution, and Wilkins's efforts to create parallel courses in the humanities and social sciences did not succeed.

Wilkins was successful, however, in securing more advising support for students; he also proposed a general plan to improve teaching by hiring more postdoctoral teaching fellows and asking the departments to be more attentive to quality in teaching.[230] Yet ultimately Wilkins did not like the job of dean, and in early 1925 he wrote to Burton asking to be relieved of the deanship in favor of a more esoteric position as a new associate dean of the faculties, where he might devote his time to studying the theoretical problems afflicting undergraduate education. Burton was not in sympathy with that idea or with Wilkins's scheme of cutting off the first two years of undergraduate work from the regular faculty, and he cautioned him that developing new theories of higher education without the pragmatic support of the next dean of the Colleges would be a dubious proposition.[231] Wilkins's impact as dean was thus limited by the structural constraints in which he found himself—namely, the resistance of the departments, which continued to exercise a stranglehold over most of the introductory courses taken by freshmen and sophomores—as well as by his evident political ineptness in dealing with Burton.[232] With little prospect of becoming a new associate dean of the faculties for higher educational theory Wilkins became disheartened. He resigned his office in February 1926, citing ill health, and he left Chicago later that year when he was offered the presidency of Oberlin College.

Upon Wilkins's resignation, the new president, Max Mason, appointed Chauncey Boucher as dean of the Colleges in June 1926. Mason himself was generally sympathetic to Burton's ideas, and although he proved incapable of exerting strong leadership to improve the situation, Mason was vocally opposed to eliminating the undergraduate program. An unlikely candidate for curricular revolutionary, Boucher was trained as a historian of the antebellum South and received his PhD from the University of Michigan in 1914. From 1924 to 1926 Boucher had served as an associate dean, which meant that he was privy to the competing curricular streams then in motion. In contrast to Wilkins, who aspired to be a theorist of higher education, Boucher had the resilience and flexibility that is indispensable for successful curricular reform at any college or university.

An excellent public speaker and well liked by both faculty and students, Boucher set about to provide the necessary initiatives that would fundamentally reshape undergraduate education.[233] Boucher began planning large-scale changes soon after he took over as dean: "I learned that President Mason and Vice President Woodward were anxious to do something really significant with the Colleges and were ready to entertain any constructive suggestions which the Dean might have to offer. I then began in earnest to study the biggest problems of college education, particularly our own problems."[234]

What problems faced the Colleges? First, rapid growth of undergraduate and graduate enrollments after 1918 led to the appointment of a large number of graduate-student teachers and other temporary instructors whose performance in the classroom was often subpar. Second, student opinion about the quality of the education that they were receiving in the Colleges became more problematic. A survey of student opinion in 1919 by the young Harold Lasswell found that "the prevailing complaint of serious undergraduates is the impersonality of their classes and the few opportunities they have for direct contact with either their own instructors or with men of prominence in their departments." Reasons cited for this shortfall included "the preoccupation of the instructor with the research work upon which his advancement depends" and peer pressure not to seek help outside class for fear that doing so might be seen as currying favor. Another complaint Lasswell heard was that "many of the [undergraduate] courses were taught by graduate assistants with little experience and buried beneath the load of graduate work."[235] The rapid increase in enrollments after the war also brought many undergraduate students to the University who were unprepared for the rigors of university work. A study of the records of 762 students who entered the University in the fall of 1919 revealed that only 308 had graduated by the spring of 1925, for a six-year graduation rate of only 41 percent. Moreover, almost 25 percent of these students had been dismissed for poor performance or were on academic probation.[236] Another study done in 1927 concluded that "in spite of the work of the Examiner's Office, there are a good many students who seem intellectually unable to meet the scholastic requirements. The greatest single cause of poor work, however, seems to be the student's own attitude, a desire to 'get-by' with the least possible effort."[237] These concerns raised red flags among the senior faculty about the University's admissions practices. A few faculty members were only too happy to use such data to discredit the undergraduate program, but most sincerely wanted to find ways to recruit more students of high academic ability to the Colleges.[238]

The most problematic issue facing students and faculty, however, concerned the rumors that the University intended, in the spirit of Judson, to abolish the Colleges. A proposal by the president of Johns Hopkins University, Frank J. Goodnow, in March 1925 to abolish the first two years of undergraduate work in Baltimore was fuel for the fire of those who wished to do likewise in Chicago.[239] Boucher was strongly opposed to such schemes, but he later recalled that, in spite of forceful public statements by Burton and Mason to the contrary, "the idea which has had currency for ten years to my knowledge, still persists among many faculty members, students, and alumni, and among the public at large, that the University of Chicago is deliberately endeavoring to kill its Colleges slowly but surely by maltreatment and become a graduate institution with only such senior college work as is necessary to supplement the graduate work."[240] Compounding these rumors was an increased disregard for undergraduate teaching on the part of key senior faculty who functioned as faculty opinion leaders. Boucher also remembered the "widely spread impression that only research and graduate instruction receive recognition in the form of promotion in rank and advance in salary.... There are many faculty members, both young and old, who consider it a mark of social and professional inferiority to be identified with the administration of, curriculum building for, or the instruction of, undergraduate students."[241]

Although many senior faculty shared Julius Stieglitz's view that the University should retain its four-year college, a noisy minority eagerly embraced the idea that the first two years of undergraduate education simply be abandoned or given away.[242] As late as 1934, William Dodd, a senior historian who played a critical role in the search committee that selected Robert Hutchins for the presidency in April 1929, would derisively warn against any plans to bring more undergraduates to campus by suggesting his distinct preference for graduate students: "Let undergraduate loafers go anywhere else, especially to Yale and Harvard where swaggy manners and curious accents can be learned easily."[243] During the planning for the new modern languages building in 1925, English professor John Matthews Manly wrote to Vice President James H. Tufts, assenting to the creation of a new library reading room for the humanities that would be connected to the main Harper Library, but making it clear that undergraduates would not be welcome in the new facility: "It was with some difficulty that some members of the Departments were brought to agree that the Modern Language Reading Room should be placed on the third floor ... [for] fear that this Reading Room would be invaded by an overflow of undergraduates from Harper. I believe that this can be prevented, but we all wish to insist that this Reading Room must be protected against such an invasion."[244]

Moreover, chronic instructional problems were glaring. A survey in early 1925 revealed that of 124 sections of 34 large departmental courses, only 30 were taught by a regular member of the faculty, with the rest being taught by graduate students or other part-timers. Of the 94 graduate-student teachers, 36 had no prior teaching experience. Moreover, 70 percent of all large courses in the Colleges were taught by individuals on one-year contracts. Many of these individuals were selected with no thought to their abilities to teach, and most departments made no effort to ascertain the quality of what they actually did in the classroom. The report gloomily concluded that "such conditions—involving instruction by teachers predominantly of low rank, a high rate of turnover in personnel, hasty appointment, selection made with inadequate or inappropriate basis, failure to ascertain the quality of the teaching done, teaching which is actually unsatisfactory, and failure to correct individual faults and promote individual abilities—are not consistent with the maintenance and development of a quality of instruction worthy of the University of Chicago."[245] As Boucher described the situation in 1928, "Departmental autonomy has been carried to the nth degree. Each Department frames its own program of course offerings as it may see fit, and the Dean of the Colleges never knows what is to be our program for any quarter until the time schedule is in print. Resulting inadequacies and inconsistencies in Departmental Undergraduate offerings, considered individually and as a whole, are frequently due to ignorance or bad judgment, but in some instances are due to deliberate intent to slight the Undergraduate work."[246]

In response to such problems, Boucher urged the University to adopt more rigorous entrance requirements that limited incoming freshmen enrollment to no more than 750 students annually, and he increased the number of prize honors scholarships. Boucher also deployed stronger and more interventionist advising resources to help struggling students, and abolished mandatory attendance at chapel.[247] But his real ambition, articulated in many position papers that he wrote between 1927 and 1930, was to begin to recruit more motivated and academically gifted students to the Colleges and then to put them in a more coherent and rigorous instructional program that was not controlled by the departments and that would be protected by an independent Office of the Examiner. He needed to construct a *completely new system* of general education for all areas of the arts and sciences at the University of Chicago, and he had to do so in a way that the influential factions of natural and social science faculty at Chicago would accept, if not actively embrace. Ernest Wilkins had run up against dogged opposition from politically formidable natural scientists like Stieglitz, and Boucher was determined not to make the same mistake.

Having been inspired by a talk that Max Mason gave to the Institute for Administrative Officers of Higher Institutions in July 1927, Boucher began to survey the state of collegiate education nationally and to consult with experts who would speak with him:

> I read more widely whatever literature would give me the current practice and progressive thought of men in other institutions; I talked with about thirty individuals in various departments and schools of the University of Chicago; in January 1928 I made a trip to learn first hand what is going on at Princeton, Columbia, and Harvard. I talked with many of the leading constructive thinkers at each of these institutions. My object was first of all to see what features of the practice at each of these institutions could be adapted to our conditions; secondly, I was anxious, if given any encouragement, to tell the main features of the plan on which I was to work, in order to get the constructive and corrective suggestion of these men whose training and experiences would make their opinions valuable.[248]

Boucher's visit to Columbia doubtlessly led him to investigate the Contemporary Civilization course launched in 1919.[249] But it would be a mistake to think that Boucher was trying to copy such models, for the political and intellectual challenge that he faced was much more radical than anything the Columbia humanists like John J. Coss and Harry J. Carman had faced in the 1920s. A critical turning point seems to have occurred in mid-February 1928, when Boucher traveled to New York City to meet with William S. Learned, a senior staff member at the Carnegie Foundation for the Advancement of Teaching and a remarkable interwar critic of secondary and tertiary levels of education in America. In 1927 Learned had published a tough critique of the state of American higher education in which he denounced "the bane of the average" that afflicted American colleges and universities. Looking over the landscape of college and university programs, Learned saw incoherence, lack of rigor, a jumble of course credits and grading practices that had no rational purpose or aim, and, most seriously, a complete disdain for "the intellectual vision, energy, and enthusiasm of young minds."[250] During the six-hour meeting, Boucher was much taken by Learned's proposals for enhancing curricular rigor and his disdain for course credits, and Learned encouraged him to pursue a set of fundamental, transdisciplinary structural reforms.[251] If any single outside influence shaped the creation of Chicago's first Core curriculum, it was the work of empiricists like William Learned and his colleagues at the Carnegie Foundation.[252]

A month later Boucher constituted and chaired a faculty committee that formulated his reform program and presented it to the University

Senate on May 7, 1928. The committee was dominated by a centrist group of scholars who, in contrast to the research-only advocates like Dodd, were sympathetic to the cause of undergraduate education but who had also spoken out against Wilkins's utopian scheme of 1924. They included Stieglitz, Carlson, Marshall, and, perhaps most notably, Charles Judd of the Department of Education. Boucher's plan called for a set of bold changes — the establishment of a junior college program that would have its own curricular structure distinct from the control of the departments but taught by the regular research faculty; the revision of the curriculum for the first two years of the undergraduate work centered on the development of broad survey courses in place of ad hoc departmental offerings, but courses that were based on research findings of the faculty (an idea that built on an earlier experiment in the natural sciences in the mid-1920s); the use of five general-education competency examinations to assess and evaluate student progress, which students might take whenever they felt ready; additional new subject-area courses designed to meet student interest in early specialization, particularly in the natural sciences; and the abolition of mandatory quarterly course examinations.[253] Nor did Boucher restrict himself to intrepid curricular changes, for his plan also presumed that several million new dollars would be invested in new residence halls, in additional endowment to pay for the upkeep of these halls, and in the construction of instructional facilities and the expansion of undergraduate library resources as well.[254] Finally, although he insisted on new resources for the College, Boucher wished to keep most of the actual instruction on the main quadrangles to avoid creating an undergraduate ghetto. For those who sought to marginalize undergraduate education at the University of Chicago, these proposals, taken in their entirety, were a declaration of war.

Boucher was conscious of the negative descriptions of the undergraduates that William Dodd and like-minded colleagues deployed to discredit collegiate work — implying as they did that the undergraduate students were not serious in their studies, that they lacked a true "University spirit," and that they thus detracted from the real work of the University — and he was convinced that a more rigorous academic program would attract even better students who would find the general culture of the University more congenial.[255] Unlike Wilkins, whose curricular prescriptions in 1924 for his junior college program looked to many faculty like a mere continuation of high school work, cast in a social regime of helping a community of young people attain the "independence of moral living," Boucher draped his plan in the aura of the research university: with the research-based content of courses; the intellectual individualism, stamina, and autonomy required of undergraduates; and the regime of "scientific" testing that would evaluate student achievement. Among his original recommendations in May 1928 was the idea that the College should make it possible "to save time for the better students, who are able to develop themselves both faster and more thoroughly than the average student, by awarding the [bachelor's] degree on the basis of demonstrated accomplishment, rather than on a required number of course credits, and thus break up the lockstep system."[256] Boucher was convinced that he had designed a system that would eliminate most of the glaring ills that Learned found evident in American higher education. But he also hoped that, in attracting more intellectually independent students who would merit the respect and admiration of the regular departmental faculties, he would be able to rescue the undergraduate program at Chicago from its politically marginal status.

Boucher's strategy for a curricular revolution stumbled badly in early May 1928 when Max Mason unexpectedly resigned the presidency of the University to take up the directorship of the Natural Sciences Division at the Rockefeller Foundation, with the informal understanding that he would then become president of the foundation within a year or two. The reasons for Mason's resignation remain murky, although subsequent rumors suggested that they involved not only Mason's personal unhappiness with the Chicago job and the appeal of a less stressful philanthropic position in New York (Mason had already extended feelers to the Rockefeller Foundation in the spring of 1928), but also the fact that a University trustee had seen him in the lobby of a hotel with a woman who was not his wife.[257] According to the historian Jean Block, who heard this account from several University trustees who had served in the 1930s, this may have been the other shoe dropping that made it urgent that Mason depart.[258] The resulting power vacuum in the summer of 1928 put Boucher's scheme in political limbo. Attempts to implement the reforms in a piecemeal fashion in later 1928 inevitably stalled, and Boucher felt isolated and unsupported, beset by powerful forces intent on thwarting his plans to strengthen undergraduate education.[259]

The fact that Mason's resignation was announced just one day before Boucher presented his reform proposals to the University Senate was also bound to influence the shape of the search for Mason's successor. The inside candidate favored by many of the trustees and, according to Charles Judd, by the majority of the faculty was Frederic C. Woodward, a professor of law and the current vice president and dean of faculties. But the faculty search committee elected by the full professors on the Senate to advise the trustees was dominated by four men—William Dodd, Charles Merriam, Henry Gale, and Gordon Laing—who held serious reservations about Woodward because of his benevolent views toward Boucher's plan and his support for Burton's housing schemes. Indeed, Woodward was stymied in his candidacy for the presidency by a group of senior faculty members who, in Judd's words, felt "terror" over the prospect that the University might make major investments in undergraduate education, a strategy that, for Dodd, meant not only a disastrous shift in material resources away from research, but also a symbolic affront to the (hoped-for) cultural hegemony of the graduate programs.[260] In September 1928 Dodd wrote to Harold Swift urging that any attempt to expand undergraduate resources would mean that "the real work of the University is doomed for the next fifteen or twenty years," and he left no doubt that by "real work" he meant graduate education and research. Moreover, unlike the often indifferent and undisciplined undergraduates, the graduate students were studious and generated no discipline problems.[261] That Dodd was himself a Wilsonian Democrat who viewed elite undergraduate colleges as being necessarily the preserve of shiftless and undeservedly wealthy youth might help to explain both his stubbornness and his anxieties, but it also showed his inability to imagine that the University of Chicago might construct an undergraduate program radically different from those of its eastern peers.[262]

As acting president and, at the same time, as the leading internal candidate for the permanent job, Woodward was in a dilemma. Over the course of 1928, alumni leaders became deeply concerned about rumors concerning the abolition of the Colleges. One committee, chaired by John A. Logan, sent a questionnaire to three hundred alumni, including questions such as "What is there to the rumor regarding the proposed abolition of the first two years of undergraduate life? If there is no reason for this rumor, as we are told, why does not the administration make an effort to destroy it by means of a definite statement to the contrary which could be given widespread publicity through the highly organized publicity office?"[263] Another group of alumni, writing anonymously, denounced the senior faculty who, in their view, held "fat" jobs with "no responsibility" and "who never would have got so far if public-spirited men had not established the institution, and parents of students paid millions in tuitions for more than thirty years. No group of educators has ever before shown such consummate selfishness, greed, and lack of principle."[264] Even more disturbing were the worries of centrist leaders among the alumni, such as Frank S. Whiting, a prominent local banker who had graduated with an SB degree in 1916. Whiting complained that it was irresponsible for the University not to resolve the issue of the future of the Colleges immediately. In measured terms he indicated that if the University *as a whole* wanted to continue to enjoy alumni support, a decision to retain the Colleges had to be made, and made quickly.[265]

Plainly, if left unanswered such views would have been disastrous for the University's public relations in the city and for its future fund-raising prospects. A committee of trustees in December 1928 urged the University administrative leaders to make "a clear and decisive statement" about "the permanence of the undergraduate college as a part of the University."[266] Faced with alumni and trustee grumbling about the bad press caused by the antiundergraduate rhetoric of senior faculty members, Woodward was forced to write to graduate deans Gordon Laing and Henry Gale in mid-January 1929, urging them (in a tone that bordered on a reprimand) to reaffirm publicly the necessity of Chicago maintaining its undergraduate college, and pointing to the growing unease that was manifest in influential alumni circles. In response, he received perfunctory reassurances of Laing's and Gale's support, but this exchange and others like it drove a knife through Woodward's chances to succeed Mason.[267] It was hardly surprising that Gale and Laing were also at the core of the opposition to Boucher's proposed curricular reforms.[268] Even though Woodward was respected by many other senior faculty members, the anti-Woodward cabalists were able to muddy the waters, and by early 1929 Woodward's candidacy was doomed, opening the way for the young, brash outsider Robert Maynard Hutchins.[269]

Barry Karl has rightly observed that this was a battle in which neither side could be permanently victorious—the University needed undergraduates for its financial welfare if not also for its long-term institutional survival, and it also needed the research luster with which Harper had originally endowed it. Still the fight was bitter, intractable, and damaging to faculty morale, and it made Robert Hutchins's subsequent support for even more radical investments and reforms in undergraduate education all the more remarkable.[270] It was not until Hutchins assumed the presidency in the summer of 1929 that Chauncey Boucher gained a powerful ally, who, as a new man with the sovereign force of his office behind him, had the credibility to force Boucher's schemes through the faculty. As we shall see, these new curricular structures would prove to be a turning point of enormous importance to the academic culture of the University of Chicago.

STUDENTS AND STUDENT LIFE AFTER WORLD WAR I

Student life is a vital, if often inchoate, component of any university's broader academic culture, and it is thus worth devoting some time to considering the features of Chicago student life after World War I, for such features would change profoundly after World War II. Unfortunately, the University kept rather fragmentary and often disorganized records on the social backgrounds of its students, but enough information survives to present a general social portrait of the early student body at Chicago. Students seeking admission to the University of Chicago were typically expected to have graduated from a high school. Many students transferred from other universities and colleges, and the same condition probably held in their cases as well. As George Counts demonstrated in his classic study of selective secondary-school admissions in the United States, although enrollments at the secondary-school level increased dramatically between 1870 and 1910, the odds that a young boy or girl of high school age in the United States would attend high school in 1920 were not more than about 25 percent. Counts found that students attending high schools of any kind were much more likely to come from families with significant cultural and financial resources (for example, students in high schools were more than two and a half times likely to come from a home that had a telephone, and their parents were much more likely to be employed in a white-collar professional or commercial career as opposed to having a working-class job). Once students were enrolled in high school their family backgrounds continued to influence whether they would undertake a college preparatory or vocational course.[271] The population of private high schools in 1918, slightly more than 158,000 in the whole of the United States, tended to come from even more affluent and propertied classes.

The size of the total undergraduate-student population at Chicago (autumn quarter enrollments) increased from 1,488 students in 1908 to 3,401 students in 1929. Chicago was coeducational from the beginning, with the number of first-year men and women undergraduates ranging from a ratio of 54 percent to 46 percent in 1908 to 57 percent to 43 percent in 1929 to 56 percent to 44 percent in 1940. The University experimented extensively with various admissions procedures in its first several decades. Until 1911, admission to the University on the junior college level required students taking an entrance examination that presumed four years (fifteen yearlong courses) of full-time course work at the high school level. Beginning in 1911–12, the University accepted students who had graduated from a four-year high school accredited by the North Central Association of Colleges and Secondary Schools (or, in other parts of the country, by similar accrediting bodies), subject to the student's record meeting certain quantitative and qualitative requirements.[272] In 1923 the University began to require substantial personal information of applicants, including family background, academic interests and professional plans, and social interests and hobbies. A year later the Colleges instituted a minimum grade requirement in academic subjects for admission from accredited high schools, stipulating that the candidate had to have average grades 25 percent higher than the difference between a passing grade and a score of 100 percent. In 1930 this complex system was abandoned in favor of the decision to admit all students in the upper half of their graduating classes without additional examination. Once at the University, academic achievement tended to correlate strongly with prior success in high school, and with parental occupation as well. Floyd Reeves and John Dale Russell found, for example, that 84 percent of the students in 1926 whose fathers were employed in professional careers attained a satisfactory academic record during their freshman year, but that this value fell to 57 percent for children of fathers who worked in the trades.[273]

Financing an undergraduate education at the University of Chicago required significant financial commitments. Given the fiscal pressures experienced by the University after World War I, when student population surged and when the faculty argued for a massive expansion of instructional and research resources, it was understandable that the cost of attendance doubled between 1917 and 1926, with annual tuition charges (fulltime and for three quarters) increasing from $150 in 1917 to $300 in 1926. By 1933, annual tuition had increased to $306; by 1939, it had increased still further to $325. If a student did not live at home, additional expenses would be incurred by room and board costs on or off campus. Within the residential system, room and board charges varied depending on the quality and location of the dorm. The lowest cost for room and board in Burton-Judson Courts in 1937 was about $425 for a full academic year. In older residence halls like Snell and Hitchcock, room and board might be obtained for about $350 per academic year (these were minimums, and wealthier students could gain better rooms for higher fees). Students living off campus might reduce living expenses still further by cooking for themselves, although it seems very unlikely that one could rent a room, feed oneself, and buy books for less than $250 a year. Thus, assuming that a student did not live at home, the real cost of attendance at the University of Chicago at the onset of the Depression was probably somewhere between $550 and $800 a year.[274] To put this latter figure in the social context of the times, the average salary of a full-time associate professor at the University of Chicago in 1930–31 was about $4,000 to $4,500 a year. A male high school teacher with a degree from a land grant college would have earned about $2,900 after ten years of service. Professions like law and medicine did considerably better: average salaries in law, medicine, and engineering for graduates of a land grant college after ten years were about $5,900, $5,700, and $3,800, respectively.[275] In contrast, a skilled worker employed in a manufacturing industry or a railroad in the 1920s might have earned about $1,600 a year.

The University offered scholarship assistance to undergraduates from the very beginning of its history, but in very modest amounts and almost always on a competitive merit basis. Scholarships were offered on the basis of competitive evaluations of student achievement within specific fields (prize or competition scholarships) and on the basis of a student's academic record in high school or at the College (honor scholarships). About ninety tuition grants were also available to undergraduate students from the LaVerne Noyes Foundation for veterans of the armed forces during World War I or for their descendants. In 1930, the University awarded scholarship aid to 167 freshmen (19 percent of all new matriculants) and to 517 upper-class undergraduates (14 percent of all full-time upperclassmen).[276] Many of the freshmen awards covered full tuition, but a large majority of the scholarships for upperclassmen covered only partial tuition. Even students with aid encountered increasing financial pressures after their first year. Many students therefore had to earn part or all of their tuition and living expenses by working. Based on a survey of 2,065 College students in 1920, Harold Lasswell and Theodore Soares estimated that 42.5 percent of male undergraduate students and 31 percent of female undergraduates worked part- or full- time.[277] A team led by H. A. Millis surveyed 1,786 undergraduates in early 1924 and came to roughly similar conclusions: 36.6 percent of the students carrying a full load of four courses per quarter had gainful employment, while 46.7 percent of those taking two courses a quarter had outside jobs.[278] In addition, almost one-third of those polled reported that they were living under stress because of the pressures of combining their studies with work. Reeves and Russell also found in 1930 that a very large number of students with full or partial scholarship assistance (who were, in turn, a distinct minority of the total Chicago college population) had to work part-time. Since many scholarship winners came from outside the Chicago area, they often experienced higher living costs than did local students who could live at home.[279] The onset of the Depression further complicated the situation. In 1939, over 56 percent of undergraduate men and 30 percent of undergraduate women reported that they expected to be either fully or partially self-supporting during their tenure at Chicago. Equally important, 54 percent of the men and 18 percent of the women reported that they had contributed to their own support while in high school.

In spite of the extraordinary endowment support provided by John D. Rockefeller and later from the Rockefeller boards, University officials from the very beginning were forced to rely on student tuition fees as a significant source of operational revenue, a form of dependence that would grow far greater over the twentieth century. By the mid-1920s fully one-third of the annual budget of the University was covered by income from student tuition fees. Eliminating the expenses and revenues associated with the Medical School and University clinics, student fees (42 percent) by the later 1930s exceeded endowment income (36 percent) as the single largest source of revenue for the general budget of the arts and sciences.[280] Between 1918 and 1930, University enrollment grew by 59 percent, but the institution's annual operational and educational expenditures increased by 323 percent.[281]

Perhaps the most difficult factor to analyze with precision is the socioeconomic status of Chicago undergraduate students. George Counts suggested in 1922 that most high school graduates who had taken college preparatory programs came ipso facto from relatively advantaged social and cultural backgrounds, and since most matriculants at Chicago were highly intelligent students who attained strong academic records in their (predominantly) public high schools, one might expect that Chicago undergraduates, as a rule, came from solidly middle-class to upper-middle-class and occasionally even upper-class social backgrounds. The median score attained by Chicago freshmen on the American Council on Education's Psychological Examination (an early examination of intelligence) revealed that Chicago undergraduates ranked fourth in the nation out of a group of 151 colleges and universities in 1931.[282]

However, a number of other data points suggest a more complex story. First, there is reasonably good data about parental occupation and education from the 1920s and 1930s. Reeves and Russell found, based on a representative sample of 3,769 undergraduate alumni from 1893 to 1930, that a substantial majority (almost 70 percent) came from families in which the father owned a proprietary business of some kind or worked in professional services or commercial services. Only 13 percent came from families in which the father was employed as an artisan or worked in transportation, public service, building trades, or printing trades. However, these occupational designations covered a wide diversity of compensation levels and jobs within each category (for example, "professional services" encompassed social workers, librarians, and public-school teachers, as well as physicians, engineers, and pharmacists).[283] Data from the 1930s also revealed that, in terms of parental education, fathers of approximately 35 percent of Chicago undergraduates had not graduated from high school, while fathers of another 21 percent had graduated only from high school. Such data, together with the parallel data on the large number of students who needed to work, may suggest that the majority of the undergraduate population of the College came from families who were more lower-middle to middle class in terms of income status, along with a smaller number of working-class students and a still smaller number of students from wealthier families. The financial impact of the Depression after 1930 on the lives of students and their families has never been studied, but it is noteworthy that undergraduate enrollment slowly declined at Chicago between 1929 (4,097 students, a historic high point) and 1938 (3,341).[284]

If the early student body of the University was socioeconomically diverse, it was distinctly less diverse in its geographical distribution. From the beginnings of the University until well into the 1940s, the majority of undergraduates came from Chicago and its close-in suburbs. In 1902, 56 percent of first-year undergraduates came from the city of Chicago and another 15 percent from the state of Illinois outside of Chicago. Since some portion of the latter group were probably residents of one of Chicago's suburbs, the Chicago metropolitan area figure was probably slightly higher.[285] Over the next thirty-five years the University's dependence on Chicago students increased rather than decreased: by the later 1930s, almost 70 percent of first-year College students came from the Chicago metropolitan area, with only 5 percent from the rest of Illinois and 25 percent from the rest of the country.[286] Until the 1950s, therefore, an early prediction of William Rainey Harper about the University's undergraduate-student admissions pool remained truer than ever: "After due discount, it is evident that the great work of the Colleges is being done in Chicago and Illinois, and that the institutions outside of Chicago have little to fear in the way of competition for undergraduate students."[287]

Given the predominance of Chicago-based students at the College and given the absence of attractive (and affordable) on-campus alternatives such as Ernest Burton wanted to build, it is not surprising that for decades a huge number of undergraduate students lived at home, with their parents or with other relatives, or in rooming houses in the neighborhood. In the autumn quarter of 1928, only 8.3 percent of undergraduates at Chicago lived in university residence halls. Of the remaining, 59 percent lived at home, and 18 percent lived in rooms or apartments in the neighborhood. In addition, 14.5 percent (all men) lived in fraternity houses.[288] The fact that almost 60 percent of the student body lived at home in 1928 paralleled the substantially local nature of the University's undergraduate admissions pool. Twelve years later, the statistics were strikingly similar: in the autumn quarter of 1940, over 60 percent of entering College students opted (or were compelled) to live at home.[289] Student motivations for living at home were doubtless complex, and not in all cases related to finances. H. A. Millis found in 1924 that of 662 undergraduate students who lived more than thirty minutes away from the University, two-thirds had a preference for living at home, but one-third reported that they would have preferred living on or near the University's campus had they been able to find affordable and inexpensive housing.[290]

In response to such conditions, Burton's plans for a new residential college continued to percolate during the regime of Max Mason. Frederic C. Woodward published a report in 1927 that called for a radical expansion of the residential system. "We must bring together the great majority of our students, graduate and undergraduate, in comfortable and attractive residence halls, with common rooms, dining-halls, recreation space, and headquarters for student organizations," he declared. "Until this is done it will be impossible to achieve the social solidarity and *esprit de corps* which are essential to the carrying out of a well-rounded educational program."[291] These remarks signaled a seriousness of purpose that was constant and deliberative. Woodward was sufficiently shrewd to couple his plea for housing reform with a parallel plea for more money to increase faculty salaries, thus anticipating head-on possible objections that he seemed more interested in investing in students than in faculty, but Woodward's remarks on student housing would soon prove to be the controversial part of his report.

Harold H. Swift shared Woodward's commitment, and in August 1927 he seized the initiative by writing to fellow trustee Julius Rosenwald: "Many of us believe that the University of Chicago is destined to be the great University of America. If this is accomplished, it depends on three things—money for salaries, wise leadership, and coordinating of the student body, both graduate and undergraduate, which means extensive dormitories."[292] Rosenwald asked Swift for a more detailed proposal and, with the agreement of Max Mason and Frederic Woodward, Swift commissioned a prominent Philadelphia architect, Charles Z. Klauder, to begin work on a south campus plan.[293]

Klauder had a distinguished reputation in collegiate architecture, having designed residence halls at Princeton, Cornell, and Pennsylvania. In October 1927, Klauder submitted to Swift a set of drawings and a plan that imagined a new south campus designed in French Gothic Style on the site between Ellis and University Avenues and Sixtieth and Sixty-First Streets (eliminating Greenwood Avenue) and consisting of a three-hundred-foot tower, a central office and classroom building with one hundred rooms, a library with 44,000 square feet of space, and a series of residence halls surrounding the tower—those on the eastern side of the block for women and those on the west for men. Klauder proposed that the University accommodate two thousand students on the south campus. Klauder also explicitly modeled the size and layout of the quadrangles he proposed on the Harkness Quadrangle at Yale. Klauder estimated the cost of his proposal at $12.5 million.[294]

Klauder's initial plans were scaled back over the next year to focus on dormitories and not an office and classroom building and library.[295] Max Mason's resignation as president in the spring of 1928 delayed a final decision. But with the bold support of Woodward, who, as acting president of the University, was willing to stand up to the bullying of the College haters like Dodd and Laing, Swift continued his lobbying campaign. In

May 1928 Swift urged Rosenwald to agree to support the plan, not only because "it would be a feather in Mr. Woodward's cap" but also because "it would greatly reassure the public to have them know that the University does not stop even if there is no incumbent in the President's chair."[296]

The maneuvering of Swift and Woodward paid off by the autumn of 1928, when Woodward announced that the board of trustees had approved a plan that deferred the idea of an office and classroom building and library but committed up to $5 million to the development of new residence halls for men and for women, which would eventually accommodate about 1,400 undergraduate students on the south side of the Midway.[297] At some point in the deliberations the board decided to change architects, dropping Klauder and hiring instead another Philadelphia-based firm— Zantzinger, Borie, and Medary. Julius Rosenwald agreed to provide up to $2 million of the needed funds, with the University investing $3 million from its endowment reserves to cover the balance.[298]

The first and only building built under the Woodward plan was Burton-Judson Courts, which opened in the autumn quarter of 1931. Designed with Harvard and Yale models explicitly in mind, this hall offered a high-quality, well-constructed home to 390 men. On June 24, 1930, the trustees had approved preliminary drawings for the women's residence hall, to be located next to the men's hall, and authorized the architects to proceed with working plans. The hope was to have the women's hall open by December 1, 1931, but on July 9, 1931, the trustees voted to defer construction of the women's hall for a period of one year, setting a new completion date of October 1, 1933.[299] This delay was fatal, given the ravages of the Depression; in July 1933, the University settled its accounts with the architects and engineers for their preliminary work (a sum of $109,488).[300] The plan for a women's residence hall on the south campus was dead, and with its demise went any possibility of additional investments in undergraduate housing. Burton's "dream of the Colleges" was abandoned, and the campus remained heavily commuter in nature.

The fact that so many of the undergraduate students were commuter students, and transfer students at that, living at home and in many cases preoccupied with part-time or even full-time work, defined the scope of student activities on the campus before and immediately after World War I. Many activities were informal and based on small-group voluntary associations subject to the vagaries of student-based leadership.[301] Moreover, the University had a benevolently hands-off attitude toward student life. One frustrated campus activist commented in 1937, "While it is true that student activities have been granted a liberal amount of freedom by the administration, it also holds true that there has been little encouragement.... So wary is the administration of coddling paternalism toward student activities that there has never been a positive statement (in the knowledge of at least two faculty members concerned) on just what if any value they have."[302]

The arts provided a good example of this microlevel voluntarism. The practice of the arts focused mainly on small amateur productions and on institutions like the University choir and band, which existed to perform at University religious and athletic events. Blackfriars was an early example of a student theater group; created in 1904 by fourteen students as an order of imaginary friars, it offered productions of cleverly written spoofs by local students and faculty every year until 1941 (except 1918), often focusing on local issues or contemporary concerns of students. The early members developed a camaraderie and folksy self-assurance that became part of alumni memories. Many of the early leaders went on to highly successful professional careers, some in the arts, and others in business, law, and medicine.[303] Most of the Blackfriars productions were comic operas with musical numbers interposed with humorous dialogue. Titles varied from "The King's Kalender Keeper" in 1905 to "The Lyrical Liar" in 1909 to "Pranks of Paprika" in 1913. Blackfriars was supported by private contributions from (mainly) senior faculty and staff, ticket sales, and advertising revenue. A list of its patrons from the 1930s included many members of the board of trustees and prominent senior professors. At first Blackfriars was organized only by students, but after 1918 professionals were hired to direct and stage the shows, and to provide musical accompaniment, while students continued to be the primary actors. A few other arts-related student groups also came together. A student-dominated University band had existed from Harper's era. Women students organized an annual dance and music revue called the Mirror Revue, run by the Mirror Board, and the Tower Players, also operating under the aegis of the University of Chicago Dramatic Association, staged one dramatic work each year beginning in the 1920s until World War II.[304]

The most prominent exceptions to this culture of small-group voluntarism were Greek life and mass athletics. In contrast to the current University, where Greek life plays only a modest role in the student culture, before 1940 it was quite prominent, and largely because fraternities functioned as a kind of ersatz housing system for a university that had such poor residential facilities. Indeed, for many years before 1945 more men lived in fraternity houses than lived in undergraduate residence halls. A parallel organization of women's clubs monopolized social life among many women, but lacked housing resources.[305]

In both cases the result by the late 1920s was a balkanized campus culture divided between an influential minority of students who belonged to private organizations, and the majority who were not.[306] A prominent professor of English and faculty adviser to many women's groups, Edith Foster Flint, complained in 1929 that the fraternities and women's clubs were having a deleterious impact on the creation of a unified student culture: they had become a "solid obstacle" to campus cohesion, such that "when the point has been reached at which it becomes necessary to discriminate between University and secret organization, they put club or fraternity first." Flint was especially critical of the fraternities, accusing them of "records of financial irresponsibility" that Flint found "really appalling."[307] Similarly, Charlotte Montgomery Grey, a recent alumna who knew the campus culture well, reported that attendance at general campus dances and parties had fallen off significantly in the 1920s, as clubs and fraternities refused to engage in the public-service work of organizing them.[308] Harold Lasswell's research confirmed that social life on campus in the early 1920s was dominated by the older and wealthier fraternities and social clubs, whose members lived close to campus and "who monopolize[d] the strategic social positions on the campus." In contrast, students who lived at home were "cut off from participation in full campus life," a situation that many students who lived in rooms beyond walking distance of the Quadrangles also probably endured. In his survey of student time allocations from 1924, H. A. Millis found a minority of students "who are addicted to a 'social life'" on campus, with "a considerable percentage of the men and women participat[ing] little or not at all in college affairs." The general portrait that emerges from these studies is of a student culture bounded by two extremes: a minority of students with more financial resources living in fraternities or residence halls (or, for women, who joined the pledge-based social clubs) and dominating the campus social culture, set against another minority who had almost nothing to do with student life outside the classroom, and with the majority of students, most of them commuters, having occasional interactions in campus social events. Many students spent time commuting to and from home, all the while trying to balance their studies with the burden of work obligations, and had little time for campus student life.[309]

The gingerly attitude of the University toward the fraternities was starkly revealed when L. R. Steere, the business manager, proposed in March 1929 that all freshmen men be required to live in dormitories if they did not reside at home. Steere's position was supported by Dean of the College Chauncey Boucher, who believed that deferred pledging would be better for freshmen, both academically and culturally.[310] Vice President Frederic Woodward rejected Steere's proposal, however, noting that "to require freshmen to live in dormitories would immediately antagonize the fraternities and their alumni at a time when we are using every effort to increase the goodwill of everyone toward the undergraduate college."[311]

Privately, many faculty may have agreed with Max Mason, who once accused fraternities of being places of "intellectual poverty," but for the most part the University tolerated their foibles.[312]

As valuable as the fraternities may have been in their ability to provide a parallel system of on-campus housing and to foster campus-based friendship groupings, the impact of fraternity membership on the academic success of the students was a matter of concern to the faculty. As part of another survey of student housing conditions in 1926, College officials included a comparison of the academic performance of students living in fraternity houses with that of students living in rooming houses or at home. Of the 198 male students who pledged a fraternity in 1925–26, 36.9 percent failed to assemble a satisfactory academic record and were not in good standing at the end of the year. Within a parallel group of 213 men who did not pledge a fraternity, only 25.4 percent were found to have a deficient academic record. The authors of the report then examined psychological achievement test results for both groups, finding that the fraternity and nonfraternity men had relatively similar median test scores. They concluded that since the men were of equal ability, the greater failure rate of the fraternity men "was due to other factors, and may possibly be connected with the fact of fraternity membership."[313] The University of Chicago Survey Project undertaken by Floyd Reeves, John Dale Russell, and others during 1930–32 also investigated the relationships between housing and student academic achievement more broadly, using two cohorts of freshmen students entering in 1929–30 and 1930–31. This survey found that students who were most likely to achieve high grades lived in University residence halls but were not members of a fraternity. The authors concluded, "The results indicate that, for men, the type of living environment associated with the highest average grade points for the Spring Quarter of the freshman year was residence in dormitories combined with the absence of fraternity connections."[314]

The situation with athletics moved in a parallel, but oddly occlusive direction. Edith Foster Flint wrote in 1929 that, in contrast to the state of affairs before 1914, athletics had become a mass spectator sport on the campus that involved both students and strangers: "In the old days—really old days—the football crowd was a college crowd.... Now with the huge stadium and the swollen popular interest in the game this has changed."[315] Yet it was precisely the fact that football had become a culture of mass spectacle that may have made athletics an even more powerful stream of student-identity formation during the interwar period. Mass athletic spectacles became an easy way for students, especially commuters, to achieve emotional identification with the school without having to involve themselves in the actual workings of student-life organizations.

The University of Chicago may have profited from its cultural spectacles, but this would prove to be a short-lived adventure. The increasingly pathetic record of the football team in the late 1920s—during the 1928 season, Chicago lost to South Carolina, Iowa, Minnesota, Purdue, Pennsylvania, Wisconsin, and Illinois—caused a minority of highly vocal alumni to rally to demand more investments, but their pleas fell on deaf ears. The logic of the University's cultural and educational values during the 1930s would move in a very different direction, and Robert Hutchins closed the sport down in 1939.

The ambient student culture symbolized by intensive Greek life on the one hand and big-time athletics on the other would change radically in the decades after 1940, as the University abandoned its attempts to sustain semiprofessional athletic operations with high-profile, citywide visibility, and as the numbers of fraternities and women's clubs significantly dwindled over the course of the 1950s. These shifts, like the curricular revolution of the 1930s and 1940s, would have a profound impact on the academic milieu of the University of Chicago in the second half of the twentieth century.

* 4 *

One Man's Revolution:
Robert Maynard Hutchins,
1929–1951

Opening Moves

Robert Hutchins was born on January 17, 1899, in Brooklyn, New York. His father, William J. Hutchins, attended Yale and the Union Theological Seminary, and after serving as a Presbyterian minister in Brooklyn and a professor of homiletics at Oberlin, became president of Berea College in Kentucky in 1920. William Hutchins was the first in the family to establish a personal connection to the University of Chicago: while at Yale, he took classes from William Rainey Harper. Robert Hutchins grew up in an enlightened, Protestant (Presbyterian) evangelical home that encouraged "habits of work and a fundamental thirst for righteousness."[1] Hutchins attended Oberlin College (1915–17) and enlisted in 1917 in the ambulance service of the US Army, serving in Italy during the last stages of World War I. He then transferred to Yale College in 1919, receiving his BA in 1921. After college Hutchins taught history and English for eighteen months at the Lake Placid (now the Northwood) School in Lake Placid, New York, a last-chance institution for wayward boys of wealthy families who had failed at other high schools.

While at Yale, Hutchins had made a name for himself as class orator and bright young man about campus, and in October 1922 the president of Yale, James Angell, recruited him to be secretary of the Yale Corporation. The position was a high-level administrative clerkship responsible for the official correspondence of the corporation and also included extensive public relations duties (he was charged with "keeping the University in right relations with the alumni and the press").[2] Well positioned to observe the inner workings of university decision making, Hutchins took to the job and developed a warm working relationship with Angell (he described his job for Angell as being "the leading University whooper-up and ballyhoo man in America").[3] Angell even allowed him to study part-time for his law degree while working as secretary, and Hutchins received his LLB in 1925. Hutchins was soon appointed a part-time lecturer in the Law School, teaching courses on trade regulation and public service law.[4] He became interested in the role that psychological theory and empirical testing might play in illuminating thorny issues of evidence and proof in courtroom trials, and began a collaboration with a young psychologist interested in criminology at Yale, Donald Slesinger, that resulted in a series of six articles on psychology and the law of evidence between 1928 and 1929.[5] In February 1927 Hutchins was named acting dean of Yale Law School to replace Thomas W. Swan, who had resigned to accept appointment as a US circuit court judge. Swan recommended Hutchins to Angell, citing the fact that "the practice of appointing an acting dean for a temporary emergency is a common one. Mr. Hutchins, though young, had had considerable experience in administrative work and the members of the Faculty have confidence in him. It would be difficult to secure unanimity on the part of the faculty in the selection of an older member."[6] Given the high level of factionalism within the law faculty, Hutchins claimed that his nomination meant only that "they dislike everyone else more than they do me," but he was enormously flattered and proceeded to lobby for new forms of instruction (small honors classes), new substantive courses on legal psychology and legal anthropology, higher admissions standards, and a curriculum restricted to graduates with baccalaureate degrees (as opposed to allowing Yale seniors to begin law school during the final year of college).[7]

A majority of his colleagues thought well enough of Hutchins's provisional efforts that in late December Angell named him the permanent dean at the age of twenty-eight.[8] Hutchins proved to be an adept, if highly opinionated, dean, an *enfant terrible* of jurisprudence. His interest in integrating medical, social, and behavioral sciences in the rules of evidence and procedure and his alliance with the legal realist faction of Yale Law School against the more conservative colleagues who relied on tried-and-true casebook methods marked him as a legal reformer committed to new scientific perspectives in modern jurisprudence, even if his own ideas had no immediate impact on the implementation of the rules of evidence.[9] Hutchins expanded the Law School faculty from fifteen to twenty-four (a sign of the wealth that was available to Yale in the mid- and later 1920s), recruiting William O. Douglas and Underhill Moore from Columbia. Given the prominence of Yale's alumni networks in elite worlds of the federal bar, big law firms, and commercial institutions in New York City, and the higher echelons of government service in Washington, DC, the Yale deanship was an ideal, if highly circumscribed, venue for Hutchins's considerable talents as a charismatic, witty speaker.[10] When he left Yale, his colleagues warmly commended his record, praising his "clear-sighted, bold and consistent" leadership.[11]

Starting with his appointment as secretary at Yale, it must have seemed that every door stood wide open for him. Hutchins's circumstances bolstered his resolve and self-confidence, but they did not teach him the virtues of strategic negotiation and watchful patience that he would need in Chicago to deal with a large, complex, and (from a faculty perspective) conservative institution, filled with entrenched departmental interests and distinguished senior faculty who were (among other things) proud, self-indulgent, and wary of change imposed from above. In such contexts smartness and cleverness (which the young Hutchins had in spades) counted for perhaps 20 percent of successful leadership, but the other 80 percent involved the strong and slow boring of hard boards that Max Weber talked about as defining the nature of politics.

THE YOUNG MAN FROM YALE BECOMES PRESIDENT

When Max Mason suddenly resigned in May 1928, Chicago needed a new president. As noted in chapter 3, the inside candidate was the acting president, Dean of the Faculties Frederic Woodward, who had the support of the majority of the faculty and who, in the spirit of Ernest Burton, favored strengthening the Colleges. Prominent senior faculty members, led by William Dodd, Gordon Laing, and Henry Gale, strongly opposed Woodward's candidacy, which served to muddy the waters in the eyes of key trustees like Harold Swift, Ernest Quantrell, and Charles Gilkey. Although Swift and his fellow trustees conducted the search proceedings collectively with the faculty committee, the fact that Dodd, Laing, and Hale mainly wanted Woodward stopped, as opposed to uniting on behalf of an alternative candidate, allowed the trustees to dominate the search process.[12] Visiting with possible candidates and soliciting expert opinion around the nation, trustee chairman Harold Swift played a supremely decisive role, and it is no exaggeration to say that he was the driving force behind the final decision. Having observed one presidency (Burton) that was brilliant but short-lived for health reasons, and a second, disappointing presidency (Mason) whose implosion left the faculty divided and demoralized, Swift was now determined to hire a president for the long haul, someone who would bring the energy of Burton but also re-create more of the foundational excitement of the early Harper era.

Gilkey and Swift admired Raymond Fosdick, the brilliant lawyer associated with the Rockefeller Foundation, and had Fosdick been willing to consider the job, the search might well have ended in the summer of 1928. As in 1922, Fosdick again said no, and the committee rumbled forward. A short list of five names had finally congealed by March 1929 (Lotus D. Coffman of the University of Minnesota, Ernest M. Hopkins of

Dartmouth, Harold Mouton of the Institute of Economics, Henry Suzzallo of the Carnegie Foundation, and Edmund E. Day of the Rockefeller Foundation), but none proved sufficiently compelling or exciting to Swift.[13] Hutchins's name had first emerged in the spring 1928 in a conversation between Trevor Arnett and Swift. Arnett feared that he might be "too much of a boy wonder," but when Swift met Hutchins personally in December 1928 he was impressed with his "attractive personality." Still, given Hutchins's extreme youth and Angell's discreetly ambivalent comments about him ("he is not yet seasoned enough yet; his enthusiasms and perspectives are not yet disciplined or matured by sufficient experience"), Hutchins's name was taken off the list.[14] He reemerged as a candidate in mid-March through the intervention of Edwin R. Embree, the head of the Julius Rosenwald Fund and a longtime supporter of Berea College, where William Hutchins was president. Embree urged Swift to reconsider Hutchins as someone who could restore an aura of innovation and change to Chicago: "We are in as great need today as we were a generation ago for educational leadership. This will require youth, imagination, and courage. Hutchins has these to a remarkable degree."[15]

At this point none of the other outside candidates excited Swift or the other trustees, and as often happens in such presidential searches, simple negative (and often petty and even snide) remarks by one or another committee members began to chip away at the credibility of the other names on the short list.[16] Well liked and respected, Fritz Woodward was still available, and if they had so desired, Swift and the trustees could have pushed his name through. A week before Embree's intervention for Hutchins, Swift seem poised to do just that: on March 8, he wrote to an alumnus who supported Woodward, "Without forecasting the result, I want to say that a great many people are thinking along the lines you indicate."[17] But the more Swift pondered the situation, the more convinced he became that Embree was right in advocating a new and young outsider, and he reaffirmed a plan that he had first outlined to Quantrell in January—namely, that Woodward should return to his previous status as vice president and dean of faculties. Charles Judd's views were also influential, and while Judd respected Woodward, acknowledged that "a large majority of the faculty" favored him for president, and found the stance of the College haters like Laing and Dodd irresponsible (their behavior was "the terror of the research rooters"), he lobbied Charles Gilkey to bring in an outsider. Gilkey reported to Swift that Judd thought faculty morale had weakened under Mason and "rapidly disintegrated" after he left office. Moreover, most of the "moral confidence" built up by Burton had vanished, Judd believed. "Only a strong man coming in with real prestige and experience enough to work very fast, preferably from outside so as not to be involved in our present factions (which are worse than for a long time) can pull us out the quicksand and down the highroad," he insisted.[18]

In early April, Swift cut bait and moved for Hutchins. Using his authority as president of the board, Swift pushed Hutchins's name back onto the short list and then brokered the assent of his fellow committee members to recommend him to the board, citing abbreviated, slightly ambiguous, but seemingly favorable endorsements from Raymond Fosdick and George Vincent. Hutchins visited Chicago twice in April, meeting with the search committee and with a majority of the trustees and favorably impressing them with his "clearheadedness," his educational ideas (according to Swift, he had "more ideas" than most of the other candidates), and his bravado, while reassuring them as to his "stability and sanity."[19] At the last moment, the strategy almost derailed when Swift asked Quantrell to contact Angell in mid-April for one final comment, and Angell responded on April 16 with a devastating critique of Hutchins's unreadiness for the job, warning Swift that Hutchins was "temperamentally rather impatient of men who disagree with him—and possibly a bit intolerant." Having worked closely with the Young Turk for six years, Angell averred that additional seasoning might well make Hutchins a plausible and successful candidate for president but that he was not yet prepared for the task.[20] At this point, having already achieved consensus within the search committee, Swift made the crucial decision to push ahead, ignoring Angell's warnings (which do not seem to have been shared with other members of the committee).[21] The only board member left uneasy was Thomas Donnelley, who continued to doubt Hutchins's readiness. But Hutchins's confident presence, his winsome personality, and his likely ability to "instill enthusiasm in the University and in the city" tipped the balance. Even the age issue receded as Swift stressed that Harper too had been a young president at thirty-five, the implication being that Hutchins at thirty was in fact a second coming of Harper, perhaps even better.[22]

Hutchins was inaugurated in November 1929, at the onset of the Great Depression. Hutchins remained at Chicago until 1951, the last six years with the title of chancellor. At a time when the University had few faculty interested in playing the role of a public intellectual in either Chicago or the nation at large, Robert Hutchins became the University's most prominent and versatile critic of higher education.[23] Hutchins presented his views on education and other public issues in a series of notable short books, including *No Friendly Voice* (1936), *The Higher Learning in America* (1936), and *Education for Freedom* (1943). These collections were conceived as speeches and lectures in the genre of intelligent, high-level populist rhetoric.[24] Hutchins came to Chicago with powerful rhetorical skills from his time at Yale, where he had developed a strong bent toward oratory, winning the DeForest Prize as a senior. Over the course of the 1930s Hutchins essentially turned himself into a national intellectual figure whose writings presented, in the words of one sympathetic Chicago trustee, a "pungent method of expression [that] is good reading."[25] The early essays and speeches led logically to the crusade of the Great Books in the 1940s and 1950s. Hutchins's speeches were carefully crafted, but delivered extemporaneously. Many were given from the high pulpit of Rockefeller Chapel, a setting that resonates with the proposition that, like his father, Hutchins was at heart a preacher as well as an orator, if a secular one.

The Higher Learning in America, given as the Storrs Lectures at Yale in 1935, was Hutchins's most important attempt to diagnose and provide a cure for what he called the "information disease" afflicting higher education in America. His diagnosis centered on the claim that only in the universities does society have a hope of pursuing truth for its own sake. We ask universities to do this, but we also ask them to train their students for productive work beyond the academy. Hutchins argued that such vocationalism tends to drive out the pursuit of truth, substituting the gathering of useful information for genuine inquiry. With vocationalism removed, universities could devote themselves to the cultivation of the intellectual virtues for the sake of the pursuit of truth through direct study of mankind's greatest achievements. Hutchins seemed fixed on the university's responsibility to protect a discursive tradition of what Joe Schwab later called "ultimate goals," a culture of permanent moral values.[26] Hutchins's program was highly intellectualist because Hutchins presumed man to be a strictly rational being. He insisted on a highly intellectualist university because, he believed, that was what a university and only a university had the resources to be. This vision was driven by a conviction that the alternative was truly dangerous: a university without a guiding purpose, forever lobbied by commercial and specialized interests and forever neglecting the intellectual for the sake of the useful. Such a university might claim that it was devoted to learning and research, but Hutchins thought that in practice it would simply do the bidding of professions, corporations, and governments, sacrificing culture to the main chance.[27]

Hutchins would find the pace of institutional change at the University to be frustrating. A brash, if precocious, young lawyer with no knowledge of the central disciplines of the arts and sciences that had given Chicago its institutional gravitas and intellectual prominence from 1900 to 1930 and with no natural allies such as he had on the Yale law faculty, Hutchins came to Chicago aiming to offer a strikingly different leadership style than his patron James Angell at Yale, about whom he had little favorable to say.[28] Angell's motto for university presidents—"grow antennae, not horns"—was the exact opposite of Hutchins's management style. Some contemporaries saw such bravado as unmitigated arrogance, and not a few interpreted it as a compensatory tactic driven by Hutchins's personal insecurity in a university filled with distinguished scholarly professionals.[29] Inevitably, Hutchins's iconoclasm ran up against both inertia and outright resentment on the part of key senior faculty. As early as 1932 he protested to his father, "I am getting more and more irritated with academic stupidity, and fear that I shall bite somebody in the ankle before long. Perhaps this is better than an attitude of resignation and adjustment."[30] By 1938 Hutchins was complaining that the university faculty were "notoriously hostile to change," operating on a "ward basis" and privileging particularistic divisional and departmental interests.[31]

The patterns of quixotic, lashing-forward leadership that Hutchins had first demonstrated at Yale continued at Chicago. John Schlegel's reflections on Hutchins's behavior in New Haven are relevant for Chicago as well:

> At times, as in curriculum reform toward which he made three starts in little over a year, the style could verge on a kind of educational guerrilla warfare. Then, movement, keeping the enemy—old, tired ways of thinking and teaching—off balance, became more important than the careful planning that may be essential to any success at the endeavor.... The style carried with it the risk that those left behind to work out the details would find that the pieces of Hutchins' abandoned projects made up something no one would have wanted in the first place.[32]

THE REORGANIZATION OF THE UNIVERSITY IN 1930–1931

Robert Hutchins faced enormous challenges in the fall of 1929, which are intelligible only if one remembers that he came to Chicago wanting both to make a name for himself and to improve the University's fortunes and prestige but immediately ran into the brick wall of the Great Depression. Given that most of his regime took place in the Depression and the Second World War, Hutchins, unlike Harper and Burton, never had the opportunity to fashion a comprehensive strategic plan for the future of the University. Charles Judd and others had fretted about faculty factionalism at the University in January 1929. With Chicago still flush with cash, Judd was convinced that "our greatest need just now is for an educational leader rather than a money-raiser, and the faculty com[mittee] are all wrong in seeking the latter first."[33] But as the national drama of October 1929 began to play out, such concerns quickly paled into insignificance. By 1931 the University desperately needed money raisers of all kinds. As for educational leadership, Hutchins brought this in spades, but like many anxious search committees intent on fighting yesterday's wars, the men who chose Hutchins completely underestimated their candidate's capacity for sweeping and unpredictable change.

The earliest and most notable of Hutchins's accomplishments was to reorganize the administrative and budgetary structures of the University of Chicago. Essentially, Hutchins gave the University a new constitution, which has had powerful repercussions for the intellectual work of the institution down to the present day. On November 13, 1930, the board of trustees voted to create the four graduate divisions and the College as new faculties, the changes to go into effect immediately. Among peer institutions in American higher education, this five-headed structure— which deliberately avoided a central nexus of curricular authority and administrative power that is usually lodged in the office of a dean of the arts and sciences—remained uncommon. The University has routinely celebrated the virtues of this confederated system, but it has also given rise to many bottlenecks and frictions over the decades.

The story of Hutchins's reorganization of 1930–31 is a drama involving money, prestige, and research prowess, combined with a quest for scientific efficiency and intellectual innovation. Unlike other interventions that Hutchins later pursued, it drew on strong institutional and faculty groundwork from the 1920s that gave it a solidity and plausibility that helped it endure. In the first decades after the University was refounded in 1890, the institution's administrative organization reflected the autocratic propensities of William Rainey Harper and his urgent focus on recruiting top-ranked scholars who would, in turn, establish distinguished scholarly departments.[34] For academic purposes the faculty and students of the arts and sciences were grouped into several complementary units—three undergraduate colleges of (respectively) arts, literature, and science, and two graduate schools, the Graduate School of Arts and Literature and the Ogden School of Science.[35] The regular faculty members of each department in the arts and sciences were simultaneously assigned to the Colleges and to one of the graduate schools. After 1920 the various curricular constituencies of the Colleges were united under a single dean, whose formal title was Dean of the Colleges of Arts, Literature, and Science, parallel to the governance structure of the two graduate schools, which were also directed by a dean. These executive officers supervised the academic affairs of their respective student bodies and did not focus on faculty matters. Under Harper's administration the core administrative unit of the new University was the department, and the early departments were ruled by "heads" who until 1910 were virtual petty presidents in their own right. Even after department heads were replaced with more democratically selected chairs, real financial and political authority relating to the hiring, retention, and promotion of faculty remained a subject of direct negotiations between the individual departments and the Office of the President.[36] At the same time faculty had little input in general budget planning or institutional priority setting: when Rockefeller's final gift arrived in late 1910, Judson agreed to consult with the Committee on Development and Relations consisting of twelve faculty members to review possible allocations of the money, but the faculty were unable to agree on priorities, and neither Judson nor the trustees took such intramural faculty interventions seriously.[37]

The University was administratively both top and bottom heavy, with few intermediary structures of financial or budgetary mediation and control in between. Each expense—large or small—had to be approved by the president's office, via an administrative Committee on Expenditures, the work of which was superintended by a young graduate of the Colleges, Trevor Arnett, who served as auditor of the University from 1902 until 1920.[38] Arnett proved so capable at his task of managing the University's accounting systems that he soon began to consult with other colleges and universities about ways to improve higher education finance, gaining a national reputation in this field.

Hutchins was to discover that as the University had grown and as the number of students and faculty increased, this dual system of extremely centralized financial control and extremely decentralized personnel decision making had become very unwieldy. Initial proposals for a new administration building as a "flagship" for the University, first put forward in 1925 (but only built in 1946), reflected the fact that the administrative apparatus necessary to govern a large university, whose assets had increased from $17 million in 1900 to more than $100 million in 1926, had grown significantly since Harper's times.[39] Max Mason had been unable to find the money to create this new administrative center, but the fragmented budgetary and administrative systems of the University did become the subjects of considerable scrutiny in the 1920s.

The agent of this scrutiny was Harper's former auditor, Trevor Arnett. Arnett had resigned from the University in 1920 to become the secretary of the General Education Board, having been asked by Wallace Buttrick and Abraham Flexner to superintend the $50 million that John D. Rockefeller gave in December 1919 to help American colleges and universities improve teachers' salaries. While at the GEB Arnett solidified his national reputation by publishing *College and University Finance* (1922), thousands of copies of which were distributed gratis by the GEB. Upon Judson's resignation as president in 1923, Ernest Burton persuaded Arnett to return to Chicago to become the chief financial officer of the University—his titles included both vice president and business manager, as well as part-time professor of educational administration.[40]

Arnett returned to a campus in 1924 that was caught up in several simultaneous transitions. Now responsible for the entire economy of the University, Arnett soon became convinced that his job bordered on the impossible. In January 1925 Arnett prepared a memorandum for the board of trustees describing his frustrations with the University's financial organization. He reported that "the University of Chicago has grown so rapidly, practically doubling its size every ten years, and has nearly doubled its expenditures in the past five years and is now setting as its goal the duplication of its resources in the next fifteen years.... I know of nothing more important than that it should immediately make an intensive study of its organization and functions."[41] He urged the board of trustees to add some additional support personnel to his office so that he would be free to conduct a systematic study of operations of the University.

To undertake his survey Arnett procured a grant of $25,000 from the General Education Board, part of a larger effort by the GEB to help colleges and universities come to terms with the problems of modern budgetary management.[42] The board approved Arnett's proposal with alacrity, but unfortunately Arnett's health was unsteady, and the unexpected death of Burton in May 1925 removed the primary attachment keeping Arnett at Chicago. He soon put out feelers about returning to Rockefeller's service, and in mid-1926 accepted reappointment to the staff of the GEB, of which he became president in 1928. Still, Arnett left Chicago with warm feelings about the University, which were to be critically important in the years to come.

Arnett's departure in mid-1926 eliminated the main advocate of a comprehensive survey of the University's financial practices. But Arnett's sometime sponsor and friend Charles Judd did not lose sight of the scheme, and Judd's ambitious plans for his own research empire helped keep the idea alive. Judd was one of the most influential figures in the history of the University between the two world wars, so much so that upon his death in 1946 a major building on the campus was named in his honor. Judd's forceful leadership as chair of the Department of Education between 1909 and 1938 shaped two generations of senior faculty appointments in education at Chicago. Judd was a leader of the generation of luminaries who put empirical social-science research relating to education on the national map—he was to the new science of education at Chicago what Charles Merriam was to the new science of politics.[43] Equally important, Judd's scholarly stature and extensive knowledge of the University impressed university leaders of all stripes, even one so self-possessed as the brash newcomer Hutchins. As Hutchins later admitted, Judd "played a great part in the reorganization of the University that went on in 1930 and 1931; the creation of the College and the Divisions, the establishment of the Board of Examinations and the Dean of Students' office, and the ultimate formation of the four-year college."[44]

In the fall of 1928 Judd was offered a well-endowed professorship at the Teachers College of Columbia University. To keep Judd at Chicago, Frederic Woodward, who had just become acting president, persuaded the board of trustees to agree to a substantial increase in the Department of Education's resources.[45] Not only did Judd want a new graduate education building (eventually built in 1931–32 with the support of the General Education Board, and renamed in his honor in 1948), more research assistants, better faculty salary support, and more discretionary research funds, but he also urged that Chicago expand the ranks of its education faculty to include specialists in the study of preschool children, study of abnormal children, study of college administration, study of general school administration, and study of higher mental processes.[46] Judd was not interested in teacher training (in contrast to his predecessor John Dewey), but rather thought that "the colleges of the University of Chicago and the general administrative organization of the University constitute a laboratory for the solution of the problems of higher education. If proper investigators were provided to make extended studies in the field of higher education, there can be no doubt that benefit would accrue to the University of Chicago and to all the colleges in this region."

Given Judd's friendship with Arnett and his own professional contacts at the GEB, it was natural that Judd decided that the time was ripe for his department to take over Arnett's comprehensive survey of the University. But Judd moved beyond Arnett's original concern with best business practices to clothe his survey in the regal garments of social scientific analysis and empirical investigation. Within weeks of turning Columbia down to remain at Chicago, Judd wrote again to Woodward about his vision, urging him to deploy his personal connections with Arnett to advance his broader plan.[47] To head the survey, Judd recommended Floyd W. Reeves, a 1925 Chicago PhD who had studied under Judd and who was currently a professor at the University of Kentucky, where he had participated in a number of school surveys. Later in the 1930s, Reeves gained a national reputation as an educational reformer and governmental adviser, but in 1929 he was a relative unknown.[48] Woodward was anxious to accommodate Judd, and after interviewing Reeves he quickly decided to support the plan.[49] With the appointment of Reeves, Arnett's earlier hope for a systematic study of the University of Chicago became possible, and on a level of ambition and professionalism that Arnett never anticipated. Arnett in turn not only sanctioned the use of the funds that the GEB had previously committed to the first, unexecuted survey in 1924, but he increased the total allocation by an additional $25,000.[50]

Scientific surveys of schools and colleges were much in vogue in the 1920s, reflecting a powerful belief in scientific management theories and their transferability from the world of business to the multiple worlds of education.[51] Between 1910 and 1933, no less than five hundred surveys were undertaken of US colleges and universities, and if one adds the surveys of public school systems on the primary and secondary levels, the number easily jumped to the thousands. The Department of Education at Chicago was unusually active in the school survey movement: the University's quarter system enhanced the flexibility of faculty members to do this kind of educational consulting, and this kind of work was highly lucrative.[52]

Floyd Reeves joined the faculty of Chicago in the fall of 1929. Hiring a staff of talented collaborators that included John Dale Russell and George A. Works, Reeves soon expanded the original plan by commissioning book-length studies of the university library, student admissions and retention, faculty recruitment and teaching patterns, the university press, university extension services, class size and university costs, and other areas.[53] Published in twelve volumes in 1933 and encompassing 3,157 pages, the Chicago survey was perhaps the single most ambitious undertaking of its kind before World War II.[54] Assisting Reeves in the effort was Colonel Leonard Ayres, who was one of the leaders of a broad and powerful movement to bring efficiency to American schools via the application of scientific management principles.[55] Trained as a statistician, Ayres first made a name for himself with his book *Laggards in Our Schools* (1909), which portrayed the school as a cultural institution to which commercial management principles should be applied to maximize efficiency. Walter Eells described him in 1937 as "one of the pioneers both in the social survey movement and in the educational survey movement."[56]

Commissioned to undertake a study of the problems that Arnett had identified several years earlier, Ayres visited the campus on several occasions in the winter and early spring of 1930.[57] He then prepared a long memorandum for Reeves that outlined what he had encountered, and suggested a few simple solutions. Reviewing the knotty fiscal jurisdictions that had perplexed Arnett, Ayres found serious inadequacies. First, the University's budgetary structure reflected an earlier and simpler time, since the annual budget was not based on definite appropriations specifically earmarked for each unit, but rather consisted of a series of provisional estimates, expenditures against which had to be requisitioned from the central Committee on Expenditures. In effect, this meant that department chairs had no accurate sense of the amount of money they had available to spend each year, and, in turn, the University had no way to hold them accountable to stay within an allocated budget. Second, too many units reported directly to the president, overwhelming the central administration with routine transactions based on "an enormous volume of petty detail." Moreover, because the existing system was overwhelmed by the volume of transactions, some units had made "reciprocal accords" with the Committee on Expenditures that gave them virtually blanket authority to make expenditures, thus moving from one extreme—extreme centralism—to another—extreme decentralism. Nor was the way in which the annual budget of the University prepared any more satisfactory. Because the budget was based on fragmentary negotiations between the president's office and seventy-odd units, it put a "tremendous burden of budget preparation" on central authorities, who could not make appropriate and timely choices about the possible academic options and opportunities implied in these transactions.

Ayres urged that the University abandon its budget of provisional estimates, instead providing the chair of each unit with a definite appropriation. Not only would such a system be more efficient, but it would also give all units "equality of freedom and maximum freedom, within the limits of their budget appropriations, and . . . hold them all rigorously within those limits save as unforeseeable new developments within the year might render revisions necessary." Ayres's most crucial recommendation involved the University's basic administrative structure. Rejecting the ponderous process under which so many units reported directly to the president's office, Ayres recommended that the departmental budgets across the arts and sciences be coordinated by a handful of senior administrative officers who would report to the president's office.[58]

Upon receiving Ayres's memo in early May 1930, Reeves forwarded it to Harold Swift and to Robert Hutchins, who had become president of the University in July 1929. Within a month, Hutchins responded to Ayres, reporting, "Since I know how busy you are and with how many important things, I am very deeply grateful for your kindness to us. I hope it will be some compensation to you to know that the principles of the report have been accepted by the officers of the University."[59] In a private letter to Swift several months later, Hutchins pithily summarized what he saw as the main virtue of reform proposals: "We are too much organized for safety and not enough for action. I think we can get safety without so many checks and balances."[60]

Even before Ayres had filed his report, signs of changes were in the wind. As early as January 1930 Hutchins was discussing a possible restructuring of the University in personal interviews in New York City with both Trevor Arnett of the GEB and with Hutchins's predecessor, Max Mason.

In summary notes to Harold Swift, Hutchins reported that Arnett had "great enthusiasm" about the idea of "a quadruple division of the University above the junior college." Mason was even more candid: "He thought the deans at Chicago [were] the worst problem and applauded [the idea of creating] a dean of the junior college plus four divisional deans."[61] Although Hutchins was contemplating bold administrative and structural changes, it took an external report to force the issue and to lend public and official credibility—scientific credibility—to the move that Hutchins wished to embrace. Hutchins would recall several years later to Walter Eells that "the work of the survey staff largely contributed to the academic reorganization of 1930 which abolished almost all the existing categories and substituted a new administrative scheme for them."[62]

The idea of vertically segmented administrative units like the future divisions, as opposed to horizontal units like the then-existing schools and faculties, also fit well with emergent trends toward interdisciplinary work at Chicago, particularly in the social, physical, and biological sciences. The 1920s had seen remarkable expansion of research projects reflecting the general enthusiasm, financial prosperity, and self-confident professionalism that characterized the University and its faculty under the leadership of Ernest Burton. Burton explicitly sought to encourage senior faculty of various departments to learn more about the material needs and intellectual ambitions of their neighboring units as a way of mobilizing the faculty's support for his fund-raising campaign of 1924. These broader horizons had a discernible impact on the views of senior faculty.[63] The new interdisciplinarity was most pronounced in the social sciences, which gave rise to a series of new research projects. The scholars who were housed in the new Social Science Research Building that opened in December 1929 represented a set of departments that, in turn, constituted a natural and obvious grouping for the Division of the Social Sciences created in November 1930. Yet while the new building housed individual scholars and their research workshops and seminars, it did not (yet) house their departments as administrative entities.[64] The point was a fine but significant one, and it suggested that new administrative entities beyond the traditional departments might not only be possible but also desirable as real scholarly, collegial, and intellectual collectives. That Robert Hutchins came to Chicago from Yale, where he was already predisposed to supporting interdisciplinary research and teaching, proved crucial to his thinking about the creation of the divisional research structure. In April 1929 Harold Swift had repeatedly cited Hutchins's collaboration with Milton G. Winternitz, the dean of Yale Medical School, in obtaining $4.5 million from the Rockefeller Foundation to create the new Institute of Human Relations at Yale—which made possible "close cooperation between many departments at his University"—as a major achievement that helped to qualify him for the Chicago job.[65]

The outcome of these tactical interventions and strategic opportunities—Ayres's proposal for a new administrative structure in May 1930; the success of key distinguished colleagues in the mid- and later 1920s in launching collaborative research enterprises that went beyond conventional departmental boundaries; and Boucher's urgent pleas for more curricular coherence above departmental parochialisms and for additional investments in undergraduate education—congealed into the master plan that Hutchins took to the University Senate on October 22, 1930, and that was subsequently approved by the board of trustees on November 13. Under Hutchins's plan, the arts and sciences were divided into five jurisdictional units led by faculty deans: four divisions that were "Ruling Bodies" licensed to recommend degrees and a College, also a Ruling Body," whose faculty was mandated "to do the work of general higher education at the University." Each of the existing departments was assigned to one of the four divisions, which were authorized to recommend candidates for baccalaureate as well as for graduate degrees, whereas the College, which became responsible for the first two years of undergraduate education, would draw on departmental faculty to staff its general-education courses, but do so as an autonomous faculty and curricular unit. Undergraduate students could not enter a division until they had fully met the curricular requirements of the College. By grouping the heretofore semisovereign departments under the leadership of a division, Hutchins hoped that genuine divisional cultures of research cooperation *and* interdisciplinary educational work would emerge. He also wanted the divisions to become curricular units for at least the upper level of undergraduate education (and possibly for some areas of graduate education as well), a realm of authority that would curb what Hutchins felt to be the parochialism and narrowness of the departments.[66] An equally vital impulse behind the reforms was the expectation that it would eliminate the many financial transactions, often on petty issues, between department chairs and the president's office, and force them to negotiate with their divisional deans for financial resources. Hutchins thought that this would result in strong rather than weak deans who would be able to bring departments into coherent regimes of resource allocation and common planning.

The outcome proved more complex, for the financial impact of the Great Depression on the University as a whole gave Hutchins more discretionary power than his predecessors had either claimed or tried to exercise. Moreover, Hutchins was not content with allowing the departmental faculties under the new decanal structures to make senior appointment decisions in a political vacuum. As Hutchins later recalled to George Dell,

"The standard view of departments is what I call without disrespect the Harvard attitude. You simply get the 'best' man. We weren't trying to be a collection of the 'best' men, we were trying to be a collection of the best people to do what we thought ought to be done, which is a different thing in some respects."[67] At the same time, Hutchins's efforts to mold the departmental cultures into higher-order educational unities within the divisions on the curricular front beyond the College's general-education courses went nowhere. Hutchins's appointment of Beardsley Ruml, the philanthropic patron of the new social sciences building and of its collaborative research spirit, as the first full-time dean of the Division of the Social Sciences in 1931 was an early signal of Hutchins's hopes to force serious educational as well as research-driven interdisciplinarities.[68] Yet Ruml came to dislike the foibles of academic administration and stubborn faculty, many of whom were uninterested in Hutchins's and his schemes for transdepartmental curricular reform. When Ruml tried to further such a goal by persuading the Department of History to appoint Charles Merriam, Frank Knight, and John U. Nef to its faculty, the department rejected the idea out of hand.[69] Ruml later recalled, "We wanted to achieve unity in the several disciplines including the social science field. But I had trouble with a handful of distinguished professors, and after three years of effort, my progress was microscopic. Those professors wouldn't work together. They wouldn't even play together."[70] Ruml resigned from the University in February 1934 to become the treasurer of Macy's Department Store in New York City.[71] Ruml's successor, Robert Redfield, had no greater luck. When Redfield tried to persuade the various departmental faculties to create a set of new interdisciplinary courses for upper-level undergraduates, he encountered stubborn resistance. He wrote ruefully to Hutchins in 1936 that "the stirrings as to curriculum in this Division are nothing to shout about. The mountain labored and brought forth a few grasshoppers."[72]

The ironic result was that the 1930s and early 1940s became as much a "presidential regime" as a confederate decanal regime, especially in the selection of senior appointments and approval of promotions to tenure. A number of scholars have commented on Hutchins's seeming distrust of empirical social science and the negative impact of this animus on the fate of several departments in the 1930s and 1940s. But this could cut both ways, and in the case of the young Subrahmanyan Chandrasekhar, whose appointment to the faculty of the physical sciences was held up in 1936 by a recalcitrant dean, Henry Gale, for racist reasons, Hutchins's willingness to override divisional deans was a happy outcome of his readiness to act imperiously.[73] The era of deep financial stringency after 1931 enhanced Hutchins's opportunities for ruthlessness, since it gave him many circumstantial opportunities to work around the resistance of faculties whom he already thought were "notoriously hostile to change." As Hutchins would insist in 1937, "Clearly the President's Office is the only place from which the University may be seen as a whole. If the same standards are to prevail throughout the institution they must be applied from that office."[74] Hutchins's own leadership team made such imperiousness all the more probable: when Hutchins took over in 1929 he asked Frederic Woodward to stay on as vice president, but Woodward's heart was no longer in the job, and many of his duties were taken up by Emery T. Filbey, a conscientious, intelligent administrator who was neither a scholar in his own right nor a person capable of standing up to Hutchins's commanding personality. Ironically, as David Riesman shrewdly observed, Hutchins became the same kind of publicly charming but autocratic leader that Harper had been, an imperial president who would have encountered the displeasure of Hutchins's distant alter ego, Thorstein Veblen.[75] The 1931 reorganization was a powerful exercise in presidential authority. It would not be Hutchins's last attempt to play institutional revolutionary.

THE COLLEGE AND THE NEW PLAN

Another front of interdisciplinarity emerged on the heels of the new constitutional structure: the creation of a single undergraduate College as a separate faculty with a uniform curriculum, in place of the topical / area colleges that Harper had installed. The University that Hutchins took over in the summer of 1929 was deeply conflicted over the future of the Colleges, and if this was a challenge, it was also a huge opportunity for the young president to make his own mark and to do so quickly. Immediately after Hutchins was appointed, Chauncey Boucher wrote two back-to-back letters to him, duly praising his appointment but also lobbying Hutchins about his (Boucher's) plans.[76] Boucher proved an able advocate, and Hutchins slowly came to embrace the basic substance of Boucher's plan. Even before he officially took office, Hutchins had written to Swift, arguing that "we must do something about undergraduate education" and asking Swift to investigate how much additional money would be required to implement Boucher's plans, in the hopes that this might be put before the General Education Board for support.[77] At first, Hutchins considered other options, such as creating a dual-track program under which departments would offer honors classes for students most interested in their subjects, along with parallel classes for students who had merely passing interests, both spanning the then-existing Junior and Senior Colleges. As we will see, this plan paralleled an equally bold proposal to reform graduate education that Hutchins put before the deans of the graduate schools in December 1929, in which he suggested that the existing PhD degree be reserved for graduate students who would go on to teaching careers and that a new degree be fashioned for those who wished to become "productive scholars."

An exact chronology of what happened between January and September 1930 is difficult to reconstruct based on the surviving sources, but it seems likely that after wide consultation with Reeves, Judd, Boucher, Swift, and others, Hutchins realized that the new organizational plan suggested by Ayres could be used to create an independent organizational and jurisdictional space to solve the College problem as well. Judd's role in the final decisions—to which Hutchins later alluded—is plausible by virtue of the fact that, unlike Dodd and Merriam, Judd was a distinguished scholar of educational theory who was on record as favoring both the retention of the first two years of college work on campus *and* strengthening the research resources of the University. The final structure also followed from Hutchins's own conviction—to which he was nudged by Boucher—that general education needed special and different kinds of organizational controls and that the divisions would be best left with the custody of "specialized" knowledge. He asserted in 1931 that "the more we considered the matter in the light of the University's history and of the needs of American education, the more we were convinced that a sharp break should be made at the end of Sophomore year. The problems of general education and the problems of specialization seemed to us different, requiring different attention and separate organization."[78] Several of Hutchins's public speeches at other colleges in the spring of 1930 suggested that he was well on his way to adopting Boucher's ideas, but with a public flair that the sober dean could not match. At a conference in Ohio in April 1930 Hutchins defended the idea of a junior college as a necessary and permanent part of a research university, and insisted that all that was needed was "an intelligent faculty, a flexible course of study, and a system of general examinations for which the student may present himself when in his opinion he is ready for them. This means, of course, the abolition of credits, grades and attendance records, and the substitution for them of an intimate knowledge of the individual and an enlightened program of examinations."[79]

The implementation of Boucher's ideas thus took place coterminously with Hutchins's decision to restructure the governance of the arts and sciences. Boucher was no longer dean of the Colleges, but dean of the College, and it was this new "College," created with the explicit mission of "doing the work of general education in the University," that became the operational site of the new curriculum. The final revisions to Boucher's plan took place in January and February 1931, during weeks of intense debate as to what curricular elements would be presented to the faculty for a formal vote in early March.[80] Mortimer Adler reported, "The place is still bubbling. The volcanic quality is still discernible in the many round table discussions at the [Quadrangle] Club. On all sides you hear discussion of 'the plan', or 'a plan', or 'our plan' or 'their plan'."[81] From Adler's reports, it is clear that colleagues from the Department of Education and the Department of Psychology, particularly George Works and Louis Thurstone, played major roles in the behind-the-scenes politicking to push through the new general-education curriculum, which helps explain the prominence of the role of those departments in the College over the next twenty years.

The results of the final negotiations were a victory for Boucher and his fellow revolutionaries. The new curriculum put into effect in the fall of 1931, called the "New Plan," created a powerful curricular expanse not controlled by the departments, based on five yearlong common courses (biological sciences, English composition, humanities, physical sciences, and social sciences) to be taken by all students and subject to end-of-the-year examinations that were not designed by or graded by the faculty members who taught the courses. In addition, students were required to take at least two more specialized courses in the same knowledge areas represented by the general-education survey courses, thus creating pathways to their later specializations in the last two years of college.[82] The New Plan called for students in the first two years to be registered in the College. Upon completing all of their general-education requirements, they would choose and register in a division for the final two years of collegiate study. The divisions thus became the sites for undergraduate teaching in the junior and senior years, and until 1942 baccalaureate degrees were awarded by the divisions, not the College. For the first twelve years of the New Plan, most faculty teaching in the general-education courses had regular departmental appointments, and it was not until after 1942 that the College began to accumulate a separate body of faculty who had no connections with the departments.

Along with the new interdisciplinary general-education courses came a new system of grading, testing, and credit allocation that was significant in the history of learning assessment in the United States. Henceforth, students would not receive quarterly course grades, and courses themselves ceased to count for the graduation requirement. Instead, each student would be obligated to sit for a six-hour "comprehensive" examination that would test his or her knowledge of the fields covered in the survey courses. These examinations would be developed by the Board of Examinations, a set of full-time professionals who would attend the lectures given by the faculty in the survey courses and develop sets of questions for the exams, working in consultation with faculty teaching the courses. The board was headed by a new university examiner and given statutory force when the university statutes were revised to give it an official, university-wide legal status. Nor were the comprehensives restricted to the first two years, for the New Plan called for senior College students to sit for two additional comprehensives, one in his or her major field of specialization and a second reflecting the study of a related field or knowledge of a cluster of introductory departmental courses. A crucial feature of the New Plan was that class attendance was made voluntary. Students could attend the lectures and discussion sessions, but they could also study the syllabus and its recommended readings by themselves on their own time and take the six-hour examination whenever they felt sufficiently prepared.

Boucher thought that the comprehensive system and the new freedom given to students to pace themselves through the curriculum would accomplish several crucial objectives. First, he wanted to make students more responsible, more autonomous, and more flexible, and facing such year-end comprehensive examinations would impose, he believed, discipline, orderliness, and seriousness on the behavior of undergraduate students that was heretofore lacking in American higher education. Second, the comprehensives and the new yearlong survey courses would create patterns of intellectual coherence instead of the jumble of random course credits, which Boucher derisively called the "book-keeping" mentality that had dominated colleges. Boucher averred, "I sometimes think that it is a cause for wonder that a respectable number of students do achieve as much as they do and develop their powers as far as they do, in spite of the obstacles and positive inducements to do otherwise which are inherent in our present system in which book-keeping in terms of numerous small course units is the only common denominator."[83] The new comprehensive examinations were, in Boucher's mind, absolutely critical to the logic of the New Plan, and great care would need to be taken in designing them.[84] As Richard Shavelson has recently observed, Boucher's comprehensive examinations "tested for a much broader range of knowledge and abilities: the use of knowledge in a variety of unfamiliar situations; the ability to apply principles to explain phenomenon; and the ability to predict outcomes, determine courses of action, and interpret works of art."[85]

The leader of the Board of Examinations from 1931 to 1938 was Louis L. Thurstone of the Department of Psychology. If Boucher conceived the idea of comprehensive exams, in the critical work of implementation he was guided by Thurstone. The new board began as a modest affair, and in its initial staffing drew heavily on younger men who were either graduate students or postdocs from the Department of Education and the Department of Psychology. Thurstone also began to develop research protocols based on the huge amount of data that the new examination system generated about student performance.[86]

After securing the approval of the new curriculum by a 65–24 vote at a general meeting of the faculty of the College on March 5, 1931, and after conferring with the newly appointed divisional deans and with key department chairs, Chauncey Boucher organized planning groups to create the new survey courses. The groups worked quickly and assembled necessary course materials. Each course produced a detailed syllabus, which included a prose outline of the major arguments and material of the course together with detailed bibliographical citations for further reading. Boucher also held several meetings for staff leaders in the spring of 1931 to work out logistical and scheduling issues. A unified curriculum slowly emerged.

In the natural sciences Boucher had the advantage of being able to drawn on a group of men who had already participated in "The Nature of the World and of Man" course that was launched in 1924. The world of the natural sciences at Chicago in the late 1920s was filled with ambitious scholars, led by luminaries like Frank R. Lillie and Anton J. Carlson, who were optimistic about the progress of their disciplines and certain that the research-based findings of modern biological science could be made appealing to a general undergraduate audience. The primary architect of the biology course was Merle C. Coulter of the Department of Botany. Coulter was the son of John M. Coulter, the founder of modern botany at Chicago, with whom the younger Coulter had collaborated in writing a book defending modern evolutionary theories in 1926.[87] In 1930 he was an associate professor of botany, a man of considerable diplomatic skill, and an inspiring teacher. The opportunity to design the general biology course enabled him to pull together a group of distinguished scholar-teachers to create a panoramic view of the biological sciences, based on the latest scientific research of the later 1920s, and thus make a significant professional contribution at the University.

Coulter's course was intended to cultivate "the scientific attitude of mind" among students by exposing them to various examples of the application of the scientific method, to provide a level of basic knowledge of biology as would be needed by "a modern citizen," and to encourage among students an interest in "the grand machinery of the organic world and in the major concepts of biology." The course was divided into four major parts: a survey of the plant and animal kingdoms; an analysis of the dynamics of living organisms, including physiology and psychology; studies in evolution, heredity, and eugenics; and the adaptation of living organisms to their environment and to each other.[88] Coulter was assisted in his lectures by a team of younger biologists, several of whom would go on to distinguished scholarly careers in the Division of Biological Sciences. He also secured the cooperation of a number of other senior biologists, including A. J. Carlson, popularly known as Ajax, who became one of the most beloved general-education faculty teachers in the College before World War II.

The parallel course in the physical sciences was organized by the Chicago-trained physicist Harvey B. Lemon, a scholar of wide-ranging interests with a flair for the dramatic. Lemon was deeply committed to improving the teaching of physics, and from 1937 to 1939 served as the president of the American Association of Physics Teachers. Lemon was joined in the course by a distinguished chemist, Hermann Schlesinger, and other eminent scholars, thus giving young College students a chance to encounter prominent researchers from across the division.[89] The new course sought to integrate basic introductions to modern work in astronomy, physics, chemistry, and geology into one yearlong survey.

Both the biological sciences and the physical sciences general courses were organized in lecture/discussion format, having three lectures plus one discussion a week. Both courses styled themselves as "state of the art" in scholarly terms, and both profited from the confidence about the contributions of the natural sciences to the betterment of human life that was common in American research universities after World War I. The war had given American scientists powerful opportunities to demonstrate the practical impact of modern science, not only for human destruction but also for human regeneration and reconciliation. Harvey Lemon was confident that science was on the threshold of enormous changes that educated men and women must understand, if only to prevent the kind of misuse of science that had (to his mind) taken place between 1914 and 1918: "Clear heads and sober minds are needed, as never before, to watch lest the genie prove to be an evil one providing us with the weapons for our own destruction.... We must keep pace with science; and, taking the warning from the fate of [Henry] Moseley, prevent the repetition of another such orgy of destruction as that which recently was detonated by the monumental stupidity of our so-called civilization."[90]

If the two natural science survey courses emerged from curricular projects and current faculty research in the 1920s, the new general humanities course had a deeper institutional history. The main architect was an elderly history professor, Ferdinand Schevill, who had been recruited by Harper to join the faculty in 1892. Schevill was an amiable colleague and a brilliant teacher. He was a member of a remarkable social circle of young humanists in the later 1890s, including John Matthews Manly, Robert Herrick, Robert Lovett, and William Vaughn Moody, who met regularly to discuss their scholarly and literary work.[91]

The new humanities general-education survey was a collaborative effort, but Schevill provided its intellectual architecture.[92] When Schevill died in 1954, Norman Maclean remembered of the founding of the course in 1931 that "in the history of our university, this moment itself was a Renaissance and the atmosphere was charged with excitement, defiance, and promise of adventure." For Maclean, Schevill's humanism lay at the heart of the course, a humanism that was itself "a form of art. He was a historian of man's creative activity."[93]

Schevill, along with historian Arthur P. Scott and linguist Hayward Keniston, fashioned a course that exposed students to "the cultural history of mankind as a continuum and a whole."[94] Framing lectures provided key chronologies, but much of the course was devoted to the history of European ideas as represented by significant writers and thinkers. Students were expected to read substantial parts of classics like the *Iliad* and the *Odyssey*, the Bible, and works by Herodotus, Thucydides, Dante, Chaucer, Molière, Luther, Shakespeare, Voltaire, Rousseau, Goethe, Darwin, and Walt Whitman. The logic of the course was to convey the rich tapestry of the European cultural tradition, but a tradition that had experienced profound rupture between 1914 and 1918. The course dealt with the First World War and its aftermath in only two lectures, most certainly because Schevill himself was so disillusioned by it.[95] The course consisted of ninety lectures of fifty minutes each over three quarters, with one discussion session a week for twenty-five students. Schevill and Scott gave most of the lectures and recruited other luminaries from the humanities to speak on subjects close to their research competency. The lectures did not duplicate the reading assignments, but were meant as introductions to broad debates or as portraits of a *Weltanschauung* of a historical era, combining narrative social and political history with studies of novels and works of art. By the mid-1930s the course had settled into a pattern of assigning one notable work—a novel, a poem, or a piece of nonfiction—each week for discussion, thirty in all through the academic year. The course was replete with facts and dates, but also aimed to encourage analytic study skills and intellectual self-confidence among its students.[96] Much of this happened outside of class, in small groups run by young instructors such as James Cate and Norman Maclean.

The yearlong social sciences course for first-year students was organized by three young professors, each of whom represented a different discipline and had personal connections to the "real" world of social science praxis that already defined the agenda of university research in the 1930s. Economist Harry D. Gideonse served as the chair of the course; an acerbic, scrappy person, with an outgoing personality and quick wit, he was the course's most articulate spokesperson. One of Gideonse's recruits was Jerome G. Kerwin of the Department of Political Science. Throughout his career, Kerwin encouraged his students to become involved in local politics, and he took pride that his former students, who were as diverse as Leon Despres, Charles Percy, and Robert Merriam, had followed his lead. Chicago-trained sociologist Louis Wirth was the most distinguished scholar of the group. By the early 1930s Wirth was emerging as one of the most important urban sociologists of his generation, and his strategy for teaching social science to beginning undergraduates was profoundly shaped by his research interests in large cities like Chicago.

The primary goal of the new social sciences course was to help students understand the complexities of urban industrial civilization of the 1930s. The course focused on three large problems and approached them with the theoretical apparatus of three different disciplines, a strategy that the organizers believed to be superior to existing introductory courses that they deemed "superficial and unsatisfactory."[97] The first quarter, taught by Gideonse, stressed the role of industrial change in England and in contemporary America. Students were asked to read R. H. Tawney's *The Acquisitive Society*, Lewis Mumford's *The Story of Utopias*, Herbert Hoover's *American Individualism*, and Norman Thomas's *America's Way Out* in order to explore the development of the present economic order. The second quarter, taught by Wirth, took up questions of the impact of scientific and technological progress on modern society, studying population movements from rural to urban areas, the ways in which the new industrial-technological order had accelerated large-scale social change, the growth of large cities, and the emergence of new kinds of cultural patterns in societies with strong traditions. This quarter used books such as W. G. Sumner's *Folkways*, Franz Boas's *The Mind of Primitive Man*, and the classic work by Robert and Helen Lynd, *Middletown: A Study in Contemporary American Culture*. The final quarter, taught by Kerwin, focused on the modern state—and especially central government—as a premier locus of political and economic control, with students exploring the growth of governmental authority and bureaucratic control in the industrial world.[98] In this quarter students read Charles A. Beard's *American Government and Politics*, Harold Laski's *Politics*, Graham Wallas's *Human Nature in Politics*, and Gilbert Murray's *The Ordeal of This Generation*. The course ended with six lectures offered by Gideonse that tied the various themes together. In addition to these books, students were assigned essays by (among others) Adam Smith, Karl Marx, Immanuel Kant, T. R. Malthus, Thomas Paine, Ruth Benedict, Charles Beard, Charles H. Cooley, Robert E. Park, William F. Ogburn, Edward Sapir, and John Dewey—a who's who of modern social and political thought. Given the inclination of Gideonse, Kerwin, and Wirth to use Chicago as field site, they integrated visits to the stock exchange, the board of trade, Armour and Company, and the International Harvester Company, as well as unemployment offices, slums, and housing projects.[99]

Seen three-quarters of a century later, the social sciences course was an enterprise invented during the vast displacements of the Depression. Ostensibly about the origins of industrial society, the course focused on the fate of individualism and personal freedom in face of the challenges that communism and fascism presented to European liberalism and American democracy. Intellectual pluralism, within a schema broadly sympathetic to industrial capitalism, would contrast with the mistaken hopes of utopians, whether on the left or the right. In an inadvertent claim that revealed much about curricular tensions on campus, Gideonse later insisted that "a course that pulled *everything* together quite systematically would not be true to life, and could only exist on the basis of some totalitarian philosophy of the Marxist, Thomist, or Fascist type."[100] As we will see, the invocation of Thomism as a "totalitarian philosophy" was for local consumption in Hyde Park.

For the College, the new curriculum was the beginning of an extraordinary odyssey. With its self-styled combination of intellectual rigor and scientific efficiency, the New Plan (as the new curriculum quickly came to be called) garnered hugely favorable publicity for the University, most of it relating to the bold and rigorous changes in the first two years of the undergraduate program. Robert Hutchins was touted as the young, visionary president of a young, revolutionary university, and the only fears vouchsafed were that the new programs might be too difficult and too challenging for average students. The *Literary Digest* proclaimed that "those who go to college for a good time, for social advantages, and for a meaningless diploma will not select Chicago University, when the proposed reorganization takes place." The *Chicago Tribune* quoted Boucher with approval to the effect that "we desire to give meaning to the bachelor's degree—that the student has passed through a stage of real educational development, and has really achieved intellectually." For the *New York Times*, the reforms embodied a bold arrangement that "goes the whole way in throwing on the student responsibility for his own education. Where some universities are trying tidbits and spurs in the way of honors systems and house plans, Chicago has begun to treat the undergraduate as though he really desired an education and needed only the sign-posts to help him get it."[101]

Student reaction to the program was positive, with students admiring the new survey courses and the freedom that they had to prepare for the comprehensive exams. Research data collected by the admissions office as well as qualitative reports from the faculty in the 1930s confirmed that Boucher's gamble about attracting more intellectually able students had paid off.[102] The median score on the American Council on Education's Psychological Examination taken by students matriculating in the fall quarter of 1932 was seventeen points higher than the class admitted in

1931, and the latter's score was, in turn, substantially higher than any of the classes admitted during the 1920s.[103] Louis Thurstone reported to Boucher in 1932, "It seems quite certain that we are attracting brighter students under the New Plan than the Old Plan. The exact reason for this may not be evident, but it is probably associated with the publicity for the New Plan."[104] William Halperin, later a distinguished historian of modern Europe who as a young man taught one of the discussion sections of the social sciences course, commented, "Many of the students are surprisingly alert and sophisticated, and at times the discussions were extremely suggestive and outspoken.... A very considerable number of them have responded to the challenge by developing very excellent study habits. It is my impression that the New Plan students not only do more work than their old-plan predecessors, but approach their academic problems with greater alertness and understanding."[105] Gideonse was proud of the fact that the New Plan had recruited a "higher caliber of students" and that students found his social sciences course deeply challenging: whereas in the 1920s social science courses were seen as "snap" courses, they now rivaled or even surpassed their counterparts in the other divisions in terms of the difficulty of mastering the material presented.[106]

Within the broader context of American higher education in the 1930s, Chicago's approach to the general-education movement was distinctive, not so much in any of its individual elements but in the coherence of the model as a whole, especially given the fact that the new courses were so closely linked to the new scholarly research trends that had taken hold in the later 1920s and early 1930s. Boucher and the other New Plan reformers conceived of their work in pragmatic ways, seeking to recruit better students to the University and to introduce those students to broad realms of knowledge, based on the best contemporary research, and key analytic skills in the first two years of college study that would logically flow into the greater specialization that students would encounter in the second half of their college careers.

By folding a solution to the problem of the College into a broader reorganization of the arts and sciences, Robert Hutchins (temporarily, at least) avoided being typecast as overtly "pro-undergraduate," a stance that Harold Swift warned him against as early as May 1929.[107] At the same time, it was profoundly ironic that the president usually associated with the founding of the Chicago Core curriculum soon came to challenge the general-education courses that Boucher's teams had put together, and that so many of the leaders of these courses became ardent opponents of Hutchins's leadership by the 1940s. Many American universities struggled in the 1930s and 1940s to revise their undergraduate curricula to achieve greater intellectual coherence and social relevance, but few tried to do so with the senior faculty and the university president at daggers drawn in a brawl for pedagogical power.

This struggle began in the fall of 1930 when Hutchins collaborated with a young, brash, and highly controversial scholar from Columbia University, Mortimer Adler, to launch a Great Books honors course taught over a two-year cycle. Modeled on a similar course taught at Columbia University by John Erskine, the seminar was called "General Honors 110" (in 1934 it was renamed "Classics of the Western World") and assigned readings from the works of Homer, Herodotus, Thucydides, Aristophanes, Plato, Aristotle, Cicero, Virgil, Plutarch, Marcus Aurelius, Saint Augustine, Thomas Aquinas, Dante, Cervantes, and other worthies as well as from the New Testament; the second year then ran from Duns Scotus to Freud.[108] The course met two hours a week on Tuesday evenings, with no formal lectures, and enrolled twenty freshmen, the students being responsible for doing all of the assigned reading for each class. Their evaluation consisted of an oral exam, administered by outside testers, as well as an essay exam based on the analysis of selected quotes. The reactions of the outside examiners were effusive, with Richard McKeon of Columbia University suggesting in 1932, "To judge by the examinations of the sixteen students who appeared before me, I can think of no more effective course in collegiate education than that which resulted in the training of those students." Similarly, Stringfellow Barr of the University of Virginia observed, "I can hardly overstate my admiration for the intellectual poise with which your students have taken hold."[109] The College Curriculum Committee eventually voted to allow students to use the final examination in this course as a substitute for one of the elective sequences beyond the general-education survey courses that each Chicago undergraduate was required to take under the New Plan.

Hutchins first came in contact with Adler in the summer of 1927 when Hutchins, on the recommendation of the British philosopher C. K. Ogden, corresponded with and then met with Adler to discuss his interest in the psychological logic of evidence.[110] Hutchins was clearly fascinated by Adler's compendious knowledge of philosophy and his volcanic intellectual temperament, and decided in the summer of 1929 to bring him to Chicago. Adler's arrival on campus in the autumn was hardly fortuitous, since Hutchins's failed attempt to impose him (as well as Scott Buchanan of the University of Virginia) on the Department of Philosophy during the 1929–1930 academic year proved to be a political disaster.[111] Hutchins eventually found Adler a berth in the Law School as an untenured associate professor, and with his abrasive personality and his habit of conducting conversations in rhetorical overdrive Adler immediately began to make waves. By early 1931, when Chauncey Boucher was organizing his teams to plan the new general-education courses, he wrote to Hutchins, "Nearly every day I encounter an expression of distrust or fear regarding the selection of men to be put in charge of the four general divisional courses provided in the report of the Curriculum Committee—namely, that Mr. Adler will be put in charge of the Humanities course, and that others of his ilk will be brought in for the other courses. In each instance I think I have convinced the person that such fears are unwarranted."[112]

Little did Boucher know what lay ahead.

Liberal Education in the Service of Society

THE THOMISTIC *FRONDE*

Adler proved a potent influence on Hutchins, especially as a model of a working intellectual grounded in broad scholarly erudition, a capacity that Hutchins envied but sorely lacked. Adler's first book, *Dialectic*, and many of his other writings of the 1930s already had the encyclopedic and Aristotelian character that later became identified as Adler's Thomism. Adler found the work of Saint Thomas Aquinas particularly attractive, since for him Thomas's *Summae* provided a model for both the encyclopedic treatment of philosophical problems and the engagement with all accessible traditional learning. As early as 1927, Adler was trying to provide a theoretical framework for the kinds of discussions that were already taking place in Erskine's General Honors course at Columbia. Adler's philosophical writings at Chicago and his teaching with Hutchins carried this work forward.

In Adler, Hutchins found a man nearly his own age who possessed substantial learning, contentious eloquence, and intense intellectual ambition. It was a natural collaboration. Both men aspired to traditional philosophical learning of great seriousness and scope, and both, for better or worse, aspired to remake the University in pursuit of that ideal. Adler had a more dogmatic temperament and panoramic mind, but both men ended up associating themselves with a fundamental attack on the forms of intellectual and scholarly pragmatism, informed by experimental science, represented by earlier generations of Chicago opinion leaders, such as John Dewey, George Herbert Mead, James H. Tufts, James R. Angell, and Addison W. Moore.[113] By 1941 Adler would proudly proclaim that the Chicago School had been succeeded by the Chicago Fight, of which Hutchins and he were the primary combatants against forces of darkness and ignorance.[114] But for Hutchins the stakes were much higher. While his prior administrative positions at Yale had taught him something about how to govern men (however tentatively), they did not endow him with the kind of educational vision that one would expect of the president of a major research university. To the extent that by the later 1930s Hutchins was able to articulate a cohesive, systematic approach in education, he owed a great debt to Adler and to their shared conflicts with the faculty.

The Adler-Hutchins Great Books course, which Adler conceived as a radical alternative to the curriculum that Boucher had instituted and which had received glowing reviews from men like McKeon and Barr, was one ongoing challenge to the New Plan. A second challenge came from Ronald S. Crane, a distinguished literary critic and editor of *Modern Philology*. Crane played a critical role as department chair in reconstituting the doctoral programs of the Department of English in the mid-1930s into problem- and theory-based learning focused on linguistics, philosophical and rhetorical analysis, and criticism; and he soon emerged as the intellectual leader of the new "Chicago School" of literary criticism.[115] For Crane a general-education program could not solely or even primarily be justified by the amount of substantive knowledge anchored in the "great fields of human thought" that was conveyed to the student. Rather, the true essence of general education was the development of what Crane called basic intellectual habits: "the ability to see problems, to define terms accurately and clearly, to analyze a question into its significant elements, to become aware of general assumptions and preconceptions upon which one's own thinking and that of others rests, to make relevant and useful distinctions, to weigh probabilities, to organize the results of one's own reflections and research, to read a book of whatever sort reflectively, analytically, critically, to write one's native language with clarity and distinction."[116] Crane believed that the best way to engender such habits was through active learning by students in small groups. This required more discussion-based teaching and learning, more focused participation, and more regular feedback and criticism than the general lecture courses of the New Plan could provide. Implicitly, it also privileged humanistic knowledge over empirical scientific inquiry, at least in the early stages of a student's career.

The circle around Crane was substantially enriched the following year by the addition of Columbia professor Richard McKeon, first in the Department of History and then in the Department of Greek, and soon thereafter Hutchins selected him to be dean of the humanities division. Immediately after arriving in Chicago, McKeon began to teach a joint seminar with Crane on the philosophy of history, a collaboration that further influenced Crane in the direction of a neo-Aristotelian approach to literary criticism. Crane generated considerable controversy in the spring of 1934 by writing a memorandum after the Department of History announced its decision to join the Division of the Social Sciences for administrative purposes in January 1933—a move that caused considerable unhappiness among faculty in the humanities division.[117] "It has come to be widely assumed among professional historians that their proper domain is coextensive with the history of culture or civilization, and that they ought to give increasing attention in their teaching and writing to subject matters, such as economics, philosophy, science, and even art which are already organized elsewhere in the University as special historical disciplines," Crane wrote. In his mind, social and political history were the legitimate province of the "professional historians," but other domains of historical inquiry and teaching should properly be left to experts in the relevant substantive fields.

Crane's demarche against the history department came at the same time that he was formulating new theoretical agendas for the study of English literature—represented in his famous essay of 1935 "History versus Criticism in the University Study of Literature."[118] But it also had a second, local target in that Crane viewed Schevill's and Scott's general humanities course to be a latter-day replica of old fashioned literary-history courses that Crane found intellectually anachronistic.[119] Since the Department of History was Chauncey Boucher's home turf, and since two prominent historians—Schevill and Scott—were the primary leaders of the humanities general course, Crane's intervention was a direct attack on Boucher and the New Plan.

As his contacts with Adler, Crane, and McKeon grew more intense, Hutchins drifted away from whatever commitment to the New Plan he had had in 1931. This shift is apparent in his confidential report to the board of trustees in early 1935: "The whole course of study suffers greatly from a disease that afflicts all college teaching in America, the information disease. I have never favored survey courses in the usual sense. A hasty look at all the facts in a given field does not seem very useful from any but a conversational point of view." Hutchins then continued by advocating the Great Books approach: "I am sure, too, that a college course which is based largely on the reading of great books, with lectures on them and discussions of them, is more likely to produce understanding, even of the contemporary world, than a vast mass of current data."[120] Hutchins thus aspired to a much more radical vision. The College might be the beginning of a university education that would be completed by the specialized work of the divisions, but it also might be the end of a university education, depending on the social efficacy and intellectual significance one accorded to the idea of general education.

From the first days of his presidency Hutchins suggested that some students might reasonably opt to finish their university work at the end of their two-year general-educational program.[121] In his hugely influential tract *The Higher Learning in America* (1936), he took it for granted that many students would not progress beyond this point: "It is highly important that we should develop ourselves and encourage the junior colleges to develop an intelligible scheme of general education under which the student may either terminate his formal education at the end of the sophomore year or go on to university work."[122] Perhaps, general education should not be viewed merely as the natural and logical academic terminus for some students; perhaps, it should rather be viewed as the proper and justified end of a four-year educational process for *all* students, a process that would begin in the third year of high school and terminate in the second year of college. When Hutchins persuaded the University Senate in mid-November 1932 to authorize an experimental four-year program that combined the last two years of the University high school and the first two years of the College for local lab school students, he launched a small but important precedent that, within a decade, would transform the academic landscape of the University.[123] Hutchins's long-term solutions to the perceived shortcomings of the New Plan were to create a real faculty for the College and to encourage that faculty to develop a full-time, fully required curriculum in general education that would span grades eleven to fourteen for all of its students.

Tensions came to a head in 1934 and 1935, when the New Plan sustained a series of embarrassing public collisions. At the December convocation of the University in late 1933, Hutchins launched a rhetorical salvo by denouncing those who would inundate the young with facts as opposed to concepts in undergraduate teaching: "The gadgeteers and the data-collectors, masquerading as scientists, have threatened to become the supreme chieftains of the scholarly world." In contrast, the University should really be a "center of rational thought," which was the "only basis of education and research." The current system of education was unfortunately designed "to pour facts into the student with splendid disregard of the certainty that he will forget them, that they may not be facts by the time he graduates, and that he won't know what to do with them if they are.... Facts are the core of an anti-intellectual curriculum." Instead of collecting evidence, the "gaze of the University should be turned toward ideas," which would "promote understanding of the nature of the world and of man."[124]

Hutchins continued this theme in early January 1934 at the annual trustee-faculty dinner, where he attacked those University teachers who "offend us ... in filling their students full of facts, in putting them through countless little measurements, in multiplying their courses, in insisting that they must have more of the student's time so that they can give him more information."[125] The discursive framework that Hutchins deployed—

"ideas" as being more important than "facts" and learning more important than memorizing—may have been grossly simplistic, and it certainly betrayed a fundamental misunderstanding of the way in which modern scientific research was conducted, but it gave Hutchins the moral high ground, accusing universities of a thoughtless disregard for the essential features of liberal education.

Hutchins's discursive bravado, which could be easily read as targeting the New Plan courses and impugning the curricular imagination of the faculty who had organized them, encouraged the undergraduate editor of the *Maroon*, John Barden, to launch a frontal assault on the New Plan. Barden was a New Plan student with a modest academic record (he had received Cs in his comprehensive exams) who had first met Mortimer Adler when he audited the Hutchins-Adler General Honors course and also enrolled in the fall of 1933 in a class Adler taught entitled "Law in Western European Intellectual History." Barden quickly fell under Adler's intellectual sway.[126] In early January 1934 Barden wrote an editorial in which he slammed Boucher's New Plan curriculum as purveying facts and not ideas: "If we assume that a general education does consist of a collection of ideas rather than a collection of facts, the new plan is not administering a general education."[127] Barden continued this theme in weekly commentaries throughout the winter and spring quarters of 1934.

On one level Barden's critiques of the New Plan as providing facts and not ideas were farcical, given the heavy theoretical superstructures offered by Gideonse and his colleagues to justify their curricular project, but his real target seems to have been the New Plan's basic assumption that scholarly professionalism *and* current faculty research should inform the teaching of general education. Barden had a clear bias against the natural sciences, and against the structure of the comprehensive exams that tested a student's mastery of such research. In a subsequent essay, in the form of a dialogue between Socrates and Exercon on the ideal of the university, Barden portrayed Socrates as arguing that "many people believe that general education consists of exposition of the latest results of modern research."[128] Barden also attacked the New Plan lectures as mainly recounting facts that could easily be obtained in textbooks.[129] Instead of teaching "great" general ideas, based on original sources that were presumably easily accessible to an undergraduate, the faculty were presenting highly technical courses based on advanced research in which students were overwhelmed with empirical data before any larger syntheses could be offered.

Within a month of Barden's attacks and Hutchins's speeches, the student biology club Alpha Zeta Beta invited Mortimer Adler and Anton J. Carlson to a public debate in Mandel Hall before seven hundred students on February 9, 1934, on the theme of facts versus ideas. This uproarious event consisted of Carlson taking the stage and reading a series of propositions defending the scientific method and attacking Hutchins, followed by Adler's witty and ironic replies, which defended Hutchins's ideas as coherent and reasonable and, by implication, criticized Carlson's presentation as an example of the obfuscations of a kind of scientific research that seemed to deny the importance of conceptual abstractions in the articulation of the scientific method.[130]

Emboldened by Adler's rhetorical brinksmanship, Barden commissioned four College seniors to write critiques of the four general survey courses in March 1934, based on their published syllabi. Because they had matriculated in 1930, the four essay writers were studying under the requirements of the old curriculum, and none of them had taken any of the New Plan general-education courses. What they had in common was that all four had been students in the Hutchins-Adler Great Books class, which in effect had become a rival general-education curriculum. Janet Kalven attacked the humanities course as an exercise in intellectual history offered by nonphilosophers, when, to her mind, only philosophers were competent to undertake such an assignment. She claimed that the humanities syllabus was "sophistical, dogmatic, anti-intellectual, inaccurate, misleading, inconsistent, sentimental, and slovenly." James Martin criticized the social sciences course as filled with a covert Comtian positivism, the theoretical structure of which he proceeded to critique. Ignoring most of the material taught in the course, Martin then opined that the course as a whole was based on "bad scholarship." Darwin Anderson thought that the physical sciences course suffered from too heavy a reliance on evolutionary theory and "mechanistic" theories of the origins of the universe, and urged that the course spend more time investigating the "fundamental principles of natural philosophy." Finally, Clarice Anderson attacked the biological sciences course as having a "mechanistic bias" and being too dependent on evolutionary frameworks, and then spent the rest of her essay explicating Aristotle's theory of human nature and its relevance for modern science.[131]

The four critiques were gratuitous, poorly argued, and naive, and other College students enrolled in the New Plan courses quickly mounted a counteroffensive.[132] One pro–New Plan student, Marie Berger, gathered 250 signatures on a petition accusing Barden of conducting an authoritarian crusade that was out of touch with the majority of student opinion. Berger pointed out that the four writers had no direct knowledge of the courses they were writing about and that Barden and his friends had behaved irresponsibly.[133] Still, the attacks in the *Maroon* got under Chauncey Boucher's skin, who viewed Barden as a "smart aleck" who had demonstrated "bad taste." Stunned by the negative publicity generated by the *Maroon*, Boucher had the College's Curriculum Committee issue a memorandum denouncing the criticisms of the New Plan as the work of "rationalistic absolutism which brings with it an atmosphere of intolerance of liberal, scientific, and democratic attitudes" that was "incompatible with the ideal of a community of scholars and students recognizable as the University of Chicago."[134] Upon receiving a copy of this statement, Barden wrote a deeply insulting letter to Boucher wondering why Boucher would have taken the views of students in the *Maroon* so seriously and adding, "I don't care how good or bad a college newspaper may be, it is *never* worth official notice by any division of the faculty. I feel that the College faculty have immeasurably degraded themselves by officially recognizing the *Daily Maroon* even exists."[135] What Barden failed to appreciate, of course, was that Boucher's real worry was that Hutchins not only had agreed with the attacks but had, with Adler, encouraged the students to press them.

The debate about facts versus ideas had a fascinating afterwash among faculty suspicious of Hutchins's ideas. Economist Frank H. Knight, a voluble and assertive personality, entered the fray with a strident attack on Adler's alleged medievalism, accusing those who would attack modern thought (presumably Adler and Hutchins) of engaging in "absolutistic verbalism," "'wish-thinking' as a substitute for truth," and "intellectual dictatorship." Throwing Thomism in the same class of "isms" as Marxism, Knight insisted that both were "social reform propaganda."[136] After trying to publish his broadside, "Is Modern Thought Anti-Intellectual?," in the *Maroon*, where Barden torpedoed it, Knight sent it in samizdat fashion to key faculty leaders around campus. To Boucher, Knight complained, "The very sources of intellectual integrity are being systematically poisoned in the University as a whole.... It seems to me impossible to believe that the President is not consciously conniving at, if not deliberately pushing, the whole uproar."[137] In response Boucher put on a brave face by reassuring Knight that he would never retreat, but the experience was deeply painful, and Boucher's final comment to Knight—"If the Faculty will but stick together and present a nearly united front, they can 'get' any damned Dean or even a President who can be shown to be a nuisance rather than an aid"—said much about how depressing the situation had become. In frustration, Boucher resigned from Chicago in September 1935 to become president of the University of West Virginia, moving in 1938 to become chancellor of the University of Nebraska.

Harry Gideonse kept a bulletin board outside his office in Cobb Hall filled with clippings from the *Maroon*, to which he added derisive commentaries for students to see. He also submitted a commentary to the *Maroon*

in June 1934 asserting that Adler and his followers were "pathic and pathetic" in their search for "certainty" in knowledge and values, presenting
themselves as a group of "tired young men [who] are rejecting the tentative
groping for truth that is characteristic of modern science."[138] Gideonse's
role as a leader of the disloyal opposition to Hutchins grew rapidly after
1935 with Gideonse appointing himself as the defender of the traditions of
experiential pragmatism espoused by earlier Chicago figures such as John
Dewey and James H. Tufts. Indeed, Dewey's critiques of Hutchins's work
The Higher Learning in America have considerable intellectual affinity with
Gideonse's own diatribes.[139] Maynard Krueger later recalled that Gideonse
was "the chief vocal leader of an opposition to Hutchins," not in the least
because he was respected by the faculty of physical sciences and biological
sciences. Gideonse believed that Hutchins's and Adler's search for general
categories to organize all knowledge reflected a muddled understanding
of what the practice of social science really involved. In a pungent essay
in 1936 Gideonse attacked the pervasive search for systems of certainty in
contemporary intellectual and political practice, ranging from "the absolutism of fascism to that of communism, and cover[ing] in its broad sweep
the curious antics of those who have found a 'Road Back' by retiring to the
'rational order' of Aristotle and St. Thomas of Aquinas." Gideonse did not
deny the need for overcoming the disjointedness of modern knowledge,
but he believed it could be done only by embracing modern science and
seeking problem-oriented solutions drawn from the experimental knowledge of the various disciplines. Rather than training "fixed person[s] for
fixed duties" with incantations of past dogmas, it was the obligation of
the modern college to educate flexible, scientific minds who would see
through the allures and temptations of the "systems."[140]

Gideonse's trenchant opposition to Hutchins doomed his career at
Chicago. By early 1935 Hutchins had decided to force Gideonse off the
faculty, telling Boucher that he had informed Gideonse that he was "not
prepared to say that we should increase his salary as the income of the
University improves or to assure him that he would be placed on permanent tenure."[141] In the spring of 1936 the Department of Economics sought
to make good on their prior commitment to Gideonse that he would be
offered tenure and a full professorship, and formally recommended such
to Hutchins. Hutchins rejected the proposal out of hand. In July 1936 the
full professors of the department then sent a respectful but forceful plea
to Hutchins to reverse his decision, but Hutchins would not bend. The
department insisted that Gideonse had been hired to be a superb teacher
of college-level economics and had been assured that distinguished teaching, rather than research, would be the primary qualification used to measure his future advancement and promotions. Now, exactly the opposite

had happened, and this from a president who claimed to be interested in high-quality undergraduate teaching.[142]

Gideonse's attacks came during the controversial attempt of Hutchins and Adler to import Scott Buchanan and Stringfellow Barr from the University of Virginia to create a Committee on the Liberal Arts at the University, whose mandate was (among other things) to think about how a Great Books curriculum might be planned at Chicago.[143] Hutchins toyed with the idea of imposing Barr as the new dean of the College, even though he admitted to Adler that it would be "hellish hard" to do so.[144] These tactics had provoked deep faculty opposition and contributed to Richard McKeon's growing reservations about Adler's schemes.[145] Gideonse then published a thirty-four-page pamphlet called *The Higher Learning in a Democracy* that excoriated Hutchins for the latter's call for a new metaphysics that would bring intellectual and moral order to the chaos of American university education, insisting that this was nothing short of imposing an "absolutistic system."[146] Gideonse was especially troubled by Hutchins's alleged disrespect for modern science, and he argued that "acceptance of the curricular primacy of a set of first metaphysical principles would reduce science to dogma and education to indoctrination.... If these are times of confusion and disorder, the results and the methods of science also make them times of unparalleled promise. Now—as never before— educational leadership calls for a persistent and critical emphasis upon the significance of present achievement and its promise for the future."[147] The pamphlet was sufficiently arresting that Hutchins asked Adler to comment on it, which he promptly did. Adler candidly noted that Gideonse had rich opportunities for intellectual subversion precisely because of Hutchins's imprecise and vague use of words and concepts about "philosophy," "metaphysics," "knowledge of first principles," and the like.[148]

Coming from an untenured professor, Gideonse's attack on the president of the University was both impudent and imprudent, but his chances for tenure at Chicago were already nil. When Gideonse resigned in the spring of 1938 to accept a professorship at Barnard College (the following year, he was elected president of Brooklyn College), Louis Wirth brought an unusual motion before the faculty of the College recognizing Gideonse's contributions and expressing regret that he had been forced to leave the University.[149] The motion passed unanimously, with each of the sixty faculty members present rising to signify approval. Most problematic was the failure of Aaron J. Brumbaugh, the acting dean of the College who had succeeded Boucher, to support Gideonse, but Brumbaugh was not a scholar and, unlike Boucher, was eager to please Hutchins.[150] Gideonse's friends felt him to be the victim of a political purge, and Hutchins's answers to student protesters that he had never rejected a recommendation of the deans that Gideonse be promoted, while technically correct (he rejected on several occasions a direct recommendation brought to him by the Department of Economics), sounded hollow.

With Gideonse's forced departure for New York City, Hutchins had eliminated a formidable public intellectual who had the leadership skills to derail Hutchins's plans to create an all-general-education College.[151] In the end, in the struggles between the forces represented by Gideonse and Hutchins we see the collision of two competing curricular revolutions in general education. The one sought to use the most auspicious work of modern social and natural science, grounded in a strong historical and developmental perspective, to create a world of general knowledge useful for the thoughtful practice of modern citizenship. The other sought to recover from the classic works of the past a more coherent but also more introspective vision of learning, stressing the skills of the individual knower and motivated by active forms of educational connoisseurship. Both constituted vast improvements over the curricular chaos of the 1920s, and both would continue to have powerful resonances in the decades to come, on Chicago's campus and in the American academy at large.

If mass higher education in the twentieth century was to do more than train the technical and professional elites for their careers, then it would need a cultural and intellectual mission to replace the classical learning of the nineteenth-century curriculum. Growing enrollments, the development of modern science, and the professionalization of scholarship had already killed off the classical curriculum. Both Gideonse and Hutchins represented systematic attempts to preserve and to protect the intellectual culture of the modern university against a "collegiate" culture that stressed adolescent amusements more than serious intellectual engagement. In this sense, both men signified a radical break from the conventional culture of the American college, and both wanted to enhance the level of intellectual seriousness expected of undergraduates at a modern university. Both began and ended with exemplary texts, subjected to critical scrutiny by teacher and student alike. Both addressed what Edward Purcell has characterized as the two crucial, but often antagonistic ambitions that informed interwar views of the science of society: the technical ideal of formulating an "objective science of society" and the moral ideal of creating a just and ethical democratic order.[152] The new century needed new alternatives, and the collision of the ideals represented by Gideonse and Hutchins under the aegis of the New Plan made the 1930s a particularly fruitful and memorable time at the University of Chicago.

At the same time, the texture of this debate, as with the larger national debate that Hutchins carried on with John Dewey in the later 1930s and early 1940s, revealed significant fissures as to how rigorous systems of liberal education could be retrofitted and integrated *into* the intellectual project of the modern research university as it evolved after 1918. Gideonse and Hutchins also conveyed different blueprints for the role of the liberal arts as they would putatively prepare young students to be democratic citizens. Gideonse was not a distinguished scholar, but he esteemed the modern social and natural sciences as they had evolved at Chicago and elsewhere in the aftermath of World War I, and his views of liberal education aligned closely with the empirical milieu of a large research university. Gideonse's approach was thus more palatable to the faculty members being hired by American research universities in the 1930s and 1940s. In contrast, with his concerns for ethical responsibility, preexistent truths, and the intellectual patrimony of "great" texts, Hutchins was bound to be frustrated by the "scientism" and pragmatic experimentalism that governed the teaching of most academic departments at Chicago. He was particularly unhappy that "although the four survey courses are general, the faculty has unconsciously tried to make the total effect of the curriculum the improvement of preparation for advanced work" in the departments.[153] These frustrations would lead Hutchins to try to engineer massive structural changes on both the undergraduate and the graduate levels at Chicago, creating a College faculty that would be totally divorced from the rest of the research university, and to divide doctoral programs into separate tracks that would train liberal arts teachers as opposed to university-based researchers. Hutchins succeeded in the first, but was fought to a standstill on the second.

THE HUTCHINS COLLEGE, 1942–1951

By the end of the 1930s the senior founding members of the 1931 general-education courses were either disillusioned or distracted in the face of Hutchins's public *fronde* against their programs. Boucher's decision to resign removed one major opponent of Hutchins's schemes, and Gideonse's purge had removed a second key obstacle. Initially Hutchins allowed the College to drift under the management of a weak interim dean, Aaron Brumbaugh, but Hutchins never viewed Brumbaugh as anything other than provisional. After searching for several years for someone with the character and political savvy to lead his intended revolution, Hutchins finally found the man he needed in the person of Clarence Faust, a young professor of American literature in the Department of English. Faust was a protégé of Richard McKeon and Ronald Crane and the leader of a group of young literary scholars who admired Hutchins's curricular goals. In August 1941 Hutchins dismissed Brumbaugh and appointed Faust as dean of the College.[154]

Then, early in January 1942, in the aftermath of the American declarations of war on Japan and on Germany, Hutchins suddenly and with considerable drama proposed that the BA degree be transferred from the jurisdiction of the divisions to the College and that it be conferred upon completion of a four-year program in general education beginning with grade eleven, thus making it possible for Chicago to graduate eighteen- or nineteen-year-olds with BA degrees.[155] The College would exercise the rights of a ruling body of the university on par with the divisions and professional schools and have its own faculty. After protracted discussion, the University Senate approved this proposal on January 22, 1942, creating the opportunity for Hutchins's supporters, led by Faust, to formulate a wholly mandated general-education curriculum that excluded any departmental majors. In addition, with Hutchins's encouragement and under the exigencies of wartime, Faust began to take advantage of the previously little-used proviso of 1932 that the College could appoint its own faculty members without divisional coappointments. Then, in November 1943, Faust obtained Hutchins's approval to interpret the statutes of the University in a way that made membership in the College faculty contingent on a person's teaching throughout all three quarters of the academic year.[156] This led to the automatic disenfranchisement of a number of divisional faculty members who had formerly also been members of the College. The effects of this change were much debated at the time, with Faust's opponents viewing it as tantamount to vote rigging (which it was).

A last-ditch effort in early April 1942 to rescind the Senate's approval of the transfer of the BA degree to the College deadlocked in a 58–58 vote, with Robert Hutchins casting the tie-breaking vote and ruling that the motion for recision had failed. At the same time, given the bitter resistance that his plans encountered from the old guard of the New Plan, Faust was forced to accept a compromise in formulating the curriculum for his new degree program. The committee in charge of formulating the curriculum produced a contested document, in which a majority report argued that students should be held to a full load of general-education courses, including two full years of humanities sequences and two years of social sciences sequences, and a minority report signed by five committee members asserted in a New Plan–like refrain that "the common core of general education expected of every student should not be expanded beyond the point which in the experience of the College advisors has proven to be the optimum. Beyond that optimum students derive more benefit from courses freely chosen than from those prescribed in fields which may be unrelated to their particular interests." The majority report encountered stiff resistance from senior faculty leaders of the humanities, physical sciences, and biological sciences divisions, many of whom wrote protest letters urging greater flexibility for post–high school entrants. On March 19–20, 1942, at a marathon meeting of the College faculty that lasted nearly five hours over two days, Faust had to settle for a compromise that created two undergraduate degrees: a BA that would be the result of a four-year and prescribed general-education curriculum, largely for students entering without a high school diploma, and a PhB that would allow students entering the College after having completed high school to take a program that included departmental electives in addition to a (now-reduced) number of prescribed general-education sequences. The PhB of 1942 was essentially the continuation of the New Plan, stripped of its former luster and innovative élan.

The second and final struggle between the College and the divisions took place between February and April 1946. Having set in place the new structure of a four-year baccalaureate degree program spanning (in theory) grades eleven through fourteen and run solely by the College, having articulated the goal of a four-year curriculum focusing almost exclusively on general education as the educational telos toward which the College should move, and having begun to construct an autonomous faculty to assume the proprietorship of that program, Clarence Faust was ready to take the final step of killing off the vestiges of the New Plan by eliminating the PhB degree. This fateful decision engendered passionate support and equally zealous opposition across the University. The conflict that followed led to a divisive constitutional struggle culminating in a collision between the University Senate and the president of the University and a subsequent appeal to the board of trustees. Again leading the fight were senior faculty from several divisions. While acknowledging the value of a systematic program of general education, these critics challenged both the philosophical and organizational assumptions that undergirded the plan, arguing that the normal undergraduate program in grades thirteen and fourteen should take cognizance of students' interests beyond general education, and that it should provide opportunities for more specialized learning. The latter point seemed to be on Norman Maclean's mind when he asked his colleagues to distinguish between "what is indispensable and basic, and what is desirable and admirable" in a general-education program. For Maclean the indispensable and basic had to remain, but colleagues might honestly differ about what was desirable and admirable. Maclean believed that "originally the problem with the College was one of having too many courses; now it is a problem of too few; and under the [1946] proposal the student would be given no choice to develop his gifts or special interests."[157]

The fundamental issues at stake during the constitutional crisis of 1946 were, thus, not only the sovereignty of the College vis-à-vis that of the divisions, but basic intellectual and pedagogical claims. These questions were nicely summarized in a pair of contesting memoranda submitted in February 1946 by Clarence Faust and Hermann Schlesinger, the one representing Hutchins's vision of prescriptive general education, the other defending the spirit of flexibility in Boucher's New Plan.[158] Faust's most emphatic argument was one of structural integrity: a program of general education had to be both internally coherent and consistent in its purpose, with various elements working with and reinforcing one another. Hence, the PhB with its optional departmental courses harmed the integrity of the program by substituting courses that could not possibly provide sound general education. Schlesinger rejected the premises of Faust's arguments, stating that Faust's plan introduced too sharp a break between the first two College years and the last two years, that electives were "an integral part" of even a general education, and that the work of the College and the divisions had to be symbiotic, lest the College become separated from the rest of the University.

Faust's opponents also argued that curricular flexibility was actually *preferred* by most College students. According to Schlesinger, 80 percent of students matriculating in 1945 chose the PhB rather than the BA because it allowed more free electives, and an informal poll of student opinion by the *Maroon* showed 58 percent of College students favoring the retention of the PhB, with a minority of 42 percent favoring its abolition.[159] But in the end, with no one wanting the board of trustees to impose a solution, a compromise was cobbled together in May 1946 under which Hutchins and Faust essentially prevailed, and the new curricular framework went into effect in the autumn of 1947.[160]

The logic of the curricular legislation of January 1942, which effectively eliminated the departments and their specializations from the undergraduate curriculum, was fiercely opposed by many senior faculty members who had taught under the New Plan. For men like Schlesinger, Wirth, and Scott the issue was not, as the proponents of the all-general-education College would later try to argue, one of rote memorization in the 1930s survey courses against conceptual learning in the curriculum installed in 1942. Rather, the division of opinion had to do with the linkage of general education to more advanced learning offered by the research faculties in the departments as an integral component of a baccalaureate degree program, and with the parallel assumption that the faculty who taught general education should have the same kinds of scholarly credentials and career aspirations as those who taught more specialized departmental courses. In contrast to the College curriculum created in 1942 and strengthened in 1946, the New Plan was conceived not as a curricular end unto itself but as a period of intellectual preparation and transition leading to the higher and more specialized learning offered in the divisions and the professional schools for the BA or BS degree.

Arthur P. Scott kept a private list of faculty who opposed Hutchins's educational ideas, and the names of most of the faculty leaders of the 1931 survey courses were on it, along with Scott himself.[161] A memorandum drafted in April 1944 by Ronald Crane and others, which challenged Hutchins's style of governance as president and his putative interest in weakening the authority of the departments (more on that below), was signed by Merle Coulter, Alfred E. Emerson, Ralph W. Gerard, Harvey B. Lemon, Hermann I. Schlesinger, Arthur P. Scott, Louis L. Thurstone, and Louis Wirth—full professors who had played decisive roles in organizing the 1931 general-education curriculum.[162] Yet the decision to evict specialized courses from the College troubled even some of Hutchins's supporters.

The changes of 1942 and 1946 led, in turn, to a radical revision of the relationships between the divisions and the College. Whereas before 1942 the award of the baccalaureate degree had remained a divisional prerogative and most members of the College faculty also held membership in the faculty of a division, now the College assembled a faculty larger (on paper at least) than three of the four divisions, and in gaining control of the baccalaureate degree it could create educational programs that afforded no place for the specialized research knowledge represented by the departments. What had been the "upper" divisions between 1930 and 1942 now became the "graduate" divisions that continue to mark the mental and political map of Chicago's local academic world. Instead of the BA degree that included specialized work, the first degree offered by the divisions would now be the MA, with the College's program focusing exclusively on general education.

Victorious in the 1946 showdown, Faust soon resigned from the deanship, exhausted by what Lawrence Kimpton called the "terrific administrative grind" Faust had endured since 1941.[163] His successor, F. Champion Ward, a young philosopher trained at Oberlin and Yale who taught at Denison University from 1937 to 1945, aggressively continued the process of assembling a separate College faculty. Ward was a courageous, defiant leader determined to protect the College from unwarranted incursions from the divisions. As late as 1958, 108 of the 160 faculty members in the College had appointments only in the College. Their presence was to have a considerable impact on the history of the University. The tensions involving the College's relations with the graduate divisions (and vice versa), which stretched well into the 1980s, derived in part from the frustration experienced by those who were appointed as faculty members in the autonomous College and who thought themselves authorized to create a unique curriculum, but then saw both the political mandate and the demographic logic of that effort being stripped away over time. At the same time, the separate College faculty engendered extremely mixed emotions in the divisions. Some divisional colleagues admired the tenacity, vision, and dedication of the (new) College faculty. But others resented the loss of faculty lines and the expulsion of their departments from any role in the undergraduate curriculum. Still others found Champ Ward's aggressive attempts to create rival pedagogical enterprises in the College that deliberately ignored the expertise of the graduate departments to be outrageous. Nor were voices absent complaining about the (in their mind) scholarly inferiority of the College appointees. Marshall Stone, chair of the Department of Mathematics, wrote to Lawrence Kimpton in 1952 that "it can be stated categorically that … no mathematician of superior creative powers will entertain a post on the College Staff, or remain with it, if he can obtain employment under normal academic circumstances.… The narrowness of the task assigned to the College Staff cannot in the long run help but have a stultifying effect on the intellects and talents of its members."[164]

The new curriculum put in place in 1942 expanded the number of required general-education sequences from five to fourteen, with an attendant growth in the number of comprehensive examinations that had to be offered on an annual basis. At its high point in the early 1950s the College's curriculum included fourteen general-education comprehensive exams: three in humanities; three in social sciences; three in natural sciences; and one each in history, foreign language, mathematics, English, and OII ("Observation, Interpretation, and Integration"), the latter course perhaps the most characteristic symbol of the Faust-Ward College and the one most indebted to the intellectual proclivities of Richard McKeon and his protégés, such as Joseph Schwab.[165]

The new College program also brought a host of new tests, especially placement tests designed to put new students in exactly the right combination of learning experience and courses of study. By the late 1940s, the examiner's office was preparing entrance tests, scholarship tests, placement tests, advisory examinations, comprehensive examinations, and various other tools of evaluation. Entrance tests were required of all applicants to the College, including a psychological test, a test of reading comprehension, and a test of writing skills, all meant to "give a good prediction of the candidate's degree of success in the academic work of the College." Thus, by the early 1950s, the examiner's office had become a veritable empire of testing. In 1950 Robert Woellner, an official involved in the testing program, could claim that "the University of Chicago uses standardized tests to a greater extent than any other institution of higher education in the country. Students are admitted, classified, counseled, evaluated in foreign language reading ability for advanced degrees, given scholarships, and awarded baccalaureate degrees upon the basis of standard tests."[166]

Woellner's views certainly reflected those of Ralph Tyler, a young educational psychologist from Ohio State University who replaced Thurstone in the position of examiner in 1938. A former doctoral student of Charles Judd who was appointed as a professor in the Department of Education, Tyler served as the University examiner from 1938 to 1953, assembling a large staff to run his organization.[167] Tyler was an articulate defender of the centralized assessment system. In a statement of February 1950 explaining the eleven different steps taken in the construction of the comprehensive examinations, Tyler portrayed the examination system as widely accepted and approved by faculty in the College. But in fact this was not the case, for two central components of the 1931 New Plan revolution—the general-education courses and the examiner's office—had serious collisions after 1950, leading ultimately to the death of the latter.

The survey courses before 1940 had been structured in a large lecture format, taught by a small number of regular faculty with departmental appointments, with discussion sessions added on to supplement the weekly lectures. But during the 1940s most general-education courses in the College shifted to become largely or primarily discussion based, and taught as small seminar classes. As the number of discussion sections and general-education sequences grew, the need for more faculty increased. It was natural that as more College faculty were hired to teach the seminars, and as discussion methods became more hegemonic, a commitment to fostering analytic skills became even more central to the Chicago project. Over time, this led to a disregard for what the general-education staffs derisively termed "factual information" and a shift away from viewing their courses as vehicles for comprehensive examination preparation (which was the central rationale of the 1930s survey courses) to a more diverse set of teaching strategies that empowered teachers with the authority to design exams and to grade their own students.[168] The new "History of Western Civilization" Core course, which emerged in 1948, presented an example of this shift in emphasis and in method, having been designed to emphasize original documents and seminar-style discussions as the primary structure of the new Core course. As discussions became more prominent, faculty became unhappy with the practice of the 1930s that allowed students to skip class and prepare for the comprehensives by themselves. These trends made the status of the independent comprehensive examinations created by Boucher to much national acclaim in

1931 politically fragile, and they soon became the victim of the curricular gang wars of the 1950s between the graduate divisions and the College.[169]

Students who matriculated under the 1942 curriculum were passionately loyal to it, both during their tenure at the University and in subsequent decades as alumni of the College.[170] For many the "Hutchins College" was an experience so transformative as to define their identities throughout their professional and adult lives. As Aaron Sayvetz put it in 1978, "Those of us who developed, as students or teachers, under the spell of Robert Maynard Hutchins and the educational environment he created, are, I suspect, irrevocably shaped by that experience."[171] Joseph Gusfield, a distinguished sociologist who entered the College in 1941, reminisced, "The University of Chicago seemed charged with an electric current that made every question a matter of analysis and argument, in which the intellectual exchange seemed to me to be as keen as possible. We all felt ourselves to be among the smartest and the brightest. Later many colleagues of mine would speak disappointedly of their undergraduate days, and I have felt very privileged to feel otherwise."[172]

Nor did the new curriculum lack impressive pedagogical achievements. A survey of 866 graduates of the College in the fall quarter of 1951 by John P. Netherton, assessing the readiness of Chicago undergraduates for advanced study in professional and graduate schools, found that most alumni felt that they had received a superior preparation in the ability "to read and think critically" and to "understand scientific methods," and that their undergraduate training in these capacities was stronger than that of the peers whom they encountered in graduate or professional schools who had attended other colleges and universities. Netherton also noted that the same alums felt significantly less well prepared in writing, oral expression, knowledge of subject matter in a major field, and the use of mathematics or statistics, and he concluded that "the large gap between the first two ratings and the remainder can be taken as a result of our planned emphasis on criticism and the understanding of methods."[173]

The situation for faculty was more complex. For many young instructors the intensity of staff-based teaching and the chance to work with intellectually curious students in the later 1940s was exhilarating even if, as David Riesman later noted, the young faculty often enjoyed speaking to one another more than to the undergraduates.[174] Henry Sams remembered about the humanities course that "the weekly staff meetings were crucial. People of differing temperaments derived different degrees of pleasure or anguish from them, but nobody deliberately stayed away. At the meetings the teachers were learners, though seldom passive ones."[175] Similarly, Joe Gusfield later recalled about the staff meetings of a sociology course, in which young luminaries like Riesman, Daniel Bell, Lewis Coser,

Benjamin Nelson, Martin Meyerson, C. Wright Mills, and Sylvia Thrupp participated as teachers, that "these meetings were less conferences about pedagogy than seminars about many scholarly matters, seminars marked by intense debate and rancor, pyrotechnical displays of ego and erudition, and great flashes of insight, wit, and critical analysis."[176] Both Clarence Faust and Champ Ward wanted not only dedicated teachers but also colleagues devoted to the study of general education as a professional career. Ward articulated these values in 1949 when he stipulated the criteria for the award of permanent tenure in the College, which contained no reference to scholarly publications.[177] Moreover, Ward and his colleagues were confident that the College would be able to continue to recruit talented professors interested in general education. Ward wrote to Hutchins in February 1947, "As the theory and practice of general education widen in the nation, we may anticipate a lessening of the difficulty of finding prospective teachers of ability who already possess some interest in and experience with the problems of general education."[178]

But even among those most loyal to the faculty ideal of Hutchins College, pressures pulled in the direction of specialization because of the prestige that the research university afforded. Some colleagues, such as Christian Mackauer and Gerhard Meyer, did make successful careers as honored teachers, but others, including Riesman, Bell, and Mills, had formidable intellectual ambitions that quickly lured them back into the big departments at Chicago and at other leading research universities. This was evident in the career of Milton Singer, a young philosopher turned social theorist, who during the 1950s became an important collaborator with Robert Redfield in the creation of a series of civilizational studies programs at the University.[179] As Redfield's successor as chair of the social sciences staff between 1947 and 1952, Singer helped David Riesman and others refashion the Social Sciences 2 course into a broad interdisciplinary project whose principal theme became the comparative study of personality and culture. In October 1951, Singer sent F. Champion Ward a long memo in which he wrestled with several problems associated with the College, focusing especially on staff morale. "I do not think that high ranks and salaries, lush offices and secretaries are going to help us much if our best people lose the sense of being involved in a vital intellectual adventure in which they can grow and be creative," Singer warned. "To the extent that these teachers lose touch with the development of their subject matters and themselves have little sense of what is involved in the growth of science and scholarship, to that extent we may expect their teaching, whether they use discussions or any other devices, to degenerate to a level of empty pedagogical 'tricks.'"[180] In 1955 Singer was invited to join the Department of Anthropology, and he soon became a founding father of the Committee on Southern Asian Studies, a group dedicated to faculty and graduate-student research. As the years passed, his connections to the College's Core social science program attenuated, and his teaching interests shifted in the direction of research-based area studies.

Unfortunately for Champ Ward's dream, Singer's behavior was emulated by many of the young instructors who had proper research credentials and could not resist the allure of specialized research and the desire for professional advancement in their disciplines. As Louis Menand has pointed out, the 1960s became a time in which "analytic rigor and disciplinary autonomy became important to an extent they had not before the war.... Scholarly tendencies that emphasized theoretical or empirical rigor were taken up and carried into the mainstream of academic practice; tendencies that reflected a generalist or 'belletrist' approach were pushed to the professional margins."[181] In such a milieu, teaching for its own sake, and general-education teaching at that, were bound to find fewer and fewer devotees in the leading doctoral programs. By 1975 Richard McKeon admitted privately,

> One of the things that we were convinced of was that the faculty giving this education [in the 1940s] didn't have this kind of education ... [but that] in the future the faculty would have this kind of education and it would be easier. We were wrong about that.... When we recruited junior faculty [in the College] we would get Ph.D.'s from Harvard, Yale, or Columbia, and they would come and they thought it would be a monstrous job to learn how to do this.... With each new set of faculty it eventually got to be a campaign against the programmed course, and a plea for freedom. Freedom to do what you do best.[182]

Like Burton before him, Hutchins had tried to solve the problem of undergraduate education at the University of Chicago, and like Burton, he would ultimately come up short. Burton had sought to divert large material resources away from the "research" university to create a separate and vibrant College residential community; Hutchins had tried the even more radical step of expelling the departments from any curricular or teaching roles in collegiate education and creating the College as a sovereign island in the sea of the larger university. Both were fascinating plans, and both left powerful traces. Burton's hopes crashed on the rocks of the Great Depression, and Hutchins's dreams would falter on the profound crisis of enrollments after 1952, which left the College exposed to hostile forces eager to launch a counterrevolution.

HUTCHINS AND THE STRUGGLE FOR ACADEMIC FREEDOM

Hutchins's rise to prominence as a pundit defending liberal education in the later 1930s, via his writings *The Higher Learning in America* and *No Friendly Voice*, was further amplified by his courageous defense of academic freedom during decades when such views were routinely scorned in many sectors of American society. It might be strange to see Hutchins's defensive stance as a "positive" contribution to the University's development, but that is exactly what it was, for Hutchins's rigor on this issue reinforced Chicago's identity and reputation as a place for serious, independent students and faculty whose educational and research programs demanded that the intellectual and cultural autonomy of the faculty and students be respected.

Challenges to the idea of academic freedom usually involved both a faculty member's teaching on campus and his right to work in the outside world. One colleague who tested these rights was Paul H. Douglas, a temperamental and opinionated liberal economist.[183] During World War II, Douglas served with distinction as an officer in the Marines, winning several medals for his valor in combat, and he returned home to run for the US Senate in Illinois as a Democratic reform candidate in 1948. Once elected, he settled into the role of a centrist liberal—strong on defense, but also for civil rights and social welfare programs. But in the 1920s and early 1930s Douglas had had a different reputation as an ardent labor activist, a socialist, and a tough-minded urban reformer. Douglas openly supported the candidates of the Socialist Party, Norman Thomas and James H. Maurer, in the 1928 presidential election, and he gave lectures expressing his admiration for the Soviet Union's welfare policies and pressing for the diplomatic recognition of the Soviet Union. One of Douglas's special targets was Samuel Insull and Insull's interlocking structure of utility companies in Chicago. Favoring the municipalization of key utilities, Douglas helped to create the Illinois Utility Consumers and Investors League, a body that sought to expose what its supporters felt to be the corruption of Insull's empire.[184]

Douglas was hated by key business interests in the city, who saw his activities as subversive and embarrassing the University. He was particularly disliked by Bernard Sunny and Albert Sprague, Loop businessmen who had professional interests in the traction companies. In 1929 Sprague threatened to resign from the University's citizens committee because of his irritation with Douglas, insisting, "I do not see how I can urgently recommend people to give consideration to an organization [the University] that sponsors work which I feel is very detrimental to the best interests of the city."[185] Woodward and Swift responded with forthright defenses of

Douglas's right to speak his mind and to engage in civic work.[186] Douglas continued his opposition to Insull's empire into early 1932, when before a stormy meeting of the Illinois Commerce Commission he challenged an attempt by Insull to float a $40-million bond issue that would have transferred money from a solvent Commonwealth Edison to several insolvent holding companies. Douglas was again tagged as embarrassing the University in the eyes of the local business community. Sunny wrote to Hutchins in July 1932, complaining, "As open minded and generous as you are, I don't think you can look over the record that Douglas has made in this case and decide that it reflects credit on either him or the University. Nor would I trust him to instruct a class of students in such matters. After working with him for several months I should expect them to be a batch of first class 'nuts.'"[187]

The impact of Douglas's radical activities was compounded in late spring of 1932 by two other spurs. First was the decision of a local socialist club on campus to invite William Z. Foster to lecture at the University. Foster was the national candidate of the Communist Party on the fall 1932 presidential ballot, and his appearance on campus in late May 1932 led to consternation in many local business circles. At the same time, Amos Alonzo Stagg agreed to allow a socialist-sponsored Counter-Olympics— the International Workers Athletic Meet—to be staged on Stagg Field in late July 1932, believing that the organizers' motives were sincere: "I could not see that any harm could come to the University."[188]

These random but converging incidents led to protests by local alumni and others, and Hutchins and Swift found themselves confronting a precedent-setting situation. In the case of Foster, Hutchins prepared a standard letter to the protesters that was uncompromising in its defense of the faculty's and students' academic freedom. He argued that Foster had been invited to the University by a recognized student organization; that the students had a right to hear his views as a presidential candidate; that Foster was not a criminal, and that, in more general terms, "as long as our students can be orderly about it they should have freedom to discuss any problem that presents itself and in which they are interested.... I am convinced that [the] cure lies through open discussion rather than through inhibition and taboo."[189] Hutchins's explanations did not sit well with various local notables, not a few of whom were also prominent members of the Republican Party. A prominent local lawyer, Arthur Galt, thought that Hutchins "personally wants the spread of at least pink ideas," whereas Silas H. Strawn, another Chicago lawyer, complained that while he otherwise admired Hutchins, he did not like "lending encouragement to the milling around of liberal minded students, aided and abetted by such creatures as Foster."[190]

Perhaps inevitably, the three cases converged into a discussion of the idea of academic freedom among members of the board of trustees. The relevant standing committee of the board with jurisdiction over faculty issues was the Committee on Instruction and Research. On July 12, 1932, this committee had a protracted discussion of academic freedom, and the conversation was so controversial that Harold Swift not only marked the minutes confidential, but also gave the participants letter codes ("A," "B," etc.) instead of using their full names. The high point of the debate came in an exchange between Hutchins ("A") and Thomas Donnelley ("B"), the vice president of the board of trustees and a prominent Chicago businessman:

"A" referred to the fact that a number of communications had been received within the past few weeks with respect to the following:

(1) A speech in Mandel by Foster at a meeting held under student auspices at which ... Foster had advocated overthrow of government by violence.
(2) Alleged radical statements made before a commission recently by a member of the faculty ("X" [Paul Douglas]).
(3) An application for the use of Stagg Field July 21 for Counter-Olympic games.

... "A" indicated that thus far he had been unable to confirm through testimony of members of the faculty attending the meeting the report that the speaker had advocated overthrow of government by force.

As to (3), he had referred the application to Mr. Stagg ..., [who] thought it wise to allow the field to be used for this purpose and thus give the persons who had illusions about the conduct of the Olympic Games a chance to explode in an athletic way. In view of the fact that Mr. Stagg is by nature conservative and is also a director of the Olympic Games, it seems proper to proceed upon his advice.

As to "X", ... he is on permanent appointment and, therefore, can be removed under the Statutes only for incompetence or misconduct. The best method of determining whether "X" is guilty of either of these two respects would seem to be to have any charge considered by persons in his field who are able to give competent judgment. If charges are brought forward by any competent person, "A" proposed to have such charges considered, including all the evidence on both sides, and later reviewed by this Committee....

"A" stated that as to the appearance of extremists in the gatherings at the University, he felt that it is in the interests of education to permit any person to present his case rather than to incur the possibility of seeming to prevent students and others in the University community from hearing all sides on an issue; that the effect on students of Foster's talk seemed anything but favorable to the speaker, and that the best way to dispose of illusions of this sort is to let people see them in person rather than merely to read their writings or hear them over the radio.

As to the application for use of Stagg Field, he believed that Mr. Stagg's judgment is correct, and that the occasion is likely to prove to be entirely harmless and merely an expression of the belief of this group that the Olympic Games are run on class lines.

"A" stated that he was reporting these matters for the information of the committee and inquired as to whether there was any desire to have the situation reviewed by the Board.

"B" stated that he felt strongly that there was a difference between academic freedom and academic license; that Foster was openly recognized as advocating the overthrow of government by force; that he thought it was all right to say to the students that the University has no objection to their listening to extremists of this sort if they insist upon it, but that in so doing they should arrange for other places than University buildings or grounds for such meetings, and that the University does not desire to give such persons the publicity which arises from meetings announced to be held in University buildings or to encourage them through permission to use the buildings, for the purpose of advocating destruction of government by force; and he believed that members of the faculty as citizens have a perfect right to do as they wish as individuals but not as members of the staff and thereby utilizing the name of the University to help them to give publicity to and spread their individual ideas; that at this time when everyone is trying desperately not to rock the boat, it is important to ask members of the faculty to avoid getting into the press in this fashion. He expressed his opinion that the fact might just as well be frankly recognized that the University must of necessity avoid the enmity of those who are in a position to aid the University.

"A" inquired as to what "B" would do if after making a request of members of the faculty as indicated, they should refuse either to accede or resign. "B" replied that in that event their services should be dispensed with.

"A" stated that it would, of course, be perfectly possible for him to have conversation with "X" as suggested, but that in such an event "X" would then have the further weapon to use that the University is a capitalistic institution and was trying to muzzle him. He stated that the head of a corporation had sent a representative to see him on the "X" matter and that he, "A," had recommended that the head of the organization in question might very properly invite "X" to lunch someday and talk the situation over with him, pointing out to him where his information was incorrect and his stand on these questions indefensible; this suggestion had been accepted but nothing had come of it. He called attention to the fact that the University had an opportunity to pass upon the desirability of "X" as a member of the staff at the time he was recommended for permanent appointment....

"C" [William Bond] emphasized the point made by "B" on the difficulty of faculty members disassociating themselves from the University. He also suggested that stenographic reports be made of talks given by persons of extreme views in University halls.

"D" [Harold Swift] suggested that he thought it would be entirely proper for "A" to make the Board just such a report as he had made to the Committee and recommended that this be done.[191]

This exchange is significant, not the least because Donnelley's and Bond's concerns about the seeming excesses to which academic freedom had led were shared by other members of the board. This meant that the leadership role of the board president, Harold Swift, became critical.[192] Swift not only managed to bring the July 1932 debate to a civil conclusion, but already in these earliest incidents emerged as a staunch defender of the idea of academic freedom. In 1929, when the first protests had arisen concerning Douglas's political advocacy, Swift insisted that Douglas "is a citizen of the United States and has a right to express his views. I don't think any one has a right to discipline him for so doing, least of all a University that stands for liberty, a search for truth and fairness. If that is so, I don't think you ought to condemn the University and on that account refuse to cooperate with it."[193] Granted that this did not match the programmatic rhetoric of Hutchins—Swift was given to softening up opponents, rather than hitting them over the head—but it lent legitimacy and protection to the young president's more doctrinaire arguments.

The effects of the 1932 collisions soon died down. In truth, Douglas was but a small thorn in the side of Chicago capitalism. Hutchins himself had managed to alienate many more potential contributors in the early 1930s, with his opinionated editorials in a local newspaper denouncing the municipal school board for political jobbery, his condemnation of unfair labor practices, and various speeches in 1932 (including a notable address to the Young Democratic Clubs in June, on the eve of the presidential convention) defending deficit spending and higher taxes as a way of coping with the Depression.[194] In his private papers Harold Swift kept a list of Chicagoans alienated from the University of Chicago, "chiefly in connection with Hutchins's speeches or socialism, or both."[195] Hutchins's perceived flippancy, his wisecracking, and his discreetly pro-Democratic and pro-labor sympathies rubbed many members of the board of trustees the wrong way, and the situation apparently came to a head at a board meeting in mid-March 1935. After the meeting, trustee James Stifler surveyed the opinions of a number of other trustees about Hutchins, and many voiced the opinion that Hutchins's views alienated the public and that he tended to ignore the fact that when he spoke, it was on behalf of the institution and not just himself.[196]

But if Hutchins was the bane of some on his own board, he would soon become a hero for academics and foundation officials around the country.[197] In the late spring of 1935 a convergence of remarkable events brought the University into the national spotlight as the target of an investigation of sedition, giving Hutchins an auspicious platform to emerge as a national spokesperson for academic freedom. In early 1935, Hamilton Fish III, congressman from New York, delivered a national radio address in which he claimed that the University of Chicago and other leading universities were "honeycombed with Socialists, near-Communists, and Communists, teaching class hatred, hatred of religion, and hatred of American institutions, including the American flag."[198] A decorated war veteran in World War I who had helped to create the American Legion in the early 1920s, Fish was a resolute isolationalist who opposed US recognition of the Soviet Union and who went on to oppose American involvement in World War II. Forced into retirement from Congress in 1944 by a coalition of Democratic and Republican forces, including Republican governor Thomas Dewey, because of his isolationist sentiments, in the early 1930s Hamilton Fish became a darling of the Hearst press because of his strident anticommunism.[199]

Fish's accusations were greeted with derision by local University representatives, but his statements were covered closely by one of the newspapers in Chicago owned by William Randolph Hearst, the *Chicago Herald and Examiner*, and thus gained notoriety. Like its sister publications in the Hearst syndicate, the *Herald* specialized in high-volume, flamboyant journalism, and when Hearst launched a crusade against communism in March 1934, the *Herald* and its sister publication, the *American*, followed their owner's lead. In the wake of Fish's radio address, the local Hearst newspapers initiated their own anticommunist crusade by publishing accusatory stories about the political views of two Chicago faculty members, Frederick L. Schuman and Robert Morss Lovett.[200] The former was a young, ambitious international relations scholar, and protégé of Charles Merriam; the latter, a venerable English professor with a penchant for left, liberal, and socialist causes. Neither was a communist, but each had strong left-wing sympathies, and both were members of so-called front organizations, and to many fearful people such distinctions were confusing and perhaps even irrelevant.[201]

Hutchins responded to Fish's accusations in an eloquent speech on February 21, 1935, at an annual dinner for Chicago-area alumni at the Union League Club: "The answer to such charges against a university is not denial, nor evasion, nor apology. It is the assertion that free inquiry is indispensable to the good life, that universities exist for the sake of such inquiry, that without it they cease to be universities, and that such inquiry and hence universities are more necessary now than ever. The sacred trust of the universities is to carry the torch of freedom."[202] The Union League speech was the first of several notable addresses that Hutchins was to make in 1935 on the issue of academic freedom, and if alumni opinion was its object, it had the desired effect.[203] Leaving nothing to chance, the University's alumni magazine also published an urbane response to Fish written by John P. Howe, class of 1927, citing the work of faculty members such as Paul Douglas, Charles Merriam, Harry Gideonse, and others in a positive and affirming manner.[204] If well-intentioned rhetoric urging the alumni to join the faculty in a solidarity of pride could reassure the wider world, surely this was the stuff to do it. However, neither Hutchins's nor Howe's self-confident words prepared the University for the jolt from the world of yellow journalism that was about to hit it, in the person of Charles R. Walgreen and his self-appointed patrons in the local Hearst press.

On April 10, 1935, the owner of a chain of drugstores headquartered in Chicago, Charles R. Walgreen, wrote to Hutchins, informing him that he was withdrawing his niece, Lucille Norton, from the University because she had been insidiously exposed to "Communistic influences." Walgreen further asked why "one of our country's leading universities … should permit even to a limited degree, seditious propaganda under the guise of academic freedom."[205] Within twenty-four hours, copies of Walgreen's letter had found their way to the editorial offices of all major Chicago newspapers. The two Hearst papers—the *Herald* and the *American*— treated the story as front-page news, with headlines screaming, "Walgreen Takes Niece from U. of C. to Avoid 'Communistic Influences,'" followed the next day by "Walgreen Offers to Prove U. of C. Red 'Influences' at Open Inquiry." Lucille Norton was an eighteen-year-old student who had come to Chicago from Seattle some months earlier to live with Walgreen and his family and attend the University. She enrolled in three courses— Social Sciences I, Music, and English Composition. In the first and last courses she encountered texts authored by communists or Soviet authors. Marx's *Communist Manifesto* was the subject of one of the lectures in the autumn quarter of the social sciences sequence, and one exercise of the

English composition course used a short selection from Ilin's *New Russia's Primer*, the purpose being to encourage students to think critically about the exaggerated claims, false assumptions, and sensational rhetoric used in that text.[206]

In both courses students were expected to read a large number of other original documents and texts, so that these exposures to "communism" were little more than episodic, and from subsequent testimony that emerged during the investigation it is absolutely certain that the instructors used both texts in a scholarly manner with no intention of propagandizing on behalf of the Soviet system.[207] According to Walgreen, however, even these small doses were far too much for his naive, innocent niece, who, before she had enrolled in the University, had not a clue about communism, but who, after attending these lectures and discussions, came back to Walgreen's house and his dinner table and began to express herself in ways that Walgreen found shocking, telling him that the family was a disappearing institution and that communism versus capitalism was the essential question of the day.

Hutchins replied to Walgreen's letter, asking whether he would provide concrete information about "the instances of communistic influence and seditious propaganda by the faculty to which your niece has been exposed." This letter too found its way to the newspapers. When Walgreen responded by asking for a public hearing, open to the press, before the board of trustees to elaborate his accusations, Hutchins peremptorily rejected this demand, insisting that for forty-three years the University had "a clear record of public service and educational leadership. In view of that record, it sees no necessity of holding a public hearing when vague and unsupported charges are made against it. The University will ignore your criticism until it receives the evidence it has asked for."[208]

Now the *Chicago Tribune* and the Hearst newspapers, especially the *Herald*, quickly fanned the dispute into a real fire. Hearst's hatred of Roosevelt made Hutchins an all-the-more attractive target, given Hutchins's public support for various New Deal labor and fiscal reforms. Hutchins's refusal to engineer a public hearing led a group of conservative Republican politicians in Springfield, Illinois, to take the matter into their own hands. On April 17 the Illinois Senate passed by a vote of 28–11 a resolution submitted by Senator Charles W. Baker of Monroe Center, Illinois, forming a special committee to investigate "subversive communistic teachings and ideas advocating the violent overthrow of the established form of government of the United States and the State of Illinois" in "certain tax exempt colleges and universities in the State of Illinois." Since private universities also enjoyed tax-exempt privileges, the commission saw fit to make the University of Chicago its first (and only) target. What Walgreen himself could not compel—a public hearing—Baker, with full endorsement of the Hearst press, would now provide.

On May 13 the first of three investigative sessions held by the committee took place in Chicago.[209] Charles Walgreen opened the hearings by testifying to the decline and fall of his niece's morals and reciting the following dinner-table conversation:

> We were discussing Communism and capitalism, and lately I said to Lucille, "you are getting to be a Communist." And she said, "I am not the only one, there are a lot more on the campus."
>
> I said to Lucille, "Do you realize that this means the abolition of the family, the abolition of the Church, and especially do you realize that it means the overthrow of our government?" And she said, "Yes, I think I do, but don't the ends ever justify the means?"
>
> "Don't you realize that this means bloodshed?" Again, she said, "Yes, but how did we get our independence, wasn't it by revolution?"
>
> "Well, Lucille, are they really teaching you these things over at the University?" And she said, "No, I don't think they are teaching it to us."
>
> "Are they advocating these things?" And she said, "No, not exactly."
>
> "Well," I said, "where do you get all these radical ideas?" "Well," she said, "we have a lot of reading on Communism"; and I said, "More than on about our own government?" and she said, "Oh, yes, much more, so far we haven't gotten much of that."
>
> "Well, how about collectiveness, fascism, syndicalism, anarchy—did you get all those?" And she said, "Yes, they were explained to us in our classes and we were given much reading but mostly on Communism." And she said, "Anyway, isn't communism vs. capitalism the issue? At least it is at the University."

Walgreen was particularly distressed that students in the English composition course had been assigned passages from the *New Russia's Primer*, concluding, "I am persuaded that the methods used in the Social Science and English courses already referred to, evidence a subtle and insidious design to impress by indirection, Communistic views on the student mind."[210]

Following Walgreen, and after a brief introduction from Harold Swift, Robert Hutchins gave a forceful defense of the faculty, arguing that he had examined all of the curricular materials in question and found them balanced and lacking in any intent to indoctrinate any political or social point of view, that the University and its faculty had a long and distinguished record of civic service, that Chicago also had the best social science group in the nation, and that its good name must not be besmirched lest the quality of the University suffer. Hutchins was followed by Charles E. Merriam, who cited his extensive involvement in city government and civic affairs in general and then delivered a trenchant attack on the University's accusers: "I charge these persons, wittingly or unwittingly, with attacking one of the strongest forces for the stabilization and maintenance of our civilization—our University. I charge them with efforts to break down and destroy one of the greatest centers of civic instruction and governmental research in America. I charge them with attempted grand larceny of human reputation and achievement."[211]

The second and third hearings of the investigation were all downhill. The second session on May 24 began with Joseph B. Fleming, the attorney for Walgreen, reading several passages from the *Chicago Maroon*, which, he claimed, showed the campus as a hotbed of communism, and offering political handbills, pamphlets, and newspaper clippings to prove that Schuman and Lovett were communist sympathizers. Schuman, Gideonse, and Lovett then took the stand, with Schuman and Lovett defending their progressive political views and Gideonse explaining that to use the *Communist Manifesto* in class did not make the teacher a communist, and that out of 5,987 pages of assigned reading in the social sciences course, no more than 55 pages (less than 1 percent) could possibly be associated with communist theory or communist authors. Moreover, contra Walgreen, Gideonse proved that more than half of the readings (about 3,000 pages) directly related to American government and institutions. Then, in a much-awaited appearance, Lucille Norton testified. Under oath she agreed with her uncle that before coming to Chicago she "had little knowledge of or interest in communism," but that she had been exposed to communism in lectures and readings. Under questioning by the committee's attorney, Russell Whitman, she admitted that she had encountered no specific efforts to induce her into believing in communism:

RUSSELL WHITMAN: Now, you have spoken about this business of indoctrinating. I suppose, when you began to favor communist trends, you did not detect that any special effort had been made to induce you to favor them, is that so?

NORTON: That is true, and I did not know that when I was taken out of the University.

WHITMAN: And, therefore, you cannot point out particular incidents?

NORTON: No, I cannot....

WHITMAN: Now, among that list of professors, can you identify any one whose instruction had this influence on your mind, or did they all have it, or, can't you tell?

NORTON: Well, Wirth had nothing to do with it, because the second quarter's work had nothing to do with it. [Harry Gideonse taught the first quarter, Louis Wirth the second quarter, and Jerome Kerwin the third quarter of the social sciences course.]

WHITMAN: That eliminates him, then.

NORTON: That eliminates him. But as to the others, I could not say.

WHITMAN: With reference to the disintegration of the family, do you attach your instruction on that point to any particular professor or his lecture?

NORTON: I don't believe I could say that. We had that in readings, and it was, I would say, one of the threads running through the whole course.

WHITMAN: And would you ascribe any of the feeling or judgment that you formed there to your talks with groups of young gentlemen and young ladies in your class?

NORTON: Yes, I would, with communism.

WHITMAN: But that you do not refer to as indoctrinating in the sense in which we are using it here, do you?

NORTON: I do not.[212]

This gripping testimony was followed by that of a fifty-eight-year-old returning student, J. W. Clarke, who described himself as "an American born citizen of American parents of Scotch extraction," who "give[s] way to no man in real patriotism and love of" his country. After mentioning that he had four children, that he was the assistant manager of a large department in a nationwide corporation ("that shows I have a job"), that he was a lieutenant in the Illinois militia, and that he despised the Reds and was "for American individualism and against all forms of forced regimentation," Clarke proceeded to report that he was a student in Harry Gideonse's course. He then cited "voluminous" class notes to prove that Gideonse (whom he admired) was highly critical of communism and that "Mr. Gideonse has tried to get his classes to think and not soak up like a sponge the things they hear and read."[213]

During the third hearing, on June 7, the atmosphere often bordered on the ludicrous, with a bored Hutchins sitting through verbose denunciations of the University by Harry A. Jung, the founder and chair of the "American Vigilante Intelligence Federation," and Elizabeth Dilling, whose publicity handouts described her as a modern "Joan of Arc" of Kenilworth, Illinois. Dilling, a self-anointed crusader against world communism, presented the committee with a 102-page pamphlet called *How "Red" Is the University of Chicago?* (compiled by one Nelson E. Hewitt). Reading a long list of random references that, she alleged, demonstrated that the University was a hotbed of communism, she proceeded to denounce Hutchins, along with Walter Dill Scott of Northwestern, Senator William Borah, Louis D. Brandeis, William Dodd, John Dewey, Harold Swift, and Jane Addams as communist sympathizers. She was convinced that "it is certain that the University of Chicago is diseased with Communism and that its contagion is a menace to the community and the Nation." Comic relief, in the form of fisticuffs, came when one bored audience member leaned over to the gentlemen next to him and asked if Mrs. Dilling should not be more accurately named Mrs. Dillinger, whereupon the second man, who turned out to be Mrs. Dilling's gallant husband, punched the first in the nose. General mayhem ensued, much to the delight of the newspaper reporters assigned to the story.

After further testimony from dubious witnesses, and a brief reappearance of Hutchins, who was asked by the senators how much Rockefeller Chapel had cost to build, the hearings ended, having exhausted the subject and certainly the participants.

The Walgreen hearings elicited a united front of support for the position taken by Hutchins. During alumni reunion weekend in early June 1935 five senior faculty spoke eloquently on the issue of academic freedom, and student leaders also rallied. Eleven seniors in prominent positions (the editor of the *Maroon*, the captain of the football team, the president of the Interfraternity Council, etc.) wrote a joint letter asserting that they had never encountered a faculty member who sought to "impose upon students communist beliefs." "We believe that the University of Chicago has a reputation for intellectual tolerance and superior education equaled by few institutions of higher learning,"[214] they wrote. Still, Hutchins inevitably became the central voice of the University's defense, and his tough-minded rhetoric, which played well in liberal media circles, afforded everyone else an anchor point of defense. Even before the Walgreen hearings opened, Hutchins went on the offensive by delivering an eloquent speech on NBC radio on April 18, 1935, titled "What Is a University?" This speech, together with the articulate defenses later provided by the faculty themselves, won considerable public acclaim in academic and in progressive political circles. On July 1 President Roosevelt sent Hutchins a "private and confidential" note of support: "You must have had a vile time with that inquisition. I sometimes think that Hearst has done more harm to the cause of Democracy and civilization in America than any other three contemporaries put together."[215]

Hutchins's words and deeds in the Walgreen affair garnered him a spot on the cover of *Time* magazine in late June 1935, where he was idolized as one of the "handsomest" university presidents in the country and as having "the courage and vision to effect new plans." Moreover, in a surprising turn of events, Hutchins had the further satisfaction in 1937 of seeing a now somewhat repentant Charles Walgreen give the University $550,000 to establish a visiting professorship/lectureship in American institutions.

Beyond Hutchins's own efforts, Harold Swift's role as chairman of the board of trustees was also of crucial importance. Simply put, he stood solidly behind Hutchins and the senior faculty. Swift's many letters to detractors and supporters had a naturalness and thoughtfulness about them that rang true, and his decency, intelligence, and courage were freely visible. Moreover, Swift was shrewd in his assessment of Lucille Norton: "My own analysis is that Mr. Walgreen is honest, a sturdy character and quite stolid, and the Niece Lucille discovered soon after entering the University that there were several points which got a rise out of Uncle. I think that she took him for several rides without his knowing it, and she probably enjoyed it hugely. Her only statement has been that she felt no attempts at indoctrination nor any insidious propaganda, but that she thought the University of Chicago was a very good place to go if a person wanted to know about communism or anything else."[216]

But Harold Swift was not the board, and the cover of *Time* magazine was not necessarily considered a place of honor. Throughout the crisis, the board was polarized about Hutchins and his impact on the reputation of the University. In public, of course, there was no dissension. The presence of trustees Laird Bell and James Douglas as attorneys for the University at the hearings gave the impression of a united front with the president and the faculty, and several trustees were openly supportive. But other trustees were deeply unhappy about the adverse publicity, and they worried about damage to the University's reputation because of the outspoken views of its young president.

The negative attitudes of some trustees reflected larger currents among wealthy elites in Chicago. A survey of local opinion in the city undertaken by the John Price Jones Corporation in April 1936 in preparation for a new capital campaign indicated that the University projected discordant images. While most of those surveyed affirmed the high intellectual standing and prestige of the University, many were also critical of its teaching "radicalism." The authors concluded (among other things) that "there is a widespread feeling that certain elements within the University are unjustifiably stirring up social discontent, and that the University itself has not been sufficiently diligent in controlling this," that "the giving public is not sufficiently sold on the case for academic freedom," that "although public opinion concerning him is improving, there is a widespread feeling in Chicago that the President is a 'dangerously independent' thinker who speaks with 'no friendly voice' and with a flippant disregard for the established order," and that "adverse public opinion already appears to have influenced adversely the entrance of high school students into the University and to have retarded recovery of giving." At the same time, the authors found that the recent controversy had exactly the opposite effect on the students and alumni: "The general feeling on the Campus was that alumni, students, and faculty were united in defense of the University by this attack as they had never been before."[217]

William Benton, commissioned to review the University's public relations problems in 1936, produced his own survey, which he distributed confidentially to the trustees in January 1937. Benton asserted that "wide acclaim would Mr. Hutchins win in some quarters if for New Year's he resolved to fire, or to attempt to fire, certain members of the faculty on the charge of radicalism. These are influential quarters, including some of Chicago's wealthiest citizens, many potential donors to the University." Benton admitted that such a purge was unacceptable, since it "would violate the most deeply embedded tradition in the world of higher education," but as a public relations expert Benton urged the University to hold special meetings for faculty to orient them on the need of the University to have friends and to ask them to refrain from overtly radical statements.[218]

The Walgreen affair thus ended on a mixed note. Four of the five senators on the Illinois Senate's committee issued a majority report in late June 1935 that exonerated the University of seditious practices but slammed Robert Lovett for his "unpatriotic course of conduct for a period of eight or ten years." In addition, two of these same senators—Barbour and Graham—also issued a supplementary statement that was positive about the University but also rebuked Lovett for outside activities that were "not conducive to effect[ive] or helpful service on his part as a member of the faculty of the University of Chicago," and recommended that he be given early retirement because of his embarrassing behavior. Particularly unfortunate in the eyes of the committee was a letter that Lovett had written in 1926 to a former acquaintance in which he casually observed that all governments are rotten.[219] Lovett's fate came before the board of trustees in mid-July. On behalf of his fellow trustee participants in the hearings, James Douglas and Harold Swift, Laird Bell gave a detailed report to the full board on the reports issued by the investigating committee. There was "no evidence whatever of inefficiency in [Lovett's] work or of any attempt to indoctrinate [his] students," Bell remarked, but he stopped short of advocating a public defense of Lovett.[220] In the end, the University maintained a studied silence on the denouement of the affair, and although Lovett retired as he normally would at the age of sixty-five in September 1936, he never received the vindication that he felt he deserved.

The opposition had no such scruples. When the committee's majority and minority reports were released in late June, the *Herald* published a vicious editorial on June 27 entitled "Red Propaganda at the U. of C. To the Fathers and Mothers of the United States" whose first sentence read, "If you want your children to become Communists, send them, if they are of collegiate age, to the University of Chicago." Hutchins thereupon received dozens of telegrams from alumni and others who were outraged at the Hearst press's insults.[221] Hutchins was experiencing a classic case of being caught in the middle—angry alumni (and a faculty member whose good name had been besmirched) who wanted the mud slung back, and the decision of Swift, Bell, and their colleagues to take their sizable, if partial, victory and walk away.[222] Universities have difficulty coping with such controversies, for their very strengths—their commitment to intellectual diversity, their culture of tolerance, and their self-assigned feelings of dignity—easily become tactical obstacles when they find themselves trapped in ideological skirmishes with opponents who refuse to play by the same rules of deference and dispassion.

After the conclusion of World War II new challenges emerged involving direct allegations of communism on the campus, amid the tense postwar confluence of fear and paranoia in the era of McCarthyism. In June 1947 the Illinois General Assembly approved legislation creating another special public commission to investigate seditious activities, but this time the committee had an open-ended mandate to look for instances of sedition in "any activities of any person or persons, co-partnership, association, organization or society, or combination thereof which are suspected of being directed toward the overthrow of the Government of the United States or the State of Illinois."[223] Created in the atmosphere of paranoia about communism that was sweeping American society in the late 1940s and in spite of strong opposition from liberal lobbying groups such as the AAUP and from several Chicago newspapers, the commission was chaired by a little-known state senator from Mt. Vernon, Illinois, Paul W. Broyles, who had made a fortune selling photo enlargements to Illinois farmers. The Broyles Commission had a two-year mandate and a budget of $15,000. By the end of its tenure in 1949, Broyles and his colleagues managed to craft five bills designed to eliminate any potential Red menace in the state of Illinois, including the mandatory registration of all political groups of twenty or more with the Illinois secretary of state; the use of loyalty oaths for all public school teachers, elected officials, and civil servants; the mandatory dismissal of all subversive teachers who taught "any doctrine to undermine the form of government of this state or of the United States"; and the prohibition of membership in communist organizations.

The drafts of the proposed legislation came before the General Assembly in February 1949, and they immediately provoked a spirited debate in the press and on campuses. The bills were a mishmash of imprecise and ill-defined wording, and they deserved the hostile scrutiny they received. At the University of Chicago the response to the Broyles bills was particularly vocal, so much so that on March 1, 1949, 106 students led by a campus group called the Young Progressives of America journeyed to Springfield to lobby against the legislation. They were joined by students from Roosevelt College and from other institutions, for a total of about 350 individuals, including representatives of the Illinois Communist Party, the Meadville Theological Students Association, the University of Chicago Republican Club, the Students for Democratic Action, the Illinois CIO, and sundry other groups. In the words of one student leader, the students felt these bills to be "police state measures" wrought by a "police-state method."[224]

What exactly transpired during the students' visit to Springfield on the afternoon and evening of March 1 was later contested.[225] The students who testified against the Broyles bills at the hearings of the Illinois Senate's Judiciary Committee were reasonably civil, and the audience boisterous but not out of control. Some students, mainly those from Roosevelt College, did get involved in a demonstration against racial segregation at a local restaurant, however, and proponents of the bills cleverly manufactured the claim that all of the visiting students had behaved with rowdiness, rudeness, and general arrogance (even those, as seems to have been the case of the Chicago students, who were already on a bus returning home). The next day two Republican representatives in the Illinois House launched an attack against the students from the University of Chicago as well as those from Roosevelt, denouncing them as having been indoctrinated by "Communistic and other subversive theories contrary to our free systems of representative government."[226] Representative G. William Horsley then introduced a resolution charging the Broyles Commission to undertake a special investigation of the University of Chicago and Roosevelt College. Horsley's resolution received unanimous support in the House on March 2, with the approval of the Senate coming a week later. Thus the second state-sponsored scrutiny of the University of Chicago came to be set in motion. As unpleasant as the investigation soon proved to be, the University had at least one distinct advantage over its situation fourteen years before. Unlike Walgreen's accusations in 1935, the Broyles controversy centered initially on allegedly unruly and unpatriotic students at the University, and did not at first involve the behavior of faculty members.[227] This gave the University a chance to seize the high ground of academic freedom without having to defend its flanks against specific accusations that individual faculty members had indoctrinated their students.

In response to an invitation of the Broyles Commission to testify, University notables were forced to go to Springfield in late April. Robert Hutchins testified on April 21, and performed brilliantly, combining moral outrage with disdain and mordant wit:

The danger to our institutions is not from the tiny minority who do not believe in them. It is from those who would mistakenly repress the free spirit upon which those institutions are built. The miasma of thought control that is now spreading over the country is the greatest menace to the United States since Hitler. There are two ways of fighting subversive ideas. One is the policy of repression. This policy is contrary to the letter and spirit of the Constitution of this country.... The policy of repression of ideas cannot work and has never worked. The alternative to it is the long and difficult road of education. To this the American people have been committed. It requires patience and tolerance, even in the face of intense provocation.[228]

Interrogated by J. B. Matthews, a professional Red-hunter who had previously worked for the House Committee on Un-American Activities, Hutchins deftly parried Matthews's questions, making Matthews look petulant and foolish. Hutchins's comments about Maud Slye and mice have entered the lore of the University for good reason:

MATTHEWS: Dr. Maud Slye was an Associate Professor Emeritus—this is [from] the latest obtainable directory.

HUTCHINS: "Emeritus" means retired.

MATTHEWS: She is retired on pension?

HUTCHINS: Oh, yes.

MATTHEWS: And [she] has at least the prestige of the University of Chicago to some degree associated with her name, in as much as she is carried in the directory of the University?

HUTCHINS: I don't see how we could deny the fact that she had been all her life a member of the faculty of the University. She was one of the most distinguished specialists in cancer we have seen in our time.

MATTHEWS: She was studying cancer when she was studying mice, is that correct?

HUTCHINS: Correct.

MATTHEWS: Are you acquainted with the fact that Dr. Slye has had frequent affiliations with so-called communist front organizations?

HUTCHINS: I have heard that she has had so-called frequent associations with so-called communist front organizations.

MATTHEWS: Is it the policy of the University to ignore such affiliations on the part of the members of the faculty?

HUTCHINS: To ignore them?

MATTHEWS: Yes, ignore them.

HUTCHINS: As I indicated, Dr. Slye's associations were confined on our campus to mice. She could not, I think, have done any particular harm to any of our students, even if she had been so minded. To answer your direct question, however, I am not aware that Dr. Slye has ever joined or advocated the overthrow of the government by violence.

MATTHEWS: May I ask if in your educational theory there is not such a thing as indoctrination by example?

HUTCHINS: Of mice? [laughter][229]

In the course of the April hearings an itinerant journalist by the name of Howard Rushmore testified that numerous University of Chicago professors were guilty of communism, mentioning the names of eight in particular. Laird Bell seized on Rushmore's unsubstantiated accusations to arrange for detailed affidavits by seven of these faculty members to be forwarded to the commission and simultaneously released to the newspapers in late April. This barrage compelled the commission to hold a second round of hearings on May 19, 1949.[230] Not only did Bell speak on behalf of the University, but five of the Chicago faculty members (Ernest Burgess, Robert Havighurst, Malcolm Sharp, Rexford Tugwell, and Harold Urey) attacked by Rushmore also appeared. Each performed in a credible and persuasive manner, with Urey, a Nobel Prize-winning chemist, arguing in his closing comments that the University of Chicago "is regarded the world over. In my years there I have intimately associated with the members of the staff of that organization and it is strictly loyal and American and a great University and deserves better of the people of Illinois than this investigation."[231]

As in 1935, the campus pulled together, with students and faculty on the same side of a hotly controversial issue. Three thousand students signed petitions affirming that they had not been indoctrinated and defending the University's culture of academic freedom.[232] Campus ministers—a Catholic chaplain, a Jewish rabbi, and two Protestant ministers—drafted letters defending the University and its students and denying that there was a widespread communist influence on campus.[233]

Yet, if Hutchins was again the University's star witness, this time he was not its principal advocate. When the crisis first broke, Laird Bell, who had succeeded Harold Swift as the chairman of the board of trustees in January 1949, assumed direct responsibility for coordinating the University's response. On March 10 Bell arranged for the board to establish a special "Counseling Committee" to advise Hutchins and the University on the investigation. Bell became the chair of this committee.[234] Having lived through the public relations nightmare of the Walgreen investigation, in which Hutchins's comments—however valid they were on points of principle—seemed to polarize the board of trustees, Bell was determined to design a more carefully scripted role for Hutchins.[235] In managing the

University's response strategy, Bell combined a strong defense of academic freedom with the political acumen needed to control the situation and not let it get out of hand. Throughout the crisis he followed some simple advice that he received from a friend early on—take the investigation seriously, allow no wisecracking, and show the public respect by respecting the investigation, since "the great body of citizens have heard this charge so often that they are interested in it."[236] Most significantly, believing that it was urgent to present the University's side of the story, Bell put his name on a pamphlet called *Are We Afraid of Freedom?* that Lynn Williams and his staff had crafted. This pamphlet provided a cogent and eloquent defense of the idea of academic freedom by both explaining the nature of the current controversy and invoking quotes from assorted worthies like Thomas Jefferson, John Stuart Mill, Woodrow Wilson, Oliver Wendell Holmes, Charles Evans Hughes, and Dwight D. Eisenhower in support of academic freedom. Within two months the University had distributed more than 69,000 copies of this pamphlet to University alumni, to other academic institutions around the country, and to various notables, including over one thousand college presidents. *Are We Afraid of Freedom?* prompted a cascade of congratulatory letters, many of them from academic leaders at other institutions.

In view of the effective presentations of the University, which discredited the motives and procedures of the commission, the investigation collapsed of its own weight. As for the Broyles bills, they languished in the Illinois House and eventually died by virtue of not being called up for a final vote in late June 1949.

Ellen Schrecker has speculated that the University of Chicago was able to weather crises like the Walgreen and Broyles affairs because Chicago was "a uniquely independent and cohesive institution," and that "had other academic leaders been as outspoken as Hutchins in opposing off-campus investigations, they might have mitigated the damage."[237] Such cohesion was amply demonstrated at the end of the Broyles investigation by one of the senior faculty members who testified in Springfield, Rexford Tugwell. Tugwell was a veteran of New Deal politics (he had been an adviser to Franklin Roosevelt in the early years of the New Deal, undersecretary of the Department of Agriculture, and later the governor of Puerto Rico), and he was familiar with the political dynamics that inform the work of legislative committees. Following his appearance with Laird Bell in Springfield, Tugwell wrote to the latter, thanking him for his support: "Freedom has a great price which someone has to pay, and in a university like ours you fellows have to do a lot of the paying.... For what it is worth, you can put it down that one of your faculty appreciates you and your fellow trustees and resolves to repay you in the only possible way he can—by producing all the academic results he is capable of. He only hopes you won't be called on too often to go to bat for his right to express himself."[238]

HUTCHINS AND GRADUATE EDUCATION

Hutchins's courageous defense of academic freedom was one of his most appealing features in the eyes of most senior faculty. But his propensity to advocate fundamental changes in policies involving the sacrosanct arena of graduate education had exactly the opposite effect. The challenge of reforming graduate education reemerged in 1929 at the University of Chicago when Robert Hutchins appeared on campus. Just as he was committed to improving collegiate instruction, Hutchins was concerned about the quality of the education received by doctoral students and particularly the training (or lack of training) that they received to be capable teachers. In early December 1929, the young president wrote a stunning memorandum to the graduate deans advocating radical changes in graduate education, including deeper preparation in teaching methods, the awarding of the existing PhD only to graduate students planning teaching careers, and the creation of new doctoral degrees, such as the ScD and the LHD, for researchers who would be "productive scholars."[239] In essence, Hutchins urged that the departments view the training of teachers as a formal and separate component of their mission, thus challenging the conventional structure of doctoral education established at Chicago during the early twentieth century.

Hutchins's probing took place after several interventions by liberal arts college presidents in the later 1920s urging that American graduate schools pay more attention to the training of college teachers.[240] As discussed in chapter 3, Raymond M. Hughes of Miami University criticized the narrowness of graduate education and the lack of interest that graduate programs in the United States had shown in preparing their students to be effective teachers. In 1927 the Association of American Colleges, representing more than four hundred teaching institutions in the United States, created a Commission on Enlistment and Training of College Teachers that issued a report in 1928 urging that graduate schools pay more attention to training for students who aspired to teaching careers.[241] Hutchins specifically cited this report in his missive to the deans.

The deans' responses to Hutchins's intervention were all over the map. Gordon Laing of the humanities argued against the creation of a new degree and proposed instead that PhD candidates simply take a couple of education courses and that they be given more teaching experience in the undergraduate College. Henry Gale of the physical sciences suggested that course requirements and research expectations for the PhD be reduced to seven or eight quarters of residence, that doctorates be awarded on the basis of shorter and less ambitious research exercises, and that graduate students interested in teaching careers be required to take an additional year of educational theory and discipline-based courses to certify them as college teachers. Charles Judd, the dean of the School of Education admitted that, lacking a system of selective admissions, the University had many graduate students who were "wholly incompetent to carry on high-grade work," and proposed creating a system of postdoctoral fellowships to reward graduate students who were especially talented at research. Finally, on behalf of the College, Chauncey Boucher, who was not opposed to Hutchins's scheme of creating two doctoral degrees, observed that Hutchins might accomplish the same result and still retain the single PhD degree if the departments were willing to build into their curricula a serious component dedicated to training in the methods of undergraduate teaching. Boucher also argued that "in some departments little attention seems now to be given to what is actually a graduate course, once the title of the course is announced.... Some graduate students complain that they have had too many graduate courses which were little more than senior college lecture courses in subject matter."[242]

Hutchins continued to probe, however, and in mid-January 1930 he pushed the deans to agree to a set of general principles to the effect that "we shall graduate nobody with a higher degree whom we cannot unqualifiedly endorse either as a research worker or a college teacher or both; we should devise different curricula for the two groups, in the expectation that a few students might pursue both; we should give different designations to those who are prepared for college teaching."[243] In February 1930 Hutchins asked the University Senate to create a high-level committee to explore basic questions involving the future of graduate education, including the preparation for teaching, in hopes that his general principles would be codified in legislation.[244]

The committee was headed by Harlan H. Barrows, chair of the Department of Geography and a man of energy and initiative.[245] His committee launched three surveys to inform their work: one for all departments, with fifty-one questions about their curriculum, teaching practices, and learning outcomes; one for former graduate students who had received their doctorates from the University between 1900 and 1929; and one for university and college presidents who employed Chicago graduates in academic positions, the students having graduated between 1920 and 1928. The committee found that few presidents had any concerns about the scholarly credentials of the graduate students whom they had hired, but many noted problems of teaching preparation or performance. As for the survey of individual graduates, on the basis of 1,065 responses the committee found that the great majority of respondents had jobs that required either research and teaching (39 percent) or teaching exclusively (29 percent), and only 10 percent were engaged in research activities with no teaching responsibilities. These data demonstrated that more than two-thirds of graduates had a positive view of the University and the research training that they had received, but that a significant minority wished that they had had more formal training in teaching ("no other suggestion was made by so many graduates as the one that 'more attention be given to the problems of teaching'"). Finally, the responses of the individual departments revealed vast differences in actual course work requirements, in admissions practices, and in other key policy areas.[246]

Based on these results, Barrows and the committee crafted a report recommending that admissions criteria and standards for the admission of graduate students be both increased and made more systematic. The committee also recommended that graduate programs be made more flexible so that graduate students could opt for different ways to prepare themselves for their desired careers, assuming that all students would receive a minimum of necessary training in research skills and substantive knowledge. Essentially, Barrows had accepted Boucher's idea that departments allow students within the same doctoral program to develop different training tracks, based on future career outcomes. On the issue of preparation for teaching, the committee declined to support Hutchins's proposal for the creation of new doctoral degrees, assuming that its call for greater flexibility and individuality within existing PhD programs would respond to the problems that Hutchins and the college presidents had identified. Given that a majority of graduate students aimed at careers that combined teaching and research, creating two separate degrees would result in the absurd situation that students would have to meet the requirements of both. The committee suggested that each department hire at least one faculty member competent to provide teaching training, and that the Department of Education be asked to create a course on the contemporary system of American higher education to "orient the prospective university or college teacher in the *general field* of his future work. It should prove of value to all departments in preparing students for careers in universities and colleges." At the same time, the committee rejected Laing's scheme to increase the number of graduate students teaching in the College, insisting that "undergraduates should be protected from an undue amount of practice teaching by graduate students; they, too, are entitled to the best training that the University can provide."[247] In the end, apart from their call for more rigorous admissions criteria, Barrows and his colleagues came down firmly in favor of strong departmental autonomy while urging the departments to assemble more flexible programs.

With the filing of the Barrows report, the academic departments at Chicago had resisted reform from above, as they generally would for the remainder of the century. The divisional structures of 1931, while impressive for their administrative efficiency, did not generate the campus-wide authority over graduate-student life that conventional, arts-and-sciences graduate school structures came to have at most other American research universities, the result being that the curricular and professional fate of doctoral students at Chicago was left to the caprice of the individual departments. Hutchins's proposals for the reform of graduate education had come out of the blue with no precedents on campus, unlike the New Plan reforms for which Boucher had been lobbying since 1927. Confronted with the laborious procedures of the Barrows committee, Hutchins must have realized that his chances of forcing the departments to accept radical reforms were next to nil.

Barrows's suggestions, however, had little impact. The constraints of the Depression became particularly acute after 1932, with budget reductions and hiring freezes, and this atmosphere of growing constraint may have played a role in the lack of new initiatives and innovations. Still, Hutchins remained frustrated about the departments' unwillingness to consider serious reforms in the operations of their graduate programs: in a report to the board of trustees in 1935 Hutchins argued that "no candidate for the Ph.D. should be allowed to graduate without some training in research. It does not follow, however, that his whole course of study should be based on the idea that he is going to be a scholar."[248] Hutchins then repeated his proposal that the University use the PhD primarily for teachers. He added laconically, "So far, I have yet to find a member of the faculty who agrees with me."

Flush with his victory on the College's curriculum and degree program in 1942, in early 1944 Hutchins returned to the problem of the (in his mind) indifference of the departments toward training their graduate students to become teachers. Hutchins did this in the context of broader frustrations about university governance and particularly about the scope of his powers as president vis-à-vis the full professors who dominated the University Senate.[249] In January 1944 he used his annual speech to the trustees and faculty at the South Shore Country Club to pose broad claims about the dire state of higher education in America, set in a highly moralistic framework. The speech contained many provocative statements, including a questioning of the system of academic rank, a critique of course-based credit for degrees, and even a proposal to replace the university's motto, *Crescat scientia vita excolatur* (Let knowledge grow that life may be enriched), with a new one drawn from Walt Whitman's *Leaves of Grass*: "Solitary, singing in the West, I strike up for a new world."

But Hutchins's most controversial proposal was that the University create a new Institute of Liberal Studies that would be licensed to give PhD degrees to graduate students interested primarily in teaching careers, with the departments then left to award a new doctoral degree to a smaller number of specialists in research. "If we are to show the way to liberal education for all," he said, "we shall have to get ready to educate teachers who are to undertake this task.... At that time we shall have to reconsider our advanced degrees and think once more whether we ought not to award the Ph.D. to those who have prepared themselves to teach through a new Institute of Liberal Studies. If we did so, we should have to confer new degrees, say the Doctor of Science and the Doctor of Letters, upon those who had qualified themselves primarily for research."[250]

This speech was a political disaster. The idea of a new graduate school of liberal studies was potently controversial, but coming in the context of Hutchins's broader attempts over the previous two years to enlarge the executive authority of his office and to create new academic programs without the assent of the senior faculty, the speech set off a firestorm of faculty protest that soon became an object of scrutiny in the *Chicago Daily News*. Several of the most vocal opponents of Hutchins's ideas on the graduate level cited what Hutchins had done with the BA degree as evidence of his propensity to irresponsible actions, which meant his willingness to deprecate the departments as sole custodians of educational wisdom involving graduate education. Hutchins's supporters made the situation worse by giving public interviews to the press, arguing that many departments at Chicago faced intellectual "stagnation" because of lack of strong local leadership.[251] Hard feelings and vitriolic language followed, with economist Frank H. Knight threatening to resign if Hutchins pursued his plans.[252] Knight and others saw Hutchins's meddling with doctoral education as an attack on the core values of research and investigation to which the University had been dedicated since its founding. Hutchins in turn viewed the departments as controlled by small cliques of full professors who opposed any meaningful educational progress and who also ignored the views of younger faculty because they had no role in university governance.

The result was a memorial petition by the University Senate to the board of trustees, signed by ninety-one full professors of the faculty, denouncing Hutchins and his motives and ideas.[253] The faculty rebellion of May 1944 was an uneasy coalition of several sources of disgruntlement: many were outraged by Hutchins's attack on the departmental graduate programs and his evident sense that the University had direct moral responsibilities to society, but others who supported the protest did so because they believed that Hutchins had gone too far in his reforms of the

College.[254] Student opinion, in contrast, was solidly behind Hutchins: the *Maroon* condemned the "memorialists" as "men interested only in their petty prerogatives, their rank, and their salaries."[255] Still, the substantive issue that Hutchins had raised in 1944 was identical to that which he had articulated fifteen years earlier. Having succeeded in the early winter of 1942 in pushing the College experiment to the limit, perhaps Hutchins thought the force of history was on his side in provoking serious reforms in graduate education and in wider university governance. But if the resulting furor did force the board to impose a new structure of faculty governance at the University in late 1944—the membership of the University Senate was broadened to include associate and assistant professors, with the Senate then electing a representative, fifty-one-member Council of the Senate, which would have the authority to approve the creation of new academic programs, and a seven-person Executive Committee that would speak on behalf of the council—it also resulted in the board's clear reaffirmation of the faculties' traditional power to recommend (or not recommend) candidates for faculty appointments and to operate academic programs.[256] In the context of graduate education this essentially meant that the individual departments would continue to make decisions about who was qualified for a PhD degree and about who would teach doctoral students, and that the PhD would remain a research-based degree par excellence.

What is more remarkable about the dustup over faculty and departmental prerogatives was that it came only a year before Robert Hutchins boldly supported the creation of two new interdisciplinary institutes, the Institute for Nuclear Studies and the Institute for the Study of Metals, in 1945. Renamed the Enrico Fermi Institute in 1955 and the James Franck Institute in 1967, respectively, these interdisciplinary institutes responded to a long-standing quest on the part of faculty from the physical sciences for more transdisciplinary support, but they also came to have a profound impact on the funding of research in the physical sciences in ways that encouraged, if not necessitated, the individual academic departments to adjust themselves to new forms of collaboration and cooperation, and that had a powerful influence on the training of their graduate students. Hence, the collision of 1944 should not be read as evidence that the faculty were unwilling to create new and flexible methods for organizing their research and graduate programs, but that such changes had to occur in a more organic and more self-directed way, with the departments having the chance to come to terms with new modes of structured collaboration. That said, graduate education at Chicago remained locked in deeply customary patterns, with no central authority, like a dean of graduate education who could look out for the interests of graduate students and set time-to-degree expectations for graduate programs across the individual departments. It was not accidental that by the late twentieth century Chicago had problematic time-to-degree records for many of its doctoral programs. Part of this problem was owing to limited resources for graduate financial aid, but also to the fact that no central authority existed to regulate the size of doctoral admissions or to insist on adequate mentoring for graduate students. In essence, Robert Hutchins had thrown dice in a crapshoot seeking a revision in authority over graduate education and had come up short, with the departmental faculties retaining as much, if not more, academic power after 1945 as before.

Institutional Pressures, the War, and the Aftermath

The Hutchins era was legendary for its cultural revolution in undergraduate life and learning, which also had a profound influence on the wider academic culture of the University. Hutchins undertook this revolution under sorely trying circumstances, for within several months of taking office Hutchins faced the greatest economic challenge in the University's history. The Depression hit the University hard, yet Chicago's experience was less traumatic than that of many other institutions because of the substantial reserves it had accumulated in the 1920s.

PUBLIC RELATIONS AND BUDGETS

Hutchins initiated an austerity program that cut administrative costs by 20 percent. He reported to his parents in November 1931, "We woke up one morning and found that we had an estimated deficit of seven hundred fifty thousand dollars. We proceeded by main force to cut four hundred and twenty thousand dollars out of the budget."[257] Three hundred and fifty courses were eliminated, faculty teaching loads were temporarily increased, and the mandatory retirement age of sixty-five ruthlessly enforced. Many clerical staff and day workers were dismissed from their jobs.[258] The general budget (which covered the costs of the nonmedical areas) was cut from $6 million to $4.5 million from 1930 to 1933. Faculty salaries were frozen, but not reduced, and attrition and retirement reduced the full professorial ranks from 160 in 1930–31 to 116 in 1939, with few replacements being hired, even at junior levels. Total salary expenditures for full professors declined by almost 20 percent between 1930 and 1940. Some departments felt decimated—by 1936, the Department of English had lost five professors, one associate professor, and six instructors, all of whom were replaced by three instructors. Departments were required to cover summer quarter and extension teaching from their regular ranks, putting more pressure on those who remained on staff. The annual income available from the endowment declined from $3.4 million in 1929–30 to $2.1 million in 1938–39, as the rate of return dropped from 6.2 to 4 percent. Student enrollments in the 1930s varied according to unit, but total University matriculations were slightly greater in 1938–39 than in 1931–32.[259]

To cover the budget shortfalls that remained even after these austerity measures, the trustees approved the use of $12 million between 1929 and 1939 from gifts, endowment reserves, and cash funds. By 1939 both the general and medical budgets were in chronic deficit ($370,000 and $500,000, respectively), with the General Education Board's $1 million grant for clinical operations in medicine from 1929 totally depleted and a $3 million general grant from the GEB half gone. Hutchins was particularly proud that he was able to protect the salaries of those who remained, even in the face of skepticism by the board: "So far we have not cut salaries and do not propose to do it."[260] As Hutchins put it to the board of trustees in September 1935, "I trust that we shall not be so preoccupied with the future that we shall sacrifice the present, and because of our desire to pass on to our successors an institution financially strong, pass on one that is educationally weak. . . . Or as another officer of the University has put it, we have threatened to carry so many life preservers that there would be no room for cargo."[261]

In the spring of 1933 Hutchins attempted a bold stroke that might have alleviated major budgetary pressures when he opened secret negotiations with President Walter Dill Scott of Northwestern University for a merger of the two institutions, to be called "The Chicago-Northwestern Universities" (although Fritz Woodward admitted privately to the Chicago trustees that the ultimate name would be "The Chicago University" or "The University of Chicago").[262] Given the substantially stronger financial position of Chicago, the merger was in fact a cleverly disguised takeover of Northwestern by Chicago.[263] The negotiations for the merger went far and collapsed only at the last moment because of pressure from Northwestern alumni and faculty on their trustees.

Hutchins's real plans were intentionally elusive, but the records of the negotiations in the Harold Swift Papers and the Walter Dill Scott Papers suggest that he hoped to consolidate a major part of the doctoral/research programs from Evanston at Hyde Park, allotting approximately five hundred new graduate-student positions to the Quadrangles. At the same time (according to Addison Hibbard, the dean of liberal arts at Northwestern) only a "small experimental college" of four to five hundred students was to remain on the Quadrangles, while the preponderant share of college teaching would be given over to the faculty on Northwestern's Evanston campus.[264] The two institutions would have one dean of students, one tenured faculty, one athletic program, one university press, one alumni organization, one library, one school of business, and one law school.

Had the merger gone through, its advocates believed that, as Beardsley Ruml put it, it would have been of "enormous value to American [higher] education."[265] Yet it was precisely the fear of being typecast as a branch-like teaching facility, with no clear institutional identity or historical legitimacy, that led to massive fears on the part of the Northwestern faculty and alumni and made the "deal" less than appetizing. In mid-August 1933 Hutchins reported to his father that he was "satisfied that the Northwestern merger will go through."[266] But the autumn brought fierce resistance from Evanston loyalists, and Dean Hibbard found among his colleagues at Northwestern "a very general feeling that no matter how sincerely the plan may be outlined at this time, eventually the two campuses would grow apart and we would have a *graduate* faculty on the South Side and an *undergraduate* faculty in Evanston.... Obviously, should this division later become rigid, the best interests of the undergraduate school in Evanston would suffer since we would not enjoy the benefits from having prominent scholars come into contact with undergraduate classes."[267] With the Northwestern board of trustees "seriously divided," its leaders decided to terminate negotiations in late February 1934.[268]

His bold scheme in shambles, Hutchins was left facing increasingly grim financial prospects. By 1938–39 the University had exhausted all easily available austerity measures, and a budget gap that could not be closed remained at about 10 percent of the annual budget. Further cuts would have meant a still greater reduction in faculty size, which Hutchins was loath to carry out. In the face of this fiscal misfortune, the specter of urgent new fund-raising loomed on the horizon.[269] The target of $12 million set for the 1940–41 campaign was intended to generate sufficient income to cover a significant part of the University's operating deficit for ten years.

Between 1926 and 1936 little changed in the organization of fund-raising. The board of trustees continued to have the standing Committee on Development (it was basically dissolved in 1926 but reestablished in 1928).[270] The committee languished, with James Stifler complaining to Swift that it was "doing a little better than marking time."[271] When the committee finally met in February 1932, Stifler reported that the members "deprecated any direct advances in solicitations for money at this time. It was their view that it would be prejudicial to the interests of the University, that while the unemployment campaign was in such serious condition and the state warrant was finding it so difficult to secure a market, to ask people to give money to these things was not wise."[272]

Hutchins's first step to try to stabilize the finances of the University had been to tread the well-worn path from Chicago to New York City. In the autumn of 1929, he had confidential meetings with the officers of the Rockefeller boards.[273] In early March 1930, he submitted a massive joint request to the GEB for $2.5 million and the Rockefeller Foundation for $4.5 million toward the first stage of a general financial program consisting of $28 million.[274] The application was originally intended to be part of a larger scheme that included gifts from Julius Rosenwald and Edward Harkness for $5 million each, but the prospects of those gifts had disappeared in early 1930. A prominent addressee of the March 1930 appeal was none other than Max Mason, who had become president of the Rockefeller Foundation in 1929. This was the beginning of a series of appeals to the Rockefeller boards for financial support, which became more urgent as the Depression deepened. The University seemed well placed to enter these negotiations, since Mason was not the only ex-Chicagoan involved: Trevor Arnett was president of the GEB; David H. Stevens, a former faculty member at Chicago and assistant to Mason, was the vice president of the GEB and then director of the Humanities Division of the Rockefeller Foundation.[275] But such intimacy also had its dangers, especially in times of financial distress, when all universities were scrambling for whatever support they might find. Mason was candid with Hutchins that his and Arnett's close association with Chicago was an issue of some awkwardness.[276] When Harold Swift tried to push Chicago's cause by writing a flattering, but grossly inflated letter to Mason telling him that his presidency was, along with Burton's, part of a "renaissance of the University," the situation became even more awkward.[277] Privately, Mason resented what he called Hutchins's "smart boy" presumptuousness toward the foundation, warning Swift that "Hutchins' attitude ... is—Here are our plans, what would you like to do about them? Thinks [it is] very poor policy to put babies on their doorstep and imply—they are your children, what are you going to do about it? ... Hutchins needed to guard himself against the 'bright boy' administration and to recognize the value of experience and an outside point of view."[278]

The boards' initial response to Hutchins's appeal was equivocal. In May 1930 the GEB agreed to a $1 million grant to assist in the construction of new buildings for anatomy and hygiene and bacteriology, but the general omnibus request was deferred, with Mason urging the University to undertake systematic budget reductions.[279] Hutchins was able to secure a five-year grant of $275,000 from the GEB in April 1931, however, to implement the College's New Plan curriculum between 1931 and 1936, covering faculty and administrative salaries, scientific equipment, and the costs of the new comprehensive examinations.[280] The spectacular academic success of the College in the 1930s was thus deeply indebted to New York support. Then, after further remonstrations, the GEB agreed in

December 1936 to give the University an emergency grant of $3 million to support both the Medical School and the University's general budget.[281] The success of this appeal rested largely on an eloquent presentation about the national importance of the University that Hutchins made personally in May 1936, which local staffers subsequently christened "Bob Hutchins's $3,000,000 Speech."[282]

Among the Rockefeller officers, however, there was a growing concern that the University needed to find other sources of support, and David Stevens wrote a gentle note to that effect to Fritz Woodward in 1931.[283] The directors of the GEB drafted a more direct memorandum in late 1936 that was sent to the University authorities. This memo, most likely authored by the Rockefeller Foundation's new president, Raymond B. Fosdick, insisted that the GEB had no "peculiar responsibility" to the University: "We emphasize this point because in some quarters it has been intimated ... that the Rockefeller Boards bore a peculiar and unique relationship to the University that was not shared by other educational institutions. For the sake of the University itself, and the necessity which it faces of developing a broad basis of financial support, we would want emphatically to disavow this opinion."[284]

Fosdick's message was conveyed more bluntly three years later by Warren Weaver, the director of natural sciences at the Rockefeller Foundation. In an informal conversation in January 1939 with Dean William Taliaferro of the Division of Biological Sciences, he reported that "certain members of the Board of Trustees of the Foundation seem to resent what they conceive to be a feeling on the part of the University officials that the University of Chicago has a special claim on Rockefeller funds," and that the Rockefeller trustees "would probably not be favorable to any large grant to the University at the present time."[285] That the Rockefeller staff's resentment had some basis in fact was reemphasized by Hutchins's own cavalier attitudes toward their future giving: in a conference with University fund-raisers in July 1939 Hutchins jokingly asserted that he would tell the General Education Board, "You gave us this money [in the past] because you felt some sort of obligation toward the University. That obligation still persists, and we still can't raise any funds." Harold Swift learned about this episode and warned Hutchins, "I feel strongly that we must be in the role of suppliant, and if we talk in terms that put responsibility or initiative on them, they will be extremely irritated."[286]

As the 1936 grant slowly evaporated, Hutchins tried again with another appeal in May 1940 for major endowment support for the University and the Medical Center, arguing, "Vocational training, practical or short-term research, and 'college life' are easily understood and are relatively cheap. Liberal education, long-term research, and experiments in organization and instruction are not easily grasped and are likely to be expensive." This time Hutchins's eloquence failed to work its magic.[287] Fosdick was deeply unenthusiastic about giving Hutchins more Rockefeller Foundation money, which led a clearly agitated Hutchins to claim that it was impossible to raise money in the city of Chicago because "Chicago is too unsophisticated about higher education to distinguish between the good and the excellent and to be willing, at least in times like these, to pay for the cost of the difference." In response, Fosdick angrily replied that Hutchins's rhetoric was "disturbing," for it seemed to suggest that "when Mr. Rockefeller and Mr. Gates were choosing the site of the new university they made a big mistake. I cannot really believe that this is true. If it is true, it is a disaster." Fosdick then repeated his negative decision: "The simple fact is that the Rockefeller boards cannot now come to the rescue of the situation in Chicago.... If the University of Chicago after fifty years is not rooted in the soil, no hothouse treatment by outside organizations is going to do any good."[288]

Undaunted, Hutchins delivered another appeal in January 1941, pitched at the need to defend the core activities of the five or six best private American universities, and urging that the Rockefeller boards allocate $3.5 million a year over five or even ten years to strengthen these institutions. Hutchins reported, "At the end I was thanked very nicely. Several members spoke about how interesting the meeting had been. I have no way of knowing what the effect of this conference was or may be."[289] Sadly, it did not have the outcome that Hutchins wanted. Robert Kohler has rightly noted that the 1930s brought a general reorientation of foundation giving, with the "linkage of research and training" losing its magic as "plummeting income from foundation endowments forced foundations to reassess the actual results of programs aimed at expanding the capacity of the research system."[290] Not only did this trend adversely affect Chicago, but the University's reliance on the foundations for basic operating support became even more precarious.

There was, moreover, a distinctly personal motive behind the decision to limit support — namely, the Rockefellers' judgment by the late 1930s that the University would never assemble a solid base of alumni and Chicago supporters as long as it could rely on huge handouts from New York City. Barry D. Karl has shrewdly commented on the "basic defects" of the University in not developing a vibrant community of alumni supporters early on, in large part because of the University's historic failure to develop strong residential life communities for undergraduates on campus: "Rockefeller did not want a University dependent on him and his name for fear that it would not attract that local support he felt necessary. From the perspective of his business practices, that meant that Harper and conceivably his successors would continue to come to the Rockefellers for support. When Rockefeller finally cut the University's endowment out of his support and that of all of his family thereafter, it was the failure of the University to create a Chicago community that would follow that of other universities."[291]

As long as personal visits to New York City continued to generate needed support, there was no motivation for onerous fund-raising campaigns. John Price Jones captured this psychological dilemma well when he shrewdly observed in 1936 that "over a long period of its history, this [fund-raising] function of the Board [of Trustees] was to some extent dulled by the large gifts from Rockefeller sources."[292] Fosdick's goal—to nudge the University into "developing a broad basis of financial support"— could be accomplished only by a strategic fund-raising plan, and as the flow of money from New York City began to slow, it was natural that the idea of a general fund-raising campaign again reared its head. As early as February 1936, anticipating that some kind of campaign would eventually be necessary, the board of trustees had commissioned the John Price Jones Corporation, which it had used a decade earlier, to prepare a detailed report on the prospects of fund-raising at Chicago. Jones and his staff produced a thoughtful analysis of the University's circumstances, including its fiscal difficulties and the impact of the accusations of radicalism generated by the Walgreen affair. It argued that the University required a campaign for at least $15 million to stabilize its finances, but that it also needed to mobilize a much larger body of civic leaders than in 1924–25 to attain this goal. "The University has grown great not through dependence on student fees and current gifts, but on independence born of endowment," the report stated. "If this independence is to be preserved, endowment must be the main objective of fund-raising."[293]

At first Jones's 201-page report had little impact, but an alumni campaign in the context of the upcoming fiftieth anniversary of the University's founding did gain support when two Chicago trustees returned in September 1936 from a similar campaign at Harvard that raised $2.5 million. When James Stifler reported to Swift in December 1936 that he believed the board "should hop to it at once,"[294] Swift responded that the board felt bound by a decision to commission another report by a talented public-relations expert, William Benton, whom Hutchins had known since his days on the intercollegiate debate team at Yale. In a confidential report to the trustees in January 1937 Benton came to conclusions not very different from those of John Price Jones.[295] With this report as additional evidence, the Committee on Development of the board met on January 25, 1937, and voted that the University should try to raise at least $15 million over the next five years, culminating in a celebration of the fiftieth birthday, the latter to be patterned after the Harvard Tercentenary. Benton also agreed to join the University in October 1937 as a part-time vice president to help with the campaign planning and execution.

The committee's recommendations were approved by the full board of trustees on February 3, 1937. The next eighteen months, however, were given over to more debate over exactly what kind of a campaign should be undertaken. Finally, to break the inertia, the committee recommended in late December 1938 that the University should reengage the John Price Jones Corporation to assist in planning both a general fund-raising campaign and the anniversary celebration.[296] As the Jones Corporation's officer who was most familiar with the University of Chicago, Robert Duncan was assigned to the case and returned to the University in the winter of 1939 to begin planning the second great campaign in the University's history.[297]

General consensus emerged about the content of an alumni campaign, but less agreement was evident about the focus of the general, public campaign, with some trustees worrying about cost and the University's poor reputation among some segments of the local business community. The University's standing among business elites was not the only roadblock. Trustees such as Herbert P. Zimmerman (class of 1901) who were interested in undergraduate education worried about reactions to a questionnaire that an alumni leader, Charlton Beck, sent to two hundred local and national Chicago alumni about their receptivity to a fund-raising drive for the University's fiftieth anniversary. Twenty-three percent were opposed to a drive, and a further 18 percent were noncommittal, while the opinion of those who gave the most generous gifts in 1924–25 was solidly negative; further, many of these same alumni expressed an "unhappy feeling" about the University.[298] Zimmerman was quoted in Benton's report: "The Alumni feel like hell. They think they've been badly neglected, that the University is indifferent to them. This is a bad time to ask them for money even though the time is near when people will have money to give."[299]

Eventually, reacting to the dismal state of the budget, the Committee on Development forced the issue, voting in June 1939 to proceed with campaigns both for the alumni and for the wider Chicago public.[300] But the committee cautioned that these interventions would not succeed unless each trustee took "an individual part in the campaign." The committee's recommendations were approved by the full board on July 13, 1939.[301] The campaign sought $12 million under the guise of an "Anniversary Fund" and would be launched on September 1, 1939. Final planning for the campaign then ensued during the summer of 1939.[302] Since the University had extended its contract with the Jones Corporation, Robert Duncan played a key role in the shaping of campaign strategy. Duncan asked Hutchins to outline his vision for the University over the next ten to fifteen years. Hutchins responded that this question was misleading, given no one in 1939 was in a position to justify any new initiatives. Rather, the only purpose of the campaign could be to control the deficit problem, or as Hutchins put it, "Keep what we've got!" This rattled Duncan as well as John Howe and John Moulds (who sat in on the session), since it would force the University to raise money to cover deficits, patently violating all conventional wisdom about why people might give money to any charity. When Duncan pressed Hutchins as to what he would really like to do with the University in the next decade, Hutchins admitted that if it were up to him he would stress integration and consolidation to a much greater degree than heretofore. Howe and Duncan thought this was the angle they were looking for, but Hutchins then torpedoed that possibility with the comment that what he thought about the University's future and what the faculty thought were two radically distinct things. The exchange revealed the paradoxical situation in which Hutchins found himself. He could not try to "sell" a new program of integration because the faculty would disown it.[303] Instead, he had to raise money to keep the status quo alive and well, and do so via a conventional booster's argument that the University of Chicago was the best university in the United States, and it was important to the nation that it remain so. Duncan also asked Hutchins if he intended to go back to the GEB for another large grant. Hutchins answered yes and with seeming confidence that he could talk Rockefeller officials into another round of largesse. In this he was, as we know, mistaken.

Three months later Hutchins published a lucid, but controversial essay, titled "What Good Are Endowments?," in the *Saturday Evening Post*. In the essay he insisted that private universities faced a terrible dilemma, having fierce competition from state schools on the one hand and falling revenues from investments on the other, and deftly raised the possibility that it might be desirable to begin to draw down endowments to sustain their operations. Coming at the beginning of a campaign that was intended to raise new capital for the University, this essay provoked still more controversy among an already skittish board, with Clarence Randall writing angrily to Benton that the essay had a desperate and unhelpful quality about it, since it gave him and his alumni friends "the impression that Bob thinks the University cannot raise money." Randall not only resented Hutchins's argument about taking money out of the endowment, but also found the very discussion of the subject to be of "doubtful wisdom" when the University was planning a new fund-raising effort.[304]

The message of the campaign was thus not radical innovation—a theme the public would have expected from Hutchins—but continuity of an intellectually distinguished but financially encumbered status quo.

The final campaign pamphlet, on which Howe and Duncan collaborated, developed this theme brilliantly, but only by concealing the real agenda harbored by the president. *Your University and Its Future* argued that endowed universities like Chicago enjoyed a special and privileged role within the system of higher education in America, and that they deserved to be sustained and protected, especially in a time of severe financial problems (which were discussed at length and with candor).[305] Invocations of American national interest and the greatness of the research university as a guarantor of the future of civilization in time of war ("At least until a more peaceful order is restored America has a special responsibility to future generations everywhere") replaced bold new ideas on the future of the university. In contrast to Burton's forward-looking campaign of 1923, the campaign of 1939 became a defensive exercise in rhetorical recidivism.

Hutchins's tensions with the senior faculty were overshadowed by two other muddles that undermined the success of the campaign—discontent with the University among members of the downtown business elite, which paralyzed many of the trustees, and continued grumbling among key segments of the alumni leadership. As discussed, the survey of local opinion in the city undertaken by the Jones Corporation in 1936 encountered numerous leading citizens who affirmed the high intellectual standing of the University but who were also critical of its teaching "radicalism." Nor did Hutchins's subsequent espousal of isolationist rhetoric in January 1941 go down well with pro-British leaders in the city. Harold Ickes, FDR's secretary of the interior and a Chicago alumnus, recorded in his private diary in April 1941, "Hutchins has jeopardized the endowment drive that comes to a head early next fall. [Charles] Merriam thought that he was looking for a large sum of money from Marshall Field, and Field is quite distinctly on the other side. Dr. Fosdick had remarked to Merriam that it seemed curious that ever since he was appointed president at Chicago, Hutchins had made no statement on a political subject but that now he should take the position that he has. The Rockefellers are also against him on this issue."[306]

The campaign also generated gratuitous commentaries from alumni leaders with a bone to pick. Hutchins could count on the solid support of most of the current students in the College, and those students who were mobilized to meet with alumni during the campaign made an excellent impression. The situation among the older alumni was more complex. Duncan had warned the trustees in April 1939 that "these [negative] feelings on the part of influential alumni, if left as they are today, will be a big handicap in any campaign."[307] Yet from the University's earliest days the feelings of independence afforded by Rockefeller's gifts had resulted in university leaders neglecting opportunities for sustaining personal or professional relationships with the undergraduate alumni. That a considerable number of the alumni were graduates of MA or PhD programs complicated the issue still more. In 1936 Herbert Zimmerman, who joined the board of trustees a year later, wrote to Paul Russell, urging that the University spend more money on alumni information. By the later 1930s the University was in a bind: it desperately needed alumni and especially undergraduate alumni backing, even though it had made little effort to sustain the connections that would have led to such support.

A survey of 1,085 students in 1938 who studied under the New Plan between 1931 and 1935 found most of them positive about their educational experiences in the College and about the University's culture of tolerance and liberalism, but a majority (78 percent) felt that their education had not helped them select a job or a profession, and almost half (46.7 percent) thought that there was too little "college spirit" at the University. When asked to compare the opportunities for social contacts at Chicago with those at the college or university they had subsequently attended, exactly half (50 percent) of the 179 students who transferred to another institution said there were fewer opportunities (as opposed to 26.4 percent who found opportunities to be the same, and 23.6 percent who found greater opportunities).[308] But the real problems for campaign organizers related to the alumni who had graduated before Hutchins came to the University. A list of the local and regional chairs of the University of Chicago Alumni Foundation in October 1939 indicated that of 214 men and women across the country, only 35 had graduated since 1931. Almost all of these were undergraduate alumni, suggesting the reliance on College graduates to carry the fund-raising torch for the University.[309] Yet it was precisely among the pre-1930 alumni cohorts that the University had the most troubles, with older alumni resenting that Hutchins's innovations had cast doubt on the efficacy of their degree programs. When Ernest Quantrell held a luncheon meeting with senior alumni representatives at the University Club in January 1940, he encountered a flood of criticisms of the recent decision to end intercollegiate football and of a perceived indifference to the fact that many children of alumni were no longer interested in attending the University.[310] Hutchins was seen as flippant and smart-alecky to these senior alums, but Quantrell was careful to note that during the five hours of "picking the University to pieces, communism was not mentioned once." Given the extraordinary publicity with which Hutchins and Boucher launched the New Plan in the early 1930s, it was understandable that older alumni felt consigned to a form of academic second-class citizenship.

Football was a crucial issue. Chicago had been an early powerhouse in intercollegiate football, enjoying the enthusiastic support of Harper.

Harper's successors seemed resigned to maintaining some kind of football program, even if many senior faculty felt ambivalence about the financial investments that a successful program demanded. But by the 1930s the ability of the school to mount effective teams to play such huge competitors as Michigan or Ohio State had vastly diminished. After consulting with key members of the board of trustees, Hutchins decided on drastic action and eliminated football at Chicago in December 1939. The story of the rise, decline, and fall of big-time football has been well told in Robin Lester's excellent book, and it is relevant to this story only in the sense that many older alumni were, by and large, opposed to Hutchins's decision, thus creating yet another communications barrier and another set of misunderstandings that the fund-raisers had to cope with on the eve of the fiftieth anniversary celebrations.[311]

To meet such criticisms head-on, campaign officials organized alumni meetings around the country in the early winter of 1940 featuring senior faculty as guests of honor. The alumni seemed honored to meet senior faculty up close and to spend time with them.[312] Hutchins too went on the road, and—given his charisma and eloquence as a public speaker—he was usually able to win his audiences over, at least temporarily. The early 1940 regional meetings and lectures generated some goodwill, but the campaign staff in Chicago still found it difficult to generate effective participation among professionally successful alumni. From September 1, 1939, to September 30, 1941, the University received $6,092,987 in new gifts.[313] The alumni gave $510,072, significantly less than in 1924–26, and all the more troubling in view of the fact that the University in 1941 had 49,300 alumni, as opposed to 27,000 in 1926.[314] The aggregate results fell vastly short of the original target of $12 million, but given the circumstances under which the campaign was launched, the results were as good as could be expected. As in 1924–25, the weakest part of the campaign was the lack of major gifts from members of the civic elite who were not alumni or trustees. The largest single gift by a nonalumnus was $250,000 from the Rosenwald family, given on the condition that the University would raise at least $5 million in pledges from other sources for the campaign. The two next largest gifts were for $150,000 and $100,000. Gifts of this level, while generous, could not resolve the structural budget difficulties of the University, however.

Robert Duncan's extensive involvement in the campaign gave him an insider's view of decision making at the University, and he was not shy about criticizing Chicago's blunders in several candid reports for the trustees. In November 1939 Duncan observed that the alumni component of the campaign had come together more effectively than the general campaign or the anniversary celebration. But he cautioned that this momentum could unravel, and in another report in early January 1941, Duncan worried that the board of trustees did not seem convinced of the need for reaching the campaign goals, and warned that the University had given hostages to future misfortune in the inept way in which it had explained recent policy changes to the alumni, particularly the absence of football and Hutchins's perceived negative attitude toward Greek life: "Many alumni, several of them influential, whether or not interested in football, still feel that the Administration's attitude on football and fraternities dooms the type of undergraduate life to which they are devoted and which would prompt them to give."[315]

The final celebration of the campaign took place in September 1941, which also marked the fiftieth anniversary of the University's founding. A high point of the celebration was the return of John D. Rockefeller Jr. to Chicago. As a courtesy to Hutchins, Rockefeller sent him a first draft of the speech that he intended to deliver before a dinner of prominent guests, many of whom were members of the Citizens Board. In this speech, which was otherwise friendly to the University, Rockefeller signaled that Chicago would not receive any additional family money, and conflating the gifts from his family and gifts from Rockefeller funds and boards, he also seemed to suggest that the University would no longer receive foundation money either. Upon receiving a copy of this speech Hutchins wrote to Rockefeller delicately but urgently requesting that he differentiate between family gifts and board gifts, that he make clear that the University had received the latter on the merits of its proposals, and that, at least potentially, it would be free to apply for more such gifts. Hutchins worried that a public statement coming from Rockefeller, at a banquet for local citizens, that no further gifts would be forthcoming would be read by other wealthy donors as indicating that the family was leaving the University in the lurch, and as having a "somewhat negative ring." Instead, Hutchins wanted Rockefeller to create a "positive challenge by telling the group what you told me in New York, that the Family was not 'abandoning' the University because of lack of faith or interest in it; it was doing so because it wanted no suspicion to lurk in the minds of the community that it could evade its responsibility to keep the University great and strong."[316]

Rockefeller responded graciously and tried to accommodate Hutchins, all the while insisting that the University had now become the responsibility of the people of Chicago and no longer of his family. The anxiety of the University authorities (Fritz Woodward also wrote to Rockefeller, urging him to soften his remarks) was underscored by Hutchins's comment to Rockefeller that "every word you say will receive the closest attention."[317] These exchanges, filled with amicable comments by Rockefeller and Hutchins about each other, signaled the final end of the Final

Gift of 1910. But they also demonstrated how acutely sensitive Hutchins had become about the standing of the University before the local civic community. Given that many potential major donors were sitting on the fence, Rockefeller's original formulations would have been a public disaster for the University. But even in the form in which they were delivered, Rockefeller's remarks made it clear that the only source of future support for the University would be the civic community. Speaking of himself in the third person, Rockefeller insisted:

> Though they [his father's and his own gifts] have been completed and it is not to be expected that further gifts from the same source will be forthcoming, this does not mean that the founder's son is any less interested in the University or its future than his father was for that is not the case. He rejoices in its present attainment and is eager for its increasing usefulness. It simply means he also feels that in one way alone can the University achieve the purposes for which it was created; that is, as the university not of a family, but of the people; wholly administered and supported by them; resting squarely on their shoulders; their responsibility alone; theirs to make as great as they will; its successes redounding to their credit exclusively.[318]

The Rockefeller era was over; and although Robert Hutchins could not know this, the era of large-scale general support from the Rockefeller boards was over as well.

THE UNIVERSITY AND THE WAR

The young radical Louis Wirth was right about the flawed peace treaty signed at Versailles in 1919, if for the wrong reasons. Whatever one thinks about Woodrow Wilson's goals in Paris in 1918–19 or about the justice or injustice of the final peace settlement, the Treaty of Versailles ushered in neither an era of stable democracy nor an epoch of lasting peace. Instead Europe in the 1920s and early 1930s became the scene of enormous social turmoil and dangerous political extremism, and out of this squalid mixture of class and racial hatred erupted renewed international violence in the mid-1930s. The failed heritage of the Great War led, on the part of many Americans, to a revulsion against mass killing and to an ardent desire to avoid entrapment in another major conflict. Yet the rise of fascism and National Socialism created the preconditions for a second, even more deadly round of international conflict that was to draw America into its vortex of horror in late 1941.

World War II was, however, a different kind of war, and the University

had a different kind of war president. Whereas Judson embraced World
War I, believing it a just and noble cause, Hutchins took exactly the opposite view, becoming an eloquent spokesperson for nonintervention in the
European and Asian wars of the later 1930s. In the 1930s, American college
campuses were marked by strong antiwar and pacifist movements, and the
University of Chicago was no exception, with students organizing peace
strikes, rallies, and parades from 1934 through 1941.[319] Reacting against the
horrors of the first war, many college-age students rejected the prospect
of fighting in what they felt to be another round of futile and immoral
conflicts. In his excellent survey of public opinion in the city of Chicago in
the late 1930s, James C. Schneider has suggested that students at Chicago
were probably more anti-interventionist and isolationist than the faculty,
a situation remarkably similar to the campus climate in 1917–18.[320] In late
January 1941, for example, the *Maroon* undertook a sample poll of 600
students, finding a majority (315 to 236) supported the proposition that
America should stay out of armed conflict with Germany or Japan.[321]

Unlike students advocating nonintervention in 1914–17, antiwar students at Chicago in 1940–41 had an eloquent university leader urging
neutrality. Having served as a young ambulance driver in Italy in 1917–18,
Hutchins had seen "the suffering caused by the war and its devastation"
at first hand, and remarked that the experience "made me into as much
a pacifist as I am. It gave me a deep suspicion of the military."[322] Unlike
Judson, Hutchins found nothing to admire or justify about any war, and
especially World War I.

Hutchins's controversial speeches against Lend Lease and American military support for Britain in the winter and spring of 1941 evoked
a conception of America's naturally limited role in the world. In both
addresses—"America and the War" (January 23) and "The Proposition
Is Peace" (March 30)—Hutchins brilliantly commingled his personal
aversion to World War I, based on its disastrous political consequences,
with deeply felt pleas for isolationism. For Hutchins the peace that World
War I had promised was a phantom, one that had led to violations of civil
liberties at home and to disastrous international consequences abroad.
The conflicts of the 1930s were the unintended offspring of the First World
War. To lure young Americans into a second military crusade was to invite
them to create a national disaster by destroying all possibility for a just,
free, tolerant, and well-cared-for civil society, according to Hutchins: "We
Americans have only the faintest glimmering of what war is like. This war,
if we enter it, will make the last one look like a stroll in the park. If we go
into this one, we go in against powers dominating Europe and most of
Asia to aid an ally, who, we are told, is already in mortal danger. When we
remember what a short war did to the four freedoms, we must recognize

that they face extermination in the total war to come."[323] American society had made some progress in achieving freedom from want and fear, freedom of speech, and freedom of worship, but those increments of progress had come at great cost and were still fragile. In its present state, America was "morally and intellectually unprepared to execute the moral mission to which the President calls us." What America needed was a "new moral order," but that was a state of collective ethical being that only America could give to itself, for itself, and by itself.

When war finally came to America on December 7, 1941, it came with a suddenness that cut through the conflicted emotions of 1939 to 1941. By rupturing history the attack on Pearl Harbor created the condition for a classic just war. The campus mobilized for war, and, unlike World War I, the scope of the conflict made it inevitable that the war would drastically reshape the campus's enrollment patterns. In the autumn of 1941, 5,315 students were matriculated on campus. By the autumn of 1942 this number had been reduced to 4,939, and by 1943 the Quadrangles had only 3,515 students. Among male students in the College and the graduate divisions the drop was quite significant: in 1941 the University had 1,561 male undergraduates, but by 1943 this had shrunk to 658.[324]

The effects of total war were soon seen throughout the campus. The University agreed to host a variety of military training programs, and by 1942 all available dormitory space had been consigned to military programs.[325] International House became a military residence hall, filled with cadets enrolled in the Institute for Meteorology and hundreds of Red Cross volunteers. Other college residences met the same fate. The Reynolds Club ceased to be a student clubhouse, becoming the headquarters for the meteorology program. However, the military training programs of 1942–44 were different from the 1918 SATC model, which Hutchins and other university leaders despised. In June 1940 Hutchins had joined with six other midwestern university presidents to write a memorandum outlining the appropriate roles of the university in time of war. The presidents affirmed that the universities should do what they could do best—namely, provide substantive knowledge-based training programs—and not become substitute army encampments.[326]

On the eve of war, in late November 1941, Emery Filbey stated that in the event of war the University would cooperate fully with the government and would participate fully in the national defense, but that it would "attempt to avoid doing a lot of the foolish things we undertook to do at the beginning of the first World War" and that "the best interests of defense would be served if, among other activities, the University undertook to maintain the integrity of its teaching and research programs, and that this in itself was no mean contribution to national defense."[327]

Hutchins himself had urged as early as 1936, when the War Department closed down the ROTC program, that the University might best serve the national defense by focusing on its capacities for "advanced training and research."[328] After 1941 Hutchins enforced these propositions, and programs like the Civil Affairs Training School for the Far East, launched in August 1943, and the Institute for Meteorology, started in October 1940, became the University's standard model of wartime support.[329]

The University hosted other military training programs as well, including a navy radio and signal training school that began in 1942 and enrolled six hundred trainees. By 1943 approximately 2,600 soldiers and sailors were taking special instruction, including such subjects as medical hygiene, optics, electronics, nursing supervision, and Japanese.[330] Ironically, in numbers of service personnel on campus, Hutchins presided over a wartime mobilization of the campus far greater than anything Judson could have imagined. As Hutchins put it to the faculty in early January 1942, "We are now an instrumentality of total war."[331] Hutchins also allowed the establishment of a special training program for civilian students that would blunt the danger of an SATC-like militarization of the curriculum. This was the Institute of Military Studies, organized in fall of 1940 as a preemptive response to the reactivation of a peacetime draft via the Selective Training and Service Act of 1940. This institute provided voluntary, after-hours, and weekend training in military subjects to thousands of civilian students before it was closed down at the end of 1944, and in so doing it helped to shield the core academic programs of the University.[332] Alongside these special military programs, regular instruction continued at the University for civilian students enrolled in degree programs. Hutchins insisted that the basic functions of the University—to cultivate liberal education and to undertake basic research—were centrally relevant to the war effort, and the timing of Pearl Harbor provided him with a unique opportunity to push through his long-desired reforms of the undergraduate curriculum, and to do so by touting their relevance to a mobilized nation in arms.[333]

Two features of the University's experience of the war were of enduring significance. The first was the recruitment of refugee scholars from Hitler's Europe. Beginning in the later 1930s and continuing during and immediately after the war, about forty-five refugee scholars, the majority of them from Germany, gained appointments to the faculty of the University. In selected fields individual scholars had a considerable scientific and pedagogical impact—witness the later influence of Hans Morgenthau and Leo Strauss in political science; James Franck, Enrico Fermi, and Antoni Zygmund in the physical sciences and mathematics; Gerhard Meyer and Christian Mackauer in the College; Edgar Wind, Hans Rothfels, Ulrich

Middeldorf, Ludwig Bachhofer, Rudolf Carnap, and Otto von Simson in the humanities; and Max Rheinstein and Friedrich Kessler in law, among many others.[334] It would be an exaggeration to argue that their collective influence was equivalent to the transposition of the hierarchical model of the nineteenth-century German *Ordinarienuniversität* onto the fledging American research universities in the 1870s, 1880s, and 1890s. Too much domestic political and economic water had flowed under the bridge of American higher education after 1900 and especially after 1918 to permit that. Still, Chicago profited from an infusion of extraordinary talent from the refugee scholars who brought new ways of thinking about venerable problems and who, in a few cases, established major schools of thought at Chicago. The refugees were not necessarily better teachers, for Chicago had many examples of homegrown success stories. But the combination of broad erudition, anchored often in classical learning and humanistic sciences, and the personal experience of having crossed deeply painful boundaries, gave these men a sense of fate and of the all-too-fragile fabric of intellectual tolerance and civility that they conveyed to their students at Chicago in powerful, if often subtle, ways. Like their nineteenth-century predecessors, this generation of European *Gelehrten*, now citizens of Hyde Park, affirmed the dignity of the academic calling and reinforced the University's sense of its intense academic mission. A university like Chicago, whose faculty culture once looked to Germany for the ideals of scientific learning and scholarly prestige, was now sufficiently mature to be able to incorporate leading European refugees into its ongoing programs of study, as well as to profit from the intellectual capital and cultural values that these scholars brought with them to the New World. This was a chance for the heirs of the first faculty to reaffirm the early internationalism so manifest in the first two decades of the University, but on terms of benefactor and patron, and not simply as advocate and consumer.

The refugees' arrival and integration was a public phenomenon, and the way that Chicagoans welcomed and quickly treated them as personal friends on a first-name basis often astonished the more reserved Europeans.[335] But the second notable wartime change on campus was a much more private, secret process, one about which few students and faculty knew anything: the atomic research project led by Arthur H. Compton, Enrico Fermi, and other major scientists. Fermi was perhaps the most distinguished of this group, and a man whom Hutchins respected not only for his scientific brilliance but also, as Ralph Tyler later recalled, for the fact that he was a "widely educated person with a tremendous devotion to mankind."[336] Laura Fermi remembered the conditions of secrecy and near quarantine under which her husband and his colleagues—most of them physicists relocated to the neighborhood from the coasts to work in the Metallurgical Laboratory—had worked. Members of the Met Lab learned quickly to avoid attention and dissimulate as they walked to work, and to limit their socialization to other members of the lab and their wives:

> In the fall Mr. and Mrs. Arthur Compton ... gave a series of parties for newcomers at the Metallurgical Laboratory. Newcomers were by then so numerous that not even in Ida Noyes Hall, the students' recreation hall, was there a room large enough to seat them all at once; so they were invited in shifts. At each of these parties the English film *Next of Kin* was shown. It depicted in dark tones the consequences of negligence and carelessness. A briefcase laid down on the floor in a public place is stolen by a spy. English military plans become known to the enemy. Bombardments, destruction of civilian homes, and an unnecessary high toll on lives on the fighting front are the result. After the film there was no need for words.[337]

At its zenith, the Metallurgical Laboratory employed hundreds of scientists and other staff, and it signaled a new pattern of cooperation between the government and the University that would extend far beyond the conclusion of the war. In accepting the plutonium research project that Compton organized in early 1942, Hutchins found himself caught between his own negative feelings about the military and his unease about government involvement in University affairs on the one hand and his responsibilities as the chief executive officer of the University on the other.[338]

Given the secrecy with which the Met Lab was organized, it is difficult to reconstruct exactly what Hutchins knew about the project and how he felt about it at the time.[339] It seems likely that Hutchins was given detailed briefings on the project, and it is instructive that one of his key lieutenants, Emery Filbey, was invited by Compton to tour the Clinton Laboratories in Oak Ridge, Tennessee, in December 1943.[340] Filbey is also reported to have assured Compton in early 1942, "We will turn the University inside out if necessary to help win this war. Victory is much more important than survival of the University." If Filbey actually said this, he would not have done so with the explicit approval of Hutchins.[341] Nor was Hutchins sheepish about exploiting the considerable human resources that the Manhattan Project had assembled in Chicago and elsewhere for the postwar advancement of scientific research at the University, since on August 9, 1945, he announced that two large research institutes would be founded at Chicago for postwar research in nuclear physics and in the study of metals.[342]

Still, Leo Szilard reported in his memoirs that as late as April 1945 Hutchins was not aware of how close the scientists had come to producing an atomic bomb, a process that had begun at Stagg Field in December 1942 when a team of scientists led by Enrico Fermi had engineered the first self-sustaining nuclear chain reaction.[343] Many years later, in May 1976, Harry Ashmore described to George Dell a conversation he had had with Hutchins on the atomic bomb project: "He said that he didn't feel guilty ... about his role as a representative of the University, but as a human being and [in] his private role, he did indeed feel guilty." To which Ashmore responded, "That's right, and that's fairly characteristic. You see, again, that's the old puritan wasp sense of obligation to the country, to the institution, [the] decision was made to do this so then he had to do it, and he did it extraordinarily well. Since it had to do with mass destruction, he dreaded the fact that it had to be done, had serious doubts about whether it should be done. One time he gets into this is when he talks about the effort to keep Truman from dropping the bomb, in which he was very highly engaged."[344]

With the atomic attacks on Hiroshima and Nagasaki, the end of World War II left the campus in an uneasy mood. Many of the Met Lab scientists involved in the atomic bomb project were profoundly disturbed by the terms on which the war had ended. A report authored by James Franck, Eugene Rabinowitch, and other leading nuclear scientists at Chicago in early June 1945, urging that the United States not use the atomic bomb against Japan without first organizing a demonstration of the new weapon "on the desert or a barren island," probably represented the opinion of the majority of Chicago scientists then working at the Met Lab.[345] Compton's poll of the attitudes of the Met Lab scientists on July 12, 1945, and Leo Szilard's petition of July 17 signed by sixty-nine scientists urging a delay in the use of the bomb, confirmed that a significant number of the project researchers had serious doubts about the deployment of the weapon against a civilian population center. Alice Kimball Smith has suggested that Hiroshima was in fact a "shattering blow" to the scientists of the Met Lab, who hoped that the bomb would not be used straightaway on a civilian target.[346] This was no less the case for Robert Hutchins.[347] To the end of his life Hutchins insisted that Truman's use of the bomb had been "incorrect and improper."[348]

The way the war ended—and, perhaps, his own feelings of culpability as war president—made it logical for Hutchins to return to the dialectical relationship between national progress and international warfare he had articulated in 1941 and to open a discussion about the future contours of a world peace in the new context of atomic terror. In "The Proposition Is Peace" in April 1941, Hutchins had observed:

Fear and ignorance wrote the last peace; the fear of the French and British, the ignorance of all nations. From this fear and ignorance sprang a peace that made this war inevitable. There is no less fear and certainly no less ignorance today. Have we the courage and the wisdom to bring the world to a peace that shall establish the four freedoms everywhere? ...

If we go to war, and preserve the British Empire, and crush Germany, our fundamental problems will remain. We do not face our fundamental problems by going to war, we evade them. We do not make a just and lasting peace by writing into another treaty the fear, ignorance, and confusion that have marred our efforts to build a democratic community at home.[349]

For those haunted by memories of 1918–19 who, in the summer of 1945, now opposed the use of atomic weapons, the stakes were particularly high. Ironically, what Robert Hutchins had feared in the winter and spring of 1941—that a new war would end in a peace even more ominous than the Peace of Versailles in 1919—seemed imminent. Within days of the bombing of Hiroshima, Hutchins participated in a University of Chicago roundtable discussion on NBC radio entitled "Atomic Force: Its Meaning for Mankind." During that program he rejected the use of the bomb, arguing that "all the evidence points to the fact that the use of this bomb was unnecessary.... The United States has lost its moral prestige [by using it]." Later in the same discussion Hutchins observed that "the only hope ... of abolishing war is through the monopoly of atomic force by a world organization." William Ogburn, a distinguished Chicago sociologist who defended the use of the bomb, replied laconically, "But that is a thousand years off," to which Hutchins rejoined, "Remember that Léon Bloy, the French philosopher, referred to the good news of damnation, doubtless on the theory that none of us would be Christians if we were not afraid of perpetual hell-fire. It may be that the atomic bomb is the good news of damnation, that it may frighten us into that Christian character and those righteous actions and those positive political steps necessary to the creation of a world society, not a thousand or five hundred years hence, but now."[350]

A month after this exchange, Hutchins was approached by two other senior faculty members, Richard McKeon and Giuseppe Borgese, who urged Hutchins to sponsor a study group to do in reality what he had advocated in theory—to write a constitution for world government. They argued that the atomic bomb had ushered in a new era in human history, one in which the future involved a stark choice between "world rule— with supreme authority vested in a global organism—[and] world ruin." The University of Chicago was a particularly appropriate place to launch a movement for global rule, since it played "a decisive role in ushering in the atomic age, whose birth-place and date might well be put in Stagg Field, December 2, 1942.... There is more than a symbolic value in the suggestion that the intellectual courage that split the atom should be called, on this very campus, to unite the world. An Institute of Nuclear Physics has been founded. We propose an Institute for World Government."[351]

Hutchins agreed to underwrite the effort, and a committee of Chicago faculty—Robert Redfield, Mortimer Adler, Richard McKeon, Rexford Tugwell, Giuseppe Borgese, and others—joined with leading academics from elsewhere to craft the outlines of a government for the world. The committee met monthly at the Shoreland Hotel and in two locations in New York City between February and October 1946 and again from February to July 1947 and assessed a variety of political and legal issues, such as those involving federalism and centralism, human rights, electoral representation, and executive power. The debates were heady and acerbic, and intellectual disagreements between Borgese—who favored a unitarist world regime that might suppress state-based nationalism—and McKeon—who favored a more federalist structure that would preserve authority for the nation-states—led McKeon to refuse to sign the final document.[352]

After eighteen months of deliberations, Hutchins's committee published its design for a world government, the *Preliminary Draft of a World Constitution*, in September 1947. The *Draft* was an elegant document that established the Federal Republic of the World. This republic was constituted by a federal convention, made up of delegates from nine electoral colleges, which, in turn, comprised regional societies of the various "kindred nations and cultures" of the world. Each electoral college had the right to nominate candidates for the office of president of the World Republic, who was then elected by the vote of the full convention for a single six-year term. The colleges also elected representatives to a ninety-nine-person world council, which exercised legislative power for the republic. The president of the World Republic was charged with the responsibility of appointing a government, including a chancellor and a cabinet, and a grand tribunal of sixty justices organized in five benches, each serving fifteen-year terms (although the world council could veto a nominee to the tribunal by a two-thirds vote). The grand tribunal in turn would elect a seven-member supreme court, which functioned both as an executive authority for and an appellate jurisdiction over the decisions taken by the tribunal. In addition to these and several other organs of world governance, the *Draft* also provided a declaration of duties and rights for the people of the world. Among its bolder and more farsighted propositions was the assertion that the four elements of life—earth, water, air, and energy—are "the common property of the human race," a postulate that merited committee members the unenviable tag of being crypto-socialists (or worse) in 1948. The *Draft* was also forward looking in that it sought to displace the electoral power of individual nation-states with regional federations, which, the authors hoped, would experience and profit from shared economic and cultural interests over time.

The *Draft* was translated into forty different languages, including Chinese, Arabic, Hindi, and Russian, and it is estimated that its final circulation ran to over a million copies. Reactions to the Chicago world government group came from all over the world, and they were of sufficient interest to justify the University of Chicago Press publishing a special monthly journal, *Common Cause*, as a venue where world government proponents could debate with their many interlocutors. Hutchins's public advocacy for world government to control atomic weapons generated interest among amateur internationalists of all walks of life. Many correspondents wrote simple, congratulatory messages. Harold E. Fackert of Jersey City, New Jersey, hoped that Hutchins would do everything he could "to encourage a world constitutional convention," predicting, "You can be a great influence toward everlasting peace and happiness for all mankind, if you will";[353] and Walter Piakowski of Chicago wrote Hutchins, "I am moved to express my admiration for your plan to effect an international organization.... If you succeed in bringing about this organization, this truly will be a miracle of the twentieth century."[354] James L. Reed of Omaha, Nebraska, confessed, "I have read of your efforts toward a one World Government with profound interest. Perhaps we who have long been proponents of a united world will take renewed interest upon finding men of your standing and ability lending efforts to the dream of so many little people, men like myself, who have not the education or stations in affairs to properly implement our hopes of a sound international order."[355] Other advocates of world government submitted their own schemes for Hutchins's review and evaluation. Most, even those that bordered on the crackpot, were acknowledged with polite responses. Hutchins had clearly touched a nerve.[356]

The project encountered both admiration and excoriating criticism. Not only was the Soviet Union militantly opposed to world government, but it was by no means clear that such a scheme bore any reasonable relationship to America's or Western Europe's vital interests in the later 1940s. The *Chicago Tribune*, a bastion of America-first loyalties, condemned the project as a "super secret constitution" generated by "one of a rash of militant globalist organizations which have sprung up in the United States and England since the United Nations has demonstrated its uselessness."[357] For the *Tribune*, the bill of rights contained in the *Draft* "appears to be a combination of Franklin D. Roosevelt and Karl Marx." The *Draft* encountered an equally venomous reaction from the spiritual home of Karl Marx: Moscow Radio condemned the *Draft* as an effort "to justify the American Empire plan for world supremacy," concluding that "the program of the Chicago world government embodies the ambitions of the American war-mongers."[358]

The energy and anxiety impelling the many world government movements in Europe and in the United States in the postwar world were driven by a palpable fear that the human race faced the possibility of not only perpetual war, but atomic war at that. The peace that had arrived in August 1945 was precarious; Hutchins and his colleagues wanted a more permanent peace, grounded in international law protected by international sanctions. Seen from the perspective of recent decades of nationalist terror, the committee's dream of a world order guaranteeing universal justice beyond the proclivities of nationalism (and national self-interest) may not be as irrelevant as it seemed in the heady days of the early Cold War. Yet it says much about the increasingly far-off frames of reference that preoccupied Hutchins after 1945 that he would sponsor the writing of a constitution for the world, designed to secure international peace and to give world governmental authorities the power to fight against racist practices, while at the same time he was unable to imagine a "constitution" for Hyde Park that would address the grave problems in urban deterioration and dislocation that had begun to afflict both the local neighborhood and the University of Chicago community. It was left to Hutchins's successor, Lawrence Kimpton, to provide such leadership, and to do so in a realpolitik style that eventually achieved the local peace that had eluded his predecessor.

YEARS OF TRANSITION, 1945–1951

In June 1945 Hutchins proposed a significant restructuring of the central administration of the University, arguing that the administrative and regulatory burdens of managing the University would grow significantly in the postwar world. Hutchins himself would become the chancellor of the University, with the title of president shifted to Ernest C. Colwell, who had served as dean of the Divinity School since 1939.[359] Hutchins would continue to chair various governing bodies and represent the University to outside constituencies and to the board of trustees. Significantly, the heads of major financial operations would continue to report to Hutchins. As the number two official in the new hierarchy, Colwell would be responsible for "the educational supervision and operations" of the University, with the unit deans reporting to him on faculty appointments and day-to-day academic affairs, and for lesser representational functions, such as giving speeches to organizations like the Englewood Kiwanis Club (an example provided by Hutchins himself).[360] The new dual system reflected Hutchins's exhaustion with having had to deal with quotidian administrative matters during the war and the bruising fight that he had had with senior faculty the previous year over the scope of his authority. Reuben Frodin may have been correct when he argued that Hutchins was demoralized by "the feeling that 'he'd lost it', i.e., botched too many budgets, etc."[361] Having failed in his struggle to gain outsize executive powers in 1943–44, Hutchins decided to divide his office into two parts, reserving those powers for himself that were more publicly notable (and that the board insisted he retain). Later observers reflected that the dual system never operated as planned, given that the lines of authority between the chancellor and the president were not always clearly observed, with most senior faculty with grievances or demands continuing to insist on meeting personally with Hutchins. Nor was the efficiency of the University's administrative operations improved. By 1949 Lynn Williams, who served as a very overworked vice president for public relations, complained, "The members of the Central Administration are so overwhelmed with minutiae as not to find the time for reflection and study which is required if we have to have an intelligent and orderly approach to meet our major difficulties. . . . We need to develop clear and regular channels for doing things so that most decisions can be handled in groups or classes, and so that we do not treat every instance as new and special. . . . As matters stand now we have no organization chart and no schedule of responsibilities."[362] Hutchins's successor, Lawrence Kimpton, deliberately avoided appointing a successor to Colwell, who left Chicago in 1951 to become vice president and dean of faculties at Emory University, given the hostility of the faculty to the arrangement.[363]

In the summer of 1946 Hutchins's personal crises with his wife, Maude, overwhelmed his capacity to deal with his professional duties. Robert Hutchins's unhappiness in his domestic life was a central, if carefully obscured, feature of his presidency. In 1921 Hutchins had married a young art student, Maude Phelps McVeigh, whom he had met during his first year at Yale. The marriage seemed happy and stable until they moved to Chicago in 1929. Maude was viewed as a distinct asset to Hutchins during the 1929 search, with Swift and others finding her "charming, attractive, capable," in contrast to the spouses of several other candidates, who had various liabilities.[364] But the reality soon proved quite different. Maude was a wealthy orphan who was a vibrant member of the flapper generation. Ensconced in the president's house, Maude thought of herself as a prominent artist whose time was rightfully her own; she hated social affairs and refused to entertain at university functions (the similarity to Max Mason's case is obvious, for different reasons). Maude and Hutchins in turn disappeared for long stretches to Europe, Florida, and Arizona, leaving Harold Swift or various nannies to care for their three daughters.[365] As Terry Castle has recently observed, Hutchins's later biographers, all of whom painted complimentary portraits of him, tended to blame Maude's dreadful temper and endless demands for money for their marital problems and for the disruptions she caused Hutchins in the exercise of his official duties.[366] But it is also true that Hutchins himself spent a lifetime unsuccessfully trying to manage his financial affairs, constantly overspending, and running into debt.[367]

From this distance it is neither plausible nor creditable to sort out guilt or innocence, but the turmoil of the marriage, eventuating in a bitter divorce in 1947–48, did have a powerful effect on Hutchins's incapacity to become a socially habitual member of an academic community dominated by (often old-school) full and associate professors and their spouses. When rumors circulated around campus in October 1934 about Hutchins's impending departure for a job in Washington, DC, the historian William T. Hutchinson recorded in his private diary, about conversations at the Quadrangle Club, "The subject of most interest about the campus is the apparent intention of Pres. Hutchins to take a year's leave of absence to accept a government post. Altho he deserves much better, I have not heard a regret expressed over his going. Quite the contrary, the few who talk seem afraid he won't go. As a matter of fact, however, the silence is the most impressive thing—seemingly most hesitate to express their real feeling for fear that he won't go, and they will thus speak 'out of turn'."[368] It might well be fair to assay that both of the Hutchinses' cavalier way of raising their children revealed personality types who had the audacity and imperviousness to flout ordinary social conventions, in much the same way that Robert Hutchins seemed to relish challenging and even affronting senior faculty and conservative trustees. William Benton once observed of his friend that he had the tendency "to take the extreme position and the strong dramatic step."[369] So too, apparently, did Maude. In this sense their marital life and the public life based on it melded together in melancholy but predictable ways.

In August 1946 Hutchins felt near to a breaking point, and he gave serious thought to resigning from the presidency, telling Harold Swift, "I have been around too long; people are lined up on one side or the other; the things I might do my personal situation prevents me from doing. At the same time my interests have become more and more concentrated on a few aspects of what is called the intellectual life; I do not do well on those aspects that do not interest me."[370] Swift and Bell talked Hutchins out of the resignation, and in a confidential meeting of the board in September, they were authorized to work out a deal under which Hutchins would be given a sabbatical for the 1946–47 academic year to permit him to get his personal life in order.[371] (Hutchins abruptly abandoned Maude in the spring of 1947, moving into a hotel and then staying with friends, including the young Edward Levi. Maude never saw Hutchins again.) In spite of Hutchins's tumultuous relations with the senior faculty between 1942 and 1946, the great majority of the board wanted him to stay on as president in 1946 (in contrast to the situation that would obtain four years later), and their private assurances of enhanced financial and moral support tipped the balance.[372] During that year Hutchins worked out of the offices of the Encyclopaedia Britannica in downtown Chicago, and while the year proved salutary from a personal standpoint—William Benton assigned an especially amiable young woman, Vesta Sutton Orlick, as Hutchins's secretary and assistant, who would soon become his second wife—he found the work at Britannica and the Great Books expedient but too small bore for his own longer-term ambitions. Moreover, the leave simply postponed the postwar governance challenges with the faculty that lay ahead if he intended to return to Chicago. As Mortimer Adler counseled him, "The Board's meeting your requirements does not change in the least the character of the Faculty, and the barriers they set up against any educational advances."[373] While Hutchins appeared filled with reforming zeal for the first conflict-ridden decade of his tenure, by the late 1940s, after having gotten what he wanted with the curricular reforms of 1942 and 1946, he seemed to have become weary (or just bored).

The last years of the Hutchins presidency thus project a fascinating but contradictory set of images. On the one hand, these were years of great pedagogical excitement and curricular drama at the University. Alumni of this era remembered with great fondness the excitement that defined the intellectual culture of the campus. Hutchins's College, based on a uniform general-education curriculum, reached its zenith during these years. The budget of the College exploded upward, growing from $79,000 in 1939 to $631,000 in 1949, and remarkable standards for teaching excellence in small discussion classes were established for the general-education programs. The University also made the transition to peacetime research in nuclear energy, metallurgy, and solid state physics, retaining or recruiting scientists of the caliber of Enrico Fermi, Harold Urey, and James Franck, establishing the Institute for Nuclear Studies and the Institute for the Study of Metals, and constructing the research institutes buildings. The new institutes had a profound impact on the quality and scope of interdisciplinary research in the physical sciences at Chicago, and also enabled key intellectual and financial linkages to the new Argonne National Laboratory, which the wartime Met Lab at Chicago had spawned in March 1943.[374] If the faculties and graduate programs in the social sciences had constituted the most prestigious cluster of departmental research programs in the later 1920s and 1930s at Chicago, after World War II that role was now shared with the physical sciences.

On the other hand, these were also years of deteriorating financial solvency, with heavy pressure on Hutchins to put the University's fiscal house in order. In order to finance the postwar expansion of the University, including the construction of the new research institutes and the administration building, Hutchins persuaded the board to draw on the endowment principal of sixteen Rockefeller funds for four years at a rate of 5 percent and a fifth year at 2.5 percent, for a total of $3.3 million, all of which was technically legal but which, as a later observer put it, "caused disappointment among the Rockefellers that the University used for current purposes funds which were intended as permanent endowments."[375] Such practices, coupled with the spending of other endowed funds and various suspense accounts to cover operating deficits, negatively affected the University's endowment growth and grated on key trustees, including Hutchins's long-term sponsor and protector, Harold Swift. Swift's once warm relationship with Hutchins had cooled in the years after the war, perhaps affected by Swift's sense that Hutchins's separation from Maude in April 1947 and their divorce in July 1948 had not enabled Hutchins to fully reengage with his responsibilities to the University. As late as the summer and fall of 1948 Swift forcefully defended Hutchins when eight alumni leaders from the class of 1922 circulated a semipublic letter to the trustees denouncing various sins of omission and commission in Hutchins's regime that, if left uncorrected, would bring "serious repercussions and further injury to the reputation of our Alma Mater."[376] By mid-1950 Swift was no longer as certain about the future. In two letters to Laird Bell in June 1950 Swift forcefully criticized Hutchins's overspending and his half-hearted work as a fund-raiser: "Since the war the University has spent or appropriated unprecedented amounts of capital (endowment) and other University funds for postwar building projects and for underwritings to finance current operations.... The University's greatest need is money, and raising it should be the Chancellor's chief concern, and his time should be dedicated to it until the situation ceases to be precarious."[377]

Nor did the trustees seem deeply committed to supporting the University in these years. To help respond to the financial crunch Laird Bell suggested in the spring of 1947 that the board members take responsibility themselves to raise money for the new administration building that the board voted to launch in 1944, which ended up costing $1.5 million. In the end, each trustee gave some contribution, but half of the $550,000 raised was provided by Swift, Bell, and Marshall Field, with the others giving extremely modest, if not paltry, amounts.[378] When Walter Paepcke complained in December 1947 that the building scheme was a bad idea, noting, "I, for one, would not be disappointed if we found some way to postpose the Administration Building until other financial requirements have been taken care of," Swift had to admit ruefully, "I, too, would be happy if we hadn't started the Administration Building, but that seems to be our own bear that we have by the tail."[379] With other resources lacking, the largest portion of the money needed for this building had to be taken from the remaining balance of John D. Rockefeller's Final Gift from 1910. The administration building was thus, ironically, Rockefeller's last gift to the University of Chicago and, sadly, an aesthetic disappointment of the first order.

In late 1950 the board commissioned Kersting, Brown & Company, a new fund-raising firm of which Robert F. Duncan had just become president, to survey the development situation. The results were predictably mixed.[380] Many alumni were unhappy with the University's alleged left-wing activities, and resented the fact that (in their minds) the College was "not getting a fair cross section of youth" and that the College was appealing to "prodigies to become 'long-haired' geniuses." They also felt that little social prestige was attached to the school; and they echoed the sentiments of alumni a decade earlier, sending their children elsewhere and observing that the abolition of football and "the fraternity situation" precluded sentimental attachment and took away "any reason for return to campus to keep up ties." Finally, some felt the chancellor to be an unnecessarily controversial figure.[381] Even so, these individuals almost always admired the University as an institution of higher learning, and many wished "to know about what the University is doing and, as one put it, be 'made to feel proud of having gone to Chicago.'" These ambivalences translated into giving rates by Chicago alumni substantially below those of private peer institutions. The average participation rate in the annual fund for Chicago alumni was 14 percent, compared with an average of 37.5 percent for five other top private American universities, resulting in $135,304 in cash contributions compared with the average of $484,320 attained by peers. As a result, Kersting found that "there seems to be on the part of some members of the Administration a sort of defeatist attitude toward the University's alumni, a feeling that they are not to be counted on, especially those in the earlier classes who should be more able to give."[382]

Most striking, Kersting found that the growth of the University's endowment was almost flat from 1939 to 1949, whereas the endowments of eight other top private universities had an average growth rate of 34 percent. The University had taken $10 million out of the endowment in this period to cover building costs and underwrite deficits. The University was especially deficient in gifts from individuals for current use. Chicago received $466,884 in gifts from individuals for 1949–50, representing 14 percent of the total gifts for current operations. In 1948–49, Harvard had received $1,043,379 in gifts from individuals (28 percent of the total gifts it received), Yale $545,764 (27 percent), Columbia $616,560 (31 percent), and Princeton $598,766 (54 percent).[383]

As time went on, contemporaries were willing to talk about the financial problems of the last years of Hutchins's presidency. In a confidential memorandum in November 1955 the University's chief financial officer, John I. Kirkpatrick, noted that expenditures had exceeded income by approximately $1 million a year since the end of World War II. Whereas the University's budget increased from $8.75 million in 1939–40 to $18.4 million in 1949–50, sufficient new income to finance these increases was not apparent, with the result that Hutchins was forced to carry large deficits. Moreover, Kirkpatrick insisted that Hutchins thought deficits were a good thing: "Mr. Hutchins proclaimed publicly that a great university operates in the red. He went on the theory that there are always more things to do than a university can afford and hence a balanced budget is an indication that a university is not progressing enough."[384] In a subsequent oral history interview George Watkins, a leading fund-raiser in the Kimpton era who admired Hutchins's intellectual style, admitted that the trustees "were scared to death of what this guy might do fiscally."[385]

As the next decades of the University's history would reveal, these negative trends in endowment growth were impossible to undo. The real value of the University's endowment slowly declined against key peers, encountering even more severe competition in the 1970s and 1980s. Adverse economic realities have a powerful impact on the life of any university. The university is not a business, but it has to pay its bills. Moreover, universities do not become or remain great because of their revenue streams, but what Hutchins failed to grasp was that without robust streams of *new* revenue in the hypercompetitive world of higher education after 1945 it would be difficult, if not impossible, to recruit and retain the eminent faculty and the talented students who do make universities outstanding.

Hutchins's eloquent defense of intellectual values shaped the University's culture in powerful ways that endure to this day. Hutchins's cultural imprint still influences the collective self-understanding of the University, not in the least because his emphasis on the vital intellectualism of the academic community accorded so well with the way in which the faculty conceived the fundamental purposes of the University. But to his critics Hutchins's academic successes came at a serious cost to the endowment and to the image of the University among key sectors of alumni and influential elements of Chicago's civic elite. At the end of his presidency, in January 1951, mixing ruefulness and deep frustration, Hutchins insisted that "the only problems that money can solve are financial problems, and these are not the crucial problems of higher education. Money is no substitute for ideas."[386] Yet the reality and depth of the financial crisis were unmistakable, and stirring rhetoric, laden with self-justifying pity, would not make it go away. As late as 1952 Hutchins would trivialize the need for effective external relationships with local elites by arguing, "I sometimes get the feeling that the University of Chicago, which can properly be compared only with Oxford, Cambridge, Harvard, and the Sorbonne, thinks of itself as a little local school, dependent on the passing whims of the local forms of animal life."[387]

Via his fascination with truth and ideas—and with his still-charming, Depression-era, the university-is-not-a-country-club rhetoric—Hutchins helped to reinforce and strengthen the University's image as an intellectual hothouse, which it still enjoys today. Hutchins turned Veblen's critique back on Harper, using it to root out or at least dampen those elements of the original Harper plan that were less "pure" (e.g., big-time athletics), while preserving the ethical urgency and the self-confident sense of scholarly independence that Harper had set in place. In fact, there are remarkable parallels between Veblen's *The Higher Learning in America* from 1918 and Hutchins's collection of speeches of the same name from 1936.[388] Hutchins did not abandon Harper's sense of democratic purpose, but he radically recentered it in a more internalist, self-reflective way by impelling the new curricular reforms of undergraduate education that he helped bring about. General education on a classical model, a curriculum marked by fourteen comprehensive exams that heavily privileged great works of art and culture, the four-year degree for very young students who, perforce, would have little to do with the wider community even in Hyde Park—all these could be justified by the same kind of impulse to citizenship and the need to save time and increase efficiency that had originally informed Harper's quarter system, correspondence schools, and extension schooling. They had little to do, however, with concrete applications in civil society or with bettering the civic environment in which the University was located.[389] The new College curriculum served as a sign of renewed intellectual vitality and, Hutchins hoped, intellectual unity for the University, but his was a more hermetic understanding of the purposes of the University than Harper would have embraced.

Hutchins was forced to spend much of his political capital in aggressive defenses of the ideal of academic freedom, a hotly controversial policy arena in the 1930s and 1940s, and one in which Harper had trod ever so gently. Harper protected the faculty (or, at least, most faculty) against the political (and denominational) realities of his nineteenth-century world. But he operated within an elite-driven civic world with more normative consistency between the senior faculty of the University and business elites of the 1890s than their counterparts in the 1930s and 1940s enjoyed (a consistency that lay at the heart of Veblen's worries before World War I). Hutchins, in contrast, had to defend the University when the ideological and social fracture lines of the 1930s were beginning to affect the student and faculty culture of many American universities.[390]

Although he had ambivalent feelings about development, Robert Hutchins might have been an effective fund-raiser had he faced more sympathetic constituencies.[391] After all, Hutchins believed in the fundamental importance of the University, and, for all its faults, he was genuinely certain that the University of Chicago was the closest example of what a real university should be. Moreover, Hutchins and the University as a whole had much to be proud of, for the 1930s and 1940s were among the most exciting decades in the University's history if measured by the scholarly attainments of the faculty and the educational progress of the students.[392] But, perhaps tragically, Hutchins did not enjoy the privilege of negotiating only with the converted. Instead, key members of the senior faculty opposed his educational reforms, important pockets of the alumni resented his institutional reforms, more conservative members of the Chicago's civic elite believed the myths that his University was filled with "Red" students and faculty, and members of his own board of trustees feared his budget practices, even if they also acknowledged his intellectual brilliance and personal charm.

Faculty memories of Hutchins were divided and conflicted. Ralph Tyler, a former dean of social sciences who was an unabashed admirer, felt that Hutchins had the virtue of always meeting problems head-on in an uncompromising and decisive way: "He was the best administrator that I have ever worked with, in the sense that he wanted to know the purpose of an activity; he wanted to understand just how what was proposed would contribute to that purpose ... and then if it looked good in those circumstances, he was strongly behind it.... He didn't have some of the problems of most administrators such as: Can you get the money? Will it alienate somebody?"[393] In contrast, for critics like Thomas V. Smith, a prominent member of the Department of Philosophy who served short stints as a state senator and a congressman from Illinois, Hutchins had a tragic, "Greek quality to his career." A man of "deep conviction, [with a] gift for maneuvering, and intelligence, shown in [his] ability to express himself, [and] clarity of mind," Hutchins habitually offended even his friends with an insecurity and quest for "triumphs" that marked him, in Smith's view, as a product of the war, as a "member of the lost gener-

ation," who desperately wanted moral certainty in all things.[394] Robert
Streeter, former dean of the College and the humanities division, argued
that Hutchins had to be seen as a nineteenth-century "cultural critic" *re-
divivus* as much as a modern university administrator, whose ideas had
a "rhetorical flare" that became a "remarkable substitute" for the money
and glittering appointments that the University lacked during the Great
Depression.[395] Hutchins's larger-than-life reputation as a moralizing
skeptic and critic, particularly his role as a national orator on behalf of
an exceedingly didactic view of higher education, generated a peculiar
combination of filial devotion and charismatic awe among his most loyal
supporters down to the end: Beardsley Ruml would fondly refer to him
as "H.R.H. Hutchins" in 1950. Others who profited from his patronage
had more ambivalent views, like Reuben Frodin, who saw him as a heroic
figure with political "feet of clay" who in his later years seemed to behave
in almost self-destructive ways.[396]

Hutchins's supporters spoke gratefully of the "intellectual ferment"
that he generated about significant educational questions, wistfully remembering the battles that Hutchins had provoked as genuinely exciting
campus-wide events.[397] But Hutchins's own memories of his administrative experience at Chicago were filled with disappointment and even failure. To F. Champion Ward, his ally in creating the Hutchins College in the
later 1940s, Hutchins insisted in 1964, "My mistake was that I thought that
I was a successful evangelist, when I actually was the stopper in the bath
tub. I thought that I had convinced everybody, when all I had done was to
block a return to 'normalcy.' I shall never cease to regret all the pain that
this mistake of mine caused you."[398] He recalled in 1972, "All the University
President has to do is to start an argument on as an important question as
he can and involve everybody in the place, and he has to figure out how
to keep this argument going. But of course, as I said before, University
Presidents are not selected with that purpose in view. They are selected
with the purpose of maintaining the public relations of the institution."
He ruefully noted in November 1964, in response to a program sponsored
by the American Council on Education to train future college presidents,
"The program is self-defeating. My observation is that good men become
college and university presidents only because they do not know any
better.... If a man knows what it is like to be a university president and
still wants to be one, he is not qualified for the job. He is interested in
salary and perquisites, publicity and prestige, and not in education and
scholarship. The president of an American college or university ... will be
judged, like every other Big Executive, by the state of his balance sheet
and public relations."[399]

Ironically, public perceptions of Hutchins outside of the University often ran in exactly the opposite direction, and it is striking that Clark Kerr's famous description of Hutchins in his *The Uses of the University* (1963)—Hutchins "was the last of the giants in the sense that he was the last of the university presidents who tried to change his institution and higher education in any fundamental way"—suggests a kind of heroic, utopian ideal of leadership to which all college presidents should aspire, but which the self-interested, self-indulgent worlds of the multiple faculty, trustee, and alumni status quos would never again allow.[400] Even today, invocations and memories of an idealized Hutchins, fighting for the noblest soul of an antivocationalist higher education, populate various "prof-scam" and "decline of the liberal arts" books criticizing what the critics assume to be the myopia, narrowness, and self-indulgence of American academics and academic life.[401] Set against this adulation was the frustration conveyed by Milton H. Thomas, a librarian and historian at Columbia University, who confessed to Richard Storr in 1953 that "the name of Hutchins always stirs me to a violent frenzy; it is astonishing that a whipper-snapper could be allowed to do as much damage to a great University as he was allowed to do."[402]

Hutchins's was a revolutionary presidency, but his revolution came in fits and starts, a bricolage of stunning interventions made all the more fascinating because they were fashioned out of strange tensions with the faculty, the alumni, and even the board of trustees. Some of these interventions failed, like Hutchins's bold attempt in 1934 to merge Chicago and Northwestern into one large metropolitan research university and his attempts to restructure graduate education by reducing the authority of the departments over their doctoral programs, while others had a stunning, if short-lived, success, the most significant of which was Hutchins's radical restructuring of the College in 1942. In The *Higher Learning in America* and other writings, Hutchins inspired others with his intellectual ideals, his witty condemnations of contemporary corruptions, and his insistence that the university and the nation not settle for the educational status quo. But he failed to connect this vision to arguments that could persuade the best minds on his own faculty and to formulate a strategy of institutional change that could sustain itself beyond a decade or two. As a result, the University of Chicago was left with the contradictory legacy of a powerful vision of intellectualism and a weakened institutional framework in which students and faculty could live out that vision.

The Age of Survival, 1951–1977

Robert Hutchins was a bold planner and aggressive risk taker. He believed that it was his obligation to raise controversial issues and force the faculty to debate these issues. But his relations with senior faculty members were often strained, and there was considerable distrust of his motives and intentions. Many notable changes in the structure and ethos of the University were products of Hutchins's audacious leadership—such as the creation of the divisions and the College as independent ruling bodies, the implementation of the first Core curriculum, and the instantiation of the University's image as a rational and intellectual milieu—but Hutchins also sowed deep political divisions within the University community, and he left the University in a severe financial and demographic crisis. The University's relations with surrounding neighborhoods, moreover, also showed significant signs of strain. Finally, although Hutchins had succeeded in giving the College a unique structure and special curricular identity, his ideas were deeply unpopular with significant segments of the divisional faculties and ultimately proved unsustainable. His successors— particularly Lawrence Kimpton and Edward Levi—were forced to deal with the consequences of his tenure on all these fronts.

Lawrence A. Kimpton, the Pragmatic Counterrevolutionary

Lawrence Kimpton was born in Kansas City, Missouri, on October 7, 1910, and attended Stanford University from 1927 to 1932. At Stanford he was an athlete, a debater, and a genial man about campus, but also a talented student who was elected to Phi Beta Kappa as a junior. Kimpton was admitted to a doctoral program at Cornell University to study philosophy, where he lived in Telluride House. In 1935 he received his PhD, writing a dissertation on the critical philosophy of Immanuel Kant. Kimpton early on decided on a career that blended teaching with academic administration, and he quickly proved that he was good at both. His connections with the Telluride Association led him to a position at Deep Springs College in California, where from 1935 to 1941 he taught philosophy, history, and German and served as the academic dean.[1] After leaving Deep Springs, he became part owner of a seven-thousand-acre cattle ranch in Nevada for a year. In 1942, he moved to the University of Kansas City, where he also served as dean.

THE MAN WHO WANTED THE JOB

During his time at Deep Springs Kimpton got to know Harvard president James Conant, who encouraged Kimpton to invite graduate students from Cal Tech to teach at the small school on part-time stints. When some of these young chemists were recruited for the Metallurgical Laboratory, the cryptic name given to Arthur Holly Compton's wartime plutonium program within the broader Manhattan Project, they recommended Kimpton for a job in Chicago, where the laboratory was located. Thus did Kimpton come to be hired at the University of Chicago in 1943 as the chief administrative officer of the Met Lab. This job gave Kimpton a broad perspective over many administrative and research domains within the University (and later, friends insisted, high doses of radiation that compromised his health). In September 1944 Kimpton began serving as dean of students and as secretary of the faculties, while holding courtesy professorships in the Department of Philosophy and the Department of Education. He demonstrated wise and fair judgment, an ability to appraise thorny political situations quickly, and a calm and friendly temperament. Kimpton was also an excellent writer, so much so that Norman Maclean would later insist that "he wrote one of the finest American prose styles ever written by a university president."[2] In sum, Kimpton came across not as an ideologue but as a literate, pragmatic problem solver.

Kimpton's talents began to be recognized nationally, and in February 1946 Arthur Holly Compton offered him the number two administrative position of vice chancellor at Washington University, which he rejected in the belief that opportunities existed in Chicago.[3] In 1947 Kimpton accepted an offer to return to his alma mater, Stanford University, where he worked as University Dean of Students from 1947 to 1950. Although he initially thought that he would like the relaxed atmosphere and slower tempo of official life at Stanford, Kimpton soon grew bored with the more languid pace of affairs, longing for the chaotic, but dynamic atmosphere at Chicago. He sent various signals to Hutchins that if the right job opened up, he would be eager to return to Chicago. From their early correspondence it seemed evident that Kimpton admired Hutchins's rhetorical boldness and his charismatic personality, and that he liked Hutchins and thought that he could learn from him. This feature of their relationship was all the more fascinating and paradoxical given that, once in power, Kimpton set about destroying many of the innovations that Hutchins had put in place involving undergraduate education and the structure of faculty appointments.[4]

Hutchins remained in touch with Kimpton on and off, occasionally expressing a hope that Kimpton would return to Chicago. Finally, reacting to pressure from the trustees to become more active on the fund-raising front, Hutchins offered Kimpton the new position of vice president for development in March 1950. Kimpton accepted with alacrity.

During the postwar years the University's finances had deteriorated, and pressure was mounting to put the University's fiscal house in order. In approving Kimpton's appointment on May 1, 1950, the trustees voiced their deep concern about the University's financial situation. Arriving in late summer of 1950, Kimpton had been warned by Lynn Williams, who was in charge of public relations, of the grave challenges that he would face: "I think you may know that there is some general dissatisfaction with the public attitude about the University, particularly in the Midwest, and I think you will very soon come to realize — if you don't already — that this presents a very serious problem in any attempt to raise funds.... As you know, not all of our alumni have been enthused about the University. Our annual fund drive with the alumni has always been disappointing."[5] But Kimpton quickly proved to be an adroit fund-raiser who was comfortable talking to both academics and wealthy private donors. Kimpton seems to have calculated that, with his own excellent interpersonal skills and his remarkable capacity for storytelling, he could parlay Hutchins's formidable fame into greater financial good for the University (with some hyperbole he called Hutchins "one of the great salesmen of all time").[6]

SUCCESSION TO THE PRESIDENCY

Only months after Kimpton returned to Hyde Park, Robert Hutchins decided to accept an offer from Paul G. Hoffman in December 1950 to assume a senior administrative position at the Ford Foundation and resigned from the chancellorship.[7] Did Hutchins leave voluntarily, or was he pushed out? In the echelons of the board there was disquiet about Hutchins's recent performance, and, in contrast to the efforts to talk him out of resigning in 1946, it was now evident that a significant faction of the trustees were prepared to let him go. Hutchins certainly knew this. At the same time, the board hesitated to force the issue, preferring to allow

Hutchins the time to make the decision himself. Given his personal sense that he had reached the limits of what was possible at Chicago and his doubts that his tenure had really changed the University in any significant way, Hutchins was looking for a way out.[8] With a supremely attractive opportunity with the Ford Foundation in hand, Hutchins made up his mind. Mortimer Adler had urged Hutchins as early as 1946 that he no longer needed the University of Chicago as a "platform from which to address the country" on educational reform.[9] Now, with the Ford Foundation's money at his beck and call, Hutchins decided that Adler was right.

Hutchins's decision created an immense power vacuum at the University, which had not conducted a presidential search since 1929. Kimpton's administrative service at Chicago, at Stanford, and again at Chicago made him a plausible candidate to succeed Hutchins. He was not a published scholar, but neither had Hutchins been. In contrast to Hutchins, Kimpton had no enemies on the faculty, he was admired by many of the trustees, and he had a close knowledge of the inner workings of the University that was appealing and credible. Kimpton was also a nationally competitive figure in that several other universities had made inquiries about his availability to become their president, so he enjoyed the aura of a rising young administrative star in whom the trustees might vest prodigious responsibility. Finally, Kimpton had suitable academic credentials, civic courage, and a genial wit. Kimpton could also be viewed by Hutchins's allies as a "Hutchins man" in his views on university governance, for Kimpton acknowledged that he had returned to Chicago to work with Hutchins.[10] For those who cared about institutional continuity this was crucial, but it would quickly prove a miscalculation.

Lawrence Kimpton's selection came at the end of a long process that saw the vetting of hundreds of names. The others on the final short list included Detlev W. Bronk, president of Johns Hopkins; Charles W. Cole, president of Amherst; Gilbert F. White, president of Haverford; and Lowell T. Coggeshall of the University of Chicago. In the end the choice came down to Kimpton and Coggeshall, the dean of the Division of Biological Sciences. According to Harold Swift, Coggeshall seemed less than enthusiastic at the prospect of leading the University, saying that he "was perfectly happy where he was and doubted whether he would do well in the proposed job but would take it if requested," whereas Kimpton said not only that he wanted the job but also that he had turned down one or more offers of other presidencies while awaiting Chicago's decision.[11] Coggeshall's equivocations tipped the choice in favor of Kimpton, and on April 12, 1951, the board officially approved his appointment. With Hutchins already gone on administrative leave, Kimpton took office immediately.

In his first months in office, Kimpton was well received by the faculty and alumni communities, so much so that the chairman of the board, Laird Bell, cautioned him about trying to please all constituencies: "You have been so well received on all fronts that it must be a temptation not to irritate anybody, but that way lies slow decay. I am anxious that though some storms be stilled and tempers smoothed the parallel with Judson's administration go no further (except that he Balanced the Budget!)."[12] Bell need not have worried that Kimpton would become a second Harry Pratt Judson, for he had no inkling of the drastic and sweeping interventions Kimpton would soon launch.

THE QUANDARY OF COLLEGE
ENROLLMENTS AND STUDENT LIFE

Although Kimpton was aware of the financial problems facing the University, he was nearly overwhelmed by them once he took office. The postwar period may have been a golden age of expansion and cresting ambition for some universities, but at Chicago it was a time of basic survival. By the fall of 1951, the yawning gulf between resources and income was all too apparent. "Hutchins left this University in a fantastic mess financially and it is going to be a hell of a job getting it squared around," Kimpton wrote to his father in early November. "I am in the process of trying to make out a budget for next year and it is inconceivable the problems one runs into."[13] Two weeks later he reiterated this theme by observing that "Mr. Hutchins very much over-extended the University, and it is my job to contract it. I've got to reduce this operating budget about a million dollars a year in reasonably short order. This is going to be a very tough thing to do and will not gain me great popularity."[14] Between 1950 and 1955 Kimpton was forced to make cuts in the regular academic budget on an annual basis by more than 5 percent, with the largest single cut of almost 10 percent coming in 1952–53.

Yet the chaotic budget situation would serve only as backdrop to Kimpton's hotly contested interventions in the College. Early in his presidency Kimpton confronted a dramatic drop in undergraduate enrollments that severely aggravated the fiscal crisis. By the autumn of 1953 enrollment in the College had sunk to 1,350 students. The entering class in the fall of 1953 — 275 first-year and 39 transfer students — was less than half its size two decades earlier. Kimpton and other critics of the College program that Robert Hutchins had created in 1942 believed the declining number of undergraduate matriculants indicated not merely admissions or marketing failures but more fundamental problems involving the College's curriculum and its governance. This downward trend put Chicago at a significant

FIG. 1. Comparative undergraduate enrollments for Chicago, Harvard, Princeton, Stanford, and Yale, 1920–2012

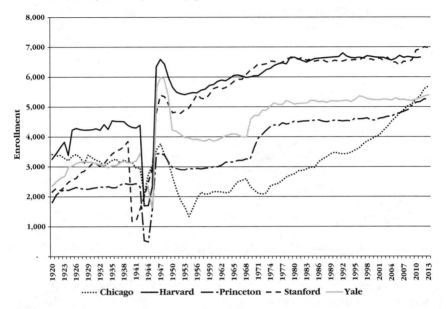

Source: Office of Registrar, University of Chicago.

disadvantage with respect to its top private peers in demographic resources and in corresponding levels of net tuition revenue and alumni philanthropy. Whereas before World War II the University had a large undergraduate college compared to most of its peers—larger than Princeton, very similar in size to Yale and Stanford, but smaller than Harvard—after the war a growing divergence occurred, with Chicago falling far behind all of its peers for almost five decades (see fig. 1). This meant that the University "lost" tens of thousands of potential alumni supporters during this period.

The collapse of enrollments had several causes, including the stereotype of hyperintellectualism as the only trait sought by the University in prospective applicants and increasing concerns about safety in the neighborhood. But among the most important factors was the University's attempt to recruit the best high school sophomores and juniors under Robert Hutchins's early admissions program. As George Watkins, the vice president for development in the 1950s, later recalled, "No program instituted by Robert Maynard Hutchins was more controversial than the Early Admission Program as it developed—and it finally became a disaster." According to Watkins, early admissions programs were not new at the time, but the program launched by Hutchins allowed qualified students to be admitted after two years of high school and be awarded an undergraduate degree at the end of their sophomore year of college. "This may have made excellent educational sense," Watkins said, but it provoked "violent criticism" in all quarters, "nowhere more vehemently than from other academic institutions and faculties." He noted that "high school teachers among our alumni ... were outraged at the notion that the last two years of high school were a waste."[15] William Warren, a young admissions counselor at Chicago in the early 1950s, echoed this view. "The attitude of many high school staff, including guidance personnel, teachers, and principals, was extremely negative on early entrance because we were trying to take away their best students.... In most high schools we were not permitted to speak with sophomores and juniors, although we asked to do so."[16] The collapse of trust among local high school officials, alumni, and parents in the University's traditional markets meant admissions officials had to try to expand the applicant base of the College by recruiting more students from distant and unfamiliar areas, putting Chicago in competition with cities and towns already dominated by other elite colleges and universities. By 1958 the number of undergraduate students from the Chicago area had declined to 33 percent, compared with 70 percent in 1940; by 1970 it had declined still further to 26 percent.

Facing these brutal facts, Kimpton came to agree with the divisional faculty who objected to the basic premises of the 1942 revolution wrought by Hutchins and Faust and maintained a profound skepticism about a curriculum that claimed that a first-rate liberal arts education could consist only of general-education sequences. Arguing that the College and its faculty had arrogantly divorced themselves from the basic research culture of the University and alienated legions of high school teachers, they demanded that opportunities for more specialized study be given greater weight and prominence in student programs.[17] In siding with the graduate divisions, Kimpton confronted an articulate, if embattled group of College professors who, since the mid-1940s, had come to feel themselves to be a genuine faculty and who acted as such. "I am trying to change the whole quality and nature of the student body, and this is not an easy job," he wrote in December 1952. "I have also been trying to get something done on this College of ours.... I am trying to ... get it into a more conventional pattern, so that it will be more attractive to students, and have a better standing in the country as a whole."[18] This letter underscores that Kimpton's hard-nosed fears about the survival of the College were not rooted in a partisan preference for one or another theory of liberal education. As a student of philosophy Kimpton certainly understood the contours of the "pragmatism versus classicism" debates that animated the collision

328 * CHAPTER FIVE

between the New Plan forces and Hutchins and his allies in the 1930s. But those debates seemed stale and irrelevant in the face of the survival of the University as an institution of the first rank.

Kimpton was also concerned about the perception that the Chicago bachelor's degree was undervalued by the outside world, even for those who entered after finishing high school, forcing College graduates to obtain additional specialized training before they were credited with having achieved a four-year college education. The reputation of the College as a demanding and intense place also limited the admissions pool. As a faculty committee on enrollment observed, "High school principals on occasion have told our representatives that there was no one in their student body of the quality required to succeed in the College."[19] Kimpton's critical views were confirmed by outside consultants hired to evaluate the public relations problems facing the University. Their report attributed the decline in enrollment to "the disaffection of important segments of the public, including particularly secondary school educators, alumni, and parents of college-oriented young men and women."[20]

As secretary of the faculties Kimpton had objectively recorded the bitter fights over the undergraduate curriculum that had transpired in the mid-1940s. Now he launched a presidential counterrevolution. His first step was to appoint a committee in February 1953 chaired by a veteran administrator, Emery T. Filbey, to review the location of the BA degree. Not surprisingly, given Filbey's instinctive respect for whoever held the reins of administrative power, in April 1953 the Filbey committee released a report recommending that control of the curriculum leading to the BA degree be removed from the exclusive authority of the College faculty.[21] In the future, the BA degree would be "relocated" by converting it into a joint degree that would be shared with the faculties of the various graduate divisions, with each side obtaining control over approximately half of the undergraduate's four-year program. This recommendation was tantamount to killing off the original Hutchins College plan and was seen to be so by all concerned. After an acrimonious debate, the report was adopted by the Council of the University Senate on May 7, 1953, by a 29–16 vote, with 375 undergraduate students standing in silent protest outside of the Law School building, where the meeting was held.

In the aftermath Champ Ward resigned as dean of the College, and although Kimpton persuaded him to stay on temporarily, it was the end of the line for the all-general-education curriculum.[22] Ward accused Kimpton of playing politics, of currying favor with powerful divisional interests, and of acting in bad faith, while Kimpton thought Ward rigid, doctrinaire, and oblivious to the fundamental threats that the University faced if undergraduate enrollments continued to stagnate.[23] Privately, Kimpton not only lacked patience with Ward but rather enjoyed the drama. "Deans are resigning all over the place and all that sort of thing, but I really like a good fight, and this is a good one," he wrote. "I only hope that I am right in what I am doing."[24]

The College crisis marked a turning point in Kimpton's relations with the board. Most trustees sided with him against the few remaining Hutchins loyalists, such as William Benton, and fence sitters, such as Laird Bell, who had imagined a happy continuity between the two regimes in early 1952, were forced to accept the logic of Kimpton's changes. Hutchins for his part was outraged, complaining to friends that "this is all part of the general movement now going on—everybody should be like everybody else. This of course means that every college should be like every other college."[25] But Hutchins knew that Kimpton had both the sovereign force of his office and the trustees on his side. The end result was a stunning rupture of the status quo.

Kimpton recognized that he was damaging his formerly cordial relations with Hutchins, but he saw no other way forward. If there was bad feeling, it was because Kimpton was doing to Hutchins what Hutchins had done to Boucher, using presidential authority to upend a program of liberal education that one faculty faction had imposed against the will of another. Leadership manuals from the 1950s on the role of university presidents warned that proposing significant change in institutional structures would always provoke opposition from faculty, who were, by nature, conservative and status preserving.[26] What made the curricular clashes of the 1950s at Chicago so heated (and so fascinating) was that none of the faculty saw themselves as status quo preservers. Rather, after the struggles of the late 1940s, all sides were convinced that their way, and only their way, was not only the most honorable but also the most innovative.

The second installment of Kimpton's strategy for restructuring undergraduate education came in 1957–58 and was a necessary, if unplanned, modification of the first. The system of individually negotiated treaties between the graduate departments and the College that had been prescribed by Filbey in 1953 had quickly proven to be a failure. When Kimpton made the decision in 1953 to recenter the demographic basis of the College from grades eleven through fourteen to grades thirteen through sixteen, this meant that in the future the high school graduate would become the normal, if not exclusive, client of the University's undergraduate programs. Now the crucial question became, for how many years of college study would the normal high school graduate be held accountable? Even after the adoption of the Filbey report in May 1953, the College faculty insisted on the necessity of almost three years of general-education course work for undergraduates, but most of the graduate divisions wanted close to

two years (or at least more than one year) of specialized and elective
course work. Rather than willing and happy cooperation between the
College faculty and the faculty of the departments, observers saw endless
wrangling and turf wars—which Kimpton himself characterized as taking
place on "an arms-length, hostile negotiating basis" defined by "skill in
poker and power politics"—the final outcome of which was that some
College students found themselves forced to take almost five years of
courses in order to fulfill the demands both of the College and of their
respective departments.

Going back to the drawing boards in early 1957, Kimpton appointed
another committee, chaired this time by himself, to sort out these clashes.
He found the process somewhat easier than in 1953, perhaps because the
College loyalists were becoming exhausted.[27] The Executive Committee on Undergraduate Education (ECUE) proposed in April 1958 that
sole control over the content and structure of the BA be returned to the
College, but that the faculty of the College be almost doubled in size by
adding ninety-one members selected from the graduate divisions, and
that in the future joint appointments between the College and a division
would be the norm. Rather than divide the undergraduate program in
two parts—Filbey's scheme of 1953—the plan of 1958 proposed a slow
but deliberate merger of the graduate divisional faculties and the College
faculty. The old College of the 1940s and early 1950s would now be replaced with a "new College," where two years of general education plus
two years of specialization and electives would become the curricular
norm and where power would be lodged in a "new" faculty that would
increasingly consist of those who held joint, codivisional appointments.[28]
The status of the College and the divisions as independent ruling bodies
would be protected, and faculty members would hold two independent
but coordinated appointments, teaching graduate students by virtue of
their membership in a division, and teaching College students by virtue
of their membership in the College.

The two-plus-two paradigm (i.e., two years in general-education
courses and the remainder divided between a student's concentration
and free electives) that emerged from the late 1950s continued to shape
the College's curriculum until the late 1990s. But with the perspective
of sixty years, two features about this diplomatic settlement should be
stressed. First, and most obvious, it was not driven by pedagogical considerations so much as by the need to cobble together a deal to end the
faculty bickering.[29] Second, while the settlement's institutionalization of
joint departmental-College appointments repudiated Hutchins's conviction about the necessity of an autonomous College faculty, it also assumed
that this new joint faculty would be able to sustain Chicago's traditions

of non-department-based general-education courses and that the College would continue to function as a curricular whole greater than any departmental parts.

It was precisely these issues that worried many colleagues in the College in 1958. Would the unique structure of interdisciplinary general-education courses developed at Chicago in the 1930s and 1940s—courses that were not beholden to individual departmental patronage—survive? Some colleagues feared that the 1958 reforms would lead to the divisions and their departments grabbing fragments of the undergraduate program that related to their own parochial interests, making the College, as the dean Robert Streeter put it, little more than "a collection of undergraduate extensions of the four Divisions."[30] Hutchins openly warned that Kimpton's paradigm empowered the very faculty who sought "to undermine the College."[31] Unfortunately, Kimpton had few plausible answers to such concerns. His overriding conviction was that Hutchins's separation of the faculty at Chicago into those who taught undergraduates and those who did research and taught graduate students—which was the fundamental logic of the College's plan between 1942 and 1953—had been a disaster. As he put it in 1960 to Alfred Romer, "To my mind, at least, the most serious mistake that he [Hutchins] made was separating teaching and research.... It created a group of second-class citizens who became more and more remote from the rest of the University and indeed from the discipline of the subject matter. I hope that we have cured that at the present time by re-establishing the College as something that everyone at the University participates in."[32]

Kimpton's interventions also reflected grave concerns about the University's negative image. Over the course of 1953, Kimpton and his staff traveled thousands of miles around the United States, meeting with hundreds of college counselors and high school principals to learn why they were not recommending the College to their students. Then in early January 1954 Kimpton gave a forceful address to the trustees and faculty that amounted to a public declaration of war on Hutchins's heritage:

> It isn't that they just don't like us—they dislike us.... For some reason, a high school principal resents being told that he doesn't know what he is doing and that half his program must be lifted from his inept hands if the youth of America is not to suffer.... But in addition to this personal resentment toward the University of Chicago, we discovered another interesting phenomenon.... Every high school principal and college counselor knows precisely the kind of student they think we want, and they endeavor conscientiously to urge these students to come to the University of Chicago. The stereotype varies a bit in different parts of the

country, but it adds up pretty well into a certain kind of youngster. First of all, he must be odd and not accepted in games and social affairs by the other students. He must be bright, not necessarily in the conventional sense of high I.Q., but in some extravagant and unusual way. He must have read and pondered esoteric things far beyond his years. He draws a sharp breath when reference is made to Aristotle, St. Thomas, John Donne, and James Joyce. He wears glasses, does not dance, deplores sports, and has advanced ideas on labor and the theory of relativity. But he is confident that he would have been happier had he lived in the age of Pericles or during some obscure period of the Middle Ages. The converse of this stereotype is also the case. As one college counselor phrased it to me, "it simply does not occur to any of our normal students to go to the University of Chicago." As one tries to get to the causes for the creation of this stereotype, many things are mentioned. It is widely understood that we read only the Great Books at the University of Chicago and ponder the 102—no more, no less—Great Ideas. We have insisted that the purpose of a university is to train the mind, and the inference has been drawn that the rest of the person may go hang so far as we are concerned. We have deplored fun, snorted at anyone who wanted to develop himself physically, and sneered at anyone who conceived of a college education as having any vocational or practical significance.

Kimpton also delivered a second message, which involved the link between enrollments and the financial solvency of the University. "The bleak economic fact is that we cannot exist solely as a graduate institution," he said. "The cost of research, the costs of the training of the student for the PhD, must be borne in part at least by a substantial number of undergraduate students. There are only two sources of income that will make us secure in our precious academic freedom: one is endowment income and the other is tuition income. All other sources are precarious or corrupting or both."

Behind Kimpton's claims was his explicit desire to attract "a very broad cross-section of young Americans at our University," which essentially meant a different kind of student. "If we are [as] good as we think we are, why can't we give the life of our students outside the classroom character, depth, and distinction?"[33] Kimpton wanted more students who blended attributes that he himself admired: intellectualism coupled with a capacity to work well in the world of affairs, or, to frame the issue in the context of Kimpton's own life, students who could thrive in intellectual debates at the Telluride Association while also driving cattle on the ranch of Deep Springs College. Kimpton's frustrations with what he called "our clumsy methods of publicizing our undergraduate work" and his efforts to revamp the admissions strategies to recruit different kinds of applicants met with covert opposition from the staff of the admissions office, most of whom had been appointed during the Hutchins era.[34] Charles D. O'Connell, who served as a junior admissions officer in the 1950s, remarked that "the University's reputation was such that, although the College attracted bright young people, it was considered to be a place for oddballs. After all, A. J. Liebling, in his famous article in *The New Yorker*, referred to the University of Chicago as the greatest collection of neurotics since the Children's Crusade. That sort of publicity did not help."[35]

Kimpton's skepticism about the current student body inevitably became public, with predictably adverse consequences. As early as January 1952 he found himself in confrontations with members of student government, who, he asserted, were convinced that "any chancellor who tries to interpret the free and democratic nature of this University to the community is a bad chancellor" and that "students, by virtue of being students, have unlimited rights but no responsibilities."[36] He became famous (or infamous) for his alleged quip in June 1954 before an Order of the C alumni banquet that the problem with the College was that it was admitting too many "goddamn queer kids" and "quiz kids" as opposed to "a broad cross section of young, healthy Americans."[37] The College may have attracted too many "quiz kids" for Kimpton's taste, but it attracted them using the paradoxical rhetoric of individual freedom and personal autonomy. As is often the case in such transformations, unanticipated change soon came into view. The chaotic, social laissez-faire that underlay the hyperintellectualism of the Hutchins College created a space for the interests of some particularly self-reliant students. One saw a taste of this playfulness and theatricality on April Fool's Day in 1955, when, in response to Kimpton's anti–quiz kid rhetoric, the *Maroon* published an article bearing the headline "Last Queer Kid Leaves Campus," with an accompanying photograph that showed a down-and-out, dejected student dressed in an oversized coat and carrying two heavy bags. The article read:

> "The last queer kid has left the UC campus," the Chancellor [Lawrence Kimpton] officially announced this week. Aristotle Schwartz, a 1953 entrant under the OLD B.A. plan was escorted by three campus police Tuesday morning to the corner of 57th and Woodlawn and pointed northwest. He was given a CTA token and a warning never to return to campus again. Schwartz was the last victim in a campus-wide queer-kid proscription initiated by the administration last August. The Internal Securities sub-committee of the faculty senate notified the Chancellor last week that the purge had been successfully completed.... When asked what the criteria were for the dismissal of several hundred students by the

sub-committee, the Chancellor stated that the criteria were known only to the sub-committee members. "If they were made public," he said, "all the queer kids in the neighborhood would be sneaky and pretend to be normal to escape detection. If we must have sneaks, let them be normal ones," he emphasized.... When asked to comment upon the successful queer-kid purge, Naomi McCorn, dean of students and chairman of the Student Advisory Boors, said "Actually, it's fine. It was done carefully. I rather like it. In fact, I like everything."[38]

Among the new waves of students entering the all-general-education College after 1945 were personalities who were less conventional and more open to new forms of meritocracy, intellectual seriousness, and aesthetic self-expression, with few social "in-groups" and a high tolerance of diversity. This side of the Hutchins College is less remembered now, but at the time it was powerfully visible, and its collective values have continued to define the ethos of the undergraduate campus culture down to the present. Out of this heady atmosphere of earnest idealism and raw creativity came groups of College students and young alumni like the Playwrights' Theatre Club and Compass Players who combined theatrical talent, ironic wit, and an appetite for risk taking to make themselves famous in the landscape of American popular theater. Given the absence of strong faculty-led academic arts organizations on campus, the 1950s saw the emergence of strains of student self-help and student-generated creativity in the arts that still mark the culture of the Chicago undergraduate student body today.[39] The College also encouraged student humor and irony in wonderfully diverse ways, including student essays describing how the friends of Aristotle invented bridge playing.[40]

At the same time, with its high attrition levels and low admission rates, the College undeniably faced chronic problems in student life. During the 1940s and early 1950s the University had made an unyielding effort to uproot the "rah-rah" milieu of Greek life and spectacle athletics from the 1930s as defining features of student culture, but in their place it established few mechanisms to encourage social solidarity and feelings of belonging to a supportive community. In his survey of alumni opinion in 1951, John Netherton encountered numerous complaints about the "one-sided emphasis on the intellectual at the expense of the social and physical," about the lack of feelings of community and school spirit, and about the cold, impersonal, anomic atmosphere that many young students encountered on campus.[41] Such observations were echoed a decade later by the assistant dean of students, James Newman: "Few adults would choose to live in a social milieu which offers as little emotional support to the individual as does the College. Yet our students endure this psychological assault at a time in their lives when they are most in need of the social support that is lacking here."[42] A later dean of the College who was himself a graduate of Hutchins's College, Donald N. Levine, described the disjunction between curricular innovation and disregard for student life that marked these years:

> The Hutchins College finally secured the primacy of the intellectual ideal in the College culture, but in a way that subjected young—often very young—and emotionally dependent students to an intensely demanding and sometimes perversely abstract curricular structure in a setting that seemed to depreciate *any* kind of student achievement other than the strictly academic. Consequently, what many regard as the curricular high point of the Hutchins era—the perfection of the Faust-Ward curriculum in the late 1940s and early 1950s—was also a period of enormous discomfort and distress for a substantial proportion of students in the College.[43]

Kimpton's interventions in the College also had implications for general university planning, for he hoped to make undergraduate students the largest demographic component of the University. In March 1954 Kimpton went before key board members with a plan to increase the size of the College from 1,350 students to 5,000 students by the mid-1960s, thus making the College 50 percent of the total University population. Even this number was a compromise, since Kimpton privately stated that he really wanted 6,000 undergraduates on the Quadrangles.[44]

Kimpton struggled admirably to carry out the plan, but he had few resources to do what needed to be done on the residential and student-life fronts. As early as 1951, in a hard-hitting report on the problems of students in the College, the sociologist William C. Bradbury signaled that the University needed to expand and strengthen the College's housing system as part of a comprehensive approach to supporting student educational growth and feelings of community. Bradbury argued that "as a result of the war and the post-war boom all the Houses have become badly overcrowded and none is a place for civilized living," and he was unapologetic about the cost that such changes would incur.[45] Yet in the early 1950s, with undergraduate matriculations and tuition revenues plunging and with a faculty significantly larger than the University could afford, Bradbury's pleas fell on deaf ears.[46]

The College's residential situation was further complicated by the slow collapse of what had been an extensive fraternity culture on campus. As noted, in the 1920s the fraternities provided housing for a significant number of College men, and they also generated a strong sense of solidarity among their members. The revision of the College's curriculum in 1931, which created the more academically challenging general-education courses, led the University in 1932 to prohibit fraternities from recruiting entering first-year students until the spring quarter of their freshman year. This change in pledging practices, together with the more academically oriented interests manifested by many of the new matriculants, created a difficult recruitment environment for the fraternities. After 1945, when the College began to matriculate a large number of very young students who were not appropriate recruits and indeed who were not allowed to join, the fraternities faced even more dire challenges, and the subsequent decline in the College's enrollments in the 1950s spelled the end for many of these groups. Whereas in 1929 the University of Chicago had twenty-nine fraternities, that number fell to seventeen by 1939 and nine by the early 1950s. By 1965, the College had only seven fraternities.[47]

Given Kimpton's abiding desire to rebuild the College, he finally persuaded the board to authorize the construction of two new residence halls: Woodward Court (initially for women) opened in 1958, and Pierce Tower opened in 1960. Woodward in particular was a sine qua non for any attempt to rebuild the population of women students, which had dropped precipitously since World War II. Woodward and Pierce were serviceable but not well-constructed buildings, and both soon showed signs of wear and tear that grew more acute over the decades. Nor were they part of a well-thought-out plan that would integrate residential living with the educational ideals of the College, such as Bradbury had called for in 1951. Woodward and Pierce were the last new residential buildings constructed by the University until the opening of the Max Palevsky Residential Commons in 2002.

Despite Kimpton's efforts during the 1950s to increase admissions, balance the curriculum, and improve student morale, the College struggled to break beyond a total four-year enrollment of barely more than 2,000 students. By the autumn quarter of 1961, the College had reached a total enrollment of 2,183 students, a far cry from Kimpton's optimistic hopes. Indeed, the most potent problem facing the College in the later 1950s and 1960s was its huge dropout rate. For example, of the 458 first-year students who matriculated in the autumn of 1956, 51 percent (234) had dropped out by the spring of 1960.[48] The class of 1959 endured similar losses: within four years almost 40 percent had dropped out. Mary Alice Newman, who undertook an exhaustive study of this crisis, attributed it not to lack of academic ability but to individual personal struggles occurring in a campus environment that many found "diffuse, or cold and impersonal."[49] Upon becoming dean of the College in the late spring of 1959, Alan Simpson surveyed the condition of the academic facilities and was appalled by what he saw: "I toured the College domain yesterday—I can only say that I never saw a sterner triumph of mind over matter. There are offices with as little space for reflection and as little light as a public toilet. There are classrooms as grim as a morgue. Diogenes in his tub was a sybarite compared with the asceticism we practice here."[50]

In the midst of legitimate concerns about student life and impoverished facilities, conflicts over academic jurisdictions continued unabated. By the time of Kimpton's departure from the University in 1960, the shotgun marriage of College and divisional faculty had been carried out, but with impatience and ill grace on both sides. Kimpton warned that "the Divisions must not regard this move as a heaven-sent occasion to go down and clobber their colleagues in the general courses," but to many College loyalists the process of *Gleichschaltung* felt exactly like that.[51] Even Simpson, who as dean from 1959 to 1964 was a flexible and creative leader, complained of the danger of giving departments too much authority, "because it would be surrendering the control of undergraduate education to agencies which have given no evidence of their readiness to accept it as the first claim on their attention."[52] The state of the curriculum was also unsteady and fractured, with many of the existing College general-education staffs resenting having to accommodate divisional partners. Among the alumni and the general public, Chicago seemed to have abandoned Hutchins's righteous dreamland of high principle for an uncertain, timorous, and muddled future. The *New York Times* announced in May 1959 that Chicago was ending the "Hutchins' System" in favor of "a policy balancing brains with brawn and beauty," while *Time* magazine quoted Simpson to the effect that "the ordinary American boy who will only make a million later in life, the ordinary girl who wants a husband as well as a diploma, are as welcome here as the Quiz Kid."[53] It would fall to Provost Edward Levi in 1965 to give the 1958 plan a more enduring constitutional and a more plausible cultural basis—a story we will return to below. Still, little real progress had been made on the admissions front, which probably did not surprise Kimpton, for as an inveterate realist he had admitted privately in 1954 that "this is going to be a long time process, and it is going to be very tough going for a number of years still."[54]

THE BUDGET CRISIS AND THE CAMPAIGN OF 1955–1958

The acute decline in undergraduate enrollments was one facet of a larger and more ominous crisis: the parlous state of University finances. By 1950–51 (the final academic year of Robert Hutchins's tenure), the University was running a budget deficit of $1.8 million on a regular budget base of $17.9 million, a situation that Kimpton described to the board of trustees as having been chronic since 1938.[55] In 1953 Kimpton explained the situation in succinct terms: "In the last eight years we have spent more money than we should have, with the results: 1) We have seriously weakened our reserve position; 2) We have built buildings we can barely afford to maintain; [and] 3) We generated a staff whose cost exceeded our operating income." A year later he said, "We are working as hard as we possibly can and yet we are continually running up against this blank wall of the need for money."[56]

The University's financial situation paralleled that of most private research universities after World War II. Instructional and research costs rose steeply, and operational expenses eventually outpaced tuition revenues and endowment payouts.[57] But three factors made Chicago's experience in these decades particularly grave. First, as undergraduate enrollment shrank, the graduate-student population expanded, and given that graduate students cost three to four times more to educate, this increase put Chicago in a particularly exposed demographic-financial position.[58] Second, Chicago was badly placed to sustain the highly competitive fundraising initiatives that became crucial to the welfare of the top US universities after 1950, given the indifference with which alumni had been treated since the late 1920s. Finally, the institution faced what many outside observers believed were life-and-death perils from the surrounding neighborhood that not only made the cultural location of the University less attractive but forced the University to commit massive financial investments to urban renewal projects (real estate acquisitions, etc.) that had nothing to do with the research capacity and intellectual prestige of the institution. The question facing Kimpton and his colleagues in the early 1950s was not just whether they could find the additional resources to make strategic investments in new, innovative research programs and thus to retain top faculty, but whether the University could survive as a first-rate institution.

Kimpton acted immediately to restore financial order and to plan a major capital campaign. He began with three years of stern budget cutting, bringing the budget into balance by 1954. But he admitted to the board that "the budget had been balanced at too high a cost to morale as well as to the standards of the University," putting the University in danger of becoming a second-rate institution.[59] Kimpton's budget slashing exacerbated the outflow of top faculty from Chicago to other top institutions, and as enrollments in the College continued to worsen, Kimpton assembled a key group of trustees and senior staff at his vacation home in Lakeside, Michigan, in early March 1954 to present a hard-hitting plan to deal with the University's financial troubles and to "talk through the present and future of the University." Kimpton proposed a social reengineering of the campus, focusing on recruiting many more students to the College and launching a general fund-raising campaign that would require a "vast drive for new money."[60] Kimpton's bold strategy for returning the University to firm budgetary solvency was premised on the University's achieving a total enrollment of 10,000 students by the mid-1960s. This would lead to an increase in new net tuition income for the University from $224,000 in 1955 to $3 million by 1960.[61] Kimpton's plan also proposed raising $12 million in new money to sustain current academic operations, $3.7 million to accommodate the higher enrollment, $2 million for financial aid, and $11.4 million for residence halls for College and graduate students and other capital projects. The total of $29.3 million was later adjusted upward for an official campaign goal of $32.8 million.[62]

Compared to what many trustees felt to be Hutchins's distant and often imperious manner of dealing with the board, Kimpton's dogged, pragmatic, even folksy, management style appealed to most trustees, and during the first few years of his administration he was able to cajole the board to contribute more actively to the welfare of the University. By acknowledging the importance of improving the public relations of the University, especially in Chicago, and the need for regaining alumni support, Kimpton focused on problems that were close to the hearts of the trustees, who as corporate and civic leaders were worried about the University's reputation in the city.[63] Kimpton's presentation in 1954 thus persuaded the trustees, and soon the debate changed from whether to have a capital campaign to how to organize it and what its goal should be.

To execute his fund-raising strategy, Kimpton hired George Watkins as his chief development officer. An affable and creative College alumnus who had fond memories of his years on campus in the 1930s (he remembered with particular gratitude courses taught by Mortimer Adler and Robert Redfield), Watkins had gained considerable marketing experience in the insurance industry and was a perfect adjutant to Kimpton. Watkins recommended that the University reengage Robert F. Duncan, whom Watkins admired for having organized Burton's "classic" 1924 drive, to help run the campaign. Duncan, who had left John Price Jones in 1950 to become president of Kersting, Brown & Company, agreed to return to Chicago in early 1955 and stayed, full-time, until June 1956. Now on his third stint at Chicago, Duncan was impressed with Kimpton's vision for the future of the University but urged him to make it more public: "If a majority of the leading citizens of the City could have the understanding of the University which you gave the group last evening, I think you would have no trouble in future years in getting all the money you need."[64]

As in 1924, the campaign was a multifaceted effort, seeking support from the alumni, the trustees, foundations, corporations, and major outside donors. The campaign devised a careful publicity schedule for the alumni, with many different letters and brochures, all timed for maximum effect.[65] The alumni campaign was put in the hands of two senior alumni from the 1920s, Earle Ludgin (class of 1920) and John McDonough (class of 1928). Ludgin, a noted advertising expert in Chicago, assumed a vital role in designing letters sent to the alumni to reenlist their loyalty and support. Ludgin's alumni letters won a national award, the Time-Life Award from the American Alumni Council in 1956, which avowed that the "erudite humor and effectiveness of the copy is spectacular in its quality."[66] The letters completely ignored Robert Hutchins and his educational reforms and said nothing about the curricular controversies between the College and the divisions in the early and mid-1950s. Rather, they invoked the glories of an idealized student past. A new women's dorm, for example, would be in line with the traditions of Kelly, Beecher, and Green, which had been "charming and romantic in our day," with an additional note that "the girls on campus are remarkably pretty these days, even to these bifocal eyes—well up to the standard of Kelly, Beecher, Foster, Green."[67] These materials were an amalgam of friendly boosterism and candid financial appeals. Much emphasis was placed on improving the quality of student life, on enhancing faculty research, and on defending the general prestige of the University.

There was, thus, a clear effort to develop themes that pre-1930 alumni could understand and accept. The main campaign brochure, *The Responsibility of Greatness*, represented a sophisticated attempt to run against the record of the Hutchins administration by rejecting the unpopular facets of Hutchins's rule without publicly repudiating him. Nowhere in this booklet was Hutchins mentioned, to the extent that William Rainey Harper was given credit for formulating the program of the College. In essence, the campaign sought to reach out to and co-opt alumni who had graduated before 1930, who occupationally and professionally would have fully established their careers by the early 1950s, who were now in a position to give substantial gifts, and whose connection to the University was once positive and could now be reengaged. It was also quite likely that many of these older alumni had fond memories of Ernest D. Burton, thus linking Kimpton's revisionist efforts to the era of good feelings among the University alumni that Burton had worked so hard to achieve in the 1920s.

Watkins's restorative theme was tricky, however, since trying to hide Hutchins was like trying to squirrel away an elephant. Intergenerational tensions rose to the surface, as in the comments of alumni who wrote responses to the fund-raising letters they received. Of the forty comments about Kimpton's administration that came in, twenty-two were favorable to Kimpton and "the way things are going now," while eighteen were mildly or strongly hostile to the administration. Most interesting about these responses is that the median class year of the positive responses was

1908, whereas the median year of the opponents was 1946. What Kimpton and Watkins had clearly tried to do was to placate and reconnect with pre-Hutchins-era alumni while not further alienating the more recent graduates. They did the first brilliantly but managed to disaffect many alumni of the Hutchins era.[68] Responding to the first nexus of alumni unhappiness— among alumni who graduated before 1930—Kimpton and his colleagues inadvertently created a second nexus of alumni discontent among graduates from the later 1940s and early 1950s, many of whom resented Kimpton's trashing of the Hutchins College.

The work of the trustees and the alumni constituted bright spots for the campaign. The trustees achieved a 100 percent participation rate and raised $4.5 million, close to their original goal of $5 million. Leading the gifts from the trustees was a joint gift of Bell, Swift, and Ryerson for $1.25 million. The alumni campaign was also vibrant and creative, and generated a respectable $2.6 million. Special gifts from nonalumni remained a challenge, however. To better understand how the civic elites viewed the University, Kimpton authorized the National Opinion Research Center to conduct a survey in August 1954 on the views of almost five hundred Chicagoans about the University.[69] The survey found that opinions about the University of Chicago were in considerable flux, more so than those about Northwestern University. Of the members of the University's citizens board, as many had a favorable impression of the University of Chicago as of Northwestern, but among other prominent leaders in the city, Northwestern had the clear advantage. The study also found that Kimpton had substantially improved attitudes about the University: nearly two-thirds of the citizens board and half of the women civic leaders and other prominent persons reported that their opinion of the University of Chicago had changed for the better over the past two or three years, in large part because of Kimpton's work. But some of the findings were troubling. A majority of citizens board members agreed with the proposition that "the University of Chicago undergraduate college has too high a proportion of very bright but socially-not-well-adjusted students."[70]

When preliminary major-gift solicitations of civic leaders in Chicago began in early 1955, Duncan reported that the civic atmosphere still remained frosty. "While there are favorable comments about the Chancellor, his administrative associates, and individual members of the Board of Trustees," Duncan reported, "we hear too often dissatisfaction with the University and especially criticism of the type of student and recent graduate.... The University is attempting to raise money in an amazingly complex situation and in the face of extraordinary handicaps."[71]

Struggling with the civic elites of Chicago, Kimpton tried to take up where Hutchins had failed and reengage New York City. In March 1955, during a five-hour meeting with Rockefeller staff in New York City, Kimpton asked Rockefeller to give Chicago a large cash gift of $8 million, including $3 million to be used as a matching fund to raise other money. Kimpton's promises to restore the nearly $4 million in Rockefeller endowments that Hutchins had used in the late 1940s to cover deficits without consulting the family did little to incite enthusiasm on Rockefeller's part.[72] Two months later Rockefeller poured cold water on any hope, telling Kimpton, "The hope your presentation expresses that I will become a major contributor to the institution is one to which I regret I cannot wisely accede. While my father was for many years a major benefactor of the institution, I never have assumed any personal responsibility for it or relation to it other than my interest in the Oriental Institute, nor have I contemplated entering into any such relationship."[73]

On the foundation front, Kimpton moved to reengage the big three New York–based foundations, meeting with the heads of the Rockefeller, Carnegie, and Ford Foundations for dinner in May 1955 to present the University's case. A cordial time was had by all; and while the bids to Rockefeller and Carnegie were unsuccessful, in December 1955, the University learned that it would receive a $5 million gift for faculty salaries from the Ford Foundation.[74] Ford's support would become a new lifeline for the University over the next fifteen years. In a decade of declining enrollments and severe losses in senior faculty, it was understandable that university leaders looked to Ford as one of the most congenial solutions to current funding needs. Yet while grateful for the gift, Kimpton was disillusioned by the penchant of many foundations to restrict their giving to focused projects and to refuse general support for the core activities of the research universities. He voiced his concern in a speech before trustees and faculty the month after the gift was announced:

> As gifts in more recent years have come to the universities in increasingly restricted form, the administration of a university has become more difficult.... We have recently launched a campaign to raise many millions of dollars. If we fail, it will seriously injure the University for years to come. And ... if we succeed, it may also injure the University for many years to come, since we can be killed by restricted kindness. Our objective is to keep the University free, and unless we take careful heed, we may enslave it, for we can be degraded and disfigured by the money we seek and spend and we can lose our souls at the peak of our prosperity.[75]

By its conclusion in June 1958, the campaign had raised only $22 million of the $32.8 million required for the original campaign objectives, and 36 percent of the total raised came as grants from the Ford Foundation, including large grants for faculty salary support ($5 million) and for the Graduate School of Business ($1.375 million).[76] While the alumni and trustees segments fared quite well, as was the case in the campaign of 1924–25, the major-gifts initiative among nonalumni donors was disappointing. The University's continued dependence on large foundation support, as opposed to major gifts from individuals, was striking.

The proceeds of the campaign and the severe budget cutting of 1951 to 1955 enabled Kimpton to begin to increase allocations to the various academic units in 1955–56, and a modest recovery was evident in faculty salaries and hiring in the later 1950s. But such progress came at the cost of nearly full-time fund-raising and grant solicitation, which Kimpton found ever more frustrating. Kimpton was particularly discouraged by the fact that the campaign was $13 million short in its last year. Moreover, as early as 1956, the board realized that the needs of the University far surpassed the initial campaign goals of 1954–55. Neighborhood investments to stabilize the areas in Hyde Park adjacent to the University would be extremely costly, and much of the discussion at a second summit meeting of officers and trustees in February 1956 focused on the need to take more money from the endowment to invest in the neighborhood.

The campaign's partial successes proved frustrating for some cherished projects. At another meeting of officers and trustees in March 1957, a vigorous debate broke out over whether to start the Law School's new building on the south side of the Midway, based on incomplete fund-raising (only $2.5 million had been raised or pledged, out of a needed $3.6 million), or whether to delay it in favor of completing already launched central projects and providing for additional budget underwriting. Kimpton insisted that the needs of the neighborhood programs, student housing, the Laboratory Schools, and the regular budget ranked ahead of the Law School project, and he opposed starting construction. At a subsequent budget committee meeting Kimpton was overruled, and the board supported the idea of a new "revolving fund" to finance the building, a plan proposed by Glen Lloyd, a trustee leader who was an alumnus of the Law School and close confidant of its dean, Edward H. Levi. Kimpton warned that "such a policy is a good one if we can raise new money, but a dangerous one if we cannot."[77]

THE CRISIS IN THE NEIGHBORHOOD

Much of the huge literature on the history of US higher education after World War II is dominated by discussions of the growing role of the federal government in the financing of research and educational programs.[78] Of course, federal research support (contract and basic) was vitally important for the research programs of the Divisions of the Physical Sciences and Biological Sciences in the 1950s. But most units of the University did not share in this upsurge in government funding, and the regular academic budget covering faculty and staff salaries and student financial aid remained heavily dependent on tuition and fees, fund-raising and bequests, endowment income, and income from auxiliary services.[79] For the leaders of the University perhaps the most important action taken by Congress between 1945 and 1960 was to approve the Housing Acts of 1949, 1954, and 1959, which authorized massive federal investments in urban renewal programs.[80]

The grimness of the local environment in which the University found itself in the 1950s led university leaders to focus on the institution's unsteady relationship with its own city and its own neighborhood. Long before Lawrence Kimpton assumed the leadership of the University, it was clear that profound social changes taking place in Hyde Park, Woodlawn, and Kenwood might seriously affect the future stability of the University.[81] As early as June 1948, the New Deal planner and sometime chair of the New York City Planning Commission from 1938 to 1941, Rexford G. Tugwell, complained to Ernest Colwell that "there are disquieting signs that the neighborhood of the University might become the center of serious social conflict." Tugwell urged that the University embark on an ambitious and comprehensive urban planning process that would involve protective zoning, redevelopment of new housing, and maintenance-development contracts.[82] Muriel Beadle would later describe the state of Fifty-Fifth Street around 1950 as follows: "Economically, there had occurred a downward shift in income and buying habits. In one two-block stretch on 55th Street there were twenty-three taverns; the gutters were full of half-pint whiskey bottles; and crime was on the increase."[83]

Robert Hutchins was deeply conflicted about what the University could or should do, however. Confronted with the University's support for racial covenants, Hutchins was perplexed morally but agreed to go along with then customary practices. Writing to his father in September 1937, Hutchins argued:

> There is little doubt that if the University does not get behind these agreements, it will become in time an island in the midst of the black race, with the Negroes living all the way down the Midway as far as the Lake. On the other hand, as the descendant of a long line of Oberlinites, I am temperamentally opposed to these agreements and opposed to having the University take any part in upholding them. I finally come to the conclusion, however, that since they are upheld by the courts of this State and since the University would probably have to go out of business

if it were surrounded by Negroes, there is nothing to do but say openly that we propose to use all honorable means to protect ourselves from inundation.[84]

He later admitted to Julian Levi, "You know, this neighborhood thing, as far as I was concerned was just a disaster.... I was schizophrenic about it."[85] Few systematic efforts were undertaken during the last years of the Hutchins administration to confront these issues, and they ended up on Kimpton's desk when he assumed office in the summer of 1951.[86]

A more general problem was the seeming standoffishness of the University in its relations with the city of Chicago. Essentially, from 1890 to 1940, neither the "neighborhood" nor the "city" had been an object of serious concern for the University or its leaders. Myriad faculty lived in and paid taxes in the city, key faculty in the Division of the Social Sciences and the School of Social Service Administration had major research programs involving the city, and the majority of the undergraduate students were born and raised in the city. Why fix something that was not broken? Over the course of the 1930s and 1940s two negative trends converged to make the benign posture of the University toward the city no longer feasible. First, patterns of neighborhood deterioration became acutely visible. Second, the civic and political elites of the city knew little about the University. "Several old-style Chicago tycoons had ambivalent feelings toward the University in older days," recalled journalist and Chicago alumnus John Gunther. "They respected it—perhaps stood in a certain awe of it—but they did not really like it. They thought that it was off-beat, radically inclined, even pinko, although its Economics Department is one of the most conservative in the country.... Chicago has traditionally been 'run' by State Street and the Irish (and other immigrant-descended) ward heelers, and to most of these the University was a puzzle."[87] At the same time, the University was often its own worst enemy. When Robert Hutchins spoke out in 1941 on the issue in a speech entitled "The University and the City," he argued that the "spirit of Chicago" had helped sustain the University's independence and courage and provided a congenial home for the new enterprise beginning in the 1890s. But beyond these simple assumptions Hutchins's real message seemed to be, Admire us, but only for our intellectual and academic prowess.[88]

The problem with such formulations was that when the University found itself in the dire social conditions that obtained in the early 1950s, it was not evident to many Chicagoans and their political leaders why saving the University of Chicago was important to the city. Lawrence Kimpton was brutally frank about this conundrum when he complained in June 1952, "There is, I am convinced, a great deal of misapprehension in our community about what the University is doing, about the importance of the University, about what it has and what it can contribute. A good deal of this has been our fault, if for no other reason than our lack of contact with much of the main stream of civic life. We must be prepared to take a more active, constructive role in Chicago affairs than before." Inheriting not only a complex local policy crisis, but also wider communications problems with the political power brokers and media elites of the city, Kimpton adopted a bravely optimistic pose: "Both the city and the University have problems, some of them in common. By establishing better relations between the community and the University, it may become easier to surround these problems and annihilate them."[89] These were fine words, but it would take years for Kimpton to fashion a reality behind them.

Beginning in the early 1940s, signs of deterioration in the neighborhood around the University were evident. As a result of the Depression and the war, many buildings had not been maintained for fifteen years, and there had been little new investment in the area. In 1945, 53 percent of the buildings in Hyde Park and 82 percent of the buildings in Woodlawn were more than forty years old.[90] During the war a heavy migration of blacks from the South to Chicago resulted in severe population pressures on the South Side. These conditions, in turn, led to predatory real estate practices: slumlords illegally converting six flats into twenty-four-unit rooming houses charging exorbitant rental rates, and not maintaining buildings to code. And, perhaps most troublesome, was the appearance of racial violence between whites and blacks on the neighborhood's borders.

The situation changed even more radically after the Supreme Court's decision in *Shelley v. Kraemer* in May 1948 that racially based restrictive covenants were unenforceable, which soon resulted in powerful pressures on the traditional "lines" separating black and white in Woodlawn and Kenwood and the movement of poorer black families into the northern and western peripheries of Hyde Park. Between 1950 and 1956, 20,000 whites moved out of Hyde Park and Kenwood, and 23,000 nonwhites moved in. In 1940, the nonwhite population of these two neighborhoods was 4 percent; by 1956, it was 36 percent.[91] George Wilgram of the Medical School, who left the University for Tufts and Harvard in 1960, later recalled his experience living in Hyde Park in the 1950s: "I have never seen anything like this in my whole life, and was completely thrown out of balance by this encounter with poverty, crime, and desolation."[92] The anthropologist Sol Tax recalled in 1958:

> In 1952—a short 6 or 7 years ago—our neighborhood in Chicago was in a state of panic.... There was a rash of new crimes, burglaries and purse-

snatchings, and occasional rapes. People could not safely walk the streets in the evening, except in groups. Middle class white families who had lived for years in Hyde Park and Kenwood were moving away, seeking safety. So were middle class Negro families who had moved in only months earlier because they wanted decent housing outside of a Negro ghetto. All were being engulfed by a tidal wave of population from the segregated, long contained black belt at the borders of our neighborhood.[93]

The first of many turning points occurred on March 17, 1952, when an armed man invaded the apartment of a twenty-eight-year-old psychology graduate student in central Hyde Park, holding her hostage for five hours and attempting to rape her.[94] A huge protest meeting was called in Mandel Hall on March 27, 1952, to mobilize the community, where angry citizens condemned the failure of the police to patrol Hyde Park adequately.[95] One immediate outcome of the meeting was a decision to create the South East Chicago Commission, a powerful new community organization. In June 1952 the SECC was established with a budget of $30,000, with the University putting up an initial $15,000 on the assumption that the community would contribute the balance of the required funds. The initial goal of the commission was to force the city to provide more forceful police protection, and early pronouncements from Kimpton and the other organizers were extremely aggressive about the failings of the police, accusing the police department of archaic management and poor training practices, and of tolerating a culture of corruption.[96] But it soon became apparent to Kimpton that the policing question was merely one part of a highly complex set of interventions that needed to be undertaken, and that more fundamental steps were urgently needed involving land use, community planning, and housing occupancy.

Lawrence Kimpton had no training in or knowledge of urban planning or urban affairs, and for the first year or so he and his colleagues seemed to have constructed ad hoc responses, driven largely by desperation. Knowing his own limitations, Kimpton reached out to Julian H. Levi in the fall of 1952, asking him to take the executive directorship of the SECC. The older brother of Edward H. Levi, Julian Levi was a graduate of the College and the Law School who worked as a successful private attorney in Chicago during the 1930s and 1940s, and then as the president of a local printing company. Admired by his friends and passionately feared by his enemies, Levi was a tough-minded, virtuoso political character, with superb negotiating skills and a reputation for both fearlessness and ruthlessness that was worthy of the best Chicago ward-politics traditions.[97] Over the course of the 1950s Julian Levi made himself into a policy expert on urban renewal, proving particularly adept at marshaling federal and municipal resources, brokering deals with the civic and political elites of Chicago, and organizing University-based staff expertise. In many respects Levi was crucial to brokering and deploying to the South Side of Chicago at least three of what Christopher Klemek has recently called the "four pillars" of postwar urban renewal in big US cities: professionalized urbanist expertise, local municipal political power, and federal (and state) financial support.[98] Levi sensed the urgency of the crisis and agreed to Kimpton's plea.

Levi and Kimpton first tried to tackle the crime issue by forcing the city to commit to a more extensive police presence. Levi later recalled that the then mayor, Martin Kennelly, did not take the University's plans seriously at first, so Levi persuaded the state legislature in 1953 to revise the Neighborhood Redevelopment Corporation Act of 1947 to give the University the right of eminent domain (if a redevelopment corporation secured the approval of 60 percent of the owners of property in a specific area, the corporation could take independent legal action to remove blighted properties).[99]

Decisive change came in April 1955 when Richard J. Daley succeeded Kennelly as mayor. Combining the offices of chair of the Cook County Democratic machine with the powers of the mayor's office, Daley seized control of the heretofore splintered municipal planning, budgeting, and development functions and signaled that he was seriously committed to the redevelopment of blighted areas. Before the election Kimpton had visited with Daley, pleading the University's case. Daley was a creature of Chicago neighborhoods, and he had an instinctive grasp of the fact that a stable and prosperous community in Hyde Park would ensure the economic viability of the University as a major South Side employer. Daley proved to be a responsive partner for Levi and Kimpton, especially after 1957, and the cooperation of city agencies increased substantially with the highly professional planning staff that the University had assembled.[100]

The history of Hyde Park renewal has been controversial, but for understanding the history of the College and the wider University, the general trends—and the complexity of the initiatives—are more important than the details. Julian Levi's initial plan sought to stabilize and rehabilitate the area between Fifty-Fifth and Sixty-First Streets, from Cottage Grove to Stony Island Avenues, and to do so on the basis of economic prosperity and school stability, while seeking to avoid being cast in a racially exclusivist portrait. This meant that Kimpton and Levi consciously decided not to try to redevelop or otherwise intervene in Woodlawn or in most of Kenwood, and that the areas of Hyde Park between Fifty-First and Fifty-Fifth Streets would be less of a priority, at least initially. In August 1953, Julian Levi reported to the board of trustees:

I make four assumptions.... I'm going to assume first of all that we've got to dominate an area between 55th and 61st, Cottage to Stony. I don't think it's big enough, but I can tell you that anything smaller than that is impossible. Second of all, I'm going to assume that we're not going to get any help from anybody.... Third, I will assume that the only way that we can insist on the kind of stabilization policy we see here is to own the properties. And finally, we assume they're all going to come on the market.... There's no reason under any circumstance that the University ought to be doing any of this unless its academic mission is involved. We're not a public improvement association.[101]

Perhaps most significant about this statement was its unequivocal assertion of the primacy of the University's self-interest, which would guide Levi in the hyperaggressive tactics that he adopted in the coming years in Hyde Park and Woodlawn. Levi was convinced that muscular, centrally controlled planning and executive policy implementation were needed, and that if the University provided this leadership, it was completely justified in framing the general social interest of the Hyde Park community through the (wide) lens of the University's own needs. Over the next seven years, university leaders and the SECC proposed several waves of renewal interventions, beginning with the Hyde Park A and B project launched in April 1954, which cleared and redeveloped about 48 acres along Fifty-Fifth Street and Lake Park Boulevard, and included plans for a suburban-style shopping center, apartment towers, and townhomes along Fifty-Fourth and Fifty-Fifth Streets.[102] This program was financed with approximately $6.5 million of federal funds, and $3.6 million in city and state funds. The A and B plan was followed in 1956 by a University initiative to redevelop 14 acres in southwest Hyde Park, from Fifty-Fifth to Fifty-Sixth Streets between Ellis and Cottage Grove Avenues, under the aegis of the South West Hyde Park Neighborhood Redevelopment Corporation. A third, and much larger, intervention began in January 1956 when the city of Chicago contracted with the University to develop what came to be called the Hyde Park–Kenwood Urban Renewal Plan, which included 855 acres in 1.3 square miles bounded by Forty-Seventh Street on the north, Cottage Grove Avenue on the west, Lake Park Boulevard on the east, and Fifty-Ninth Street on the south.

The so-called Final Plan called for the clearance of 101 acres, with 630 buildings (out of a total of 3,077) to be demolished, at a total cost of $37.8 million in government and local funds.[103] The plan wound its way through various administrative reviews, and enjoyed extensive community consultation.[104] The plan was approved by the Conservation Community Council in April 1958 and by the Community Conservation Board in July 1958, and it was forwarded to the Committee on Urban Planning of the city council. As Julian Levi later summarized, the main objectives of the 1958 plan were to be "nondiscriminatory," to assure "a community which would generate a sufficiently large pre-collegiate student body that would enable the public schools to do a first-rate job of collegiate preparation," and to win the support of the city council and the mayor.[105]

In the weeks before the final vote in the council, a Catholic priest, Monsignor John Egan, tried to mobilize support against the University, arguing that masses of poor people were being displaced without proper protections. Eventually, Mayor Richard Daley intervened, and the city council unanimously adopted the plan on November 7, 1958. Yet University officials were anxious about the outcome, all the more so given that Egan, as the price for cooperation, had tried to maneuver Levi into conceding more public housing in Hyde Park to protect Catholic parishes elsewhere on the South Side from being "inundated" by black residents forced to relocate out of Hyde Park.[106]

The University's final intervention came in July 1960 in a presentation to the Chicago Land Clearance Commission involving an area in Woodlawn immediately south of the Midway. The University already owned about 60 percent of the land between Sixtieth and Sixty-First Streets, from Cottage Grove to Stony Island, and it now wanted to acquire the remaining 27 acres, most of which were filled with deteriorated buildings, for future campus expansion. This proposal generated intense opposition on the part of the newly created Woodlawn Organization, which eventually (July 1963) secured the University's and the city's commitment to support the creation of five hundred units of low-cost and subsidized housing on Cottage Grove Avenue between Sixtieth and Sixty-Third Streets as the price of approving the University's land acquisition plans between Sixtieth and Sixty-First Streets.[107]

In total approximately 925 acres of land were part of the planning process, with 14 percent of the total subjected to land clearance and with the expenditure (as of 1959) of a total of $135 million in federal, state, local, and private funds. The University's own expenditures between July 1, 1954, and June 30, 1961, involved $6.8 million to acquire neighborhood properties that were deemed to be deteriorating or substandard and to finance various campus expansion projects and an additional $3.2 million to purchase and renovate twenty-four neighborhood apartment buildings to house graduate and married students.[108] These interventions caused more than 640 small businesses to lose their premises, and only a small number of these were able to survive.

The deepest public controversies in the execution of these plans developed over the forced housing relocations, which were made necessary by the demolition of blighted properties. Under the massive 1958 renewal plan, buildings containing 4,371 families were demolished, clearing approximately 15 percent of the buildings in the plan area, in an effort to lessen the density of the neighborhood by razing substandard properties. Of these families, 1,837 were white, and 2,534 were black, making the non-white relocatees about 58 percent of the total.[109] The majority of those who were forced to move were lower-income families, and of those who did not return to Hyde Park, the percentage of blacks was substantially greater than whites. Over time those who criticized the plan targeted this statistic, accusing the University of racial discrimination in the form of "Negro clearance."[110] Kimpton for his part genuinely believed that the plan was not racist but was driven by fundamental economic and social constraints and the desire to create an interracial neighborhood with high-quality housing and good schools, a quieter, less dense, and more amenity-filled neighborhood where university faculty members would want to live and raise their families and where parents would be willing to send their children as students to local schools. Early on in the renewal planning, in December 1952, he insisted that "the problem of community deterioration is not a racial problem. The enforcement of zoning, housing, and building codes, the prevention of overcrowding, the insistence upon proper standards of maintenance have nothing to do with the race, creed or color of either the owner or the occupant of any building. A blunt insistence on effective law enforcement and effective action to prevent the deterioration and misuse of property is neither anti-white nor anti-Negro. It is simply pro-government."[111]

Subsequent critics of Lawrence Kimpton's role in urban renewal, particularly Arnold Hirsch, have accused him of public dissimulations and outright racism, judgments that seem to be unduly harsh and distorting of Kimpton's personal values and strategic intentions.[112] Other critics have suggested that the University under Kimpton's leadership overreached, acting in a precipitous and almost dictatorial fashion where more citizen participation and more civic consultation with local community groups would have been prudent. Given the extensive neighborhood deterioration and crime levels that were already apparent by the early 1950s, and what Peter Rossi and Robert Dentler have characterized as the "primitive state of governmental machinery in the city before 1956," it is hard to imagine that a cluster of more modest initiatives—less decisive, less transformational, and less interventionist—would have achieved the rapid and enduring structural changes that were needed to protect the livability of the Hyde Park neighborhood for large numbers of faculty families and students, initiating a level of sustained progress that was already apparent to longtime residents of Hyde Park by the 1970s and early 1980s.[113] Kimpton and Levi believed that if the University failed to take rapid and decisive action, the Hyde Park neighborhood would have lost a significant percentage of faculty families and students as permanent residents.[114]

As for the first objection, Kimpton's goals were both straightforward and transparent: he wanted a stable, prosperous, and substantially middle-class neighborhood because he was convinced that future faculty and students considering the University would expect such conditions in order to agree to become permanent residents of Hyde Park in the decades to come. Kimpton was less concerned that veteran faculty who had made Hyde Park their home for long tenures since the 1920s and 1930s would suddenly leave in the 1950s than that he and his presidential successors would be unable to persuade new faculty, coming to Chicago from more stable and safer residential environs elsewhere in the nation, to live in Hyde Park.[115] This may explain the fascination of University planners with suburban-like amenities (shopping centers) and green spaces, which were characteristic of 1950s urban planning. At the same time, in contrast to the experiences of Harvard and Stanford in thinking about the economic potential of their urban communities in the 1950s and 1960s, it is striking that Chicago leaders were focused on improving housing and ensuring personal security in Hyde Park, as opposed to articulating more imaginative ideas about long-range economic innovation.[116] Levi and his colleagues believed that Hyde Park should remain an exclusively residential community appended to (what they hoped would continue to be) a vibrant central business district in the Loop.[117] It is instructive to remember that in the middle of the controversy over the University's Final Plan in the summer of 1958, Richard J. Daley issued the city of Chicago's own *Development Plan for the Central Area of Chicago*, which called for massive improvements in a ten-square-mile area surrounding the Loop.[118]

The plans eventually resulted in what Rebecca Janowitz has fairly characterized as a "racially balanced community," but also a community based on substantial wealth, affluence, and even privilege.[119] In recent decades the success of the Hyde Park renewal project has been domesticated, with the current status quo (especially since Barack Obama's election to the presidency in 2008) almost taken for granted as an inevitable outcome of the struggles of the 1950s and 1960s. It is striking how, in his excellent book on urban studies and Chicago, Robert Sampson describes the current situation of Hyde Park from a kind of "new normal" perspective: "Hyde Park has been stable after its brush with rapid change in the mid-twentieth century and maintains its integrated housing with a mix of organizational and structural advantages. The most obvious is the university, but the community boasts a robust civic life, a diversity of nonprofit organizations, an educated elite, and connections to power."[120]

Kimpton's hopes for a neighborhood that would be both interracial and multiracial did eventually come to pass. But Kimpton also believed that both racial and economic balance were crucial, and he knew it was a fateful but brutal fact that many whites, including many white University of Chicago faculty, would refuse to live in a neighborhood in which poor, impoverished African Americans constituted the overwhelming majority of the residents.[121] That the University engaged in social engineering on a vast and unprecedented scale involving the lives of thousands of lower-income residents is undeniable, and the social turmoil manifested in these years was bound to elicit strident criticism of the University's policies and motives that would cast a long shadow into the decades ahead. In the end, Muriel Beadle's sober appraisal from 1964 about the tensions between various advocates for renewal of Hyde Park is instructive: "The greatest compromise of all, and the bitterest pill that the community had to swallow, was to accept the fact that the stated objectives of conservation and renewal could not be obtained unless (1) the community accepted integration; (2) treated integration as a class problem; and (3) discriminated against lower-income families and individuals. It took a long time and a colossal amount of talk before the community came to this conclusion."[122]

Given the massive scale and the precipitous timing of the University's interventions, and the conflicting opinions among Hyde Parkers themselves about the legitimacy of Kimpton's and Levi's urban renewal initiatives, it was unrealistic to expect that the wounds that had been opened in Hyde Park and Woodlawn could be healed quickly. In analyzing similar case studies, Margaret O'Mara has argued that beginning in the 1970s, urban universities across America "sought to mend the rift between town and gown that resulted from campus expansions and urban redevelopment of the 1950s and 1960s."[123] This would eventually prove true for the University of Chicago, beginning in the mid- and late 1990s, as we will discover in chapter 6.

Lawrence Kimpton provided heroic service to the University. He helped to transform and save the neighborhood of Hyde Park as a congenial place for university faculty (and many other citizens) to live and to raise their families; he enhanced faculty salaries (the median for full professors rose from $10,416 in 1951–52 to $13,257 in 1959–60) and slowed the exodus of faculty that began in the early 1950s; he negotiated a workable, if controversial, truce between the College and the divisions over the undergraduate curriculum; he presided over a generally successful fund-raising campaign; and he helped the University set out on the long, rocky road back to a reasonably sized undergraduate College.[124] In his eulogy to Kimpton in Rockefeller Chapel in January 1978, George Watkins insisted that his friend had "saved" the University of Chicago, and there is truth to that statement.

Kimpton was not simply a clever "fix-it man" struggling with awkward troubles. He was an eloquent spokesperson about the central academic mission of the University even while imposing austerities and dealing with a string of real-world problems. Kimpton's drastic attempts to solve the problem of undergraduate education at Chicago by rebuilding and expanding the College reflected urgent financial necessities. But because he failed to persuade the faculty to construct a coherent and workable educational *alternative* to Hutchins's experiment—other than ceding chunks of the curriculum to the graduate departments—Kimpton left office with little success to show. Nor was Kimpton able to make any significant progress on Ernest Burton's schemes for a more integrated culture of student life based on a substantially residential college campus. Kimpton had the courage to identify enormous problems facing the University, but his formulas for educational change were too reactive and too modest, being hamstrung by the University's need to spend massive funds on neighborhood investments. Kimpton left office having "killed off" the Hutchins College curriculum and faculty, but without putting in place an attractive substitute that could meet any of his cherished goals.

The Levi Years: "This Must Be One University"

KIMPTON'S RESIGNATION AND THE SEARCH FOR A NEW VISIONARY

Kimpton had devoted almost ten years to responding to the enormous problems facing the University. He felt completely exhausted, and in early 1960 he confided to George Watkins that he planned to leave the University. Kimpton refused genuine and heartfelt pleas from key trustees to reconsider his decision, even though Watkins warned him that if he left office in 1960 he would go down in history merely as "the guy who saved the neighborhood."[125] In March 1960 Kimpton announced that he would resign as chancellor.

The search for Kimpton's successor commenced in the spring of 1960, but proved more difficult than expected. The two top candidates—McGeorge Bundy of Harvard and Clark Kerr of Berkeley—both considered the prospect but eventually rejected it. The chairman of the board of trustees, Glen Lloyd, personally contacted Bundy, the dean of the faculty of arts and sciences at Harvard, to ascertain his possible candidacy. Lloyd was taken with Bundy, and upon Bundy's initial negative reaction he asked David Rockefeller to intervene to persuade Bundy to change his mind. Bundy did not do so, but instead wrote a detailed and highly insightful five-page critique of Chicago's predicament that is still worth reading today. Bundy argued that the University, once great, had "slipped academically in the last ten years," although he did not blame Kimpton for the slippage: "Great things happened under Hutchins, but they were done at the price of a radical disregard for the claims of the future.... The severe academic losses which Chicago has suffered in the last ten years are surely to be charged to Hutchins, not Kimpton." Although Bundy found much that was attractive about Chicago's traditions, he feared that no permanent recovery could take place without a massive recapitalization of the University: "Unless there is a really radical reinforcement of the unrestricted financial resources of the University, above and beyond the efforts that the ordinary devoted President and conscientious Board of Trustees are always making for their institutions, I see no prospect that this University can, as a whole, play for the next generation the extraordinarily important innovating role it has played in the past." Bundy's prescription was stunning: the University needed an immediate cash infusion of at least $200 million. This infusion was merely the beginning of a longer-term process of financial rebuilding, the goal of which was to put the University in a state where "with luck this time the place could be put beyond the need for another such transfusion." Bundy concluded by posing a paradox: "The Trustees are looking for academic leadership, and they are saying to themselves that this is the one thing they need.... But the Trustees of our present-day universities have come to put so much weight on the happy choice of a man that they do not look as sharply as they should at the economics of greatness." Putting the matter even more baldly, Bundy observed, "In a way it is queer that I should spend so much time on money, which is nothing, to a university, in itself. There are rich and lousy places, as there are poor and good ones. But I am persuaded, on all the evidence, that there are no poor and *great* ones, no matter who is president."[126]

Although he was taken aback by its candor, Lloyd was impressed with Bundy's missive, and later in the decade he remarked to Bundy, "Back in the 1960s you were the most helpful single person in one of my assignments. You wrote an extraordinary letter which I believe to be as pertinent today as it was then."[127] With Bundy and Kerr out of the running, the committee came up with a less-than-compelling short list, at the top of which was George Beadle, a professor of biology at the California Institute of Technology who had won the Nobel Prize in 1958 and who had served as the chair of the Division of Biology at Caltech since 1946.[128] Given the need to conclude their deliberations, the committee chose Beadle. The trustees wanted (or were persuaded by senior faculty that they wanted) a distinguished academic leader. As a prize-winning scientist with an international scholarly reputation, Beadle was chosen because he seemed to be everything that Kimpton was not. It seemed that after nine years of painful restructuring and belt tightening, many senior faculty looked to the other end of the spectrum for an inspired intellectual leader.

During the course of the presidential search, the structure of central governance emerged (or perhaps reemerged) as an issue, and Glen Lloyd and other key trustees toyed with the idea of creating a dual presidency or some other dualistic power-sharing arrangement. This issue had arisen even during Kimpton's term, and in April 1960 he broached one version of such a plan with a University Senate committee—namely, that the chancellor become a full-time salaried officer and deal with external relations and fund-raising for the University, and the president run the academic affairs of the University.[129] In the end, the board decided not to move in this direction, but the idea reflected a keen sense on the part of key board members that Kimpton had exhausted himself in trying to manage the ever more complex external relations of the institution, and that more systematic central leadership needed to be brought to the internal academic and financial affairs of the University. Another option was put forward by John J. Corson, a consultant from McKinsey & Company whom Glen Lloyd brought in during the summer of 1960 to "look over our general organizational set-up" and to advise on the presidential search. Corson strongly recommended to Lloyd that the board impose a new dual management structure by creating a provostship.[130]

George Beadle was appointed without any definite resolution of this issue, but it is clear that the idea of some kind of dual governance team was already in the minds of the trustees. Kimpton himself had thought about creating a semi-independent second officer, but given the hostility of the faculty to the Hutchins-Colwell experiment, he had decided against it. Instead, he relied on R. Wendell "Pat" Harrison as a vice president to handle day-to-day academic affairs and budgetary planning. Harrison had served faithfully and dutifully, but Kimpton later recalled that on crucial academic matters the faculty still insisted on dealing with Kimpton personally. Moreover, by 1960 Harrison himself was in poor health and was only capable of day-to-day stewardship.

The transition from Kimpton to Beadle was not an easy one. Beadle took office in May 1961. He had little relevant senior administrative experience to fall back on in taking charge of a complex campus culture that was, then as now, challenging even for locals to navigate. Given Harrison's ill health, Beadle relied on Lowell Coggeshall to assist him. Coggeshall, the dean of the Division of Biological Sciences from 1947 to 1960 who had been the runner-up in the presidential search in 1951, was a careful, methodical administrator who had established a reputation as an effective fund-raiser by negotiating a huge gift of $17.6 million from the Louis Block estate in late 1955.[131] To help shore up the day-to-day administrative functions, Beadle also recruited John T. Wilson of the National Science Foundation in July 1961 on the assurance that he would eventually hold the rank equivalent to that of a vice president, but Wilson, like Beadle, was an outsider to the faculty culture at Chicago.[132] By the fall of 1961, senior staff meetings were increasingly disjointed, and major agenda items were being dealt with in very ad hoc modes. Coggeshall and Wilson tried to bring some system to the process, but a sense of drift was apparent, and no one seemed able to generate a comprehensive strategy for rebuilding the academic prestige of the University.

George Beadle was an engaging and courageous person and a friendly colleague, but he was also a somewhat indecisive administrator. Someone was needed to take charge of the running of the academic side of the University, and it soon became apparent to key trustees that this person was not Beadle. The trustees were particularly concerned that Beadle could not develop a coherent plan for spending the $3.5 million presidential fund that they had assembled (a goodly sum in 1961 dollars) or for a more general fund-raising drive that Lloyd and others wanted to launch in 1962. The situation was further complicated by the fact that Beadle himself took a personal liking to Lowell Coggeshall, and soon proposed to Lloyd in August 1961 that Coggeshall be his new permanent second in command.[133] Lloyd was disinclined to accept this idea, sensing that Coggeshall represented more of the same gradualism, whereas the trustees wanted decisive leadership. By the early winter of 1962 disquiet on the board with Beadle's leadership style was growing.

EDWARD LEVI'S PATH TO THE CENTRAL ADMINISTRATION

In late 1961 or early 1962, Edward Levi's name emerged among influential trustees as a possible fix for their dilemma. The dean of the Law School since 1950, Levi had been a key member of the presidential search committee in 1960; he had voted for Beadle; and in early December, according to Muriel Beadle's recollections, he had lobbied Beadle to accept the job.[134] Even at the time Levi's own name had emerged as a possible presidential candidate, and, equally important, Levi in his role as dean had had a long-standing and close personal relationship with Glen Lloyd, who was an alumnus of the Law School and one of Levi's major alumni fund-raisers in the 1950s.[135]

Sometime during March, Levi was contacted by Lloyd, who informed him that the board was concerned about the drift in academic planning and lack of strong directional leadership in Beadle's team, and that they, together with Beadle, had decided that a new number-two position should be created and that he, Levi, should take it. As he later recalled, Levi told Lloyd that he did not want the job, but Lloyd was undeterred: "Ed ... you urged George to accept, and you helped to get us into this mess, and now you are going to help us get out of it."[136]

The former chairman of the board, Edward Ryerson, was asked to meet with Beadle and to convey the board's unhappiness with the lack of movement. During this meeting Ryerson urged Beadle to assume stronger and more thoughtful leadership, and stated the need to appoint a strong number two. But Ryerson was not altogether convinced that Beadle would act, and feared that "he may lack the decisiveness to get it done without a good deal of prodding and pressure from outside influences."[137] In the end Glen Lloyd himself applied the necessary pressure, meeting several times with Beadle alone and finally, in a joint meeting with Beadle and Coggeshall, engaging in what must have been an awkward conversation, in which Coggeshall was offered a place on the board of trustees as a kind of consolation prize.

Levi, meanwhile, received the job description that he wanted, which was far more than simply a senior vice president. The new position would differ from a conventional vice presidency in that the provostship would be an independent statutory authority, distinct from the president, and would be responsible for the academic administration of the University, for academic planning and faculty appointments, as well as for all budgetary matters involving academic affairs. The University's budget officer would henceforth report to the provost.[138] The decision to create this new executive authority proved to be of immense importance for the future of the University. Levi's joining the central administration gave the University a strong infusion of academic-managerial expertise that could build on the fierce defensive work accomplished by Lawrence Kimpton.

Edward Levi was a lifelong Hyde Parker and the son and grandson of Jewish rabbis. He fondly remembered his grandfather, Emil G. Hirsch, as a supporter of William Rainey Harper and as the man who had helped to broker Julius Rosenwald's huge financial support of the University.[139] Levi had received all of his formal education at the University of Chicago: he attended the Laboratory Schools for primary and secondary school, and he graduated from the College in 1932 and the Law School in 1935, where he was editor in chief of the *Law Review*. While he was in the College, Levi participated in a Great Books seminar taught by Robert Hutchins and Mortimer Adler, and he was captivated by their bracing intellectual style in class and beyond. Levi then spent a year on a Sterling Fellowship at Yale from 1935 to 1936. In May 1936, the dean of the Law School, Harry A.

Bigelow, recommended Levi to Hutchins as an assistant professor at Chicago, noting that Levi was said to be a "very good" scholar and teacher. Of Levi's personality, Bigelow commented that he was "vigorous but not unpleasant."[140]

After Levi returned to Chicago from Yale in September 1936, he reintroduced himself to Hutchins by sending him the introduction to "The Elements of Law," a set of teaching materials that he and Roscoe Steffen had prepared at Yale, and urging him in a cover letter to consider Friedrich Kessler of Yale for a faculty appointment at Chicago. The letter included a deferential notation: "I feel that the form of this communication may be a breach of etiquette, but this is a pretty important matter and I am willing to risk it."[141] Three years later, Levi made a bold proposal to Hutchins: "The proposition is that you and I write a book on the philosophy of law.... If this is an impertinent and otherwise bad suggestion, I suppose you will know what to do with it."[142] These casual notes suggest how deeply Levi admired Hutchins throughout the 1930s and 1940s, which is critical to understanding Levi's subsequent work as a university leader in the 1960s and 1970s.

Between 1940 and 1945 Levi served in the Justice Department, working with Thurman Arnold in the Antitrust Division and then as a special assistant to Attorney General Francis Biddle. He returned to Chicago in 1945, and in August 1950 Hutchins appointed Levi as dean of the Law School, where he served from 1950 to 1962. Levi's appointment was the source of considerable controversy, since several members of the board objected to the fact that Levi was a Jew. To his credit Hutchins dismissed such prejudice and offered Levi the job. Levi proved himself to be an effective and trusted dean and an imaginative fund-raiser. He was also a brilliant teacher and an incisive scholar. His little book, *An Introduction to Legal Reasoning*, remains a classic even today.

STRATEGIES FOR RENEWING THE UNIVERSITY

The University was in a fragile state in 1962. Edward Levi recognized that even with Kimpton's heroic efforts in the 1950s the University had suffered severe losses in faculty and student enrollment, and that a major intellectual and academic recapitalization effort had to be initiated immediately. Levi took action in three critical areas.

Investments in Faculty and Facilities

Levi's first priority was the rebuilding of the senior faculty. Over the course of the 1950s the University had lost a series of eminent scholars to other universities, and many departments were fighting a losing battle against pessimism and despair. Levi was particularly sensitive to the need for robust investments in faculty salaries and for aggressive faculty hiring policies. In April 1963 he argued to the board of trustees that "because of the a) many offers being made to our faculty personnel, b) the neighborhood problem, c) the fact that the University has slipped, and d) the University's other kinds of unique and unusual problems, it is necessary that the University pay higher salaries than any other academic institution in the country if it is to regain its previous position of leadership."[143] Perhaps the best symbol of Levi's audacious, if still untested, confidence was the new program of ten university professorships, first formulated in June 1962, which was designed to bring to Chicago internationally notable scholars at (for the time) outrageously high salaries of $20,000 to $30,000. As if to signal that his initiative was an uncanny reprise of Ernest Burton's extraordinary ambitions from the mid-1920s, Levi also proposed that the trustees create an additional ten Distinguished Service Professorships for senior scholars already on the faculty. Five of the new professorships were created at once and named in honor of worthy past faculty luminaries or distinguished former board members: Max Mason, Albert A. Michelson, William B. Ogden, Paul S. Russell, and Harold H. Swift. An additional five were approved but banked for future use until funds could be raised to endow them.[144] So focused was Levi on the success of these new senior faculty initiatives he also proposed that the University provide "special housing of a luxurious nature near campus" where these new luminaries might live when they arrived in Hyde Park.[145]

Over the next five years Levi succeeded in recruiting six new University Professors and a host of other distinguished senior and junior faculty.[146] Like Burton before him, Levi was monomaniacal about the competitive status of faculty salaries, wanting to be as near to the top of the national market as possible. In total, Levi increased the size of the total professorial faculty (including clinical appointments in the biological sciences) to 894 by 1965 (it had been 769 in 1959). By 1966 he could proudly announce that "unlike the situation in the 1950s when you were scared to death if a member of the faculty got an offer because you couldn't see how the institution would stand another professor leaving," now it was a question of determining "what will make the department stronger. Is he somebody we want to keep? That isn't always true ... that's bragging, but it's almost true." Levi would take pride in how well the University had rebounded: "I think that we are one of the few universities in the country that could have gone down as much as we did and come back as strong as we did, and I'm quite willing to say that this shows some kind of inner strength and inner values."[147]

Stephen A. Douglas's house on Thirty-Fourth Street, the near South Side of Chicago. Chicago History Museum.

John C. Burroughs, president of the first University of Chicago, 1859–1874. Chicago History Museum.

Douglas Hall, first University of Chicago. Chicago History Museum.

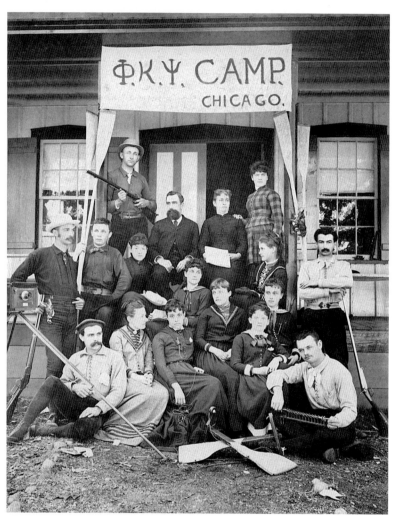

Wisconsin outing of Phi Kappa Psi fraternity, first University of Chicago, 1885.
Special Collections Research Center, University of Chicago.

Galusha Anderson, president of the first University of Chicago, 1878–1885. Special Collections Research Center, University of Chicago.

Frederick T. Gates, Baptist minister and trustee of the University of Chicago. Special Collections Research Center, University of Chicago.

Thomas W. Goodspeed, secretary of the Board of Trustees of the University of Chicago, circa 1890. Special Collections Research Center, University of Chicago.

John D. Rockefeller Sr., founder of the University of Chicago, 1880. Special Collections Research Center, University of Chicago.

William Rainey Harper, president of the University of Chicago, 1891–1906. Special Collections Research Center, University of Chicago.

Hutchinson Tower cartoon, "All Ready for John D. Santa Claus at the University of Chicago," *Chicago Herald Record*, December 2, 1902. Special Collections Research Center, University of Chicago.

"Days with People—Mr. Rockefeller," February 1900. Cartoonist and newspaper unknown. Special Collections Research Center, University of Chicago.

William Rainey Harper with a student band, circa 1900. Special Collections Research Center, University of Chicago.

Professors Delbrück, Erhlich, Herrmann, Kohler, and Meyer with President Harper and members of the faculty and the board of trustees on the occasion of the awarding of honorary degrees at the fiftieth convocation of the University, March 1904. *Chicago Tribune.*

Hermann von Holst, professor of history. Special Collections Research Center, University of Chicago.

Albion W. Small, professor of sociology. Special Collections Research Center, University of Chicago.

James H. Breasted, professor of Egyptology and Oriental history. Special Collections Research Center, University of Chicago.

James Lawrence Laughlin, professor of political economy. Special Collections Research Center, University of Chicago.

Harry Pratt Judson, president of the University of Chicago, 1906–1923. Special Collections Research Center, University of Chicago.

Vice President James R. Angell and Major Henry S. Wygant, C.O., and Adjutant, at the first assembly of the Student Army Training Corps at the University of Chicago, October 1, 1918. Major Wygant reads messages from President Wilson and War Department officials. Special Collections Research Center, University of Chicago.

Harold H. Swift, chairman of the Board of Trustees of the University of Chicago, 1922–1949. Special Collections Research Center, University of Chicago.

Ernest D. Burton, president of the University of Chicago, 1923–1925. Special Collections Research Center, University of Chicago.

Charles E. Merriam, professor of political science. Special Collections Research Center, University of Chicago.

Julius Rosenwald, trustee of the University. Special Collections Research Center, University of Chicago.

College students in front of Cobb Hall, late 1920s. Special Collections Research Center, University of Chicago.

South campus plan for the College, Charles Z. Klauder, October 1927. Special Collections Research Center, University of Chicago.

Rockefeller Memorial Chapel, 1928. Special Collections Research Center, University of Chicago.

Robert Maynard Hutchins, president of the University of Chicago, 1929–1951. Special Collections Research Center, University of Chicago.

Chauncey S. Boucher, dean of the Colleges, 1926–1930, and dean of the College, 1930–1935. Special Collections Research Center, University of Chicago.

Mortimer J. Adler, professor of the philosophy of law. Special Collections
Research Center, University of Chicago.

Photographs for FORTUNE by Oeser

Professor Harry Gideonse, chief opponent of President Hutchins, gives lecture in
Mandel Hall to students in the social sciences survey course. *Fortune Magazine*,
December 1937.

Core class in the 1950s. Special Collections Research Center, University of Chicago.

War protest, College Flanders, April 17, 1940. Special Collections Research
Center, University of Chicago.

University of Chicago Student Committee against the War, Spring 1940. Special Collections Research Center, University of Chicago.

Meteorology training, Spring 1943. Special Collections Research Center, University of Chicago.

Lawrence A. Kimpton, chancellor of
the University of Chicago, 1951–1960.
Special Collections Research Center,
University of Chicago.

Julian H. Levi, director of the South East
Chicago Commission. Special Collections
Research Center, University of Chicago.

Edward H. Levi, president of the University of Chicago, 1968–1975. Special
Collections Research Center, University of Chicago.

Joseph Regenstein Library, 1970. Special Collections Research Center, University of Chicago.

Attendees at the inauguration dinner for University of Chicago president
Edward H. Levi., Hilton Hotel, Chicago, November 14, 1968. *Left to right:*
McGeorge Bundy, Edward H. Levi, Robert M. Hutchins, and George W. Beadle.
Special Collections Research Center, University of Chicago.

Hanna H. Gray, president of the University of Chicago, 1978–1993. Special
Collections Research Center, University of Chicago.

"Salute the Sun," 1985, part of the final day of Kuviasungsnerk, a weeklong festival in celebration of winter. Special Collections Research Center, University of Chicago.

Students exercise en masse in the Henry Crown Field House for Kuviasungsnerk, January 1991. Special Collections Research Center, University of Chicago.

Hugo F. Sonnenschein, president of the University of Chicago, 1993–2000.
Special Collections Research Center, University of Chicago.

Geoffrey R. Stone, provost, and Lawrence J. Furnstahl, vice president and chief
financial officer, discuss the budget crisis at a campus informational session, 1994.
Special Collections Research Center, University of Chicago.

Joe and Rika Mansueto Library. ©The University of Chicago (Photo by Tom Rossiter).

Renée Granville-Grossman Residential Commons. ©The University of Chicago (Photo by Rob Kozloff).

Reva and David Logan Center for the Arts. ©The University of Chicago (Photo by Tom Rossiter).

Scav hunt. ©Jason Smith (Photo by Jason Smith).

The rebuilding of the faculty was one component of a larger set of goals that Levi articulated, and these dovetailed nicely with the exigencies of University fund-raising. Lacking a mega gift of the kind imagined by Mc-George Bundy, the University was forced to adopt a different strategy, to launch a major fund-raising campaign at the heart of which would be a huge grant from the Ford Foundation. During the 1960s, the Ford Foundation made available a series of giant challenge grants to leading universities and colleges around the country. This program, created in 1960 and designated as the Special Program in Education initiative, was an attempt "through special assistance on a substantial scale ... to make a significant contribution to the process by which a few universities and colleges can reach and sustain a wholly new level of academic excellence, administrative effectiveness, and financial support."[148] Between 1960 and 1967, the foundation allocated huge sums of money to sixteen universities and sixty-one colleges. In total, until its termination in 1968, the program spent $349 million, which, in turn, generated an additional $991 million in matching funds.[149]

The Special Program in Education was a splendid and even vision-ary poster child for the post-Sputnik élan, expansionism, optimism, and self-confidence of the early and mid-1960s. It was also an expression of the peculiar symbiotic relationship between a small group of elite private universities and the newly cash-flush Ford Foundation that developed during the presidency of Henry T. Heald from 1956 to 1965. A former chancellor of New York University brought in to ease the foundation out of the controversial political waters in which it had become trapped un-der the leadership of Paul G. Hoffman, Robert M. Hutchins, and Rowan Gaither, Henry Heald never met a private university president whom he did not like.[150] Under the program, Chicago, along with Stanford, Colum-bia, and NYU, was the recipient of the largest of the program's matching grants—namely, $25 million in 1965 ($189 million in 2014 dollars).[151] To secure such a grant, a university had to undergo a major long-term plan-ning process, and it had to persuade the foundation that its goals were both serious and realistic.

Immediately upon taking office as chancellor in 1961, George Beadle contacted Clarence Faust, former dean of the College and then vice pres-ident of the Ford Foundation, to explore the possibility of a gigantic gift from Ford for the University of Chicago. Chicago had already received nu-merous large grants from Ford since the mid-1950s, but a grant under the Special Program in Education could be expected to be of extraordinary proportions. Initially, the reaction of the foundation was noncommittal, since the original purpose of the Special Program in Education was to as-sist promising second-tier colleges and universities in attaining a stronger status, not to provide huge resources to the elite research universities. It required various letters and visits by Beadle, soon supplemented by those of his newly appointed provost, Edward Levi, to earn the University the chance to apply for a major challenge grant in the summer of 1964. Final approval for the University to submit a proposal came in early July 1964, and Gladys Hardy, a Ford program assistant, visited the campus later that month to assist local administrators in planning the organization of the profile.

When he assumed the provostship in 1962, Edward Levi was urged by colleagues to launch a comprehensive planning process, so Ford's planning requirements and the University's own internal political dynamics fit well together.[152] Working with the deans and the directors of all the units, Levi pulled together an enormous body of data about the University's situation and its future needs, and between the autumn of 1964 and early 1965 he almost single-handedly fashioned this material into an ambitious two-volume report, known as the Ford Profile.

Edward Levi presented a fifty-page summary of the Ford Profile on February 11, 1965, to the board of trustees, where it was debated extensively.[153] On March 15, 1965, the board voted unanimously to adopt the plan for the Ford Foundation as the University's basic strategy for the future. In presenting the plan, George Beadle emphasized that Ford expected the trustees to stand behind it: in voting for the plan, "this implies agreement in general with the projected needs for the next 10 years and the plans for raising the funds ... to meet these needs. It is tremendously important that there be substantial consensus among all of us—Board, Officers, Faculty—for this will determine the future of the University."[154]

The brilliance of Levi's plan was that it accommodated almost everything the University seemed to need, and it needed a great deal. Edward Levi would later comment to the board in October 1966 that Chicago was not a university created *ad seriatim*—if Harper had tried to do that, the University would never have come about—but this also meant that it was difficult to repair or rehabilitate it *ad seriatim*. The logic of the plan was simple. Chicago would continue to expand the total number of faculty in the arts and sciences and in the professional schools. Total faculty, including clinical ranks, would rise from 922 in 1965 to 1,227 in 1975. Faculty compensation in the arts and sciences and professional schools would rise from $10.9 million in 1965 to $26.1 million by 1975. Chicago would also embark on major capital improvements, including a new research library for the humanities and social sciences, a new science library, a new chemistry building, a new geophysical sciences building, a new high energy physics building, and new research and teaching facilities in the biological sciences, as well as new facilities for music and the arts. Also included were the remodeling of Cobb Hall and the transformation of Harper Library as an administrative center for the College. Equally important, the University would invest $21 million in new undergraduate residence halls, $13.9 million in new and remodeled graduate-student facilities, $2 million in a new student theater, $1 million in a new skating rink, and $3.5 million in a new gymnasium and a new swimming pool.

This massive recapitalization of the University would be paid for by more than doubling the level of tuition income available to the University. This doubling would result from expanding the size of the College—which would increase from 2,150 students in 1965 to 4,000 students by 1975— and from rising graduate enrollments (another 1,100 arts and sciences graduate students would also be added, who would bring in additional tuition revenue, as well as 585 additional professional school students). In addition, a massive fund-raising effort that would focus on unrestricted giving as part of a $300 million capital campaign would run from 1965 to 1975. Phase one of the campaign—with a goal of $160 million over the next three years—was launched in the autumn of 1965, concurrent with the announcement of the Ford grant.

The gamble of the Ford Plan was that it presumed a series of years of planned budget deficits, after which the University would return to stable and balanced budgets through extraordinary success in generating new, unrestricted gift income and its optimistic enrollment targets. But the real strength of the proposal lay in the way it combined detailed and thoughtful financial and programmatic analysis with a vision of what Chicago once was and what it wished to continue to be—namely, a deeply integrated university with a common culture characterized by scholarly rigor and intellectual meritocracy. Levi often invoked the Harperian image of Chicago as "one" university, and this principle was acutely visible in the logic of the Ford Plan. For Levi the stakes were high: merely to continue to survive was a recipe for failure. Rather, the tangible aim of the plan was to restore the distinction that Chicago had lost in the 1940s and 1950s.[155]

Top officials at the Ford Foundation seemed to concur. In a fourteen-page docket memorandum that Clarence Faust submitted to Henry Heald in August 1965, the staff of the Special Program in Education argued that even though the original initiative excluded institutions such as the University of Chicago, "special circumstances" at the University distinguished it from its peers: "As a relatively young institution, it does not have nearly the depth of financial support from wealthy alumni that characterizes some of the Eastern seaboard universities. Moreover, there has even been some question as to whether Chicago still belongs among the few American private universities of international renown. It is only now beginning to emerge from a series of academic and financial crises extending back over more than two decades."

Among the many features of the plan that the Ford officials found fascinating was Levi's vision for the College:

> The undergraduate student body will be grouped into five sub-colleges, four of which will mirror the four graduate divisions, while the fifth will be an inter-divisional multi-disciplinary unit.... One of the key objects of the plan is to provide units of instruction and of residence which are small enough to allow the kind of intimate association and discussion which has been of such value in the small liberal arts college and which is often lost in the large university context.... An overriding goal of the new plan is to associate the faculty of the graduate divisions more directly and more continuously in the development of the undergraduate curriculum and in undergraduate teaching.

The report concluded with the following recommendation for the members of the Ford board:

> The University of Chicago, through quiet but heroic efforts over the past decade, has extricated itself from a state of disarray which could have spelled ruin for a lesser institution with less capable leadership. The Ford Foundation's ability to make a very large grant to the University at the present time represents a rare opportunity to contribute decisively to the renaissance of what once was and may well again be one of the world's great universities.[156]

On October 15, 1965, the Ford Foundation notified the University that its request for a special $25 million grant had been approved. Five days later, the University announced the Campaign for Chicago with a goal of $160 million. The next several years were dizzying. Much of the Ford Plan was in fact realized, with faculty surging to 1,108 members by 1970–71, exceeding the number that the Ford Plan predicted by 27 positions. In 1967 George Beadle proudly reported to the foundation that the increases in the faculty were running ahead of the totals predicted in the Ford Plan.[157] Faculty salaries also increased apace. As early as 1966 Edward Levi informed the board that Chicago was now third in the country in faculty compensation, just slightly behind Harvard. Total faculty compensation for full and associate professors grew from $6.8 million in 1959 to $18.4 million in 1968, far outpacing the growth in endowment payout.[158]

Long-standing research and capital needs were also met. On the facilities front the new Joseph Regenstein Library, styled initially as a "graduate research library," was most notable for its massive size and the aggressive force of its neo-Gothic-meets-modernism aesthetic. If one building symbolized the heady optimism that reigned at Chicago in the mid-1960s, it was this magnificent edifice, the funding for which was secured in 1965, the cornerstone laid in 1968, and the official opening held in 1970. After decades in which a new central library seemed everyone's second priority, the momentum of the Ford Plan created a plausible context in which the library could rise to become the University's highest priority. It was hardly surprising that the briefing documents for Beadle and Levi to prepare for their meeting with representatives of the Regenstein family in October 1965 stressed that they should emphasize the imposing ambition of Edward Levi's planning study for Ford and that the new library would be "the cornerstone of our long-range plan."[159] Regenstein Library was thus a tribute to the efficacy of the Ford Plan, and George Beadle acknowledged to McGeorge Bundy in September 1966 that "the Ford challenge grant was a powerful factor in helping us get the ten million dollar pledge [from the Joseph Regenstein Foundation]."[160]

Many other new research buildings were authorized and completed in the later 1960s and early 1970s as well. Levi had asserted in 1965 that "the University now faces the absolute necessity for substantial plant improvement.... Three fourths of the $166,000,000 needed for plant must be available within the next five years," and a bevy of new research buildings dotting the campus landscape confirmed his ambitions: the Henry Hinds Laboratory for the Geophysical Sciences, the Searle Chemistry Laboratory, the new High Energy Physics Building, the Albert Pick Hall for International Studies, the Wyler Children's Hospital, the A. J. Carlson Animal Research Facility, the Social Services Center, and the Cummings Life Science Center.[161] All of these facilities, including Regenstein in its formal role as an intellectual home for graduate students, underscored Levi's determination to reassert Chicago's eminence in the world of scholarship.

One omission from this chronicle of successful launches was student facilities, especially student housing. The original Ford plan called for "new residence halls, a new gymnasium and other athletic facilities, additional student common rooms ... all these items will be part of a sustained move toward a brighter, more rewarding campus for the College." As we will see, this brighter campus community did not materialize.

The Reconstruction of the College

A second area of great concern to Levi was the College. Despite Kimpton's Sturm und Drang strategy, the College struggled to move beyond a total four-year enrollment of barely more than 2,000 students. Reporting to the board of trustees on his plans for the future of the College in October 1964, Levi observed that "it is anticipated that student enrollment will climb from the present 2,200 to 4,000 over the next 10-year period," and this was the goal stated in the University's submission to the Ford Foundation.[162] Levi had to confront the many ongoing problems of the College's organization and operations to give his larger vision of the future of the University any possibility of success.

Levi's most concrete intervention involving the College came when the dean of the College, Alan Simpson, resigned to take up the presidency of Vassar College. In 1962–63, Simpson and others had pushed the idea that the College should be subdivided for curricular and governance purposes into what they called "multiple colleges." Simpson's proposals came at the end of a fractious twelve years during which the College's curriculum had been repeatedly reformed. In spite of his rhetorical talents, Simpson's scheme ran into a bandsaw of faculty opposition, arising both from turf-based particularism and from fears that such a plan would fragment the undergraduate experience. By the end of 1963, Simpson was convinced that his plan had gone down in failure. But Simpson's departure for Vassar gave Levi an opportunity, and in the spring of 1964 Levi appointed himself acting dean of the College, using that unusual status to resurrect the reform idea and push it through the College faculty later the same year.

In a long programmatic memo sent to the faculty in August 1964, Levi proposed a series of structural changes.[163] The faculty of the College would no longer meet as a plenary body but would be represented by a forty-member Council. This Council, half elected and half appointed by the president of the University, would have full jurisdiction over all levels of the undergraduate curriculum. The College in turn would be subdivided into five "area colleges," four of which would parallel and be closely integrated with the four graduate divisions. The fifth college—it came to be called the New Collegiate Division—would house experimental and interdisciplinary programs that could not be accommodated in one of the other area colleges. The area colleges—eventually known as collegiate divisions—would be led by senior faculty members—the collegiate masters—and would be authorized to determine the specific components of the College's general-education curriculum that were relevant to their area and to have oversight of curricular structures in their disciplinary domain beyond the first year of the College. The first year of a student's experience in the College was declared to be a general or common year in which the student belonged to no specific departmental major or specialization.

Levi's reasons for implementing this model were driven in part by his conviction that it would be desirable to have "a kind of federalized educational program of five separate, but interdependent areas concerned with the four-year undergraduate program." Curricular flexibility was not the only reason, for Levi reported to the board of trustees in 1963 that "if five or six programs can be developed with a faculty for each program serving approximately 400 students then the opportunity would be created a) for further growth and b) of placing upon different faculties the responsibility for innovating and developing programs and recruiting from the Divisions and elsewhere the teaching personnel that was required."[164] Levi subsequently observed in 1965 that "it is assumed that the College enrollment will about double, moving from 2,100 to 4,000 within the ten years, but the plans for the reorganization of the College into collegiate divisions will preserve the small college flavor important to students, despite the doubled enrollment."[165] Levi's structural reorganization of the College was thus organically linked to the larger demographic logic of the Ford Plan.

A second, equally strategic issue involved Levi's desire to preserve the integrity of the College as a functioning faculty responsible for all levels of undergraduate education. Here Levi's personal loyalties as an alumnus of the College and his intense admiration for Robert Hutchins came into play, for Levi was insistent that some central body had to have policy authority over the undergraduate programs as a whole. Robert Streeter had raised serious questions in 1958 about the fragmentation of responsibility for undergraduate education among the departments, and Levi was determined to create agencies—the College Council and the collegiate divisions—whose robust political and administrative legitimacy would undergird the constitutional resilience of the larger College as a university-wide institution.[166]

Last, a federated College closely linked to the graduate divisions would enable the College to become, in Levi's mind, a "generalizing influence" for the University as a whole, an ideal that Levi thought essential to the future of the University. Levi also hoped that the new collegiate divisions would generate new, experimental curricular initiatives and programs that would bring together faculty from a wide variety of scholarly interests, not only enriching the general pedagogical environment but re-creating the intellectual excitement and passions generated by the original Core staffs in the 1930s and 1940s. He argued that "if the College finds its mission and its role within the University in this unifying and inquiring function, the College will gain in strength to fulfill this task only if the members of the faculties within the University are in fact willing to engage in undergraduate teaching in sufficient numbers."[167]

Edward Levi gambled that this wider engagement with undergraduate teaching across the University would, over time, enhance both the intellectual prestige and institutional prominence of the College. One cannot underestimate the boldness of this vision, for what Levi was in fact attempting to do was to blend elements of the ambitions of Burton,

Kimpton, and Hutchins into a new institutional synthesis that would, at last, ensure university-wide political legitimacy for the College.

In spite of grousing on the part of College stalwarts, who feared that the new collegiate divisions represented another power play by the graduate divisions that would lead to the disappearance of the College as a ruling body, Levi's reforms were officially adopted in November 1964. The governance changes proved salutary on the administrative front. But they did not address the many thorny and unresolved issues of the curriculum that still hung over the College from the later 1950s, and they had no impact on the equally profound student-life problems that the College faced. They were a necessary step toward more effective governance, but they operated largely on a constitutional level.

Edward Levi did have curricular views about the shape of undergraduate education, and even today they have a radicalism that echoes that of Hutchins. In a sense Levi sought to accomplish what Hutchins had tried between 1942 and 1946, but in reverse. Rather than cannibalize the high school years in favor of early college, he believed that the professional school years should be cannibalized in favor of a more creative merger of college and professional school. Yet these views were for the bully pulpit, and for better or worse Edward Levi did not try to push a specific genre of curricular reform at Chicago, although he was decidedly in favor of older undergraduates specializing in something, as opposed to continuing to study everything, and he made no bones about his approval of integrating preprofessional studies in the undergraduate curriculum in the name of making education less costly and more efficient. No one could question Levi's devotion to the liberal arts, but the history of serious curriculum reform efforts at Chicago has manifested again and again a permanent duality marked by noble and earnest ideals on the one hand and messy, political-disciplinary patronage on the other. Levi accepted the fact that the faculty should shape the curriculum, but he also knew that shaping would be a deeply political process and the results might be different from those desired by well-meaning architects. Yet Levi's vision for the College—that it become a unifying and coordinating force for the University—was an intervention that would, over time, come to have strong legs.

The Discursive Strategy: Levi's Speeches

A third and final domain to which Levi devoted considerable effort was public rhetoric about the University. Between 1964 and the early 1970s he delivered a series of programmatic speeches on higher education, fourteen of which were later compiled in a book, *Points of View: Talks on Education*, published by the University of Chicago Press in 1969. Essentially, Levi sought to reinfuse the central governing offices of the University with a stronger intellectualist aura through a series of high-level rhetorical exercises that were both aesthetic and substantive. The early speeches portrayed the university as special kind of multiversity in its several functions but also one that had a distinctive intellectual culture and great unity and ideological coherence. Over time, Levi's talks became more "externalist" and more defensive as he tried to engage the student protest movement of the later 1960s and confront what he felt to be unjustified demands made by government and key sectors of civil society to change the mission and disrupt the very identity of the universities. Levi sought to accomplish three broad purposes with these speeches—first, to rearticulate and reanimate the special cultural identity of the University of Chicago for its own constituencies, the faculty and the alumni; second, to explain how close to disaster the University had come in the 1950s and to give his audiences confidence that its leadership had now taken a step back from the precipice; and finally, to elucidate the broader purposes of the research university to the public at large at a time when, especially in the later 1960s, universities seemed to be caught in a vise between popular anti-intellectualism on the one hand and strident demands for social and political relevance on the other. Gerhard Casper, who knew Levi well in the context of the Law School, later characterized Levi's public rhetoric as "an educational effort to counter the confusion, carelessness, and folly, which, he wearily saw, too often ambushed the educational enterprise."[168] The last function became more prominent in the later 1960s, as Levi experienced the student protest culture and the political cross fire involving those in government, industry, and civil society. He complained to Thurman Arnold in December 1968, "Some years ago I would have thought that the money problems alone were enough to overwhelm us. To this we now have to add the mood of our society as it touches the universities."[169]

The addresses Levi gave then compare to the great speeches of Robert Hutchins from the 1930s, which is appropriate, given the personal ties that connected Levi with Hutchins from the mid-1930s to the end of Levi's career. "I had [a] father-son relationship with Hutchins and almost all that I now am is due to him," Levi confessed in 1977.[170] And in 1990 Levi observed, "Hutchins's legacy is an important plus for the University, and because of its continuity with the Harper influence, is a central factor to the present strength of the University."[171] Like Hutchins, Levi compiled a book of his addresses, and it was not accidental that in persuading Levi to publish his book with the University of Chicago Press, Morris Philipson would twice invoke the name of Hutchins as a former president who published with the press.[172] The warmly congratulatory letters that Levi received from loyalists of the Hutchins era, such as F. Champion Ward and Mortimer Adler, and from Hutchins himself, on the occasion of his appointment as provost in the spring of 1962 predictably hoped that Levi would return Chicago to policies more congenial to Hutchins's legacy. Indeed, Edward Levi professed deep affinity for the educational "old times" that these men represented.[173]

Yet there were limits to this comparison. One sees them openly in Levi's speech on the university and public service that he gave before the alumni gathering in Washington, DC, in June 1968. Levi argued that while universities had to be cognizant of and responsive to the social problems of the communities in which they resided, the central purposes of universities were to cultivate knowledge and to preserve an intellectual tradition, not to function as de facto government agencies. "Undue reliance upon universities as handy agencies to solve immediate problems, remote from education, can only end in corruption of the universities," he warned. "And the danger is greater because corruption is easy and attractive, particularly when it is dressed up as a relevant response to the problems of our day."[174] The speech won accolades from various senior faculty members, all of whom seemed to admire Levi's vision of universities as special bastions of a unique set of intellectual virtues.

Yet Levi's University was not the same as Hutchins's University. Levi faced a different set of external constituencies and a profoundly different public culture than had Hutchins. Hutchins's moralist certitudes came in the midst of the economic disasters of the 1930s, but that upheaval did not immediately challenge in fundamental ways either the administrative and fiscal character or the operational self-image of the American research university. Hutchins's rhetoric was "democratic" but also charmingly elitist, presuming a program of educational rigor that most American high school students could not possibly pursue. In contrast, in the later 1960s, Edward Levi found himself facing a conflict between the responsibilities of a mass-oriented higher educational establishment and what it "owed" American society at large and more traditional notions of the core purposes of research universities. As Philip Altbach has argued, having worked assiduously after World War II to assume central roles of cultural enlightenment across American civil society, American universities now found themselves dragged into the "most traumatic social crises of the period."[175] After 1945 many university leaders had welcomed the chance to reposition their institutions as engines of mass democratic citizenship, eagerly accepting the waves of federal largesse that flowed to them under the mantle of this new role in the 1950s.[176] Now the universities discovered unfriendly strings were attached to their self-articulated claims about their own magnanimity and capacities. Levi worried deeply about the dangers of powerful centrifugal forces pulling the universities away from their primary function of cultivating knowledge and generating new knowledge. These forces grew even more acute in the 1980s and 1990s.[177]

Ironically, if Hutchins was Levi's *spiritus rector*, the historical figure whom he most often invoked was William Rainey Harper. As dean of the Law School Levi had often cited Harper to bolster the idea of professional education as integral to the wider intellectual mission of the University.[178] Levi relied on Harper for his mainstay argument (what Provost John Wilson later called "Mr. Levi's catechism") about the University's oneness or wholeness. For example, in January 1969 he insisted that Harper "was demanding a unity that was not found in many institutions. . . . The thought that this must be one University, not a segmented institution, was always predominant. . . . At times it has given the institution the assurance or a feeling of necessity to go it alone."[179] This was a structural argument, but also a moral one, in that Levi insisted that the unity of the community was what had enabled it to hold together in the dark days of the 1940s and 1950s, and that it was this unified community that would now reemerge in the brightness of reform and renewal in the 1960s. By invoking this particular reading of Harper, Levi deliberately historicized the University's notability and sense of purpose, but he also challenged his contemporaries to take seriously the need for the University to survive on its own terms and not the terms of any external interest group or governmental agency. Or, as John Wilson put it, "Harvard has more money, [but] Chicago has more university."[180]

LATER CHALLENGES IN LEVI'S PRESIDENCY

George Beadle announced his retirement from the presidency in late June 1967, and the board set in motion procedures to find a successor. This time the process went quickly. The search committee was appointed in August 1967, and by mid-September the committee had agreed on a nominee, Edward Levi.[181] It was the fastest presidential appointment the University had made since the selection of Harper.

Student Unrest: The Sit-Ins of 1966 and 1969

Levi officially took office in mid-November 1968. The early months of his presidency were virtually consumed with managing the great student sit-in of January and February 1969. The history of this sit-in, as well as those that preceded it, was deeply complex. The first major sit-in at the University of Chicago had occurred in May 1966 and was directly related to the Vietnam War; some alumni from that era would argue that it was historically more influential and momentous than its younger cousin of 1969.[182] Early in May 1966 George Beadle had announced that the University would provide class ranks along with other academic information to draft boards for students seeking deferments, but that each individual student would have the right to determine whether this information would be forwarded to his draft board or not. Students opposed to the University's ranking of male students in accord with requirements of the Selective Service system quickly mobilized under the nominal leadership of Students against the Rank (SAR). Unable to force a reversal of the University's decision, they organized a sit-in in the administration building. The sit-in began on Wednesday, May 11, and ended on Monday, May 16. Initially about 400 students entered the building, but the number dwindled as time went on, with most students leaving within three days. Other students—Students for a Free Choice—rallied to the University's position, with more than 350 signing a petition in which they expressed their desire that the University be able to submit such information to the Selective Service system.

The May 1966 sit-in was one of the first major sit-ins at a university administration building in the 1960s, and it set a pattern for sit-ins that followed on other US campuses. Interestingly, the University did not discipline the students who participated, but the Council of the Senate issued a recommendation in the aftermath of the sit-in that in the future such disruptions would be subject to "appropriate disciplinary action, not excluding expulsion." The late spring of 1967 brought a second and shorter sit-in (called a "study-in") in the administration building, also over the issue of the draft and student ranking. This time the University appointed an ad hoc faculty disciplinary committee, which imposed one- or two-quarter suspensions on fifty-eight students in early June 1967. This second sit-in was to prove important, since it established the administrative, legal, and disciplinary precedents for how the administration would handle the big sit-in of 1969.

In the aftermath of the 1966 sit-in, the Council of the Senate urged that the University create a special committee on faculty-student relationships. In April 1967 the committee issued a report, but more interesting were its two supplementary statements—one written by the committee's student members, who argued that students should have substantial rights in all areas of university governance; the other by a long-serving member of the College faculty, Gerhard Meyer, who argued that in extracurricular affairs students should be given a wide range of rights, but that in academic affairs key decisions must continue to rest with the faculty. Whereas the students asserted that they "must play a significant role in the decisions made in all academic units," Meyer saw no need for such involvement.

"There is little reason to fear that giving faculty members the major or even the sole responsibility for important academic decisions would permit, or foster, arbitrary decisions unresponsive to the needs and rights of students as students and as human beings," Meyer stated.[183] The gulf between Meyer's statement and the wishes of the students could not have been wider. The exchange focused on the core realm of power within the University—namely, faculty prerogatives to determine academic policies. For Meyer, one of the most devoted teachers from the Hutchins's era, there were key aspects of institutional self-governance in which faculty authority was not only singular but supreme as well.

Beyond the two sit-ins of 1966 and 1967, the campus saw a general radicalization of student opinion that assumed many forms and seems to have escalated over time. This transformation took place within the crescendo of larger events on the scene of American higher education and American politics more generally. Alan Brinkley has characterized 1968 as "the most traumatic year in the life of the nation since the end of World War II."[184] This was, after all, the year of the Tet Offensive in January, the assassinations of Martin Luther King Jr. and Robert F. Kennedy in April and June, and the riots surrounding the Democratic National Convention in Chicago in August. It has been estimated that following a major uprising led by Students for a Democratic Society (SDS) at Columbia University in April 1968, more than two hundred student demonstrations occurred on at least one hundred American college campuses in the spring of 1968.[185] That the Columbia authorities opted to use the police to clear their occupied buildings eight days into the strike—an intervention that turned violent, with hundreds of arrests and many injuries—set an unattractive tactical precedent that was certainly available elsewhere.

The fall of 1968 saw renewed incidents of political protest, including attempts by local SDS members to disrupt Edward Levi's inaugural civic dinner in mid-November. Then, an issue emerged in December 1968 that allowed radical students to galvanize support among a broader group of graduate and undergraduate students. The Department of Sociology had two left-wing junior faculty members on its faculty roster. Richard Flacks had been hired in 1964 and renewed for a second term in 1966; Marlene Dixon came to the University on a joint appointment between the Department of Sociology and the Committee on Human Development in 1966 and was scheduled for a renewal decision in the autumn of 1968. Both became extremely popular with graduate students and undergraduates, and both became informal mentors to politically oriented students, some of whom were SDS activists or at least informally connected to SDS.

In mid-December 1968 the University informed Marlene Dixon that her contract would not be renewed, based on a negative decision of the senior faculty of the Department of Sociology.[186] Student unhappiness over this was immediately apparent. On January 9, 1969, an ad hoc group of students calling themselves the Committee of 85 met and issued "demands" that the criteria for the decision be made public, that Marlene Dixon be rehired, and that students have equal control with faculty in all future decisions on hiring and rehiring of faculty. They set an initial deadline of January 13 for their demands to be met.

On January 13 the dean of the social sciences, D. Gale Johnson, announced a meeting to discuss in general terms the procedures for appointment and promotion in the division, but not the Dixon case in particular. Attended by several hundred students, this meeting took place in Judd Hall on January 17, but Johnson, as well as William Henry and Morris Janowitz, the chairs of Human Development and of Sociology, and various other faculty members walked out after the students demanded that the meeting focus specifically on Dixon's case. The next day Dean Johnson requested that the dean of faculties, John T. Wilson, appoint a university-wide faculty committee to review the Dixon decision. This seven-person committee was chaired by Hanna H. Gray, at that time an associate professor in the Department of History and the College.

On Monday, January 27, approximately 150 students staged a two-hour sit-in in the office of Dean Johnson.[187] The students entered the office and searched Johnson's files, both actions without permission. A vote was taken to seize the files, but this was not carried out. The Committee of 85 had already sent Edward Levi a letter on January 23 renewing their demands and setting a new deadline of January 29. The deadline came and went, with Levi issuing a general letter rejecting the students' demands for co-control of the hiring process and insisting that it would be inappropriate for a president or provost to appoint someone to a department against the wishes of the faculty of that department.

On January 30, 1969, four hundred students entered and encamped in the administration building. Having occupied the building, a student "Negotiating Committee" then sent Edward Levi a four-point set of demands: the immediate rehiring of Marlene Dixon; the acceptance in principle of equal student-faculty power in the hiring and firing of professors; agreement that any pay loss suffered by employees as a result of the sit-in be recompensed by the University; and amnesty for all those participating in the sit-in, since "we consider our actions legitimate and not subject to discipline."[188]

The response of the University came through the Committee of the Council of the Senate and the dean of students, Charles D. O'Connell. The committee issued a statement strongly supporting Edward Levi on February 1, 1969, and refusing to bargain or negotiate under the threat of coercion. More important, the committee immediately appointed the nine-member University Disciplinary Committee on January 29, the day before the sit-in actually began, to be chaired by Dallin Oaks of the Law School.[189] The stalemate between the sit-inners and the central administration lasted two weeks. By February 3, the number of students in the building was rumored to be down to about 175. To bolster their efforts, some students tried to engineer a strike against classes in the social science building on Tuesday, February 11, which failed completely, given that majority opinion among the student body was unsympathetic to the sit-in. On February 12, the Gray committee's report on the Marlene Dixon case was released. The review committee found that the procedures used in the original evaluation had been fair and appropriate, but it also recommended a one-year extension of Dixon's contract in the Committee on Human Development. Later the same day, Marlene Dixon rejected the proposal and announced she no longer wished to teach at the University.

With the issuance of the Gray committee's report and with Dixon's response, the original justification for the sit-in had been eliminated. Sometime in the second week of February, two graduate-student leaders of the sit-in met privately with Julian Levi in his office in the old YMCA on Fifty-Third Street to discuss the situation. According to the recollections of one of these students, Levi was calm and dispassionate, smoking a big cigar with his feet propped up on a desk. Levi commented that the sit-inners had raised some plausible issues, and he told them that he admired their guts. But he also observed that they were going to lose, big time, and pointed out that the University's most loyal financial supporters were unaffected by the kinds of issues raised by the sit-in. Stunned by Levi's tough, realpolitik dismissal of their cause, the students returned from the meeting convinced that the administration would continue to be both immovable and totally unyielding to their demands. Soon thereafter, a vote was taken to abandon the building. The sit-in officially ended on Friday, February 14, with no police having been called.

Even more controversial than the sit-in itself were the disciplinary consequences. Forty-two students were expelled from the University. An additional eighty-one students were suspended for periods ranging from less than one to six quarters, although in some cases the suspensions were themselves suspended, and the students were permitted to register on probationary status.[190] Seven of the forty-two expelled students were not enrolled at the University in February 1969. Of the thirty-five enrolled students who were expelled, five were graduate students and thirty were undergraduates. Some of the expellees were students with radical external political agendas, for whom the University was, in their view, part of a larger system of repression and racism. Several ended up in Weathermen demonstrations later in 1969 and ran afoul of federal law. Other expellees were students with less overt political agendas but who felt strongly about student rights on campus. Still others were students who were deeply unhappy at the University for personal reasons.

Faculty attitudes during the sit-in varied widely, both as to how to deal with the initial event and how to manage the disciplinary process. Edward Levi was under substantial pressure from some senior faculty to call in the Chicago police, and the fact that he resisted this pressure was to his profound credit. Some faculty members were willing to cooperate in the process of issuing summonses and organizing the disciplinary committees, but others, while disapproving of the sit-in, refused to cooperate in any aspect of the disciplinary proceedings. Senior faculty reactions at the time can be gleaned from short position statements issued by many individual full professors. Few were sympathetic to the students' demands, and the range of rhetoric moved from the critical to the heatedly denunciatory. Several senior faculty members invoked images of Nazi storm troopers. For example, H. Stanley Bennett in his public letter of February 8 asserted that "no one can force a department or division of this University to accept a faculty member judged to be unsuitable. The principle called for by this demand was used in Nazi Germany to compel the placement of fascist professors in universities. We cannot permit the same dangerous principle to become established here."[191] A more balanced, but no less determined voice was that of the historian John Hope Franklin, who argued that "in the resort to the seizure of a building, the ransacking of official files, and the effort to disrupt classes by noisome and juvenile antics," the students "have rejected the very principles on which the University can have a healthy existence. . . . They blaspheme their predecessors, in other areas, who struggled against unjust and illegal laws to which they had no recourse. And they insult the progeny of those early fighters for justice who have had the wisdom and grace, in our own time, to understand the difference between a great seat of learning and an ordinary public hustings."[192]

Several departments and other units—economics, chemistry, education, Social Service Administration—issued collective statements of support for Levi and the Committee of the Council. At the same time, for every faculty member who wrote a public letter denouncing the sit-in, many more did not do so. Many faculty found themselves caught in the middle, and during a revolution—cultural or otherwise—the middle is an awkward and even dangerous place to be. Wayne Booth, a colleague widely respected by both faculty and students who was on the verge of concluding his term as the dean of the College in the spring of 1969, expressed this frustration at a meeting of the College Faculty on February 4:

"We meet at a moment of great crisis, and for many of us it is not the first time.... Ever since a former student called me a liar in a public meeting more than two weeks ago, I've often felt that someone was deliberately dogging my steps and distorting my motives and words."[193] Still other faculty believed that it was wrong for the University to mistake the symptoms of student rebellion for the deeper causes of student unrest, thus ignoring the sources of student unhappiness to begin with. In a statement dated February 11, 1969, forty-six faculty members encouraged the administration not to dismiss student demands out of hand: "Some of the criticisms the students make are justified, in our opinion. Other demands of theirs would harm the University and must be resisted, but failing to acknowledge the dissatisfaction with existing conditions underlying these unreasonable demands and refusing to institute needed improvements would also harm the University as a viable institution."[194] Opinion surveys and votes in various assemblies, large and small, suggested that the majority of students were opposed to the sit-in as a tactic but that many sympathized with the campus governance issues that their fellow students were raising.[195]

The sit-in was a collision over rules and procedures, but it was also a collision over values involving the constitution of authority on the campus. Moreover, the sit-in revealed serious fissures in the ethos of campus life and in student morale that went beyond the turmoil of what happened in the administration building. The most extreme student opinions and actions—such as those espoused by the most militant members of the SDS—were the easiest to disregard or even condemn. But fifty years later one is struck by the sincerity of other kinds of student sentiments that were in play—appeals for quality of teaching and for the rights of students to participate in the work of the departments and the University. Many of the students associated with or at least sympathetic to the sit-in were not political radicals or members of the SDS. These students were much more concerned about campus climate, about the quality of teaching, and about what they felt to be the University's indifference to their intellectual and personal needs. Writing much later (1999), one College alumnus from the class of 1969 reported, "The social and political life of the University we found to be in stark contrast to its intellectual life. As a classmate said, 'We were expected to be able to discuss Thucydides like an expert in class, but out of class we were expected to remain silent about matters affecting our everyday lives.' We thus found ourselves frustrated in any attempt to use our newly developed critical skills to discuss practical issues of importance to us."[196]

The sit-in thus had an elemental quality about it, made more acute since the triggering issue—the prerogative to appoint and reappoint faculty members—came as close to the academic nerve system of the University as one could imagine. Yet in defending the received hierarchy of academic authority, professional expertise, and professional identity, which many senior faculty invoked as part of a defense of their vision of the University as a venerable cultural institution, it was easy for them to be seen by the students as making themselves out to be the exclusive owners of the University and thus as being hostile or at least unresponsive to a broad range of student concerns.

The crisis of 1969 hit Edward Levi hard on a personal as well as a professional level. Indeed, Wayne Booth later recalled that Levi on several occasions threatened to resign because of the student tumults affecting his University.[197] Booth also remembered the passionate extremes that the participants in those perplexing times grappled with, from brash threats against the students and against the College itself to sincere fears about the integrity of the University, and including a level of visceral hostility evinced by a small minority of senior faculty toward the students: "The behavior of some faculty members was atrocious. One arrived at most meetings [of the senior administrative steering committee during the sit-in] wearing his army uniform with all of his badges. Another suggested, before the students actually got in [the administration building], that we leave some cash distributed about the office desks so that we could have students arrested for theft."[198]

Caught in the middle of these terrible upheavals, Levi's most powerful impulse was to find ways to hold the university community together.[199] On February 14, when the protesters decided to leave the administration building, Levi observed:

> The University has sought throughout this period, however imperfectly, to exemplify the values for which it stands. It has encouraged discussion through faculty and student groups.... In a world of considerable violence, and one in which violence begets violence, it has emphasized the persuasive power of ideas. It has sought—and the unique response of the faculty and students has made this possible—to handle its own affairs in a way consistent with its ideals. As I write these lines I cannot help but wonder what our success has been and whether the choice we made remains viable. But I do not believe success was the only measure of this choice.[200]

Contracting Budgets and Staggering Needs in the 1970s

The drama of the sit-in eventually passed, but more fundamental challenges remained. Unlike most previous presidents before they took office,

Edward Levi knew only too well the financial conditions of the University, and in November 1968 they were only somewhat promising. In spite of the infusion of cash and pledges from the campaign, the University's budget was barely balanced. Levi's conundrum was clear in private memos and correspondence that presented a depressing view of the University's financial problems. In a memo to his staff in February 1967, he asserted, "I am now convinced that we are in a major financial crisis."[201] When Morris Janowitz approached him with ambitious plans for the Department of Sociology in May 1968, Levi sharply responded, "We must keep in mind that the University is really hard up.... And we may have to cut back on basic educational enterprises."[202]

Finally, Levi decided to go public. In early December 1969, Ben Rothblatt, an administrator in the provost's office, published in the *University of Chicago Record* an unusually lengthy budget report, the main argument of which was that the University of Chicago was in fact not a wealthy institution and that its annual deficit was bound to increase unless significant new revenue streams could be identified. Noting that the Campaign for Chicago had not met its goals—"less than half of the announced goal for building funds was attained" and a "considerable portion of the Campaign funds pledged and received are for long range or other future programs and cannot immediately be put to use"—he warned that "funds for immediate needs [are] in relatively short supply" and that current operations were being paid for by unrestricted funds provided by the Ford challenge grant, the last payment of which was scheduled to be made in the current academic year.[203]

Concurrently, Levi issued his annual report to the University, and in it he alerted the faculty to a potential structural hole in the University's academic budget that amounted to nearly $6 million. Echoing Rothblatt's document, Levi explained that the Ford challenge grant, which had been used to cover the budget deficits during the later 1960s, was now about to disappear, and he indicated that it might be impossible to secure a sufficient increase in unrestricted funding to cover the margin. A budget shortfall of about $5.69 million was thus possible, accentuated by Chicago's failure to assemble unrestricted gifts anywhere near what was needed to balance the budget. Such a deficit in 1970 was the equivalent of a $35 million deficit in 2014.[204]

Of course, the challenges that Chicago was about to face were not atypical at the time. If the early and mid-1960s were a golden age for many American research universities, the 1970s proved a different environment indeed. Economic stagnation, rampant inflation, the image of cultural disarray in the later 1960s that many US universities projected to their gift-giving constituencies, the withdrawal of federal research and fellowship dollars, the detritus of student unrest—all these factors helped create a climate of budgetary austerity, if not crisis.[205]

Chicago found itself faced with a looming fiscal crisis, but the specific nature of its crisis was directly affected by the events that occurred in the spring of 1969, and by the fact that the 1950s had been years of basic survival, not exuberant expansion. The Ford Plan of 1965 was predicated on the University's capacity to increase unrestricted giving in support of current operations and to sustain increased enrollments, translating into incremental tuition revenues, with an estimated doubling of tuition dollars by 1975. The November 1969 reports were a signal that the earlier optimism about the sustainability of massive increases in unrestricted giving to cover the University's now-inflated current expenditures had been exaggerated, but what these documents did not yet confront—and what their authors may not have even been fully aware of in the late summer of 1969—was that more severe challenges lay immediately ahead because of negative trends on the enrollment front.

The vision behind the Ford Profile presumed more students and more facilities to house those students. Between 1960 and 1968, College enrollments began to grow slightly (from 2,163 to 2,598), but housing resources did not follow suit. Even though the University formulated an ambitious plan for new student facilities, the Ford campaign raised no funds toward that project, and as early as October 1966, Edward Levi expressed doubts that the University could carry the project out. Not only did the Campaign for Chicago fail to generate sufficient unrestricted gift funds to replace the Ford money, but it also failed to produce the huge sums needed to improve student life. In 1960 housing officials declared that, as a first step toward a largely residential College, they would require that undergraduate women live all four years on campus and that undergraduate men spend at least the first two years on campus. But with demand far exceeding supply, frustrated administrators in the housing service tolerated and even encouraged petitions from students who wished to opt out of the housing system. In the spring of 1964 the University acknowledged that it had overreached itself and rescinded the on-campus requirements. A faculty committee surveying the housing situation in 1961 complained that "the residence halls do not now provide living facilities consistent with the aspirations of the College. The crowding, noise, meager student-faculty contacts, relatively drab uniformity, and tone of management which prevails in much of the dormitory space contrasts with the independence, imagination, and communication which the College cultivates in the classroom."[206]

The problems were several. First, both of the new residences opened in the late 1950s—Pierce and Woodward—had been designed with many small, undersized rooms, which, when deployed as doubles, quickly became seriously overcrowded. This fact was evident when Eugene Rostow, dean of Yale Law School, wrote to Edward Levi about his son's experiences: "My son was housed in a well-designed modern dormitory at Chicago, Pierce Tower, which I regard as an educational abomination. He and a roommate shared a room about the size of my Yale bedroom, or a steerage statement on an old Cunard liner. They were expected to sleep, study and entertain in that room. Of course, they couldn't."[207] Second, the College's housing staff struggled to manage a system of older, substandard properties in which the graduate divisions and professional schools were allowed to cannibalize the older, pre-1918 dorms for faculty office space, thus shrinking the residential options for College students at the same time that Pierce and Woodward opened and undergraduate enrollments began to grow.

In April 1963 the *Maroon* criticized the decision to close down the older women's dorms on the Quadrangles and to transfer women students to an old apartment building over a mile from campus, prompting a stunning assessment from Mary Alice Newman, a young assistant dean of students in the College. She wrote to Warner Wick, the undergraduate dean of students, "The *Maroon* (for once) has accurately delineated the seeming irrationality of current decisions with regard to housing.... As one of the original proponents of a 'residential college' I presumed that it would be supported by a minimum standard of living.... However, three years later not only have positive gains not materialized, but we have actually lost ground." Wick in turn forwarded Newman's letter to the central administration, adding his own caustic commentary: "We are in trouble, chiefly because of the decisions made long ago.... Talk of our 'residential college' is a big laugh, and the world is hearing about it."[208] Frustrated staff members, asked to deal with angry parents of young women who were assigned to the Harper Surf building at Fifty-Fourth Street and Harper Avenue, vented their discontent as well: James W. Sheldon Jr., a young development officer, wrote to George Beadle, "If this is the best housing that we can provide for a female, junior undergraduate, it looks as though our claim to being a 'resident college' is no longer true. If we can't do any better, maybe we should completely eliminate the co-educational feature of the College, as we certainly won't attract many of the kinds of girls we want with this type of housing offering."[209]

Among the most agitated was Wick himself, who became increasingly frustrated about the gap between the University's lofty goals and the disoriented realities that he was forced to administer. Wick was convinced that the high dropout rate that afflicted the College's student body was directly linked to the "failure of so many students to become identified with the community," and this in turn was connected to the College's poor residential facilities.[210] In February 1964 he complained about the situation in an unusually harsh memo: "The 'residential college' we spoke of so proudly five years ago has become a rather bitter joke.... We cannot now house even two of the four undergraduate classes in dormitories. We have been forced to pretend that the privilege of 'living out' is an exception to the rule, permitted only by petition. But if the vast majority of upperclass students did not petition to live out, we would be in trouble.... This situation subverts everything I think we stand for."[211]

In response to these concerns and in an effort to gain control over the inchoate process of student residential development, Edward Levi commissioned a major faculty report in 1964 to chart the future of the housing system. The committee was chaired by Walter J. Blum, a law professor and avuncular campus loyalist given to telling the truth in nononsense language. Blum's committee deliberated from September 1964 to May 1965, soliciting a wide variety of opinions from faculty, students, and administrative staff. The final report forcefully argued in favor of the construction of new student housing on campus—focusing especially on the land between Fifty-Fifth and Fifty-Sixth Streets between Ingleside and Cottage Grove Avenues to create a student village for unmarried and married students, and including athletic facilities and space for shops and commercial services. Blum also supported the construction of a second, better-designed tower on the Pierce site. Instead of a bevy of small double rooms, Blum argued that each two-story house in the new tower should have about forty-five single rooms, together with ten suites designed for two students each. Blum also noted the possibility of expanding Burton-Judson Courts on the south campus, and he emphasized the importance of high-quality construction: "It is of the utmost importance that the University at least keep pace with the quality of housing for unmarried students which has been (and is being) built at other schools of the highest quality.... Unfortunately, the last two residences built by the University— Pierce Tower and Woodward Court—suffer badly in comparison with housing built by other schools with which the University competes for students."[212] In transmitting the final report, Blum observed that "the University, if it is to achieve its aspirations, must create the supportive facilities and the atmosphere in which a wide variety of students can feel comfortable, develop sustaining associations, and 'settle down' while undertaking their studies."[213] In thanking Blum for his report, George Beadle acknowledged the force of his arguments, and College administrators warmly endorsed the recommendations.

Unfortunately, they would not be implemented. In 1966 the University engaged Edward Larrabee Barnes to develop the student village plan.

The following year the University proudly announced a plan for a student complex, now called the North Quadrangle, for a total cost of $23.8 million, including housing for nine hundred students in a student village; art, music, and drama buildings; and an athletics center with a swimming pool.[214] Like the fate of the Burton-Woodward initiatives of the late 1920s for a new south campus residential plan, however, the Blum committee's bold vision for a new north campus complex was soon swallowed up by a combination of other urgent needs, budget crises, and planning inertia. Warner Wick was quoted by the *Maroon* in May 1966 to the effect that the costs of new housing were "staggering" and "the difficulty with money for housing is that it usually comes from unrestricted grants, the same money that is the backbone of our academic program. Thus housing is in direct competition with our most serious academic needs."[215]

Essentially, the expansion of the faculty and the array of impressive capital investments for faculty research during the 1960s had solved the "neighborhood" problem as it pertained to the senior faculty and their doctoral students. Regenstein Library may have come to function as a library for all members of the campus, but at its opening it was billed as a graduate research facility for faculty and doctoral students.[216] Yet the "neighborhood" problem of students in the College remained—they still did not have the physically and culturally welcoming place for which Burton had so passionately argued in the 1920s. To make matters worse, the solution for the faculty—prestigious appointments, academic excellence for the departments—seemed to do little to address students' concerns and unhappiness. If Levi was to achieve his goal for the College—that it serve as a powerful integrative mechanism for the whole University— more would have to be done.

The state of student housing became fiscally relevant when in mid-March 1969, less than a month after the end of the sit-in, the dean of the College, Wayne Booth, announced at a meeting of the College Council a decision to reduce the size of the College's entering class in the fall of 1969 from 730 to 500. Booth argued that "too many first-year students at Chicago have again this year been reported as miserable in their quarters, uninspired in their instruction, and unrenewed by their extracurricular life."[217] These missing students not only meant that the financial goals articulated by Edward Levi in the Ford Profile were never met, but they—by their absence—also caused havoc in the already-strained budgets of the early and mid-1970s. Between 1968 and 1973, College enrollments declined from 2,598 to 2,115 students, while total University enrollments fell from 8,335 to 7,258. The decision to reduce the size of the College was not the only cause of the failure of the Ford Plan, but it contributed mightily to it. Within a short time voices of regret were apparent—Provost John

Wilson admitted ruefully in October 1972 that "twelve hundred additional students, or even half that number, would do a great deal to alleviate the pressure on the general funds of the University"—but the damage had been done.[218] In the same vein, a report of the faculty Advisory Committee on Student Enrollment, chaired by former Dean of the College Roger Hildebrand in March 1974, stated bluntly, "Our failure to meet past enrollment projections either in the long run or the short run has been a direct cause of our present deficits.... Donors more willingly support universities with growing lists of applicants. It is urgent and imperative that we reverse the downward trend of the last four years."[219] The committee called for a concerted effort to add 1,100 additional students to the Quadrangles by 1980 and a reduction in the faculty by about seventy-five positions over the following three years. Yet both goals soon proved unrealistic.

Beyond enrollment problems, the University faced other serious financial woes that were analyzed in several detailed reports to the faculty on the University's financial situation by John Wilson between 1970 and 1975. Not only did the market value of the endowment fail to keep up with a growing pattern of inflation, but endowment payouts even in nominal dollars to the budget in 1979–80 ($16,379,000) were below those allocated in 1971–72 ($17,075,000).[220] The dreadful performance of the stock market in the mid-1970s and the University's deficit spending not only overwhelmed the current income available from University investments but compromised the future growth of those portfolios. Unrestricted gifts to the University also declined in the early 1970s, falling from $4 million in 1970–71 to a low of $3.1 million in 1974–75, returning to healthier levels only later in the decade.[221] Wilson remarked about the "gift estimate" in the 1970–71 budget that it gave him "the greatest cause for concern," arguing that meeting the gift targets needed to balance the budget that year would require a "minor miracle."[222] The miracle did not happen. Reductions of federal aid to research and graduate education made the situation still more perilous. Finally, patterns of foundation giving also changed in ways that were deeply unsympathetic to the deficit-dependent budgetary practices of research universities.[223] The difference between the generosity of the Ford Foundation toward Chicago during the fifteen years from 1956 to 1971—$95 million—and the amount it provided between 1972 and 1986—$4.8 million—is striking and reveals the massive dependence of the University on Ford support in the initial postwar period.[224]

For Chicago this was tantamount to the other shoe dropping. As the University struggled with the unceasing frustrations of budget austerity in the early 1970s, there was always the hope of one more outside intervention. Thus, in the summer of 1973, Edward Levi once again journeyed to New York City, this time in the company of two trustees and a senior faculty member, to ask for a major grant from the Ford Foundation. As before, the University followed the visit with a detailed memorandum to state its case, but this time it struck a deeply defensive tone. Unlike the buoyant atmosphere that obtained in 1964–65, Levi's intervention in 1973 was undertaken out of grave necessity and considerable apprehension, and Ford's response this time was strikingly different. The later 1960s and 1970s had been particularly hard on the investments of the Ford Foundation, and it had had been forced to retrench and curb spending habits that had eroded its endowment. Equally ominously, skeptics within the foundation questioned the wisdom of the huge grants that had been administered under the Special Program in Education.

It is not surprising that Edward Levi's appeal fell on unsympathetic ears. In a fascinating internal memo, Ford officials Harold Howe and Earl F. Cheit analyzed shrewdly and sensibly the financial difficulties of the University in the early 1970s. After acknowledging that Chicago's situation was made even more acute by its small undergraduate enrollment and by the concentration of its alumni "in employment that has rewards other than money," they concluded that the University had "special problems in raising large-scale funds." Not surprisingly the university leaders saw "only one way out of this dilemma: a $20–30 million vote of confidence by the Ford Foundation."

The desired vote of confidence, and the desired huge sum of money, however, did not come. In a subsequent letter to Levi in November 1973, Howe and Cheit argued that the University's plan for controlling expenditure growth was still "inadequately focused." What was needed, they said, was a plan that would "be directed toward establishing better control of the internal processes of the institution" and would be related "to the larger aims of the Fund Drive and the funding of the University." Later in the same letter they returned to the issue of undergraduate enrollment targets, a point that must have been of some sensitivity given Levi's commitments to Ford eight years earlier: "Given the rich mix offered by the University, we cannot understand why the University should have difficulty recruiting another thousand undergraduates. We believe that that issue bears some serious investigation."[225] The letter offered a striking repetition of the concerns that Raymond Fosdick had expressed to Harold Swift and Robert Hutchins in the later 1930s, signaling that Rockefeller Foundation support was coming to an end and urging the University to mobilize local civic support for itself. Instead of another major Ford Foundation grant, Edward Levi was advised that more expenditure controls, better planning, and larger undergraduate enrollments would surely lead Chicago to the promised land of budgetary probity.

University leaders had no choice but to launch phase two of the Campaign for Chicago in the summer of 1974—a campaign that should have been started in 1970 but had been sidetracked by the 1969 sit-in and the decline in enrollments—without a major challenge grant. The new campaign immediately ran into trouble, and, with Edward Levi's resignation from the University to become US attorney general in 1975, it had to be quietly scaled back, with the final results in 1978 painfully below the original goals.

The University's reaction to the convergence of all of these problems was renewed budget cutting, modest reductions in faculty size, and other austerities. All major US universities struggled with the collapse of stock prices and the decline of foundation giving in the 1970s, but Chicago was particularly hard hit because it had only barely recovered from the severe budget and neighborhood crises of the 1950s, and it had done so essentially with short-term cash, as opposed to creating a resilient and successful development program among its alumni and civic supporters. The 1970–71 budget had been constructed on the assumption of no growth in faculty size and a total Quadrangles enrollment of 8,300 students, but the actual number of students who showed up was 600 lower. In turn, for the 1971–72 fiscal year, the deans' Budget Committee recommended an across-the-board reduction in academic unit budgets of 5 percent, but the final reduction was actually closer to 7 percent.[226] In October 1972, Wilson informed the faculty that a serious deficit might still emerge in the 1972–73 budget, and warned that a further faculty reduction was on the horizon.[227]

During the 1972–73 cycle, it was also reported that the "condition of the stock market raises [the] question of [our] ability to meet the endowment estimate."[228] The endowment problem was worsened by the fact that unrestricted giving to the University also dropped substantially, from an annual high point of $6.8 million in 1966–67 to $3.3 million in 1971–72. Total gifts sank from $34.6 million in 1968–69 to $24.1 million in 1971–72. During the 1972–73 fiscal year, the University had to draw $3 million from the endowment to cover the operating deficit, even though such action reduced future income.

In 1973–74, the general situation was still quite serious. During the late spring of 1973, it became apparent that even the already-austere budget for 1973–74 had overestimated enrollment by two hundred students, increasing the deficit by $500,000, shares of which each of the units had to cover. In January 1974, Edward Levi released a summary of an unusually candid and tough-minded deans' budget report, which openly asserted that the deficit was harming the future viability of the University of Chicago and urged that the budget gap be closed within three years. The deans recommended further that "the size of the faculty, as of other segments of the

University, will need to be trimmed" and that "[a] rigorous examination should be made of academic units which might be eliminated *in toto*."[229]

Three years later, grave problems were still apparent. A report of the deans' Budget Committee in December 1976 warned that the University of Chicago was still facing budget problems "in especially severe terms" because of "adventuresome risk taking in budgeting.... The number of faculty members increased from 813 in 1960–61 to 1139 in 1970–71, without a corresponding increase in continuing financial resources. As a result, dangerous gaps developed between income and expenditures."[230]

The various reports of Edward Levi and John Wilson to the faculty on the miserable budgetary situation during the 1970s combined a surprising candor about the crisis with an unwavering faith in the higher destiny of the University. The increasing financial gloom and budgetary retrenchment after 1970 were perplexing and even frightening, compared to the bright days of the 1960s, when all things seemed possible.

A Balance Sheet for the Age of Survival

In what ways was the University better or worse off after Levi's service from 1962 to 1975? On the positive side, the University profited from Levi's creation of cogent forms of institutional planning and from crucial investments in key intellectual and scientific resources—above all, Regenstein Library. It also experienced a stunning increase in the size of the faculty in the early and mid-1960s, the rebuilding of key departmental leadership structures, the creation of the university professorships and the substantial expansion of the other named professorships, and investments in key new research facilities in the natural sciences. The $25 million from the Ford Foundation in 1965 was not the $200 million that McGeorge Bundy had called for, but it was a massive and encouraging gift, and it set the stage for the era of good feelings that defined the celebrations of the seventy-fifth anniversary of the founding of the University in 1967 and led popular commentators to proclaim that Chicago's "rising eminence [is] posing a challenge to Harvard as No. 1."[231] When Franklin Ford, who had succeeded McGeorge Bundy as dean of the faculty of arts and sciences at Harvard, called the University of Chicago "a giant, a 'world university'" in the spring of 1967, Levi might have felt justifiable satisfaction that he had transported Chicago back to its golden age of the 1920s and 1930s.[232]

Levi's dignified defense of the University's values chronicled a stunning recovery of nerve on the part of the faculty during the 1960s that built on the material recovery that Lawrence Kimpton had started in the 1950s. A private note that Levi drafted after Kimpton's tragic death by suicide in 1977 recalls their unity:

Lawrence Kimpton became Chancellor of the University at a crisis time when drastic and difficult action was required. Extraordinary budget problems had to be met. The area problems [in Hyde Park] were such that many persons believed that they could not be solved and the University would have to move. Kimpton ... [recognized] the historic purposes and unique qualities of the University which had to be preserved and, as is always the case, strengthened. He did not give lip service to these qualities; he made them possible by his willingness to face the issues that had to be met. He was a person of great talent and insight, innate modesty and courage, who loved the University, appreciated its past and made its future possible.

These lines could apply to Edward Levi himself. Levi then added, but deleted, a telling line that characterized Kimpton's leadership in the years of financial grimness that Levi experienced in his own presidency: "His [Kimpton's] role was not the one he would have selected, but it was the role required."[233]

On the debit side were the continuing problem of the College, the failure to meet the enrollment targets for graduate or undergraduate students that the University had established with the Ford Foundation and with the federal government, and basic structural-fiscal weaknesses that would place Chicago at a serious disadvantage against its ever-ambitious peers in the decades after 1980. During the 1970s the University began to lag behind its peers in key indicators such as size and growth of endowment and fund-raising receipts, all of which had weighty consequences for Chicago's future competitive position. Equally important, there was a continued frustration about student life and frustrations of students with student life that haunted Levi and other senior administrators in the 1960s and the 1970s. Most senior faculty believed that Edward Levi had saved the moral integrity of the University during the great sit-in of 1969. David Riesman would later argue that under Levi's leadership Chicago was the "only major research university to have come through the 1960s relatively unscathed and ... unpolarized." From a senior faculty perspective, Riesman's judgment was correct.[234] But many students and younger alumni saw things differently, and the bitter feelings that developed in the later 1960s and early 1970s became corrosive elements in the University's alumni culture for decades to come.

Edward Levi was particularly unlucky in his hopes for rebuilding and expanding the College. As a student of Chicago's history, Levi understood better than most of his contemporaries that the University's formidable perplexity relating to undergraduate education had harmed the wider welfare of the institution since the 1920s. In contrast to Burton, Hutchins, and Kimpton, Levi had fashioned a governance structure and articulated an intellectual mission for the College in 1964–65 that would, in theory, permit its effective integration with the University's lofty research traditions. Yet Levi's enormous frustrations in trying to resolve this conundrum had proved that the College could not be reborn exclusively by investing in distinguished faculty research and by writing compelling policy documents. The University had to be willing to enhance the research opportunities, the extracurricular resources, the residential facilities, and the career advising program for the undergraduates, set in the context of a formal curriculum that balanced strong general education with sufficient space for attractive specialized training programs. All this had to be undertaken with as much administrative foresight, financial courage, and creative energy as Levi devoted to rebuilding the faculty's research profile or Kimpton to saving the neighborhood.

The 1970s were years of considerable structural and cultural change in American higher education at large. Declines in student enrollment and projections of still greater demographic problems in the future, competing claims by public and private sectors of higher education for scarce federal and state support, rising fixed costs owing to steep inflation and overexpansion of facilities and programs in the 1960s, and cascading operating deficits followed by galloping tuition increases—these challenges gave rise to considerable soul searching among analysts of the postsecondary sector about the future of private colleges and universities in 1978.[235] Conventional, tried-and-true sources of new revenues had gone missing: the big private foundations were under grievous financial stress, and unlike the situation after 1945, more government largesse was improbable. As Christopher Loss has observed, "While the state had thrown money at higher education in the past, it now balked at doing so for the simple fact that there was less money to throw around.... Indeed, many policymakers and average citizens thought that the state had already done far too much."[236] The editors of *Daedalus* devoted their fall 1974 and winter 1975 issues to the theme "American Higher Education: Toward an Uncertain Future." Many voices manifested uncertainty and defensiveness. The challenges facing the leading private universities seemed particularly acute, for, as Daniel P. Moynihan noted, "Higher education has become a public utility with private standards. The political institutions of the land understand the public service function and see to its first-order requirements—that of making it available to the public. The second aspect, maintaining quality, is but little understood and little explained." For Moynihan, the top private universities were those "most associated with the maintenance of standards," but also those whose ecological profile was highly privileged, devoted to pursuing rigorous selection and sustaining intellectual elites, and thus not particularly well suited to "pressing their case for public support."[237]

In contrast to the experience of many of its peers, the decades after 1945 were hardly a golden age for Chicago. In 1965 key officials at the Ford Foundation had bluntly acknowledged that Chicago's case was both peculiar and unusual, wondering if Chicago still ranked "among the few American private universities of international renown," and Kimpton and Levi had performed a magic act in ensuring the University's survival as a first-rate scholarly institution. They had also managed to sustain a campus culture of intellectual rigor that pervaded all realms of the student experience. But the downturn of the 1970s demonstrated how fragile this process of scholarly reconstruction had been; and the student culture, while blessed with intense academic rigor, was also characterized by considerable unhappiness and outright disaffection over the failure of the University to support students and treat them with respect. If the University of Chicago was to sustain in a long-term, permanent way the national and international luster that it had enjoyed before World War II, new leadership and new approaches to educational programs and student life, along with new financial resources, were desperately needed.

* 6 *

The Contemporary University, 1978 to the Present

Edward Levi had announced in the fall of 1974 that he would retire in September 1976, but his appointment as US attorney general in January 1975 led to the need to replace him more quickly. As in the past, large numbers of nominees were put forward, and by April 1975 the list had been narrowed to ten to fifteen names. The candidate who emerged as a leading choice was Donald Kennedy, the chair of the Department of Biological Sciences at Stanford University. Kennedy visited campus in the late spring and summer of 1975 but generated only tepid enthusiasm from senior faculty and local administrators, not so much because of Kennedy's personal qualities or talents but because many committee members (and the senior faculty more generally) were evidently attempting to find a second Edward Levi. Vice President Jean Allard noted that Kennedy himself was "appropriately wary" of what Allard characterized as the "Levi legend," and one local faculty leader in his evaluation of Kennedy bluntly observed, "Donald Kennedy is knowledgeable about the affairs of his own University, well briefed about ours, and thoroughly affable. What further virtues could we expect him to display over a fancy hamburger? The trouble is that we have learned more from Edward Levi over cold scrambled eggs. And there is no escaping that trouble."[1] Local names bubbled up, including the dean of the humanities, Karl J. Weintraub, and a former dean of the College, Roger H. Hildebrand; those names were still in play in the autumn of 1975, as were outsiders such as Clifton R. Wharton Jr., Charles P. Slichter, and James Q. Wilson. The committee soldiered on, but by the late autumn it was apparent that no individual had emerged as the leading contender, with the committee stuck and the board becoming nervous. Glen Lloyd had cautioned the search committee in July 1975 that no one "had been closer to Edward Levi than he had, and warned of the danger of trying to find another Edward Levi. He thought, first, that it could not be done;

and, second, that the current needs of the University might not be fitted by an Edward Levi." But Levi's shadow still loomed large, and it was not surprising that the committee spent a substantial amount of time trying to articulate the kinds of qualities it wanted in the new leader.[2] Following Levi's resignation, Provost John Wilson had agreed to serve as acting president, but from the very first he had stubbornly refused to be considered as a candidate. In the face of board chairman Gaylord Donnelley's urgent pleas, Wilson now agreed to continue in this role but only until the summer of 1978.[3] Believing that it was important for the morale of the faculty and for the capacity of the institution to conduct serious fund-raising that Wilson not be lodged in a pro tem position, the board appointed him to the official status of president, even though the arrangement was agreed by all parties to be a temporary one.

Wilson was a thoughtful administrator who had a broad knowledge of the University's administrative structures and financial liabilities and excellent working relationships with the deans of the individual units. During his brief service as president he initiated plans to strengthen student life and athletic and instructional facilities on campus (the remodeling of Haskell / Walker / Rosenwald complex, the renovation and naming of the Henry Crown Field House in 1976–78) and gave special priority to the quality of teaching resources. Still, the brittle state of faculty opinion at the University was manifest in a pungent "minority report" submitted by the chair of the Department of Mathematics, Felix Browder, to the Council of the Senate in January 1977 that accused Wilson of not supporting the academic excellence of the institution and turning Chicago into an aimless "multiversity" run by a "special administrative caste without real responsibility to the faculty" and pursuing "projects fashionable in the educational and foundation bureaucracy."[4] Most faculty dismissed Browder's report as intemperate and lacking in evidence, but a few took it as a sign that Wilson had failed to communicate effectively with the faculty about how to best respond to the ongoing financial problems facing the University. Wilson himself was concerned that it was a sign that some faculty did not yet understand the fragile nature of the University's economy and the fact that the University was deeply dependent on new fund-raising to permit additional faculty appointments.[5] The dustup was a classic case of faculty getting on each other's nerves after nearly a decade of grating cost reductions, a significant drop in the real value of faculty salaries, and endless worrying about short-term fiscal adjustments. The University desperately needed a permanent leader with excellent communication skills who could reframe the quandaries of the moment into a new forward-looking narrative and instill hopes of a more promising future for the institution.

The search for the successor to Edward Levi resumed in February 1977, under the direction of a new board chairman, Robert Reneker. This time the search proceeded with even greater determination, and the committee soon returned to a nominee whose name had been in play in the early stages of the 1975 search, the provost of Yale University, Hanna H. Gray. Gray was a distinguished scholar of Renaissance history who had worked with Myron Gilmore at Harvard University, receiving her PhD in 1957. In 1961 she was appointed to the faculty of the University of Chicago as an assistant professor of history, and served as the leader of the College History Group. She gained campus-wide attention during the sit-in of 1969, when she deftly chaired a senior faculty committee reviewing the controversial Marlene Dixon appointment. Her report on the Dixon affair was a model of perspicacity and sound judgment, and it signaled the emergence of a talented faculty leader who was able to work through the messiness of complex and emotionally wrought issues and to frame solutions in cogent, fair, and transparent terms, and who also was unusually effective in reaching consensus through rational discussion.[6] In 1972 Gray left Chicago to become the dean of the arts and sciences at Northwestern University, and in 1974 she moved to Yale, where she was named provost. In 1977–78 she was also acting president of Yale. By the fall of 1977 Gray had emerged as the top choice of both the faculty and the trustees at Chicago. Her appointment was announced on December 10, 1977. Typical of Chicago, with its emphasis on merit, no fuss was made over the first full-term appointment of a female president at a major research university in the United States.

Toward a New University Demography

PLANNING AND THE PURSUIT OF EQUILIBRIUM IN THE GRAY YEARS

When she assumed the presidency in the summer of 1978, Hanna Gray inherited a budget that was (just) in balance because of economies and reductions imposed during the interim Wilson administration. Within six months, however, the University's continuing stresses became apparent, including a projected deficit of nearly $3.8 million for the 1979–80 academic year. In the summer of 1979 Gray began to construct a four-year plan to achieve financial equilibrium for the University by 1983, focusing not only on controlling expenditures but on creating more accurate estimates of the University's income expectations and on launching new development efforts to increase the University's income from gifts and grants. To do so Gray had to create more effective, professional systems

of budget planning, financial oversight, development, and institutional research. Indeed, the origins of the University's current budget and planning
systems date from the early years of Gray's tenure, and her presidency was
particularly notable for the management systems she deployed to conduct
the University's affairs. Gray immediately hired several key administrators, such as Jonathan F. Fanton, Arthur M. Sussman, and William R.
Haden, to help professionalize and systematize key planning processes
and to create a stronger development office.

Until Gray's appointment, the preparation of the university's budget
had been a somewhat informal affair, developed by the provost's office
in consultation with the university comptroller, Harold E. Bell. An ac-
countant by training, Bell had struggled to implement efficient budgetary practices in the face of relatively primitive ledger and card-punch
systems. To gain greater clarity over a budgetary and policy landscape
that was much more complex than it had been in the 1950s and 1960s,
Gray commissioned a major survey of the University's financial systems
and fiscal resources by an outside consulting firm, Cambridge Associates,
in early 1979.[7] Based on the firm's recommendations, Gray announced
the appointment of a professional budget director, Alexander E. Sharp,
in October 1979 to restructure the University's budgeting and financial
information systems. When Sharp was named vice president for financial affairs in July 1980, Ralph Muller succeeded him as budget director.
Sharp and Muller became responsible for long-range financial planning,
recasting current budget practices, developing more effective information
systems, monitoring budget trends within the central university and the
units, and preparing the annual budget itself.

Gray made a concerted effort—in numerous reports to the faculty—to
communicate detailed information about the University's financial challenges and to enlist faculty in identifying possible solutions. She was aided
by several talented provosts—D. Gale Johnson, Kenneth W. Dam, Robert McC. Adams, Norman M. Bradburn, Gerhard Casper, and Edward O.
Laumann. The budget reports issued to the trustees and the faculty during
the 1980s revealed more sophisticated metrics for gauging the longer-
term financial prospects of the University, not merely for the purpose of
balancing the budget but also to strengthen the University's capacity for
basic research and liberal learning.[8] Gray believed that the highest value of
an independent private research university like Chicago lay in its unique
community of scholars. A tough-minded focus on enhancing the University's scholarly creativity and pedagogical ambitions, while conserving and
renewing its financial resources, was a primary theme of Gray's leadership
in the 1980s. Gray sought to strengthen the real value of faculty salaries and
thereby improve their competitiveness (in general, faculty compensation

at Chicago had lost about 20 percent of its real value during the 1970s); she also supported the hiring of a significant number of distinguished new senior faculty. And she launched new graduate fellowship programs in the arts and sciences to try to reverse declines in applications and enrollment on the graduate level. Gray successfully navigated a perceived crisis in graduate education, treating it as an opportunity to reassure senior faculty anxious about the survival of their doctoral programs.

Gray's tenure saw major investments in new buildings for Court Theatre, the John Crerar Library, and the Kersten Physics Center; major renovations in many other campus buildings, including Mandel Hall, the Kent Chemical Laboratory, Cobb Hall, Midway Studios, the Jones Laboratory, and the Walker Museum; and the construction of the new cinema in Ida Noyes Hall, named in honor of Max Palevsky, and a new Film Studies Center in Cobb Hall. In 1993 the University opened the Biological Sciences Learning Center, imagining it as a "one-room schoolhouse" for undergraduate, graduate, and medical school classes in biology. The Department of Computer Science was established in June 1983, and the Committee on Public Policy Studies, which had been created in January 1974, was made into an independent professional school in February 1987, supported by a $7 million gift from Irving B. Harris. Major investments were made in university-wide computational systems and facilities and in efforts to support faculty use of personal computers. Gray devoted special attention to the university library system, adding major financial resources to compensate for the inflation in book acquisition costs and the loss of the dollar's purchasing power for foreign book and serial acquisitions, as well as advocating the construction of a new science library. Against these new investments she cut costs by consolidating administrative offices, reducing nonessential staff, closing some centers and programs, and shortening the standard workweek for employees from 40 to 37.5 hours in 1983–84.

The Gray years were marked by serious debates among the faculty, the Council of the Senate, and the trustees about the character of the University as represented by enrollments and by resources invested in the College and professional schools versus the graduate divisions. How large should the University be, and at what cost? How could Chicago improve the amenities of the campus and the neighborhood in times of tight budgets? Another concern was both the size and the age distribution of the faculty. Within its peer group Chicago had one of the largest arts and sciences faculties and the smallest undergraduate college, resulting in significantly lower net tuition revenue to cover faculty salaries compared with other major institutions. This situation grew more acute as government and foundation support for faculty dwindled, forcing the University to cover an ever-larger share of the regular academic budget from unrestricted revenues. In addition, federal legislation increasing the retirement age from sixty-five to seventy added millions in additional salary costs after 1982 and reduced the number of vacancies that might be available to hire younger faculty. Given these variables, could Chicago continue to afford a faculty of the arts and sciences that was larger than that of most of the Ivy League universities, MIT, or Stanford? If not, could it sustain its national and international distinction with a slightly smaller faculty base? This was a topic of much discussion among senior administrators, culminating in the decision, as part of the deficit reduction plan of 1987–88, to reduce the arts and sciences faculty size by about 5 percent through attrition over a five-year period.

The discussions about the faculty dovetailed with concerns about undergraduate teaching responsibilities (would the established faculty be willing to teach a larger College?) and key recommendations of the Baker Commission on graduate education from 1982 that (potentially) challenged the prerogatives of senior faculty with regard to how they supervised (or failed to supervise) their graduate students (see below). These years were also marked by concerns about social issues involving race and gender, and discussions of diversity within the faculty and the student body came forward more powerfully and prominently than before. Significant progress in increasing the number of women enrolled in the College from 34 percent to 42 percent between 1979 and 1989 was welcome, but rates of matriculation by African American and Hispanic students remained quite low.

During Gray's tenure, two major and related national developments in admissions and tuition had a lasting impact on the University's finances and on the demography of the student body. First, the 1980s saw the full implementation of need-blind admissions and need-based aid—the idea that universities should guarantee all qualified students, regardless of economic status, sufficient resources to be able to attend. This model was itself a policy outcome and social construction of the late 1960s and the 1970s and closely tied to the new federal regime of guaranteed student loans and grants.[9] Second, Chicago's undergraduate tuition rate, which had been set significantly below that of peer institutions in the 1960s and 1970s, was increased to achieve parity with other top private institutions, on the assumption that need-based aid would rise in tandem.[10] As a result, the University participated in what Roger Geiger and others have termed the "high tuition–high aid" paradigm to enhance unrestricted university revenues.[11] Already in the 1970s the University's financial dependence on tuition had become apparent, and it became more prominent over time: by 1990–91, tuition revenue constituted almost 62 percent of Chicago's unrestricted academic budget, compared to 42 percent in 1970–71. As tuition increased, so did the pressure of financial aid on the unrestricted budget. At the same time, federal and private grant support per student grew more slowly over the 1980s, and the University had to devote more of its own resources to fill the gap. Inevitably, all private universities felt compelled to raise tuition substantially in the 1980s to cover mushrooming costs, and Chicago with its large and increasingly tenured faculty in the arts and sciences (82 percent tenured in 1985) was no exception.[12] According to Charles Clotfelter, between 1900 and 1980 the University of Chicago's tuition had increased annually at an average of 1.6 percent faster than price inflation, but between 1980 and 1990 tuition doubled in constant dollars, giving Chicago an increase of 6.2 percent over inflation in this decade.[13]

The large tuition increases of the early and mid-1980s, together with the College's increased size (3,000 students by 1984), various cost-cutting measures, and an adjustment in the payout formula for the endowment helped achieve budgetary equilibrium in the mid-1980s. By 1982–83 the University's budget was finally balanced and remained so through 1985–86. But significant financial pressures caused by high inflation, large reductions in federal research support and student loan funds, rapidly increasing financial aid costs, and soaring utility costs and fringe benefits rates soon jeopardized the new status quo.[14] Gray estimated in 1987 that had the federal government simply sustained the funding rates that had been in place in 1978, the University would have received $13 million more in annual revenue than it actually did. Equally disconcerting was the fact that by 1992 it cost US research universities three times as much in constant dollars to support faculty researchers in the natural sciences as it did in 1962, and much of that burden fell to the unrestricted budget.

In her annual report to the faculty in 1986, Gray reflected on some of the peculiar challenges that distinguished Chicago from other first-tier universities:

> Compared to our peer institutions in the private sector, the University is quite small, especially in its numbers of undergraduates. It has, as we all know, a higher proportion of graduate to undergraduate students than do most, but an equivalent diversity and scope of academic programs and centers, a higher faculty-student ratio, a generally smaller class size, a lesser dependence on graduate students for its College teaching, and a smaller endowment than Harvard or Princeton or Yale or Stanford or Columbia, which means a smaller endowment per faculty member. The proportion of tenured faculty is relatively higher, and total faculty com-

pensation expenses are higher relative to the total budget, to the number
of students, to the level of federal support, and to the size of the endowment. Tuition in the College and in the Divisions has been relatively
lower than in comparable institutions. The proportion of undergraduate
students receiving financial aid has been higher.[15]

By 1986–87 the University again faced acute deficits, almost $5.5 mil-
lion in the unrestricted budget in that year alone. Beginning in 1987–88,
Gray and the provost at the time, Norman Bradburn, launched a multiyear
plan to reduce the deficit, this time by shrinking the size of the arts and
sciences faculty, increasing undergraduate enrollment further, freezing
graduate enrollment, and imposing additional reductions on administrative expenditures and nonacademic staff. These measures had mixed
results: the deficit reached a low of $1.3 million by 1990–91 but again rose
to $4.6 million in 1991–92.[16]

The recession of 1990–92 hit all universities hard, and Chicago particularly so. By the fall of 1992, the University faced the specter of annual
deficits reaching over $13 million by 1994–95. A host of factors were to
blame for this bleak scenario: reduced investment income, new maintenance costs, rising student aid requirements, the uncapping of mandatory retirement for senior faculty, changes in federal guidelines relating
to health and safety on campus, increasing costs of health care for faculty
and staff, loss of state support, and a continuing decline in federal support.
Meanwhile, the University felt committed to continue investment in new
research programs in several key areas, such as the biological sciences,
and to maintain competitive faculty compensation, which put even more
pressure on the strained budget. None of these factors was deadly, and
none reflected unwise or imprudent decisions by the board of trustees.
Most top US private universities found themselves in similar financial
straits between 1991 and 1993.[17] But at Chicago these negative trends,
coming so soon after the restoration of equilibrium in the first half of
the 1980s, converged to create renewed uncertainty about the structural
elements undergirding the political economy of the University. Chicago's
pronounced undercapitalization in the face of high ambitions is crucial to
keep in mind in understanding the policy options faced by the Sonnenschein administration after 1993.

In comments to the Council of the Senate in November 1992, Gray
alluded to the fact that the University now faced serious choices, including
the size of its graduate programs. "It will be necessary to decide if we want
a certain number of well-supported students or a larger number of less-
well supported students," she said. Gray further argued, "If the University

will be willing to be mediocre, the choices would not be difficult. But to remain a great research university, we must be willing to identify the most important purposes and to become more differentiated. Although we are in a strong position today, these are issues that this institution will need to deal with again and again."[18]

On the bright side, development efforts in the 1980s were significantly more successful than in the 1970s. From 1977 to 1981 fund-raising increased from $26.2 million to $45.5 million, giving planners confidence to set their sights high. Instead of a general campaign on the model of past decades, Gray and the board launched targeted appeals, one for the arts and sciences and one each for law, business, and medicine, geared toward alumni in those areas. The goal for all four campaigns was $350 million between 1982 and 1987. Planning documents for the campaign for the arts and sciences, targeted at $150 million, were explicit in emphasizing the need to balance investments to protect the quality of current programs as well as to support new ventures. The board was particularly interested in expanding the portfolio of major gifts, where the University had historically been weak. In the end, each of the campaigns was successful in generating substantial new revenues— $151.7 million for arts and sciences, $25 million for law, $23 million for business, and $36 million for medicine—and proved critical to reestablishing budgetary stability between 1983 and 1986.

Upon the conclusion of these campaigns, planning ensued in 1988–89 for a $500 million university-wide campaign that would run from July 1991 to June 1996, marking the University's centennial. The trustees had hoped for a higher goal, but given the size and nature of the alumni body and the state of the economy, they settled for what they believed to be a more manageable target. Planning documents for the campaign noted the relatively low value of average alumni gifts in the 1970s and 1980s compared to those given to peer institutions (Chicago alumni gave an average of $117 compared to $200 and more at peer institutions) and the difficulties Chicago had encountered in raising very large, transformational gifts. Moreover, the number of College Fund alumni prospects between the ages of fifty-five and sixty-four had dropped precipitously, from nearly six thousand in 1984 to fewer than three thousand by 1994—a result of the deep collapse of undergraduate enrollments in the 1950s. The goal for faculty chairs, junior faculty fellowships and instructorships, and faculty development awards was set at an ambitious $219 million, nearly 45 percent of the overall goal. Another $102 million was designated as unrestricted support for current operations of the University and as unrestricted endowment, a crucial goal given the shrinking percentage of endowment income available for unrestricted purposes.

RECENTERING THE COLLEGE IN THE 1980S

Both Kimpton and Levi had projected substantial increases in the size of the College, but because the political controversy between the College and divisional forces in the 1950s and 1960s had focused on the control of the curriculum and the right to appoint faculty, and because the initial efforts to meet Kimpton's target of a College of 5,000 students proved so inept, the "size" issue never emerged as a hot-button *politicum* during those decades. Given its small applicant pool and other liabilities, it seemed as if Chicago was fated to have a small undergraduate college, almost as an act of providence, but this was to change dramatically after 1980. In 1979 a detailed report authored by a committee chaired by Norman Bradburn analyzed why the University had had such a difficult time meeting its enrollment targets in the 1970s and presented a cogent case of pros and cons for a future expansion of the student body, offering scenarios under which the College might increase from 2,700 to 3,000 or even 3,200 students. But the report was also concerned about the size of the graduate-student population and acknowledged the sensitivity of maintaining a rough balance of power between the two sets of enrollments, asserting that Chicago was "traditionally a graduate university." To bolster that characterization, the report suggested that prior to World War II the University had more graduate than undergraduate students in the arts and sciences. But in doing so the report failed to acknowledge the real status of juniors and seniors prior to 1942: because college students graduated from a division and not the College before 1942, they were listed as divisional students in the registrar's statistics, but they were still the same undergraduates that all other four-year colleges enjoyed. In fact, throughout the 1930s Chicago had more college than graduate students in its regular academic-year programs.[19]

In response to the Bradburn report, the dean of the College, Jonathan Smith, argued that the increase would be "extremely difficult" to achieve, noting that although the applicant pool was of high quality, the College was forced to admit nearly 80 percent of all applicants to get a class and that "as a rule we tend to get as matriculants the bottom part of the admitted pool rather than the top."[20] Smith also worried about the educational consequences of the University's decision to staff and revitalize Core courses by shifting faculty to the divisions. Still, the report's measured tone and careful options gave a plausible justification for increasing the number of undergraduate students. Faculty reactions were diverse, but enlightened leadership by the deans offered a pragmatic perspective: Robert McC. Adams of the social sciences suggested that if expanding the College could help protect the extensive size of the regular faculty, the option should be seriously considered.[21] Gray and her colleagues inched enrollments forward, investing in various College programs, improving the work of the admissions office by the appointment of Dan Hall as dean of undergraduate admissions in 1980, and strengthening the mandate of the dean of the College as a university officer whose position, in Barry D. Karl's words, inevitably had "quasi-provostial" features.[22] Gray also used the intense discussions about graduate education that preoccupied many of the divisional faculty in the early 1980s (discussed below) to remind the faculty that "regardless of the degree of success a Department has in securing good graduate students, it is clear that the College is playing a part of increased importance in the well-being of the University as a whole."[23] By 1986 undergraduate enrollment reached the goal of 3,000 students. Provost Robert McC. Adams had admitted in 1984 that "the growth of the College at a time when graduate enrollments were falling, has been of inestimable importance for the maintenance of the University's financial, but also scholarly strength during the 1970s and 1980s." But Adams also feared that "we are approaching an upper limit of undergraduate enrollments that will obtain for some time to come, resulting from both the limits of our applicant pool and on space in our dormitories." Adams concluded that "the only way to sustain the University in the years immediately ahead, therefore, is to commit greater efforts to finding supplementary sources of revenue."[24]

The issue of size was not, however, dead. In the autumn of 1984 Hanna Gray decided to formally revisit the question by commissioning a second major report on the status of campus enrollments and the size of the University. A committee chaired by J. David Greenstone of the political science department recommended in early 1986 that the University increase undergraduate enrollments to 3,400 students if financial considerations demanded this step.[25] Along with this recommendation the committee suggested that doctoral students, who heretofore had few teaching opportunities during their tenure, be allowed to assist the faculty in teaching the Core curriculum. The leaders of the College believed that the projected increase in enrollment could be accomplished by improving retention rates of existing students rather than enlarging the applicant pool.[26] During the discussion in the Council of the Senate on the report, Gray remarked candidly that "no solvent institution among the great research universities has so small a number of undergraduates with so large a faculty in the arts and sciences as the University of Chicago."[27] The debates in the Council articulated concerns about preserving the qualities that many faculty believed were attractive about the existing programs (small classes, etc.), but also reflected worries about the admissions pool, about institutional resources, and the need to grapple with traditions that allowed for immense variation in faculty teaching commitments.

Over the next six years the report's recommendations were fully implemented. Support for the College increased substantially in these years, with the College's budget growing annually by 10 percent at a time when general university expenditures increased only by 5 percent. By the end of Hanna Gray's presidency, the College had reached and slightly surpassed the enrollment goal of 3,400, having thus increased by almost 800 students since the time Gray had taken office. The issues that informed the Greenstone debates would reemerge, however, in different and more acrimonious forms in the later 1990s, until a rough political consensus accepting the need for a significantly larger College population gradually took hold among the arts and sciences faculty in the decade after 2000.

Significant progress on the student-life and curricular fronts began to be made in the mid-1980s under the leadership of Donald N. Levine, whom Gray appointed as dean of the College in 1982. Levine was a loyal alumnus of the Hutchins College, but he was under no illusions about the deficiencies to which Jonathan Smith had bluntly alluded in 1980. Levine undertook major initiatives to reform the curriculum, to cultivate a more balanced and sympathetic student environment, and to create more extracurricular opportunities for students.

Kimpton's attack on the Hutchins College had produced curricular disarray, with Core staffs no longer having the right to control a BA program filled only with yearlong general-education sequences. During the 1960s, several attempts were made to broker compromises that would lead to one unified curriculum, the last one, in 1966, essentially giving each of the five new collegiate divisions the right to design its own version of a general-education Core, under which students would be required to take certain Core courses but would be free not to take others. This was a political compromise (Wayne Booth called it "a hodge-podge that can be justified largely on political grounds"), but it did lower the threshold of conflict and cooled tempers somewhat. It also had the virtue of sustaining a robust, if slightly uncoordinated, set of Core courses into the later 1960s, 1970s, and early 1980s at the University of Chicago at a time when many other American universities were abandoning their general-education programs.[28] Chicago maintained its commitment to general education as a defining principle of liberal education after 1960—a state of affairs that was increasingly rare in American higher education—and the "heritage" effect of the continuing Core structures that rolled inexorably forward from the 1950s onward ensured the survival of general education at the University.[29]

Upon becoming dean, Levine set about stripping the collegiate divisions of their separate prerogatives and reassembled a genuinely common Core for all students. The result was a new curriculum passed in early 1985, which required the equivalent of twenty-one Core courses out of a total of forty-two courses for a baccalaureate degree. The 1985 reforms created a common curricular platform for all students, thus reestablishing the unity of the Core that was part of its original mandate in 1931 and 1942.[30] At the same time these reforms faced three major challenges. First, they assembled a large general-education component, amounting to 50 percent of a student's total course work in the College, at a time when many of the older faculty who were most dedicated to the spirit of the Hutchins Core felt increasingly marginalized. The challenge was that many newer faculty appointed in the 1970s and 1980s came to Chicago from universities where there was no tradition of general education, and they themselves had graduated from colleges without a core curriculum. While willing to participate in the Core, many of these colleagues valued upper-level undergraduate courses in the area of their research specializations as much, if not more, than Core teaching.

Second, and even more troubling, teaching loads for arts and sciences faculty nationwide had begun to decline precipitously from those of the prewar and immediate postwar periods.[31] The normal teaching load at Chicago had been at least five or six quarter courses a year as late as the 1950s and 1960s, but by the mid-1980s it had contracted to four courses a year in many social science and humanities departments, allocated equally between graduate and undergraduate teaching. These reductions had an inordinate impact on faculty teaching in the College's general-education programs, leaving College administrators with severe staffing issues for their very large Core curriculum. The problem at Chicago was less a crisis of intellectual confidence in the idea of general education per se—as occurred at many other colleges and universities—than a profound shift in relative teaching time that most faculty members devoted to undergraduate teaching at all. As early as 1975, the dean of the College, Charles Oxnard, admitted that "participation in undergraduate [Core] teaching by tenured faculty presents a mixed picture," and recommended the creation of a new category of postdoctoral fellows (the Harper Fellow program) to help teach the Core sections that regular departmental faculty were either unwilling or unable to teach.[32]

A third problem originated in the constant nature of the Core sequences left over from the Hutchins College. Many of these courses, excellent in their design, were associated with College faculty who had created or sustained them in the 1950s and 1960s. But as new faculty joined Chicago's ranks in the 1970s with joint appointments in both a department and the College, many were unwilling to participate in older courses over which they had no intellectual control. As the master of the social sciences collegiate division, Bernard Silberman, put it candidly in 1979,

The problem would not arise if there was an orderly succession of [Core] courses—old ones dying and new ones emerging in a regular pattern. This doesn't occur. The result is that a course exists that becomes institutionally responsible to a number of undergraduates but which has relatively little appeal to a new group of social scientists. New recruitment of regular faculty fails since the course in its founding reflected the interests of a small group. Potential new recruits cannot view the course as an accurate reflection of what they do and what they think social science is about.[33]

Such critiques did not mean that general education had lost legitimacy, for Chicago did not experience the curricular meltdown of general-education programs that afflicted many other institutions, but they did signal that if the Core was to survive, it would have to become more flexible and open to intellectual renewal and conceptual revision.

The University also faced a vicious circle: the small size of the College's resident student population had made it difficult to generate the resources needed to remedy critical student-life issues, and the failure to remedy these problems stunted the positive effects of the Core. Levine himself was candid with the faculty about "the emotional hardships experienced by our students that produced palpable waves of depression and demoralization, resulting in suboptimal learning, unjustifiably high attrition rates, a discouraging stance toward prospective students, and disaffected alumni."[34] In August 1986 the admissions office surveyed students who were admitted to the College but chose to go elsewhere, and many of the comments involved negative perceptions of student life on campus, as well as the poor state of College residence halls.[35] Many alumni from this era later reported that they received a superb academic education in the College, one like no other, but also that they disliked the grimness of the place and would not want their children to attend Chicago.

In response, Levine, in collaboration with his associate dean, Richard P. Taub, and with the dean of students, Herman Sinaiko, launched several student-life initiatives that were significant for their precedent and impact, if not for the controversy they engendered. Levine secured changes in the academic calendar to create a winter-break day and a two-day reading period in each quarter. The College also sought to eliminate the many hassles that students faced in dealing with multiple and often confusing administrative jurisdictions. In 1983 the College created Kuviasungsnerk Winter Festival, a weeklong series of activities to raise spirits in the coldest and darkest months of the year. The spring Festival of the Arts was revived to create an anchor for late spring student activities, along with student-organized festivals in later May. Stagg Field was expanded with a new soccer field and new baseball and softball fields with permanent dugouts. New food services were provided in Hutch Commons and the C Shop, and the capacities of the student-run cafes were also enlarged. Herman Sinaiko and English professor Frank Kinahan did heroic service in creating a genuine student theater program, merging existing groups—Blackfriars, Concrete Gothic, and others—to establish the student-dominated University Theater Committee to manage the affairs of theater on campus. The "reborn" University Theater immediately gained traction, and by December 1984 student theater claimed to be the second largest student activity (measured by participation) on campus, next to intramural sports.[36] Gradually, an undergraduate subculture developed during the 1980s and 1990s that meshed the performance of theater and the study of theater in creative ways. Resources for intramural athletics were strengthened, and in 1986 the College joined the University Athletic Association, a new Division III conference, along with Brandeis, Rochester, Washington University, Emory, New York University, Johns Hopkins, Carnegie Mellon, and Case Western Reserve—a sign that varsity athletics had reemerged over the 1970s and 1980s as a student activity of substantial interest to a large number of men and women in the College. For the first time in its history the College established formal and informal channels to communicate with parents, including an annual fall weekend where parents were invited to campus to attend model classes and meet College faculty and staff. In the larger universe of university activities, such events might seem modest, but over time they created much goodwill among parents of College students.

Over the course of the 1980s, student satisfaction with the College clearly increased, if measured by first-year retention: whereas the freshman dropout rate had been as high as 20 percent in the early 1970s, by 1983–84 it had declined to about 13 percent.[37] Student academic preparation remained impressive, and employment surveys during the later 1980s revealed that most graduating seniors gained admittance to leading graduate programs or found highly desirable first jobs. On the other hand, even though applicants to the College had slowly increased in the early and mid-1980s (from 2,253 in 1978 to 2,469 in 1985), the College's applicant pool was still quite small: for the eight years between 1978 and 1985 it averaged 2,299, and admissions rates were exceedingly high—for the same eight years an average of 81 percent of all applicants were admitted. Among leading universities in the Ivy Plus group, Chicago was dead last in applications and in yield.[38] Signs of significant change came in 1986–87, when the applicant pool increased from 2,606 to 3,212 and the acceptance rates declined from 78 percent to 69 percent, an indication that the initiatives to improve student life that Gray, Levine, and their colleagues had

instituted were beginning to bear fruit. These changes continued resolutely after 1987 under the deanship of Ralph W. Nicholas, who succeeded
Levine in 1987. The growth, although very welcome, still left Chicago
woefully behind most of its peers, who enjoyed high-quality applicant
pools two or even three times the size. More important, little progress
was made in planning for new residence halls for College students or new
athletic facilities for the university community, since they would have
required huge financial investments.[39]

THE SONNENSCHEIN YEARS: A TEST OF
CHICAGO'S MYTHS AND TRADITIONS

In April 1992, after nearly fifteen years of service, Hanna Gray announced
that she would leave the presidency of the University in mid-1993. Despite
her and her senior leadership team's laudable work, many challenges remained on the horizon at the end of her tenure. Gray and her colleagues
sustained the academic integrity, research luster, and financial stability
of the University, and Gray herself had offered an eloquent national
voice defending the mission of the University as a place to generate new
knowledge and to cultivate liberal arts learning. Gray was also a vigorous
defender of the University's traditions of academic freedom and strongly
resisted political or ideological influences to tinge the workings of the
University. Under her leadership the College had come back from the
margins, with increased enrollment and a significantly improved quality
of life for undergraduates. By forcing disciplined discussions about priorities and investment choices within a regime of coherent, university-wide
budget planning, Gray had also made it possible to sustain and enhance
the research profile of the arts and sciences faculty and the professional
schools. The academic stature and reputations of most departments and
schools at Chicago were higher at the end of the Gray administration than
at the beginning, and given the continuing budget pressures under which
the University operated, this was an extraordinary achievement. The size
of the University and its student and faculty demography were still live
issues, however, and it is striking that even with the progress that had
been made during the 1980s, the University's undergraduate population
was still far short of the goal of five thousand to six thousand that Lawrence Kimpton had recommended four decades earlier as necessary for a
healthy institutional economy to undergird the arts and sciences.

In December 1992 the trustees elected Hugo F. Sonnenschein to succeed Hanna Gray. Sonnenschein was a distinguished economist trained at
Rochester and Purdue who had served as the dean of the arts and sciences
at the University of Pennsylvania and as provost at Princeton University.

Sonnenschein devoted his first year to a systematic examination of the state of the University and its future prospects. He was assisted by his newly named provost, Geoffrey R. Stone, the former dean of the Law School, who was also a bold and decisive administrator. The team was effective and forward thinking.

Soon after taking office in mid-1993, Sonnenschein and Stone faced a worsening of the financial trends that had become apparent in the early 1990s. The 1992–93 academic year had closed with a $10 million deficit, followed by $14.8 million in 1993–94. By 1994–95 the worst-case predictions of 1991–92 seemed to become true, as the University faced a $26 million budget deficit for the new academic year.[40] The budget for 1995–96 projected a deficit of $23 million. To understand these deficits (which were brought under control by the 1996–97 and 1997–98 budgets) more fully, the new vice president and chief financial officer, Lawrence Furnstahl, decided to assemble a series of data from the 1950s to the 1990s to gauge Chicago's competitive position vis-à-vis its private university peers. Believing that the recurrent deficits were symptoms of Chicago's low rate of capital formation (a combined measure of endowment, temporary funds functioning as endowment, and cash on hand), Furnstahl produced an extensive set of data showing that Chicago was falling behind many of its peers in a number of ways: demand for the College, patterns of lifetime alumni giving, size of the inflation-adjusted endowment, the real growth of the endowment, real growth in fund-raising, philanthropic support per faculty member, capital accumulation in physical assets, relative investment in physical plant and research facilities, and investment in libraries and library budgets. Perhaps the most troubling finding was that Chicago's real endowment growth since 1958 was far below any of its peers—its endowment had increased by 32 percent whereas most other top private schools enjoyed thirty-five-year growth rates far exceeding 100 percent and even 200 percent (see table 1). Inflation-adjusted fund-raising and endowment payout were equally low compared to leading peer institutions (see table 2). Furnstahl argued that "in the 1930s Chicago had one of the largest undergraduate colleges [compared to the Ivy group]. The relative decrease in undergraduate enrollment (compared to peer institutions) over the past six decades has been paralleled by a relative decline in capital capacity." A particularly arresting comparison looked at the ratio of undergraduate tuition to the regular faculty's salary and benefits costs. At Chicago's peers, net undergraduate tuition significantly exceeded the cost of faculty salaries, leaving these institutions with surpluses of $20 million to more than $46 million that could be used to cover other essential academic costs such as student aid and library operations. At Chicago, the opposite was true: undergraduate tuition ($37.7 million) did not even

TABLE 1. Real endowment growth over 35 years, 1958–1993 (in millions of dollars)

If Chicago had achieved the average growth in endowment among the comparison group over the past 35 years, the University would have over $50 million more per year in endowment payout.

University	1958 Nominal	1958 Inflated	1993 Nominal	35-Year real change	35-Year real growth (%)
Harvard	535	2,674	5,778	3,104	116
Princeton	134	670	3,286	2,616	391
Stanford	103	515	2,853	2,338	454
Yale	250	1,250	3,219	1,969	158
MIT	129	645	1,753	1,108	172
Columbia	164	820	1,847	1,027	125
Pennsylvania	84	420	1,096	676	161
Cornell	112	560	1,215	655	117
Northwestern	141	705	1,308	603	86
Chicago	**186**	**930**	**1,224**	**294**	**32**
Average	184	919	2,358	1,439	157

Source: Lawrence J. Furnstahl, "Historical Review of the Economy of the University," August 21, 1996, p. 11, College Archive.

cover basic faculty salary costs ($41.6 million).[41] Furnstahl concluded that "the University of Chicago's success in balancing its operating budget, while significant, is only part of ensuring its long term health." If Chicago did not shore up its capital structure, he warned, "the University could find that it no longer had the libraries, laboratories, and faculty salary and fellowship stipend structures necessary to attract and retain the very best scholars, scientists and students."[42] Thus, even with the improvements in development and fund-raising in the 1980s, the size of the endowment in the 1990s still compared poorly with that of leading peers, underscoring the difficulty the University faced in playing catch-up.

The Furnstahl data were striking, but the material relating to Chicago itself was hardly unknown or unexpected. Furnstahl was simply updating trends that had been clearly apparent to Edward Levi and Hanna Gray and their colleagues.[43] What stood out was that when Chicago was compared with other top private research universities in several key areas, the extent to which it had failed to keep pace was undeniable.

In response to these data and the negative budgetary environment, and after consultations with the deans and other senior university officials, Hugo Sonnenschein made a crucial decision. In the fall of 1994, Geoffrey Stone had convened two committees of senior faculty to discuss the future of graduate and undergraduate education.[44] In early 1996, both committees produced thoughtful reports that addressed key issues, including the

TABLE 2. Philanthropic support per faculty member: Real change in endowment payout plus gifts over six decades

Over the past six decades, philanthropic support (both current giving as well as gifts accumulated in the endowment and generating payout) per faculty member has tripled at peer institutions, while remaining flat at Chicago.

	Six decades ago (1993 dollars)	Current (1993 dollars)	Real change over six decades (%)
Endowment payout plus gifts in aggregate			
Comparison group*	50,132,000	267,992,000	435
University of Chicago	69,659,000	138,335,000	99
Endowment payout plus gifts per faculty			
Comparison group*	61,908	180,593	192
University of Chicago	101,395	97,282	−4

Source: Lawrence J. Furnstahl, "Historical Review of the Economy of the University," August 21, 1996, p. 13, College Archive.
*Average of Harvard, Princeton, Yale, Stanford, Columbia, MIT, Cornell, and Penn

number of potential applicants, adequacy of facilities, and faculty teaching responsibilities. The undergraduate committee, however, was unable to find consensus on the question of the future size of the College; instead, it discussed concerns that would have to be considered if enrollment were to increase, while not explicitly endorsing such an increase.[45] The lack of consensus meant that a final decision on the size and timing of enrollment increases would be left to the president and the board of trustees.

Sonnenschein had been discussing the University's future demography with the board since 1994. In the spring of 1996 he proposed adding one thousand students to the College within a decade, assuming that the applicant pool could be widened to include more talented students. On April 30 he sent a formal letter to the university faculty, stating that Chicago's "brilliant past," which was a product of the University's "fierce commitment to ideas and intellectual community," would be difficult to sustain without investments in research facilities, libraries, classrooms, salaries, and financial aid.[46] It was clear, he wrote, that a financial structure in which "tuition does not cover salaries and [the] endowment does not grow at a robust rate" was not "sustainable over the long term."

But the task at hand was not simply to increase revenue; it was also to expand and improve the quality of liberal education, a social mission richly deserving of the University's resources and consistent with its history. The kind of education offered at Chicago, Sonnenschein observed, had never been more needed than in the present time of "dynamic change in knowledge and technology." Liberally educated men and women were crucial to "a world in which hope, respected leadership, and thoughtful citizenship are in short supply, and in which prejudice, fear, and the manipulation of public opinion are all too prevalent." The University of Chicago, with its reputation for education in critical thinking and the thoughtful formation of values, curricular innovation, interdisciplinarity, and carefully crafted Core, had the responsibility to communicate to the broader public "the profound worth" it had to offer, beginning with reaching the most talented students and convincing them to apply and matriculate. To begin, this required a changed disposition toward undergraduates, with recognition that "a student's life encompasses more than coursework," and that students "will pursue many career paths" and "do not fall short of their aspirations as learners when they decide to become bankers or film producers instead of professors." More broadly, it would require a curriculum that attended to students' goals and intellectual interests "both before and after graduation," as well as investments in student community through new dorms, food services, nonacademic programming, and recreational facilities. Sonnenschein closed his letter with a challenge: while this course of action was "not without risk," the greater risk was "to remain on a course that will not sustain excellence. Belief in the values that make the University of Chicago distinctive must be translated into actions that provide the necessary support for these values." Although Sonnenschein cited adverse financial trends as a major reason for the expansion, he also stressed that a larger College, with a more successful record of applications and matriculations and stronger student-life functions, would strengthen the general cultural welfare of the University as well. The decision to move beyond the threshold of 3,400 undergraduates presumed a willingness to make significant new investments in facilities and staff, given the Gray administration's earlier judgment that 3,400 was the maximum that the existing plant and teaching resources could bear.

Faculty reaction to the letter was divided and divisive. A group of senior faculty called for the creation of a Committee for a Year of Reflection to conduct a yearlong investigation of the justification and impact of the president's proposals. The committee was populated by well-known scholars and respected teachers, some of whom believed that Sonnenschein's plan endangered the identity and cultural balance of the University, not only because it stipulated a substantial increase in the undergraduate as opposed to the graduate population, but also because it came at a time when the University had little capacity for expanding an already-large arts and sciences faculty; the combination seemed to imply that existing faculty would undertake more undergraduate teaching. Other committee members were not convinced that the admissions pool could carry such an expansion, given the numbers of applications and relatively low yield ratios. If the University began admitting unqualified students, the plan would be disastrous for the College.

The committee functioned as a kind of informal grand jury to examine all facets of Sonnenschein's plan, including a remarkable session with three historians whom they consulted, hoping that the deep past of the University might inform their present concerns and possible conclusions. The historians were understandably leery of being dragged into a partisan debate between the president and a dissenting faction of faculty, with both Neil Harris and Barry Karl cautioning the committee on the complexity of the University's history. As Harris put it, "The University has had, throughout its past, a series of contested presents; it is an institution whose populace lives by myths which, quite frequently, collapse under close examination. Many on the faculty have a sense of the University's history that, while incomplete or inaccurate, nonetheless can prejudice a moment of change-making by contrasting an envisioned future with an unsubstantiated notion of a continuous past tradition." Karl added that "the history of the University [was] a long series of contests among individual members of the faculty, at the instigation of its presidents, over what the institution should be."[47]

The reports and discussions generated by the committee were a fascinating mélange of deeply held convictions about the University's mission and (in the personal view of the author of this book) an underappreciation of the ominous financial trends that Sonnenschein and his team had identified. In the end, in January 1998 the committee presented to the Council of the Senate a carefully crafted report with a number of cautionary concerns that in effect did not oppose the expansion.[48] The committee's report recalled similar debates from the mid-1920s when Ernest Burton first proposed the creation of a fully residential university. Just as Burton had put down a mutiny, thus did Sonnenschein win the battle, but like Burton, "only after great difficulty."[49] What was different in 1996, as opposed to 1925, was that Sonnenschein, Stone, and Furnstahl had publicly exposed chronic financial and developmental trends that, if left unresolved, would have fundamentally weakened the University, whereas Burton had proposed his interventions in a time of fiscal plenty.

While the issue of the size of undergraduate population was being debated among the faculty, in the media, and among the alumni, the College had also embarked on a systematic review of the Core curriculum under the leadership of the author of this book, whom Gray had appointed to the deanship of the College in 1992. The curriculum review was informed by a large survey of student opinion on the quality of life in the College, conducted by sociologist Richard Taub in 1995, which found that significant minorities of students were unhappy with the instructional quality of many of the Core sequences, particularly in mathematics and the natural sciences. A second issue for College leaders was the fact that the 1984–85 reforms, although of fundamental importance in creating a more coherent curriculum for all students, had created a very large Core that pushed many general-education sequences into the third and even the fourth years of undergraduate study. This pattern contradicted the assumptions of the original architects of the Core in the 1930s—namely, that general education should come first, not last, for it prepared younger students for the methods and learning skills necessary for higher-level university work and exposed them to broad areas of knowledge before they were expected to focus on one field of study. The deflection of parts of the Core into the later years of the College made it virtually impossible for students to study abroad in their third year, since many students were forced to spend that year taking yearlong general-education sequences that they had been unable to fulfill or had postponed fulfilling in the first two years of their studies.

Finally, the debates of the mid-1990s reflected increasing strains within the faculty itself about the importance of the Core compared to other elements of the undergraduate curriculum. The generational changes that Bernard Silberman had pointed out in the late 1970s had grown even more acute in the ensuing decades. In 1990 Wayne C. Booth, in his role as chair of the Council on Teaching, complained that "of the total number of students in the arts and sciences . . . more than half are undergraduates, but far less than half of faculty teaching time and energy goes into College teaching," fostering a dependence "on altruism and a dwindling tradition of loyalty" to maintain staffing.[50] Two highly respected faculty members in English wrote to the dean of the College in 1996, urging that the Core be shortened to entail fewer requirements and that more room be made for students to choose their own programs of study. These steps would create "stronger majors . . . that would include more faculty advising and more extracurricular contact between students and faculty," along with "a broader menu of the kinds of classes undergraduates take, ranging from large lectures to intimate junior and senior seminars," and "significantly higher stipends for graduate students coupled with significantly more teaching."[51] Their views were quietly shared by many other faculty across the four divisions. Faculty opinion on the size of the Core in fact was all over the map, with older faculty, particularly those with personal connections to the Hutchins College era, attached to the idea of a large Core, but many younger faculty impatient with what they saw as its virtual domination of the undergraduate experience.

By the fall of 1997, after an intense series of often-contentious debates involving many dozens of faculty members, a plan emerged that would reduce the size of the Core by several courses (from twenty-one to eighteen or even fifteen, depending on how a student met the foreign language requirement), substituting two-quarter Core courses—designated "doublets" by the master of the physical sciences collegiate division at the time, Sidney Nagel—in place of yearlong sequences in the biological sciences, humanities, civilizational studies, and the physical sciences. The plan was intended to allow most students to complete their Core requirements in the first two years of study, while also increasing the number of free electives to allow third- and fourth-year students greater freedom to explore advanced courses taught by regular faculty, both in the departments and in several of the professional schools. The scheme rejected any attempt by the departments to cull more courses to add to their majors, declaring that the current size of the majors would be frozen and thus enlarging the number of electives. Instead of a curriculum dominated by the Core, general education now made up a third of a student's curricular plans, similar to the share of Core courses required by the New Plan curriculum of 1931. The doublet model was structured to allow for more experimentation and the development of new options, thus addressing the problem of frozen-up courses to which Silberman had alluded twenty years earlier. The gamble of the proposal was that the slightly smaller, but more intensively focused and organized general-education curriculum would still serve the original functions of the Core with which Chauncey Boucher had first endowed it in 1930—namely, to recruit students who are more academically oriented and to give them an intense synoptic intellectual experience that would introduce them to the broader scholarly values of the University during their first two years on campus. The fundamental goal was to save the Core by bringing it closer to the size that it had originally enjoyed in the 1930s while opening it up to new intellectual impulses and scholarly movements. Given that Chicago's quarter system functioned, with the heavy workloads imposed by many professors, almost like the semester system at other top colleges, the proponents of the plan believed that there would be no net loss of intellectual "intensity." Indeed, to the extent that the new curriculum would allow students to take a few more advanced or graduate-level courses as free electives, the result might even be a bolstering of the College's famed academic rigor.

At a dramatic meeting of the College Council on March 10, 1998, this plan passed by a 24–8 vote. The new curriculum went into effect in the fall of 1999, with current students choosing by March 1999 whether to conclude their studies under the old (1985) or the new (1999) Core curriculum. About 95 percent opted to join the new curriculum immediately. The vote of March 1998 was legitimate and final, but the outcome did not sit well with some senior faculty, who believed that the central administration had somehow forced the changes in the name of creating a Chicago-lite experience that would enable the admissions office to attract more applicants who would be inclined to work with less rigor in the College. It was perhaps inevitable that both issues—the size of the College's student population and the size and structure of the Core—became flash points for critics, who believed that the present and future seemed to repudiate a hallowed and sacred past. Thanks to the aura of a distantly remembered Hutchins (who had now been absent from campus long enough to be embraced even by those who did not particularly like undergraduates) and the traditions of the Core, Chicago seemed to have a stronger tie to the notion of a shared, cultural patrimony than other universities. The critics who preferred a top-heavy doctoral university, and those who feared that Chicago would recruit the wrong kind of undergraduates in search of money, found common cause in shared anxieties. The impatience of younger faculty with the idea of fixed canonical texts, the desire of many to trim Core requirements, and the appearance of new alternatives (like gender and sexuality studies) appeared to corroborate the threat to the older traditions. The expansion of the College, meanwhile, could be seen as a large-scale acquiescence to the spirit of the times: a campus flooded with young adults who were both incapable of playing the role of scholars-in-waiting to the research faculty and inclined to challenge the authority of professors to guide them in interpreting texts. Sonnenschein would later warn of the dangers of "fear, prejudice and the manipulation of public opinion," but the stuff of such fears was already present in 1996, perhaps explaining the overreactions and intemperate rhetoric from faculty members who felt that the world that they had long cherished was about to crash and burn around them. And, in fairness to the critics who did care about the College, the assumption that the University could suddenly enlarge its application pool in such a short period of time seemed to be extremely risky.

Still, the initial controversy over both reform plans seemed to subside after the spring of 1998. The Year of Reflection committee had run its course in a final presentation to the Council of the Senate in early March 1998, and a week later the College Council approved the new Core curriculum.[52] The civic universe at Chicago seemed likely to return to a semblance of decentralized normality, filled with searches for new faculty appointments, plans for more great books and research conferences, and congeries of local-political rivalries and collaborations in the departments like those at most American research universities. But later that year, in late December, an event occurred that brought massive levels of apprehension back into play. A new vice president for public relations at the University, Al Chambers, had contacted the New York Times in November about a possible article on the recent changes on the campus. The *Times*'s national education correspondent, Ethan Bronner, became interested and decided to write an article.[53] Bronner's story, based on selective interviews with several administrators and faculty members, was a shrewdly written account of the changes in play, but Bronner framed them as if the University were in desperate straits and in a kind of survival mode.[54] The new vice president for College enrollment, Michael Behnke, was quoted as saying, "I don't know how many students we can attract if we go after those who only seek the life of the mind. . . . Kids aren't sure that they can lead a balanced life here. My job is to convince them that they are not joining a monastery." Behnke's quip would have been fully accepted in private and public conversations on campus—earlier admissions officers and staff in the dean of students office had been saying the same thing for decades. But appearing on the front page of the *New York Times*, such a comment could easily be manipulated to prove that the University was intending to make the College less rigorous and to be a more popular choice, and that this larger college would weaken the intellectual environs and standards of the wider university. One subheading even asserted that the University was "adjusting a curriculum for students who are also consumers."

The article quickly turned into a public relations disaster, empowering small but well-organized interests to attack both the College's curricular changes and the University's plans for expanding the size of the undergraduate population. One particularly ill-informed screed by the National Association of Scholars published in the *Wall Street Journal* alleged that Chicago had already abandoned its traditional dedication to the History of Western Civilization course in the name of "trendy razzmatazz" involving feminism and gender studies, and that the latest changes were a sign that "the administration has done far more than acquiesce; over the past decade it has eagerly recruited such left-wing celebrity academics as Martha Nussbaum, Homi Bhabha, and Catherine MacKinnon."[55] Two prominent department chairs, Elizabeth Helsinger of the Department of English and Kathleen Conzen of the Department of History, replied in an eloquent, measured letter, citing the need for curricular renewal and reform, stating that such changes were both necessary and healthy for any institution of higher learning, and arguing that the recent revisions to the curriculum were signs of Chicago's "intense intellectualism and the energetic re-envisioning of its programs." Another letter, drafted anonymously but signed by ten prominent conservative intellectuals, including Walter Berns, Seth Benardete, and Gertrude Himmelfarb, warned the trustees that "changing the curriculum to attract less intellectual students jeopardizes the moral core of a great university. Making academic decisions on the basis of marketing is itself a crime against the mind." The letter went on to invoke Robert Maynard Hutchins's warning that great universities should not lose their souls in the pursuit of money.[56]

The logic of such interventions was all the more ironic, given that Hutchins's cavalier attitude about university finances was the source of many of the chronic financial problems with which later presidents of the University had had to cope. The situation quickly became a slugfest of accusations, rumors, and wild allegations among small groups of highly vocal alumni who protested the alleged dumbing down of the College and its putative exploitation by the larger university for crass financial reasons. Reacting to what they felt to be negative and embarrassing images of the University now filling the press, but also sensing that recent events had opened yet another chance to stop the expansion of the College, a group of senior faculty drafted a letter of protest to the board of trustees in February 1999, stating that "the plans of the present administration to change the image and the substance of the university are alienating faculty, students, and alumni alike. The idea that the University of Chicago is abandoning its distinctive intellectual values is spreading among our academic colleagues around the country, indeed around the world." The provost, Geoffrey Stone, responded to the draft with a point-by-point rebuttal, arguing that it was filled with "serious misstatements and half-truths that fall far below the standards of discourse at this University."[57]

To address the crescendo of rumors and fears, the College bound three monographs on the history of the University authored by the dean of the College into one volume, entitled *Three Views of Continuity and Change*, and mailed it in March 1999 to thousands of alumni households. The book explained that the changes to the curriculum and the efforts to increase the size of the College were compatible with earlier policy developments and intellectual traditions in the history of the University, and that both decisions were intended not to violate university traditions but to strengthen them. Yet paperback history books sent by the dean via first-class mail were no match for misinformation and rumors traveling via e-mail.[58] Hot-button curricular issues took on a life of their own with a suddenness that was unprecedented in the history of the University's curricular struggles, most of which had been conducted quietly, out of the view of the alumni and even the student body at the time. Sonnenschein and other administrative leaders were accused of "cutting the Core," when, in fact, no one in the central administration had had any significant role in the final decisions voted in March 1998 about the future of the Core curriculum, which were laboriously worked through by the College's faculty in dozens of politically charged meetings between 1996 and 1998.[59]

Ultimately, the board of trustees closed the debate by announcing that the expansion of the College would go forward. Whereas student and alumni protests were seen as short-term problems based on misunderstandings that would soon dissipate, the unhappiness of senior faculty was taken more seriously. At the same time, the board had become convinced that the University faced dire consequences without radical changes in the size and makeup of the College. That these changes were proposed in the late 1990s in a time of rapid economic growth for the city of Chicago and a booming housing market in Hyde Park also gave the board confidence that the University was now working with the market and the city, rather than against them, and that the city's bright future under the leadership of Mayor Richard M. Daley made it possible for the University of Chicago to become a nationally competitive "school of choice" both politically and culturally. The whole episode, with its combination of hysteria among alumni, dyspeptic fears among senior faculty, and ad hominem rhetoric, revealed the complexity of instituting major structural changes at a research university—even one like Chicago, which had always touted its openness to innovation—when fundamental issues of identity were seen to be at stake.

Outside commentators offered widely different appraisals of the controversies. David Kirp of Berkeley, writing in April 2001, was perhaps the shrewdest when he observed that Sonnenschein's emphasis on the urgent need for financial viability was bound to run up against faculty fears, especially on the part of faculty who were longtime residents of the University, who had a particularly close affiliation with the (historically discordant) images of the University as *either* a post-1960s PhD imperium *or* the organic descendant of the values of Robert Maynard Hutchins, and who worried that the frank and open pursuit of financial solvency would dilute the intellectual culture of the institution. Kirp wisely predicted that only time would tell which view would end up on the right side of history.[60]

In the end, the wisdom of Sonnenschein's decisions bore itself out, and the fears about the degradation of the College and its applicant pool proved groundless. Indeed, the opposite happened: the academic preparation and intellectual quality of both the applicant and matriculation pools increased as the number of students applying to the College grew enormously. But it would take years of deliberate implementation before most came to accept the fact that the University had not abandoned its niche intellectualist identity by becoming "like everybody else."[61] In the case of complex institutions like the great private universities, dominated by tenured faculty who cherish the status quo rather than rapid innovations, such readjustments are not simple. If anyone should be "blamed" or "praised" in all of this, perhaps it was Lawrence Kimpton, who understood better than anyone (and said so publicly on many occasions) that the University of Chicago needed a large, thriving undergraduate college to sustain itself financially over time.

The Sonnenschein years also saw significant improvements in the University's fund-raising and alumni relations capacities. When Sonnenschein assumed office in 1993, about $290 million of the centennial campaign's $500 million goal had been raised. Both Sonnenschein and Stone were particularly engaged fund-raisers and sought to infuse more dynamism into the University's development operations.[62] They also sought to step up the involvement of unit deans in the campaign by allowing them to retain the new revenue that they were able to raise via gifts up to $250,000.[63] In February 1995, in a debate filled with expressions of their sense of their own obligations and regrets about the missed opportunities that the University had endured in the past, the trustees reversed their earlier hesitations and voted to raise the campaign target to $650 million. By mid-1996 the campaign had brought in $676 million.

Hugo Sonnenschein sought to compel the faculty to confront unpleasant realities and to drive fundamental change, and he did so with a directness that provoked controversy. But his administration and the Gray administration shared basic strategic goals and mission-oriented values. Just as the Kimpton-Levi years have to be seen as one historic period, the Gray-Sonnenschein years also constitute an integrated historic period of substantial transformation and strengthening of the University. Each president's leadership style differed. Gray never ignored the big financial picture at moments of crisis, but the discussions about raising new revenues, increasing enrollments, controlling costs, and planning for new expenditures took place at a deep, granular level. As a leader, she grappled with the complexity of decisions and carefully evaluated what seemed possible and what was not. Toward the end of her presidency, she too was faced with the need to consider more fundamental, structural changes to enhance the University's budget base and to make possible more renewal and replacement of the physical plant. Sonnenschein was new to the University, and profoundly influenced by a sense that he had been asked to lead a great institution that still suffered from a weak competitive position with roots in the late 1940s. Some critics believed that the money was Sonnenschein's *only* agenda and that he cared only about financial issues, but this analysis is simplistic and unfair. It would be more accurate to say that precisely because he was an outsider, Sonnenschein found himself confronting congeries of financial, investment, and development problems that had plagued the University since the final years of the Hutchins regime and were now merging into a perfect storm of *structural* disadvantages that would weaken Chicago vis-à-vis its peers. Facing what he perceived to be a genuine crisis, Sonnenschein had to do something to preserve the special academic mission and intellectual-ist values the University had cherished for so long. He often framed the question by challenging trustees and faculty to imagine how they would ensure that the second hundred years of the University's history would be as fine as its first hundred.

Both presidencies were transformative. By the end of her adminis-tration, Hanna Gray had added almost as many students to the College (2,600 to 3,400) as Hugo Sonnenschein proposed to do in 1996 (3,500 to 4,500). Gray also began the work of slashing unnecessary adminis-trative costs and improving fund-raising and development, which were Sonnenschein's goals as well. Both leaders sought to make the campus a more attractive and livable place; both had exceedingly high standards for new faculty appointments, believing that the luster of the University depended above all on the scholarly distinction of its senior faculty; both were staunch defenders of Chicago's traditions of academic freedom; and both were seriously concerned with improving the welfare and experi-ence of students. In this light, Gray's strategic interventions set the stage for the more radical reforms of the late 1990s and early 2000s in a way that was appropriate to the late 1970s and 1980s. Kimpton had wanted a Col-lege of 5,000 almost by fiat and divine providence, and this simply did not work. It would have been impossible for Sonnenschein to have called for the expanded College in 1996 without the careful and highly efficacious work that was done by Gray between 1978 and 1993. If his reforms were still almost unthinkable to many skeptics in 1996, they were much more possible than in 1977 because of Gray's work.

Perhaps most significant, the changes in the College initiated by Gray and Sonnenschein, together with the growing prominence of the profes-sional schools described below, made it possible for Chicago to join with other top private universities in preserving the fiscal capacity for future progress despite the slow decline in federal funding during the 1970s and 1980s, which was followed by an even more radical decline in state fund-ing for public universities in the 1990s and 2000s.[64] The doctorate-heavy American research university of the 1950s and 1960s, deriving much of its support from federal and state funding and from major private foun-dation gifts, became increasingly difficult to sustain after 1980. But be-cause of the onset of the high-tuition-increases/need-based-aid model, massive private philanthropy, and continuing levels of massive federal support in the biomedical, physical-mathematical, and computational sciences and engineering, the elite private universities recalibrated the earlier model and continued to excel.[65] These schools created a new mix of resources — including steeply rising levels of unrestricted revenue from their undergraduate colleges and their professional schools and alumni gifts—that helped them fulfill and even enhance their ambitions. But after 2000, with the slowing growth in median incomes of American families, shifts in public opinion about cost of attendance and student debt, and the massive decline in state funding for public universities, it became difficult for many institutions to sustain both the aspirations for eminence in doctoral research and the earlier practices of the pre-1940 teaching institutions.[66] Roger Geiger has recently argued that "one of the salient characteristics of the current era has been the growing differentiation of the selective sector from the rest of American higher education."[67] Had Chicago not undertaken the demographic changes initiated by Gray and Sonnenschein in the 1980s and 1990s, with their long-term philanthropic consequences and with the corresponding success of the College after 2000 in becoming a school of first choice for most of its students, the University's reputation for top-ranked scholarship and desirability for the most qualified students, undergraduate as well as doctoral, would have been severely undermined.

TRANSITIONS IN LEADERSHIP AND STUDENT LIFE AFTER 2000

In early June 1999 Hugo Sonnenschein announced his intention to resign the presidency in mid-2000. At the time a small and vocal minority of faculty were actively unhappy with the policy directions Sonnenschein had outlined, but the majority realized that the University had no realistic alternative than to move forward with these plans, even if many were uncertain as to how successfully they could be executed. The board of trustees elected Don Michael Randel as the University's twelfth president in December 1999. Randel was a prominent senior musicologist at Cornell University, where he had served with distinction as dean of the College of Arts and Sciences and as provost. Randel served until July 2006, when he left Chicago to become president of the Andrew W. Mellon Foundation. Randel's tenure was marked by increased support for the arts on campus, stronger efforts to create effective lines of communication with civic and business leaders in the city, investments in major campus facilities, and the launch of a new $2 billion capital campaign. Randel provided thoughtful, highly reflective leadership of the University in a time of substantial institutional change. He was succeeded in mid-2006 by Robert J. Zimmer, a distinguished mathematician who had first joined the faculty of Chicago as a Dickson Instructor of Mathematics in 1977. He had served as associate provost for education and research from 1995 to 1998, as deputy provost for research from 1998 to 2000, and vice president for research and for the

Argonne National Laboratory from 2000 until 2002, when he left to become provost of Brown University. Zimmer's return to Chicago brought a leader of prodigious energy, vision, and visceral impatience with status quo thinking.

The Sonnenschein administration had anticipated in 1996 that College enrollments would increase from approximately 3,500 to 4,500 over a ten-year period. At the end of Sonnenschein's tenure in mid-2000, undergraduate enrollments had grown to about 4,000 students. In the years that followed, the leaders of the College, in concert with Provosts Richard Saller and Thomas Rosenbaum and Presidents Don Randel and Robert Zimmer, decided to take Sonnenschein's plans further. By the autumn quarter of 2013, the College at Chicago had a full-time population of 5,700 undergraduate students, an increase of nearly 63 percent over its size in 1992.

This strategy was driven by four exigencies. First, the College believed that Lawrence Kimpton had been right in aiming for an undergraduate population of 5,000 to 6,000 students, since it aligned more closely with the Ivy Plus schools with which Chicago aggressively competed for the most distinguished scholars and students in the arts and sciences. Columbia University, for example, had 6,100 undergraduates; Harvard University, 6,500; Stanford University, 7,000; and Yale University, 5,400 (with plans to increase to 6,200 by 2017). Only thus could the University have the necessary resources to maintain the large and distinguished arts and sciences faculty that the Greenstone report and many other commentators had highlighted as characteristic of Chicago. Yale, the alma mater of both William Rainey Harper and Robert M. Hutchins and the school from which Hanna H. Gray had come to Chicago, seemed to constitute a particularly appealing demographic model of an outstanding, midsize liberal arts college set in the midst of a distinguished research university with rigorous scholarly traditions.

A second reason for pushing forward with this strategy was the hope that an on-campus college population of 5,000 or more would help enormously in creating a more vibrant, self-starting milieu of student life—the complex matrix of student clubs, organizations, causes, initiatives, and even occasional protests—that would give Chicago a more appealing ambient social culture for academically gifted younger students and help to remedy the sense of college students as constituting a kind of marginal population within a graduate-heavy campus. An in-depth study of the College's attrition problem by Jeffrey S. Slovak in late 1997 had highlighted the importance of the density of campus organizational activity and involvement as a key to successful retention, noting,

Over approximately the last decade and a half, the size of the College has grown by about one-third. Many observers believe that this growth helped to create a critical mass of undergraduates who were ready and willing to participate in extracurricular activities and who, by that participation, have created a richer, more collegiate orientation at the University. Over the next decade the College is slated to grow by another third.... It would behoove us to be on the lookout for ways and means to encourage the further development and elaboration of student organizational life as it occurs.[68]

Slovak's report proved very influential in developing the strategy for student-life issues that was articulated after 2000.

Third, a larger undergraduate student body would provide the means to move forward in a number of areas, including long-overdue reforms in the financing of doctoral education (the Graduate Aid Initiative described below), new instructional programs, and new housing. Sweeping improvements in campus housing—the construction of new and attractive residential facilities on campus and the elimination of the older, substandard off-campus halls—would require significantly more students than the original target of 4,500. And finally, from a political perspective, it seemed a mistake to struggle toward the 4,500 threshold, as if this was all that the University could accomplish, even as its top competitors easily sustained undergraduate colleges that were significantly larger. To inch up to the target of 4,500 and stop would have been the equivalent of Patton's forces exploiting the Avranches breakthrough in Normandy and then stopping halfway to Paris. The goal was to reach Paris.

To reach a target of 5,000 or more, it would be critical to enlarge the applicant pool while reassuring the faculty that student quality was increasing, not decreasing. Many of the earlier apprehensions about a larger undergraduate population focused on the worry that the University was stuck in a scenario in which only a small number of "self-selected" students wanted to come to Chicago. This assumption was misleading, given the high attrition rates among these "self-selected" students after they arrived in Hyde Park.

To address these concerns, the College launched several interventions. First, Michael Behnke, the dean of admissions at MIT, was appointed vice president for College enrollment at Chicago in 1997. Behnke was able to break the cycle of high-acceptance and low-yield rates that had plagued the College since the 1950s and to undermine the assumption that "self-selection" necessarily translated into fatefully small, encumbered numbers of applicants. Behnke bluntly insisted that the University had become a backup school for many students: "In admitting between sixty and seventy percent of the applicants in recent years, the College has brought in a number of students for whom it was their third or fourth choice. These students are not likely to have looked as carefully at Chicago as those to whom the faculty point as 'self-selecting' Chicago. They, in turn, contribute to the College's relatively high attrition rate."[69] Behnke increased applications from 5,522 to 12,397 and reduced the admissions rate from 61 percent to 28 percent. Yield rates increased from 30 percent to 38 percent. Upon Behnke's retirement in 2009, James Nondorf of Rensselaer Polytechnic Institute and Yale dramatically revitalized admissions by deploying a series of imaginative communications strategies, and by the fall of 2012 Chicago experienced a huge increase in interest from academically qualified students across the nation. The results were not only a stunning uptick in inquiries and applications, with more than 30,000 applications in 2013, but a pronounced increase in the yield rate for admitted students (60 percent in 2014) and a substantial increase in the academic quality of the matriculation pool as measured by SAT scores (see figs. 2 and 3).

Over time, these trends, which transformed Chicago into a school of first choice, led to significant improvements in student retention as well: the College's freshman retention rate was 90 percent in 1994, but had

FIG. 2. Comparative applications to Chicago and peer institutions, 1972–2013

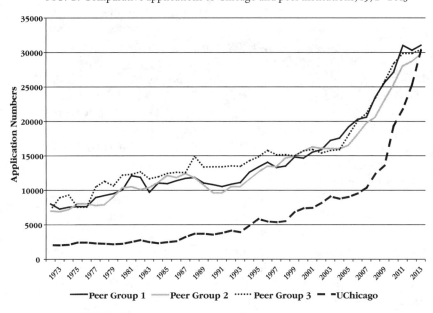

Source: Office of Admissions, University of Chicago.

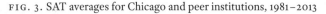

FIG. 3. SAT averages for Chicago and peer institutions, 1981–2013

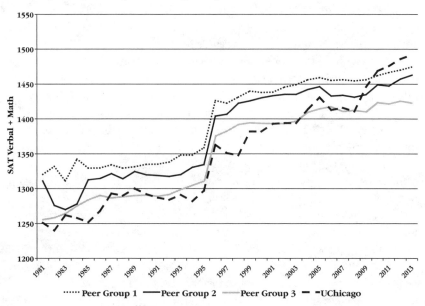

Source: *Office of Admissions, University of Chicago.*

increased to almost 99 percent by 2012. Second, the College sought to adopt a series of new interventions to address problems of campus climate and student life. In May 1996 a faculty committee chaired by Susan Kidwell had called attention to a host of problems that hindered a positive sense of belonging and personal success among College students.[70] Kidwell's report drew on the results of the earlier survey on the quality of campus life undertaken by Richard Taub, which found that as many as 35 percent of current students had given serious thought to leaving the College at one time or another, as well as on many qualitative interviews with current students and staff. The findings of the Kidwell and Taub reports underscored the need to create a more supportive and friendly campus environment while preserving the highly intellectual nature of Chicago student culture. The idea was not to change or weaken that culture but to surround and infuse it with a much more student-friendly set of interventions and institutions, on the assumption that what would be most distinctive about Chicago graduates in the future would be their genuine intellectualism, their love of the University and its community, and their commitment to their own and their fellow students' personal and professional success during and after college.

To that end the University invested large sums of money to construct new facilities, including a transformed student center in the Reynolds Club and a major new athletic center and swimming pool named in honor of alumnus Gerald Ratner. Most significant, two new residential facilities were constructed, the Palevsky Residential Commons on land surrounding Regenstein Library and a second new residential commons south of Burton Judson Hall, named in honor of an alumna of the College, Renee Granville-Grossman. Ground has since been broken for a third large residential complex of eight hundred beds in place of Pierce Tower on Fifty-Fifth Street, and a fourth residential commons is likely to emerge on the eastern side of the south campus. These new halls were not simply dormitories but sites for the endless conversations about academic issues and intellectual controversies that have traditionally fascinated and engaged Chicago students beyond the classroom. Equally important, the College set as a firm goal the desire to house at least 70 percent of its students in new, well-designed, and well-equipped residence halls that would be located on or adjoining the central campus. These residences would strengthen student engagement with the physical campus and deepen social ties and friendships among students during their entire time at Chicago; they would also foster a new sense of loyalty and support among alumni communities. This decision was a direct repudiation of the University's earlier strategy of acquiring older properties off campus to house students, which had turned masses of College students into de facto commuters.

Responding to the criticisms articulated in the Kidwell report and in many alumni polls about the inadequacies of the University's career services, beginning in the late 1990s the College focused on creating robust career planning and advising programs and internship opportunities. Over the next fifteen years Chicago developed one of the most coherent and ambitious sets of programs in career planning for undergraduate students in the United States, not only investing heavily in internships and mentoring programs but also engaging alumni and faculty from across the University (including the professional schools) to help students think about and prepare themselves to fulfill their professional ambitions.

Another major site of innovation was the College's new international programs. For reasons of financial expediency the University was slow to acknowledge the educational legitimacy of study-abroad programs, even as other US universities were aggressively entering the domain of international education in the 1970s and 1980s. Many faculty believed that the University of Chicago was the greatest institution of higher learning in the Western world, and that students would be crazy not to spend all four years in Hyde Park. Beginning in the mid-1990s key groups of younger faculty in the humanities and social sciences argued for a radically different approach that emphasized the intrinsic value of in situ cross-cultural learning. Within a decade, the College would go from having no international programs to possessing a rich palette of faculty-taught programs in major cities around the world. The idea was simple: for many decades the College had taught its famous History of Western Civilization course in an intensive, total immersion format during the summer quarter. Why not deploy the same format during the regular academic year and offer Western Civilization, together with an intensive course in the local language, in a series of major historic European cities to groups of twenty-five students taught by three regular members of the faculty?

The program began with one-quarter intensive experiments in Barcelona and Tours, and soon expanded to encompass Athens, Paris, Rome, and Vienna. Students and faculty found the new courses highly appealing, and soon the concept spread to places outside of Europe, including Jerusalem, Cairo, Istanbul, Cape Town, Pune, Beijing, Hong Kong, and Oaxaca. As a way of strengthening the College's capacity to provide high-level international educational opportunities to still more students, plans were also developed to establish a new permanent center in Paris. Funded largely by gifts from College alumni and located in the midst of the massive Paris Rive Gauche urban renewal project in the thirteenth arrondissement, two city blocks from the new National Library, the Paris Center celebrated its opening in 2004. The center grew rapidly and offered a series of intensive courses in the humanities, social sciences, and natural sciences, and by 2012 almost 250 College students, along with a dozen or so doctoral students, were studying in France each year, the largest overseas population of the entire University.

The new international strategy of the College also included large numbers of direct study grants and research fellowships to permit Chicago undergraduates to undertake research and foreign-language training abroad; these qualities made the program a valuable tool for the admissions office, which presented the College's venerable educational programs as grounded in tradition but also open to rapid and flexible change, in ways that intellectually serious high school seniors found attractive. The success of the Paris Center served, in turn, as a model and precedent for other recent university initiatives abroad, including the creation of new international centers in Beijing and Delhi. And, to bring this story back to the "crisis" of the late 1990s, if the Core curriculum had not been shortened to permit third-year students to study abroad, the international programs and centers would not have been plausible or perhaps even possible.

Finally, the increase in the size of the undergraduate population had to be accompanied by an expansion in faculty. The University authorized the hiring of twenty-two new tenure-track assistant professors, as well as many new senior lecturers and full-time lecturers, positions held by PhDs who were distinguished teachers and in many cases active scholars. The two-year Harper Fellow program of the 1970s was expanded to a four-year program, with almost forty postdoctoral Fellows appointed as collegiate assistant professors at salaries closely pegged to those of beginning tenure-track faculty in the humanities and social sciences nationally. This transformation itself became the subject of local controversy, also in 1999, since it gave official faculty status to the Harper Fellows. But the research prowess of the new professors, the high quality of their scholarship and teaching, and their natural inclination to join the graduate workshop program along with the regular tenure-track faculty quelled any criticism.

By 2012 the size and academic strength of the College's applicant pool had dramatically improved, the University's reputation was much more attractive to prospective applicants and their families, students were more satisfied with their educational and social experiences, and the undergraduate student body reached a more competitive size of 5,700 students. The attractiveness of the College also led to enhanced visibility for many of Chicago's doctoral and professional programs, since many of the leading applicants to the graduate divisions and professional schools had applied four or five years earlier to the College and been the subject of intense cultivation.

The Evolution of Postgraduate Study

GRADUATE STUDIES AFTER THE GOLDEN AGE

Before 1940, undergraduate degrees in the arts and sciences significantly outnumbered graduate degrees at Chicago. Between 1918 and 1931 the University awarded 11,088 BA degrees, 4,409 MA degrees, and 1,616 PhD degrees.[71] This pattern continued in the 1930s: in 1933–34, for example, the four divisions and the College graduated 736 BAs, 248 MAs, and 145 PhDs. Twenty years later, the ratios had almost reversed: in 1954–55 the University awarded 324 BAs, 399 MAs, and 221 PhDs. In part this reversal reflected the radical decline in College enrollments discussed in chapter 5. But it also reflected an absolute and relative expansion of graduate education after 1945 that had many streams and causes, some local, others national. In the 1950s, Lawrence Kimpton had viewed the expansion of graduate education as a way to counteract the decline of undergraduate enrollment, given that graduate students were routinely expected to finance much of their own studies and were thus a source of net tuition revenue.[72]

In this strategy Chicago was following national trends: between 1950

and 1958, the top twelve research universities increased doctoral enrollments by nearly 40 percent, and PhD production at the same schools
more than doubled. In the wake of Sputnik, the early and mid-1960s became a golden age of graduate study, as new federal and private fellowship and scholarship resources became available.[73] The annual number
of doctorates in the United States had gone from 6,000 in 1950 to 10,000
in 1960, increasing to almost 30,000 by 1970.[74] The early 1970s saw the
historical zenith of numbers of PhDs granted at the University of Chicago,
as the number of doctorates awarded annually went from 258 doctorates
in 1960–65 to 444 doctorates annually in 1970–75, before sinking back to
an average of 337 in 1980–85 and 349 in 1990–95. The largest number of
PhDs was awarded in 1972 (477), which constituted an 83 percent increase
over 1962 (261).

Enrollment trends, as opposed to degrees, began to sink in the 1970s,
when applications and matriculations in the four graduate divisions began
to decline, reaching a low point in 1981: the number of degree candidates
for graduate degrees in the divisions was 37 percent smaller in 1981 than in
1968.[75] Even with the short-term crisis of the early 1980s, the prominence
of graduate and particularly doctoral programs remained central to the
identity of the faculty who joined Chicago in the 1960s and 1970s, and in
many years the total number of graduate (MA and PhD) degrees awarded
in the arts and sciences continued to exceed undergraduate degrees until
the early 2000s. Well into the new century Chicago had more registered
graduate students in the humanities and social sciences than any of its
private peers.[76] In the natural and mathematical sciences, in contrast,
Chicago's enrollments were at the lower end of the mean of other top
private universities.

Traditionally, Chicago had fewer resources for financial aid for doctoral
students than its peers, a point acknowledged by the Bradburn committee
in 1979: "It is clear that Chicago ranks low compared with other universities in the amount of unrestricted university aid it has offered to graduate
students."[77] The Baker Commission found in 1982 that "graduate students
at Chicago pay a larger proportion of average financial requirements from
personal and loan funds than do graduate students at most other private
universities."[78] This gap in financial aid led to two trends. First, in order
to provide some level of in-house funding for at least some doctoral students, and as a necessary device to bolster university revenues more generally, the University continued to urge departments to admit substantial
numbers of unfunded or underfunded students. During the 1960s new
sources of outside fellowship support became available from the federal
government and from private sources such as the Ford Foundation, the
Woodrow Wilson Foundation, and the Danforth Foundation, but even in

those years large numbers of unfunded graduate students were admitted to the various doctoral programs. In the early 1970s, once federal grants and private support from Ford and others began to dry up, the funding situation became even more problematic.[79] Aristide Zolberg of the Department of Political Science estimated that by 1982, 30 to 40 percent of social science graduate students at Chicago were admitted without aid: "Large numbers of mediocre students were admitted because their tuition money was necessary for institutional survival."[80] Nor did Chicago and most of its peers revise their burgeoning graduate programs to reduce attrition and increase completion rates. Roger Geiger has argued that much of the money spent to improve and restructure doctoral programs in the 1960s had little positive impact, since university faculties resisted changes that would improve time to degree, the end result being that the leaders of the Ford Foundation, who had hoped to increase completion rates and force programs to become more efficient, "later complained that the universities had not embraced the goals of the program but had cynically taken the money as a form of general support."[81]

But the inflow of large entering graduate classes also had a second, equally powerful consequence in that as faculty members in the 1950s and 1960s became accustomed to having large graduate cohorts and (with the decline of undergraduate enrollments) limited responsibilities in the undergraduate College, they began to define their professional responsibilities and identities in the context of their doctoral programs. This led some departments to adopt what one colleague in the history department characterized in 1978 as a "collective image of itself as a graduate research center."[82] Even though departmental majors in the College were reconstituted in the mid- and late 1950s, the total enrollments in the College had collapsed to the point that in many departments the numbers of in-resident doctoral students in the first three years of graduate study (generally, the period in which such students were taking formal coursework) often exceeded the number of college majors. For example, in 1974 the Department of History had twenty-seven history majors writing senior papers, but in the same year it admitted an entering class of seventy-five doctoral students (and had also admitted eighty-one the year before). Given the College's traditional focus on Core courses, and the natural affinity that departmental faculty had toward teaching their (now well-populated) graduate classes, the history major threatened to become a "sizable no-man's land" without faculty support or curricular coherence.[83] History's experience may have been typical of other large departments, with some juniors and seniors experiencing a liminal status as academic lost souls. President John Wilson complained with considerable candor in 1978 that "too many of our concentration offerings appear to be perfunctory in design and execution and reflect little discernible evidence of well-thought-out educational purposes."[84] Equally noteworthy, the claims of senior faculty that Chicago was now (and should remain) largely a graduate university were bound to harm prospects of enlarging the size and deepening the quality of the College's applicant pool, for they reinforced the image of the University as "an institution dedicated wholly to graduate and professional training, with a few hardy undergraduates tagging along."[85]

One of the most significant developments in the history of graduate education at Chicago took place in 1980 and 1981. Graduate enrollments had mushroomed during the 1960s, and the faculty quickly became accustomed to this state of affairs. When in the aftermath of the Vietnam War graduate applications and enrollments began to drop in the mid- and late 1970s (a decrease that all top research universities faced but that was particularly acute at Chicago), a sense of crisis emerged, with genuine fears that, as colleagues in the Department of Anthropology put it, "symptoms of a general malaise in graduate education" would have a profound, negative impact on the stature and culture of the University.[86] These anxieties were short-lived—graduate enrollments recovered somewhat in the later 1980s at all top US graduate schools, and the annual number of PhDs at Chicago regained healthy levels in the 1990s—but the fears were real and deeply felt nonetheless.

In May 1980 President Gray appointed a high-level faculty committee, chaired by Keith M. Baker, to investigate the causes of the decline and to recommend possible responses to improve the attractiveness and effectiveness of the graduate programs. The Baker Commission undertook a searching, candid, and comprehensive study of graduate education at Chicago. It discovered several trends, including the fact that "overall, doctoral students at the University of Chicago tend to be among the slowest to receive their degree," compared with students at ten peer institutions, and identified negative features of the graduate-student environment, such as failure of faculty to evaluate student work in a timely way, students' feelings of isolation from the faculty, and high attrition rates.[87] The commission formulated new strategies for graduate recruitment and new funding mechanisms to provide more competitive doctoral fellowships. The commission also recommended that university-wide registration requirements be divorced from the actual programs of instruction designed by the individual departments, creating a common system of registration under which all graduate students would work. A new system of residence would help students progress toward their degrees in more efficient and transparent ways. The commission also proposed that the formal course work requirement for the doctorate be reduced from twenty-seven to

eighteen courses. The commission's most controversial proposal, however, was that the University create a new postdepartmental structure for
the humanities and the social sciences—a research institute—into which
doctoral students would move after they had completed formal course
work in their departments. The institute would then supervise and mentor
the PhD students during their dissertation writing and support a system
of workshops in which advanced students could present their dissertation
chapters for feedback and support.

The idea of the research institute was quite radical and became the
subject of intense discussions within the commission itself. Had it been
implemented it might have had a powerful impact both on the broader
structures of graduate-student identity and on faculty governance at the
University. Perhaps understandably, neither the graduate divisions nor
the individual departments showed much enthusiasm for the idea of a
supradivisional research institute, and some departments, particularly
in the social sciences, reacted strongly against it. The idea died quietly,
without the public Sturm und Drang that Hutchins had engendered in
his attempt to monkey with the structures of graduate education in 1944.

One of the commission's innovations that did gain acceptance was the
new system of registration.[88] The new system created a two-year unit of
scholastic residence, followed by a second two-year unit of research residence and then a third unit of advanced residence, with tuition charges
decreasing with each change of status. The system was designed to eliminate the problem faced by hundreds of "ghost" graduate students who
were unregistered after their third year because their financial support
(and tuition charges) had ended with their course requirements. Although
the new system required much debate, given the great variety of existing
departmental requirements, it eventually passed the Council of the Senate
in April 1984 with strong support across the divisions.[89]

Another idea championed by the commission was a series of new graduate workshops in the humanities and social sciences designed to foster
greater intellectual and social support for advanced graduate students
writing their dissertations. The idea for the workshops first emerged at
Chicago in the economics department in the late 1940s, and in the early
1960s it spread to the Business School as well.[90] The workshop program
was created in 1983–84 and overseen by a standing committee named
the Council on Advanced Studies in the Humanities and Social Sciences,
which was drawn from faculty in the humanities, social sciences, and the
Divinity School. The workshop program grew rapidly, and as of 2012 there
were more than five dozen workshops each year involving hundreds of
faculty members and doctoral students. The workshops proved politically palatable and worked well within the extant governance structures

precisely because they did not challenge or infringe on the control of the individual departmental doctoral programs of their graduate students.[91] The program was voluntary: teams of faculty members were invited to apply for support on behalf of discrete groups of graduate-student dissertation writers. The workshops were gradually embraced by most of the departments in the humanities and the social sciences, and some even cut across traditional disciplinary boundaries. In many cases the workshops became vehicles for mentoring and professionalizing doctoral students within their existing graduate programs, going beyond simply providing moral support for nervous dissertation writers to becoming a testing ground for new and often controversial ideas and a training ground for public speaking and conference presentation skills. To the extent that Chicago graduate students gained a reputation for their poise at scholarly conferences, the workshops played a role in enhancing their self-confidence without stoking the departmental fears and paranoia that had doomed the idea of a research institute. Perhaps most important, the workshops helped to establish less formal means of communication between faculty and graduate students, moving closer to the kinds of egalitarian cultural practices that already obtained in smaller interdisciplinary graduate programs like the Committee on Human Development.

Yet these attempts to enrich the educational opportunities of doctoral students did not fully address the basic issues raised by Robert Hutchins in 1930 and 1944. Although the University had put in place mechanisms to help advanced doctoral students prepare themselves as young researcher-scholars, little was done to help students become collegiate teachers, even though most Chicago PhDs spent much of their professional career in predominantly teaching institutions. The Baker Commission estimated that 82 percent of the students who received a PhD in 1970–71 went on to jobs involving teaching and research at the college and university level.[92] Data on PhD employment placement are scarce for the decades before 2000 (and not only at Chicago), but a detailed study of doctoral recipients between 1998 and 2000 estimated that only about 5 percent of students who earned PhDs at Chicago immediately found tenure-track jobs in the top departments in their field; within two years of obtaining the degree, a majority of students in the biological sciences (54.9 percent), the humanities (69 percent), the physical sciences (70.4 percent), and the social sciences (59.6 percent) were lodged in academic positions or postdocs, while the minority pursued nonprofit work outside the academy or worked in for-profit industries.[93] More recent data show that almost 85 percent of those awarded PhDs in the humanities between 1997 and 2012 took academic positions, indicating that the vast majority of Chicago's doctoral students in the humanities (and likely social sciences) seek academic teaching and research careers. A breakdown of the institutions where they teach is instructive: over 80 percent of those in tenure-track appointments teach in liberal arts colleges or in universities where undergraduate teaching will be the major component of their everyday professional responsibilities, as opposed to top-ranked research universities.[94]

The Baker Commission's report in 1982 renewed the call to prepare graduate students for careers as teachers. The small size of the College in the 1960s and 1970s had made it unnecessary to use graduate students in instructional positions, but the growth in the College since the late 1990s expanded the range of meaningful teaching opportunities for advanced doctoral students. The larger issue of the way in which Chicago prepared its graduate students for their professional careers as teachers, however, was addressed only in ad hoc and often idiosyncratic ways. The University created a Center for Teaching and Learning in the late 1990s that, with a modest budget and a dedicated but small staff, created some helpful mentoring and training programs. Individual Core staffs in the College organized mentoring and apprentice programs to help introduce doctoral students to the concepts and practices of general-education teaching. In the domain of writing instruction, Chicago developed a particularly innovative program, the Little Red Schoolhouse, which with its core principles focusing on the questions and expectations of readers has had an outsize impact on the graduate and undergraduate students who have participated in its training programs. Since the 1990s a few departments also took formal steps to create structured programs of serious teaching preparation, but as of 2014 more work needed to be done.

In the mid-1980s less than a third of admitted graduate students at Chicago received aid, whereas for most other top graduate schools the percentage was greater than two-thirds. In the humanities and social sciences, almost 60 percent of the offers of admission to graduate students in 1986 contained no aid. Whereas doctoral programs in peer institutions awarded aid packages consisting of fellowship support in the first two years and teaching assistantships in the third and sometimes fourth years, Chicago, with its small undergraduate College, offered graduate students few teaching opportunities and sources of support. The disparity grew in the late 1990s and early 2000s, as peer universities—most of which had smaller doctoral programs, larger tuition-generating undergraduate colleges, and more fund-raising resources—offered full fellowship support for all matriculating doctoral students, leaving Chicago at an even greater disadvantage. By the early 2000s Chicago was significantly behind in the resources it offered doctoral students. Most other top private universities had adopted standard fellowship packages in the humanities and social sciences for graduate students ranging from $17,000 to $19,000 annually,

plus tuition waivers and special summer study grants, and most expected
some significant level of teaching as part of these arrangements. Chicago,
in contrast, had a complex bricolage of some full fellowships (many of
which were below the peer average), some partial fellowships, and some
tuition waivers, and it was the only institution in its peer group that was
still admitting a small number of doctoral students with no aid and that
had no systematic teaching expectation for doctoral students (except for
students receiving full fellowships, and even then the requirement was
very modest and not always systematically enforced). In the physical and
biological sciences the funding situation for students was traditionally
more favorable, with almost all entering students having stipendiary support or teaching assistantships, although recent cutbacks in federal funding in the natural sciences have created constraints in that domain as well.

Chicago's success in recruiting top graduate students has always varied
by department and field, and has most often been influenced by the availability of competitive financial aid. On the basis of yield rates of 28 percent
in the humanities and 34 percent in the social sciences, the Baker Commission investigated why students declined Chicago's offer of admission
in favor of other leading institutions, and found that "among students who
declined admission to the Humanities and Social Sciences Divisions, a
higher proportion received smaller awards here than elsewhere and
a lower proportion receive larger awards here than elsewhere." Of the
general quality of the final matriculants, the report cautiously observed
that "while the overall quality of the students admitted to the University
for graduate study in 1980–81 may not have been as high as the faculty
might wish, it appears to have been fairly high."[95] In the mid-1980s Chicago regularly admitted more than 60 percent of all graduate students
who applied, compared to less than 30 percent at the other top private
universities. Yield rates for Chicago were also substantially lower than
for its peers. Over the next two decades the yield rates improved, but
Chicago was still at a serious disadvantage in the first decade of the new
millennium. For 2006–7 Chicago had (combined) acceptance and yield
rates of 17 percent and 37 percent for the humanities and social sciences,
but most of its top peers were at or below 10 percent in acceptance and
above 50 percent in yield.[96]

In February 2007, in an effort to make Chicago more competitive by
eliminating partial funding and reducing loan indebtedness for doctoral
students, President Zimmer and Provost Rosenbaum announced the
Graduate Aid Initiative. The initiative was intended to fully fund all new
entering doctoral students in the humanities, the Divinity School, and
the social sciences for five-year terms and to reduce both attrition and
time to degree.[97] Initial planning projected that additional graduate aid

costs would increase from $2.3 million to nearly $12 million by 2013. As of 2014–15 the initiative depended on an annual direct subsidy of almost $18 million from the provost's office, made possible by larger undergraduate enrollments in the College. In contrast to earlier interventions, however, this program was not designed to increase doctoral enrollments. Quite the opposite—given its heavy new costs, it presumed constraining doctoral cohorts to a more manageable size, emphasizing both a higher level of competitiveness for top-ranked doctoral matriculants and an improved educational experience for students once enrolled. The program initially raised the hackles of a small minority of the faculty who prized large numbers of PhD students, but it was welcomed by the great majority of the faculty as a significant improvement in Chicago's competitive capacity to recruit and retain the best young scholars.

Crises and corresponding hand-wringing in American graduate education have come and gone over time. As David Riesman put it to Bernard Berelson in 1958, debates about the future of graduate education were "one of those familiar, insoluable discussions in American life, like that about liberty and equality." Riesman's response was ironic resignation: "To each period, its own crisis."[98] The doctorate for research and teaching has proven to be a durable professional goal, but its long-term viability is bound to depend on future employment prospects for PhDs in the arts and sciences. Whether universities should regard PhD training as suitable for nonacademic careers is a politically charged question. The push in the late 1950s to expand doctoral numbers arose not only from reasons of national prestige and desires to enhance the research capacity of the nation, but also from the need to provide more college teachers to educate the expanding population of baby boomers. The former goals will remain, but if the national teaching market for PhDs continues to shrink, it will affect the relevance of many of these degrees. The Baker Commission argued—with considerable eloquence—that the University should expand the legitimacy of the doctorate for nonacademic employment, but most faculty at Chicago continue to consider academic careers as the most prestigious ones for their students. The Committee on Social Thought's unvarnished declaration in 1983 was probably typical of the private feelings of faculty in many departments: "The Committee strongly believes that no change should be made to alter the meaning of the degrees it offers. We aim to train learned and skilled scholars and teachers who will continue to occupy positions of leadership in the academic world."[99] The logic of Chicago's deepest values—dedication to university-based and academically grounded research—not only defined the self-understanding of the faculty but also encompassed their most cherished (and prestige-generating) hopes for their doctoral students. This should not suggest that all Chicago

PhDs seek academic careers. It has long been customary, for example, for some PhDs in the natural sciences and quantitative social sciences such as economics and political science to pursue industry, government, or nonprofit research careers. Still, a large number of Chicago PhDs, and particularly those in the humanities and qualitative social sciences, want employment as professors in colleges and universities. The internal logic of the graduate programs themselves fit this paradigm. That logic was one of natural selection (for lack of a better term)—students proved that they belonged at Chicago by surviving increasingly severe challenges, filled with qualifying papers and oral exams. Each accomplishment confirmed that one was worthy of having gained entry, particularly when so many of one's peers could not do so. It was (and continues to be) difficult for most doctoral students to see how training for a "career plan B" could fit into a system where the students were asked to throw everything into a race to the scholarly top. It would sound like bet hedging from the start.

In 2001 John Mark Hansen, as associate provost for research and education, urged departments to "consider how well their programs train students for the jobs that most of them will actually have."[100] Yet this very formulation raised the question of the connectedness between the existing models of doctoral training and future employment options. Graduate schools afford doctoral students valuable research skills, and few leaders in US higher education seem interested in reviving Hutchins's schemes for offering teaching as opposed to research doctorates. But given that doctoral students pay no tuition and enjoy a highly subsidized status, is it wise for universities (and fair to the students themselves) to subsidize large-volume doctoral programs—which can last eight or more years—to train students for nonacademic careers when a shorter period of formal graduate study might suffice? Almost twenty years ago Louis Menand suggested that serious thought be given to three-year doctoral programs without dissertations or required teaching obligations.[101] His suggestion went nowhere, but less drastic options might be possible. In response to Bernard Berelson's survey of graduate education in the late 1950s, the philosopher Roderick Chisholm argued that doctoral dissertations might properly be understood to fall "somewhere between 'an original contribution to knowledge' and a 'research exercise.' The dissertation should not be thought of as a definitive treatment of its topic; its primary purpose is offer the graduate a sense to prove himself."[102] Might not the exercise of dissertation writing be foreshortened for those who are not seeking academic-research careers, thus abbreviating for some the time needed to obtain the degree? This and similar questions are likely to (or at least should) be faced by US graduate schools in the decades to come.

THE BOUNDARIES OF PROFESSIONAL STUDY

Harper's conception of the University included professional education from the start. The Divinity School was the first professional school on the scene, followed by the College of Commerce in 1898, the School of Education in 1901, the Law School in 1902, the School of Social Service Administration in 1919, and the Graduate Library School in 1928.[103] Harper and the board of trustees opted not to create a stand-alone scientific medical school in the late 1890s, much to Frederick Gates's disappointment; instead the University brokered an affiliation agreement with Rush Medical College in 1898, not developing its own medical school until 1927.[104] Harper's dream of a technical-engineering school was never implemented, though the University did establish the Institute for Molecular Engineering in 2011. The University came to have its School of Public Policy only in 1987.

Demographics tell an ambivalent story. Although the increase in enrollments in the professional schools from 1903 to 1931 paralleled that of the arts and sciences, the number of professional graduate degrees awarded was extremely small compared with those of the academic departments, and faculty size was equally modest.[105] The Depression and war years hit most of the professional schools hard, and down to the Second World War the predominant weight of prestige and investment at the University lay in the research programs in the arts and sciences. When Edward Levi formulated his master plan for the revival of the University in the mid-1960s, as a former dean of the Law School he gave careful and sympathetic attention to the professional schools, but he still conceived of the University's prestige as being rooted in the larger academic departments in the graduate divisions. As late as the 1970s, concerns that the expansion of professional education might tip the cultural balance on campus were clearly apparent, similar to the worries about a further expansion of the undergraduate College.[106]

Over the next forty years this portrait changed drastically. By the fall of 2013, of the new degree-seeking (and tuition-paying) graduate students in MA and doctoral programs matriculating at Chicago, 68 percent were enrolled in one of the professional schools. Indeed, the new students entering the four Booth School of Business degree programs outnumbered the new (terminal) MA and doctoral students matriculating in all of the graduate divisions. Even allowing for the fact that some percentage of the latter were in programs that required longer time frames than twenty-one months of study, the balance of financial power and physical presence had shifted substantially. More striking was the rate of change in these

FIG. 4. New matriculants in the College, divisions, and schools, by calendar year, 1979–2012

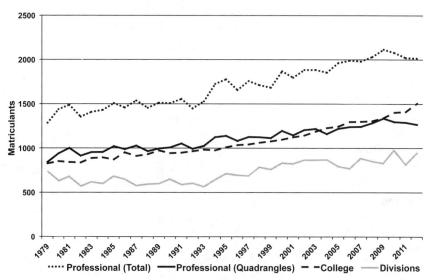

Note: "New matriculants" excludes students who have previously been enrolled at the University of Chicago at any level. Source: Office of the Registrar, University of Chicago.

numbers since the late 1970s. In 1979 the four graduate divisions had 727, the College 827, and the professional schools 1,285 new degree matriculants. The corresponding numbers for 2012 were 946 new matriculants for the graduate divisions, 1,506 for the College, and 2,015 for the six professional schools (see fig. 4). Over the past thirty-five years a significant shift in the demographic mix of the student population of the University had taken place.

Professional education was not a thing apart, and it came to constitute and be shaped by the broader contours of the general faculty culture at Chicago.[107] The Law and Business Schools offered strong examples of curricular interdisciplinarity and intellectual interconnectivity. The Law School was older and had for many decades the more distinguished patrimony. Harper wanted a law school from the first, which he saw as an intellectual and cultural pendant to the Divinity School, and he insisted that, like the Divinity School, it be an integral part of the fundamental mission of the University.[108] Yet it required a decade to assemble the necessary funding and find a donor for a proper building. John D. Rockefeller was persuaded to finance most of the cost of the Law School building at $250,000, and its cornerstone was laid by President Theodore Roosevelt on April 2, 1903. Harper also struggled to assemble the right faculty and gain consensus on the curricular and professional identity of the school. From the first Harper was particularly influenced by Ernst Freund, a distinguished jurist and expert in administrative law first appointed to the Department of Political Science in 1894. Freund urged that Chicago should embrace a mission that included nonlegal subjects (as electives), such as diplomatic history, finance, comparative politics, and sociology, as part of its curriculum, a view that Harper enthusiastically endorsed. The issue became tangled up in the politics of providing early leadership of the school, given that Harper asked Harvard Law School to lend a senior faculty member to help establish the fledgling Chicago operation. In the end Harvard lent Joseph H. Beale for a two-year visiting appointment as interim dean, who in turn agreed to compromise with Freund's "heretical" views involving the boundaries of legal education, and the school began to organize itself. Harper then raided Stanford to obtain James Parker Hall for a top salary of $5,500, and he became the school's first permanent dean in 1904.

The faculty at Chicago held different views on the scope and methods of legal education than their purist Harvard colleagues, a fact that became obvious in the 1930s.[109] Harper also insisted that a program of prelegal studies be created for College seniors, given his systematic disregard for the formal boundary that many institutions had created between the last two years of college and the first years of graduate school. In contrast to the practices at other institutions at the time, this meant that students could double count their senior year as part of the first year of Law School, and hence from the very beginning of its history the school drew a heavy percentage of its students from the undergraduate colleges at Chicago (almost half in the 1920s), the great majority of whom entered the school at the end of their junior year. As late as 1958 more than half of the alumni of the Law School had BA degrees from the College as well as JD degrees.[110]

The Law School faculty were thus attuned to decisions about the shape and content of the undergraduate curriculum.[111] Following Boucher's reforms that created a Core curriculum in the early 1930s, the Law School, led by Wilbur Katz, Malcolm Sharp, and the young Edward Levi, put together a four-year plan in 1937. The plan allowed students to enter the Law School after completing the two-year Core curriculum in the College, and it expanded the program of studies to include subjects other than conventional law disciplines, such as business, accounting, and psychology.[112] Levi's famous course on the elements of law (first titled Legal Methods and Materials) originated as a key component of the first year of the new program for undergraduate law students.[113] Four years later Levi commented that one of the plan's primary objectives was to incorporate "non-legal materials into the law program when these non-legal materials were relevant."[114] Katz was convinced that the new curriculum would also have a bracing and stimulating effect on the faculty: "Students who have been studying economics and political theory as part of such an integrated program can be relied upon to task embarrassing questions in law courses, questions which will stimulate the law instructor to broaden his equipment. Stimuli should develop in the other direction as well; the social science instructor also will be 'on the spot.'"[115] Also in 1937, the school created a tutorial program of individual legal writing for first-year students, hiring teaching fellows (named in honor of former Dean of the Law School Harry A. Bigelow in 1947) to assist new students with the skills of legal exposition.[116] This spirit of intellectual breadth and curricular experimentation was especially important after Levi gained the powers of the school's deanship in 1950, and it is not surprising that throughout the 1950s Levi urged his colleagues to consider programs that linked law with other social science disciplines and research perspectives. The radical interdisciplinary experiments of the 1930s in the College found their analogues in the four-year plan of the Law School before World War II and in the social science–based research agendas of the school in the 1950s and 1960s. Or, put slightly differently, Edward Levi's admiration for Robert Hutchins had long legs.

World War II took a heavy toll on the Law School, according to Dennis Hutchinson, who remarked that the school "had a near-death experience ... as enrollments plummeted and University facilities were commandeered for training programs supporting the armed services." President Hutchins even considered closing down the Law School in 1943, when only nine students graduated.[117] The appointment of Levi as dean in September 1950 gave the Law School a leader who was shrewd in defending the interests of the school during the budget-cutting era of the early Kimpton administration. Slowly the Law School rebuilt its enrollment (it reached 310 students by 1955), although it remained small compared to other top law schools in the United States. Levi aggressively hired younger and established stars from other schools (Roscoe Steffen, Karl Llewellyn, Soia Mentschikoff, Allison Dunham, Francis A. Allen, Kenneth Culp Davis, Brainerd Currie, and Nicholas Katzenbach), creating a distinguished faculty who by the end of the 1950s had attained the dubious honor of being among the most heavily targeted for outside raids by other peer universities.[118] But Levi also launched a center- and research-institute-based strategy to enhance the scholarly visibility of the Law School, in large part with the support of the Ford Foundation. Levi urged his colleagues to consider programs that linked law with other social science disciplines and research perspectives, beginning with the Law and Behavioral Science Program, which netted Levi more than $1.4 million in support from Ford. With these funds Levi launched the American Jury project led by Harry Kalven and other research programs on commercial arbitration and on public attitudes about the fairness of taxation—initiatives that enabled him to hire promising scholars like Hans Zeisel in 1952 and Philip Kurland in 1953.[119]

The appointment of Aaron Director in 1946 to head up the Free Market Study project at the Law School proved critical to the establishment of the law and economics movement at Chicago, which was initially supported by grants from the Volker Fund.[120] A structural parallel to the behavioral science programs launched with Ford money, law and economics eventuated in even more powerful strategic directions, enabling subsequent leaders of the school to attract a series of scholars with strong connections to the social sciences in the 1960s and 1970s (such as Ronald Coase, William Landes, Richard Posner, and Gary Becker), all of whom also had reputations for heavy levels of productivity.[121] Remarkably between 1958 and 1972 the school came to have a portfolio of three high-powered, faculty-edited journals that still help to define its national research reputation today: the *Journal of Law and Economics*, founded by Director in 1958; the *Supreme Court Review*, founded by Philip Kurland in 1960; and the *Journal of Legal Studies*, founded by Richard Posner in 1972. In the 1960s and early 1970s the school began to adopt the workshop system that the Department of Economics and the Graduate School of Business had already embraced, and by the later 1970s and 1980s the workshops had become a permanent fixture in the faculty culture of the Law School.[122] International legal perspectives were also fortified via Max Rheinstein's Foreign Law Program, established in 1956 with $375,000 from the Ford Foundation, which also included course work in history and the social sciences.[123]

Even with a small faculty, the school gained an outsize reputation for scholarly distinction, especially for open-ended basic research that might not have what Levi later called "immediate or unambiguous application[s]," and in the coming decades this portrait helped to undergird and sustain its competitive reputation.[124] Moreover, the school always maintained a serious view of the importance of rigorous faculty teaching for careers in legal practice. The trio of Levi and his close friends Bernard Meltzer and Walter Blum (both of whom were hired in 1946 and, like Levi, were alumni of the College and the Law School), along with other distinguished teachers like Mentschikoff and Llewellyn, was particularly important in the 1950s and 1960s in setting high standards of teaching and engendering pride among the faculty in educating future leaders of the bar. The Law School's dedication to high-quality faculty teaching was further reinforced during the deanships of Gerhard Casper and Geoffrey R. Stone in the 1980s and 1990s. A small number of alumni went on to distinguished teaching and research careers in academic law, but the vast majority of the school's alumni each year became practicing attorneys.[125] The school's impact on the legal profession was thus bimodal—lacking a PhD program, as the Graduate School of Business came to have, its student progeny tended to staff top law firms much more than academic law schools, while the faculty sustained a distinctive collective personality characterized by intense and combative scholarly values that often cut across conventional legal disciplines.

The professional school that both endured and prospered from the greatest level of change was the Graduate School of Business (now the Chicago Booth School of Business). As noted in chapter 2, the Business School was created in 1898 as the College of Commerce and Politics and underwent several name changes before being called the School of Business in 1932. Its most important early dean, Leon C. Marshall (appointed in 1909), saw the school as "a place for truly scientific work" and a "community of scholars," not merely a vocational training institute.[126] The school obtained the right to offer postbaccalaureate degrees in 1914, and in 1920 Marshall established the first PhD program in business in the United States; it issued its first doctorate in 1922. In 1935 the school replaced its MA degree with the MBA, a sign of growing professional ambition. It was also the happy recipient of an unexpected (and unsolicited) gift in 1916 from Hobart W. Williams, a local businessman who decided to leave real estate worth $2 million to the University for the purposes of "instruction in commercial or business studies."[127] By 1917 the school began to focus on training executive managers based on specific business functions, but during the Hutchins administration its scholarly ambitions gained little support.[128] The school remained heavily undergraduate from the later 1890s up to the Second World War, and as late as the 1939–40 academic year it awarded a total of 141 degrees, 94 of which were baccalaureate degrees.

The early faculty consisted of some fundamental researchers like Paul H. Douglas, William H. Spencer, Theodore O. Yntema, and Garfield V. Cox, but also talented practitioners and consultants like James O. McKinsey, who founded McKinsey and Company in 1925, and James L. Palmer, who was later the president of Marshall Field and Company.[129] Joint faculty appointments between the Department of Economics and the Business School were more common before 1940, and at one time or another leading economists such as Frank Knight and Jacob Viner were associated with the school. Marshall launched a series of important business textbooks, called the Materials for the Study of Business, that eventually included over forty titles and proved influential in undergraduate business education nationally before World War II. But starting in the 1930s and especially during the 1940s, the school lost faculty whom it could not easily replace. As Allen Wallis argued in 1957, "Lacking budgetary support, the School could not, in the post-war period, regain the distinction which it had earlier enjoyed."[130] By the 1950s Jamie Lorie recalled that "the business school was in a very bad situation. There was no money, no zeal, no imagination, not even telephones anymore."[131]

In 1950 the school redefined its mission and became an exclusively graduate operation (its title changed to the Graduate School of Business in 1959). A major impetus for reconceiving the identity and mission of the school and reviving its financial fortunes began in the late 1950s. The larger national context was defined by major programmatic intervention by the Ford Foundation that in 1959 published a comprehensive critique of current business schools authored by Robert Gordon and James Howell. Gordon and Howell severely criticized the haphazard teaching and curricula that constituted business teaching and advocated a more rigorous and integrated curriculum based on the adoption of modern social-scientific research methods for American business schools.[132]

Lawrence Kimpton's appointment of W. Allen Wallis as dean of the school in 1956 proved central to the broadening of the school's intellectual mission and developmental horizons.[133] In October of that year, under the leadership of Wallis and his associate dean, James H. Lorie, the Business School faculty submitted to Kimpton "a preliminary blueprint of a long-range development program designed to change profoundly the scale and nature of activities of the School."[134] The plan was striking for its commitment to fundamental research in the social sciences as the paradigm of the school's new identity, even if this research was focused primarily on accounting, economics, statistics, and law. To accomplish this agenda the school would seek "outstanding scholars" who were "interested in and capable of doing original research." The most promising faculty would be derived from "the faculties in the social and physical sciences in other leading universities," not from graduates of other business schools. In addition the school would undertake an aggressive marketing campaign to attract top students, and "develop a program of public and press relations which will bring the activities of the School to the favorable attention of a very much wider audience than we have enjoyed in the past."

Lawrence Kimpton's view of the Business School was more sympathetic than that of Hutchins, and by the mid-1950s, when the University's budget crisis had slowly been brought under control, he was willing to channel new financial support to the school. He provided a cash infusion of $375,000 and authorized seven new faculty appointments between 1955 and 1957, more than in any comparable period in the school's history. Between January and May 1957 the school then formulated a major application to the Ford Foundation, requesting a $9.5 million grant to finance new classroom and office buildings and to secure more faculty positions and research programs, with the goal of developing new instructional and research strategies anchored in the formal study of social and behavioral science. In the end Ford awarded Chicago a more modest grant of $1.375 million for new faculty appointments and doctoral fellowships, both designed to encourage the training of future business school faculty members at other US institutions.

Wallis wanted a school with three foundational pillars—economics, quantitative methods, and behavioral sciences. The first two came easily and with rapidity, while the third took some time to mature. Critical to Wallis's strategy was his decision to begin to recruit top scholars to the school while developing the school's relationships with the Department of Economics and other social science departments. To establish preliminary links Wallis created the Social Science Advisory Committee, chaired by Edward Shils of Sociology and Social Thought, to advise him on appointments from the disciplines of the social sciences.[135] George J. Stigler, who won the Nobel Prize in Economics in 1982, was a key figure in making the Business School into a powerhouse for economics when Wallis persuaded him to leave Columbia University and accept the Charles R. Walgreen Chair of American Institutions in the Business School in 1958. Stigler would play a role of enormous significance in the intellectual transformation of the Business School in the 1960s and 1970s, not in the least because he controlled substantial research funding that could be allotted to other faculty and graduate students.[136] Along with Stigler, Wallis also recruited George P. Shultz in labor economics, Sidney Davidson in accounting, and many other prominent scholars. This trend continued under Wallis's successor, George Shultz, creating within the Business School "an economics department that rivaled the top graduate economics departments in the United States."[137] Assembling a formidable reputation for theoretical research in economics and finance, the Business School became one of the few in the United States that could compete effectively for top talent among the best young economists.

The result was momentous not only for the Business School but for the status of economics at Chicago and nationally. Marion Fourcade and Rakesh Khurana have recently argued not only that the formidable cluster of leading scholars devoted to neoclassical economics at the Business School had a powerful effect in shaping the priorities of the school toward financial economics as a premier field of study, but that the combination of the Business School's resources with those of the Department of Economics was of fundamental importance in the creation and diffusion of the law and economics movement.[138] Over time, fruitful but also competitive relationships developed between the Department of Economics and the Business School, with economics doctoral students working as research assistants for faculty in the Business School, a few prominent faculty joint appointments (most notably George Stigler and Robert Fogel), and, more recently, Business School faculty staffing part of the curriculum for economics doctoral students. At the same time, the two were often competitors for top talent and university resources, even as they jointly helped create the Chicago School of neoclassical economics, with several faculty members winning a Nobel Prize in Economics.[139] The 1960s and 1970s saw the implementation of a rigorous but flexible curriculum that deemphasized inductive approaches in favor of deductive, conceptual styles of teaching that were dependent on advanced mathematical analysis and quantitative problem solving.

Wallis's term was highly charged with change. In 1961 the school proudly issued a report titled "What's Going On" to its alumni, stating that the "quality of the School's faculty, students, teaching, research, publications and services to business has improved so greatly in the past three or four years that information about this progress has lagged far behind, particularly in business circles."[140] Expenditures were five times what they were in 1956, with a $2 million budget and with student enrollment three times greater. Wallis expanded the still small PhD program, providing generous fellowships for a targeted group of students funded by foundations and firms as well as private donors. Wallis and Lorie also sought to spread the word about the school among liberal arts colleges, seeking better applicants to all of the school's programs. In 1960 the school launched a three-week summer training program for teachers of economics at small liberal arts colleges, in cooperation with the Department of Economics. Under the program, which was paid for by the General Electric Corporation, forty professors were invited to visit Chicago for intensive workshops in monetary theory and labor employment policies.[141] Perhaps taking a page from Kimpton's ambitions for expanding the College, Wallis wanted to increase the on-campus population of MBA students from 250 in 1957 to 1,000 by 1966. Downtown and executive programs would increase the numbers dramatically, giving the school a total population of 2,450 instead of 1,000.

The school made a point of reaching out to the Chicago business community for financial and moral support, and invited business leaders as well as alumni to join the Council on the Graduate School of Business. The council advised school leaders on administrative and policy problems and helped formulate new programs, such as the associates program, management conferences, and an annual business forecast luncheon. Council members also helped to fund various research and publication initiatives by the faculty.[142]

The Wallis-Lorie model of business education straddled and deliberately blurred the line between a professional school and a high-powered, social-science research institute. In the 1970s, surveys of business school deans published in the *MBA Magazine* and *Change Magazine* were highly favorable toward Chicago: Chicago ranked third nationally in 1974 and again in 1977.[143] A slightly different survey of 74,000 business executives by Standard and Poor in 1976 ranked Chicago sixth.[144] The Business School's reputation also compared well with that of the Department of Economics at Chicago, which, in a survey of economics departments in 1975, tied for first in faculty quality and for second for the effectiveness of the doctoral program.[145] The Business School faculty themselves took pride in the fact that their intellectual connections to other parts of the University were closer and more integrated than at other American business schools.

This happy state of affairs suffered a serious jolt a decade later, when the first national rankings of business schools based on student satisfaction and reputation among corporate recruiters, and not primarily on faculty prestige, were published by *BusinessWeek* magazine in November 1988. Against all expectations of the faculty, the University of Chicago ranked eleventh in the nation, and Northwestern garnered the top spot.[146] Even more troubling, Chicago students themselves rated their program twentieth in the nation, complaining that the professors were "too research oriented." This state of affairs was a bitter pill, given that the rankings reflected student and alumni attitudes about the quality of education and their cultural experiences as opposed to academic recognition, and it set off considerable self-reflection and soul searching among the Business School faculty.

The Business School dean, John P. Gould, and his fellow deans commissioned a detailed survey of current student views of the school, and the results were not altogether flattering.[147] Based on a poll of 681 students in the campus MBA program and 710 in the downtown program, analyst Francis Fullam reported that "many students have issues with the basic theoretical orientation" of the Business School "and would like to see more emphasis on applications," and desired "improvements in teaching style and greater access to faculty." A more detailed analysis of the data suggested that "in both the teaching/curriculum and student services/placement areas, students are satisfied with some aspects and dissatisfied with others. In the social environment area, there is widespread dissatisfaction." The latter domain included insufficient social events, difficulty in developing friendships, an unfriendly social environment, a lack of school spirit, and inadequate facilities for students. This analysis concluded that students viewed the Business School's strengths as cultivating "thinking skills and analytic skills," and weaknesses as teaching "industry conventions and practices" as well as "leadership, entrepreneurship, and public speaking skills."[148] Alumni, meanwhile, appreciated the high value of their classroom education but criticized the lack of emphasis on how to use theory to resolve real-world problems.

Wallis had dismissed attempts to teach leadership in an academic context, arguing that "to claim that a student will be trained in a school of business in the actual processes of decision-making is at best naïve or ignorant, and at worst deceptive."[149] But voices soon emerged arguing for a more balanced approach. During deliberations on possible reforms to the curriculum in 1970, a faculty panel chaired by John Jeuck raised the issue of the "relevance" of the education provided to MBA students, admitting that "although alumni, on balance, express general satisfaction with the curriculum they also argue for doing more than we have done to help them 'see the relevance' of the concepts and methods material to business problems."[150] In a report released six years later, alumni leaders on the school's council, then chaired by Irving B. Harris, echoed these concerns: "The faculty of the Graduate School of Business might be even better known and students better taught if more individuals with a practical orientation could be attracted to the faculty."[151]

No action was taken until the early 1980s, when Deans John Gould and Harry Davis urged the school to invest more systematically in leadership training and to encourage more social solidarity among students. Gould and Davis commissioned a survey in 1986 on the status of the school among local and national business executives, and the message was essentially that Chicago graduates were reputed to be strong analytical thinkers but not action-oriented leaders. Of the five top business schools, Chicago was ranked second in the quality of its faculty research but last in the ability of its students to earn leadership positions and be well prepared for their first jobs. Business executives surveyed also said that Chicago MBAs were often missing key skills, such as the ability to persuade others, to demonstrate perseverance in the face of obstacles, to appreciate the value of quick and decisive actions, and to adapt to changing circumstances effectively.[152] In response, Gould and Davis organized a series of dinners with small groups of faculty in 1987–88 to try to persuade them to pay more attention to business leadership. They argued that "the reputation of the GSB among business leaders is increasingly important to the long-term success of the School" and that "further gains on academic excellence *per se* will not materially increase the School's current reputation among business leaders." Gould and Davis proposed a range of experimental interventions, including new links to other parts of the University, serious curriculum modifications, more clinical experiences for students, and a "more imaginative use of practitioners within the MBA program."[153] Then, as if by an act of providence, came the *BusinessWeek* rankings of 1988, making the issue of leadership, set in the context of student life, of paramount importance.

Gould appointed a senior faculty task force—the Dean's Advisory Committee on MBA Students and Curriculum, chaired by Professor Kenneth R. French—to examine all aspects of the student and academic programs.[154] French's committee not only used the survey of current students, but held focus groups and discussions with students and alumni and examined the course evaluations of alumni who had graduated during the 1970s. Released in May 1989, the report noted that "many students believe that teaching is not important to the faculty or administration. In particular, there is a perception that the quality of a faculty member's teaching is almost irrelevant for promotion and tenure. This perception is interpreted as evidence that the faculty and administration do not care about the students."[155] French was candid in arguing that the problems could not simply be addressed by more clever public relations. The right way to change the ranking, he said, "is not to go bribe *Business Week* so they say we're number one next time. I would much rather earn the number one ranking than simply go and change the perceptions."[156]

French's committee proposed a number of interventions, but the one that had the most immediate and long-lasting traction was the Leadership Education and Development (LEAD) program, designed principally by Harry Davis in cooperation with some stalwart students. A particularly gifted teacher who had joined the Business School faculty in 1963, Davis founded the New Product Laboratory in 1978, to give students pragmatic development and marketing experience in introducing new consumer products.[157] Davis championed experiential education as a complement to the highly theoretical framework of the Wallis-Lorie curriculum, and for him the crisis of 1988–89 opened a window of opportunity. The LEAD program, designed for incoming students, would encourage them to assess their interpersonal and communications skills, capacities for taking and implementing action, and ability to manage conflict, thus launching a process of self-knowledge, insight, and intuition that students would refine and strengthen as they proceeded through the MBA program.[158] LEAD initially counted as an experimental course in the curriculum and was tuition-free, so that Davis and Gould did not have to seek faculty approval for their scheme (the faculty voted to make it part of the regular curriculum in 1991–92). Davis believed it was crucial to mobilize the backing of current students in designing and implementing the new program, and he received strong support from then first-year students, who were worried about their school's ranking and who were willing to participate as second-year facilitators in the fall of 1989. This support in turn created an ongoing pattern of student co-ownership of LEAD, since each year new cohorts of student leaders had the chance to revisit and revise past practices, making the program their own.

Harry Davis and Robin Hogarth would soon codify many of the principles that informed the LEAD program in a now-classic position paper, "Rethinking Management Education: A View from Chicago," published in 1992, in which they argued that in addition to teaching conceptual knowledge, the Business School had to cultivate "action skills" and "insight skills" in students, and that this effort should become an integral part of the curriculum: "An educational setting provides time and opportunities that are difficult to find in a job: to practice different skills explicitly, to reflect on levels of achievement, and to spend time remedying deficiencies that would be difficult to examine in actual job settings."[159]

LEAD's formal mission was to promote individual leadership development and experiential learning skills as well as community building, but it also ended up creating social solidarity and fostering feelings of loyalty to the school. Given the Business School's open curriculum, students found few mechanisms to foster connectedness and group activities outside the academic curriculum. LEAD set in motion changes on both fronts. At the end of LEAD's first year, Gould could report that "student interaction with faculty increased, and student philanthropic organizations provided important community service such as food and clothing drives and tutoring in neighboring schools."[160] Over time LEAD gained the respect of senior faculty, and with additional programmatic adjustments under the leadership of Stacey Kole and Jeffrey Anderson in 2008 the Booth faculty decided to expand LEAD to include students in all the school's part-time MBA programs in addition to the full-time program in Hyde Park.

Changes continued to accelerate. In the fall of 1989 the school developed plans for a new downtown center on a site on the Chicago River, just north of the Loop, later named the Gleacher Center. During the 1990s the school also launched new international executive MBA programs in Europe (first in Barcelona in 1994, but transferred to London in 2005) and in Asia (launched in Singapore in 2000, but then moving to a large new campus in Hong Kong to be shared with the College), which now provide opportunities for 180 students annually. At the time, the Business School's international strategy, first conceived by Harry Davis and fully implemented by Robert Hamada, was unique in that it was the first top-ranked business school in the United States to organize stand-alone degree programs not in cooperation with local European universities. In 2004 a huge new building (415,000 square feet) became the new home of the Business School one block away from its previous dwelling. Designed by Rafael Vinoly at a cost of $125 million, this facility won aesthetic acclaim when it opened, and in 2007 it was named in honor of Charles M. Harper. The building is one of the largest and most visually impressive new structures constructed on Chicago's campus since World War II, and it was deliberately designed with the needs of students as well as faculty in mind, alleviating long-standing complaints by students about severe overcrowding in Walker and Stuart Halls. A year later, in 2008, alumnus David Booth, the cofounder of Dimensional Fund Advisors, provided a leadership gift of $300 million to name and endow the Graduate School of Business. Although student-informed rankings are imprecise measures of academic quality, under the recent leadership of Deans Ted Snyder and Sunil Kumar, Booth has been consistently ranked among the top business schools in the United States, and its assemblage of research centers has underscored its image as a place of advanced research in economic science as well as business practice.

Since the 1990s, relations between the Booth School of Business and the Department of Economics have grown steadily deeper. A key turning point was the launching of a new course, "Economic Analysis of Major Policy Issues," taught by Gary Becker, Ted Snyder, and Kevin Murphy, which led to Becker's joining the faculty of the Business School in 2002 and to the creation of the Initiative on Chicago Price Theory in 2004, renamed the Becker Center on Chicago Price Theory in 2006. The new Becker-Friedman Institute for Research in Economics—a merger of the Becker Center with the Milton Friedman Institute (itself the subject of campus controversy for several years)—is permanently housed with the Department of Economics in the former Chicago Theological Seminary at 1160 East Fifty-Eighth Street, beautifully renovated and renamed the Saieh Hall for Economics.[161] At the same time, student support for the school has been robust and enthusiastic, judging from recent surveys of graduates and the alumni's support for the school.

With the transformation of the Business School from a modest vocational operation housed in rather run-down quarters to an international center of research housed in a majestic new building with two ambitious extensions in London and Hong Kong, it was possible to see how the practices of original research and scholarly acumen could be successfully combined with high-quality collaborative teaching and experiential training for the professions. Success in the future will depend on the capacity of Booth and other top US business schools to sustain themselves if interest in attending graduate business school should flag. A decline in the

Business School's fortunes would affect not only the school but also the broader University, which has depended since the early 1970s on significant tuition revenues from Booth.[162]

The other professional schools at Chicago combined fundamental scholarship with practical training and encountered success on both fronts, but it remains to be seen if they will enlarge their demographic footprint within the University in ways that follow the GSB's model. The Law and Business Schools both underwent profound changes in their instructional and research profiles during the 1950s and 1960s (the Law School, beginning in the later 1930s) that broadened the impact of their faculty cultures outward and engaged other parts of the University's intellectual community, particularly the social sciences. The Business School and the Law School had different experiences, however, with bringing interdisciplinarity into their curricula. Both fused instruction with social sciences methods, but the Law School did so gradually, in a way that does not seem to have created challenges for its fundamental teaching mission. In contrast, for Booth, the strategic shift into the world of the professional social sciences of the late 1950s and 1960s led to cultural unhappiness among its own students, which required readjustment on the part of the school in the 1980s and 1990s.

Harper had anticipated that the professional schools would be defined and managed by leading research scholars, and he had insisted that their curricular identities and programs be linked to other knowledge communities in the University. But he had probably not expected that the student matriculants and degree recipients of the schools would outnumber those of the graduate programs in the arts and sciences. Given that many of the faculty who teach in the professional schools practice research that blurs conventional disciplinary boundaries, however, the formal shift in student demography may ultimately reinforce older, university-wide cultural values—the intense intellectualism associated with Harper's idea of the University as a single, organic whole—but in new formats and new venues of instruction.

Chicago as an Academic Community in the World

REENGAGEMENT WITH THE CITY

During the recession of the 1970s the urban renewal projects undertaken in previous decades were no longer plausible or affordable. The University came to view its role in less controversial ways, seeking to improve the quality of life in Hyde Park through efforts to prevent crime and improve access to transportation and launching a number of outreach and service programs.[163] The Office of Community Affairs was established in 1974, and it soon founded the neighborhood schools program, under which hundreds of students served as volunteer tutors and teaching assistants in local public schools. The scholarship program for children of police and firefighters also dated from the mid-1970s. Larry Hawkins organized a clutch of supplementary enrichment initiatives under the aegis of the Office of Special Programs, founded in 1968, including Upward Bound, the summer youth programs, the Pilot Enrichment Program, and the open tutorial program, helping youth from inner-city schools prepare for college.

Individual initiatives continued in the 1980s, such as Paul Sally's Young Scholars Program in Mathematics, which brought dozens of Chicago high school students to campus during the summer for intensive math training. Laura Bornholdt organized a similar enrichment program of summer seminars for Chicago public school teachers in 1985 with the support of the Lloyd A. Fry Foundation. Hawkins also initiated a partnership program with Harold Washington College in 1988 to assist its students in transferring to selective four-year colleges.[164]

The role of the campus police continued to grow in importance as a guarantor of public safety throughout Hyde Park, and not just the close perimeter of the campus. The University's vice president for community affairs in the 1980s, Jonathan Kleinbard, played a major role in assisting Chicago developer Bruce Clinton to stabilize and revive the Regents Park apartment complex at Fifty-First Street and South Lake Shore Drive. Working with the North Kenwood–Oakland Conservation Community Council and local public officials, Kleinbard also helped to facilitate the redevelopment of North Kenwood–Oakland in the late 1980s and early 1990s, which led to the construction of a new shopping center along Forty-Seventh Street and new single-family homes and condominium and rental buildings between Thirty-Ninth and Forty-Seventh Streets.[165] Kleinbard played a key role in collaborating with community leaders to create the Woodlawn Preservation and Investment Corporation and the Fund for Community Redevelopment and Revitalization. In 1993–94, construction began on the first of twenty-eight new market-rate homes in Woodlawn, south of Sixty-First Street, with blighted apartment buildings in the area being rehabbed.[166] Kleinbard was also a hawk in urging the improvement of dilapidated or badly managed commercial stores and restaurants.[167]

In the decades after 1980 the University's relations with the city of Chicago slowly changed in significant ways, as the University launched a series of initiatives intended to reverse the unfortunate image of isolation and indifference to broader community concerns. Hyde Park had deteriorated almost beyond recognition in the 1940s and 1950s, and it had taken several decades to rehabilitate it, even in a generally flush economy.

Slowly, the population size and density of the neighborhood stabilized, and by the late 1970s Hyde Park was trending toward a stable, racially integrated, and visually pleasant area, with growing median family income levels and property values. Reported crime rates also slowly declined. Yet these positive trends brought ironies as well: Jonathan Kleinbard noted in 1978, "As the neighborhood became more stable ... property values increased and the number of rental units declined. Younger faculty are unable to compete for the better housing units in this market, when such are available. Students are finding fewer and fewer places to rent and those they do find are at prices few of them can afford."[168]

Given Hyde Park's proximity to Chicago's central business and cultural districts, most members of the university community continued to view the Loop and Near North neighborhoods as convenient destinations for shopping and entertaining. When asked about the issue of the lack of vital commercial development in Hyde Park in the Council of the Senate in 1983, Hanna Gray reminded faculty that changes in retail and entertainment options in Hyde Park depended on free-market forces. Some progress was made in June 1993 when the University sponsored a major renovation of the Hyde Park Shopping Center, with new management, new tenants, and more attractive landscaping.

These initiatives notwithstanding, the University was still perceived by many in the community as being isolated within the broader South Side, and the level of amenities in the neighborhood of Hyde Park itself remained modest. What had not changed, moreover, were the negative memories of the University's interventions in the local African American communities, many of whose leaders still regarded the University with suspicion, even after the era of urban renewal was over.[169]

Town-gown relationships in Hyde Park experienced dramatic changes over the course of the 1990s and early 2000s. Perhaps the most critical point of contact became public education. In 1998 the University created a system of charter schools in North Kenwood–Oakland and eventually Woodlawn that would serve as leverage points and pathway mechanisms for the development of more outward-looking civic strategies. The origins of the new interventions lay in the work of Tony Bryk and his colleagues in the Center for School Improvement and a parallel organization, the Consortium on Chicago School Research. The center was organized in 1989 in the wake of major reforms in public school governance in Chicago that created local school councils and gave them the power to hire and dismiss principals (and, in 1995, transferred responsibility for the public school system to the mayor, Richard M. Daley).[170] Bryk believed that Chicago would make a fascinating and comprehensive laboratory for investigating what was wrong and right in current school policies and for designing new interventions based on detailed survey research and statistical analysis that might significantly improve the educational outcomes and achievements of pupils in public primary and secondary schools.[171] The initial proposals for the center envisioned it as a place where public school principals and administrators, teachers, the University (through faculty from the Department of Education), and research practitioners could discuss common problems and formulate strategies to strengthen instruction in the primary grades in reading, writing, and mathematics. One of the center's driving principles was that local practitioners rather than distant bureaucrats or theoreticians should direct reform. Toward that end, the center sponsored workshops, summer institutes, and professional development programs for public school staff in selected local schools in Chicago, particularly school principals, who played key roles in implementing the new administrative structure. The center was also focused on early childhood literacy, that is, teaching the youngest students to learn from reading and to express their own ideas creatively in language.[172] The Consortium on Chicago School Research, meanwhile, looked for ways to break through the boundaries that separated researchers and educators in the hope that more "place-based" research integrated into local schools would lead to more effective policy outcomes.[173] The scholars associated with the center and the consortium published many empirical studies, culminating in the important book *Organizing Schools for Improvement: Lessons from Chicago* in 2010.[174] Among the key concepts that originated from this research were Tony Bryk's and Barbara Schneider's theories of social trust as an element of collective action in schools.[175] The goal of creating social trust not only defined the charter school project itself but also the broader dynamics of university-neighborhood relations in North Kenwood and Oakland.

The opening of the first charter school in 1998 emerged as an initiative by the center to create a professional-development school for its work in Chicago.[176] Supported with an initial $300,000 subsidy from the University, the school aimed to develop a curriculum that had literacy as its cornerstone: "The core of our curriculum across the grades is literacy. Our literacy framework emphasizes a balanced approach to literacy—the use of real books combined with skills instruction growing out of the assessed needs of the students. This requires a school brimming with books, stimuli for writing, and projects in which these skills and interests are put to use through authentic applications."[177] Its curricular design and implementation were owing to the leadership of Marvin Hoffman, a skillful, no-nonsense reformer who had worked as a teacher, administrator, and school psychologist in a variety of challenging rural and inner-city educational programs. Noted for his effectiveness in training language arts teachers and in working with communities that housed and sustained reformist schools, Hoffman had been invited by Bryk, via the Center for School Improvement, to come to Chicago in 1996 to lead a program that prepared teachers to be literacy coordinators in the local schools. But Hoffman, Bryk, and Sara Spurlark became frustrated with the obstacles they faced in implementing the kind of literacy instruction they envisioned within the Chicago public school system, and they decided that a charter school might be the answer.[178] University officials led by Henry Webber, the vice president for community affairs, and Richard Saller, then dean of the Division of the Social Sciences, strongly supported the charter school venture, not only for reasons of social good but because they believed that it was in the University's self-interest to promote the revitalization of the surrounding communities to the south and north, and a successful charter school was about as promising a new option as they were likely to find.[179] The charter school project reinforced patterns of civic engagement that were already stirring at the University in the late 1980s and early 1990s, but Hugo Sonnenschein's decision to proceed with an application for the first charter school in October 1997 was a decisive enlargement of this trend. As Bryk recalled, the decision "committed the University to a new institutional presence in the city and to a revitalized commitment to research and teaching in education." When one of the trustees asked Sonnenschein what the University's exit strategy was, Sonnenschein replied, "We have none. We will make this work."[180]

The first K–8 charter school, soon to be housed in the vacant Shakespeare Elementary School at 1119 East Forty-Sixth Street, opened in August 1998. The school gained immediate traction in the community and soon saw impressive success rates in student performance indicators.[181] By 2003 it was clear not only that additional campuses would respond to strong public demand in the community but that to realize its full ambitions the Center for School Improvement needed a high school. Hence between 2005 and 2008 three other charter school campuses were added with a total annual enrollment of more than 1,700 low-income students.[182]

The success of the University's charter schools led to a second ambitious initiative in 2004, the Urban Teacher Education Program (UTEP), for training young teachers working in urban primary and secondary schools.[183] An eight-quarter program, UTEP arose from the New Teacher Network, another venture of the Center for School Improvement, to provide pragmatic mentoring for new, inexperienced teachers working in inner-city schools. UTEP generated a stunning record of placement success, with almost 90 percent (as of 2014) of its graduates in teaching positions still teaching in the Chicago Public Schools, as opposed to moving to wealthier suburban school districts. In 2008 the University created a new governing and administrative apparatus to coordinate and administer UTEP and the charter schools, as well as the Consortium on Chicago School Research, and to advance the cause of empirical research on schools across the nation. This was the Urban Education Institute (UEI), led by Timothy Knowles, who had directed the Center for Urban School Improvement and the University's programs in teacher preparation since 2003.[184] UEI collaborated closely with a new multidisciplinary faculty Committee on Education, created in 2006 under the leadership of Stephen W. Raudenbush, that signaled the reemergence of the University of Chicago as a major national force in educational research. In recent years UEI has embarked on an ambitious national reform strategy, under the aegis of the UChicago Impact program, now active in twenty-three states and fifty-five major cities, to provide diagnostic and research tools and training modules for schools and school systems across America. But this time practice drove theory, with greater relevance for teachers and students alike.[185]

Beyond enhancing the educational success of many hundreds of young students, the charter schools enabled the University to begin to develop more reciprocally balanced relationships with community groups in North Kenwood–Oakland and in Woodlawn, which slowly mushroomed into interactions on other policy areas of mutual concern. The University's work in public education and school research over the 1990s also helped to strengthen its relationship to Chicago's city government, which regarded public education as a major policy concern. As Bryk explains,

> Conceptually, I always thought that the work we were doing tapped into the deep history of the University of Chicago; this great university arising on the shores of Lake Michigan amidst the problems of urbanization, industrialization and immigration. The problems of this emergent metropolis were grist for the development of much of the social sciences at the University and fueled the University's emergence as the premier institution in multiple social science disciplines. Over time however, these field connections atrophied and the disciplines became more inward looking. So our work in education returned to the taproot of the University itself.[186]

The University's efforts on the education front complemented and reinforced other strategic interventions in the civic realm. One such effort was the new Community Service Center, focused on student volunteerism and service opportunities throughout the city, that was established in 1996–97 under the leadership of a young Harvard-trained lawyer named Michelle Obama. University leaders also sought to establish closer partnerships with local political and nonprofit leaders in Woodlawn and North Kenwood to promote economic development and residential improvements. Among their initiatives was an employer-assisted forgivable loan program launched in May 2003 to encourage university employees to purchase homes in North Kenwood–Oakland and other South Side neighborhoods. Moreover, the University made concerted efforts to hire minority-owned businesses on the South Side of Chicago in the construction, merchandise, and service industries, committing millions of dollars in its role as one of the primary drivers of economic development in Chicago south of the Loop. Another initiative signaling what the *Chicago Tribune* characterized as the "growing partnership between the University of Chicago and the Woodlawn community" was the expansion of the patrolling area of the University's campus police force from Sixty-First to Sixty-Fourth Street in October 2001.[187]

The most recent urban strategy of the University has focused on improving neighborhood amenities. It began by encouraging the closure of the financially defunct Hyde Park Coop in January 2008 and opening the Treasure Island grocery store in the Hyde Park Shopping Center in March 2008, and then launching a major commercial revitalization of Fifty-Third Street in 2009–10.[188] Given that Hyde Park remains a less densely populated neighborhood than communities with similar property values and household income levels on the north side of the city, the challenge represented by the neighborhood's collective per-capita net purchasing power—which is key to attracting commercial ventures—has been pronounced. By investing in the redevelopment of the old Harper Court Shopping Center site between Fifty-First and Fifty-Third Streets, restoring the old Harper Theater complex, constructing a twelve-story office building and hotel on the corner of Fifty-Third Street and Lake Park Avenue, and sponsoring a large residential complex with 276 rental apartments between Kimbark and Kenwood Avenues on Fifty-Third Street, the University created a stronger consumer base for more restaurants and shops and generated more employment on Fifty-Third Street.[189] The University has also embarked on new programs to respond to community health needs on the South Side (the Urban Health Initiative, sponsored by the university medical center), research on crime prevention (the Crime Lab, sponsored by the School for Social Services Administration), new efforts to support neighborhood artists and art organizations as incubators of community redevelopment (the Arts and Public Life initiative, the Arts Incubator, and the many programs of the Reva and David Logan Center for the Arts), new programs sponsoring economic innovation and local entrepreneurship (the Chicago Innovation Exchange), and new initiatives to provide intensive experiential learning opportunities for College students in Chicago (Study Chicago, a structure that is parallel to the Civ-Abroad model developed on the international level).

The University was able to develop these partnerships only because of the hard-won successes of the initial urban renewal efforts of the Kimpton administration. The University sponsors a wide range of faculty research and teaching involving urban history, policy, and culture that will continue to be driven by individual or small group investigations. Yet as a huge institution with many thousands of employees who live and work in the city, with budgets, investments, and contracts that encompass large-scale expenditures in the city, and with educational programs sponsored by UEI that are now helping to reshape the landscape of contemporary urban education in Chicago, the University is more than the sum of its individual departmental or school parts. Will the University take the opportunities, but also the corresponding risks, of rising expectations, to develop a more integrated strategy to interact with its community and the wider city? The experiences of the University over the past fifteen years suggest that it would be optimal to do so, while remaining mindful of the dangers of unintended consequences and of overpromising. Many of the most successful recent programs started as modest, experimental efforts and required patience, determination, and considerable luck to reach full fruition.

CODA

Universities and Their Identities

Every generation since the 1890s has had its Jeremiah in regard to higher education (this fact itself says something about the profound civic meaning of higher education in the United States). There was Veblen in Harper's generation, then Hutchins/Adler on the left and Walgreen et al. on the right in the 1930s and 1940s, then Earl J. McGrath in the 1970s, and more recently Andrew Hacker on the left and Charles Sykes et al. on the right—and this list only scratches the surface. In our day this tradition is also alive in the complaints about how expensive and administratively top-heavy universities are and how college professors refuse to teach (or at least teach in ways the critics find congenial), and in the push for technological quick fixes like online courses, which will someday yield their own scandal literature and look a lot like a computerized revision of Clark Kerr's Multiversity of the early 1960s.[190] The practices of an institution like Chicago, with its strong traditions of thoughtful, if contested, curricular change, provide fascinating case studies to test and evaluate many of these critiques.[191]

As mentioned in chapter 5, observers in the 1960s and 1970s worried about the emergence of forces that pulled universities away from their traditional mission of cultivating and generating new knowledge. Given the University of Chicago's formidable sense of its academic mission, built on rigorous meritocracy and intellectual analysis—however contested the mix of elements in that mission might have been between the 1920s and 1960s—these forces proved less of an immediate danger to Chicago than to other institutions. The most serious threats that Chicago faced in the 1970s may have arisen from the opposite direction and on a different front—namely, the isolation of the University and the faculty from its own student and alumni constituencies. In the case of the College and the Graduate School of Business, both units had to confront a disjunction between the value that alumni placed on intense and exciting learning practices and the serious inadequacies of what the Business School reformers of the later 1980s called the academic "social environment" in which students lived.

Yet identities and traditions do not endure forever, not without constant regeneration. Two cases that arose in the 1950s and 1960s raised questions about the intellectual mission and identity of the University and resolved them in ways that had a lasting effect on the history of the institution. One involved the Kalven report (the Report of the Committee on the University's Role in Political and Social Action), a classic statement of the University's disinterestedness in the face of political or ideological advocacy. In late January 1967 President George Beadle appointed a committee of senior faculty to reflect on the boundary between individual and collective political opinion at the University. The chair of the committee was Harry Kalven, a distinguished law professor who specialized in studies of the First Amendment. The time was both propitious and contentious, filled with student demands that the University take institutional positions on providing draft boards with the class rankings of male students, on making investments in South Africa, and on the state of race relations in the United States. Two weeks before the committee was formed, the Committee of the Council of the Senate had a frustrating meeting with student leaders over the extent to which—or whether—the University should provide class rankings to Selective Service draft boards when students requested that this be done. This issue had already provoked a major student sit-in in the administration building in mid-May 1966, and it was a hotly debated topic during the 1966–67 academic year. On another, but parallel political front, in late January 1967, just before the committee began its work, two hundred University of Chicago students organized by the Students for a Democratic Society (SDS) picketed the offices of Continental Illinois National Bank in the Loop, demanding that the bank divest itself of investments in South Africa, and two days later they staged a rally on the steps of the administration building, demanding that the University cease doing business with the bank. The tides of radical protest engendered by such issues seemed inexorable, and within two years the University would endure one of the most bitter crises in its history—the sit-in of January 1969. Many of the issues that divided faculty and students, as well as faculty and faculty, would relate precisely to the boundary issues involving not only the University's role in civil society but its simultaneous responsibility to protect the right to full academic freedom of its individual members in a climate in which the logic of collective interest politics often seemed to overshadow the legitimacy of individual moral autonomy.

Through several meetings, consensus emerged on the scope of the document, with the main axis of debate focusing on protecting the individual rights of the faculty and students and on the ways that the University would understand and interpret its corporate standing and its collective actions so as to enhance and protect those individual rights. This dualism was anchored in the expectation that only an ideologically neutral university could guarantee each individual member's rights to full self-expression.

A particularly challenging issue for the committee was not the scope of rights of the individual faculty member or student, but rather the status of the University as a corporate agent that would inevitably have economic or professional relationships with other groups or institutions (the University as a landlord, as a corporate neighbor in the city, etc.). In early March 1967 one member of the committee, Gilbert White, wrote to Kalven, urging that a paragraph be incorporated in the report to the effect that "wherever the University through its ownership of property or act of delegation and membership exercises a positive role in the life of the larger community it has a responsibility to consider the ethical implications of its stand."[192] White's proposal sat badly with another committee member, George Stigler, who believed that while the University should act honorably in its material dealings, it should refrain from expressions of social or political values, for these might compromise the independence of individual faculty members.

The final draft of the committee's report prepared by Kalven incorporated several arguments. On one hand, the report staunchly defended individual rights to complete academic freedom. In fact, so obvious were these rights that the report did not elaborate in detail on this proposition, other than to suggest that such rights were the principal means by which the University might fulfill its core responsibility of discovering, improving, and disseminating knowledge. Kalven argued that the University's vision was "for the long term" and that it had a special responsibility in being "the home and sponsor of critics." To fulfill its mission, the report said, the University needed to "sustain an extraordinary environment of freedom of inquiry" and had to embrace and defend "the widest diversity of views within its own community." That community was of a special and limited sort: it existed "only for the limited, albeit great, purposes of teaching and research"—it was not a club, trade association, or lobby. Since the University was a community "only for these limited and distinctive purposes," it was not authorized to "take collective action on the issues of the day without endangering the conditions for its existence and effectiveness," nor was it a community that could "resort to majority vote to reach positions on public issues."

The end of the report was trickier, however. Kalven responded to tensions between White and Stigler by inserting compromise language in the final draft: "Of necessity, the university, however it acts, must act as an institution in its corporate capacity. In the exceptional instance, these corporate activities of the university may appear so incompatible with paramount social values as to require careful assessment of the consequences." Stigler challenged this compromise formulation, preferring a purer notion of the University as behaving "with honor" in its dealings with outside constituencies, but refraining from using its corporate activities "to foster any moral or political values."[193]

The Kalven report also reflected the coming of age of the University's faculty as the agent of its own defense and identity. The board of trustees was not consulted in the process of drafting the statement, even though it addressed general university policy with broad implications for the future positioning of the University toward the outside world. Provost Edward Levi merely informed the board in June 1967 that the faculty had approved the statement.[194]

The line between the university as an intellectual community of robust free opinion and the university as a social community of ethical moment was extremely difficult to draw. William Rainey Harper's understanding of the university as a community was more multifaceted but less easily explainable. Harper believed that the university was called on to defend a rational principle, and that for its community to sustain free inquiry and research, it could not afford the imputation of partisanship on the part of any of its members. For an individual to say that he or she did not wish to implicate the university via partisan or ill-informed statements, and thus exempt the university beforehand of any responsibility, might not be enough, for Harper (as Richard Storr rightly suggested) viewed the university as a community whose corporate legitimacy was a necessary and prior condition for the effective freedom of each member.[195] In contrast, the image of the university in the Kalven report was more deliberately circumscribed, but also more readily defensible—a community of individuals whose strength comes from the a priori authority and intellectual freedom of each of its individual members. Kalven's report, endorsed by all the members of his committee, was submitted to the Council of the Senate in June 1967, where it met with general approval.

Crafted in the turbulence of the later 1960s but still relevant for the contemporary university, the Kalven report gave Chicago a sturdy stake in the ground of ideological neutrality as it sought to ward off unwanted political interventions and partisan temptations from outside the University's walls. Since that time the report has come to have an almost canonical standing in the civic culture of the University, and has been repeatedly cited and invoked by subsequent administrations as a first principle in defining the University's role in civil society. Its impact has been so powerful precisely because it fit in well with and reinforced the status of scholarly independence rooted in the faculty culture of the early university, dating from the advocacy of Hermann von Holst, J. Laurence Laughlin, and others. As President Robert Zimmer argued about the impact of the Kalven report in 2009,

> The University of Chicago holds these as its highest values and we seek to reinforce them at every turn. The Kalven report is a component of this culture. Many other institutions push other values forward as legitimate competing interests, and their culture may not support such a strong position on this particular set of values. Every institution needs to come to its own conclusion as to what it is and what it wants to be. It needs to decide how much weight to give to various competing interests. Kalven only works at the University of Chicago because of these common values at the University, and can only be fully understood as a part of the realization of these values.[196]

The issue of cultural relevancy also had a lasting impact on the University's sense of identity in a second case, as new scholarship in cultural studies and ethnic studies in the 1980s and 1990s challenged the alleged hegemony of Western culture as the source of intellectual patrimony in the humanities and social sciences.[197] Chicago had thought through the complex issues of culture and civilization in the 1950s and 1960s in ways that could be transferred into the curricular reforms of the 1980s and 1990s and that respected the legitimacy of cultural diversity while ensuring that scholarly values based on a spirit of skepticism, not ideological sentiments, governed the curriculum.

In the 1950s, Robert Redfield and Milton Singer had created new analytic approaches to the comparative study of world cultures, with substantial support from the Ford Foundation. Robert Redfield had undertaken his graduate work in anthropology and sociology at Chicago in the 1920s. He had been dean of the Division of the Social Sciences in 1943, when the University established an Army Specialized Training School for language and area study and a Civil Affairs Training School.[198] In late April 1944 Redfield participated in a Social Sciences Research Council conference in New York on the future of area studies. He was critical of the intellectual narrowness of the wartime projects, and he urged that the postwar continuation of area studies be placed on a more solid scholarly footing. "The ends of universities are not the same as the ends of the wartime area programs," he wrote. "The ends of a university are education and research. The ends of the wartime area programs are training and more training." Redfield also considered the possibility of using an area studies approach in collegiate general-education programs, weighing the costs as well as the benefits of inviting young American students to study other parts of the world in lieu of or in addition to American culture and history at an institute established for the purpose:

> Such an enterprise would look to the long future, and would be content to develop a few first-rate scholars dealing with one aspect or another of the region chosen, and talking often with each other about their work. Such an enterprise would combine the study of books and texts with field study of the people living in the area today. The organization would include both representatives of the humanities and social scientists. For the conception which would give unity to the effort would be not so much the spatial fact that China or Russia or Latin America is one part of the earth's surface, as the fact of culture. These students would all be concerned with a traditional way of life that had maintained a distinguishing character over long time, to great consequence for mankind. A literate people expresses its traditional way of life in what is written; and every people expresses it in institutions and customs and everyday behavior. Ultimately the conception of culture as a naturally developed round of life and the conception of culture as enlightenment through mental and moral training, go back to the same reality: a people with a way of life that is or can be a subject of reflective study. The regional program of research may take the form of long study of the great world cultures.[199]

Redfield had been a close collaborator and admirer of Robert Maynard Hutchins throughout the latter's presidency at Chicago. Once Hutchins left Chicago in early 1951 for the Ford Foundation, he encouraged Redfield to apply for Ford support to undertake a new intercultural studies project. In June 1951 Redfield sent Hutchins a detailed letter sketching the operational outlines of the project he had in mind, and less than three months later the board of the Ford Foundation agreed to provide an initial $75,000 grant to permit Redfield to launch his program. The project was designed to prime a worldwide pump of comparative cultural studies through the energy of the Chicago faculty and for the sake of nothing less than world peace and the education of a generation that would make world peace possible. Milton Singer, the young philosopher turned social theorist discussed in chapter 4, joined with Redfield to codirect the project. The Annual Report of the Ford Foundation for 1951 listed the grant under the rubric of awards in support of "Peace" as opposed to awards in support of "Education" or "Strengthening Free Institutions."[200] Between the initial award in 1951 and the official conclusion of the project in 1958, the Ford Foundation approved grants totaling $375,000 in support of the Redfield-Singer intercultural studies research project. In 2014 dollars this amounted to more than $2 million.

Conceived during the early Cold War, Redfield and Singer's project in comparative civilizations encompassed a series of interconnected ventures that, in their words, would "affect the work of scholars and scientists so that their characterizations and comparisons of the great contemporary civilizations become more valid and significant. The resulting good will be improvement of understanding of the persisting and influential characteristics of the principal cultures of mankind and of the humanity that is common to all of them." The project would also hold "a hope of modifying in some degree the separateness with which study of Western Civilization has been carried on, and of supplementing, through a more central vision, the efforts made in UNESCO and elsewhere to develop a world community of ideas."[201]

The project was defined by Redfield's interest in furthering research that would "help the study of the 'great traditions' and of other cultures to develop toward greater comparability."[202] But just beneath the surface was a more programmatic and "practical" concern for international understanding. In Singer's words, the project's central intellectual problem was to evaluate and develop methods "to characterize and explore living civilizations, with a view to improving international understanding and international security."[203] On the one hand, Singer and Redfield wanted to explore ways by which civilizations might be compared and classified, with a goal of establishing a comparative approach to the study of cultures and civilizations; on the other, the project immediately supported research ventures in the study of specific historic civilizations. This duality between the general and the specific, the comparative and the regional, provided the flexibility to support a variety of different approaches.

On campus, the central activity of the project was the now-famous

Redfield-Singer seminar. This biweekly seminar, "Anthropology 342," was taught at least annually and brought together both local and visiting faculty and graduate students to discuss and evaluate concepts and methods for characterizing and comparing civilizations like "world view," "total cultural pattern," "ethos," and "national character." In addition to the seminar, Redfield and Singer also sponsored scholarly conferences that resulted in major book publications, edited by such distinguished scholars as John K. Fairbank, Gustave von Grunebaum, Arthur Wright, Harry Hoijer, and others, some of which were included in the series Comparative Studies of Culture and Civilization. The grant also supported the work of scholars like Marshall Hodgson, McKim Marriott, Surajit Sinha, M. N. Srinivas, Edward Kracke, and Bernard Cohn, all of whom were to go on to distinguished scholarly careers and to complete major publications on various aspects of cultural studies.

In 1955, at Milton Singer's urging, the two directors focused the project's resources on India.[204] As early as 1953, Singer had argued that "India is a particularly good place to pursue such a study since it has a very ancient civilization and contains a variety of subcultures of distinct world views sufficient to permit controlled comparison and the testing of hypotheses concerning cultural change."[205] The excitement of intellectual discovery and Singer's eagerness to see the results of his and Redfield's work translated back into the classroom were not long in revealing themselves. In the 1955–56 academic year, a joint committee of the Division of the Social Sciences and the College (whose members included Milton Singer and William H. McNeill) proposed a new baccalaureate degree program in which students would study both Western civilization and a non-Western civilization. The committee argued that the program would "not only familiarize a student with a civilized tradition other than his own, and thus permit him to glimpse the world and his own civilization as others see them, but might also enable him to understand better his own cultural heritage by comparing it with another."[206]

With the support of a second major grant, this one from the Carnegie Corporation and running from 1956 to 1959, the College was able to launch sequences in Islamic civilization, Chinese civilization, and South Asian civilization during the 1956–57 academic year. The links between the Ford cultural studies research project and the Carnegie-sponsored teaching project were many and varied. Singer's role was critical, and the first years of the Indian Civilization course were profoundly influenced by his leadership. In May 1957, Singer and Redfield organized a national conference—"Introducing India in Liberal Education"—to celebrate their work in course design. The University of Chicago Press printed the proceedings, which included papers on contemporary society, anthropological fieldwork, philosophy, music, pedagogy for courses on Indian civilization, and general reflections on civilizational studies.

Another key figure in intercultural studies was Marshall Hodgson, who became the principal architect of the new course on Islamic civilization. Hodgson was hired in March 1953 by Redfield and Singer as a research associate on the Ford project as well as to continue work on revising his doctoral dissertation on Islamic sects for publication as a book.[207] From the first, Hodgson thought the Redfield-Singer project sounded "very, very noble," and when the time came to develop the syllabus for Islamic Civ, it was natural that Hodgson would perform most of the work. The Ford Foundation underwrote Hodgson's salary in 1955–56 so that he could prepare to launch the course in the autumn of 1956.[208] Hodgson's three-volume masterpiece, *The Venture of Islam*, emerged from the syllabus he developed for Islamic Civ.[209]

The Redfield-Singer project thus led organically to the development of a set of powerful courses in the various (non-European) world civilizations that matured and gained legitimacy over the course of the 1960s and 1970s. By the early 1980s the anthropologist Bernard Cohn would call them "one of the jewels in the College crown."[210] Soon groups of relevant faculty developed other world civilization courses involving Latin America, Africa, and Russia. By the 1960s various area study committees or centers had been created, encompassing South Asia, the Middle East, Africa, East Asia, and Latin America—many of which controlled substantial research resources from the Ford Foundation[211]—and the University slowly assembled a large and distinguished faculty in various world civilization areas beyond Europe and America. When the College was forced to decide on the standing of these courses during the Core curriculum changes enacted in 1984–85, the faculty declared all of the world civilization sequences valuable in the critical skills and substantive knowledge that they contributed to a student's liberal education. Hence, instead of a scenario in which "History of Western Civilization" claimed (or expected) a privileged status by virtue of its putative representation of Western values, Chicago's approach to general intercultural understanding from the 1950s fundamentally shaped the decision thirty years later to declare all world civilization courses to be of equal scholarly value in the Core curriculum. A student would be obliged to choose one such sequence for his or her Core program, giving relative priority or absolute privilege to none. The tradition of scholarly engagement with non-European civilizations in the 1950s and 1960s enabled the College in the 1980s and 1990s to avoid asymmetrical power struggles or turf claims in favor of intercultural pluralism. This decision did not deny the intrinsic importance of the European tradition, which continued to dominate the intellectual framework of most of the Core sequences in the humanities and social sciences and which, as Hanna H. Gray has recently argued, is a tradition that itself is "intensely self-critical and intensely self-conscious, characteristically interested in coming to know other cultures in part as a way to define its own, to question its own assumptions and enlarge its own experience," thus in turn shaping "the basic life and vigor of the university itself, at every level."[212] But it did illustrate the wisdom of pedagogical change based on new scholarly paradigms in cultural studies developed in scientific ways rather than in response to outside pressure. David Hollinger has observed of the hotly politicized situation of cultural studies at many universities that "in the 'multiculturalist' ethos of the 1980s and 1990s, cultural programs led by canon-changing academic humanists were sometimes assigned extravagant power to make society more egalitarian and democratic."[213] Chicago largely escaped the temptation of using the curriculum in these ways both because the massive scholarly grounding of the civilization courses made them inappropriate for overt or even covert political ends and because the very structure of the Core presumed that all cultural knowledge was ultimately comparative and that the greater the cognitive distance that students were forced to move to engage other cultures, the more profound their understanding of their own culture would become.

The Redfield-Singer initiative underscored the importance of linking fundamental research with innovative teaching as a central feature of Chicago's best self. The comparative cultures project was a classic example of the fortuitousness of original scholarship for the development of new teaching strategies and intellectual agendas. Moreover, the Kalven report and Redfield-Singer initiative shared a powerful, if unspoken, link. The report presumed the right of diverse individuals to assert their views, however radical, within a university community that would collectively remain steadfastly neutral. The initiative defended the right of diverse civilizations to be fairly and equitably scrutinized, deeming each world culture authentic and equally deserving as an object of study. In the American university of the 1980s and 1990s, the kind of enlightened cultural diversity that the initiative presumed and sponsored was crucial to protect the exercise of individual rights articulated by Kalven. That is, without the formation of a campus academic community that manifested a *scholarly* commitment to cultural diversity, programmatic declarations of the right of free expression would have proved much less effective to sustain. John Stuart Mill's justified fear of the "tyranny of opinion" could best be met by a community that was itself robustly dedicated to the "eccentricity" of diverse views. Only by grounding rights to academic freedom, and indeed the very presumption of such rights, in a matrix of resiliently tolerant cultural beliefs in the community as a whole, demanding objectivity and open-mindedness from all in the study of controversial cultural questions, could these rights be efficaciously practiced.

The University of Chicago has a robust history of fostering self-understanding and curricular regeneration. The Kalven and Redfield-Singer projects were two of the more relevant episodes that continue to define the University's tradition of renewal, a tradition that is the best answer to the recurrent Jeremiads about decline. The goal of the universities should be to protect and even enlarge the space needed for such efforts, not to respond under pressure to the particular change or "corruption" the latest Jeremiah is lamenting.

A Sustained Cultivation of Sensitivities, Taste, and Judgment

When the reforms of November 1930 creating the divisions and the College were adopted, Robert Hutchins presented them to the alumni and to the world at large as an experiment, suggesting, "If after a period of trial and error we conclude that we have been mistaken in beginning it, we shall have the courage to end it." Hutchins also insisted, though, that much was at stake and that many good things would come of success: "By attempting it now we lay ourselves open to the attack as dreamers and fanatics. But we also commend ourselves, I hope, to the sympathy of those interested in earnest efforts to improve education and advance knowledge. For though our attempt may be futile, you may be sure that it is earnest.... We submit our program, not for your congratulation but for your criticism in the belief that only by experiment constantly criticized and revised shall we produce in this country a generation more educated than our own and individuals better educated than ourselves."[214]

The past eighty-five years have encompassed exactly that process of an "experiment constantly criticized and revised." The University's basic constitutional structures have proved sturdy and resilient, but they have also been part of—and at times even the agents for—a history often marked with serious conflict. Since World War II and especially since the 1960s the graduate divisions have fostered opportunities for collaboration among faculties that have helped to ensure the strength, distinction, and effectiveness of their member departments, even if they did not become the independent curricular entities over and above their member departments that Hutchins hoped for. Changes in funding and employment patterns for PhDs in many fields of the arts and sciences have made it necessary to conceive of the PhD programs as smaller to midsize, stressing the quality of the graduate experience for a smaller number of students and a substantial improvement of their performance in time to degree.

In contrast to the marginal status of the small College between 1950 and 1975, undergraduate education and life now stand at the center of the institutional culture of the University, charged with protecting a style of liberal education that respects and draws from but is not limited to the disciplinary knowledge of the individual departments and other clusters of specialized knowledge. Since the 1930s, the College has helped to foster the culture of interdisciplinary work and curricular innovation that is one of the most distinctive educational norms of the University. This work has been critical to protecting the intellectual rigor of the University more generally, because it has helped to constitute and sustain an undergraduate campus culture that is based on merit, self-discipline, and rigorous inquiry. With its jointly appointed faculty, the College retains the responsibility to govern the undergraduate curriculum, to staff that curriculum as best as it can, to formulate a broad range of other policies influencing and supporting undergraduate life, to establish admissions and aid guidelines, and, in the past two decades or so, to develop a coherent and sustainable program of alumni relations and of fund-raising.

One challenge that remains is how to integrate and reconcile the competing needs of college and doctoral education. The moral, intellectual, and financial welfare of the University depends on the success of its College, whose traditions of liberal education are as important to the identity of the University as any of its doctoral or professional programs. If Robert Hutchins was correct in arguing that it is a basic purpose of the University to be not merely a collection of the best men and best women, but rather "to be a collection of the best people to do what we [think] ought to be done," how can the University ensure that it will continue to have a faculty who are both able to sustain the luster of the research and prepared to do what "ought to be done" about the College's traditions of nondepartmentally based, interdisciplinary liberal education?[215] On the other hand, as the Bradburn committee observed in 1979, a substantial increase in the population of the undergraduate student body, compared to graduate students, would lead to "other changes in the life of the University, most particularly in the teaching responsibilities of the faculty."[216] Will the faculty culture at Chicago, rooted in the decades after 1945 in the mirage of a small college and an overt privileging of graduate education, adjust to the realities and responsibilities of this century, especially given the fact that College students now account for about 75 percent of the students in the arts and sciences who need classroom instruction on a daily and weekly basis? Roger Geiger and Donald Heller have warned that large public universities face severe financial pressures that "have forced an 'unbundling' of university tasks: universities have increasingly utilized non-tenure track faculty for undergraduate teaching so that regular faculty can engage in research, scholarship and advanced instruction."[217] Such a trend would have devastating consequences for the long-term intellectual welfare and cultural coherence of the private American universities, and none more so than the University of Chicago.

Another vital question that remains unresolved is the future of graduate and particularly doctoral education. How can the University most effectively prepare its doctoral students for the demands of teaching that await many of them in their own professional careers? And how can the doctorate itself be modified to take into account the employment challenges awaiting young PhDs? The past is not a reservoir of good tips for the present, but it is striking how prescient Hutchins and Baker were in arguing that preparing graduate students to be effective teachers should be a central concern of graduate education, on par with training them to be successful researchers.

At the same time, conversations about the preparation of graduate students for teaching should reemphasize the importance that the faculty themselves place on their *own* teaching. To be a teaching and research university does not mean that Chicago is a university filled with some who do research and others who teach, or with some who only teach small numbers of advanced students and others who teach larger numbers of younger students. It means that the research faculty should understand themselves as what William Rainey Harper wanted them to become— namely, a community defined by the high value of teaching on all levels and at all times to all of the University's members. A commitment to teaching informed by research is perhaps the best defense against critics who decry the foibles of contemporary higher education, particularly for those beasts of intellectual prey that we call research universities. As Gerhard Casper has observed, what makes the university "irreplaceable" is "the link between teaching and research in the laboratory and the classroom, the working environment for professors and students that requires a particular brand of camaraderie that both assumes and makes possible this environment."[218] But Casper's dictum is plausible only if universities recognize that supporting distinguished teaching and fashioning coherent curricula for their students must be among their highest priorities, as opposed to allowing their faculties to become agents of fragmentation in the name of "research excellence"—which, while appealing in itself, weakens the fundamental mission of teaching and thus of a great university.

Some of the most eloquent statements about the fundamental values of the University have come in rhetoric celebrating the University of Chicago's teaching mission. Responding to the question of "why we teach" as a way of introducing the "Report of the Committee on Teaching" in 1972, the distinguished English scholar Stuart Tave responded, "We speak here not of teaching and not of teaching at a University but of teaching at a University of a certain sort.... It is a University that conceives highly of itself and with these pretensions it must be judged severely, for if it is not what it claims to be then it has no valid claim; it becomes not merely good in another kind but an inferior version of a thing that has value only when it is superior."[219] Tave's admonition found a splendid analogue in the more individualistic claim that Karl J. Weintraub made in 1974 in his lecture "In Behalf of the Humanities." For Weintraub, an eminent instructor in the History of Western Civilization for many years, teaching was not simply a way of valorizing the University's institutional mission: "A teacher finds his satisfaction simply in having raised consciousness by one little notch; it may make all the difference between mediocrity and excellence. The quality of a culture depends ultimately on this long, this sustained cultivation of sensitivities, of refined taste, and of sound judgment.... In this invisible labor lies the great contribution a university makes to all that is visible to the larger public."[220] Both Tave and Weintraub understood that the vocation of teaching has defined the highest and best nature of the University. Rigorous and demanding teaching has given the University of Chicago a singular identity of intellectual transformation, and teaching has also made the University a powerful agent in the constitution of the quality as well as the integrity of the broader culture in which we live.

Yet the understandings of this teaching mission as both a private good, for the enrichment of the individual student, and a public good, for the service of the University's context, have evolved over the past century. The University's purposes today are the result of ambitions that have built on, but also reinforced, one another from one generation to the next. Harper, Hutchins, and Levi each served as a touchstone in the ongoing history of thought about the university's mission. Harper's deployment of the search for truth in a quasi-religious mode in the 1890s enabled him to define higher education as both a private and a public good simultaneously. It was private, because the University enabled individual students to enhance and enrich their personal and professional lives, and it was public because in searching for and learning the truth, students and scholars of the University helped create a stronger, more enlightened, and more virtuous public culture for the nation.

Hutchins drew on Harper's devotion to truth telling as a near-sacral cause in the 1930s, but his antivocationalist rhetoric denigrated the practical or professional value of education for the individual learner. Instead, to the extent that individual students and scholars searched for truth, they would do so above all to reaffirm the public efficacy of the university as a moral force. Collapsing the boundary between the individual and the University community, Hutchins's intellectualist holism focused on the idea that the University as a body was responsible for articulating and transferring the values and discernment that were vital for democracy. He hoped that the University could achieve a kind of unity of purpose that the diversity of knowledge and the independence of scholarship would, in the end, not allow. Where Harper sought to shape an institution united by devotion to inquiry, Hutchins tended to conflate higher education as a private and as a public good into one grand whole, with little air or space between institutional moral purpose and the individual pursuit of knowledge.

Edward Levi sought to meld together elements of Harper and Hutchins in the 1960s and 1970s in a historicist mode that looked backward as well as forward, for he had the advantage of having direct contacts with both eras while being beholden to neither of them. Levi understood that Hutchins's devotion to truth telling, to academic freedom, and to a singular devotion to the culture of learning could survive, but that Hutchins's desire to create a University with a moral unity was an illusion that had to be abandoned. An ardent secularist, Levi also deliberately stressed Harper's idea of the structurally unified University, but now that goal became a norm for the purposes of intellectual enrichment and professional success in the world, not a license to spread liberal Protestant virtue outside the University or to inculcate moral sensibilities among the University's individual members. Today's University manifests elements of all three visions, intermixed in varying proportions and executed with mutually productive tensions.

In 1924, Ernest D. Burton argued that the greatest gift University founders had given to succeeding generations was an institution with "a long future." He was referring not only to physical buildings and research programs but also to the ideals of merit-based achievement, intellectual self-actualization, and scholarly dispassion that have now defined the institution over the past 125 years. The first University of Chicago—which lasted from 1857 to 1886—collapsed for want of a clear academic purpose. The second University of Chicago has a distinctive academic mission, to elevate and enrich the social worlds in which we live via the intense cultivation and spread of new knowledge as a private and a public good. The University's academic purpose focused the minds of the early leaders and the early faculty, students, alumni, and trustees, and this academic purpose, at the core of an institutional history filled with impressive success and considerable failure, remains important to this day. It is still what gives the University of Chicago's controversies their meaning, and it is what makes working through their historical genesis and significance worthwhile on the 125th anniversary of the University's founding. The grandeur of the University, that which shines forth to each person who visits Chicago even for a short time, that which graces all who have had the privilege of joining its community as permanent members, is that it is a courageous and fearless place, a place of strong liberty and vibrant convictions, and out of all those convictions, out of all the generations of free and open debate that they have sponsored and protected, has arisen an institution truly worthy of the meaning and the promise of the higher learning.

Acknowledgments

Many colleagues have assisted me over the years in the researching and writing of this book. For insightful discussions and conversations about various facets of the history of the University, I am grateful to Andrew Abbott, Susan Art, Mitchell Ash, Leora Auslander, Peggy Bevington, Leon Botstein, Dominic C. Boyer, Norman M. Bradburn, Bill Brown, Gerhard Casper, James Chandler, Thomas Christensen, Terry N. Clark, Kathleen N. Conzen, Edward M. Cook, David Crabb, Harry L. Davis, Constantin Fasolt, Martin E. Feder, Lawrence Furnstahl, Michael Geyer, Jan E. Goldstein, Hanna H. Gray, Adam Green, David Greene, J. Mark Hansen, Neil Harris, Tony Hirschel, Marvin Hoffman, Emile Karafiol, Katherine Karvunis, Timothy Knowles, Stacey Kole, John R. Kroll, Sunil Kumar, Ralph Lerner, Donald N. Levine, Charles A. Lewis, John Lucy, Daniel Meyer, Bill Michel, Robert J. Morrissey, Janel Mueller, David L. Murphy, Deborah L. Nelson, David Nirenberg, Andrew Patner, Moishe Postone, Bob Riesman, Thomas F. Rosenbaum, Richard A. Rosengarten, Martha T. Roth, Marshall Sahlins, Allen Sanderson, Michael Silverstein, Joel Snyder, James T. Sparrow, Geoffrey R. Stone, Lorna P. Straus, Richard A. Strier, Richard P. Taub, William Veeder, Katy Weintraub, and Robert J. Zimmer, as well as my late colleagues Wayne C. Booth, Bert Cohler, Barry D. Karl, Friedrich Katz, Edward H. Levi, Charles D. O'Connell, and Herman L. Sinaiko. I am also grateful to Jim Sparrow and Richard F. Teichgraeber for helpful bibliographical suggestions about the history of American higher education, to Mark Hansen, Debbie Nelson, and Allen Sanderson for extremely valuable discussions about the history of graduate education, to Tim Knowles and Chuck Lewis for vital information about the early history of the Urban Education Institute and its various programs, and to John J. MacAloon for an insightful conversation about civilizational studies and the social sciences.

Special thanks to Anthony S. Bryk, Harry L. Davis, Lawrence Furnstahl, Marvin Hoffman, Donald N. Levine, Alexander E. Sharp, and Ted Snyder for offering perceptive reflections about their administrative roles at the University.

Many former graduate students have helped me with my archival inquiries, including John Deak, Rachel Feinmark, Patrick Houlihan, Alison Lefkovitz, Mihir Pandya, Gerard Siarny, Peter Simons, Thomas Sutton, and Naomi Vaughan. I am particularly indebted to Daniel Koehler for his excellent support and astute counsel over many years, and to Scott Campbell, William Greenland, and Peter Wilson for their help with admissions and enrollment statistics. My colleagues Michael R. Jones and Martha L. Merritt have given me constructive criticisms and discerning suggestions about many components of this book, as well as providing outstanding examples of enlightened academic leadership. My fellow historian Dennis J. Hutchinson has been a stimulating interlocutor and wise informant about many details of Chicago's history.

The archivists in the University's Special Collections Research Center, led by Daniel Meyer and Eileen A. Ielmini, have been laudable models of help and encouragement over the many years required to research this book. At the University of Chicago Press, Leslie Keros has been an outstanding editor of a very large and complex manuscript. The perspicacious and wise judgments and rigorous counsel of Timothy Mennel, senior editor at the Press, have made this a much better book.

I am particularly grateful to President Hanna H. Gray for first appointing me as dean of the College in May 1992. When describing the responsibilities to me, she remarked that the position was in fact more like being the president of a college than that of a regular academic dean. Either way, it has been a fascinating experience for a historian to be able to observe, from the inside out, the self of a remarkable university in times of significant transformation.

Finally, Barbara Boyer's shrewd and generous assessments of human nature have been crucial to my understanding of the paradoxes of a university that is stunningly and confidently cosmopolitan and, at the same time, profoundly and resolutely home-grown.

Chicago, January 2015

Notes

Introduction

1. Electronic copies of these monographs are available at http://college.uchicago .edu/about-college/college-publications.

2. Christian Meier, *From Athens to Auschwitz: The Uses of History* (Cambridge, MA, 2005), pp. 1–33, esp. pp. 20–23.

3. Robert B. Strassler, ed., *The Landmark Thucydides: A Comprehensive Guide to "The Peloponnesian War"* (New York, 1998), p. 14.

4. Arlette Farge, *The Allure of the Archives* (New Haven, CT, 2013), pp. 8, 12.

5. Alexander Gerschenkron, *Continuity in History and Other Essays* (Cambridge, MA, 1968), pp. 21, 38–39, 44.

6. Robert M. Hutchins, interview by George W. Dell, January 13, 1977, Robert M. Hutchins and Associates, Oral History Interviews, Box 1, folder 12.

7. I owe this formulation to one of the anonymous outside readers of this manuscript, commissioned by the University of Chicago Press.

8. Ernest D. Burton, "Charles L. Hutchinson and the University of Chicago," in *Charles Lawrence Hutchinson, 1854–1924* (Chicago, 1925), p. 24.

Chapter One

1. Christopher Jencks, "The Next Thirty Years in the Colleges," *Harper's Magazine*, October 1961, pp. 121–28. Jencks's essay caught the attention of Chicago staffers who summarized its arguments for the University's administrative leadership. See Carl Larsen to Alan Simpson, September 28, 1961, College Archive. At the time of the writing of this book, the College Archive encompassed both archives of the College organized in boxes under the series title Dean of the College Records in the Special Collections Research Center and archives that were working files in the Office of the Dean of the College and would eventually be sent to the Special Collections Research Center.

2. The literature is enormous and highly varied, but see particularly Bill Readings, *The University in Ruins* (Cambridge, MA, 1996); Dominick LaCapra, "The University in Ruins?," *Critical Inquiry* 25 (1998): 32–55; Charles T. Clotfelter, *Buying*

the Best: Cost Escalation in Elite Higher Education (Princeton, NJ, 1996); Thomas Bender and Carl E. Schorske, eds., *American Academic Culture in Transformation: Fifty Years, Four Disciplines* (Princeton, NJ, 1998); William F. Massy and Robert Zemsky, "Faculty Discretionary Time: Departments and the 'Academic Ratchet,'" *Journal of Higher Education* 65 (1994): 1–22; Roger L. Geiger, *Knowledge and Money: Research Universities and the Paradox of the Market* (Stanford, CA, 2004); David L. Kirp, *Shakespeare, Einstein, and the Bottom Line: The Marketing of Higher Education* (Cambridge, MA, 2003); Derek C. Bok, *Our Underachieving Colleges: A Candid Look at How Much Students Learn and Why They Should Be Learning More* (Princeton, NJ, 2006); Andrew Delbanco, *College: What It Was, Is, and Should Be* (Princeton, NJ, 2012); Robert Zemsky, *Making Reform Work: The Case for Transforming American Higher Education* (New Brunswick, NJ, 2009); and Zemsky, *Checklist for Change: Making American Higher Education a Sustainable Enterprise* (New Brunswick, NJ, 2013).

3. Louis Menand, "College: The End of the Golden Age," in Stephen J. Gould and Robert Atwan, eds., *The Best American Essays, 2002* (New York, 2002), pp. 219–31; Menand, *The Marketplace of Ideas: Reform and Resistance in the American University* (New York, 2010), pp. 63–77. See also the important discussion in Roger L. Geiger, *Research and Relevant Knowledge: American Research Universities since World War II* (New York, 1993), pp. 198–229; the perceptive "Introduction" in Wilson Smith and Thomas Bender, eds., *American Higher Education Transformed, 1940–2005: Documenting the National Discourse* (Baltimore, 2008), pp. 1–11; and the helpful survey in Richard M. Freeland, *Academia's Golden Age: Universities in Massachusetts, 1945–1970* (New York, 1992), pp. 70–119.

4. Christopher Jencks and David Riesman, *The Academic Revolution* (New York, 1968), pp. 8–27, 38–40, esp. pp. 23–24. For a useful critique of this book, see the review by F. Champion Ward in *Ethics* 80 (1969): 74–75.

5. Robert Herrick, "The University of Chicago," *Scribner's Magazine* 18 (1895): 399–417.

6. *The Responsibility of Greatness: A Statement Presented by the Board of Trustees of the University of Chicago* (Chicago, 1955), p. 5; *Great University Memorials, with a Reference to the Plans for the Development of the University of Chicago* (Chicago, 1925), p. 12.

7. Edward P. Brand, *Illinois Baptists: A History* (Bloomington, IL, 1930), p. 165; Perry J. Stackhouse, *Chicago and the Baptists: A Century of Progress* (Chicago, 1933), pp. 81–83.

8. Robert W. Johannsen, *Stephen A. Douglas* (New York, 1973), pp. 335–36.

9. William W. Everts, "History of the University of Chicago," p. 1, Old University of Chicago, Records, Box 9, folder 4. Unless otherwise indicated, all archival collections cited in this book are in the Special Collections Research Center, Joseph Regenstein Library, University of Chicago.

10. J. C. Burroughs, "Benefactors of the University: Stephen A. Douglas," *Volante*, December 1872, p. 28; Everts, "History of the University of Chicago," p. 2; Justin A. Smith, *A History of the Baptists in the Western States East of the Mississippi* (Philadel-

phia, 1896), pp. 281–82. Douglas had traveled to Europe between May and October of 1853 to meet prominent European political leaders (including Napoleon III and the Czar Nicholas) and to gain firsthand knowledge of British and continental political institutions. See Johannsen, *Stephen A. Douglas*, pp. 382–86.

11. "Address of Thomas Hoyne," in *Addresses and Appeals in Behalf of the University of Chicago and the Baptist Theological Seminary* (Chicago, 1867), p. 12; Daniel Meyer, *Stephen A. Douglas and the American Union* (Chicago, 1994), pp. 29–30.

12. J. O. Brayman, "Stephen A. Douglas Gift," n.d., Old University of Chicago, Records, Box 9, folder 5.

13. *Chicago Tribune*, July 8, 1857, p. 2.

14. Minutes of the Board of Trustees, September 2, 1857.

15. Ibid.

16. *Chicago Tribune*, January 28, 1874, p. 7.

17. *Christian Times*, October 1, 1856, p. 2.

18. Jones gave $30,000 in general support, including Jones Hall, whereas Scammon gave $30,000 for the Dearborn Observatory.

19. Johannsen, *Stephen A. Douglas*, pp. 620, 702, 870–71.

20. Burroughs was born in Stamford, New York, in December 1818 to a pioneer farm family. A bookish youngster who was an avid reader, his early education was literally in a log schoolhouse. He was appointed a part-time teacher at the age of sixteen and then apprenticed in a law office in Medina, New York, at the age of nineteen. He attended the Brockport Collegiate Institute and then Yale College, from which he graduated in 1842. He graduated from Madison Theological Seminary in 1846, served as a pastor in West Troy, New York, for five years, and then moved to Chicago, where he became the pastor of the First Baptist Church in 1852. He was offered the presidency of Shurtleff College in Alton, Illinois, in 1855, which he refused. After leaving the old University of Chicago, Burroughs served as a member of the city Board of Education and in 1884 was elected assistant superintendent of public schools. He died in April 1892. See "John C. Burroughs," in *Biographical Sketches of the Leading Men of Chicago* (Chicago, 1868), pp. 583–89.

21. Smith, *A History of the Baptists*, p. 287.

22. Minutes of the Board of Trustees, July 15, 1858.

23. Thomas W. Goodspeed, "The Founding of the First University of Chicago," *University Record* 5 (1919): 248.

24. Frederick Rudolph, *The American College and University: A History* (New York, 1962), pp. 177–200; Donald G. Tewksbury, *The Founding of American Colleges and Universities before the Civil War, with Particular Reference to the Religious Influences Bearing upon the College Movement* (New York, 1932), pp. 23–28; and more recently, the excellent survey of Roger L. Geiger, "The Era of the Multipurpose Colleges in American Higher Education, 1850–1890," in Geiger, ed., *The American College in the Nineteenth Century* (Nashville, 2000), pp. 127–52.

25. *Christian Times*, July 10, 1857, p. 2. The ceremonies were delayed inordinately because proper equipment to maneuver the cornerstone into place had not been summoned, but following a ceremony managed by a local Masonic lodge, all the

guests were well fed at tables loaded with "bountiful provision" by local Baptist ladies.

26. See Frederick Rudolph, *Curriculum: A History of the American Undergraduate Course of Study since 1636* (San Francisco, 1977), pp. 61–65; Arthur M. Cohen, *The Shaping of American Higher Education: Emergence and Growth of the Contemporary System* (San Francisco, 1998), pp. 73–83; Geiger, "The Era of the Multipurpose Colleges," pp. 128–29, 139–42. For an earlier, and contrasting view of the liberal arts from 1828, see David B. Potts, *Liberal Education for a Land of Colleges: Yale's Reports of 1828* (New York, 2010), esp. pp. 33–47.

27. See David B. Potts, *Baptist Colleges in the Development of American Society, 1812–1861* (New York, 1988), pp. 323–32; and Richard Hofstadter and Wilson Smith, eds., *American Higher Education: A Documentary History* (Chicago, 1961), 1: 334–75, esp. p. 358. Wayland had recently published another tract, in 1855, *The Education Demanded by the People of the United States: A Discourse Delivered at Union College, Schenectady, July 25, 1854, on the Occasion of the Fiftieth Anniversary of the Presidency of Eliphalet Nott, DD, LLD* (Boston, 1855).

28. See John C. Burroughs, "Benefactors of the University—Dr. Wayland," *Volante*, January 1873, pp. 42–43.

29. Richard Hofstadter and C. DeWitt Hardy, *The Development and Scope of Higher Education in the United States* (New York, 1952), p. 13; as well as Laurence R. Veysey, *The Emergence of the American University* (Chicago, 1965), pp. 21–25, 32–40.

30. Thomas W. Goodspeed, "Frederick A. Smith," in *The University of Chicago Biographical Sketches* (Chicago, 1922–25), vol. 1, p. 320.

31. See *First Annual Catalogue of the University of Chicago: Officers and Students for the Academic Year 1859–1860* (Chicago 1860), p. 19.

32. The *First Annual Catalogue of the University of Chicago*, pp. 12–22 provides an overview of the various options. The literature on pre-1870 colleges in the United States is huge and quite varied. I have found most helpful Cohen, *The Shaping of American Higher Education*, pp. 9–97; Rudolph, *The American College and University*, pp. 44–286; the revisionist account in Colin B. Burke, *American Collegiate Populations: A Test of the Traditional View* (New York, 1982); the detailed analysis in Potts, *Baptist Colleges in the Development of American Society*; and the various essays in Geiger, *The American College in the Nineteenth Century*.

33. *Volante*, March 1873, p. 1.

34. Another, more sympathetic student writer commented that the weakness of the sciences reflected the simple fact that "the want of money is the root of the evil." *Volante*, May 1873, p. 78. As late as 1886–87, 62 percent of all students enrolled in colleges in the United States were taking classical courses of study. See Thomas D. Snyder, *120 Years of American Education: A Statistical Portrait* (Washington, DC, 1993), p. 64.

35. See Veysey, *The Emergence of the American University*, pp. 40–56.

36. *Chicago Sunday Record-Herald*, October 6, 1912, part 5, p. 2.

37. The student newspaper was strongly opposed. See *Volante*, June 1873, pp. 95–96.

38. *Volante*, May 1884, p. 152; March 1885, p. 5.

39. Snyder, *120 Years of American Education*, p. 64.

40. Ibid., pp. 75–76. The contrast with today's proportion is striking: in 2011, 42 percent of Americans aged eighteen to twenty-four attended degree-granting postsecondary institutions.

41. For the norm at many other colleges, see Helen L. Horowitz, *Campus Life: Undergraduate Cultures from the End of the Eighteenth Century to the Present* (New York, 1987), pp. 23–55.

42. "The Passing of the Old University of Chicago," *Chicago Sunday Herald-Record,* October 6, 1912, part 5, p. 2. On the contests, see *Volante,* December 1873, pp. 29–30.

43. "Many students pay their entire expenses by engaging in clerical and manual labor of various kinds. No young man desirous of a liberal education need be deterred by lack of means." *Twenty-Seventh Annual Catalogue of the University of Chicago, including the Union College of Law* (Chicago, 1886), p. 25.

44. *Volante,* December 1873, p. 27; November 1877, pp. 24–25.

45. Minutes of the Board of Trustees, June 12, 1883.

46. For example, James R. Boise, *Exercises in Greek Prose Composition, Adapted to the First Book of Xenophon's "Anabasis"* (New York, 1867); Boise, *First Lessons in Greek, Adapted to the Grammar of Goodwin, and to That of Hadley as Revised by Frederic D. Forest Allen* (Chicago, 1891); and Albert H. Mixer, *Manual of French Poetry with Historical Introduction, and Biographical Notices of the Principal Authors, for the Use of the School and the Home* (New York, 1874).

47. Judy A. Hilkey, *Character Is Capital: Success Manuals and Manhood in Gilded Age America* (Chapel Hill, NC, 1997), p. 60.

48. Frederick Rudolph, "Who Paid the Bills? An Inquiry into the Nature of 19th-Century College Finance," *Harvard Educational Review* 31 (1961): 144–57; Rudolph, *The American College and University,* pp. 193–200.

49. Kenneth W. Rose, "John D. Rockefeller, the American Baptist Education Society, and the Growth of Baptist Higher Education in the Midwest" (unpublished manuscript, 1998), p. 8.

50. Edson S. Bastin to Anna Bastin, July 31, 1878, Bastin Papers, Box 1, folder 1.

51. Old University of Chicago, Records, Box 2, folder 14.

52. The denominations that founded these small colleges were often unwilling to provide money, given the urgent press of other priorities. Geiger, "The Era of Multipurpose Colleges," p. 151.

53. On Everts's influence, see Stackhouse, *Chicago and the Baptists,* pp. 58, 68–69, 81; and "William W. Everts," in *Biographical Sketches of the Leading Men of Chicago,* pp. 141–47, here 146.

54. Smith, A *History of the Baptists,* p. 285; *Standard,* July 7, 1864, p. 2. In June 1888, after the University went bankrupt, the observatory's telescope was removed to a site on the campus of Northwestern University.

55. See the long article by Everts's son, W. W. Everts Jr., in the *Chicago Tribune,* February 7, 1874, p. 7. A total of $25,000 was eventually raised for this professorship. See Minutes of the Board of Trustees, December 20, 1865.

56. W. W. Everts, *The Life of Rev. W. W. Everts, DD* (Philadelphia, 1891), pp. 99–100.

57. William Everts to his wife, September 10, 1888, p. 4, Old University of Chicago, Records, Box 9, folder 4.

58. Everts, *The Life of Rev. W. W. Everts*, pp. 96–97. Everts later wrote an unpublished manuscript attacking Burroughs and his fellow trustees for all manner of irresponsible and irresolute behavior, alleging that out of indifference or laziness they deliberately refused to find ways to strengthen the University's finances. See Everts, "History of the University of Chicago" [1889 or 1890], Old University of Chicago, Records, 1856–1890, Box 9, folder 4.

59. Arthur A. Azlein, "The Old University of Chicago" (course paper, University of Chicago, 1941), pp. 34–35; Minutes of the Board of Trustees, October 11, 1864.

60. *Chicago Tribune*, September 7, 1873, p. 7. Ogden "felt a lively interest in the institution, and was understood to be pledged to erect the north wing of the great university building as soon as the institution should free itself from debt. This it never did, and the troubles which broke out among the Trustees and for many years paralyzed their efforts so discouraged Mr. Ogden that any benevolent intentions he had cherished toward the institution were never carried out." Thomas W. Goodspeed, "William Butler Ogden," in *The University of Chicago Biographical Sketches*, vol. 1, p. 52; Everts, "History of the University of Chicago," p. 5.

61. Minutes of the Board of Trustees, July 7, 1863; June 30, 1865.

62. Minutes of the Board of Trustees, July 19, 1865.

63. Azlein, "The Old University of Chicago," p. 37.

64. Sawyer to the Board of Trustees, April 20, 1869, Old University of Chicago, Records, Box 2, folder 5.

65. Minutes of the Board of Trustees, July 2, 1869.

66. Everts later claimed that, at the urgent request of the trustees, he had undertaken an emergency fund-raising campaign in the East to dispose of the land, netting $60,000 that enabled the board to finance the commitment Burroughs had made to the investors. Everts, *The Life of Rev. W. W. Everts*, pp. 101–3.

67. See Azlein, "The Old University of Chicago," p. 47. Much of the early financial history of the University emerged during the proceedings of the foreclosure suit filed by the Union Mutual Insurance Company. These proceedings are reprinted in "The Chicago University," *Chicago Tribune*, November 27, 1884, p. 9.

68. Minutes of the Board of Trustees, October 1872. In 1877, the board again reported that "all that had been relied upon for Endowment of professorships before the great fire of 1871 was literally swept away by that calamity." Minutes of the Board of Trustees, January 11, 1877.

69. *Volante*, February 1872, p. 4.

70. *Chicago Tribune*, October 3, 1872, p. 5; October 4, 1872, p. 6; October 10, 1872, p. 7; September 7, 1873, p. 7; January 13, 1874, p. 3; January 23, 1874, p. 3; and January 30, 1874, p. 7.

71. Minutes of the Board of Trustees, October 1872; Everts, *The Life of Rev. W. W. Everts*, p. 103.

72. *Chicago Tribune*, April 10, 1874, p. 2; July 1, 1874, p. 4; July 3, 1874, p. 2. In addition to teaching at Crozer and Lewisburg, Moss was the secretary of the United States Christian Commission from 1863 to 1865. From 1868 to 1872 he served as the editor of the *National Baptist*. He died in 1904.

73. Moss's own account is in the *Standard*, August 26, 1875, p. 4.

74. *Standard*, August 19, 1875, p. 2.

75. Minutes of the Board of Trustees, July 13, 1875. *Standard*, August 19, 1875, pp. 2, 4, contains a detailed account of these maneuvers of the board.

76. *Standard*, July 29, 1875, p. 4. A meeting of alumni of the University on July 26 manifested divided opinions, but in the end a majority approved resolutions demanding that Moss be reinstated. *Chicago Tribune*, July 27, 1875, p. 1. On the history of the *Standard*, see Myron D. Dillow, *Harvesttime on the Prairie: A History of the Baptists in Illinois, 1796–1996* (Franklin, TN, 1996), pp. 274–75.

77. *Standard*, August 19, 1875, p. 2.

78. *Standard*, July 22, 1875, p. 4.

79. He said as much in a letter to the board. See Minutes of the Board of Trustees, June 28, 1876. After resigning, Abernethy became president of the Cedar Valley Seminary at Osage, Iowa in 1881.

80. *Chicago Tribune*, July 31, 1875, p. 8; August 10, 1875, p. 3; August 15, 1875, p. 14; October 23, 1877, p. 2. The *New York Methodist* proclaimed, "The Chicago University (Baptist) has for some time been a seat for an incompetent President." Quoted in *Chicago Tribune*, August 1, 1875, p. 16.

81. *Chicago Tribune*, December 9, 1875, p. 8.

82. *Chicago Tribune*, April 8, 1878, p. 2. In addition to the debt to the insurance company, the University had another $35,000 in floating debt.

83. Everts, "History of the University of Chicago," pp. 5–6; Azlein, "The Old University of Chicago," p. 51.

84. Minutes of the Board of Trustees, February 19, 1873.

85. Minutes of the Board of Trustees, January 11, 1877.

86. Kathleen D. McCarthy, *Noblesse Oblige: Charity and Cultural Philanthropy in Chicago, 1849 to 1929* (Chicago, 1982), pp. 53, 62.

87. Ibid., p. 65.

88. Helen L. Horowitz, *Culture and the City: Cultural Philanthropy in Chicago from the 1880s to 1917* (Chicago, 1989), pp. 84–85.

89. David A. Hollinger, "Inquiry and Uplift: Late Nineteenth-Century American Academics and the Moral Efficacy of Scientific Practice," in Thomas L. Haskell, ed., *The Authority of Experts: Studies in History and Theory* (Bloomington, IN, 1984), pp. 142–56.

90. The early history of the seminary is charted in C. E. Hewitt, "Twenty-Five Years, History of the Baptist Union Theological Seminary, 1867–92," Baptist Theological Union, Records, Box 2, folder 8.

91. *Christian Times and Witness*, October 11, 1866, p. 3. Classes officially began in the fall of 1867.

92. *Standard*, July 8, 1869, p. 4. After the seminary moved to Morgan Park, the

building was converted into a hospital, called the Chicago Baptist Hospital at 3410 S. Rhodes until 1912.

93. W. W. Everts Jr. claimed that Dwight L. Moody, the young preacher who would eventually go on to create a powerful rival evangelical movement in Chicago, was an early student at the seminary. See Everts, *The Life of Rev. W. W. Everts*, p. 111.

94. For the early student body, see "Special Report of the Executive Committee on Character of Students" [1876], Baptist Theological Union, Records, Box 2, folder 7.

95. D. B. Cheney, "Report of the Board of Trustees of the Baptist Theological Union Located at Chicago, Made to the Union, May 8, 1877," p. 1, Baptist Theological Union, Records, Box 2, folder 11. See also the explanation in the *Standard*, October 19, 1867, p. 4.

96. Cheney, "Report of the Board of Trustees ," pp. 2–3.

97. See Thomas W. Goodspeed, "George Clarke Walker," in *The University of Chicago Biographical Sketches*, vol. 1, pp. 112–15.

98. The total gift comprised forty-five acres of land. The original gift document is filed in Baptist Theological Union, Records, Box 2, folder 9. A second hall, named in honor of Nelson Blake, was built in 1886–87 for $38,000. See "Annual Report of the Board of Trustees, April 19th, 1888," pp. 3–4, ibid., folder 11.

99. Walker's insistence on this issue was one of the motives behind the decision of the university administration to build a classroom building immediately adjacent to his museum for the geology and geography departments, Rosenwald Hall.

100. Blake to Goodspeed, June 8, 1881, Baptist Theological Union, Records, Box 2, folder 1; Thomas W. Goodspeed, "E. Nelson Blake," in *The University of Chicago Biographical Sketches*, vol. 1, p. 73.

101. Thomas W. Goodspeed, *The Baptist Union Theological Seminary, Morgan Park, Ill.: A Great Opportunity* (November 1885), pp. 1, 5, Baptist Theological Union, Records, Box 2, folder 10.

102. Ibid., pp. 7–8.

103. Hewitt, "Twenty-Five Years, History of the Baptist Union Theological Seminary."

104. The Hengstenberg Library was secured with the leadership of William W. Everts, who used his son, William Jr., as a purchasing agent (his son was studying at the University of Berlin at the time).

105. *The Hebrew Student: A Monthly Journal in the Interests of Old Testament Literature and Interpretation* 1 (July 1882): 71–72, 79.

106. Thomas W. Goodspeed, *A History of the University of Chicago: The First Quarter-Century* (Chicago, 1916), p. 25.

107. Merrill to Goodspeed, December 9, 1886, Baptist Theological Union, Records, Box 2, folder 1.

108. See James F. Findlay, *Dwight L. Moody, American Evangelist, 1837–1899* (Chicago, 1969), pp. 54–135; Bruce J. Evensen, *God's Man for the Gilded Age: D. L. Moody and the Rise of Modern Mass Evangelism* (New York, 2003), pp. 123–63; Dar-

rel M. Robertson, *The Chicago Revival, 1876: Society and Revivalism in a Nineteenth-Century City* (Metuchen, NJ, 1989), pp. 17, 41, 48; Timothy George, ed., *Mr. Moody and the Evangelical Tradition* (London, 2004), pp. 3–4.

109. See Lawrence B. Davis, *Immigrants, Baptists, and the Protestant Mind in America* (Urbana, IL, 1973), pp. 51–52, 58–59, 158–59, 193. Local Baptist leaders like George Lorimer and Eri B. Hulbert were known for their hostility to immigration. The Baptist newspaper in Chicago, the *Standard*, was outspoken in its condemnation of the Haymarket rioters, for example.

110. See Arthur H. Wilde, ed., *Northwestern University: A History, 1855–1905* (New York, 1905).

111. *Standard*, January 31, 1884, p. 4.

112. Gates to Harper, November 19, 1888, University of Chicago Founders' Correspondence, 1886–1892, Box 1, folder 4.

113. *Chicago Tribune*, February 1, 1878, p. 7, which delicately noted that Burroughs was now "regarded as not altogether suitable in a financial way."

114. *Chicago Tribune*, April 8, 1878, p. 2.

115. Frederick L. Anderson, *Galusha Anderson: Preacher and Educator, 1832–1918* (privately published, 1933), pp. 17–18.

116. Minutes of the Board of Trustees, June 29, 1881; June 13, 1882.

117. *Chicago Tribune*, May 14, 1878, p. 8; March 16, 1879, p. 7.

118. Rockefeller to Anderson, April 20, 1882, "John D. Rockefeller, Private Letterbook, 'Pledges, Donations, Family, etc.', May 20, 1881 to April 3, 1886," p. 2, Storr Papers, Box 6. Rockefeller rejected Anderson's further appeals in January and March 1883 and February 1885.

119. Anderson to Mrs. Marsh, December 8, 1884, Old University of Chicago, Records, Box 2, folder 12.

120. Anderson, *Galusha Anderson*, pp. 18–19.

121. *Chicago Tribune*, June 5, 1877, p. 2; June 15, 1877, p. 8.

122. Ibid., July 1, 1877, p. 8; July 3, 1877, p. 8.

123. See "Oral Argument of Mr. Swett in Foreclosure Case," in the *United States Circuit Court, Northern District of Illinois: The Union Mutual Life Insurance Co. vs. the University of Chicago; Argument for Complainant, Swett, Haskell and Grosscup Complainant's Solicitors* (Chicago, 1884), p. 52; as well as the coverage in the *Chicago Tribune*, November 27, 1884, p. 9.

124. "Opinion of Judge Blodgett in Foreclosure and Scholarship Cases," in the *United States Circuit Court, Northern District of Illinois: The Union Mutual Life Insurance Co. vs. the University of Chicago*, p. 5.

125. *Hyde Park Herald*, July 25, 1885, p. 1. What Harper actually thought of Galusha Anderson is uncertain. After 1892 Harper was always solicitous of Anderson and the old faculty both in public and in private, and the alumni reciprocated. On Lorimer, see A. H. Newman, ed., *A Century of Baptist Achievement* (Philadelphia, 1901), pp. 384–85.

126. *Standard*, February 11, 1886, p. 5; Francis W. Shepardson, "Recollections of First Things at the University of Chicago," pp. 6–7, Goodspeed Papers, Box 4, folder

12; "An Historical Sketch," *President's Report, July, 1897–July, 1898, with Summaries for 1891–97* (Chicago, 1899), p. 1.

127. *Chicago Tribune*, January 25, 1874, p. 8; as well as February 1, 1874, p. 8.

128. *Hyde Park Herald*, April 17, 1886, p. 4.

129. Northrup to Rockefeller, December 10, 1888, University of Chicago Founders' Correspondence, 1886–1892, Box 1, folder 4.

130. Bastin to Anna Bastin, April 9, 1882, Old University of Chicago, Records, Box 2, folder 12.

131. *Standard*, July 11, 1878, p. 4.

132. Blake to Goodspeed, July 2, 1888, Baptist Theological Union, Records, Box 2, folder 1.

133. "The Pursuit of Order in Late Nineteenth Century Education," p. 4, Storr Papers, Box 4, folder 12.

134. Minutes of the Board of Trustees, June 15, 1886.

135. Rockefeller to Goodspeed, April 13, 1886, University of Chicago Founders' Correspondence, 1886–1892, Box 1, folder 1.

136. Goodspeed to Rockefeller, April 7, 1886; April 22, 1886; May 7, 1886.

137. Goodspeed to Rockefeller, June 15, 1886, and June 16, 1886.

138. See *Standard*, September 16, 1886, p. 4; September 23, 1886, p. 4. A committee of five alumni, led by trustee David G. Hamilton, drafted a last-minute proposal that the University negotiate a deal with the insurance company under which it would continue to lease the Thirty-Fourth Street building and try to pay off its debt via a new subscription drive, but this was too little and too late. Hamilton, curiously, was a director of Union Mutual. See Minutes of the Board of Trustees, May 8, 1886. *The Watchman*, the Baptist newspaper in Boston, characterized Hamilton's scheme as "delusive," and rightly so. *Watchman*, October 21, 1886, filed in George C. Walker Scrapbook, 1873–1903, Box 1, folder 1.

139. P. S. Henson, T. W. Goodspeed, and J. A. Smith, "To the President and Directors of the Blue Island Land Company," October 1, 1886, George C. Walker Scrapbook, Box 1, folder 1.

140. See the letters of October 27, 1886, November 16, 1886, November 24, 1886, and November 29, 1886, George C. Walker Scrapbook, Box 1, folder 1.

141. By 1917 he had given $275 million to charity. See Ron Chernow, *Titan: The Life of John D. Rockefeller, Sr.* (New York 1998), p. 623.

142. "John D. Rockefeller, Private Letterbook, 'Pledges, Donations, Family, etc.', May 20, 1881 to April 3, 1886," p. 11, Storr Papers, Box 6.

143. Edgar J. Goodspeed, *As I Remember* (New York, 1953), p. 34.

144. Editor's note attached to a transcript of Rockefeller to Goodspeed, June 14, 1886, University of Chicago Founders' Correspondence, Box 1, folder 1. Later in his life, Gates described Rockefeller's deflections of Augustus Strong's constant pleas as "as fine a disclosure here, as elsewhere, of his superb mastery of the art of fencing." Gates to Goodspeed, March 17, 1914, Goodspeed Papers, Box 1, folder 21.

145. Goodspeed to Rockefeller, October 15, 1887, University of Chicago Founders' Correspondence, 1886–1892, Box 1, folder 2.

146. Goodspeed to Rockefeller, June 16, 1886, folder 2.

147. Goodspeed to Harper, October 15, 1888, folder 3.

148. Henson to Rockefeller, June 4, 1888, folder 3.

149. "Your long letter with respect to the university I have read and re-read and think it is a very important question but have not been able to see my way clear to give you any encouragement. I will still further investigate." Rockefeller to Goodspeed, February 14, 1887, folder 3.

150. Rockefeller to Lorimer, February 6, 1888, folder 3.

151. Rockefeller to Henson, June 19, 1888, folder 3.

152. See Grant Wacker, *Augustus H. Strong and the Dilemma of Historical Consciousness* (Macon, GA, 1985), p. 5.

153. Strong to Rockefeller, February 22, 1887, University of Chicago Founders' Correspondence, Box 1, folder 2.

154. Augustus Strong, "A University—What It Is and Why We Need One," University of Chicago Founders' Correspondence, Box 1, folder 2. In October 1888, Strong gave a long lecture that presented his plan in considerable detail: *The Church and the University: A Detailed Argument and Plan* (Rochester, 1889), filed in American Baptist Education Society, Records, Box 1, folder 1.

155. Strong first contacted Harper in September 1887. See Strong to Harper, September 21, 1887, Office of the President, Harper, Judson, Burton Administrations (hereafter HJB Administrations), Box 78, folder 28; Wacker, *Augustus H. Strong*, p. 61; and Lars Hoffman, "William Rainey Harper and the Chicago Fellowship" (PhD diss., University of Iowa, 1978), pp. 34–41.

156. Strong to Rockefeller, September 24, 1887, University of Chicago Founders' Correspondence, Box 1, folder 2.

157. Strong to Rockefeller, September 25, 1887.

158. Strong to Rockefeller, September 28, 1887.

159. Strong to Harper, October 4, 1887; October 11, 1887; October 17, 1887; October 25, 1887; October 26, 1887; November 2, 1887; November 7, 1887; November 12, 1887; November 17, 1887; November 26, 1887; December 5, 1887; December 9, 1887; December 19, 1887; February 16, 1888; February 26, 1888; April 23, 1888; April 26, 1888; April 30, 1888, HJB Administrations, Box 78, folder 28; Strong to Harper, March 1, 1888; March 14, 1888; March 26, 1888; March 29, 1888; April 13, 1888, American Institute of Sacred Literature, Records, Box 4, folder 1. It is telling that Harper was insistent on Strong launching the whole plan immediately, and not simply starting with a divinity school. See especially Strong to Harper, October 26, 1887, HJB Administrations, Box 78, folder 28.

160. Strong went so far as to urge Harper not to confuse Rockefeller by even mentioning the Chicago project: "But it would not be wise to complicate the matter just now by asking Mr. R. to establish even a small institution in Chicago, much less to undertake the harmonizing of Baptist interests throughout the land.... Now we must divide in order to conquer. One thing at a time. Like Napoleon, mass your forces at the critical point." Strong to Harper, October 26, 1887, HJB Administrations, Box 78, folder 28.

161. Strong to Rockefeller, February 15, 1887; February 17, 1887, University of Chicago Founders' Correspondence, Box 1, folder 1. Henry Morehouse also reported to Frederick T. Gates that Strong "would like the influence of yourself and of myself if it could be used with Mr. Rockefeller to induce him to commit himself to this measure without delay." Morehouse to Gates, October 6, 1888, Gates Papers, Box 1, folder 2.

162. See Harper to Rockefeller, December 2, 1887, University of Chicago Founders' Correspondence, Box 1, folder 2.

163. Crerar Douglas, ed., *Autobiography of Augustus Hopkins Strong* (Valley Forge, PA, 1981), p. 249. Strong confessed to Harper, "I have a little fear that my last letter to Mr. R. may have been too plain. It was intended only to be honest. As many times before, I took my life in my hand to write it and risked a great deal." Strong to Harper, December 5, 1887, HJB Administrations, Box 78, folder 28.

164. Strong eventually apologized to Rockefeller for his pushy, heavy-handed behavior. Strong to Rockefeller, December 23, 1887, University of Chicago Founders' Correspondence, Box 1, folder 2. Gates thought that Rockefeller "is not convinced that Dr. Strong's scheme is on the whole now the most needful thing." Gates to Morehouse, October 9, 1888, Gates Papers, Box 1, folder 2.

165. After much politicking, the final vote was 188 in favor, and 34 opposed. "It was really a popular victory of the moneyless and educationally destitute West and South, over the moneyed and educationally well-provided Eastern and New England states." Frederick Taylor Gates, *Chapters in My Life* (New York, 1977), p. 91. The debates over the society are reprinted in *The National Baptist Convention and Organization of the American Baptist Education Society held in the Calvary Baptist Church at Washington, D.C., May 16 and 17, 1888* (Washington, DC, 1888), esp. pp. 70–75.

166. H. L. Morehouse, "A Seven Years' Survey," in *Fifty-Fourth Annual Report of the American Baptist Home Mission Society, Convened in Educational Hall, Asbury Park, NJ, May 27, 28, and 29, 1886* (New York, 1886), pp. 151–52.

167. *The National Baptist Educational Convention and Organization of the American Baptist Education Society*, pp. 63, 70. On Morehouse's later advocacy of immigration restrictions, see Lawrence B. Davis, *Immigrants, Baptists, and the Protestant Mind in America* (Urbana, IL, 1973), pp. 75–77, 86–87.

168. Kenneth W. Rose, "John D. Rockefeller, The American Baptist Education Society, and the Growth of Baptist Higher Education in the Midwest" (unpublished manuscript, 1998), pp. 6–7; as well as Rose, "Why Chicago and Not Cleveland? The Religious Imperative behind John D. Rockefeller's Early Philanthropy, 1855–1900" (unpublished manuscript, 1995).

169. The poll was sent by Dr. P. S. Henson, George Lorimer, A. K. Parker, W. M. Lawrence, Everett D. Burr, J. Wolfenden, and J. B. Thames. A copy of the appeal is filed with Gates to Morehouse, July 14, 1888, Gates Papers, Box 1, folder 1. For a contemporary survey of the most important Baptist churches in Chicago, see Alfred T. Andreas, *History of Chicago from the Earliest Period to the Present Time* (Chicago, 1884–86), vol. 3, pp. 811–18.

170. Blake to Goodspeed, July 2, 1888, Baptist Theological Union, Records,

Box 2, folder 1; Van Asdel to George Lorimer, P. S. Henson, et al., June 11, 1888, Gates Papers, Box 1, folder 1.

171. Quoted in Lathan A. Crandall, *Henry Lyman Morehouse: A Biography* (Philadelphia, 1919), p. 128.

172. Morehouse to Gates, June 12, 1888, Gates Papers, Box 1, folder 1. Morehouse described Gates's early conceptions in the following way: "Your comprehensive view of the educational situation in the west shows that you have grasped the idea thoroughly and I hope you may live to see your plans realized, namely, a great institution at Chicago with academical feeders in adjacent states."

173. See Gates, *Chapters in My Life*, esp. 77–121.

174. Soma Hewa, "The Protestant Personality and Higher Education: American Philanthropy beyond the 'Progressive Era'," *International Journal of Politics, Culture and Society* 12 (1998): 150–51, 154–55.

175. Gates later observed that Rockefeller "was not for his part prepared to lead off in such an undertaking until he could act on the unassailable ground of denominational authority and united denominational support. He was not prepared to act in favor of Chicago until he heard the voice of the entire Denomination calling upon him so to act and uniting with him in the work." Gates to Goodspeed, January 9, 1915, HJB Administrations, Box 45, folder 12.

176. Gates to Morehouse, July 14, 1888, Gates Papers, Box 1, folder 1.

177. Gates to Morehouse, July 29, 1888; August 23, 1888, University of Chicago Founders' Correspondence, Box 1, folder 3.

178. Gates attended the meeting held on July 2, 1888, at the Grand Pacific Hotel where Lorimer and a group of ministers officially voted to launch a fund-raising campaign to secure $500,000 for a new University of Chicago. See Lorimer to Walker, July 3, 1888, George C. Walker Scrapbook, Box 1, folder 2.

179. Gates to Morehouse, July 29, 1888, University of Chicago Founders' Correspondence, Box 1, folder 3.

180. Gates to Morehouse, June 21, 1888, Gates Papers, Box 1, folder 1.

181. "The Need of a Baptist University in Chicago, as Illustrated by a Study of Baptist Collegiate Education in the West," Gates Papers, Box 1, folder 2. Gates subsequently wrote to Morehouse explicitly arguing against the Morgan Park option: "The fact is that the thing to do is to locate in the city and not at Morgan Park. Both the Presbyterians and Methodists are out of the city. The city is the place and no mistake." Gates to Morehouse, October 17, 1888, Gates Papers, Box 1, folder 2.

182. Gates to Morehouse, October 9, 1888.

183. Gates to Rockefeller, January 21, 1889, HJB Administrations, Box 45, folder 12.

184. Gates to Morehouse, October 16, 1888, Gates Papers, Box 1, folder 2.

185. Gates to Morehouse, October 23, 1888.

186. Morehouse to Gates, October 26, 1888.

187. Goodspeed to Gates, October 15, 1888.

188. Goodspeed to Harper, October 25, 1888, University of Chicago Founders' Correspondence, Box 1, folder 3.

189. As late as April 1888, Harper was still advocating Strong's scheme to Rockefeller. See Harper to Rockefeller, April 28, 1888, University of Chicago Founders' Correspondence, Box 1, folder 3; and the correspondence from late March and early April 1888 in the American Institute of Sacred Literature, Records, Box 4, folder 1.

190. Harper to Goodspeed, October 13, 1888; Goodspeed to Harper, October 15, 1888, University of Chicago Founders' Correspondence, Box 1, folder 3. Goodspeed sent Harper a copy of Gates's report in late October, requesting that Harper send it on to Rockefeller, which Harper did on October 30. Goodspeed to Harper, October 25, 1888.

191. Harper to Gates, November 13, 1888, as well as Harper to Goodspeed, November 5, 1888, University of Chicago Founders' Correspondence, Box 1, folder 4. Later in his life, Gates reflected that Harper's reports of these conversations were likely to have been exaggerated and overly optimistic. See Gates to Goodspeed, December 13, 1926, Office of the President, Mason Administration, Records, Box 7, folder 8; and Gates, *Chapters in My Life*, p. 100.

192. Goodspeed to his sons, November 11, 1888; Goodspeed to Rockefeller, November 13, 1888; November 22, 1888, University of Chicago Founders' Correspondence, Box 1, folder 4. Gates too now bought into the idea of a university in Chicago with an endowment of "four to ten millions." Gates to Harper, November 26, 1888, ibid. To Morehouse he advocated not a college but a "university in the highest sense of the term." Gates to Morehouse, November 26, 1888, Gates Papers, Box 1, folder 3.

193. Strong to Harper, November 18, 1888, HJB Administrations, Box 78, folder 28.

194. Douglas, *Autobiography of Augustus Hopkins Strong*, p. 250. This manuscript was written after 1896 for the private use of Strong's family. It was not published until 1981.

195. "You must tell him [Strong] that if you conveyed the impression that his great University was to be built in Chicago, it was a mistake, or the matter has taken a different shape, that we have in mind a very different sort of institution and such a one as he approves for Chicago." Goodspeed to Harper, November 24, 1888, University of Chicago Founders' Correspondence, Box 1, folder 4.

196. Goodspeed to Harper, November 30, 1888.

197. Harper to Goodspeed, November 28, 1888. Of Rockefeller he wrote, "We want to keep him up to high-water mark, and when we see that there is danger that he is going to throw up the whole thing we can come down, and not until then."

198. Harper to Goodspeed, December 5, 1888.

199. Harper was present at this meeting and "intimated to the Board in a semi-confidential way his reasons for believing that Mr. Rockefeller was deeply interested in the movement and would take an active part in the establishment of the institution." Editorial note by Gates, on a report of the decision of the board, dated December 13, 1888, University of Chicago Founders' Correspondence, Box 1, folder 4.

200. Strong to Rockefeller, December 25, 1888, University of Chicago Founders' Correspondence, Box 1, folder 4.

201. Harper to Morehouse, December 28, 1888.

202. "As matters stand today Mr. Rockefeller still has confidence in me and he is waiting simply to see whether the brethren will stand by me or whether—accepting Dr. Strong's charges—they will brand me as a heretic and throw me overboard." Harper to Goodspeed, December 28, 1888.

203. Northrup wrote to Rockefeller, assuring him that Harper's "intellectual abilities are of the highest order, his scholarship is accurate, thorough and wide; he possesses a remarkable genius for organization, has extraordinary power of creative enthusiasm, and is a born leader of men." Northrup to Rockefeller, January 1, 1889, University of Chicago Founders' Correspondence, Box 1, folder 5.

204. Gates to Morehouse, January 3, 1889.

205. Gates to Morehouse, January 6, 1889; Gates to Goodspeed, January 11, 1889; Harper to Rockefeller, January 13, 1889.

206. Gates to Goodspeed, October 8, 1914, Goodspeed Papers, Box 1, folder 21.

207. Gates to Rockefeller, February 23, 1889; Harper to Rockefeller, February 25, 1889, University of Chicago Founders' Correspondence, Box 1, folder 6.

208. Rockefeller to Gates, February 26, 1889.

209. "Report of Committee on Proposed Institution of Learning in Chicago, April 12, 1889," University of Chicago Founders' Correspondence, Box 1, folder 7.

210. Harper visited Rockefeller in late January and reported that Rockefeller had been approached by Broadus of the Louisville seminary for $50,000 as well as by Gilman of Johns Hopkins, Welling of Columbia, and several others. Rockefeller was also "more tired than ever" of Strong's New York plan. Harper to Goodspeed, January 27, 1889, University of Chicago Founders' Correspondence, Box 1, folder 5.

211. Gates, *Chapters in My Life*, pp. 111–12.

212. Barry D. Karl and Stanley N. Katz, "Foundations and Ruling Class Elites," *Daedalus* 116 (1987): 14–15.

213. Goodspeed to Gates, December 7, 1888, Gates Papers, Box 1, folder 3.

214. See Goodspeed, "The Founding of the First University of Chicago," pp. 257–58.

215. Gates to Rockefeller, January 13, 1889, University of Chicago Founders' Correspondence, Box 1, folder 5.

216. Harper to Goodspeed, November 28, 1888, folder 4.

217. Statement of Gates to the Board of Trustees, July 9, 1890, Gates Papers, Box 1, folder 7.

218. Goodspeed to Harper, June 22, 1889, University of Chicago Founders' Correspondence, Box 1, folder 8.

219. Gates to Morehouse, February 2, 1890, folder 9.

220. Gates to Harper, February 17, 1890, folder 9.

221. Gates to Harper, October 23, 1889, folder 8.

222. Gates to Harper, November 12, 1889, folder 8.

223. On the gift from the Jewish businessmen, see Goodspeed to his sons, April 20, 1890, and Gates to Morehouse, April 25, 1890, University of Chicago Founders' Correspondence, Box 1, folder 9. That gift originated in a meeting that Goodspeed had with Mr. B. Loewenthal, a local Jewish banker. Loewenthal offered

to use his contacts and also suggested that Goodspeed contact Rabbi Emil Hirsch, who would do likewise. Goodspeed to his sons, February 23, 1890, ibid.

224. Harper to Gates, January 7, 1889; Harper to Goodspeed, January 8, 1889; Goodspeed to his sons, January 13, 1889, University of Chicago Founders' Correspondence, Box 1, folder 5. This letter suggests that Harper had been asked to give Yale a six-year commitment.

225. Harper to Rockefeller, January 13, 1889, University of Chicago Founders' Correspondence, Box 1, folder 5. Morehouse wrote to Gates that "he has peremptorily declined to take the presidency of the proposed University of Chicago and says he has told Mr. Rockefeller so." Morehouse to Gates, January 4, 1889, Gates Papers, Box 1, folder 4.

226. Gates to Morehouse, January 6, 1889; Harper to Goodspeed, January 19, 1889, University of Chicago Founders' Correspondence, Box 1, folder 5.

227. Goodspeed to Harper, June 1, 1890; Goodspeed to Harper, June 8, 1890; Gates to Harper, June 9, 1890, folder 10.

228. George S. Goodspeed to Thomas W. Goodspeed, May 26, 1890, folder 10. The negative currents at Yale that Goodspeed refers to very likely involved the strident reaction of President Dwight to Harper's toying with the idea of leaving New Haven. Dwight considered Harper's behavior as bordering on the unethical.

229. Gates to Rockefeller, July 28, 1890, University of Chicago Founders' Correspondence, Box 1, folder 10.

230. Rockefeller to Harper, August 6, 1890, folder 11.

231. "This, I suppose, means a good deal for him but is, of course, not very distinct." Harper to Gates, August 9, 1890, University of Chicago Founders' Correspondence, Box 1, folder 11. This was the beginning of a fateful, and perhaps deliberate, set of misunderstandings about the extent of Rockefeller's future support. Frederick Gates later asserted that each man viewed Rockefeller's commitment to provide sufficient resources for the new institution from a very different perspective.

232. Harper to Rockefeller, August 9, 1890, folder 11.

233. Goodspeed to his sons, April 28, 1889, folder 7; Strong to Harper, December 23, 1890, folder 12.

234. "Editor's Note" [1915], attached to the letter of August 5, 1890, University of Chicago Founders' Correspondence, Box 1, folder 11.

235. Karl and Katz, "Foundations and the Ruling Class Elites," pp. 21–22.

236. Gates to Henry Morehouse, February 7, 1891, University of Chicago Founders' Correspondence, Box 2, folder 1.

237. Harper to Goodspeed, September 6, 1890; Harper to Morehouse, September 10, 1890; Northrup to Harper, September 10, 1890, University of Chicago Founders' Correspondence, Box 1, folder 11.

238. Harper to Morehouse, September 6, 1890, folder 11.

239. Broadus to Harper, October 13, 1890, folder 12.

240. "Dr. Goodspeed and myself have written to Dr. Bright asking him to discontinue [our subscription to] *The Examiner*. I have no use for a paper that deliberately ignores such a magnificent gift to denominational education as that of Mr. Rocke-

feller. The hostility to Chicago is too manifest.... I rejoice in the thought that the new University will be so powerful as to defy such arbitrary, tyrannical, and brutal papers. They are a curse to the denomination." Northrup to Harper, October 15, 1890, folder 12.

241. Harper to Rockefeller, January 8, 1891, University of Chicago Founders' Correspondence, Box 2, folder 1.

242. Gates to Morehouse, February 6, 1891, Gates Papers, Box 1, folder 8. At the same time, Gates's frustration over Harper's intellectual acrobatics was evident: "Is there not danger that in announcing your iconoclastic views, you will sow doubts which you can by no means destroy? I have been more and more concerned to observe your tendency to 'speak out'. I can understand how a desire to be honest, and candid, and particularly not to deceive the public, now calling you to a lofty office, seems to you to demand frankness of speech on these points. You have stated your views to the leading brethren. That is enough it seems to me." Gates to Harper, January 11, 1891, University of Chicago Founders' Correspondence, Box 2, folder 1.

243. Goodspeed to Harper, January 14, 1891, folder 1.

244. Mark S. Massa, *Charles Augustus Briggs and the Crisis of Historical Criticism* (Minneapolis, 1990), p. 99; as well as Gary Dorrien, *The Making of American Liberal Theology: Imagining Progressive Religion, 1805–1900* (Louisville, 2001), pp. 335–65.

245. Harper to Morehouse, February 7, 1891, University of Chicago Founders' Correspondence, Box 2, folder 1.

246. Morehouse to Harper, February 2, 1891, folder 1. This letter was written with Rockefeller's explicit approval.

247. Harper to Whitney, March 21, 1892, William D. Whitney Papers, Yale University Archives.

248. Ira M. Price, "Some Personal Recollections of W. R. Harper Prior to 1892," p. 14, Price Papers, Box 6, folder 2.

249. Walker to Culver, December 17, 1895; and Culver to Walker, December 19, 1895, George C. Walker Scrapbook, Box 1, folder 9; Thomas W. Goodspeed, "Helen Culver," in *The University of Chicago Biographical Sketches*, vol. 2, p. 95.

250. Goodspeed, "William Butler Ogden," pp. 55–56.

251. Henderson's career straddled the old and new universities. A dedicated moralist and booster of Chicago, he also developed an impressive scholarly persona that gave his social reform activities in the city the aura of professional legitimacy. See Andrew Abbott, "Pragmatic Sociology and the Public Sphere: The Case of Charles Richmond Henderson," *Social Science History* 34 (2010): 337–71, here 365, as well as Daniel T. Rodgers, *Atlantic Crossings: Social Politics in a Progressive Age* (Cambridge, MA, 1998), pp. 243–44.

252. *Chicago Tribune*, February 23, 1907, p. 6.

253. Anderson, *Galusha Anderson*, p. 24.

254. Gates Papers, Box 1, folder 5.

255. Mabie to Gates, May 28, 1889, University of Chicago Founders' Correspondence, Box 1, folder 7.

256. See Gates to Morehouse, October 23, 1889, Gates Papers, Box 1, folder 5.

257. Morehouse to Gates, October 18, 1889.

258. Harper to Gates, October 21, 1889.

259. Gates to Harper, November 12, 1889.

260. Goodspeed to his sons, January 12, 1890, University of Chicago Founders' Correspondence, Box 1, folder 9. Field was first approached by George Lorimer in early November 1889, but made no commitment. Goodspeed to his sons, November 10, 1889, ibid., folder 8. Goodspeed sent Field a detailed proposal on January 8, 1890, and Gates and Goodspeed met with him a week later, on January 15. Field claimed that he was influenced by Rockefeller's example and by a letter that Harper had also sent to him: "He had not fully made up his mind when we went in, but the thing that brought him to time seemed to be our desire to telegraph Mr. Rockefeller his favorable answer." Gates to Harper, January 15, 1890, ibid. The estimated market value of both plots together was $250,000, so Field's gift was significant in scope. See the original gift documents in Gates Papers, Box 1, folder 6; and Goodspeed's recollections in "Marshall Field," in *The University of Chicago Biographical Sketches*, vol. 1, pp. 17–20. The exact scope of the land given by Field changed slightly between 1889 and 1892. For the general background, see Robin F. Bachin, *Building the South Side: Urban Space and Civic Culture in Chicago, 1890–1919* (Chicago, 2004), pp. 34–43.

261. Gates to Morehouse, January 1, 1890, Gates Papers, Box 1, folder 6.

262. Gates to Morehouse, January 17, 1890. The "grip line" refers to the mechanical grip that enabled tramway cars to latch onto the cables that operated the system.

263. *Standard*, January 23, 1890, p. 4.

264. Field to Gates, May 26, 1890, quoted in Goodspeed, *A History of the University of Chicago*, p. 93.

265. The insurance company demolished the old University building in January 1889 in order to clear the site for new development. The stone was sold to a saloon keeper who used it to build his house and to the Calvary Baptist Church at Thirty-Eighth Street and Wabash Avenue, whose building was largely constructed from these materials.

266. See Richard Hofstadter, *The Age of Reform: From Bryan to FDR* (New York, 1955), pp. 153–54; as well as Roger Geiger, *To Advance Knowledge: The Growth of the American Research Universities, 1900–1940* (New York, 1986), pp. 20–39; Richard Hofstadter and Walter P. Metzger, *The Development of Academic Freedom in the United States* (New York, 1955), pp. 274, 404–12; Burton J. Bledstein, *The Culture of Professionalism: The Middle Class and the Development of Higher Education in America* (New York, 1976), pp. 269–96, 323–31; Veysey, *The Emergence of the American University*, pp. 121–79; Steven J. Diner, *A City and Its Universities: Public Policy in Chicago, 1892–1919* (Chapel Hill, NC, 1980), pp. 4–10; Mary O. Furner, *Advocacy and Objectivity: A Crisis in the Professionalization of American Social Science, 1865–1905* (Lexington, KY, 1975), pp. xi, 2, 107–8, 125–26, 144–45, 289; and Thomas Bender, "The Erosion of Public Culture: Cities, Discourses, and Professional Disciplines," in Haskell, *The Authority of Experts*, pp. 99–101; Andrew Abbott, *The System of the Professions: An Essay on the Division of Expert Labor* (Chicago, 1988), pp. 53–58.

267. William Rainey Harper, "The University and Democracy," in *The Trend in Higher Education* (Chicago, 1905), p. 8.

268. Gates to Goodspeed, March 6, 1914, Goodspeed Papers, Box 1, folder 21.

269. Gates to Goodspeed, May 19, 1914, folder 21.

270. Gates Papers, Box 1, folder 7.

271. Small to Goodspeed, August 2, 1915, Goodspeed Papers, Box 4, folder 12.

272. See Bender, "The Erosion of Public Culture," pp. 94–96.

Chapter Two

1. For further reading on Harper, see Richard J. Storr, *Harper's University: The Beginnings* (Chicago, 1966); and Daniel Meyer, "The Chicago Faculty and the University Ideal: 1891–1929" (PhD diss., University of Chicago, 1994).

2. Undated memoir by Harper's sister, Mary Harper, Goodspeed Papers, Box 4, folder 12.

3. E. H. Sherman to Goodspeed, June 5, 1927, folder 12.

4. See Edgar S. Furniss, *The Graduate School of Yale: A Brief History* (New Haven, CT, 1965), p. 18. Yale awarded its first PhDs in 1861.

5. R. H. Robins, *A Short History of Linguistics* (Bloomington, IN, 1967), p. 169.

6. Louise L. Stevenson, *Scholarly Means to Evangelical Ends: The New Haven Scholars and the Transformation of Higher Learning in America, 1830–1890* (Baltimore, 1986), esp. pp. 1–13, 37–38, 59, 81, 90–93; Laurence R. Veysey, *The Emergence of the American University* (Chicago, 1965), pp. 59, 125–58, 173, 182–83, 312; Julie Tetel Andresen, *Linguistics in America, 1769–1924: A Critical History* (London, 1990), p. 167; Michael Silverstein, ed., *Whitney on Language: Selected Writings of William Dwight Whitney* (Cambridge, MA, 1971), pp. x–xxiii, 1–6; Stephen G. Alter, *William Dwight Whitney and the Science of Language* (Baltimore, 2005), pp. 211–12.

7. Veysey, *The Emergence of the American University*, pp. 370–71.

8. Charles R. Brown, who knew Harper in the early 1880s, later recalled the "reticence and self-distrust that distinguished him in that period … his clinging dependence upon his friends, and his confidence in the efficacy of their prayers." "William Rainey Harper as a Friend: An Appreciation," *Watchman*, January 18, 1906, p. 9. Similarly, Paul Shorey suggested that as a young man Harper was "extremely susceptible to the influence of strong personalities among his teachers and friends." "William Rainey Harper," *Dictionary of American Biography*, vol. 8, pp. 287–92, here p. 287. Shorey's short essay is an elegant appreciation.

9. Willard C. MacNaul to Thomas W. Goodspeed, November 26, 1927, Goodspeed Papers, Box 4, folder 12.

10. Hoffman, "William Rainey Harper and the Chicago Fellowship," pp. 68–70; William R. Hutchison, "Cultural Strain and Protestant Liberalism," *American Historical Review* 76 (1971): 403.

11. Edgar J. Goodspeed, *As I Remember* (New York, 1953), pp. 22–36 offers a charming portrait of life in this small suburb in the 1880s.

12. Chandler memoir, undated [1927], Goodspeed Papers, Box 4, folder 12.

13. C. F. Castle memoir, undated, Goodspeed Papers, Box 4, folder 12.

14. Kenneth N. Beck, "The American Institute of Sacred Literature: A Historical Analysis of an Adult Education Institution" (PhD diss., University of Chicago, 1968), pp. 27–81.

15. "Editorial Notes," *Hebrew Student*, April 1882, p. 11. This journal went through five different names: the *Hebrew Student* (1882–83), the *Old Testament Student* (1883–89), the *Old and New Testament Student* (1889–92), and the *Biblical World* (1893–1920). It is still published as the *Journal of Religion* (1921–present).

16. Robert L. Carter, "The 'Message of the Higher Criticism': The Bible Renaissance and Popular Education in America, 1880–1925" (PhD diss., University of North Carolina, 1995), pp. 94–147, esp. p. 107.

17. Shailer Mathews, "President Harper as a Religious Leader," *Standard*, January 20, 1906, p. 10.

18. Virginia L. Brereton, "The Public Schools Are Not Enough: The Bible and Private Schools," in David L. Barr and Nicholas Piediscalzi, eds., *The Bible in American Education: From Source Book to Textbook* (Philadelphia, 1982), pp. 52–58; Brereton, *Training God's Army: The American Bible School, 1880–1940* (Bloomington, IN, 1990), pp. 160–61.

19. It was renamed the *American Journal of Semitic Languages and Literatures* in 1895 and the *Journal of Near Eastern Studies* in 1942.

20. Harper's editorials are carefully surveyed in Maria Freeman, "Study with Open Mind and Heart: William Rainey Harper's Inductive Method of Teaching the Bible" (PhD diss., University of Chicago, 2005).

21. "Editorials," *Old and New Testament Student*, October 1889, p. 197.

22. William Rainey Harper, *A Critical and Exegetical Commentary on Amos and Hosea* (New York, 1905), p. vii. Harper intended this book as the first of three volumes on the minor prophets, but this was not to be.

23. James H. Tufts, "Graduate Study," pp. 4–5, in his "Unpublished Autobiography," Tufts Papers, Box 3, folder 11.

24. Freeman, "Study with Open Mind and Heart," pp. 115–16. For an excellent overview of Harper's stance as biblical critic, see James P. Wind, *The Bible and the University: The Messianic Vision of William Rainey Harper* (Atlanta, 1987), pp. 49–86.

25. Carter, "The 'Message of the Higher Criticism'," pp. 185–220.

26. William Rainey Harper, "The Pentateuchal Question, I: Gen. 1:1–12:5," *Hebraica* 5 (1888–89): 18–73; W. Henry Green, "The Pentateuchal Question," ibid., 137–89. For the background, see Dorrien, *The Making of American Liberal Theology*, pp. 348, 360, 362; Marion A. Taylor, *The Old Testament in the Old Princeton School (1812–1929)* (San Francisco, 1992), pp. 233–38.

27. Harper's sometime mentor, the elderly John A. Broadus of the Southern Baptist Theological Seminary in Louisville, Kentucky, rebuked him thus: "I am scared at the very idea of your undertaking such an advocacy. I dread it for the sake of what I believe to be vital truth." Broadus to Harper, February 17, 1888, University of Chicago Founders' Correspondence, Box 1, folder 3.

28. "Editorials," *Old and New Testament Student*, July 1889, p. 2.

29. Harper to J. M. Taylor, September 18, 1895, Harper Papers, Box 2, folder 17.

30. William R. Hutchison, *The Modernist Impulse in American Protestantism* (Cambridge, MA, 1976), p. 194.

31. Ernest D. Burton, "Memoranda of Conversations with President Harper in December, 1905," Burton Papers, Box 2, folder 7.

32. Seymour to Harper, July 20, 1890, University of Chicago Founders' Correspondence, Box 1, folder 10.

33. Edgar J. Goodspeed, *As I Remember*, p. 54.

34. Harper to Rockefeller, September 22, 1890, University of Chicago Founders' Correspondence, Box 1, folder 11. To Morehouse he wrote, "I have a plan for the organization of the University which will revolutionize College and University work in this country. It is 'bran splinter new,' and yet as solid as the ancient hills." Harper to Morehouse, September 22, 1890, ibid.

35. Lewis Stuart to Harper, November 28, 1890, University of Chicago Founders' Correspondence, Box 1, folder 12.

36. *University of Chicago. Official Bulletin No. 1, January, 1891* (Chicago, 1891), p. 6. The plan was presented to the full board of trustees on December 15, 1890, having been earlier approved by the board's Committee on Organization and Faculties. On December 26, 1890, the plan was officially adopted, and on December 27, 1890, the board decided to issue the plan in a series of bulletins, the first to be published in January 1891. For a good overview of the plan, see Meyer, "The Chicago Faculty," pp. 66–80.

37. This scheme may have reflected in part Harper's local experience at Yale, which had a curriculum in the 1880s that involved high levels of compulsion in the first two years, followed by significantly enhanced elective opportunities in the second. See George W. Pierson, *Yale College: An Educational History, 1871–1921* (New Haven, CT, 1952), pp. 73–94, 708. George Goodspeed reported to Thomas Goodspeed in May 1890, "I am surprised at his clear grasp of great university problems. He has been closely studying Yale for the past year." Letter of May 26, 1890, University of Chicago Founders' Correspondence, Box 1, folder 10.

38. Edward H. Levi, "The Critical Spirit," *University of Chicago Magazine*, October 1965, pp. 2–5.

39. *University of Chicago. Official Bulletin No. 1, January, 1891*, pp. 15–16.

40. Samuel N. Harper, *The Russia I Believe In: The Memoirs of Samuel N. Harper, 1902–1941* (Chicago, 1945), p. 5.

41. Angell to Goodspeed, April 14, 1915, Goodspeed Papers, Box 4, folder 12.

42. Tufts, "A University with a New Plan," p. 8, in his "Unpublished Autobiography," Tufts Papers, Box 3, folder 14.

43. Harper, *The Russia I Believe In*, p. 3. Harper argued elsewhere that western universities (including Chicago) were more likely to manifest the "modern democratic spirit" and to make "the student and the professor brothers in the pursuit of knowledge." Harper, "Higher Education in the West," *North American Review* 179 (1904): 585–86.

44. I owe this insight to Dan Meyer.

45. Shailer Mathews, "As an Editor," *Biblical World* 27 (1906): 205.

46. *University Record* 2 (1897–98): 14–15.

47. *University Record* 1 (1896–97): 6.

48. *Chicago Tribune*, September 9, 1894, p. 13. Between 1892 and 1902, nearly 87 percent of those who had enrolled in correspondence courses were classified as "educators." See *The President's Report, July, 1892—July 1902: Administration, The Decennial Publications, 1st ser., vol. 1* (Chicago, 1903), p. 314.

49. When he completed his study trip to Europe in the early autumn of 1891, Harper wrote to Gates, "Give me America and American institutions." Harper to Gates, October 3, 1891, University of Chicago Founders' Correspondence, Box 2, folder 4. The European model is of special interest. Harper did not study at a German university, although his mentor at Yale had done so. It was only after his plans were published that he set off on his study tour of English, German, and French universities in the late summer and early autumn of 1891. Harper was particularly interested in the extension activities organized by British universities.

50. *Chicago Tribune*, December 6, 1903, p. 1.

51. Albert Bushnell Hart, "William Rainey Harper," *Boston Evening Transcript*, January 11, 1906, p. 11.

52. Harper to Gates, December 26, 1891, University of Chicago Founders' Correspondence, Box 2, folder 4.

53. J. Laurence Laughlin, "Recollections of the Founding of the University," Goodspeed Papers, Box 4, folder 12. For an excellent survey of the early faculty of the University and the arrangements for their appointments, see Meyer, "The Chicago Faculty," pp. 81–130.

54. The earliest and most important faculty deliberative body was the University Senate, which originally consisted only of department heads but by 1908 included all full professors. In 1892 the trustees created a single general Faculty of the Arts, Literature, and Science, which in 1895 was divided into separate faculty bodies: the Academic College Faculty, the University College Faculty, the Faculty of the Graduate School of Arts and Literature, the Faculty of the Ogden School of Science, the Faculty of the Divinity School, and the Faculty of the University Extension. Subsequent modifications occurred in 1902 and 1907, when the faculties of the Senior College and the graduate schools of the arts and sciences were merged. This system was again modified in April 1908 when independent Faculties for the Colleges and the Graduate Schools of Arts and Literature and of Science were established, as well as Faculties for the Divinity School, the Law School, and the College of Education, all subject to the legislative authority of the University Senate.

55. For the details, see Meyer, "The Chicago Faculty," pp. 214–20, 226–33.

56. "There was a tragic incident when the Trustees themselves unitedly, here in New York, refused to back up Harper in his request for another million dollars. The Trustees were polled, and each individual, from Ryerson down—and there were five or six of them present—declined to back Harper in any further requests for money until the University could demonstrate its ability to live within its budgets. This was the origin of the long barren period. It was faithfully adhered to by both sides. No further money was given. Meantime, Harper sickened and died." Gates to Goodspeed, June 11, 1915, Goodspeed Papers, Box 1, folder 21.

57. Harper, *The Russia I Believe In*, p. 5.

58. Gates to Goodspeed, May 22, 1915, Goodspeed Papers, Box 1, folder 21.

59. Emery Filbey, interview by Richard Storr, May 7, 1954, Storr Papers, Box 6, folder 8. Trevor Arnett, who served as Harper's assistant for budgetary matters after 1902, offered the same kind of argument to Storr. See "Conversation with Trevor Arnett," July 2, 1953, ibid.

60. Mathews, "As an Editor," pp. 204–5.

61. "Conference with R. M. Lovett," February 15, 1955, Storr Papers, Box 6, folder 8.

62. Handwritten but unpublished note for Harper's memoir, *The Russia I Believe In*, Samuel N. Harper Papers, Box 75, folder 11.

63. Minutes of the Faculty of Arts, Literature, and Science, October 1892 to February 1896, pp. 1–2.

64. *The First Annual Report, President Harper, 1892*, p. 147 (unpublished manuscript; hereafter Harper, *The First Annual Report*).

65. Goodspeed to Harper, December 7, 1892, University of Chicago Founders' Correspondence, Box 2, folder 7.

66. Harper, *The First Annual Report*, p. 147.

67. *University of Chicago Weekly*, January 11, 1894, pp. 2–3.

68. Willard J. Pugh, "A 'Curious Working of Cross Purposes' in the Founding of the University of Chicago," *History of Higher Education Annual* 15 (1995): 93–126, esp. 116–20.

69. J. Laurence Laughlin, *Twenty-Five Years of the Department of Political Economy at the University of Chicago* (Chicago, 1916), p. 20.

70. *The President's Report: Administration*, pp. cv, 11.

71. *The President's Report, July, 1897–July, 1898, with Summaries for 1891–97* (Chicago, 1899), pp. 77, 85.

72. Tufts, "A University with a New Plan," pp. 22–23.

73. "The chief reason … is that we may better prepare students for the graduate work which we wish to develop. The student who comes from nine out of ten [college] institutions is in no sense fitted for graduate work." *The First Annual Report*, p. 138. Fifteen years later, Albion W. Small, in his role as the dean of the Graduate School, raised similar concerns about the quality of the training that newly matriculated graduate students had received at various colleges in the United States. See "The Graduate School of Arts and Literature," in *The President's Report, July, 1904–July, 1905* (Chicago, 1906), pp. 13–14.

74. Harper, *The First Annual Report*, p. 138; C. S. Boucher, "Some Studies of Freshman Admissions at the University of Chicago," November 3, 1932, College Archive, Box 1, folder 1. For the local and national contexts more generally, see Harold S. Wechsler, *The Qualified Student: A History of Selective College Admission in America* (New York, 1977), pp. 3–13, 215–58.

75. Harper to Gates, September 26, 1892, University of Chicago Founders' Correspondence, Box 2, folder 7.

76. See Storr, "College Program to 1906," pp. 12–18, Storr Papers, Box 4, folder 24; and Floyd W. Reeves and John Dale Russell, *Admission and Retention of Univer-*

sity Students (Chicago, 1933), pp. 13–15. For an early commentary by Harper himself, see "Dr. Harper Talks of Admissions," *Chicago Tribune*, January 7, 1895, p. 3. A slight modification occurred in 1895, when the University agreed to allow well-qualified teachers in various high schools to serve as "advisory examiners" who would supervise the preparation of special test units for students in their schools and who would then forward these test papers to the relevant departments at the University for grading. A major change to the University's admissions procedure came in 1911 when the University agreed to admit graduates of secondary schools accredited by the new North Central Association of Colleges and Secondary Schools, subject to a review of their high school transcripts and on the basis of quantitative and qualitative achievement standards. After 1923, applicants to the University also had to submit detailed information on their family background, their academic goals and plans, and their extracurricular achievements. In addition, in the same year the University began to require two letters of recommendation from high school teachers.

77. Storr, "College Program to 1906," p. 18.

78. *The President's Report: Administration*, pp. 92, 117.

79. Storr, *Harper's University*, p. 127.

80. *The President's Report: Administration*, p. 13.

81. *Chicago Tribune*, July 31, 1894, p. 3.

82. To one prospective student he wrote in 1898, "I am quite sure … that life in connection with a great University will be of real and marked profit to you. The atmosphere of a University is different from the atmosphere of a college." Harper to E. C. Herrick, February 23, 1898, Harper Papers, Box 4, folder 2.

83. *Chicago Tribune*, January 7, 1895, p. 3.

84. William Rainey Harper, "Ideals of Educational Work," in *National Educational Association, Journal of Proceedings and Addresses, Session of the Year 1895* (St. Paul, 1895), pp. 987–98.

85. *Chicago Tribune*, November 9, 1902, p. 35, as well as November 5, 1902, p. 16.

86. William Rainey Harper, "The Educational Progress of the Year 1901–02," *Educational Review* 24 (1902): 252.

87. See Harper's "The Situation of the Small College," in his *The Trend in Higher Education* (Chicago, 1905), p. 377. Similar evolutionary discourse is found in Harper's "Higher Education in the West," pp. 584–90.

88. *The President's Report: Administration*, pp. 67–68.

89. See Reeves and Russell, *Admission and Retention of University Students*, pp. 79, 129.

90. *The President's Report: Administration*, p. 84; Floyd W. Reeves and John Dale Russell, *The Alumni of the Colleges* (Chicago, 1933), pp. 65–66.

91. Ibid., p. 65.

92. *The President's Report: Administration*, p. 68; see also Reeves and Russell, *Admission and Retention of University Students*, pp. 129–30.

93. "Report of an Interview with Mrs. Weherley, May 4, 1961," Storr Papers, Box 6, folder 7.

94. For the early history of women at the University, see Janel M. Mueller, "Co-

education at Chicago—Whose Aims?," in John W. Boyer, ed., *The Aims of Education* (Chicago, 1997), pp. 107–47; Lynn D. Gordon, *Gender and Higher Education in the Progressive Era* (New Haven, CT, 1990), pp. 85–110; and "'On Equal Terms': Educating Women at the University of Chicago," online web exhibit, Special Collections Research Center, University of Chicago Library.

95. Gordon, *Gender and Higher Education*, pp. 88, 118–19.

96. Pugh, "A 'Curious Working of Cross Purposes'," pp. 11617.

97. Harper to Moore, March 1, 1899, Harper Papers, Box 4, folder 24. He also disagreed that all professors needed to be scholarly producers: "In my opinion, it is as important to have good teachers as to have good producers, and in my opinion there are good teachers who are not good producers."

98. Harper had tried to segregate some classes in the junior college by gender in 1902, arguing that younger men and women would learn more effectively in separate academic settings, but operationally his plan was doomed to failure and never gained serious traction. It was effectively dead by 1907. See Mueller, "Coeducation at Chicago—Whose Aims?" pp. 107–47, esp. 123–24; Storr, *Harper's University*, pp. 324, 338; Gordon, *Gender and Higher Education,* pp. 112–20; and Harper's arguments in *The President's Report: Administration*, pp. cviii–cxi.

99. The files on this plan are in HJB Administrations, Box 34, folder 8.

100. *University Record* 10 (1905–6): 15, as well as pp. 68–70.

101. *Chicago Tribune*, February 22, 1894, p. 8; December 18, 1894, p. 3; December 5, 1895, p. 1.

102. "'Mr. Stephens, you are working too hard and do not take enough exercise.' When I told him of my outside work for self-support which I thought gave me some exercise, he said 'But that is not enough. Now I want you to go through these exercises every day.' Then he got up, took off his coat, went through several calisthenics right there in his office." Frank F. Stephens to Richard J. Storr, December 10, 1953, Storr Papers, Box 6, folder 11.

103. *University Record* 1 (1896–97): 256.

104. "I am inclined to think that a university ought to control the department of physical culture and athletics, just as it does the department of Latin." Harper to D. E. Brown, April 20, 1899, Harper Papers, Box 4, folder 26.

105. This story is wonderfully told in Robin Lester, *Stagg's University: The Rise, Decline, and Fall of Big-Time Football at Chicago* (Urbana, IL, 1995), pp. 1–65.

106. Lester, *Stagg's University*, pp. 19, 48–50, 81–86.

107. *The President's Report: Administration*, pp. cxxxi-cxxxii; *Chicago Tribune*, February 25, 1894, p. 39.

108. Harper to his daughter, Davida, December 23, 1897, Harper Papers, Box 3, folder 21.

109. Harper, *The Russia I Believe In*, p. 8. The transcripts for both students are on file in the microfilm collection of the registrar's office at the University of Chicago.

110. *Chicago Tribune*, March 2, 1902, p. 4; March 6, 1902, p. 9.

111. *Chicago Tribune*, February 22, 1894, p. 8; April 9, 1901, p. 5; December 6, 1903, p. 1; January 29, 1905, p. 8.

112. *The President's Report: Administration*, p. xxxiii.

113. Ibid., p. 68.

114. Tufts, "A University with a New Plan," p. 19.

115. James R. Angell, "The Curriculum: Excerpts from a Report to the President by the Dean of the Faculties of Arts, Literature, and Science," *University Record* 1 (1915): 35–36.

116. A good example is W. Carson Ryan, *Studies in Early Graduate Education: The Johns Hopkins, Clark University, the University of Chicago* (New York, 1939), pp. 106–38, which contains little information on the actual operations of the graduate programs, but a great deal of historical background on the distinguished nature of the faculty.

117. For the national context, see John S. Brubacher and Willis Rudy, *Higher Education in Transition: A History of American Colleges and Universities, 1636–1976* (New York, 1976), pp. 193–97; Bernard Berelson, *Graduate Education in the United States* (New York, 1960), pp. 6–24; Richard J. Storr, *The Beginnings of Graduate Education in America* (Chicago, 1953), pp. 129–34.

118. McLaughlin to Small, January 9, 1917, Department of History, Records, Box 1, folder 3.

119. See the "Report of the Committee on the Precise Formulation of the Recommendations for the Reorganization of Departments, Presented to the University Senate," Minutes of the University Senate, October 29, 1910. The report was drafted by James H. Tufts.

120. Reeves and Russell, *Admission and Retention of University Students,* pp. 141–42.

121. Edwin E. Slosson, "University of Chicago," in *Great American Universities* (New York, 1910), p. 432. Reeves commented in 1933 that "there appears to be little doubt that the Summer Quarter entrants were inferior to the Autumn Quarter entrants in degree-earning ability." Reeves and Russell, *Admission and Retention of University Students,* p. 167.

122. James R. Angell, "Special Report of the Dean of the Faculties of Arts, Literature, and Science to the President of the University, October 1913," p. 35, HJB Administrations, Box 34, folder 1. In 1910 a total of 409 PhDs were awarded by US graduate schools. See Walton C. John, *Graduate Study in Universities and Colleges in the United States* (Washington, DC, 1934), p. 19. A brief overview of the status of US graduate programs at the end of World War I can be found in George E. Zook and Samuel P. Capen, *Opportunities for Study at American Graduate Schools* (Washington, DC, 1921).

123. Floyd W. Reeves, Ernest C. Miller, and John Dale Russell, *Trends in University Growth* (Chicago, 1933), pp. 96, 104. Angell argued in 1913 that the departments producing the largest numbers of doctorates also had the most eminent records of faculty publications: "Chemistry, mathematics, botany, and zoology which show so excellent a record in the conferring of doctor's degrees are also most creditably represented in publication." See Angell, "Special Report," p. 37.

124. "The Seminar is sharply distinguished from ordinary class exercises. The

method of instruction is that of individual investigation or immediate preparation for investigation by the student." *The Regulations of the University of Chicago* (Chicago, 1903), p. 33. Andrew Abbott has recently explored the history of these early libraries in his essay "Library Research Infrastructure for Humanistic and Social Scientific Scholarship in the Twentieth Century," in Charles Camic, Neil Gross, and Michèle Lamont, eds., *Social Knowledge in the Making* (Chicago, 2011), pp. 49–53, 56–59.

125. Harper, *First Annual Report*, pp. 148–49.

126. Thomas W. Goodspeed, *The Story of the University of Chicago: 1890–1925* (Chicago, 1925), p. 61.

127. See Reeves and Russell, *Admission and Retention of University Students*, pp. 133–35.

128. Prospective graduate students were only required to submit "testimonials as to character and scholarship. Such testimonials may take the form of diplomas, or of written or printed theses." See *The Regulations of the University of Chicago*, pp. 19–20. As late as 1930 the graduate deans resisted the idea of imposing selective admission on their programs. Gordon Laing argued that "to adopt a stricter system would result in still larger numbers of students going to the neighboring state universities," while Henry Gale insisted, "I think that it would be very unwise in view of the increased tuition for graduate students to adopt any legislation which would complicate the question of admission at this time. I think that we should be especially careful to make graduate students feel that they are welcome and offer them no difficulties or hurdles in the matter of admission." Memos to Hutchins of February 3 and 8, 1930, Office of the President, Hutchins Administration, Records, Box 96, folder 2.

129. H. Foster Bain, "Some Changes in Graduate Studies," *Dial*, August 6, 1903, p. 84.

130. This may explain the fact that what passed for Wissenschaft in the "seminars" in American research universities before the 1920s was often quite different from the rigorous and intense intellectual ambience that obtained in the best German and Austrian university institutes. See Anthony T. Grafton, "In Clio's American Atelier," in Camic, Gross, and Lamont, *Social Knowledge in the Making*, pp. 93–97.

131. Gordon J. Laing, "The Graduate School of Arts and Literature," in *The President's Report, Covering the Academic Year July 1, 1927, to June 30, 1928* (Chicago, 1929), p. 3.

132. Laing, "The Graduate School of Arts and Literature," in *The President's Report, Covering the Academic Year July 1, 1929, to June 30, 1930* (Chicago, 1931), p. 5.

133. Carl F. Huth to Norman Beck, August 26, 1924, Department of History, Records, Box 1, folder 4. See also Herrick, "The University of Chicago," p. 409.

134. Reeves and Russell, *Admission and Retention of University Students*, p. 158.

135. Angell, "Special Report," p. 33.

136. This meant about ten to twelve hours of teaching each week. See Floyd Reeves, Nelson B. Henry, Frederick J. Kelly, Arthur J. Klein, John Dale Russell, *The University Faculty* (Chicago, 1933), p. 94. Berelson argues that that this was a

"radically light teaching load," signifying Harper's dedication to giving faculty time for research. Berelson, *Graduate Education in the United States*, p. 12.

137. Floyd W. Reeves, Nelson B. Henry, and John Dale Russell, *Class Size and University Costs* (Chicago, 1933), p. 38.

138. Herrick, "The University of Chicago," pp. 410–11.

139. Albert H. Tolman, "English at the University of Chicago," *Dial*, June 16, 1894, p. 356.

140. McLaughlin to Boucher, January 25, 1918, Department of History, Records, Box 5, folder 1.

141. Percy Gardner, "Impressions of American Universities," *Living Age*, February 25, 1899, pp. 470–71.

142. Quoted in Berelson, *Graduate Education in the United States*, p. 18.

143. "Wife Part of Ideal: Dr. Harper Says Professors Should Be Married and Fathers," *Chicago Tribune*, January 29, 1904, p. 1.

144. McLaughlin to William Dodd, October 3, 1913; Dodd to McLaughlin, October 18, 1913, Department of History, Records, Box 1, folder 1.

145. Some evidence remains that graduate students were concerned with the indifference of departments relating to their professional placement, especially as other graduate schools began to produce increasing numbers of doctorates. The leader of a graduate-student club in the Department of Sociology, H. Warren Dunham, wrote to William F. Ogburn in 1939, urging, "The past few years have shown a marked increase in the number of universities granting doctorates in sociology. Concomitantly, the vocational opportunities have not increased in proportion. In view of the more rigorous requirements at the University of Chicago, we recommend that the department become more positive in securing vocational placements for graduate students." Dunham to Ogburn, December 19, 1939, Burgess Papers, Box 33, folder 5.

146. Judson to Ryerson, February 11, 1908, HJB Administrations, Box 82, folder 23. Abbott decided to go to Princeton.

147. Herrick, "The University of Chicago," p. 409. On early regulations for the doctorate, see Storr, *Harper's University*, pp. 154–59.

148. Albion W. Small, "The Graduate School of Arts and Literature," in *The President's Report, Covering the Academic Year July 1, 1922, to June 30, 1923* (Chicago, 1924), pp. 4–5.

149. Goodspeed, *The Story of the University of Chicago*, pp. 60–61.

150. *University Record* 2 (1897–98): 11.

151. Harper to Boyd [no first name], July 20, 1898, Harper Papers, Box 4, folder 10.

152. Bacon to Bolza, April 23, 1936, Department of Mathematics, Records, Box 12, folder 1.

153. The personal memoirs that Richard Storr collected from early alumni in the 1950s are filled with tributes to their teachers. Alma Hirschberg, who graduated in 1901, recalled that "Lovett and Robert Herrick, Von Holst, Chamberlain, Salisbury, Ferdinand Schevill, and von Klenze were scintillating members of a faculty that inspired many students who still remember the interesting vistas opened to them for

future enjoyment. To me that is the greatest contribution college education makes to the average layman … the incentive to delve into the real values in literature, science and history and to keep up those interests all through the years." Letter of November 9, 1953, Storr Papers, Box 6, folder 11.

154. Laughlin's *Twenty-Five Years of the Department of Political Economy at the University of Chicago, pp. 18–19,* contains a list of PhD holders from 1894 to 1916.

155. *The President's Report: Administration,* pp. 141, 303–4.

156. Storr, *Harper's University,* pp. 134–41, 304–6.

157. Reeves et al. commented in 1933, "Two of the professional schools, Business and Law, attract relatively large numbers [of undergraduates] for specialization by reason of the flexible curriculum requirements permitting a combination of liberal arts and professional work for the bachelor's degree." Floyd W. Reeves, W. E. Peik, and John Dale Russell, *Instructional Problems in the University* (Chicago, 1933), p. 35.

158. Storr, *Harper's University,* p. 306.

159. Albion W. Small, "The Graduate School of Arts and Literature," in *The President's Report, Covering the Academic Year Ending June 30, 1913* (Chicago, 1914), p. 47.

160. Angell, "The Curriculum," p. 38.

161. Slosson, "University of Chicago," p. 433.

162. Harper to Charles Hutchinson, February 19, 1894, HJB Administrations, Box 82, folder 12.

163. Oskar Bolza, *Aus meinem Leben* (Munich, 1936), p. 27.

164. Slosson, "University of Chicago," pp. 425–26.

165. Herrick, "The University of Chicago," p. 415.

166. *The President's Report, July, 1897–July, 1898, with Summaries for 1891–97,* p. 75.

167. Angell would later comment to Thomas Goodspeed that many of Harper's educational structures were not, in fact, all that revolutionary, but that "he was distinctly responsible for attracting public attention to them in this part of the world." Angell to Goodspeed, April 14, 1915, Goodspeed Papers, Box 4, folder 12.

168. Goodspeed to Harper, June 1, 1890, Harper Papers, Box 9, folder 7. Most trustees honored their original obligations, and several, including Ryerson, Hutchinson, and Walker, gave buildings to the University.

169. Hutchinson to Harper, January 26, 1896, HJB Administrations, Box 82, folder 12.

170. Thomas J. Schlereth, "Big Money and High Culture: The Commercial Club and Charles L. Hutchinson," *Great Lakes Review* 3 (1976): 25–26. See also Horowitz, *Culture and the City, pp. 70–92.*

171. See his private diary, a partial transcript covering the period 1881 to 1911, with several large gaps, Charles L. Hutchinson Papers, Newberry Library.

172. James Gilbert, *Perfect Cities: Chicago's Utopias of 1893* (Chicago, 1991), p. 38; as well as McCarthy, *Noblesse Oblige,* pp. 53–96.

173. Frederick Gates informed Harper that he had used the contributions of men like Ryerson and Walker to reassure Rockefeller. Gates to Harper, April 27, 1891, Harper Papers, Box 8, folder 19.

174. Field to Gates, January 22, 1890, Gates Papers, Box 1, folder 6; Field to Gates, May 26, 1890, HJB Administrations, Box 43, folder 9.

175. This narrative is described by Thomas W. Goodspeed in his "Charles Lawrence Hutchinson," in *The University of Chicago Biographical Sketches*, vol. 2, pp. 41–42; as well as Goodspeed, *A History of the University of Chicago*, pp. 83–88.

176. "I deem this matter of electing Mr. Ryerson of great importance, for altho' not a Baptist, he is a worthy man and once enlisted heartily in University matters, he would be a tower of strength." Blake to Harper, October 16, 1890, HJB Administrations, Box 82, folder 2. To Gates a few days later Blake wrote of Ryerson, "He is young, smart, deeply interested, well educated, liberal and wealthy, also of ability." Blake to Gates, October 20, 1890, Gates Papers, Box 1, folder 7.

177. Goodspeed to Harper, October 1, 1890, Harper Papers, Box 9, folder 7. Four days later Goodspeed insisted, "Ryerson it seems to me is the man.... I do not see why he should not be worth half a million to us during the next five years." Goodspeed to Harper, October 5, 1890.

178. Alonzo Parker reported to Harper in late October 1890 that he had been assailed by angry Baptist ministers worried about the fact that Ryerson was not a Baptist. Parker to Harper, October 21, 1890, University of Chicago Founders' Correspondence, Box 1, folder 12.

179. Blake to Harper, July 4, 1892, HJB Administrations, Box 82, folder 2. By the end of 1892 the $1 million fund for the first round of campus buildings derived almost entirely from non-Baptists, except for a last-minute pledge from Henry Rust. Harper commented to Gates, "Do you realize the significance of Mr. Rust's gift—a million with almost not a Baptist cent, yet saved by a Baptist gift." Letter of July 10, 1892, Gates Papers, Box 1, folder 11. Unfortunately, Rust was unable to make good on his promise, thus confirming the importance of the decision to broaden the base of the board.

180. Stefan Germer, "Traditions and Trends: Taste Patterns in Chicago Collecting," in Sue Ann Prince, ed., *The Old Guard and the Avant-Garde: Modernism in Chicago, 1910–1940* (Chicago, 1990), p. 181.

181. Ryerson also bought directly for the museum, and during his lifetime many of his purchases were sent to the Art Institute on long-term loan. Martin A. Ryerson Papers, Box 11, Collections Records, Archives of the Art Institute of Chicago. Ryerson's mansion in Kenwood, at 4851 South Drexel Boulevard, is owned by the Croatian Franciscan Friars. For Ryerson as a collector, see the excellent analysis by Neil Harris, "Midwestern Medievalism: Three Chicago Collectors," in Isabella Stewart Gardner Museum, *Cultural Leadership in America: Art, Matronage, and Patronage* (Boston, 1997), pp. 105–10.

182. See Goodspeed, *A History of the University of Chicago*, pp. 85–86, 169–73, 258, 336; and, in general, Jean F. Block, *The Uses of Gothic: Planning and Building the Campus of the University of Chicago, 1892–1932* (Chicago, 1983), pp. 8–13; and Bachin, *Building the South Side*, pp. 34–61. The original tract donated by Marshall Field was to be located between Fifty-Sixth and Fifty-Seventh Streets east of Ellis Avenue, but subsequent negotiations shifted the site to the area between Fifty-Seventh and

Fifty-Ninth Streets. This site included Field's gift as well as the additional land that he offered to sell to the University. Ryerson's and Hutchinson's intervention extended the University's boundary along the Midway to the full extent from Ellis to University Avenue. The University was able to lease the block north of Fifty-Seventh Street in 1892 for an athletic field, named appropriately Marshall Field, which it then purchased in 1898. The name was changed to Stagg Field in 1914.

183. Ryerson to Harper, June 15, 1892; Ryerson to Harper, November 7, 1892, HJB Administrations, Box 82, folder 23. In July 1910 he then contributed an additional $200,000 to expand and refit the physics building to meet the changing research needs of the faculty of the department. The process by which individual donors came to be associated with specific buildings was slightly chaotic and only took final shape over the course of 1892.

184. Minutes of the Board of Trustees, 1890–95, pp. 99, 228–29; Goodspeed, *A History of the University of Chicago*, pp. 271–72, 276. A major purpose of this initiative was to retire $400,000 in debt that the University faced in the aftermath of its explosive beginnings. See Harper to Gates, October 23, 1893, Gates Papers, folder 12.

185. Ryerson to the Board of Trustees, September 6, 1898, HJB Administrations, Box 82, folder 23.

186. Dorothy Michelson Livingston, *The Master of Light: A Biography of Albert A. Michelson* (New York, 1973), p. 295. Albert Einstein observed in 1952 of Michelson, "I always think of Michelson as the artist in Science. His greatest joy seemed to come from the beauty of the experiment itself and the elegance of the method employed." Ibid., p. 6. Einstein's appraisal of Michelson may help to explain why Ryerson, who had the eye of a connoisseur in evaluating artistic achievement, was impressed with the work of this great scientist.

187. Nor was Ryerson's philanthropy restricted to the physical sciences, for he also supported the research work of scholars in the humanities. See Manly to Ryerson, July 28, 1924, Acquisitions File, Bacon Mss.; and Manly to Ryerson, July 1, 1930, Acquisitions File, Ms. 564; *Calendar of the Martin A. Ryerson Collection of Court and Manorial Documents from the Estate of Sir Nicholas Bacon in the University of Chicago Library* (Chicago, 1974).

188. *University Record* 2 (1897–98): 247.

189. *University Record* 6 (1901–2): 104.

190. *University Record* 1 (1896–97): 579–80.

191. Hutchinson's private diary, on deposit at the Newberry Library, provides a charming if cursory record of some of the world excursions the two couples took together. Just as they traveled together, they collected art together as well. For the story of their collaboration on the Art Institute, see Celia Hilliard, *"The Prime Mover": Charles L. Hutchinson and the Making of the Art Institute of Chicago* (Chicago, 2010), pp. 42–44, 54–69.

192. Schlereth, "Big Money and High Culture," p. 19; as well as Hilliard, *"The Prime Mover,"* pp. 13–16.

193. McCarthy, *Noblesse Oblige*, pp. 88–89; and Hilliard, *"The Prime Mover,"* pp. 19–35.

194. Quoted in Henry Justin Smith, *Chicago: A Portrait* (New York, 1931), p. 304.

195. "Art: Its Influence and Excellence in Modern Times," *Saturday Evening Herald*, March 31, 1888, p. 3; as well as Hutchinson to Harper, April 4, 1900, HJB Administrations, Box 82, folder 13.

196. Burton, "Charles L. Hutchinson and the University of Chicago," p. 24. Ryerson too was deeply involved in architectural oversight. As late as 1920, Harry Pratt Judson would use Ryerson's close involvement with the plans for Rockefeller Chapel as a way of reassuring John D. Rockefeller Jr.: "I may add that Mr. Ryerson has spent a great deal of time with the architect in working on these plans and the artistic and practical adjustments are, we think, very complete." Judson to Rockefeller, December 3, 1920, HJB Administrations, Box 14, folder 10.

197. Ryerson to Harper, February 28, 1894, HJB Administrations, Box 82, folder 23.

198. Ryerson to Harper, March 7, 1897.

199. Ryerson to Harper, February 23, 1896. For the context of this observation, see Meyer, "The Chicago Faculty," pp. 208–9.

200. "General Observations," pp. 9–11, HJB Administrations, Box 13, folder 14.

201. Gates to Harper, May 13, 1892, Harper Papers, Box 8, folder 20.

202. See the appendix to the letter of Gates to Harper, June 25, 1904, Harper Papers, Box 9, folder 3.

203. Gates to Harper, November 25, 1903, Harper Papers, Box 9, folder 2.

204. Report of Starr J. Murphy, February, 1904, quoted in Storr, *Harper's University*, pp. 345–46.

205. "Report to the Trustees," February 9, 1905, pp. 1, 5, Rockefeller Archive Center, Pocantico Hills, Sleepy Hollow, NY.

206. For local reactions to Murphy's 1905 report by Goodspeed and others, see the letters and memoranda in HJB Administrations, Box 61, folder 10.

207. In 1904, Murphy insisted, "I should, however, be extremely loath to attribute such motives to the Trustees. It must be remembered that they are busy men of the highest standing, and they are devoting a great deal of most valuable time gratuitously to this work." Quoted in Storr, *Harper's University*, p. 344. But in 1905 he insisted, "There is a tendency to expend money of the University without authority," and demanded that Rockefeller have now a local agent "on the ground" (in Chicago), "without whose approval no obligations could be incurred or expenditures made." Report of February 9, 1905, pp. 28, 31, Rockefeller Archive Center. The latter comments were certainly a rebuke to the board of trustees.

208. Frederick Gates reported in 1897 that Ryerson and Harper insisted that the deficit had arisen "in part on the ground of inadvertence and in part on the ground that the policy of erecting beautiful and costly buildings and of securing a numerous and expensive corps of instructors had been a policy which had brought to the institution vast sums of money from the city of Chicago, and attached the city to the University as nothing else could have done." "Report of [a] Conference between Messrs. F. T. Gates, T. W. Goodspeed, and H. A. Rust, with Reference to the University of Chicago, February 10, 1897," p. 2, HJB Administrations, Box 43, folder 11.

209. "Reminiscences of Thomas W. Goodspeed," pp. 300–301, Goodspeed Papers, vol. 1.

210. Hutchinson to Harper, January 26, 1896, HJB Administrations, Box 82, folder 12.

211. Ryerson to Harper, March 18, 1900, HJB Administrations, Box 82, folder 23.

212. "Conversation between President W. R. Harper, Mr. Martin Ryerson, Maj. H. A. Rust, Mr. John D. Rockefeller, Jr. and Mr. F. T. Gates on the Budget of the University of Chicago for 1899–1900 and Collateral Questions, December 5, 1898," pp. 31–32, HJB Administrations, Box 13, folder 14.

213. Gates, *Chapters in My Life*, p. 196; Storr, *Harper's University*, pp. 346–48.

214. Ryerson to Gates, November 10, 1903, Rockefeller Archive Center.

215. Ryerson to Harper, July 18, 1892, HJB Administrations, Box 82, folder 23.

216. Hutchinson to Harper, January 3, 1892, HJB Administrations, Box 82, folder 12. See also Meyer, "The Chicago Faculty," pp. 87–88.

217. One of Murphy's prescriptions for budgetary economies in the area of faculty salaries should be mentioned. Rather than reward deserving faculty members with regular salary raises and promotions, thus increasing the University's deficit, he suggested that the University organize its faculty like the army did its officer corps—so many generals, colonels, and captains, all at fixed salary levels and in a predetermined number of slots. Neither time in grade nor distinguished service per se would merit one either a promotion or a salary increase unless a slot opened up, and since the number of higher slots would be controlled, the need for substantial salary increases would be avoided. "Confidential. To the Trustees of the University of Chicago," February 9, 1905, pp. 26–27, Rockefeller Archive Center.

218. "Reminiscences of Thomas W. Goodspeed," pp. 301–2, Goodspeed Papers, vol. 1.

219. Between 1906 and 1907, Rockefeller contributed $3.7 million in additional endowment support: $1 million in January 1906 for the 1906/7 fiscal year and another $2.7 million in January 1907 for the 1907/8 fiscal year. This was followed by another $1.54 million gift in January 1908 and an additional gift of $928,000 in January 1909. See Minutes of the Board of Trustees, 1904–7, pp. 350, 478; Minutes of the Board of Trustees, 1907–9, pp. 149–50, pp. 309–13. Judson noted in his annual report for 1908–9 that "the gift by the founder in January of one million dollars for endowment, to take effect July 1, 1909, will, it is expected, in the next fiscal year wipe out the last of the recurring annual deficits." *The President's Report, July 1908–July 1909* (Chicago, 1910), p. 5. In mid-December 1910, Rockefeller then announced a $10-million concluding gift that would be paid in $1 million installments over the next ten years, beginning January 1, 1911. For Rockefeller's letter announcing the gift, see Goodspeed, *A History of the University of Chicago*, pp. 291–92.

220. Karl and Katz, "Foundations and Ruling Class Elites," p. 34.

221. See Morehouse to Harper, December 12, 1890, University of Chicago Founders' Correspondence, Box 1, folder 12; Dr. L. A. Crandall to Harper, September 24, 1890, Storr Papers, Box 3, folder 26.

222. When Frederick Gates tried to persuade John D. Rockefeller to give yet

another huge gift to the nascent University in February 1892, Gates wrote that he stood "in awe" of the University: "God is in it in the most wonderful way. It is a miracle.... Think of the significance of that. Harper, Goodspeed, and myself, as we look into the great future of this land and consider what seems certainly to be the great part God is raising up this institution to fill, uncover our heads and walk very softly before the Lord." Gates to Rockefeller, February 1, 1892, University of Chicago Founders' Correspondence, Box 2, folder 5.

223. William Rainey Harper, "Some Features of an Ideal University," in *Third Annual Meeting of the American Baptist Education Society, Held with the Southern Baptist Convention, Birmingham. Ala., May 8 and 9, 1891* (Chicago, 1891) pp. 49–60, here 58, 60. On Harper's religious values and the University, see Wind, *The Bible and the University*, pp. 133–46.

224. *Chicago Tribune*, March 16, 1891, p. 2.

225. Goodspeed to Harper, September 9, 1890, University of Chicago, Founders' Correspondence, Box 1, folder 11.

226. Goodspeed to Harper, February 16, 1891, Box 2, folder 1.

227. "The University always will be a Christian institution, and will stand for the great principles of broad Christianity. But the University is not Baptist. It is not kept up by Baptists alone. It is not attended by a majority of Baptists. Its professors are elected without regard to their religious beliefs." *Chicago Tribune*, January 28, 1904, p. 12.

228. HJB Administrations, Box 49, folder 8.

229. The speech was later published as a pamphlet, "The University and Democracy," in *The Trend in Higher Education*, pp. 1–34. Harper gave a similar address in Chicago at the winter baccalaureate service of the University on December 18, 1898. See *Chicago Tribune*, December 19, 1898, p. 4.

230. Democracy was "the highest ideal of human achievement, the only possibility of a true national life, the glorious and golden sun lighting up the dark places of all the world." Harper, "The University and Democracy," pp. 1, 19.

231. Among many critics, see especially James T. Burtchaell, *The Dying of the Light: The Disengagement of Colleges and Universities from Their Christian Churches* (Grand Rapids, MI, 1998), pp. 842–51, here 846. From a different perspective, see also D. G. Hart, *The University Gets Religion: Religious Studies in American Higher Education* (Baltimore, 1999), pp. 54–56, 250–51.

232. Wacker, *Augustus H. Strong and the Dilemma of Historical Consciousness*, p. 11.

233. W. Clark Gilpin, *A Preface to Theology* (Chicago, 1996), p. 90; as well as Conrad Cherry, *Hurrying toward Zion: Universities, Divinity Schools, and American Protestantism* (Bloomington, IN, 1995), p. 13.

234. *Chicago Tribune*, July 30, 1894, p. 4.

235. Harper to Andrew H. Green, January 1891, University of Chicago Founders' Correspondence, Box 2, folder 1.

236. Strong to Harper, December 23, 1890, HJB Administrations, Box 78, folder 28.

237. Harper to Gates, May 18, 1892, University of Chicago Founders' Correspon-

dence, Box 2, folder 6. Gates, ever the pragmatist, told Rockefeller that if "our Baptist Brethren" were so worried about the Universalists building the chapel, "let them bestir themselves to raise the funds, if possible to build it." Gates to Rockefeller, May 21, 1892, ibid. Hutchinson changed his mind, eventually funding the Commons that is named in his honor.

238. *Chicago Tribune*, April 26, 1896, p. 4.

239. Carter, "The 'Message of the Higher Criticism'," pp. 209–10.

240. *Chicago Tribune*, October 2, 1898, p. 7; William Rainey Harper, "Shall the Theological Curriculum Be Modified, and How?," *American Journal of Theology* 3 (1899): 45–66; and the outside responses, ibid., pp. 324–43.

241. On Foster in general, see Gary Dorrien, *The Making of American Liberal Theology: Idealism, Realism, and Modernity, 1900–1950* (Louisville, 2003), pp. 151–81. For this collision, see Edgar A. Towne, "A 'Singleminded' Theologian: George Burman Foster at Chicago," *Foundations* 20 (1977): 36–59, 163–80.

242. Harper to MacLeish, March 16, 1905, HJB Administrations, Box 82, folder 16. Copies of the subscription form for the building drive are in Divinity School, Records, Box 9, folder 2.

243. Warren Cameron Young, *Commit What You Have Heard: A History of the Northern Baptist Theological Seminary, 1913–1888* (Wheaton, IL, 1988), pp. 10–15; Stackhouse, *Chicago and the Baptists*, pp. 169–70, 187–88.

244. Gates to Rockefeller, March 10, 1914, Goodspeed Papers, Box 1, folder 21; Fosdick to Richard J. Storr, September 20, 1956, Storr Papers, Box 6, folder 14. Accomplishing this task was an incremental process and a slower one than Gates may have hoped. Changes were made by the board in 1923 and 1930, reducing the dominance of the Baptists, and by April 1944, all denominational requirements for trustees and the president were eliminated, with the exception that the board of the Baptist Theological Union always had to have a representation on the board of the University. Essentially, this meant that only one member of the University of Chicago Board of Trustees had to be a Baptist. No other religious tests or stipulations were retained, although the board stipulated that all future trustees would receive a statement indicating the board's "sincere desire 'to insure the continuance of the University forever as a *Christian* institution.'" Minutes of the Board of Trustees, April 13, 1944.

245. David A. Hollinger, *After Cloven Tongues of Fire: Protestant Liberalism in Modern American History* (Princeton, NJ, 2013), p. 108, as well as pp. 218–19.

246. Angell to Judson, December 7, 1911, HJB Administrations, Box 78, folder 22.

247. Henderson to Gates, December 20, 1892, HJB Administrations, Box 70, folder 11.

248. Theodore G. Soares and Harold D. Lasswell, "Social Survey of the Undergraduates of the University of Chicago," HJB Administrations, Box 78, folder 1. The survey was conducted among students enrolled in the 1919–20 academic year.

249. An informal survey of 187 faculty in 1923 resulted in 122 listing a religious affiliation, 63 listing no affiliation, one listing agnostic, and another listing "none," the latter word underscored several times. Again, it is important not to overinterpret

such data, but it is interesting that 65 percent of the faculty apparently expressed some personal religious affiliation. See "Committee on Religious, Moral, and Social Welfare of Students, Conference, March 15, 1923," HJB Administrations, Box 60, folder 23.

250. First Baptist Church of Hyde Park, November 28, 1900, Records, April 1, 1896–April 29, 1903, Archives of the Hyde Park Union Church, Chicago.

251. "J. M. Jackson reported on behalf of the Advisory Committee on the recommendation of Dr. W. R. Harper in reference to a church building. The report recommended that immediate and decisive steps be taken towards [the] building." The motion was adopted. First Baptist Church of Hyde Park, March 1, 1893, Records.

252. Charles H. Arnold, *God before You and behind You: The Hyde Park Union Church through a Century, 1874–1974* (Chicago, 1974), p. 28.

253. See Harper's comments in *Biblical World* 3 (1894): 307–8; as well as Carter, "The 'Message of the Higher Criticism'," pp. 113–19, 135–37, 218–19.

254. "Editorial," *Biblical World* 6 (1895): 164.

255. Copies of Harper's annual printed reports are filed in the handwritten minutes of the church, First Baptist Church of Hyde Park, Records, April 1, 1896–April 29, 1903.

256. *Chicago Tribune*, September 20, 1900, p. 6.

257. "How Dr. Harper Wins," *Chicago Tribune*, January 19, 1896, p. 26; "Dr. Harper's Rapid Rise," March 8, 1897, p. 9; Hollis W. Field, "How W. R. Harper Works," ibid., October 30, 1904, p. E2; George T. B. Davis, "The Career of a Great Educator: The Rapid Rise and Remarkable Achievements of William R. Harper, President of the University of Chicago," *Our Day* 17 (1898): 387.

258. Elizabeth Wallace, *The Unending Journey* (Minneapolis, 1952), p. 97.

259. See especially John D. Rockefeller, *Random Reminiscences of Men and Events* (New York, 1909), pp. 179–80.

260. *Chicago Tribune,* March 8, 1900, p. 3.

261. *Chicago Tribune,* January 11, 1906, p. 1; also reprinted in J. M. P. Smith, "President Harper as the Christian Scholar," *Standard*, January 20, 1906, p. 10.

262. Harper to Rev. W. J. Stewart of Canton, IL, December 24, 1897, Harper Papers, Box 3, folder 21.

263. The honorary degree for McKinley was proposed by the Departments of Political Science, History, Political Economy, and Sociology. Minutes of the University Senate, September 20, 1898.

264. "Tuesday evening I received returns at the Auditorium but honestly after the first fifteen minutes, the figures were so overwhelming that Republican as I am, I was almost more sorry for the Democrats than I was glad for myself." Harper to Leo F. Wormser, November 11, 1904, Harper Papers, Box 7, folder 14. Of course, Harper did not share Roosevelt's views of John D. Rockefeller, but he admitted that the attacks were having an impact on the University: "There is no question that the public feeling has been greatly aroused within the last six months against the Standard Oil and monopolies in general. This has resulted in part from President Roosevelt's attitude and is the outgrowth of the magazine articles.... It is hurting

the University very seriously." See Harper to Ryerson, April 18, 1905, Harper Papers, Box 15, folder 13.

265. Harper to Samuel N. Harper, November 8, 1900, Samuel N. Harper Papers, Box 1, folder 2.

266. "A few of our professors do not think that the war ought to be continued in the Philippines. This is all they have ever thought, or have ever said. You may be sure that the University of Chicago is all right." Harper to P. H. Ellsworth, May 9, 1899, Harper Papers, Box 4, folder 27; *Chicago Tribune*, June 20, 1898, p. 10; September 20, 1898, p. 6. Holst presented a stirring condemnation of American imperialism in remarks before the Junior College Assembly on February 6, 1899. See his "Some Lessons We Ought to Learn," *University Record* 3 (1898–99): 299–304.

267. Harper to Ryerson, April 15, 1898, Harper Papers, Box 4, folder 5; *Chicago Tribune*, April 2, 1898, p. 6; September 19, 1898, p. 7; May 1, 1899, p. 2.

268. Harper to C. P. Linzee, May 9, 1899, Harper Papers, Box 4, folder 27.

269. Harper to Ferdinand Peck, February 21, 1901, HJB Administrations, Box 61, folder 7.

270. Dorothy Ross, *The Origins of American Social Science* (Cambridge, 1991), pp. 226–27; Diner, *A City and Its Universities*, pp. 31–33. Like Small, both Henderson and Merriam had strong connections to the world of pre-1914 German urban social policy. See Rodgers, *Atlantic Crossings*, pp. 243–44; and Barry D. Karl, *Charles E. Merriam and the Study of Politics* (Chicago, 1974), pp. 37–38, 61–83.

271. *Chicago Tribune*, July 31, 1894, p. 3.

272. Robert L. McCaul, "Dewey's Chicago," *School Review* 67 (1959): 258–80.

273. Harper to Andrew MacLeish, April 7, 1896, Harper Papers, Box 2, folder 24.

274. McCaul, "Dewey's Chicago," pp. 263–64. By 1900 the University had affiliation agreements with Des Moines College, Kalamazoo College, Stetson University, Butler College, Bradley Polytechnic Institute, Morgan Park Academy, Frances Shimer Academy, South Side Academy, Harvard School, Princeton-Yale School, Kenwood Institute, Wayland Academy, Rugby School, Chicago Manual Training School, Culver Military Academy, Elgin Academy, Dearborn Seminary, Burlington Institute, and University School for Girls. See *Annual Register, July, 1900–July, 1901*, pp. 152–65.

275. Andrew MacLeish to Harper, April 15, 1896; and D. G. Hamilton to Harper, March 13, 1896, HJB Administrations, Box 11, folder 13.

276. *Chicago Tribune*, June 30, 1896, p. 5; Harper to MacLeish, April 18, 1896, Harper Papers, Box 2, folder 24.

277. E. L. Rosseter to Harper, January 16, 1897, HJB Administrations, Box 11, folder 14.

278. A. A. Sprague to Harper, January 10, 1898, HJB Administrations, Box 11, folder 14; Albert G. Lane to Harper, March 28, 1898, ibid.

279. *Chicago Tribune*, May 8, 1899, p. 7.

280. Statement of A. F. Nightingale, April 17, 1896, Harper Papers, Box 2, folder 24; *Chicago Tribune*, December 6, 1897, p. 5.

281. Harrison to Harper, July 8, 1898, Harper Papers, Box 4, folder 9.

282. *Chicago Tribune*, June 30, 1898, p. 5. Anti-Harper sentiment was expressed

by a board member who thought that Andrews's nomination was yet another effort to make the public schools "subservient to the University of Chicago" and "an adjunct to a private enterprise." Harper was not reappointed to the board in July 1898, largely because Harrison was under pressure from those who feared Harper was trying to take over the schools. Ibid., July 12, 1898 p. 7. Harper wrote to Andrews in June 1898, urging him to take the job on the grounds that "the time is ripe. With the Mayor back of us we can introduce a great number of reforms." Harper to Andrews, June 16, 1898, HJB Administrations, Box 8, folder 10.

283. "Memorandum of Proposition to E. Benjamin Andrews from Univ. of Chicago," undated [most likely spring or summer of 1893], HJB Administrations, Box 8, folder 10. Harper seemed to suggest that he and Andrews would each run the University for six-month intervals, spelling each other in a regular cycle. See also Meyer, "The Chicago Faculty," pp. 110–12.

284. See "Dr. Andrews's Unpopularity," *Chicago Teacher and School-Board Journal*, 1 (1899): 377–78: "It is many years since a superintendent of schools in Chicago so completely lost the good will of teachers and trustees."

285. For Harrison and the Union League Republicans, see Marjorie Murphy, "From Artisan to Semi-Professional: White Collar Unionism among Chicago Public School Teachers, 1870–1930" (PhD diss., University of California at Davis, 1981), pp. 38–39.

286. *Report of the Educational Commission of the City of Chicago* (Chicago, 1899), pp. xxi–xiii, 11–17, 21–57.

287. See John C. Pennoyer, "The Harper Report of 1899: Administrative Progressivism and the Chicago Public Schools" (PhD diss., University of Denver, 1978), esp. pp. 255–71; Murphy, "From Artisan to Semi-Professional," pp. 34–54; David J. Hogan, *Class and Reform: School and Society in Chicago, 1880–1930* (Philadelphia, 1985), p. 197; Diner, *A City and Its Universities*, pp. 81–86; Robert L. Reid, "The Professionalization of Public School Teachers: The Chicago Experience, 1895–1920" (PhD diss., Northwestern University, 1968), pp. 44–57; and Julia Wrigley, *Class Politics and Public Schools: Chicago, 1900–1950* (New Brunswick, NJ, 1982), pp. 92–104.

288. See Pennoyer, "The Harper Report of 1899," pp. 90–92.

289. *Chicago Tribune*, June 19, 1899, p. 3.

290. Reid, "The Professionalization of Public School Teachers," p. 53.

291. *Chicago Tribune*, March 5, 1899, p. 13; September 26, 1899, p. 1; April 18, 1900, p. 1; April 19, 1900, p. 1; Joseph W. Errant, "The Chicago School Situation," *Educational Review* 18 (1899): 119–37.

292. Harper to Andrews, December 15, 1898; Andrews to Harper, December 16, 1898, HJB Administrations, Box 8, folder 10.

293. Mary J. Herrick, *The Chicago Schools: A Social and Political History* (Beverly Hills, CA, 1971), p. 87.

294. See David Hogan's comments in *Class and Reform*, pp. 196–97 and 312 n. 57; and Reid, "The Professionalization of Public School Teachers," p. 41.

295. See Robert L. Reid, ed., *Battleground: The Autobiography of Margaret A. Haley* (Urbana, IL, 1982), p. xx. For Haley, see Cherry W. Collins, "Schoolmen, School-

ma'ams, and School Boards: The Struggle for Power in Urban School Systems in the Progressive Era" (PhD diss., Harvard University, 1976), pp. 153–87, 207–31.

296. See Maureen A. Flanagan, *Charter Reform in Chicago* (Carbondale, IL, 1987), esp. 110–35; Flanagan, *Seeing with Their Hearts: Chicago Women and the Vision of the Good City, 1871–1933* (Princeton, NJ, 2002), esp. pp. 59–70.

297. Diner, *A City and Its Universities*, p. 87; John T. McManis, *Ella Flagg Young and a Half Century of the Chicago Public Schools* (Chicago, 1916), pp. 95–100, 103–22, 156–99; Joan K. Smith, *Ella Flagg Young: Portrait of a Leader* (Ames, IA, 1979).

298. When Harper complained that the board's own teacher training institute, the Chicago Normal School, was luring (or forcing) teachers into taking their extension courses instead of the University's courses, Edwin G. Cooley, who succeeded Andrews as city schools superintendent, became outraged, writing to Harper, "We are every day conscious of antagonism, to the Normal School in particular, manifested by people connected with your institution. We hear criticism of our methods of work, of the character of the people employed as instructors, and we are inclined to believe that a part of this abuse comes from the fact that the extension movement is headed by the Normal School." Cooley to Harper, October 14, 1903, HJB Administrations, Box 12, folder 1.

299. *University Record* 4 (1899–1900): 141–51, here 151. Spalding was one of the founders of the Catholic University of America in 1887.

300. In this sense, what happened to Chicago after 1906 fits well with the general pattern of developments articulated by Thomas Bender in his "The Erosion of Public Culture," where he argues that the research universities were perfectly willing to have their academic specialists study the city but also insisted on becoming "intellectual refuges" set apart from the "complexity and disorder" of the city. See Bender, "The Erosion of Public Culture," pp. 100–101.

301. The most stunning exception, of course, was the salutary work undertaken by the University's School of Social Service Administration, formerly the Chicago School of Civics and Philanthropy, which was integrated as an official part of the University in 1920–21 with the support of trustee Julius Rosenwald and later the Laura Spelman Rockefeller Memorial and the Rockefeller Foundation. But it was characteristic of the lure of research surrounding the new school that the dean of SSA, Edith Abbott, would frame the mission of her new school in 1925 first and foremost as stressing the "importance of research work in the social service field," whose "greatest need is for funds for research and publication." *The President's Report, Covering the Academic Year July 1, 1924, to June 30, 1925* (Chicago, 1926), pp. 19–20.

302. John M. Coulter, "The Contribution of Germany to Higher Education," *University Record* 8 (1903–4): 348–53. Coulter received an honorary PhD from Indiana University in 1884. He did not study in Germany, but as the chief editor of the *Botanical Gazette* Coulter maintained professional contacts with various senior German botanists.

303. *Maroon*, October 8, 1904, p. 2.

304. Small to Harper, April 27, 1903, HJB Administrations, Box 42, folder 16.

305. This debate is nicely summarized in Roy Steven Turner, "Humboldt in

North America? Reflections on the Research University and Its Historians," in Rainer Christoph Schwinges, ed., *Humboldt International: Der Export des deutschen Universitätsmodells im 19. und 20. Jahrhundert* (Basel, 2001), pp. 289–302. For the general background, see Walter Ruegg, ed., *A History of the University in Europe*, vol. 3, *Universities in the Nineteenth and Early Twentieth Centuries (1800–1945)* (Cambridge, 2004), pp. 163–77.

306. Henry Geitz, Jürgen Heideking, and Jurgen Herbst, eds., *German Influences on Education in the United States to 1917* (Cambridge, 1995), p. 17; as well as Mitchell G. Ash, ed., *German Universities: Past and Future; Crisis or Renewal?* (Providence, 1997); and Ash, "Bachelor of What, Master of Whom? The Humboldt Myth and Historical Transformations of Higher Education in German-Speaking Europe and the US," *European Journal of Education* 41 (2006): 245–67.

307. Gabriele Lingelbach, "Cultural Borrowing or Autonomous Development: American and German Universities in the Late Nineteenth Century," in Thomas Adam and Ruth V. Gross, eds., *Traveling between Worlds: German-American Encounters* (College Station, TX, 2006), p. 111; and Lingelbach, "The Historical Discipline in the United States: Following the German Model?," in Eckhardt Fuchs and Benedikt Stuchtey, eds., *Across Cultural Borders: Historiography in Global Perspective* (Lanham, MD, 2002), pp. 184–85.

308. Charles E. McClelland, "Die Universität am Ende ihres ersten Jahrhunderts— Mythos Humboldt?," in Heinz-Elmar Tenorth and Charles E. McClelland, eds., *Geschichte der Universität unter den Linden, vol. 1, Gründung und Blütezeit der Universität zu Berlin 1810–1918* (Berlin, 2012), vol. 3, p. 640.

309. Lingelbach, "Cultural Borrowing or Autonomous Development," p. 105. See also Lingelbach, *Klio macht Karriere: Die Institutionalisierung der Geschichtswissenschaft in Frankreich und den USA in der zweiten Hälfte des 19. Jahrhunderts* (Göttingen, 2003).

310. Thomas W. Goodspeed, unpublished original manuscript of his *History of the University of Chicago*, p. 43, Goodspeed Papers, Box 2, folder 7.

311. Ibid., p. 67.

312. Goodspeed Papers, Box 4, folder 7, pp. 3–4. This issue is referred to in the *Chicago Tribune*, October 25, 1891, p. 11.

313. Breasted to Harper, September 16, 1890, HJB Administrations, Box 12, folder 10. For a recent account of Breasted's experiences at Yale and in Germany, see now Jeffrey Abt, *American Egyptologist: The Life of James Henry Breasted and the Creation of His Oriental Institute* (Chicago, 2011), pp. 12–40.

314. Breasted to Harper, December 26, 1891, HJB Administrations, Box 12, folder 10.

315. "If you will pardon me for saying it myself, Dr. Joachim the translator of the 'Papyrus Ebers' told me this morning that both Erman and Steindorff (Coptic) said to him that they were 'expecting great things of me for Egyptology.'" Breasted to Harper, April 25, 1892, HJB Administrations, Box 12, folder 10.

316. Rodgers, *Atlantic Crossings*, p. 87.

317. Breasted to Harper, August 24, 1892, HJB Administrations, Box 12, folder 10.

318. Breasted to Harper, November 24, 1892, HJB Administrations, Box 12, folder 10.

319. Charles Breasted, *Pioneer to the Past: The Story of James Henry Breasted, Archaeologist* (New York, 1943), pp. 34–57.

320. Breasted to Harper, July 21, 1894, HJB Administrations, Box 12, folder 10. In the years that followed, Breasted continued to admire German academic culture, particularly the willingness of the Royal Academies to support independent research projects and the munificence with which scholarly conferences were organized. But it was also telling, and fully in line with Harper's own sympathies, that when the question came up in 1902 of appointing a scholar of Arabic at Chicago, Breasted did not urge that Harper hire a German scholar. This suggestion signaled a general and growing self-confidence in the prestige and power of the new American research university, and a willingness to repudiate the need to look to Europe for well-trained scholars. Breasted to Harper, September 12, 1902, HJB Administrations, Box 12, folder 11.

321. James H. Tufts, "Some Impressions of the University of Michigan, 1889–91," p. 4, in his "Unpublished Autobiography," Tufts Papers, Box 3, folder 11.

322. See Tufts to Harper, September 28, 1891; November 22, 1891; December 21, 1891; February 20, 1892; June 9, 1892; and July 14, 1892, Harper Papers, Box 14, folder 12. Tufts also sent Harper the names of other young Americans whom he met or heard about in Germany.

323. Tufts, "Germany," p. 8, in his "Unpublished Autobiography," Tufts Papers, Box 3, folder 13.

324. Tufts, "Wartime," p. 1, folder 19.

325. Payne went on to become an editor of the *Dial* literary magazine in Chicago. See Frederic J. Mosher, "William Morton Payne," *Newberry Library Bulletin,* 2nd ser., no. 7 (October 1951): 193–212. He was militantly anti-German during World War I.

326. Shorey to Payne, September 16, 1881; September 18, 1881; October 30, 1881; May 2, 1882; May 14, 1882; June 11, 1882; January 8, 1884, William M. Payne Papers, Newberry Library.

327. Paul Shorey, "American Scholarship," *Nation*, May 11, 1911, pp. 466–69.

328. In an interview in the *Chicago Record-Herald*, Small insisted that many Germans had told him that they thought that war with America was inevitable because they believed that America's rising hegemony in world markets deeply threatened key German interests. *Chicago Record-Herald*, September 30, 1903, p. 9; Albion W. Small, "Will Germany War with Us?" *Collier's Weekly*, December 10, 1904, p. 23. Small provided a more subtle and reasoned explanation of his concern to the German consul general in Chicago, Walther Wever. See Small to Wever, October 3, 1903, Small Papers, Box 1, folder 15.

329. Albion W. Small, "America and the World Crisis," *American Journal of Sociology* 23 (1917–18): 145–73.

330. Albion W. Small, "The Life History of Albion W. Small," pp. 16–17, Small Papers, Box 4, folder 3.

331. See Jurgen Herbst, *The German Historical School in American Scholarship: A Study in the Transfer of Culture* (Ithaca, NY, 1965), pp. 154–59, 192–96; Herbst, "From Moral Philosophy to Sociology: Albion Woodbury Small," *Harvard Educational Review* 29 (1959): 227–44; Axel R. Schäfer, *American Progressives and German Social Reform, 1875–1920: Social Ethics, Moral Control, and the Regulatory State in a Transatlantic Context* (Stuttgart, 2000), pp. 47–50; and Rodgers, *Atlantic Crossings*, pp. 89–95.

332. On this point, see the analysis in Ross, *The Origins of American Social Science*, pp. 126–27, 224–26. For a survey of Small's thought over the course of his career, see now Robert C. Bannister, *Sociology and Scientism: The American Quest for Objectivity, 1880–1940* (Chapel Hill, NC, 1987), pp. 32–63, esp. 48–49.

333. Albion W. Small, *The Cameralists: The Pioneers of German Social Polity* (Chicago, 1909), pp. vii, 586.

334. Ibid., p. 17.

335. Albion W. Small, *Origins of Sociology* (Chicago, 1924), pp. 30–36, 326–28. For the complex experiences of other young Americans with institutionalist economics in Germany in the 1880s and 1890s, see the elegant analysis in Rodgers, *Atlantic Crossings*, pp. 89–111.

336. Robert Rosenthal, "The Berlin Collection: A History," in *The Berlin Collection: Being a History and Exhibition of the Books and Manuscripts Purchased in Berlin in 1891 for the University of Chicago by William Rainey Harper with the Support of Nine Citizens of Chicago* (Chicago, 1979), pp. 1–23.

337. Karen Parshall, Moore's biographer, suggests that "the ideas which Moore encountered in Germany dominated his mathematical thinking for the remainder of his career." See Karen H. Parshall, "Eliakim Hastings Moore and the Founding of a Mathematical Community in America, 1892–1902," *Annals of Science* 41 (1984): 313–33, here 315. I am grateful to my colleague Robert J. Zimmer for helpful comments on the early history of the department, and on the ways in which its early research traditions endured well into the twentieth century.

338. Karen H. Parshall and David E. Rowe, *The Emergence of the American Mathematical Research Community, 1876–1900: J. J. Sylvester, Felix Klein, and E. H. Moore* (Providence, 1994), pp. 435–36.

339. The sequencing of the two appointments, and their tactical interconnectedness, is described in Parshall and Rowe, *The Emergence of the American Mathematical Research Community*, pp. 197–202, 286–93.

340. Raymond C. Archibald, *A Semicentennial History of the American Mathematical Society, 1888–1938* (New York, 1938), p. 145; and Parshall and Rowe, *The Emergence of the American Mathematical Research Community*, pp. 363–419.

341. See the handwritten biographical sketch of Nef by his son, John U. Nef Jr., John U. Nef Sr. Papers, Box 1, folder "Biographical Materials."

342. See the handwritten memorandum of Nef, most likely to Harry Pratt Judson, December 1906, John U. Nef Sr. Papers, Box 1, folder "1902–1906."

343. Harper to Ella Young, January 28, 1899, Harper Papers, Box 4, folder 22.

344. Benjamin S. Terry, a younger American scholar working on his PhD with

Holst at the University of Freiburg who assisted Harper in conducting the negotiations with Holst (and who was also hired by Harper as a professor at Chicago),
wrote candidly to a confidant of Harper about the personal sovereignty that the
senior German scholar brought to his vocation: "I do not believe that you will get
him to enter into any stipulation as to the number of hours per week [of teaching]
in the amount or kind of work that he is to do. He simply asks for the liberty to do
what he shall think is best for his department and for his work.... You need have
no fears that he will not earn his salary. As a simple advertisement, all that he costs
will be well spent. More than that, he is much more widely known, and has a much
more extensive personal acquaintance among the wealthy Germans of America than
I think you are aware of, to say nothing of his wide acquaintance with the eminent
men of his own department in both Europe and America." Terry to Eri B. Hulbert,
December 27, 1891, Harper Papers, Box 14, folder 8.

345. Judson to Harper, December 23, 1891, and December 25, 1891, Harper Papers, Box 9, folder 10.

346. See Eric F. Goldman, "Hermann Eduard von Holst: Plumed Knight of
American Historiography," *Mississippi Valley Historical Review* 23 (1936–37): 511–
32; as well as Jörg Nagler, "A Mediator between Two Historical Worlds: Hermann
Eduard von Holst and the University of Chicago," in Henry Geitz, Jürgen Heideking,
and Jurgen Herbst, eds., *German Influences on Education in the United States to 1917*
(Cambridge, 1995), pp. 257–74; and Hans-Günter Zmarzlik, "Hermann Eduard von
Holst," in Johannes Vincke, ed., *Freiburger Professoren des 19. und 20. Jahrhunderts*
(Freiburg am Breisgau, 1957), pp. 21–76.

347. See "Is Fiat of a Dictator," *Chicago Tribune*, December 19, 1895, p. 2; "Von
Holst Stirs Up War," ibid., December 22, 1895, p. 1. Thomas Haskell has argued per-
suasively that the most critical variables in explaining the rise of academic freedom
were the forces of professionalism and professionalization. See Thomas L. Haskell,
"Justifying the Rights of Academic Freedom in the Era of 'Power/ Knowledge'," in
Louis Menand, ed., *The Future of Academic Freedom* (Chicago, 1996), pp. 43–90,
esp. p. 54

348. Holst to Harper, December 22, 1895, HJB Administrations, Box 85, folder 2.

349. Hired over Laughlin's objections, Bemis was a man of outspoken convictions on key social causes of the day, particularly the municipalization movement
against private utilities and greater state regulation of the railroads. Bemis's first
quarter of teaching did not go well, and Laughlin's continued lobbying of Harper to
get rid of Bemis eventually led to Bemis's termination. In October 1895 Bemis went
public with a denunciation of Harper's behavior, implying that he had been fired to
please the whims of wealthy capitalists. Subsequent scholarship on the Bemis case
has found Harper's motives and actions at best confused and at worst duplicitous.
Bemis not only faced the outright hostility of Laughlin, but also received little sympathy from the head of the Department of Sociology, Albion Small, who urged him
to temper his public statements. See Mary O. Furner, *Advocacy and Objectivity: A
Crisis in the Professionalization of American Social Science, 1865–1905* (Lexington,
KY, 1975), pp. 177–82; as well as Clyde W. Barrow, *Universities and the Capitalist*

State: Corporate Liberalism and the Reconstruction of American Higher Education, 1894–1928 (Madison, WI, 1990), pp. 189–90; and Bannister, *Sociology and Scientism*, pp. 41–43.

350. In the case of a Mr. Jude, Holst wrote that "it would not be calculated to build up its reputation for a high standard if higher degrees were frequently conferred upon students of Mr. J's intellectual caliber." Holst to Harper, June 29, 1895, *HJB Administrations*, Box 85, folder 2.

351. Holst to Harper, December 24, 1895.

352. James Laurence Laughlin, "Life and Character of Professor von Holst," *University Record* 8 (1903–4): 161–69, here 161, 167.

353. Wever's program of exchange professorships eventually sent John Matthews Manly and Albert Michelson to the University of Göttingen and J. Laurence Laughlin to the University of Berlin and brought Hermann Oncken, Heinrich Kraeger, Ernst Daenell, and Lorenz Morsbach to Chicago. A signal of equality and independence, Chicago would now send "its" senior *Ordinarien* (as they were perceived by the German academic community) to Europe. No longer was the University simply dependent on German culture; it now had something to offer in its own right. For the context of these exchanges, see Bernhard vom Brocke, "Der deutsch-amerikanische Professorenaustausch: Preussische Wissenschaftspolitik, internationale Wissenschaftsbeziehungen und die Anfänge einer deutschen auswärtigen Kulturpolitik vor dem Ersten Weltkrieg," *Zeitschrift für Kulturaustausch* 31 (1981): 128–82.

354. Minutes of the Board of Trustees, July 1, 1903; February 28, 1904.

355. See Mortimer Chambers, "The 'Most Eminent Living Historian, The One Final Authority': Meyer in America," in William M. Calder and Alexander Demandt, eds., *Eduard Meyer: Leben und Leistung eines Universalhistorikers* (Leiden, 1990), pp. 105–6.

356. William Rainey Harper, "A Function of the University," *University Record* 8 (1903–4): 347.

357. Harper to Tower, March 26, 1904, HJB Administrations, Box 81, folder 5.

358. Chandler memoir, June 21, 1927, Goodspeed Papers, Box 4, folder 12.

359. Thorstein Veblen, *The Higher Learning in America: A Memorandum on the Conduct of Universities by Businessmen* (repr., New Brunswick, 1993), pp. 173–97. Veblen wrote a shorter first draft of this book while still on the Chicago faculty (he left in 1906), but completed a full text only in 1916, which was then published in 1918. Veblen never mentions Harper by name, but the "captain of erudition" (pp. 182, 189–90) is clearly modeled on Harper. The literature on Veblen's views of the universities is large, but see the insightful comments of Thomas Bender in *Intellect and Public Life: Essays on the Social History of Academic Intellectuals in the United States* (Baltimore, 1993), pp. 65–66; David Riesman, *Thorstein Veblen: A Critical Interpretation* (New York, 1953), pp. 99–110; John P. Diggins, *The Bard of Savagery: Thorstein Veblen and Modern Social Theory* (New York, 1978), pp. 172–85; and Richard Teichgraeber's excellent introduction to the new version of Veblen's work, recently published by the Johns Hopkins University Press.

360. William Rainey Harper, "The Business Side of a University," in *The Trend in Higher Education,* pp. 161–85; Harper, "The College President," in Robert N. Montgomery, ed., *The William Rainey Harper Memorial Conference, Held in Connection with the Centennial of Muskingum College, New Concord, Ohio, October 21–22, 1937* (Chicago, 1938), pp. 24–34, here 33.

361. G. Stanley Hall to John D. Rockefeller, December 18, 1905, Harper Papers, Box 17, folder 1.

362. Parker to Storr, November 3, 1953, Storr Papers, Box 6, folder 11.

363. Harper to Colwell, February 8, 1899, Harper Papers, Box 4, folder 22.

364. Mandeville to Richard Storr, November 12, 1953, Storr Papers, Box 6, folder 11.

365. See McClelland's shrewd comments in "Die Universität am Ende ihres ersten Jahrhunderts—Mythos Humboldt?," p. 646.

366. Beardsley Ruml, "The University of Chicago Program" [unpublished fragment of a book manuscript that Ruml never completed], n.d. [most likely 1956], *Beardsley Ruml Papers,* Box 1, folder 1.

367. Levi, "The Critical Spirit," p. 5.

368. Gates to Goodspeed, December 27, 1915, Goodspeed Papers, Box 1, folder 21.

Chapter Three

1. The dustup made for odd bedfellows. Robert Lovett later confessed that he and Ferdinand Schevill had lobbied for Judson as a way of stopping Albion Small, whom they felt to be unsympathetic to the humanities, but as we will see, Judson's later militarism during World War I must have given Lovett second thoughts. See Lovett's comments to Richard Storr, in "Conference with R. M. Lovett," February 15, 1955, Storr Papers, Box 6, folder 8; and more generally, Meyer, "The Chicago Faculty," pp. 221–25.

2. Goodspeed, *A History of the University of Chicago,* pp. 291–92.

3. See Judson to Henry C. Morrison, June 12, 1922, HJB Administrations, Box 56, folder 2.

4. The plan was changed to a contributory structure in 1922, with faculty required to purchase a retirement annuity by contributing 5 percent of their annual salary (up to $300 per year), an amount that was then matched by the University at the same level. In 1924 the trustees set the official retirement age for faculty at sixty-five.

5. James H. Tufts, "Chicago, 1904–1917," p. 7, in his "Unpublished Autobiography," Tufts Papers, Box 3, folder 19.

6. As Judson put it to William Gardner Hale in 1907, in rejecting the need to meet outside offers, "The university has advanced too far for the loss of any one to be 'terrible.' It has also gone too far to make it necessary to 'dicker' with people who receive other calls and to offer 'inducements' to stay with the institution." Judson to Hale, April 19, 1907, HJB Administrations, Box 48, folder 4.

7. Memorandum to H. A. W., April 10, 1915, Swift Papers, Box 119, folder 4. Swift was referring to John U. Nef, who found Judson unsympathetic to his research de-

mands and who ended up receiving some modest (and anonymous) support directly from Swift.

8. Harry Pratt Judson, *Europe in the Nineteenth Century* (New York, 1900), pp. 9, 332–33.

9. Harry Pratt Judson, *The Growth of the American Nation* (New York, 1906), pp. 353–55.

10. Meyer, "The Chicago Faculty," p. 95.

11. Ibid., pp. 171–72; Judson, "The Treaty of Peace with Spain," *University Record* 3 (1898–99): 315–21. Several months before America's entrance into World War I, Judson was asked whether he favored the permanent retention of the Philippines. He replied, "It has always seemed to me advisable to keep the Philippine Islands until the people there are sufficiently developed to be able to administer their own affairs. That time in my opinion will not come for two or three generations. It seems to me hardly necessary to interpret such a phrase as 'permanent retention.'" Judson to Walter D. Kline, October 2, 1916, HJB Administrations, Box 55, folder 6.

12. Judson to Irving Fisher, January 21, 1916, HJB Administrations, Box 55, folder 6. Judson also opposed federal aid to education, arguing that education was a matter for the states and for private foundations. Judson to O. E. Tiffany, December 16, 1915, ibid.

13. Diner, *A City and Its Universities,* pp. 18–19.

14. W. Alexander Mabry, ed., "Professor William E. Dodd's Diary, 1916–1920," *John P. Branch Historical Papers of Randolph-Macon College*, n.s., 2 (March 1953), p. 28. For Wilson and the race problem, see John Hope Franklin, "The Birth of a Nation: Propaganda as History," in *Race and History: Selected Essays, 1938–1988* (Baton Rouge, 1989), pp. 16–17, 20–21; and John David Smith, *An Old Creed for the New South: Proslavery Ideology and Historiography, 1865–1918* (Athens, GA, 1985), pp. 123–24, 198.

15. See Morris Janowitz, ed., *W. I. Thomas on Social Organization and Social Personality: Selected Papers* (Chicago, 1966), pp. xiv–xv; and Martin Bulmer, *The Chicago School of Sociology: Institutionalization, Diversity, and the Rise of Sociological Research* (Chicago, 1984), pp. 59–60; Judson to Abraham Flexner, April 1, 1919, HJB Administrations, Box 84, folder 12.

16. "Judson," p. 1, Tufts Papers, Box 3, folder 17; Theodore G. Soares, "President Judson," *University of Chicago Magazine* 19 (1926–27): 263–64.

17. Henry F. May, *The End of American Innocence: A Study of the First Years of Our Own Time, 1912–1917* (New York, 1959), p. 363; as well as David M. Kennedy, *Over Here: The First World War and American Society* (Oxford, 1980), pp. 178–79; and John Whiteclay Chambers II, *To Raise an Army: The Draft Comes to Modern America* (New York, 1987), pp. 80–81.

18. See Carol S. Gruber, *Mars and Minerva: World War I and the Uses of the Higher Learning in America* (Baton Rouge, 1975), p. 105, as well as pp. 28–30, 95.

19. C. Judson Herrick to Judson, March 16, 1917, HJB Administrations, Box 87, folder 4.

20. See, for example, his letter to Major Eugene Greathiel, March 8, 1918, com-

menting on the latter's concern about finding jobs for demobilized veterans and assuring him that just as Civil War veterans had found work immediately, so too would soldiers of this war. HJB Administrations, Box 88, folder 3.

21. Harry Pratt Judson, *A History of the Troy Citizens Corps, Troy, N.Y.* (Troy, NY, 1884), p. 3. Ironically, for all of Judson's later denunciation of Prussian militarism, the uniforms worn by his corps were described in 1879 as a "neat Prussian uniform and 'pickelhauben'" (pp. 72 and 55).

22. Harry Pratt Judson, *Caesar's Army: A Study of the Military Art of the Romans in the Last Days of the Republic* (Minneapolis, 1888), p. iv.

23. See "National Security League: Purpose, Organization, and a Few Facts as to the Preparedness of Our Country," HJB Administrations, Box 88, folder 1; Robert D. Ward, "The Origin and Activities of the National Security League, 1914-1919," *Mississippi Valley Historical Review* 47 (1960-61): 51-65; Chambers, *To Raise an Army*, pp. 81-82.

24. See "Professor William E. Dodd's Diary, 1916-1920," pp. 14-15, 21, 24, 28-29, 43.

25. Judson to A. Naumann, March 7, 1917, HJB Administrations, Box 86, folder 11.

26. Letter of December 30, 1916, HJB Administrations, Box 88, folder 1.

27. For examples of Judson's fiscalism, see Meyer, "The Chicago Faculty," pp. 343, 346, 351-52, 364, 373, 389-93. The resistance to Judson's appointment as president in 1907 also reflected his colleagues' unease about his deep fiscal conservatism. Meyer, pp. 221-25.

28. Robert Herrick, *Chimes* (New York, 1926), p. 235. Robert Herrick said of his Judson-figure Dolittle, "The war had surprisingly rejuvenated Dolittle. He was once more feeling his own importance, which was the psychological basis of youth." *Chimes*, p. 266.

29. *Maroon*, October 23, 1917, p. 3.

30. See Hartmut Pogge von Strandmann, "The Role of British and German Historians in Mobilizing Public Opinion in 1914," in Benedikt Stuchtey and Peter Wende, eds., *British and German Historiography, 1750-1950: Traditions, Perceptions, and Transfers* (Oxford, 2000), pp. 335-71. The most recent analysis of German ideological rhetoric during the war is Steffen Bruendel, *Volksgemeinschaft oder Volksstaat: Die "Ideen von 1914" und die Neuordnung Deutschlands im Ersten Weltkrieg* (Berlin, 2003).

31. Harry Pratt Judson, "The Threat of German World-Politics," *University Record* 4 (1918): 22-47. See George T. Blakey, *Historians on the Homefront: American Propagandists for the Great War* (Lexington, KY, 1970), pp. 34-56; and Peter Novick, *That Noble Dream: The "Objectivity Question" and the American Historical Profession* (Cambridge, 1988), pp. 112-28, a survey of the propagandistic excesses senior historians allowed themselves in their anti-German rhetoric.

32. *Maroon*, January 5, 1918, p. 2.

33. *Maroon*, January 8, 1918, p. 2. For midwestern attitudes about the war, which were somewhat more isolationist than those on the East Coast, see Chambers, *To Raise an Army*, pp. 84, 108-11, 176-77; Blakey, *Historians on the Homefront*, p. 77; and May, *The End of American Innocence*, pp. 370-71. The print run for the Chicago

War Papers series was 25,000 each. "War Activities," HJB Administrations, Box 88, folder 3. It is possible that the Chicago series was modeled on the Oxford Pamphlet series, which began in the fall of 1914 and reached eighty-seven by the fall of 1915. Strandmann, "The Role of British and German Historians," pp. 352–58.

34. Minutes of the Board of Trustees, March 12, 1918, pp. 387–88.

35. The best and most reliable account of the affair is that of Friedrich Katz, *The Secret War in Mexico: Europe, the United States, and the Mexican Revolution* (Chicago, 1981), pp. 350–78. See also Count Bernstorff, *My Three Years in America* (New York, 1920), pp. 380–81. For two postwar American opinions of Bernstorff, see Robert Lansing, *War Memoirs* (Indianapolis, 1935), pp. 217–18, 356–58; and Charles Seymour, *The Intimate Papers of Colonel House* (Boston, 1926), vol. 2, pp. 422–23.

36. See John Henry Hopkins to Judson, March 20, 1918, HJB Administrations, Box 50, folder 14.

37. Judson to Governor Frank Lowden, August 1, 1917, HJB Administrations, Box 87, folder 2. His official appointment was as a member of the District Board for Division 1 of the Northern District of the State of Illinois. David Robertson reported, "Since that time the President, except for one hour each morning, has given his entire time to the Government." *Maroon*, October 23, 1917, p. 3. Judson served from August to December 1917, when he resigned and found a replacement for himself from the University's law faculty. Judson to Charles Evans Hughes, December 12, 1917, HJB Administrations, Box 87, folder 2.

38. See Judson to Stanley Hall, May 18, 1918, HJB Administrations, Box 88, folder 7. On Judson's trip to Persia, see "The American-Persian Relief Expedition," *University Record* 5 (1919): 232–38.

39. Maroon, January 8, 1918, p. 1; "Officers of the University in the Service of the Nation and Its Allies," *University of Chicago Magazine* 11 (1918–19): 56–59.

40. See Stieglitz to Robertson, December 15, 1917, HJB Administrations, Box 86, folder 7.

41. "Work and Fight. Together We Win," a handout signed by Elizabeth Wallace in 1918; as well as Wallace to Angell, October 16, 1918, HJB Administrations, Box 88, folder 8; and Wallace, *The Unending Journey*, pp. 202–17.

42. *Chicago Tribune,* May 28, 1917, p. 4; May 29, 1917, p. 2; Robert Lovett, *All Our Years: The Autobiography of Robert Morss Lovett* (New York, 1948), pp. 137–50.

43. Gruber, *Mars and Minerva*, pp. 43–44, 108–17.

44. Herrick, *Chimes*, pp. 260–61. The novel was published two years after Herrick's resignation from the faculty. In his *Robert Herrick: The Development of a Novelist* (Berkeley, 1962), p. 285, Blake Nevius rightly characterizes the novel as "the history of a big business, one might call it, as seen through the eyes of a rather disgruntled former employee."

45. Small published his essay under the title "Americans and the World Crisis" in the *American Journal of Sociology* 23 (1917): 145–73. On campus, Small gave a similar lecture with the title "Why Americans Must Fight." See *Maroon*, December 11, 1917, p. 1; December 14, 1917, p. 1.

46. Unpublished lecture notes for a war address, 1917, Shorey Papers, Box 42,

folder 3, here pp. 17–19, 32. The *Maroon* published a version of this talk on May 4, 1917, p. 1.

47. Male enrollment dipped from 1,427 in the spring of 1917 to 1,007 in the spring of 1918, while female enrollment remained steady during this time (1,045 women in the spring of 1917, and 1,010 women in the spring of 1918). *Annual Register of the University of Chicago, 1916–1917*, pp. 778–81; and *Annual Register of the University of Chicago, 1917–1918*, pp. 730–33. Undergraduates declined from 999 to 754, graduate students from 428 to 253. The initial Selective Service Act of May 1917 set the age range for conscription from twenty-one to thirty. Not until August 1918 was the draft age reduced to eighteen.

48. *Maroon*, May 18, 1917, p. 1.

49. *Maroon*, October 5, 1917, p. 1; October 18, 1917, p. 1.

50. See the list dating from late May 1917, HJB Administrations, Box 88, folder 6. Over some resistance, Judson had been able to persuade the faculty to authorize an ROTC program in 1916. To encourage military training, the University allowed men to count one military science course toward their degree programs. See "Notice concerning Military Training" [1917], ibid., folder 4.

51. *Maroon*, May 1, 1917, p. 2.

52. *Maroon*, May 3, 1917, p. 2; May 7, 1917, p. 1.

53. *Maroon*, October 3, 1917, p. 1.

54. *Maroon*, December 11, 1917, p. 1.

55. *Maroon*, February 8, 1918, p. 2.

56. *Maroon*, June 4, 1918, p. 2.

57. Minutes of the Board of Trustees, December 10, 1918, p. 632.

58. *Maroon*, April 18, 1918, p. 1.

59. *Maroon*, April 16, 1918, p. 1; May 1, 1918, p. 1.

60. *Maroon*, January 31, 1918, p. 1; February 5, 1918, p. 1; February 15, 1918, p. 1.

61. In 1914, out of a total population of 2,437,526 in Chicago there were 399,977 first- and second-generation Germans, 58,843 Austrians, and 146,560 Irish, many of whom were, in Melvin Holli's term, "Anglophobic." Holli also points out that "the Scandinavians, comprising 118,000 Swedish ethnics and 47,496 Norwegians, were generally correctly neutral, but were pro-German in their basic sympathies." Peter d'A. Jones and Melvin G. Holli, eds., *Ethnic Chicago* (Grand Rapids, MI, 1981), pp. 262–63. Holli's figures probably underestimate the size of the Irish population. In addition, many of the 230,000 Poles felt ambivalence about the war, as did segments of the 750,000 "native born." Aldermanic elections in the spring of 1917 saw substantial numbers of Germans voting Socialist, in protest against the war. See Leslie V. Tischauser, *The Burden of Ethnicity: The German Question in Chicago, 1914–1941* (New York, 1990), p. 39.

62. Lovett, *All Our Years,* p. 147; *Chicago Tribune*, October 26, 1917, p. 1.

63. *Maroon*, April 27, 1917, p. 2. An editorial in the *Maroon*, March 1, 1918, p. 2, implied that there were other such students on campus.

64. *Maroon*, December 15, 1917, p. 2.

65. Elizabeth Wirth Marvick, "Louis Wirth: A Biographical Memorandum," in

Albert J. Reiss Jr., ed., *Louis Wirth: On Cities and Social Life; Selected Papers* (Chicago, 1964), pp. 335–36. According to his official transcript, Wirth was an excellent student, who merited honors in sociology and in history and was elected to Phi Beta Kappa. The only blemish was the C he received in a philosophy course called "Intellectual Background of War" in the spring of 1918.

66. *Chicago Tribune*, May 20, 1919, p. 21; June 7, 1919, p. 3; *Maroon*, May 16, 1919, p. 2. For the Cosmopolitan Club movement, see Louis P. Lochner, *Always the Unexpected: A Book of Reminiscences* (New York, 1956), pp. 33–44.

67. See the memorandum "Members of the Cosmopolitan Club Accused of Open Bolshevistic, Anti-Government Statements," in HJB Administrations, Box 87, folder 9; and the unsigned statement, written after May 14, 1919, in Burgess Papers, Box 6, folder 11.

68. "Minutes of the Faculty of the Colleges of Arts, Literature, and Science, Special Meeting, June 5, 1919," p. 1, Special Collections Research Center; *Chicago Tribune*, June 7, 1919, p. 3.

69. See the later memoir of Mary Bolton Wirth, "1916–1920 at the University of Chicago," Mary Bolton Wirth Papers, Box 1, folders 1 and 2. Mary Wirth, who was also an undergraduate at Chicago during the war, describes in graphic detail the stolid campus political atmosphere presided over by Judson.

70. Robert M. Lovett, "Democracy in Colleges," p. 6, unpublished and undated manuscript, Lovett Papers, Box 2, folder 17.

71. *Maroon*, October 9, 1918, p. 1.

72. *Maroon*, October 10, 1918, p. 1.

73. *Annual Register of the University of Chicago, 1918–1919*, pp. 741–44.

74. See Angell to the editor of the *Herald-Examiner*, September 5, 1918, HJB Administrations, Box 88, folder 3. The alumni magazine reported that the University received 1,745 applications, of which 523 were current students and 1,222 were new students attracted by the ads. *University of Chicago Magazine* 11 (1918–19): 8.

75. *University of Chicago Magazine* 11 (1918–19): 38.

76. *Maroon*, October 2, 1918, p. 1.

77. Minutes of the Board of Trustees, September 10, 1918, p. 562.

78. McLaughlin to Harper, November 5, 1918, Department of History, Records, Box 1, folder 3.

79. James R. Angell, "Report for Collegiate Section A, S.A.T.C.," HJB Administrations, Box 87, folder 7.

80. Minutes of the Board of Trustees, December 10, 1918, pp. 631–32. For Judson's support for postwar universal military training, see his letter to George F. James, March 26, 1920, HJB Administrations, Box 88, folder 3.

81. See Hutchins to Major General Frank R. McCoy, April 9, 1936, Hutchins Administration, Box 145, folder 5.

82. "A Statement regarding the Department of Military Science for the Board of Trustees," [1924]. The leader of the unit, Major Harold Mayr, insisted to Burton that he needed "the active—not passive—cooperation of every member of the faculty." Letter of July 13, 1923, HJB Administrations, Box 22, folder 9.

83. Dean Chauncey Boucher informed the chair of the Department of Military Science in 1934, "It seems to me that Military Science as a College sequence will have to sink or swim on its own merits as reflected by student interest in, and demand for, the sequence, just as any of the other College elective sequences." Boucher to Major Preston Vance, October 12, 1934, Hutchins Administration, Box 145, folder 5.

84. See Reeves, Miller, and Russell, *Trends in University Growth*, p. 212.

85. R. D. Salisbury to Judson, October 28, 1921, HJB Administrations, Box 76, folder 14.

86. Gruber, *Mars and Minerva*, pp. 113–15. Herrick captured this mood in *Chimes*, when he wrote that "the older men returned to the academic nest, discarding regretfully the uniform, their honorable khaki and spurs, feeling somehow that the great vacation of all their lives had ended, with the freedom of being 'under orders'! Now they must enter the treadmill once more and give orders to themselves. They must resume the dull tasks of study and classroom, get out of the desk drawer the old lecture notes, which looked more dingy and lifeless than after the usual vacation." *Chimes*, p. 274.

87. Karl, *Charles E. Merriam*, pp. 98–99; as well as Geiger, *To Advance Knowledge*, pp. 94–95.

88. See Ellen Condliffe Lagemann, *The Politics of Knowledge: The Carnegie Corporation, Philanthropy, and Public Policy* (Middletown, CT, 1989), pp. 33–50; Robert E. Kohler, "Science, Foundations, and American Universities in the 1920s," *Osiris*, 2nd ser., 3 (1987): 140–47. Chicago played a key role in the creation of the NRC. James Angell became one of its directors, while Robert Millikan was its vice chairman and director of research.

89. Robert A. Millikan, "The New Opportunity in Science," *Science* 50 (1919): 285–97, here 292–93, 297. For the context, see Robert E. Kohler, *Partners in Science: Foundations and Natural Scientists, 1900–1945* (Chicago, 1991), pp. 91–95.

90. The *President's Report, Covering the Academic Year July 1, 1919, to June 30, 1920* (Chicago, 1921), pp. 7–8.

91. Robert H. Kargon, *The Rise of Robert Millikan: Portrait of a Life in American Science* (Ithaca, NY, 1982), pp. 100–103; Meyer, "The Chicago Faculty," pp. 402–3.

92. "The University of Chicago: Its Needs, Immediate and of the Future; Its Plans to Meet These Needs," July 1924, p. 4, HJB Administrations, Box 60, folder 12.

93. Memorandum to the Trustees, late December 1922, Swift Papers, Box 27, folder 6.

94. For his work on the draft exemption board, see his letter to James Angell, October 2, 1917, HJB Administrations, Box 88, folder 1. In general, see Meyer, "The Chicago Faculty," pp. 389–93.

95. See the correspondence in HJB Administrations, Box 88, folder 2. Judson wrote to Frank McNair on November 12, 1919, "I have not hurried in this matter because I have been anxious that we should proceed deliberately and with a full knowledge in our minds, preparatory to making the right choice."

96. The memorial was a gift to the University from the class of 1918. See the materials in Hutchins Administration, Box 18, folder 14.

97. Swift to Glen A. Lloyd and George W. Beadle, April 17, 1961, Swift Papers, Box 119, folder 29.

98. The alumni magazine did publish a cluster of short eulogies to Judson, along with longer appreciations by Theodore Soares and Shailer Mathews.

99. Tellingly, upon receiving a draft statement prepared by a member of the University's news staff to announce Judson's retirement in January 1923, Swift edited out a large section that contained effusive praise for Judson. See Swift Papers, Box 35, folder 1.

100. When Angell received an offer from the University of Michigan of its presidency, a group of sixty-one senior faculty members petitioned Judson to try to retain Angell. Angell turned down the Michigan offer, but eventually grew tired of waiting for the Chicago job to open. See the petition to Judson, signed by Albert Michelson et al., March 27, 1919, HJB Administrations, Box 8, folder 13.

101. Harold H. Swift, interview by Richard Storr, February 11, 1955, Storr Papers, Box 6, folder 8.

102. See Angell's own account in his short autobiography, "James Rowland Angell," in Carl Murchison, ed., *A History of Psychology in Autobiography* (Worcester, MA, 1936), vol. 3, pp. 18–21. It is interesting to speculate what would have happened had Angell taken the presidency in 1919 or 1920. The interwar period would have been shaped by his personality, not that of Hutchins, and the intellectual and organizational trajectory of the University would have proceeded in profoundly different directions, not in the least because, unlike Hutchins, Angell was a staunch Republican and had a profound dislike of the New Deal. As president of Yale, Angell increased its endowment from $25 million to $107 million, doubled the size of Yale College, and expanded substantially Yale's doctoral programs. Of Angell's tenure, Brooks Kelley has observed that "even more important, nearly every department (excluding the sciences) had risen to a position among the best in the land.... He made Yale a great university." Brooks Mather Kelley, *Yale: A History* (New Haven, CT, 1974), p. 392. For a different and more negative portrait of Angell, see Gaddis Smith, "Politics and the Law School: The View from Woodbridge Hall, 1921–1963," in Anthony T. Kronman, *History of Yale Law School: The Tercentennial Lectures* (New Haven, CT, 2004), pp. 139–41.

103. For the politics of the presidential search, see Meyer, "The Chicago Faculty," pp. 405–19.

104. "I know of course that not even under the most favorable circumstances can my term of office be anything else than brief. But however brief I am looking forward with joy to sharing it with you and with hope that within it we may set things definitely forward toward our goal." Burton to Trevor Arnett, May 14, 1923, Arnett Papers, Box 1, folder 1.

105. Abraham Flexner, *I Remember: The Autobiography of Abraham Flexner* (New York, 1940), p. 271.

106. White to Margaret Burton, February 17, 1956, Burton Papers, Box 7, folder 9. White's letter came on the occasion of his nomination to the Ernest DeWitt Burton Distinguished Service Professorship.

107. Levi to John Moscow, March 1, 1968, Office of the President, Beadle Administration, Records, Box 199, folder 3.

108. On Burton's early career, see Thomas W. Goodspeed, *Ernest DeWitt Burton: A Biographical Sketch* (Chicago, 1926), pp. 15–29.

109. See David L. Lindberg, "The Oriental Educational Commission's Recommendations for Mission Strategy in Higher Education" (PhD diss., University of Chicago, 1972), pp. 41–61, 78–136.

110. Robert W. Funk, "The Watershed of the American Biblical Tradition: The Chicago School, First Phase, 1892–1920," *Journal of Biblical Literature* 95 (1976): 9–14.

111. Ernest D. Burton, *A Critical and Exegetical Commentary on the Epistle to the Galatians* (New York, 1920), pp. lxiv, lxxi.

112. "A Survey and Fundraising Plan for the University of Chicago," March 8, 1924, p. 20, HJB Administrations, Box 40, folder 1

113. See, for example, Burton to Swift, December 26, 1923, Swift Papers, Box 73, folder 3.

114. Burton to Ryerson, April 19, 1924, HJB Administrations, Box 35, folder 3.

115. Convocation Statement, June 1924, Swift Papers, Box 47, folder 4.

116. See Judson to Swift, January 30, 1923, HJB Administrations, Box 56, folder 2.

117. "Report of the Senate Committee on Research," December 18, 1922, HJB Administrations, Box 70, folder 19. The report was drafted by E. H. Moore, with whom Harper had jousted many years earlier about the value of undergraduate as opposed to graduate teaching.

118. See *Chicago Daily News*, February 22, 1923, p 1; *Chicago Tribune*, February 22, 1923, p. 3. The Faculty of the Colleges of Arts, Literature, and Science had voted on February 8, 1923, to limit the number of new matriculants "to the number that can be taught effectively in view of the facilities of the University and its major purposes of graduate instruction and research." Burton was uneasy about this stipulation and was able to secure the postponement of its implementation, subject to a wider study of the problem of selective admission and retention. See Minutes of the Faculty of the Colleges of Arts, Literature, and Science, February 8, 1923; March 8, 1923.

119. Carl F. Huth to David Robertson, January 29, 1923, Department of History, Records, Box 1, folder 4.

120. Burton issued a damage-control statement after the faculty's actions, denying that the University intended to abolish the Colleges. See *Chicago Tribune*, February 25, 1923, p. 17.

121. See Ernest DeWitt Burton, "The Relation of the Colleges and the Graduate Schools," undated [late January 1923], Swift Papers, Box 144, folder 7. Burton prepared this document as a way of confronting the antiundergraduate views of Abraham Flexner, who was an influential adviser to the Rockefeller boards in New York City.

122. Burton to Swift, February 9, 1924, HJB Administrations, Box 60, folder 12.

123. "Needs of the University," Sheet 3, February 9, 1924, HJB Administrations, Box 60, folder 12.

124. Christopher Loss has recently argued that the 1920s were a time of significant reorientation in higher education toward concerns about student social needs and the emotional health of students. Christopher P. Loss, *Between Citizens and the State: The Politics of American Higher Education in the 20th Century* (Princeton, NJ, 2012), pp. 38–51. See also Roger Geiger, "The Crisis of the Old Order," in Geiger, ed., *The American College in the Nineteenth Century*, p. 275.

125. *The President's Report, Covering the Academic Year July 1, 1922, to June 30, 1923* (Chicago, 1924), pp. xv–xviii.

126. In 1928 approximately 39 percent of the available rooms were occupied by undergraduates. Sixty-one percent were assigned to graduate and professional students. See "Student Housing—Autumn Quarter 1928," Mason Administration, Box 8, folder 3. For example, Green Hall was filled largely with women graduate students, and Hitchcock Hall had a majority of graduate students as residents.

127. John Moulds informed Burton in 1923 that "since we have rooms for only about one third of those who would like to live in the Women's Halls, it seems entirely logical to me that we ought to give the protection of the halls to the younger girls who need it most. The isolated and rather depressing type of rooms available in the neighborhood are very much less desirable for young girls who need the group life than they are for older students whose ideals and standards have become settled. Under our present system it is almost impossible for a freshman girl to obtain a room in the Halls unless she has made application more than a year in advance." Moulds to Burton, March 29, 1923, HJB Administrations, Box 41, folder 8.

128. Burton himself later explicitly linked his ideas from 1902 and those that he developed in the 1920s. See his "The Relation of the Colleges and the Graduate Schools," p. 2, 1923, Swift Papers, Box 144, folder 7.

129. "An Address Delivered by Acting President Ernest DeWitt Burton before the Chicago Alumni Club, May 31, 1923," p. 13, University Development Campaigns, Box 5, folder 3. Harold Swift applauded Burton's "dream of the Colleges" and cited alumni support for the vision. See Swift to Burton, July 24, 1923, Swift Papers, Box 47, folder 3.

130. Ernest DeWitt Burton, *The University of Chicago in 1940* (Chicago, 1925), pp. 29–30.

131. Ernest DeWitt Burton, *Education in a Democratic World* (Chicago, 1927), p. 63. It was also logical that Burton's sensitivities about the University's cultural impact on student personalities would influence his tastes in faculty recruitment. As a professor at Chicago he had insisted that the University's moral goals as a Christian community for its students could be met only by "by unfailing courage and courtesy on the part of the Christian men on the faculty and among the students, and by care in the election of men to positions on the faculty." Over time, and especially after his election to the presidency, Burton tempered the explicitly Christian tone of such rhetoric, but a strong residue remained in his articulations about the responsibility of the faculty to train young college students to serve as leaders in the world beyond the academy. Memorandum on the Role of Religion in the University, December 18, 1892, HJB Administrations, Box 70, folder 11.

132. Hugely wealthy stockholders in the Standard Oil Company, Edward S. Harkness and his mother, Anna Harkness, gave substantial gifts to Yale and Harvard to create residential housing systems. The Harvard house plan was launched with an $11 million gift from Harkness in 1929, while Yale received over $15 million in 1930 for its residential college system. See Kelley, *Yale*, pp. 373–76; and Katherine Towler, "The Men behind the Plan," *Exeter Bulletin*, Fall 2006, p. 31. For trends toward enhancing residential life, see Mark B. Ryan, *A Collegiate Way of Living: Residential Colleges and a Yale Education* (New Haven, CT, 2001); James Axtell, *The Making of Princeton University: From Woodrow Wilson to the Present* (Princeton, NJ, 2006), pp. 1–3, 16–17, 21; August Heckscher, *Woodrow Wilson* (New York, 1991), pp. 153, 157, 164–73, 203; Benjamin J. Sacks, "Harvard's 'Constructed Utopia' and the Culture of Deception: The Expansion toward the Charles River, 1902–1932," *New England Quarterly* 84 (2011): 287–93.

133. See Loss, *Between Citizens and the State*, pp. 34–52. A. Lawrence Lowell's comments to Harvard students in 1909 were typical: "I believe that the future of the country is in the hands of its young men, and that the character of its young men depends largely upon their coming to college. And in the college, I believe that their character depends not merely on being instructed, but mostly on their living together in an atmosphere of good fellowship." Henry A. Yeomans, *Abbott Lawrence Lowell, 1856–1943* (Cambridge, MA, 1948), pp. 101–2; as well as David O. Levine, *The American College and the Culture of Aspiration, 1915–1940* (Ithaca, NY, 1986), pp. 106–8; William Bruce Leslie, *Gentlemen and Scholars: College and Community in the "Age of the University," 1865–1917* (University Park, PA, 1992), pp. 240, 247–49; and Geiger, *To Advance Knowledge*, pp. 129–39.

134. Burton, *Education in a Democratic World*, p. 44.

135. Levine, *The American College and the Culture of Aspiration*, pp. 14, 123; Daniel A. Clark, *Creating the College Man: American Mass Magazines and Middle-Class Manhood, 1890–1915* (Madison, WI, 2010), pp. 181–90.

136. Tufts, "Burton," p. 14, in his "Unpublished Autobiography," Tufts Papers, Box 3, folder 18.

137. Minutes of the University Senate, May 10, 1924 and June 11, 1924.

138. "Eighth Session," p. 54, Office of the President, Kimpton Administration, Records, Box 252, folder 1. See also Meyer, "The Chicago Faculty," pp. 449–50.

139. LaVerne Noyes gave $300,000 to build Ida Noyes Hall in 1913 and an additional $1.5 million to create a scholarship fund for veterans of World War I and their descendants. Hobart Williams gave a gift of $2 million for scholarships and instruction in 1916, which was totally unsolicited. Rosenwald provided $250,000 in 1912 for a building for geology and geography, again largely of his own volition.

140. "Burton," p. 8, Tufts Papers, Box 3, folder 18.

141. Memorandum of December 1, 1922, Swift Papers, Box 27, folder 5.

142. "A Survey and Fund-Raising Plan for the University of Chicago," March 8, 1924, pp. 16, 41, HJB Administrations, Box 40, folder 1.

143. Swift to Judson, June 5, 1920, Swift Papers, Box 156, folder 25. Judson only

commissioned Goodspeed to work on the booklet a year after Swift requested it. See Goodspeed to Swift, December 24, 1920, ibid.

144. Swift to Edgar J. Goodspeed, January 4, 1921, Swift Papers, Box 156, folder 25. A few days later, Swift sent another letter in which he noted that "undergraduates and graduates of our College Department frequently feel that we are trying to stifle rather than encourage that Department." Letter of January 7, 1921, ibid.

145. *The University of Chicago in 1921* (Chicago, 1921), p. 26.

146. Dickerson to Swift, May 9, 1923, Swift Papers, Box 82, folder 12.

147. Swift to Burton, December 31, 1923, Swift Papers, Box 73, folder 3. Goodspeed's proposal for an internally organized campaign is also in this folder.

148. See "A Survey and Fund-Raising Plan for the University of Chicago," HJB Administrations, Box 40, folder 1. Jones argued that "such a survey bears to a financial Campaign the same relation that a map bears to a military Campaign or a diagnosis to medical treatment." Jones to Albert Sherer, November 14, 1923, Swift Papers, Box 73, folder 4.

149. See Scott M. Cutlip, *Fund Raising in the United States: Its Role in America's Philanthropy* (New Brunswick, NJ, 1965), esp. pp. 171–77, 480–82. Jones was also a graduate of Harvard. The Jones firm was chartered in New York State on November 23, 1919.

150. See Cutlip, *Fund Raising,* p. 481; and Morton Keller and Phyllis Keller, *Making Harvard Modern: The Rise of America's University* (New York, 2001), pp. 178–83.

151. Trevor Arnett, "A Letter to the Alumni of the University of Chicago," HJB Administrations, Box 35, folder 3.

152. Duncan to Thomas Gonser, October 24, 1955, Kimpton Administration, Box 100, folder 6.

153. Swift to Burton, February 20, 1924, Swift Papers, Box 73, folder 5.

154. See Burton's speeches of May 31, 1923, p. 13, and March 24, 1925, p. 6, in University Development Campaigns, Box 5, folders 3 and 12.

155. "The University of Chicago: Its Needs, Immediate and of the Future; Its Plans to Meet These Needs; A Memorandum for the Information of the Trustees of the University," July 1924, HJB Administrations, Box 60, folder 12.

156. The negotiations are charted in the correspondence in Swift Papers, Box 74, folder 7.

157. "Proposal to Build and Endow an Administration Building at the University of Chicago," undated, 1925, Mason Administration, Box 1, folder 2.

158. "The University of Chicago: Its Needs, Immediate and of the Future," p. 4.

159. See Burton to Ryerson, April 19, 1924, HJB Administrations, Box 35, folder 3.

160. Distinguished Service chairs were given by Sewell L. Avery, Charles F. Grey, Frank P. Hixon, Morton D. Hull, Andrew MacLeish, and Charles H. Swift. In addition the board created a chair in honor of Ernest D. Burton based on subscriptions by the senior classes of 1925, 1926, 1927, and 1928 and special donations by John D. Rockefeller Jr. and Harold H. Swift in 1930. Finally, a chair to honor the mathematician Eliakim Hastings Moore was created by the board at the urging of Max Mason in May 1927 without any endowment to honor the memory of "renowned professors."

This was a practice the board later regretted, and a subsequent report prepared for Robert Hutchins in 1936 suggested archly that "it is a question as to whether it should be referred to as a distinguished service professorship."

161. On the history of the chapel, see Edgar J. Goodspeed, *The University of Chicago Chapel: A Guide* (Chicago, 1928); and Sara M. Ritchey, *Life of the Spirit, Life of the Mind: Rockefeller Memorial Chapel at 75* (Chicago, 2004). Construction costs were covered by a part of Rockefeller's final gift from December 1910, which allocated $1.5 million for the project. The building was initially called the University Chapel and renamed in honor of John D. Rockefeller only in 1937.

162. Burton to Goodspeed, September 21, 1924, Edgar J. Goodspeed Papers, Box 2, folder 2.

163. Minutes of the Board of Trustees, April 20, 1925, pp. 136–38. In 1898 the University signed an affiliation agreement with the Rush Medical College, a local medical school organized in 1837. The relationship with Rush led Harper to refuse the chance to obtain the independent medical research institute that Frederick Gates persuaded the Rockefellers to support the creation of the Rockefeller Institute for Medical Research in 1901. See E. Richard Brown, *Rockefeller Medicine Men: Medicine and Capitalism in America* (Berkeley, 1979), pp. 105–9; and Gates, *Chapters in My Life*, pp. 179–89. The trustees' decision to proceed with an independent academic medical school and a teaching hospital came in November 1916, with the two million-dollar gifts from the Rockefeller Foundation and the General Education Board, pledged as part of a $5.3 million project to which Martin A. Ryerson, Julius Rosenwald, and other trustees also contributed.

164. For the creation of the academic Medical Center in the 1920s, see Ilza Veith and Franklin C. McLean, *The University of Chicago Clinics and Clinical Departments, 1927–1952: A Brief Outline of the Origins, the Formative Years, and the Present State of Medicine at the University of Chicago* (Chicago, 1952), esp. pp. 14–15; Edwin F. Hirsch, *Frank Billings, the Architect of Medical Education, an Apostle of Excellence in Clinical Practice, a Leader in Chicago Medicine* (Chicago, 1966), pp. 103–9; and Cornelius W. Vermeulen, *For the Greatest Good to the Largest Number: A History of the Medical Center, the University of Chicago, 1927–1977* (Chicago, 1977), pp. 8–20.

165. See Jane Maienschein, "Whitman at Chicago: Establishing a Chicago Style of Biology?," in Ronald Rainger, Keith R. Benson, and Jane Maienschein, eds., *The American Development of Biology* (Philadelphia, 1988), pp. 151–82; Philip J. Pauly, "The Appearance of Academic Biology in Late Nineteenth Century America," *Journal of the History of Biology* 17 (1984): 382–87, 392–93, who argues that before 1918 "medicine exerted only a minor influence on the shape of biology at Chicago. The biology division, housed in magnificent surroundings, was left largely undistracted in its choice of faculty and research programs." Lily E. Kay, *The Molecular Vision of Life.: Caltech, the Rockefeller Foundation, and the Rise of the New Biology* (New York, 1993), notes that Whitman and Lillie were adamant in preventing fundamental research in the biological sciences becoming merely a "service to medicine." (pp. 80–81).

166. See Robert E. Kohler, *From Medical Chemistry to Biochemistry: The Mak-*

ing of a Biomedical Discipline (Cambridge, 1982), pp. 303–10; and Kohler, "The Management of Science: The Experience of Warren Weaver and the Rockefeller Foundation Programme in Molecular Biology," *Minerva* 14 (1976): 279–306, who describes these new structural trends for the 1930s.

167. See especially Bulmer, *The Chicago School of Sociology*, esp. pp. 129–50, 190–224; Bulmer, "The Early Institutional Establishment of Social Science Research: The Local Community Research Committee at the University of Chicago, 1923–1930," *Minerva* 18 (1980): 51–110; Karl, *Charles E. Merriam*; and Andrew Abbott, *Department and Discipline: Chicago Sociology at One Hundred* (Chicago, 1999).

168. Swift's standard solicitation letter left the recipient with little choice but to give a gift: "I dislike soliciting funds, especially from my good friends, but [I] believe you will realize that this is the feasible way to handle [the matter]. To that end, I enclose herewith two pledge cards, one of which I should appreciate you filling in with the amount of your subscription." Swift to Robert Lamont, November 21, 1924, Swift Papers, Box 76, folder 4.

169. The lists are in Swift Papers, Box 76, folders 4 and 8.

170. Dean James H. Tufts identified this problem as a chronic challenge for fundraisers employed by Chicago in 1925, and it would remain such for many decades to come. See his comments in *The President's Report, Covering the Academic Year July 1, 1924 to June 30, 1925* (Chicago, 1926), p. xviii.

171. "Alumni Campaign Book," p. 8, Swift Papers, Box 75, folder 23.

172. If one includes the additional 4.8 percent of the alumni who were in the ministry, and another 2.2 percent who were categorized as being "scientists," it is clear that well over half of Chicago alumni in 1924 were in occupations in some way related to learning and education. See University Development Campaigns, Box 2, folder 5; and Reeves and Russell, *The Alumni of the Colleges*, pp. 64–91.

173. "University-Alumni Relations: A Survey and A Suggested Plan" [1926], p. 21, Swift Papers, Box 156, folder 27.

174. Robert P. Lamont to Swift, May 29, 1925, Swift Papers, Box 76, folder 21.

175. "Eighth Session," p. 54, Kimpton Administration, Box 252, folder 1.

176. See Warren Weaver, "Max Mason, October 26, 1877–March 22, 1961," in *National Academy of Sciences Biographical Memoirs* (Washington, DC, 1964), pp. 205–32.

177. The files on the search are in Swift Papers, Box 36. See also Meyer, "The Chicago Faculty," pp. 458–70. Burton and Swift were largely responsible for the push to revise the statutes in May 1923, which in my view was the result of the fiasco over Angell's failed candidacy. The report to the Northern Baptist Convention, requesting approval of the change, noted that the management of a large university was a complex and challenging task, that the number of men qualified for such a position was always very limited, and that "the difficulty of finding a man for the presidency of the University has greatly increased since the Articles of Incorporation were framed in 1890." Minutes of the Board of Trustees, June 14, 1923, p. 207.

178. See Swift's public autobiographical statement of April 1955 in Swift Papers, Box 78, folder 2.

179. Kohler, *Partners in Science*, p. 274. That said, Mason's charming personality continued to impress interlocutors to the end of his career. The young historian Richard Storr, when undertaking research for his history of the Harper era, was invited to meet with Max Mason in 1953 when Mason visited Chicago. Storr, who did not deal with senior foundation officials (or university presidents) on a regular basis, was astonished by the insouciant banter between Kimpton and Mason about the enormous discretionary power such individuals held in their hands: "Seeing Mason with the others of the Central Administration I realized more sharply than before that there is a class of men whose job it is to make policy for the life of the mind—to decide if classical archaeology has about run its course, etc." Storr Papers, Box 6, folder 8.

180. Swift's memo to C. H. S., February 19, 1930, Swift Papers, Box 73, folder 13.

181. Swift Papers, Box 74, folder 6.

182. The Eckhart gift came as a result of trustee Julius Rosenwald's intervention. The Jones gift originated from an intervention by David Evans. The Wieboldt gift resulted from cultivation by Ernest Burton and Julius Rosenwald.

183. "Memorandum on New York Trip of Max Mason, January 4, 1927," Swift Papers, Box 175, folder 6. An interesting exchange occurred on this visit between Abraham Flexner and Mason. Flexner decried the influence of undergraduates at a research university, but Mason pointed out that the best way to change the attitudes of American society about the importance of scholarly research was to expose undergraduates to scholarship during their years in college.

184. Bulmer, "The Early Institutional Establishment of Social Science Research," pp. 94–98. The memorial provided $1million for the building, and an additional $1 million for faculty and research support.

185. See Abt, *American Egyptologist*, p. 341.

186. Woodward to Arnett, March 29, 1929, forwarding "The General Medical School Budget and the University Clinics," March 27, 1929, Development and Alumni Relations, Records, Box 48. The awards from the Rockefeller boards to the Medical School amounted to more than $12.8 million by 1932. Plimpton to Swift, March 4, 1932, Swift Papers, Box 85, folder 13a.

187. Kohler, "Science, Foundations, and the American Universities in the 1920s," p. 140; Kohler, *Partners in Science*.

188. Robert Duncan reported to Albert Sherer in February 1926 that after Burton's death "there was a noticeable slowing up in Campaign activity, and the momentum of the early spring 1925 was never regained. The result is that the possibilities of gifts from citizens of Chicago have hardly been scratched." "The Campaign for Development of the University of Chicago, August 11, 1924–February 6, 1926," University Development Campaigns, Box 2, folder 9. This report provides a comprehensive overview of the strategies of the campaign.

189. See the list of Rockefeller-associated gifts to the University of Chicago from 1890 to 1932 in Swift Papers, Box 85, folders 13a, 15, 17. See also "Conditional Gifts-University of Chicago," July 21, 1927, ibid., Box 75, folder 28; and the data from 1938–39 in Office of the Vice President Records (hereafter VP Records), Box 6, folder 13.

190. Raymond M. Hughes, *A Study of the Graduate Schools of America* (Oxford, OH, 1925). The American Council on Education issued a similar set of rankings in 1934, in which Chicago was found to have twenty-one "distinguished" programs, tied with California and Columbia, and exceeded only by Harvard, which had twenty-three. See the findings in the "Report of Committee on Graduate Instruction," issued by the American Council on Education (Washington, DC, 1934), as summarized by Laurence Foster, *The Functions of a Graduate School in a Democratic Society* (New York, 1936), pp. 19–20.

191. Brubacher and Rudy, *Higher Education in Transition*, p. 195.

192. Hughes, *A Study of the Graduate Schools of America*, pp. 7–8.

193. See the discussion G. Stanley Hall, in "How Can Universities Be So Organized as to Stimulate More Work for the Advancement of Science?," at the AAU's annual meeting in November 1916, reported in the *Journal of Proceedings and Addresses of the Eighteenth Annual Conference of the Association of American Universities*, 1917, pp. 25–54; as well as the overview in Berelson, *Graduate Education in the United States*, pp. 16–24.

194. Woodbridge to William A. Nitze, May 16, 1918, Nitze Papers, Box 13, folder 22.

195. Albion W. Small, "What Should Be the Ideal of Our Own Graduate School of Social Science?," February 28, 1923, HJB Administrations, Box 47, folder 6. For the background to this memo, see Bulmer, *The Chicago School of Sociology*, pp. 130–34.

196. For Small's relationship to his own department after 1918, which played a role in this *crise de conscience* about the future of graduate education, see Bannister, *Sociology and Scientism*, pp. 55–63.

197. William James, "The Ph.D. Octopus," *Harvard Monthly*, March 1903.

198. Lawrence K. Frank, "The Status of Social Science in the United States," manuscript, Laura Spelman Memorial, Records, Series, 3.06, Box 63, folder 679, Rockefeller Archive Center.

199. Ibid., pp. 5, 8, 23.

200. Martin Bulmer and Joan Bulmer, "Philanthropy and Social Science in the 1920s: Beardsley Ruml and the Laura Spelman Rockefeller Memorial, 1922–1929," *Minerva* 19 (1981): 371–78; as well as Donald Fisher, *Fundamental Development of the Social Sciences: Rockefeller Philanthropy and the United States Social Science Research Council* (Ann Arbor, MI, 1993), pp. 31–39.

201. For the status of graduate programs in the United States on the eve of World War II, see Marcia Edwards, *Studies in American Graduate Education* (New York, 1944), who commented that "in spite of all the growth and expansion ... the underlying structure and basal characteristics of graduate education have changed comparatively little since 1900" (p. vii).

202. Laing explicitly mentioned his concern that graduate education not be left behind as the University debated ideas for strengthening the undergraduate program: "It seems to me important that this study of the Graduate School should be carried on at the same time as the study of the undergraduate situation by the

Commission which is already at work." Laing to Burton, January 15, 1924, HJB Administrations, Box 47, folder 6.

203. Laing to Burton, March 5, 1924, folder 6. Laing married the daughter of Harry Pratt Judson, Alice C. Judson, in August 1903, so it was perhaps not accidental that the son-in-law shared his father-in-law's dislike of undergraduates.

204. "Report on the Graduate Schools," pp. 4–6, 7–8, 47–49, 53, folders 7–8.

205. Laing's real goal, about which he was publicly vocal, was to reduce senior faculty teaching loads by 50 percent, from six courses a year to three per year. See "The Graduate School of Arts and Literature," in *The President's Report, Covering the Academic Year July 1, 1923, to June 30, 1924* (Chicago, 1925), p. 9.

206. *The President's Report, Covering the Academic Year July 1, 1929, to June 30, 1930* (Chicago, 1931), p. 5.

207. Bender, *Intellect and Public Life*, p. 77. The humanities did receive some support from the Rockefeller boards in the later 1920s and 1930s for projects such as William Craigie's Dictionary of American English project, William Nitze's Arthurian Romances project, and John M. Manly's Chaucer edition project. See the Division of the Humanities, Research Grants, Records, 1926–44. However, most of these projects were of modest scale, and few involved new analytic methods or approaches to the training of doctoral students. In general, see Kathleen D. McCarthy, "The Short and Simple Annals of the Poor: Foundation Funding for the Humanities, 1900–1983," *Proceedings of the American Philosophical Society* 129 (1985): 3–8.

208. Fisher, *Fundamental Development of the Social Sciences*, pp. 27–66; Ross, *The Origins of American Social Science*, pp. 402–4; Karl, *Charles E. Merriam*, pp. 149–52; Bannister, *Sociology and Scientism*, pp. 179–81, 190–95; Bulmer, "The Early Institutional Establishment of Social Science Research," pp. 70–110. Karl notes that the Local Community Research Committee at Chicago followed logically from Albion Small's earlier "efforts to persuade the social scientists to listen more to one another." Karl, Charles E. Merriam, p. 150.

209. Kimpton to Ruml, February 17, 1955, on the occasion of inviting Ruml to participate in a twenty-fifth anniversary celebration of the dedication of the Social Sciences Research Building in November 1955, Ruml Papers, Box 3, folder 9.

210. Melvin W. Reder, "Chicago Economics: Permanence and Change," *Journal of Economic Literature* 20 (1982): 5, 9; Ross B. Emmett, "Entrenching Disciplinary Competence. The Role of General Education and Graduate Study in Chicago Economics," in *History of Political Economy* 30 (1998): 134–50; Ross, *The Origins of American Sociology*, pp. 449–58; Bulmer, *The Chicago School of Sociology*, pp. 95–96, 117, 130–31, 172, 215; Mary Jo Deegan, "The Chicago School of Ethnography," in Paul Atkinson et al., *Handbook of Ethnography* (Thousand Oaks, CA, 2001), pp. 12–14; Bannister, *Sociology and Scientism*, pp. 174–87; James T. Carey, *Sociology and Public Affairs: The Chicago School* (Beverly Hills, CA, 1975), pp. 153–59; Karl, *Charles E. Merriam*, pp. 147–56; Michael T. Heaney and John Mark Hansen, "Building the Chicago School," *American Political Science Review* 100 (2006): 589–96.

211. Kenton W. Worcester, *Social Science Research Council, 1923–1998* (New York, 2001), pp. 25–27; Fisher, *Fundamental Development of the Social Sciences*, pp. 59–61.

Not surprisingly, Merriam influenced Ruml's thinking on the key issue of graduate-student fellowship support. Karl, *Charles E. Merriam*, pp. 133–34.

212. Heaney and Hansen, "Building the Chicago School," p. 591.

213. Ruml's original "General Memorandum" of October 1922 for the new directions in which he wanted to lead the Spelman Memorial emphasized graduate scholarships and fellowships as levers to "enlarge the possibilities of minor investigations by graduate students." See Bulmer and Bulmer, "Philanthropy and Social Science in the 1920s," p. 365.

214. The history of teaching loads at Chicago, as at other major research universities, would require its own lengthy monograph. For a survey of the state of play by the late 1920s, see Floyd Reeves et al., *The University Faculty* (Chicago 1933), pp. 93–113.

215. Charles Merriam reported in 1934 that "the International House continues to be a very important center for interchange of ideas among students, particularly on the graduate level. A considerable proportion of our students have made their residence in the House and have found this of very great value to them." *Annual Report of the Political Science Department* (Chicago, 1934), p. 2. See also Herbert Blumer's comments to James Carey about his experiences as a doctoral student in sociology in the interview of May 22, 1972, p. 16, *University of Chicago, Department of Sociology, Interviews, 1972.* Blumer recalled that "those who were engaged in that type of work in the late twenties particularly, in the very beginning of the thirties were constituted as a group of graduate students with a tremendous amount of camaraderie and a tremendous amount of close contact with one another, due in large measure to their actual working setting."

216. Charles E. Merriam, "A Word in Conclusion," Merriam Papers, Box 120, folder 4.

217. SSRC fellowships were among the most important. Fisher observes that "by the end of the Second World War a whole generation of social scientists occupying responsible academic posts and research positions owed the critical part of their training and their professional development to the SSRC." *Fundamental Development of the Social Sciences*, pp. 200–201.

218. Margit Szöllösi-Janze, "Science and Social Space: Transformations in the Institutions of 'Wissenschaft' from the Wilhelmine Empire to the Weimar Republic," *Minerva* 43 (2005): 355.

219. Lasswell to Merriam, November 5, 1923, Merriam Papers, Box 34, folder 4.

220. See "Report on Foreign Student Work at the University of Chicago, Autumn Quarter 1923," HJB Administrations, Box 44, folder 6.

221. John Matthews Manly to Ernest D. Burton, October 31, 1924, HJB Administrations, Box 58, folder 13.

222. Karl, *Charles E. Merriam*, pp. 37–38.

223. Ibid., pp. 169–85, here 171. Merriam's own contribution to the series, *The Making of Citizens: A Comparative Study of Methods of Civic Training* (Chicago, 1931), provided the theoretical overview.

224. Quincy Wright, "International Affairs: International Law and Totalitar-

ian States," *American Political Science Review* 35 (1941): 743. On Wright, see also Steven J. Bucklin, "The Wilsonian Legacy in Political Science: Denna F. Fleming, Frederick L. Schuman, and Quincy Wright" (PhD diss., University of Iowa, 1993), pp. 17–76.

225. See "The Report on the Commission on the Future of the Colleges," April 22, 1924, HJB Administrations, Box 34, folder 10. The commission was nominally chaired by Henry Prescott of Latin, but Wilkins was the primary author of the main report and the sole author of "A Theory of Education."

226. See Wilkins to Tufts, October 23, 1924, including "A Theory of Education" as an enclosure, HJB Administrations, Box 34, folder 2.

227. See Minutes of the Faculty of the Colleges of Arts, Science, and Literature, February 21, 1925; March 7, 1925.

228. Burton to Swift, May 10, 1924, Swift Papers, Box 144, folder 7. Swift himself urged Burton to create a "a College Department which will put emphasis on real development of boys and girls into fine men and women rather than exclusively on the academic interests of the University field." Swift to Charles W. Gilkey, August 28, 1923, ibid.

229. The report and rejoinders from Stieglitz and other scientists were debated at several faculty meetings in early 1925 and again in January 1927. See part 5 of the set of documents marked "Material for Discussion and Action by the Faculty of the Colleges of Arts, Literature, and Science," College Archive, Box 1, folder 15, and also filed with the Minutes of the Faculty of the Colleges of Arts, Science, and Literature, January 31, 1925, and January 19, 1927. At the January 1927 meeting a committee representing both the Graduate and College faculties filed a response to Wilkins that essentially disemboweled his ideas. Chauncey Boucher was a member of this group, and the experience of serving on it must have been instructive for him as he began to formulate the revolutionary curricular plans that he would soon push forward.

230. See the memorandum "Improvement of Instruction," in Wilkins to Burton, December 6, 1923, HJB Administrations, Box 85, folder 31.

231. See Wilkins to Burton, February 18, 1925, and Burton to Wilkins, February 28, 1925, HJB Administrations, Box 85, folder 31.

232. Burton distanced himself from Wilkins's plan in a letter to Swift, May 10, 1924, Swift Papers, Box 144, folder 7.

233. "He is one of the most versatile personalities on the faculty, and his eloquence, his ready wit, his ease of address have made him the most sought after speaker on campus." *Hyde Park Herald*, January 9, 1931, p. 1.

234. Chauncey S. Boucher, "Suggestions for a Reorganization of Our Work in the College, and a Restatement of Our Requirements for the Bachelor's Degree," pp. 53–54, December 1927, College Archive, Box 27, folder 6. Boucher gave this long appeal to Max Mason in January 1928 and sent it to his colleagues in the University Senate on March 12, 1928.

235. Theodore G. Soares and Harold D. Lasswell, "Social Survey of the Undergraduates of the University of Chicago," pp. 19–20, 1920, HJB Administrations, Box 78, folder 1.

236. Edward Potthoff and George R. Moon, "A Statistical Study of the Records of 762 Students Who Entered the University of Chicago as Freshmen in the Autumn Quarter of 1919," College Archive, Box 15, folder 1.

237. George R. Moon, "A Study of Students Reported Doing Unsatisfactory Work," 1927–28, College Archive, Box 15, folder 1.

238. See Wechsler, *The Qualified Student*, pp. 222–26.

239. Frank Johnson Goodnow, "Johns Hopkins Plan for Real University," *New York Times,* March 1, 1925, p. 10.

240. Chauncey S. Boucher, "Thoughts and Suggestions Regarding an Educational Policy, and Its Successful Administration, in the Colleges of Arts, Literature, and Science, of the University of Chicago," pp. 3–4, December 1928, Mason Administration, Box 3, folder 7.

241. Boucher, "Report on the Conditions in the Colleges of Arts, Literature, and Science, December 21, 1928," p. 14, Mason Administration, Box 3, folder 7.

242. See Meyer, "The Chicago Faculty," pp. 445–50, 474–76. One of the most notable proponents of this view was an influential outsider, Abraham Flexner, who was the secretary of the General Education Board. See Flexner, "A Proposal to Establish an American University" [1922], pp. 8–9, Swift Papers, Box 144, folder 7.

243. Dodd to Bessie Louise Pierce, February 3, 1934, Pierce Papers, Box 9, folder 10.

244. Manly to Tufts, July 1, 1925, Department of Buildings and Grounds, Records, 1892–1932, Box 34, folder 4.

245. "See the report "Instruction in Large Junior College Courses," filed with the Minutes of the Faculty of the Colleges of Arts, Literature, and Science, January 31, 1925.

246. Boucher, "Report on the Conditions in the Colleges of Arts, Literature, and Science," December 21, 1928, p. 18, Mason Administration, Box 3, folder 7.

247. See Chauncey S. Boucher, "The Colleges of Arts, Literature, and Science," in *The President's Report, Covering the Academic Year July 1, 1927, to June 30, 1928*, pp. 24–31. Boucher's decision to support a limit on entering students was a clearly a tactical move, taken to blunt the antiundergraduate agitation of men like William Dodd. Ultimately, Boucher hoped to increase undergraduate enrollments, but only after he had put in place his new curricular schemes, which, he was convinced, would enable the University to attract a higher caliber of applicants.

248. Boucher, "Suggestions for a Reorganization of Our Work," pp. 51–52.

249. See John J. Coss, "A Report of the Columbia Experiment with the Course on Contemporary Civilization," in William S. Gray, ed., *The Junior College Curriculum* (Chicago, 1929), pp. 133–46; Justus Buchler, "Reconstruction in the Liberal Arts," in Dwight C. Miner, ed., *A History of Columbia College on Morningside* (New York, 1954), pp. 48–135; Gary E. Miller, *The Meaning of General Education: The Emergence of a Curriculum Paradigm* (New York, 1988), pp. 35–41; and Timothy P. Cross, *An Oasis of Order: The Core Curriculum at Columbia College* (New York, 1995).

250. William S. Learned, *The Quality of the Educational Process in America and in Europe* (New York, 1927), pp. 42–48, 98–125. Learned was chiefly responsible

for organizing the famous Pennsylvania Study, which examined learning outcomes for large numbers of high school and college students in that state between 1928 and 1932 on the basis of systematic assessment testing. He was also the architect of the first Graduate Record Examination, created in 1937 on a trial basis with the cooperation of Harvard, Yale, Princeton, and Columbia.

251. Boucher reported that he considered Learned "to be the one man in the country, if there is any such one man, best prepared and best qualified to give a critical judgment on any such plan as the one proposed." After going over his plan with Learned, he was pleased to report that Learned "sincerely hoped the University of Chicago would adopt the plan and carry it into successful operation in the immediate future, ... because if the University of Chicago were to inaugurate such a system of work and requirements, it would be more significant in its effects on both secondary and college education in this country than if it were done by any other institution." Boucher, "Suggestions for a Reorganization of Our Work," pp. 52–53; as well as Learned to Boucher, March 3, 1928, in which Learned commented about Boucher's plan that "few things have ever crossed my desk that seem to me more significant than this either in themselves or in the promise that they contain of authoritative guidance for American education at a moment of great uncertainty." College Archive, Box 27, folder 6. On Learned's opposition to course-based credit and grading, see Paul F. Douglass, *Teaching for Self Education—As a Life Goal* (New York, 1960), pp. 82–89. See also Ellen Condliffe Lagemann, *Private Power for the Public Good: A History of the Carnegie Foundation for the Advancement of Teaching* (Middletown, CT, 1983), pp. 101–7.

252. In his 1932 Inglis Lecture at Harvard, Learned spoke approvingly of "the recent revolution at the University of Chicago," signified by its use of new comprehensive examinations. See William S. Learned, *Realism in American Education* (Cambridge, MA, 1932), pp. 27–28.

253. "Report of the Senate Committee on the Undergraduate Colleges (Presented to the University Senate, May 7, 1928)," Mason Administration, Box 13, folder 19. This report contains as well a "Supplementary Statement" by Boucher. The May 1928 report was based on a long document that Boucher prepared in December 1927, "Suggestions for a Reorganization of Our Work in the Colleges, and a Restatement of Our Requirements for the Bachelor's Degree," College Archive, Box 27, folder 6.

254. "Suggestions for a Reorganization of Our Work," pp. 53–58; as well as "Bait, Cut by C. S. Boucher," January 7, 1930, pp. 18–19, Hutchins Administration, Box 53, folder 4. In mid-December 1928 the University announced a $2 million gift from Julius Rosenwald (matched by a $3 million commitment from the University) for the construction of new undergraduate dormitories for men and women. "Proposal for a Dormitory Development on a 40% Gift and 60% Investment Basis" [1928], Department of Buildings and Grounds, Records, *1892–1932,* Box 12.

255. After investigating retention and attrition in the 1920s as part of the general university survey, Floyd Reeves and John Dale Russell concluded that the quality of students had improved in that decade and that the continuing high attrition rates might be owing to the fact that "year after year certain instructors and certain de-

partments have followed the same curve of grading, irrespective of the increased ability of the entering classes.... There is some question whether it is desirable for the University to continue to raise its standards and at the same time to continue to fail from one-fourth to one-third of those whom it admits." See Reeves and Russell, *Admission and Retention of University Students*, pp. 25–26, 55.

256. "Supplementary Statement," May 7, 1928, pp. 1, 11.

257. I have this information from Daniel Meyer, the archivist of the University of Chicago, who discussed the issue of Mason's resignation with historian Jean Block. Harold Swift gave Richard Storr a parallel account in 1953: "After deciding to re-marry, M[ason]. came to S[wift]. and asked to be fired. S. said: this isn't [a] matter of you over there and me here and of my firing you. We are a committee to work out a situation. You may withdraw but I won't fire you. The Rockefeller job opened up and M. left." Harold H. Swift, interview by Richard Storr, February 13, 1953, Storr Papers, Box 6, folder 8.

258. As a public rationale for his resignation, Mason reported that he was keen to be able to fund large-scale scientific projects involving key frontier areas in astron-omy and astrophysics and in biology and the behavioral sciences. See "Max Mason Quits U. of C.," *Chicago Tribune*, May 6, 1928, p. 1; May 22, 1928, p. 1.

259. The plan that Boucher brought before the University Senate was not a for-mal legislative proposal for that body, but rather a series of recommendations that would have to be considered first by the Faculty of the Colleges of Arts, Literature, and Science. This faculty met on May 15, 1928, and agreed to create two boards—one for the Junior College curriculum and one for the Senior College curriculum—to evaluate Boucher's proposals and then report back to the full faculty. The boards began to meet in the fall quarter of 1928, but it soon became apparent that, lacking the presence of the new (and, as of yet, unnamed) president, it would be difficult to establish sufficient political consensus as to how to proceed.

260. Karl, *Charles E. Merriam*, pp. 157–61. Dodd was worried that the trustees were solidly behind Woodward's ideas for the College: "This morning speech of F. C. Woodward, before a group of men brought together by Trustees, declared himself candidate for the presidency of the University. All his speech had to do with the Undergraduate Colleges—my interpretation of that is: Trustees mean to put Woodward into the presidency and then carry their programme [out]." Private diary, entry of July 27, 1928, William E. Dodd Papers, Library of Congress.

261. Dodd to Swift, September 1, 1928, Swift Papers, Box 144, folder 8. Dodd emerges from this correspondence as obsessed with an ideal of the University as a graduate-level research institute that bordered on the financially unreal, almost a caricature of a late nineteenth-century German research university that he remem-bered from his student days in Leipzig.

262. See the insightful comments on this point in Fred Arthur Bailey, *William Edward Dodd: The South's Yeoman Scholar* (Charlottesville, VA, 1997), pp. 142–43.

263. See the general letter of John A. Logan, Phyllis Fay Horton, Arthur C. Cody, Dunlap C. Clark, Frank S. Whiting, and Paul S. Russell, late 1928, Mason Adminis-tration, Box 1, folder 6.

264. Letter from a "A Group of Alumni" to Arthur C. Cody, undated [most likely early 1929], Mason Administration, Box 1, folder 4.

265. Whiting to Logan, March 7, 1929, Mason Administration, Box 1, folder 5.

266. "Joint Meeting of Trustee Committees on Alumni Relations and Alumni Contributions, December 7, 1928," Mason Administration, Box 1, folder 9.

267. See Woodward to Gale and Laing, January 11, 1929, and their guarded responses of January 15, 1929, and January 14, 1929, Swift Papers, Box 144, folder 8. More generally, see Benjamin McArthur, "A Gamble on Youth: Robert M. Hutchins, the University of Chicago, and the Politics of Presidential Selection," *History of Education Quarterly* 30 (1990): 161–86, esp. 166–73.

268. Karl, *Charles E. Merriam*, p.158. Chauncey Boucher was also the chair of the faculty committee charged with designing the new residence halls, thus giving proof positive to the College haters like Dodd and Laing that his curricular ideas were tied to Woodward's residential life scheme (which they were).

269. See chapter 4. In contrast to some other descriptions of the presidential search process, Daniel Meyer rightly observes that many senior faculty with respected research credentials favored Woodward's candidacy. Dodd and his colleagues may have been outliers, but they were in a key position to influence the outcome. See Meyer, "The Chicago Faculty," pp. 482, 486–88.

270. Karl, *Charles E. Merriam*, pp. 156, 162.

271. George S. Counts, *The Selective Character of American Secondary Education* (Chicago, 1922), pp. 72–73, 141–48.

272. In 1930 the University required that a student "shall have an average in high-school non-vocational subjects higher than the passing mark of the school by at least 25 per cent of the difference between the passing mark and 100. For example, if the passing mark is 75, the average of at least 81.25 is required." See Reeves and Russell, *Admission and Retention of University Students*, pp. 16–17.

273. Reeves and Russell, *Admission and Retention of University Students*, p. 44.

274. W. H. Harrell to W. J. Mather, June 24, 1937, Hutchins Administration, Box 70, folder 7.

275. Earl W. Anderson, "Salaries in Certain Professions," *Educational Research Bulletin*, January 11, 1933, pp. 1–9. Most of Anderson's data came from the years 1926 to 1930.

276. Floyd W. Reeves and John Dale Russell, *Some University Student Problems* (Chicago, 1933), pp. 15, 18, 30–32, 65, 70–81.

277. Soares and Lasswell, "Social Survey of the Undergraduates of the University of Chicago."

278. H. A. Millis et al., *Report of the Faculty-Student Committee on the Distribution of Students' Time, January 1925* (Chicago, 1925), p. 84. Millis also found that being a commuter was directly related to the course load that a student could carry. Students carrying a two- or three-course load (per quarter) were much more likely to be commuters than students carrying a four-course load (p. 24).

279. Reeves and Russell, *Some University Student Problems*, pp. 65–68. Using representative samples, John Kennan found in 1933 that 61 percent of entering freshmen

on scholarship aid were commuters, whereas 75 percent of nonscholarship students were commuters, presumably living at home. John C. Kennan, "A Comparison of the Two-Year Honor Scholars Winners with a Non-Scholarship Group in Respect to Finances, Study, Recreation, and Sleep," p. 3, February 1933, College Archive, Box 15, folder 7.

280. "Sources of Support for the General Budget, 1938–39," VP Records, Box 6, folder 13.

281. Reeves, Miller, and Russell, *Trends in University Growth*, pp. 176–77.

282. Reeves and Russell, *Admission and Retention of University Students*, pp. 68–69.

283. Reeves and Russell, *The Alumni of the Colleges*, p. 8.

284. These data reflect the total number of different undergraduate students who registered during these academic years and not merely autumn quarter matriculations. See *The Registrar's Report to the President, 1938–1939*, table 6, p. 10.

285. *The President's Report, July 1902–July 1904* (Chicago, 1905), p. 3.

286. "Statistics on the Freshman Class Entering Autumn Quarter, 1940," Hutchins Administration, Box 204, folder 8; Wechsler, *The Qualified Student*, pp. 228–29.

287. *The President's Report, July 1902–July 1904*, p. 3.

288. "Student Housing—Autumn Quarter 1928," Mason Administration, Box 8, folder 3.

289. "Statistics on the Freshman Class Entering Autumn Quarter, 1940."

290. *Millis et al., Report of the Faculty-Student Committee on the Distribution of Students' Time*, p. 86. My colleague Bertram J. Cohler has also suggested that ethnicity may have played a role in the decision not to live on campus, since students coming from specific ethnic backgrounds may have felt more comfortable continuing to live with their families, instead of making the (semi)clean cultural break that moving into on-campus housing would have involved.

291. *The President's Report, Covering the Academic Year July 1, 1926, to June 30, 1927* (Chicago, 1928), pp. 3–4.

292. Swift to Rosenwald, August 30, 1927, Mason Administration, Box 6, folder 12.

293. Rosenwald to Swift, September 6, 1927; Swift to Charles Z. Klauder, October 8, 1927, Mason Administration, Box 6, folder 12.

294. See Klauder to Swift, October 18, 1927, Mason Administration, Box 6, folder 12; and the sketch, dated October 15, 1927, Architectural Drawings Collection, Drawer 40.

295. Woodward to Klauder, December 20, 1927; Klauder to Woodward, January 12, 1928; Woodward to Klauder, September 20, 1928; Klauder to Woodward, October 22, 1928; Mason Administration, Box 6, folder 12.

296. Swift to Rosenwald, May 31, 1928; as well as Woodward to Swift, September 14, 1928.

297. The trustees approved the plan on November 6, 1928. See "Minutes of the Committee on Buildings and Grounds and the Committee on Finance and Investment," November 6, 1928, Swift Papers, Box 6, folder 12. The initial authorization was for two halls, but the minutes and schematic plans suggest that the board ex-

pected to proceed with the additional two buildings as part of the future program: "It has also been assumed that each dormitory group would be placed on a separate block, giving the opportunity for expansion to cover the entire block if the later experience should justify."

298. Woodward to Rosenwald, November 9, 1928, Mason Administration, Box 6, folder 12.

299. "Minutes of the Committee on Buildings and Grounds," October 8, 1931, Swift Papers, Box 7, folder 1 .

300. "Minutes of the Committee on Business Affairs," July 27, 1933, Swift Papers, Box 7, folder 6. The financial ravages of the Depression were felt in Burton-Judson Courts as well. In January 1930, the trustees reduced many original details, including eliminating many fireplaces and substituting a roof of wood instead of steel in order to reduce the cost from $1,671,000 to $1,360,000.

301. A list of on-campus student organizations from 1934 is filed in Office of Dean of Students, Records, Box 6.

302. "Curricular Extras," *Pulse*, November 1937, p. 12.

303. See Walter L. Gregory, "Twenty Years with the Blackfriars," Blackfriars, Records, Box 4. Gregory later became the president of the State Street Council and was the original organizer of the State Street Christmas parade in 1934.

304. The Dramatic Association was the successor organization to the Dramatic Club, a student group that was founded in the 1890s and that had both men and women members.

305. For these clubs, see Gordon, *Gender and Higher Education*, pp. 106–7.

306. Memoirs of student life collected in the 1950s by Richard Storr from then living pre-1914 alumni of the Colleges confirm the impression of a social life in which a minority of women (perhaps as many as one-third) were organized in social clubs, with the majority left to fend for themselves in creating their own activities. See Storr Papers, Box 6, folder 7.

307. Flint to the Alumni Council, April 29, 1929, Mason Administration, Box 1, folder 6.

308. Charlotte Montgomery Grey to the Alumni Council, April 26, 1929.

309. Soares and Lasswell, "Social Survey of the Undergraduates of the University of Chicago," p. 14; Millis et al., *Report of the Faculty-Student Committee on the Distribution of Students' Time*, pp. 88–90.

310. See Chauncey Boucher's appeal to Frederic Woodward, May 29, 1929, Hutchins Administration, Box 71, folder 4.

311. Woodward to L. R. Steere, March 6, 1929, Hutchins Administration, Box 70, folder 10. Harold Swift too was against a radical change. He wrote to Hutchins and Woodward, "Some time, too, I hope there will be less fraternities at the University than at present, but this, too, I hope to be a gradual development. After all, we owe the fraternities a lot. They have done our job in supplying housing accommodations for a good many men for a long time and I believe that we can't chuck them overboard by precipitate action." Letter of November 4, 1929, Hutchins Administration, Box 71, folder 4.

312. *Chicago Tribune*, May 18, 1928, p. 1.

313. "Preliminary Report of a Survey of Housing Conditions for Students of the University of Chicago," May 19, 1930, p. 19, Hutchins Administration, Box 106, folder 7.

314. Reeves and Russell, *Some University Student Problems*, p. 136.

315. Flint to the Alumni Council, April 29, 1929, Mason Administration, Box 1, folder 6.

Chapter Four

1. William H. McNeill, *Hutchins' University: A Memoir of the University of Chicago, 1929–1950* (Chicago, 1991), p. 18.

2. "Robert Maynard Hutchins: Secretary of Yale University," Hutchins Papers, Box 2, folder 5.

3. Hutchins to Angell, February 3, 1926, folder 2.

4. For Hutchins's tenure at Yale Law School, see the detailed analysis in John Henry Schlegel, "American Legal Realism and Empirical Social Science: From the Yale Experience," *Buffalo Law Review* 28 (1978–79): 466–91; as well as Laura Kalman, *Legal Realism at Yale, 1927–1960* (Chapel Hill, NC, 1986), pp. 107–15; Edward A. Purcell Jr., *The Crisis of Democratic Theory: Scientific Naturalism and the Problem of Value* (Lexington, KY, 1973), pp. 80–92, 139–42; and Anthony T. Kronman, ed., *History of the Yale Law School: The Tercentennial Lectures* (New Haven, CT, 2004), pp. 139–41, 154.

5. Robert M. Hutchins and Donald Slesinger, "Some Observations on the Law of Evidence—the Consciousness of Guilt," *University of Pennsylvania Law Review* 77 (1929): 725–40; Hutchins and Slesinger, "Some Observations on the Law of Evidence—the Competency of Witnesses," *Yale Law Journal* 37 (1928): 1017–28; Hutchins and Slesinger, "Some Observations on the Law of Evidence—Spontaneous Exclamations," *Columbia Law Review* (1928): 432–40; Hutchins and Slesinger, "Some Observations on the Law of Evidence—State of Mind to Prove an Act," *Yale Law Journal* 38 (1929): 283–98; Hutchins and Slesinger, "Some Observations on the Law of Evidence—Memory," *Harvard Law Review* 41 (1927–28): 860–73; Hutchins and Slesinger, "Legal Psychology," *Psychological Review* 36 (1929): 13–26.

6. Swan to Angell, February 1, 1927, James R. Angell, Presidential Records, Box 121, folder 1247, Yale University Archives.

7. Hutchins to William G. Hutchins. February 4, 1927, Hutchins Papers, Box 141, folder 8; C. G. Poore, "Yale Dean of Law Wins Post at 28," *New York Times*, March 13, 1927, p. xxii.

8. See "Report of the Committee on the Selection of the Dean of the Yale Law Faculty to the Governing Board of the Yale Law School," James R. Angell, Presidential Records, Box 121, folder 1247.

9. For the lack of impact of Hutchins's and Slesinger's work, see Jeremy A. Blumenthal, "Law and Social Science in the Twenty-First Century," *Southern California Interdisciplinary Law Journal*,12 (2002): 11–12.

10. Hutchins's rhetorical style was not to everyone's taste. John Wigmore, the dean of Northwestern University Law School, warned Angell against Hutchins's "jaunty and witty but irresponsible dismissal of the recorded experiences of judges and lawyers of the last two or three centuries," which Wigmore took to be a sign of "an unscientific and unsafe attitude towards the law." Wigmore to Angell, April 1, 1927, James R. Angell, Presidential Papers, Box 121.

11. See the resolution of the Yale Law School faculty upon Hutchins's resignation, April 1929, in Hutchins Papers, Box 231, folder 10.

12. The search committee was nominally chaired by Charles W. Gilkey, a trustee, a liberal theologian trained at Union Theological Seminary and several European universities, and the pastor of the Hyde Park Baptist Church. But Gilkey completely deferred to Swift on all significant issues.

13. Several Chicago newspapers jumped the gun on March 21, 1929, announcing that Edmund Day had been selected as the new president.

14. Swift to Gilkey, December 28, 1928, Swift Papers, Box 38, folder 11; "Memo of Discussion with Trevor Arnett," May 31, 1928; and "Memoranda of Conversations, December 29–30, 1928," ibid., Box 37, folder 4.

15. Embree to Swift, March 16, 1929, Swift Papers, Box 38, folder 11. Embree's grandfather had founded Berea College.

16. Swift to Donnelley, March 28, 1929, Swift Papers, Box 38, folder 11.

17. Swift to W. A. McDermid, March 8, 1929, Swift Papers, Box 39, folder 18.

18. Gilkey to Swift, January 18, 1929, Swift Papers, Box 37, folder 3. Judd favored Hopkins of Dartmouth and Coffman of Minnesota as leading options. Gilkey became an avid supporter of Hutchins, having known Hutchins's father for many years.

19. Swift to Donnelley, April 9, 1929, Swift Papers, Box 38, folder 11. Swift gave a sanitized account to John Gunther: "Swift Reveals Why Hutchins Heads U. of C.," *Chicago Daily News*, June 26, 1929, p. 4.

20. Swift to Quantrell, April 9, 1929; Swift internal memo of April 15, 1929; Angell to Swift, April 16, 1929; report of Ernest Quantrell of his interview of Angell, April 16, 1929, Swift Papers, Box 38, folder 11.

21. The committee report recommending Hutchins's appointment as president to the full board of trustees was dated April 17, 1929, so it was very likely drafted before Swift received Angell's letter of the day before denouncing the idea.

22. "It is said that he is further along at thirty than either Harper or Eliot taking their jobs at 35." Swift to Quantrell, April 9, 1929, Swift Papers, Box 38, folder 11.

23. On Chicago's different relationship to the cultural intelligentsia of the city of Chicago in the 1930s in contrast to Columbia University in New York City, see the insightful comments of Thomas Bender in *Intellect and Public Life*, pp. 64–65, 77–78.

24. It is striking that Hutchins began to move in this direction after his hopes for a federal appointment in Washington were dashed, a tendency that was amplified once William Benton arrived on campus in 1937. John U. Nef Jr., interview by Richard Storr, April 28, 1954, Storr Papers, Box 6, folder 8.

25. Clarence Randall to William Benton, November 20, 1939, Swift Papers, Box 49, folder 10.

26. Joseph Schwab, interview by George Dell, April 12, 1976, p. 16, Robert M. Hutchins and Associates, Oral History Interviews, Box 2, folder 9.

27. For the intellectual context, see the helpful analysis in Purcell, *The Crisis of Democratic Theory*, pp. 139–52.

28. "You want somebody who is prepared to take the initiative and be responsible for making recommendations. Everything that I did at Chicago may be regarded as the reverse of what I'd been through at Yale. I sat for six years for the Yale Corporation and the President of the University [James Angell] never made a recommendation to the Board. Not one. And they would say to him, well Mr. President what do you think? What is your recommendation? And he would say, very skillfully, he would say; on the one hand we have this and on the other we have that, and this is a matter for you to decide. Well I could see that was no way to run a University. These people didn't know anything and insofar as they knew anything, they knew what Yale had always been like, therefore they were not prepared to agree to any changes. Therefore, it seemed to me that it was irresponsible on his part. And so I always made recommendations, and always felt that if they didn't accept them that was alright, unless they were fundamental, in which case I would resign." Robert M. Hutchins, interview by George Dell, May 30, 1973, Robert M. Hutchins and Associates, Oral History Interviews, Box 1, folder 9.

29. See the perceptive comments of Laird Bell, who liked Hutchins and knew him well, in "Conversation with Laird Bell," June 21, 1956, Storr Papers, Box 6, folder 8.

30. Hutchins to his father, May 27, 1932, Box 11, folder II-10–8, William J. Hutchins Papers, Berea College Archives.

31. Mary Ann Dzuback, *Robert M. Hutchins: Portrait of an Educator* (Chicago, 1991), p. 192.

32. Schlegel, "American Legal Realism," pp. 489–90.

33. See Gilkey to Swift, January 18, 1929, p. 1, Gilkey Papers, Box 1.

34. For Harper's desire to create a strong, presidentially controlled administrative regime that would preempt vigorous traditions of faculty autonomy above the department level, see Meyer, "The Chicago Faculty," pp. 197–98, 504–5.

35. Originally, students matriculated in the Junior (Academic) Colleges of Arts, Literature, Philosophy, and Science, and then proceeded to the Senior (University) Colleges of the same titles. In 1908, a unified faculty structure was created for all of these units, the Faculty of the Colleges of Arts, Literature, and Science. For the early administrative history of the University, see Reeves, Peik, and Russell, *Instructional Problems in the University*, pp. 3–22; and Meyer, "The Chicago Faculty," pp. 214–38.

36. See Floyd W. Reeves, Frederick J. Kelly, John Dale Russell, and George A. Works, *The Organization and Administration of the University* (Chicago, 1933), pp. 45–46.

37. See "Report of the Committee on the Development and Relations of the University," Minutes of the University Senate, November 25, 1911. The trustees received the report, thanked the faculty, and filed it *ad acta*.

38. The title of "auditor" was changed to "comptroller" in the late 1920s.

39. See "The Administration Building of the University of Chicago," undated, 1927, Mason Administration, Box 1, folder 2. The new building would have enabled the move of the president's office, located on the first floor of the west tower of Harper Library, plus the consolidation of all other university administrative offices.

40. See *University of Chicago Newsletter* 16 (December 31, 1923): 1–2; and Woodie Thomas White, "The Study of Education at the University of Chicago, 1892–1958" (PhD diss., University of Chicago, 1977), pp. 266–67.

41. Minutes of the Board of Trustees, January 8, 1925, p. 30.

42. *Annual Report of the General Education Board, 1923–1924* (New York, 1925), p. 11.

43. See Merriam's comments at the dedication of Judd Hall in 1948, Merriam Papers, Box 120, folder 13.

44. Quoted in Richard O. Niehoff, *Floyd W. Reeves, Innovative Educator and Distinguished Practitioner of the Art of Public Administration* (Lanham, MD, 1991), p. 39.

45. The handwritten notes of Woodward's presentation to the board are filed in Mason Administration, Box 20, folder 6. Judd subsequently received one of the newly created Distinguished Service Professorships, which enabled Woodward to increase his salary from $8,000 to $10,000 a year. See Woodward to Judd, October 29, 1929, Hutchins Administration, Box 285, folder 5.

46. See the memorandum in Mason Administration, Box 20, folder 8. In October 1929 Judd submitted a second and similar memo to Hutchins himself. See Judd to Hutchins, October 1, 1929, ibid. Judd's negotiations came at a time when the department had lost several senior faculty members to other institutions. Judd's disdain for teacher training explains why the Department of Education at Chicago never came to play a role analogous to the Teachers College at Columbia, and why Judd ultimately had little interest in going to New York. In 1928 Chicago abolished its undergraduate BA program in education for teachers. See White, "The Study of Education at the University of Chicago," pp. 220–21; and the insightful comments of Emery Filbey to Richard Storr, May 7, 1954, Storr Papers, Box 6, folder 8.

47. Judd to Woodward, undated [February 1929], Mason Administration, Box 20, folder 6. Woodward had already alerted Arnett about Judd's plan for the future of the department the previous month. Woodward to Arnett, January 2, 1929, ibid.

48. On Reeves, see Niehoff, *Floyd W. Reeves*, esp. chaps. 2–5; and White, "The Study of Education at the University of Chicago," pp. 361–68.

49. Judd to Woodward, undated [February 1929]; and telegram, Woodward to Judd, February 25, 1929, Mason Administration, Box 20, folder 6.

50. *Annual Report of the General Education Board, 1930–1931* (New York, 1932), pp. 7–8.

51. See Raymond E. Callahan, *Education and the Cult of Efficiency: A Study of the Social Forces That Have Shaped the Administration of the Public Schools* (Chicago, 1962); Herbert M. Kliebard, *The Struggle for the American Curriculum, 1893–1958* (New York, 1987).

52. White, "The Study of Education at the University of Chicago," pp. 196, 200–201.

53. By early 1931 Reeves was contemplating a survey that would extend to sixteen separate volumes, including studies of the university hospitals and of the Laboratory Schools. See "Tentative Outline of the Survey of the University of Chicago, February 20, 1931"; the various drafts of Reeves's original outline can be found in Hutchins Administration, Box 233, folders 2 and 3.

54. In an analysis published in 1937 of the 230 surveys of American colleges and universities undertaken since 1910, Walter Eells of Stanford described the Reeves project as among the best organized and most expensive ever undertaken. When Eells conducted an informal poll of thirty-six experts, he found that the Chicago survey was rated number one in terms of its method, significance, and importance to higher education. Walter Crosby Eells, *Surveys of American Higher Education* (New York, 1937), pp. 102, 143, 153, and esp. 219–23.

55. On Ayres, see Callahan, *Education and the Cult of Efficiency*, pp. 15–18, 153–56, 165–69; Kliebard, *The Struggle for the American Curriculum*, pp. 102–4; Ellen Condliffe Lagemann, *An Elusive Science: The Troubling History of Education Research* (Chicago, 2000), pp. 80–83; and Mary B. Stavish, "Leonard Porter Ayres," *American National Biography*, vol. 1, pp. 800–801.

56. Eells, *Surveys of American Higher Education*, p. 57.

57. See Swift to Arnett, July 10, 1930, Swift Papers, Box 53, folder 5.

58. Leonard P. Ayres, "Some Aspects of the Financial Organization and Administration of the University of Chicago: A Report Prepared by Leonard P. Ayres, and Presented May 10, 1930," reprinted as an appendix in *The Organization and Administration of the University*, pp. 134–42.

59. Hutchins to Ayres, June 9, 1930, Hutchins Administration, Box 233, folder 2.

60. Hutchins to Swift, August 1, 1930, Swift Papers, Box 53, folder 6.

61. "Memorandum of Conversation with Mr. Mason," January 16, 1930; and "Memorandum of Conversation with Arnett," January 17, 1930, Swift Papers, Box 175.

62. Hutchins to Eells, January 17, 1935, Hutchins Administration, Box 233, folder 3.

63. In explaining the logic of the new divisional structures to a local alumni group, Emery Filbey would argue in November 1931 that "recent trends towards inter-departmental research in connection with such projects as child development, international relations, the dictionary of ideas for medics, mental hygiene and sex research" demonstrated the need for the new structures. "Outline of Talk before Ridge Park University Club," November 5, 1931, Filbey Papers, Box 2, folder 5.

64. "The Social Science Building is in fact a workshop where perhaps two hundred scholars and workers combine their efforts in a comprehensive research program. The layout of the rooms suggests the workshop spirit.... The building and its equipment are tools in the hands of an earnest group of social scientists who are patiently seeking better ways of life for the city and for the state." Leonard D. White, "The Local Community Research Committee and the Social Science Research Building," in T. V. Smith and Leonard D. White, eds., *Chicago: An Experiment in Social Science Research* (Chicago, 1929), pp. 27–28, 32.

65. See J. G. Morawski, "Organizing Knowledge and Behavior at Yale's Institute of Human Relations," *Isis*, 77 (1986): 219–42; Schegel, "American Legal Realism," pp. 482–88. James Angell played a major role in the architecture and implementation of this plan as well.

66. Minutes of the University Senate, October 22, 1930; Minutes of the Board of Trustees, November 13, 1930. Hutchins subsequently argued, "The aim will be to develop a divisional, rather than a departmental curriculum. Departments will not institute or maintain work duplicating that of other departments in the same division. Through a divisional curriculum the student will have opportunities denied him hitherto. Many departments have insisted on narrow specialization in departmental fields. A divisional course of study means that departmental requirements will have to have the approval of the divisions, thus guaranteeing to the student the opportunities offered by all departments in the division, and the consequent breadth of training that many of them now lack." Speech of November 20, 1930, pp. 5–6, Hutchins Papers, Box 355, folder 11.

67. Robert M. Hutchins, interview by George Dell, May 29, 1973, Robert M. Hutchins and Associates, Oral History Interviews, Box 1, folder 9.

68. Bulmer, "The Early Institutional Establishment of Social Science Research," p. 109. On Ruml, see Bulmer and Bulmer, "Philanthropy and Social Science in the 1920s"; and Earlene Craver, "Patronage and the Directions of Research in Economics: The Rockefeller Foundation in Europe, 1942–1938," *Minerva* 24 (1986): 205–22.

69. Minutes of the Department of History, March 5, 1934, Department of History, Records, Box 19, folder 6.

70. *Current Biography*, 1943, p. 648.

71. For Ruml's later career, see C. Hartley Grattan, "Beardsley Ruml and His Ideas," *Harper's Magazine*, May 1952, pp. 78–86; and Alva Johnston, "Beardsley Ruml: A Profile," *New Yorker*, February 10, 17, and 24, 1945.

72. Redfield to Hutchins, July 15, 1936, Division of the Social Sciences, Records, Box 16. For the details, see John W. Boyer, *"A Twentieth-Century Cosmos": The New Plan and the Origins of General Education at the University of Chicago* (Chicago, 2007).

73. See Donald E. Osterbrock, "Chandra and His Students at Yerkes Observatory," *Journal of Astrophysics and Astronomy* 17 (1996): 235.

74. Annual Confidential Statement to the Board of Trustees, September 30, 1938, p. 42; Report of the President, 1935–36, February 27, 1937, p. 6, Special Collections Research Center.

75. David Riesman, *Thorstein Veblen: A Critical Interpretation* (New York, 1953), pp. 101–3.

76. Boucher to Hutchins, April 27, 1929, and May 3, 1929, College Archive, Box 1, folder 8. Representing the other side, William Dodd immediately contacted Hutchins with a memorandum laying out his opposition to Woodward's and Swift's plans. Hutchins politely responded that he needed time to study the matter. See Dodd to Hutchins, May 15, 1929; and Hutchins to Dodd, Mary 23, 1929, Hutchins Papers, Box 18, folder 3.

77. Hutchins to Swift, July 3, 1929, Swift Papers, Box 49, folder 16. For Boucher's

response, see Boucher to Stevens and Woodward, October 9, 1929, Mason Administration, Box 3, folder 17.

78. Robert M. Hutchins, "The Upper Divisions of the University of Chicago," in William S. Gray, ed., *Recent Trends in American College Education* (Chicago, 1931), p. 144.

79. "The University and the Individual," address given at the Ohio Teachers' Conference, April 3, 1930, Hutchins Papers, Box 355, folder 3.

80. We know from a stream of private letters from Mortimer Adler to Hutchins in early 1931 about the rearguard action fought by several key faculty members to keep as many department-controlled courses in the first two years of the new curriculum as possible, which Adler viewed as a sign of their disdain for anything other than their own fields. The departmental advocates were "all greedily protecting their private diggings and what gets me sorest is that they are doing [so] under the false banner of educational theory." Adler to Hutchins, January 1931 [marked "Saturday"], Adler Papers, Box 56.

81. Adler to Hutchins, January 1931 [marked "Saturday afternoon"]. Charles Judd reported to William Gray as early as 1928 about Boucher's plans that "there is going to be a good deal of opposition to this report." Judd to Gray, May 9, 1928, Judd Papers, Box 10, folder 11.

82. For the details, see Chauncey S. Boucher, *The Chicago College Plan* (Chicago, 1935), pp. 43–104.

83. Chauncey S. Boucher, "Supplementary Statement by the Chairman of the Committee," p. 2, Hutchins Administration, Box 51, folder 13. This statement is an appendix to the "Report of the Senate Committee on the Undergraduate Colleges, May 7, 1928."

84. Boucher, "Suggestions for a Reorganization of Our Work," pp. 41–42.

85. Richard J. Shavelson, *A Brief History of Student Learning Assessment: How We Got Where We Are and a Proposal for Where to Go Next* (Washington, DC, 2007), p. 8.

86. Details of the methodology used in creating the comprehensive examinations can be found in Board of Examinations, University of Chicago, *Manual of Examination Methods by the Technical Staff*, 2nd ed. (Chicago, 1937). See also Louis L. Thurstone, *The Reliability and Validity of Tests: Derivation and Interpretation of Fundamental Formulae Concerned with Reliability and Validity of Tests and Illustrative Problems* (Ann Arbor, MI, 1931).

87. John M. Coulter and Merle C. Coulter, *Where Evolution and Religion Meet* (New York, 1926).

88. "The General Course in Biological Science" [1931], College Archive, Box 6, folder 9.

89. A detailed history of the course is provided by Thornton W. Page, "The Two-Year Program: Physical Sciences," November 1949, Hutchins Administration, Box 53, folder 2.

90. Harvey B. Lemon, "New Vistas of Atomic Structure," *Scientific Monthly* 17 (1923): 181.

91. Lovett, *All Our Years*, pp. 97–98.

92. See Schevill to Boucher, April 23, 1931, College Archive, Box 7, folder 2.

93. Norman Maclean, eulogy for Ferdinand Schevill, 1955, James L. Cate Papers, Box 4.

94. "Preliminary Report of the Committee in Charge of the General Course in the Humanities," College Archive, Box 7, folder 2.

95. During World War I Schevill was one of a small minority of faculty who opposed America's entrance into the war, earning the severe enmity of Harry Pratt Judson. The course's first syllabus, published in September 1931, commented that "the modern world of science and machines, of national states and world empires, has set in motion forces which seem to have got out of hand and threaten, like Frankenstein's monster, to destroy the civilization which gave rise to them." *Introductory General Course in the Humanities Syllabus* (Chicago, 1931), p. 328.

96. Maclean remembered about James Cate's discussion groups that "Jimmie pursued his students with shrewd, unrelenting questions until he caught them with the answer.... To him, you always knew the answer, if you only knew how to find it." Maclean to Frances Cate, November 6, 1981, Maclean Papers, Box 15.

97. See Gideonse, Wirth, and Kerwin to the Social Sciences faculty, May 15, 1931, p. 1, College Archive, Box 8, folder 2.

98. See Gideonse's testimony about the course during the Walgreen investigation, May 24, 1935, Bell Papers, Box 10, folder 1.

99. Mary B. Gilson to Boucher, May 11, 1933, College Archive, Box 8, folder 2. In addition to these formal visits, which were planned to illustrate lecture or discussion topics in the course, the faculty also staged smaller events away from campus, including a gathering for a group of fifty students at Druce Lake, who heard the young Reinhold Niebuhr discuss the (in his view) deeply flawed nature of American capitalism. Another group of students organized a three-day retreat on international relations at Lakeside, Michigan, which debated whether the United States should belatedly join the League of Nations.

100. Gideonse to Brumbaugh, October 31, 1935, p. 4, College Archive, Box 8, folder 2.

101. *Literary Digest*, December 27, 1930, p. 16; *New York Times*, September 27, 1931, p. E7.

102. See "Report of an Evaluation of the College Program of the University of Chicago by Students Who Entered the College in the Autumn Quarters of 1933, 1934, and 1935" and "Students at the University of Chicago," 1940–41, College Archive, Box 9, folder 12 and Box 15, folder 2.

103. W. F. Cramer to Emery T. Filbey, March 24, 1933, Hutchins Administration, Box 177, folder 7.

104. Thurstone to Boucher, March 18, 1932, as well as "General Courses: First Year Examination, Autumn Quarter 1931," College Archive, Box 15, folder 9.

105. Halperin to Boucher, May 27, 1933, College Archive, Box 8, folder 2.

106. "Sub-Committee on Curriculum," January 14, 1935, Division of the Social Sciences, Records, Box 16, pp. 2–3.

107. See the curious notes that Swift made for himself in the briefings he needed

to give to Hutchins in May 1929: "[Tell Hutchins to] Watch his step at start on research. Tell Burton's experience after Dream of Colleges." Swift Papers, Box 49, folder 16.

108. The list of readings for the General Honors course is filed in Hutchins Administration, Box 111, folder 1. On Erskine, see Gerald Graff, *Professing Literature: An Institutional History* (Chicago, 1987), pp. 133–36.

109. McKeon to Hutchins, June 12, 1932; and Barr to Hutchins, June 15, 1931, Hutchins Administration, Box 110, folder 13.

110. Mortimer Adler, *Philosopher at Large: An Intellectual Autobiography* (New York, 1977), pp. 107–10; Dzuback, *Robert M. Hutchins*, pp. 88–108; Schlegel, "American Legal Realism," pp. 479–81.

111. The events were described in detail in "A Statement from The Department of Philosophy" [1930], Hutchins Administration, Box 163, folder 12. See also Harry S. Ashmore, *Unseasonable Truths: The Life of Robert Maynard Hutchins* (Boston, 1989), pp. 85–87; Amy A. Kass, "Radical Conservatives for Liberal Education" (PhD diss., Johns Hopkins University, 1973), pp. 108–18; and Hutchins to Adler, November 11, 1929; December 4, 1929; and January 30, 1930, Adler Papers, Box 56. More recently, see William N. Haarlow, *Great Books, Honors Programs, and Hidden Origins: The Virginia Plan and the University of Virginia in the Liberal Arts Movement* (New York, 2003).

112. Boucher to Hutchins, March 3, 1931, Hutchins Administration, Box 163, folder 12.

113. On the faculty of Chicago and pragmatism up to the 1930s, see Darnell Rucker, *The Chicago Pragmatists* (Minneapolis, 1969), esp. pp. 3–27, 132–70; Brubacher and Rudy, *Higher Education in Transition*, pp. 186, 298, 303. For a good overview of the basic tenets of American pragmatists, see David A. Hollinger, "The Problem of Pragmatism in American History," *Journal of American History* 67 (1980): 88–107, esp. 96–99, 104. For the more general debate over pragmatism's fate in late twentieth-century American thought, see James T. Kloppenberg, "Pragmatism: An Old Name for Some New Ways of Thinking?," ibid. 83 (1996): 100–138.

114. Mortimer Adler, "The Chicago School," *Harper's Magazine,* September 1941, 377–88. For the immediate context of Adler's essay, see Purcell, *The Crisis of Democratic Theory*, pp. 141–52, 202–3, 218–19; and John Patrick Diggins, *The Promise of Pragmatism: Modernism and the Crisis of Knowledge and Authority* (Chicago, 1994), pp. 389–96.

115. Richard McKeon, "Criticism and the Liberal Arts: The Chicago School of Criticism," *Profession* 6 (1982): 1–18; Wayne C. Booth, "Between Two Generations: The Heritage of the Chicago School," ibid., pp. 19–26; and Graff, *Professing Literature*, pp. 145–61, 233–40. For Crane, see Elder Olson, "R. S. Crane," *American Scholar* 53 (1984): 232–38; Anna Dorothea Schneider, *Literaturkritik und Bildungspolitik: R. S. Crane, die Chicago (Neo-Aristotelian) Critics und die University of Chicago* (Heidelberg, 1994), pp. 78–93, 261–305; Wallace Martin, "The Critic and the Institutions of Culture," in A. Walton Litz, Louis Menand, and Lawrence Rainey, eds., *The Cambridge History of Literary Criticism*, vol. 7, *Modernism and*

the New Criticism (Cambridge, 2000), pp. 308–10; and the brief description in M. H. Abrams, "The Transformation of English Studies, 1930–1995," in Bender and Schorske, *American Academic Culture in Transformation*, p. 128.

116. Crane to Boucher, January 15, 1931, Hutchins Administration, Box 53, folder 10.

117. "Minutes of the Department of History, January 13, 1933," Department of History, Records, Box 19, folder 6; Minutes of the University Senate, March 11, 1933.

118. Ronald S. Crane, "History versus Criticism in the Study of Literature," *English Journal* 24 (1935): 645–67. Crane called for enhanced emphasis on "systematic work in the theory, generally of all the fine arts, and specifically of the art of literature" and more "exercises in the reading and aesthetic explication of literary texts" (p. 665).

119. For Crane's views of traditional literary history, see the insightful comments in Graff, *Professing Literature*, pp. 147–48, 234. The relevant documents in the case are R. S. Crane, "The Organization of History in a University," April 1934, and the History Department's response, "The Objectives of a Department of History," June 1934, which are filed in Department of History, Records, Box 25, folder 3.

120. *Report of the President to the Board of Trustees, The Academic Years 1930–34, February 1, 1935*, pp. 21–22, Special Collections Research Center. Hutchins also urged that English composition be abolished.

121. See "The University and the Individual," April 3, 1930, p. 3; and the untitled speeches dated November 20, 1930, p. 3, and December 5, 1930, p. 10, in Hutchins Papers, Box 355, folder 3.

122. *The Higher Learning in America* (New Haven, CT, 1936), p. 18.

123. Robert M. Hutchins, "Statement on the Recommendations of the Senate," December 9, 1932, Hutchins Administration, Box 52, folder 2. At the same meeting Hutchins was also able to confirm for the College the legal right to hire its own faculty apart from the departments.

124. The speech garnered the attention of the local press. See Edgar Ansel Mowrer, "Hutchins Stirs University by Questioning Science as a Basis for Philosophy," *Chicago Daily News*, December 27, 1933, p. 5.

125. Both speeches were later published in Robert M. Hutchins, *No Friendly Voice* (Chicago, 1936), pp. 24–40.

126. See Barden's use of the Adler-Hutchins Great Books course as a model for a future curriculum in the College in *Maroon*, March 8, 1934, p. 2. For Adler's subsequent account of these events, see his *Philosopher at Large*, pp. 149–71.

127. *Maroon*, January 5, 1934, p. 2.

128. Ibid., January 9, 1934, p. 2.

129. Ibid., February 20, 1934, p. 2.

130. Ibid., February 9, 1934, p. 1. Carlson had denounced Hutchins's views in a newspaper interview in late December 1933, insisting that "the particularly disturbing element in the present instance is that it comes from the president of a university whose main distinction has come from its achievements in science." Gifford Ernest, "Fact-Finding of Science Defended by Dr. Carlson; Denies Charges of Hutchins,"

Chicago Daily News, December 28, 1933, p. 8. Adler's notes for the February 1934 debate are filed in Adler Papers, Box 57.

131. *Maroon*, March 8, 1934, pp. 1, 3, 5–6.

132. Ibid., April 11, 1934, pp. 1–4.

133. Ibid., March 14, 1934, p. 2.

134. "The Educational Objectives of the College in the University of Chicago," April 21, 1934, Hutchins Administration, Box 54, folder 6.

135. Barden to Boucher, May 3, 1934, Adler Papers, Box 56.

136. "Is Modern Thought Anti-Intellectual?," Knight Papers, Box 61, folder 22. It was eventually published in *University of Chicago Magazine*, November 1934, pp. 20–23, with Knight complaining about the *Maroon*'s refusal to print it.

137. Knight to Boucher, July 28, 1934; Boucher to Knight, July 31, 1934, Knight Papers, Box 58, folder 6.

138. Harry D. Gideonse, "The New War of Science and Dogma," *Maroon*, June 7, 1934, p. 2.

139. John Dewey, "Rationality in Education"; "President Hutchins' Proposals to Remake Higher Education"; and "The Higher Learning in America," *Social Frontier*, December 1936, pp. 71–73; January 1937, pp. 103–4; and March 1937, pp. 167–69. For the debate itself, see now James Scott Johnston, "The Dewey-Hutchins Debate: A Dispute over Moral Teleology," *Educational Theory* 61 (2011): 1–16; Lisa Heldke, "Robert Maynard Hutchins, John Dewey, and the Nature of the Liberal Arts," *Cresset* 59 (2005): 8–13; and Thomas Ehrlich, "Dewey versus Hutchins: The Next Round," in Robert Orrill, ed., *Education and Democracy: Reimagining Liberal Learning in America* (New York, 1997), pp. 225–62.

140. Maynard Krueger, interview by Christopher Kimball, May 25, 1988, p. 13, University of Chicago, Oral History Program; Harry D. Gideonse, "Integration of the Social Sciences and the Quest for Certainty," Social Studies 27 (1936): 363–72.

141. Hutchins to Boucher, February 23, 1935, Hutchins Administration, Box 283, folder 8.

142. The writers worried that Hutchins was motivated by his personal dislike of Gideonse. "If the impression should once gain ground that those who freely objected to administrative policies were denied promotion, strong men would slowly leave the University and only the weaker and less courageous would remain. We know that this is the last thing you really want." Chester W. Wright et al. to Hutchins, April 8, 1936; H. A. Millis et al. to Hutchins, July 17, 1936, Hutchins Administration, Box 283, folder 8. This letter was all the more remarkable, as McKeon noted in a confidential advisory to Hutchins, since it manifested the "singular unanimity of a group of men who seldom agree about anything." McKeon to Hutchins, July 29, 1936, Hutchins Papers, Box 37, folder 8.

143. See Adler, *Philosopher at Large*, pp. 172–77.

144. Hutchins to Adler, September 8, 1936, as well as August 21, 1936, Adler Papers, Box 56.

145. See Minutes of the Faculty of the Division of the Humanities, May 8, 1937, and October 9, 1937. Hutchins initially sought to have Barr appointed in the College,

after vetting by the Department of History. Harley McNair was asked to poll the senior faculty in the department and concluded that Barr was an "exceptionally pleasing person," but also that Barr "makes no pretense of scholarship or scholarly productivity in the sense in which those terms are understood at the University of Chicago." McNair to Brumbaugh, November 26, 1935, College Archive, Box 2, folder 11.

146. "By constructing a university in this way it can be made intelligible. Metaphysics, the study of first principles pervades the whole.... I should insist that a university is concerned with thought and that the collection of information, historical or current, had no place in it except as such data may illustrate or confirm principles or assist in their development." Hutchins, *The Higher Learning in America*, pp. 108–9.

147. Harry D. Gideonse, *The Higher Learning in a Democracy: A Reply to President Hutchins' Critique of the American University* (New York, 1937), pp. 9, 33. Gideonse further elaborated some of his ideas about the importance of educating what he characterized as the "whole man" in "Quality of Teaching or Content of Education?," *The Preparation and In-Service Training of College Teachers, Proceedings of the Institute for Administrative Officers of Higher Institutions* 10 (1938): 65–75.

148. Adler to Hutchins, June 25, 1937, Adler Papers, Box 56.

149. See Minutes of the Faculty of the College, June 2, 1938, p. 1.

150. Ralph Tyler later remembered that Brumbaugh was "an easy going, nice guy, who could say he believed in all the things Hutchins believed in, but was intellectually, in my opinion, too lazy to think through what that meant and how to do anything about it." Ralph W. Tyler, *Education: Curriculum Development and Evaluation: An Interview Conducted with Malca Chall in 1985, 1986, 1987* (Berkeley, 1987), p. 160.

151. William Hutchinson noted shrewdly of Gideonse that "Chicago will miss him, although probably Pres. Hutchins isn't sorry to see him go." William T. Hutchinson Diary, entry of May 27, 1938. For Gideonse's later career as an educational leader, see Harry D. Gideonse, *Against the Running Tide: Selected Essays on Education and the Free Society*, edited by Alexander S. Preminger (New York, 1967).

152. Purcell, *The Crisis of Democratic Theory*, p. 46.

153. *Report of the President, 1934–35*, September 10, 1935, p. 34, Special Collections Research Center.

154. A Chicago PhD (1928), Faust joined the faculty as an assistant professor in the Department of English in 1935. Faust sent McKeon drafts of work in progress for comment. Equally important, among Faust's most influential teachers had been Ronald Crane. To the extent that Faust brought a vision for the College to his deanship in 1941–42, this was informed by the curricular ideas of the "scholastic" ginger group centered around Crane and Adler from a few years earlier. Indeed, Mortimer Adler reports in his autobiography that "among the young instructors who attended the sessions of the Crane Group [in 1933–34] were men who many years later became pivotal figures in the educational reforms that Clarence Faust,

who was one of them, instituted when he became Dean of the College in 1941." Adler, *Philosopher at Large*, pp. 160–61.

155. Hutchins first announced the plan in his report to the faculty, "The University at War," on January 7, 1942. See also *Maroon*, January 8, 1942, pp. 1–2; and January 23, 1942, pp. 1, 3.

156. Hutchins had first suggested this scheme to Faust as early as March 1942. See Hutchins to Faust, March 9, 1942, Hutchins Administration, Box 52, folder 4.

157. Minutes of the Faculty of the College, December 17, 1945.

158. See the memoranda of February 21, 1946 and February 25, 1946, filed as Exhibits B and C, in "Documents Pertaining to the College Proposal of February 6, 1946," submitted to the Board of Trustees by the Committee of the Council of the Senate, April 1, 1946.

159. In 1952 John Netherton found that alumni were more inclined to support the PhB option if they intended to pursue careers in medicine or the natural sciences. See J. P. Netherton, "Some Opinions of Their Education in the College Expressed by 866 Recent Graduates Who Continued at the U of C," pp. 44–45, College Archive, Box 101.

160. The compromise patched together in May 1946 placated the scientists by allowing College students to substitute an introductory general physics course for one of the interdisciplinary science sequences. This deal is noteworthy because it is the ancestor of the College's current system, whereby science majors are permitted to take entirely different kinds of Core science courses from those taken by nonscience majors. Another significant concession was an agreement to modify the original Faust curriculum—which had suppressed history as a distinctive (and professional) discipline—by including a general history course.

161. Scott Papers, Box 1, folder 13.

162. A copy of the memorandum is filed in the Knight Papers, Box 60, folder 14, as is Minutes of the University Senate, April 14, 1944.

163. Kimpton to Hutchins, August 22, 1946, PP Addenda, 1998-006, Box 14. Years later Faust noted, "I tend to recall my days in the College as the most exciting of days and the most futile." Faust to Ward, November 5, 1973, Ward Papers, Box 1, folder 3.

164. Stone to Kimpton, May 5, 1952, College Archive, Box 9, folder 5.

165. The curriculum, and its history between 1942 and 1946, are described in F. Champion Ward, ed., *The Idea and Practice of General Education* (Chicago, 1950).

166. Robert C. Woellner, "Administration of Tests, January through December 1951," Kimpton Administration, Box 108, folder 11.

167. See White, "The Study of Education at the University of Chicago," pp. 385–429, 482. On Tyler, see Morris Finder, *Educating America: How Ralph W. Tyler Taught America to Teach* (Westport, CT, 2004), esp. pp. 9–10, 149–52.

168. See, for example, Milton Singer, "The Social Sciences Program at the College of the University of Chicago" [1947], College Archive, Box 8, folder 3. Discussion sessions were capped at twenty-five students. Each staff still gave general lectures, and students were expected to attend them, but they slowly ceased to be the primary organizational feature of the Core courses.

169. For the details of its demise, see John W. Boyer, *"Teaching at a University of a Certain Sort": Education at the University of Chicago over the Past Century* (Chicago, 2012).

170. For a contemporary statement of student support, see Abraham Krash and Alan J. Strauss, "On the Philosophy of the College: An Unofficial Statement of the Methods and Purposes of the College of the University of Chicago as Seen by Two of Its Graduates," June 1948, College Archive. The students asserted that the educational practices of the Hutchins College were ironically similar to the ideals of John Dewey: the College "subscribed to the thesis of one of its critics, Professor John Dewey of Columbia, who argues that one learns only by doing, by actual experience. At Chicago we learn how to analyze by analyzing. The dominant technique of the classroom is not that of lecturing to the students; it is, instead, that of leading them to a discussion of significant problems" (pp. 2–3).

171. Aaron Sayvetz, "The Rational Revolutionary," *Journal of General Education* 30 (1978): 9.

172. Joseph Gusfield, "My Life and Soft Times," in Bennett M. Berger, ed., *Authors of Their Own Lives: Intellectual Autobiographies by Twenty American Sociologists* (Berkeley, 1990), p. 110.

173. Netherton, "Some Opinions of Their Education in the College," pp. 6–8. Netherton contacted 1,105 alumni and had an 83 percent response rate. Similarly positive results were evident in GRE test results from 1947–48. See Netherton's "Quality of the Later Academic Work of Graduates of the College," Ward Papers, Box 1, folder 4,

174. Riesman to Ward, February 25, 1992, Ward Papers, Box 1, folder 13.

175. Henry W. Sams, "The Hutchins College after the War," *Journal of General Education* 30 (1978): 60–61. On Sams, see James P. Beasley, "'Extraordinary Understandings' of Composition at the University of Chicago: Frederick Champion Ward, Kenneth Burke, and Henry W. Sams," *College Composition and Communication* 59 (2007): 36–52.

176. Gusfield, "My Life and Soft Times," p. 112.

177. Ward to Staff Chairmen, January 28, 1949, College Archive, Box 21.

178. Memorandum dated February 17, 1947, Hutchins Administration, Box 161, folder 8.

179. Singer received his PhD from the Department of Philosophy in 1940, and in 1941 he was hired to teach in the College's Social Sciences program.

180. Singer to Ward, October 9, 1951, Singer Papers, Box 93.

181. Louis Menand, "College: The End of the Golden Age," in Stephen J. Gould and Robert Atwan, eds., *The Best American Essays, 2002* (New York, 2002), p. 225; as well as Thomas Bender, "Politics, Intellect, and the American University, 1945–1995," in Bender and Schorske, *American Academic Culture in Transformation*, pp. 22–23, 29.

182. Richard McKeon, interview, June 3, 1975, Robert M. Hutchins and Associates, Oral History Interviews, Box 2, folders 7–8. For a similar assessment, see Bell, *The Reforming of General Education*, p. 37.

183. Douglas joined the faculty in 1920 and was promoted in 1925 to full professor. For the first ten years of his career he was a member of the Business School; thereafter he was a member of the Department of Economics, specializing in labor relations and economic theory. Douglas was an academic adviser on unemployment to Governor Franklin Roosevelt in New York State in 1930 and was appointed by Governor Gifford Pinchot to be the secretary of the Pennsylvania Commission on Unemployment. He also advised Governor Horner of Illinois in 1933 on the utilities legislation that was passed by the state legislature that year. He styled himself as a "progressive and liberal" but denied that he was either a communist or a socialist. During the Walgreen investigation, Douglas prepared a biographical and intellectual sketch, which was not used in the public hearings, but a copy of which is filed in the Swift Papers, Box 191, folder 9.

184. See Paul H. Douglas, *In the Fullness of Time: The Memoirs of Paul H. Douglas* (New York, 1972), pp. 55–65, esp. pp. 60–61.

185. Sprague to Sunny, May 31, 1929, Swift Papers, Box 85, folder 6.

186. Swift to Sprague, June 27, 1929; Woodward to Sunny, June 22, 1929, Swift Papers, Box 85, folder 6.

187. Sunny to Hutchins, July 2, 1932, Swift Papers, Box 192, folder 3.

188. Stagg to Hutchins, June 28, 1932, Swift Papers, Box 190, folder 1.

189. See the draft of a general letter, Swift Papers, Box 192, folder 4.

190. Galt to Robert L. Scott, July 5, 1932; Strawn to Sunny, June 29, 1932, Swift Papers, Box 192, folder 4.

191. "Confidential Memorandum Concerning Matters Discussed at the Meeting of the Committee on Instruction and Research, July 12, 1932," Swift Papers, Box 192, folder 3.

192. On Swift, see Dorothy V. Jones, *Harold Swift and the Higher Learning* (Chicago, 1985).

193. Swift to Sprague, June 27, 1929, Swift Papers, Box 85, folder 6.

194. See Ashmore, *Unseasonable Truths*, pp. 120–27.

195. Memo of November 25, 1932, Swift Papers, Box 49, folder 4.

196. Although one must be cautious about such a memo since it may have been colored by Stifler's own views, the results were quite striking. According to Stifler, trustee Albert Sherer felt that "we have no chance of securing gifts until we have done something to mitigate the feeling against us. He blames Robert for a great deal of it." Trustee Sewell Avery "thinks we underestimate yet the extent and depth of the prejudice against us.... He spoke pretty sharply about Robert as a man who had not lived up to his promise." Harry Gear argued that "business men can't understand academic freedom. They are used to an organization with discipline from the top down. They cannot believe that men like [Robert] Lovett exercise such freedom outside their sphere unless the President sympathizes. It will take considerable education of the public to counteract this." William McC. Blair "thinks that Robert assumes that academic freedom argues its own case which, in Mr. Blair's opinion, it does not. Robert's attitude is, 'there it is, take it or leave it.' He thinks Robert should endeavor to win his case with his own Trustees and be conciliatory."

William Bond "thinks that we are seriously handicapped by prejudice against us on account of our 'radicalism' which, in his judgment is unjust. Robert has done a great job in cutting expenses and maintaining standards. Wishes that he was more careful about giving handles to our critics." Robert L. Scott "is hopelessly prejudiced against Robert on all counts—considers him a disaster to the University." Charles Goodspeed thought that "freedom of thought and expression are essential for the advancement of knowledge. However there is a great deal of difference between academic freedom and academic license. The former is constructive, the latter de-structive. The problem of differentiating between the two is for the faculty, not for the Trustees. It is also the problem of the faculty to rectify the unjust impression the public has gained of the University because of the activities of a few of their members." James L. Stifler to Harold Swift, March 29, 1935, Swift Papers, Box 49, folder 6.

197. This is clear in the many letters that Hutchins received after his radio address in April 1935 and after his convocation address in June 1935.

198. The radio address was delivered on February 19, 1935. It was reprinted in the *Congressional Record*, February 20, 1935, pp. 2300–2302. Fish's radio talk in mid-February was a reprise of a statement he made in late December 1934, in which he asserted that Chicago was among ten leading universities (Harvard, Vassar, City College, Columbia, Smith, Wesleyan, Wisconsin, California, and the University of Washington, in addition to Chicago) that were hotbeds of subversives.

199. See Anthony C. Troncone, "Hamilton Fish, Sr., and the Politics of American Nationalism, 1912–1945" (PhD diss., Rutgers University, 1993).

200. See the *Herald* of February 24, 1935, p. 8; March 15, 1935, p. 12; and April 1, 1935, p. 2; and the *American* of March 13, 1935, pp. 1–2. In the April 1 essay, Schuman was accused of assailing President Roosevelt, Secretary of State Cordell Hull, and the Hearst press.

201. On Schuman, see Steven J. Bucklin, "The Wilsonian Legacy in Political Science: Denna F. Fleming, Frederick L. Schuman, and Quincy Wright" (PhD diss., University of Iowa, 1993); for Lovett, see his autobiography *All Our Times*. Schuman submitted four memos on his life and work for the Walgreen hearings. See Swift Papers, Box 191, folder 9.

202. The speech was reprinted in *University of Chicago Magazine*, March 1935, pp. 171–72.

203. A year later several of these speeches were published in the collection of essays entitled *No Friendly Voice* (Chicago, 1936).

204. John P. Howe, "News of the Quadrangles," *University of Chicago Magazine*, February 1935, pp. 150–54.

205. Walgreen to Hutchins, April 10, 1935, Swift Papers, Box 191, folder 5.

206. The design and purpose of the English composition course and the specific uses to which the *New Russia's Primer* were put were carefully explained by Profes-sor Edith Foster Flint during the first session of the Walgreen investigation. See her testimony in Bell Papers, Box 9, folder 9.

207. The required readings for the Social Sciences I course included works by

J. L. and Barbara Hammond, Franz Boas, Herbert Hoover, Walter Lippmann, R. S. and H. M. Lynd, H. C. McBain, Gilbert Murray, William Sumner, and numerous others.

208. Hutchins to Walgreen, April 11, 1935, and April 13, 1935, Swift Papers, Box 191, folder 5.

209. The official transcripts are filed in Bell Papers, Box 9, folders 6–9 and Box 10, folders 1–2. A good summary is provided by John P. Rowe, in "News of the Quadrangles," *University of Chicago Magazine*, Midsummer 1935, pp. 345–52.

210. Statement of Charles R. Walgreen, Bell Papers, Box 9, folders 7–8.

211. Statement of Charles E. Merriam, Bell Papers. Box 9, folder 9.

212. Statement of Lucille Norton, Bell Papers, Box 10, folder 1

213. Statement of J. W. Clarke, Bell Papers, Box 10, folder 1.

214. Letter addressed to Charles Walgreen, April 15, 1935, Swift Papers, Box 191, folder 5.

215. Quoted in David Nasaw, *The Chief: The Life of William Randolph Hearst* (Boston, 2000), pp. 514–15. Roosevelt's break with Hearst came in August 1935, shortly after this note to Hutchins.

216. Swift to Albert L. Scott, May 18, 1935, Swift Papers, Box 190, folder 4.

217. "Survey, Analysis, and Plan of Fund-Raising for the University of Chicago," pp. 49, 57, 76–77, University Development Campaigns, Box 7, folder 20.

218. William B. Benton, *The University of Chicago's Public Relations* (Chicago, 1937), pp. 23, 26, 51–52, 54.

219. See "Majority Report of Investigating Committee Authorized by Amended Senate Resolution No. 33," *Journal of the Senate of the Fifty-Ninth General Assembly of the State of Illinois*, June 26, 1935, pp. 1304–17, esp. 1308, 1316.

220. Minutes of the Board of Trustees, July 11, 1935, pp. 89–95.

221. The fifty-nine telegrams, most dated and received on June 27 and 28, 1935, are filed in the Swift Papers, Box 191, folder 10.

222. Harold Swift did try to defend Lovett privately, however. To Stanton Speer he argued, "Probably you know Lovett. If so you realize that he is an earnest, high class man, anxious to correct social injustices, and that he is typically sorry for the underdog." Letter of March 19, 1935, Swift Papers, Box 190, folder 2.

223. *Report of the Seditious Activities Investigation Commission* (Springfield, IL, 1949), p. 5.

224. *Maroon*, March 4, 1949, p. 1.

225. See Martin G. Pierce, "Red-Hunting in Illinois, 1947–1949: The Broyles Commission" (master's thesis, University of Wisconsin, 1959), pp. 42–53.

226. *Chicago Tribune*, March 3, 1949, pp. 1–2.

227. John Howe, the alumni official who had helped to shape the University's response to the Walgreen affair in the 1930s, urged the University to make a "strong direct stand on the issue of principle" of its right to admit students who might be radicals. Howe to Benton, March 24, 1949, Bell Papers, Box 4, folder 6.

228. *Special Report: Seditious Activities Investigation Commission, State of Illinois; Investigation of the University of Chicago and Roosevelt College, 1949* (Springfield,

IL, 1949), p. 21; as well as the account by E. Houston Harsha, "Illinois: The Broyles Commission," in Walter Gellhorn, ed., *The States and Subversion* (Ithaca, NY, 1952), pp. 95–108.

229. *The Great Investigation* (Chicago, 1949), pp. 10–11.

230. See Pierce, "Red-Hunting in Illinois," pp. 165–70.

231. Special Report, p. 270.

232. See *The Great Investigation*, pp. 64–65; as well as the letter of Bell to G. B. Pidot, May 12, 1949, Bell Papers, Box 4, folder 7; and *Maroon*, March 8, 1949, pp. 1, 8; March 11, 1949, pp. 3, 7; April 8, 1949, pp. 1, 10.

233. These letters are filed in Bell Papers, Box 4, folder 6.

234. The other members were Paul Russell, James Douglas, Henry Tenney, and Harold Swift, with Hutchins occupying only an ex officio status.

235. Bell's solicitude had a humorous side: he offered Hutchins $25 if he would avoid making any wisecracks during his testimony. Hutchins later observed, "He paid me—a triumph of avarice over art." See *Maroon*, October 14, 1966, p. 9.

236. Undated memorandum, Bell Papers, Box 5, folder 7.

237. Ellen W. Schrecker, *No Ivory Tower: McCarthyism and the Universities* (New York, 1986), pp. 113, 337.

238. Tugwell to Bell, May 23, 1949, Bell Papers, Box 4, folder 7.

239. Letter of December 9, 1929, Hutchins Administration, Box 96, folder 2.

240. See F. J. Kelly, "The Training of College Teachers," *Journal of Educational Research* 16 (1927): 332–41; Melvin E. Haggerty, "The Improvement of College Instruction," *School and Society* 27 (1928): 25–36; Floyd W. Reeves, "A Critical Summary and Analysis of Current Efforts to Improve College Teaching," *Phi Delta Kappan* 11 (1928): 65–71; Michael Chiappetta, "A Recurrent Problem: The Professional Preparation of College Teachers," *History of Education Journal* 4 (1952): 18–24; and Carter V. Good, *Teaching in College and University: A Survey of the Problems and Literature in Higher Education* (Baltimore, 1929).

241. See O. E. Randall, "Enlistment and Training of College Teachers," *Bulletin of the American Association of University Professors* 14 (1928): 329–37, here 335, 337; Ernest H. Wilkins, "Report of the Commission on Enlistment and Training of College Teachers," *Bulletin of Association of American Colleges* 15 (1929): 40–44, 187; Walter Crosby Eells, "A University Course on 'The American College'," *Journal of Higher Education* 9 (1938): 141–44. These interventions were part of a broader critique of teaching in the research universities that emerged in the 1920s. See Julie A. Reuben, *The Making of the Modern University: Intellectual Transformation and the Marginalization of Morality* (Chicago, 1996), pp. 202–6, 250–52.

242. Judd to Hutchins, December 12, 1929; Gale to Hutchins, December 16, 1929; Laing to Hutchins, December 16, 1929; and Boucher to Hutchins, December 18, 1929, and February 1, 1930, Hutchins Administration, Box 96, folder 2

243. Hutchins to Gale, Laing, Judd, and Boucher, January 30, 1930.

244. Gale to Hutchins, February 8, 1930.

245. Its other members, all of whom were also full professors, were Anton J. Carlson of the Department of Physiology, Harry A. Millis of Economics, William H.

Taliaferro of Biology, Algernon Coleman of French, Frank N. Freeman of Education, and James R. Hulbert of English.

246. "Report to the President and Senate of the University of Chicago, May 16, 1931," Hutchins Administration, Box 96, folder 3. A detailed, hundred-page summary of the responses of the departments was submitted by the committee to the University Senate on November 5, 1930. Barrows also prepared a separate report on the responses of the departments about teacher preparation (or the lack thereof), which he sent to Frederic Woodward on June 25, 1930.

247. "Report to the President and Senate of the University of Chicago, May 16, 1931," pp. 11, 20–21.

248. *Report of the President to the Board of Trustees, The Academic Years 1930–34, February 1, 1935*, p. 24.

249. As early as September 1938 Hutchins had complained to the board that his authority as president was not commensurate with his responsibilities as an educational and academic leader. See his *Annual Confidential Statement to the Board of Trustees*, September 20, 1938, pp. 35–49, Special Collections Research Center. By the early 1940s he suggested that the board should either change the statutes to make the president a mere chair of the faculties, with little or no responsibility for academic matters, or grant the president a much more direct and substantial level of executive authority involving curricula and academic appointments, with the proviso that if the board or the faculties strongly opposed his decisions they could be rescinded and, in extreme cases, the president would be expected to offer his resignation. The board of trustees initiated a series of conversations about these options with senior members of the University Senate in 1943 and 1944, seeking to resolve the problems of power allocation against which Hutchins was rebelling. These negotiations essentially led to no plausible resolution—the faculty opposed both options Hutchins had proposed—but the faculty did agree that the current Senate was too undemocratic and too unwieldy to function as an agency of effective governance, and they assented to the idea of creating a representative council to act on the full faculty's behalf and broadening the membership of the Senate to include associate and assistant professors who had served in rank a requisite number of years. These negotiations are summarized in "The Report of the Committee on Instruction and Research to the Board of Trustees in Relation to Proposed Administrative Changes," December 28, 1944, Knight Papers, Addenda, Box 1, folder 3. The various memos are contained in VP Records, Box 35, folder 19.

250. A full text of the speech is filed in Hutchins Papers, Box 368, folder 3.

251. See Harry M. Beardsley's interview of Emery Filbey in "Midway Feud on Old Question of State against the Individual," *Chicago Daily News*, March 7, 1944, p. 11.

252. Knight to Hutchins, June 3, 1944, Knight Papers, Addenda, Box 1, folder 3.

253. "Memorial to the Board of Trustees on the State of the University," April 1944, Knight Papers, Box 60, folder 14; Minutes of the University Senate, May 22, 1944, pp. 1–4. R. S Crane was the principal author. The vote in favor was 94, with 42 opposed. For Harold Swift's response to the memorial, urging cooperation and conciliation on all sides, see Minutes of the Board of Trustees, June 8, 1944, pp. 105–7.

254. Some faculty were agitated by Hutchins's conviction that the University was responsible for correcting the world's ills. William Ogburn asked archly in his private diary in 1946, "Is the University a promotional or propaganda agency?" Diary, January 10, 1946, Ogburn Papers, Box 46, folder 2.

255. *Maroon*, June 16, 1944, p. 3.

256. The compromise was largely crafted by trustee Laird Bell. See Minutes of the Board of Trustees, December 28, 1944, special executive session. For the whole episode, see McNeill, *Hutchins' University*, pp. 126–29.

257. Hutchins to his parents, November 5, 1931, Box 11, folder II-10–8, William J. Hutchins Papers, Berea College Archives.

258. Filbey wrote to one job seeker in 1935 that "because of the drastic budgetary reductions in all of these areas it has been found necessary to discharge workers, many of whom have been in service for a number of years." He also predicted yet more terminations in the years ahead. Filbey to Mary F. Caldwell, Filbey Papers, Box 1, folder 2.

259. See E. C. Miller to Hutchins, September 12, 1939, Hutchins Administration, Box 177, folder 7.

260. Hutchins to his father, April 4, 1932, Box 11, folder II-10–8, William J. Hutchins Papers, Berea College Archives.

261. *Report of the President, 1934–35*, September 10, 1935, p. 49, Special Collections Research Center.

262. Woodward to the Trustees, marked "confidential," July 8, 1933, Swift Papers, Box 179, folder 1.

263. See N. C. Plimpton to Swift, January 19, 1934, who charted the decidedly negative financial and budgetary position of Northwestern compared to Chicago; Swift Papers, Box 179, folder 2 ("Really there could be no favorable comparison between the positions of the two institutions"). The various position papers and memoranda generated by Northwestern faculty groups betray the fears and apprehensions of an underfunded but proud midsize business about to be gobbled up by a larger and wealthier commercial rival. See "Report of the Northwestern University Senate Committee on the Proposed Merger between Northwestern University and the University of Chicago," February 6, 1934, Walter Dill Scott Papers, Box 42, folder 1, Northwestern University Archives.

264. Hibbard to Scott, December 8, 1933, Scott Papers, Box 41, folder 4, Northwestern University Archives.

265. Ever the visionary, Ruml insisted that "no minor considerations, no matter how numerous, should be permitted to prevent the merger." Ruml to Walter Dill Scott, January 10, 1934, Ruml Papers, Box 1, folder 1.

266. Hutchins to his mother and father, August 11, 1933, Box 11, folder II-10–8, William J. Hutchins Papers, Berea College Archives.

267. Hibbard to Scott, October 28, 1933 Scott Papers, Box 42, folder 10, Northwestern University Archives.

268. Swift memorandum for the files, February 26, 1934, Swift Papers, Box 179, folder 2.

269. Detailed information on university finances in the 1930s, as presented to the board of trustees in 1939, is filed in VP Records, Box 6, folder 13.

270. See John F. Moulds to Swift, November 5, 1926, Swift Papers, Box 74, folder 6.

271. Stifler to Swift, December 1, 1931, Swift Papers, Box 82, folder 7.

272. Stifler to Hutchins and Swift, February 16, 1932, folder 8.

273. Hutchins to Swift, October 1, 1929, Swift Papers, Box 175, folder 7; "Confidential Memorandum of Conversation between Mr. Hutchins and Mr. Mason, October 13, 1929," and "Memorandum of Conversations with Mason, Day, and Ruml, December 7, 1929," Development and Alumni Relations, Records, Box 52.

274. Hutchins to the Rockefeller Foundation, March 5, 1930, Swift Papers, Box 175, folder 7; "Memorandum on the Financial Programme of the University of Chicago," March 24, 1930, Development and Alumni Relations, Records, Box 52. This memo revised the original proposal of March 5, 1930.

275. Other members of the GEB board included James R. Angell and Harold H. Swift himself.

276. "Very embarrassing [to have] so many Chicago men officers. More embarrassing to Arnett than him." "Confidential Memorandum of Conversation between Mr. Hutchins and Mr. Mason, October 13, 1929," Development and Alumni Relations, Records, Box 52.

277. Draft of a letter to Mason, November 14, 1929, Development and Alumni Relations, Records, Box 52.

278. "General Observations" [notes by Swift on a discussion with Mason, March 1931], Swift Papers, Box 175, folder 8.

279. Minutes of the Board of Trustees, June 12, 1930, p. 147.

280. Ibid., May 14, 1931, p. 59. This grant was also the result of a personal visit to New York. See "Mem. of Conversation with Messrs. Mason, Arnett, and Stevens, 13 January 1931," Development and Alumni Relations, Records, Box 52.

281. Hutchins had provided Mason with a detailed accounting of the financial distress of the University in a letter of November 7, 1931, and its intended budget reductions. Development and Alumni Relations, Records, Box 52.

282. Raymond D. Fosdick to Hutchins, November 16, 1939, Development and Alumni Relations, Records, Box 52. Hutchins's notes for the speech are in the same file. See also Hutchins to Fosdick, June 4, 1936, Development and Alumni Relations, Records, Box 48.

283. Stevens to Woodward, May 8, 1931, Development and Alumni Relations, Records, Box 48.

284. "Report of the Committee of Three of the General Education Board (Mr. Rockefeller, Jr., Mr. Young, and Mr. Fosdick) on the Chicago University Medical Project," included in a letter from Raymond B. Fosdick to Harold Swift, December 18, 1936, Development and Alumni Relations, Records, Box 48.

285. W. H. Taliaferro to Hutchins, January 24, 1939, Development and Alumni Relations, Records, Box 52.

286. Swift to Hutchins, July 31, 1939, Swift Papers, Box 49, folder 10.

287. Robert M. Hutchins, "The University of Chicago, with Special Reference

to Medicine," May 15, 1940, Development and Alumni Relations, Records, Box 48. Hutchins was forced to reply to Fosdick's ambivalent response to this memo by insisting that the University was not seeking "preferential" treatment by making these further requests. See draft of a letter to Fosdick, undated, 1940, ibid.

288. Hutchins to Fosdick, November 7, 1940; and Fosdick to Hutchins, November 20, 1940, Swift Papers, Box 182, folder 12.

289. Robert M. Hutchins, "The Rockefeller Trustees," February 4, 1941, as well as his remarks entitled "The Function of the Endowed University," Development and Alumni Relations, Records, Box 52.

290. Kohler, "Science, Foundations, and the American Universities," p. 162; as well as Patricia J. Gumport, "Graduate Education and Research: Interdependence and Strain," in Philip G. Altbach, Robert O. Berdahl, and Patricia J. Gumport, eds., *American Higher Education in the Twenty-First Century: Social, Political, and Economic Challenges,* 2nd ed. (Baltimore, 2005), pp. 433-35.

291. Barry D. Karl, "The Rockefeller Method" (unpublished essay, 2001), p. 18.

292. "Survey, Analysis and Plan of Fund-Raising for the University of Chicago," April 18, 1936, p. 119, University Development Campaigns, Box 7, folder 20.

293. John F. Moulds, "Digest of the Report of the John Price Jones Corporation," p. 13, as well as "Survey, Analysis, and Plan of Fund-Raising for the University of Chicago," April 18, 1936, pp. iv, 109, 117, 200, University Development Campaigns, Box 7, folder 20. These materials are also filed in Hutchins Administration, Box 68, folder 9.

294. Stifler to Swift, December 1, 1936, Swift Papers, Box 82, folder 13.

295. Benton, *The University of Chicago's Public Relations,* pp. 129-42; Sydney Hyman, *The Lives of William Benton* (Chicago, 1969), pp. 68-70.

296. "Committee on Development," December 23, 1938, and January 19, 1939, Swift Papers, Box 201, folder 21.

297. "The Fiftieth Anniversary Plan for the University of Chicago," February 15, 1939, Swift Papers, Box 201, folder 15.

298. Zimmerman to Paul S. Russell, April 20, 1939; Duncan to Zimmerman, April 19, 1939, VP Records, Box 22, folder 22. See also "Minutes of the Meeting of the Alumni Committee on Cooperation with the Fiftieth Anniversary Celebration, June 27, 1939," Swift Papers, Box 201, folder 6; and Swift to Moulds, "confidential," June 12, 1939, ibid., folder 2.

299. Benton, *The University of Chicago's Public Relations,* p. 66.

300. See "A Suggested Report from the Committee on Development to the Board of Trustees," in Moulds to Swift, July 3, 1939, Swift Papers, Box 201, folder 21.

301. Minutes of the Board of Trustees, July 13, 1939, p. 232.

302. Donald P. Bean (class of 1917), a former director of the University press, was installed as the executive director of both the alumni and the public campaign efforts, with assistance from John Howe, William Morgenstern (campaign publicity director), William Mather (executive director of the alumni campaign), and other staff members from Benton's office. The University opened a downtown office, and organized alumni gift committees and a special gifts committee.

303. "Proceedings, President Robert M. Hutchins Special Conference," June 19,

1939, VP Records, Box 22, folder 27, pp. 9–11, 28. For Hutchins's turbulent relations with key groups of senior faculty in the 1930s, see the balanced analysis in Dzuback, *Robert M. Hutchins,* esp. pp. 185–207.

304. Randall to Benton, November 20, 1939, Swift Papers, Box 49, folder 10, referring to Robert M. Hutchins, "What Good Are Endowments?," *Saturday Evening Post,* November 11, 1939.

305. *Your University and Its Future* (Chicago, 1941), p. 4. See the files in VP Records, Box 23, folder 11.

306. *The Secret Diary of Harold L. Ickes* (New York, 1953–54), vol. 3, p. 472.

307. Duncan to Herbert Zimmerman, April 19, 1939, VP Records, Box 22, folder 22.

308. "Students at the University of Chicago," pp. 7–9, VP Records, Box 6, folder 10.

309. Swift Papers, Box 156, folder 3.

310. "Confidential Report of Mr. Quantrell's Luncheon at the University Club," January 17, 1940, Swift Papers, Box 156, folder 10.

311. Lester, *Stagg's University.* The University's tougher stance toward fraternities was also blamed by unhappy alumni who worried about the decline of the athletic programs. One critic wrote in 1933 that "with fraternities greatly weakened by the University policy and class interests practically nullified by the new educational program, and the former athletic prestige of the University almost obliterated, there is little left in the University student life to hold the interest, protection, and loyalty of the alumni." "Memorandum re Fraternities at University of Chicago," April 20, 1933, Hutchins Administration, Box 91, folder 3.

312. Al F. O'Donnell to Mather, January 23, 1940, Swift Papers, Box 201, folder 10; D. B. Smith to Mather, February 26, 1940, ibid., folder 11.

313. "Outcome of Fiftieth Anniversary Fund Raising Reports," Swift Papers, Box 201, folder 7.

314. Out of the total alumni body of 49,300, contributions were made by 14,484 alumni. John Nuveen Jr., "Report of the Chairman of the Executive Committee," November 1, 1941, Swift Papers, Box 201, folder 7.

315. "The University of Chicago Alumni Foundation: A Report from the John Price Jones Corporation," January 2, 1941, pp. 5–8, Swift Papers, Box 156, folder 2.

316. Hutchins to Rockefeller, August 28, 1941; Rockefeller to Hutchins, August 30, 1941, Swift Papers, Box 201, folder 22.

317. Hutchins to Rockefeller, September 4, 1941; and Woodward to Rockefeller, August 29, 1941, Swift Papers, Box 201, folder 22.

318. "Remarks by John D. Rockefeller, Jr. at the Citizens Dinner of the President and the Trustees of the University of Chicago," September 26, 1941, University Development Campaigns, Box 14, folder 34.

319. Robert Cohen, *When the Old Left Was Young: Student Radicals and America's First Mass Student Movement, 1929–1941* (New York, 1993), pp. 91–97, 99, 308–18. For the University's experience, see Robert Coven, "Red Maroons," *Chicago History* 21 (1992): 20–37, esp. 26, 34–37.

320. James C. Schneider, *Should America Go to War? The Debate over Foreign Policy in Chicago, 1939–1941* (Chapel Hill, NC, 1989), pp. 100, 102, 191–92.

321. *Maroon*, January 30, 1941, p. 1.

322. Robert M. Hutchins, interview, May 26, 1976, Robert M. Hutchins and Associates, Oral History Interviews, Box 1, folder 11.

323. "America and the War," *University of Chicago Magazine*, February, 1941, pp. 5–8; and "The Proposition Is Peace," Hutchins Papers, Box 364, folder 6. Hutchins subsequently informed John U. Nef Jr. that he had received about three thousand responses to his talk, of which only 3 percent were negative. Hutchins to Nef, January 29, 1941, Nef Jr. Papers, Box 23, folder 5.

324. See *The Registrar's Report to the President, 1941–1942* and *The Registrar's Report to the President, 1943–1944*. The drop in male divisional enrollments was even greater, from 1,764 men in 1941 to 518 men in 1943.

325. Government–related programs occupied 97 percent of all available housing and food provisioning space on campus and 33 percent of all instructional and research space by the fall of 1943. See "Space Used for Government Training and Research," October 2, 1943, Hutchins Administration, Box 250, folder 2. The Institute of Meteorology alone commandeered 70 percent of the Law School, all of Reynolds Club, and 75 percent of Mandel Hall. W. B. Harrell to the Army Air Forces Materiel Command, October 2, 1943, Hutchins Administration, Box 241, folder 9

326. Memo of June 28, 1940, Hutchins Administration, Box 244, folder 1.

327. Filbey to William Benton, November 26, 1941, Hutchins Administration, Box 250, folder 1.

328. Hutchins to McCoy, April 9, 1936, Hutchins Administration, Box 145, folder 5.

329. The Institute of Meteorology was launched at the urging of Arthur Compton, who long before Pearl Harbor insisted that such a program could provide the University with a useful role in defense: "Our reason for urging this matter at the present time is solely the question of national defense." Compton to Emery Filbey, July 13, 1940, Hutchins Administration, Box 11, folder 4; and Douglas R. Allen, "The Genesis of Meteorology at the University of Chicago," *Bulletin of the American Meteorological Society* 82 (2001): 1905–9.

330. *Maroon*, October 15, 1943.

331. "The University at War," *University of Chicago Magazine, January 1942*, pp. 1–7.

332. The institute was open to nonuniversity students as well as Chicago matriculants, requiring applicants to be between sixteen and forty-eight years of age and to have finished at least two years of high school. See the materials in Hutchins Administration, Box 242, folder 3; and Ashmore, *Unseasonable Truths*, pp. 223–24; as well as Milton Mayer, *Robert Maynard Hutchins: A Memoir* (Berkeley, 1993), p. 225, for a different view.

333. See Clarence H. Faust, "How the University of Chicago Is Meeting the Emergency," in John Dale Russell, ed., *The Colleges in Wartime: New Responsibilities* (Chicago, 1943), pp. 42–54.

334. In general, see Laura Fermi, *Illustrious Immigrants: The Intellectual Migra-*

tion from Europe, 1930–41, 2nd ed. (Chicago, 1971). For Chicago's case, see John W. Boyer, *"We Are All Islanders to Begin With": The University of Chicago and the World in the Late Nineteenth and Twentieth Centuries* (Chicago, 2008), pp. 69–125.

335. See the charming memoir about her sojourn in Chicago by the wife of Otto von Simson, Louise Alexandra von Simson, *Happy Exile* (Darmstadt, 1981), esp. pp. 133–42.

336. Ralph Tyler, interview by George Dell, March 11, 1978, p. 16, Robert M. Hutchins and Associates, Oral History Interviews, Box 2, folder 13.

337. Laura Fermi, *Atoms in the Family: My Life with Enrico Fermi* (Chicago, 1954), p. 176.

338. Mayer, *Hutchins,* pp. 248, 250–52, 263, 274–76; Robert M. Hutchins, interviews, May 29, 1973 and May 30, 1973, Robert M. Hutchins and Associates, Oral History Interviews, Box 1, folder 9. In October 1941, Hutchins cautioned John U. Nef Jr. to the effect that "I might elaborate my fears about the participation of the government in education. Direct gifts mean control. Such is the state of politics in this country that control means bad education." Letter of October 31, 1941, Nef Jr. Papers, Box 23, folder 5.

339. Compton's memoirs, *Atomic Quest: A Personal Narrative* (New York, 1956), pp. 79–86, contain little specific information on his negotiations with Hutchins about the University accepting the project. Compton had already secured university approval, however, to create a project on self-sustaining fission in beryllium with National Defense Research Committee support in April 1941. See Jack M. Holl, *Argonne National Laboratory, 1946–1996* (Urbana, IL, 1997), p. 5; and W. B. Harrell to Irvin Stewart, April 14, 1941 (confidential), Hutchins Administration, Box 241, folder 6.

340. See Compton to Filbey, November 23, 1943; and L. R. Groves to Hutchins, March 10, 1943, Hutchins Administration, Box 241, folder 6.

341. Quoted in Holl, *Argonne National Laboratory,* p. 8. See also Richard Rhodes, *The Making of the Atomic Bomb* (New York, 1986), p. 399.

342. *Chicago Tribune,* August 10, 1945, p. 7; R. S. Mulliken to Hutchins, August 15, 1945, Hutchins Administration, Box 164, folder 8. A third institute on radiobiology and biophysics was soon added. An unsigned memorandum from 1945 justifying these institutes invoked as precedents the institutes of the Kaiser Wilhelm Gesellschaft in pre-1933 Germany, arguing that they made possible a level of scientific progress impossible within normal university settings; ibid., Box 212, folder 6. By 1947, the three institutes had a total budget of $1.5 million.

343. Spencer R. Weart and Gertrud Weiss Szilard, eds., *Leo Szilard: His Version of the Facts; Selected Recollections and Correspondence* (Cambridge, MA, 1978), p. 182.

344. See Harry Ashmore, interview by George Dell, May 25, 1976, Robert M. Hutchins and Associates, Oral History Interviews, Box 1, folder 3. Ashmore further mentioned that Hutchins "doesn't like to talk about it [the atomic bomb project], because he doesn't like the result."

345. Alice Kimball Smith, *A Peril and a Hope: The Scientists' Movement in America, 1945–47* (Chicago, 1965), pp. 24–72, 560–72, esp. 566–67. For Szilard's peti-

tion to stop the use of the bomb in July 1945, see Weart and Szilard, *Leo Szilard*, pp. 209–15.

346. Smith, *A Peril and a Hope*, pp. 75–76.

347. Szilard sent Hutchins a copy of his petition; Hutchins replied, "The petition looks good to me. I hope it may be effective." Hutchins to Szilard, July 26, 1945, Hutchins Administration, Box 241, folder 6.

348. Robert M. Hutchins, interview, May 29, 1973, Robert M. Hutchins and Associates, Oral History Interviews, Box 1, folder 9.

349. "The Proposition Is Peace," pp. 13–15, Hutchins Papers, Box 364, folder 6.

350. "Atomic Force: Its Meaning for Mankind," transcript of the Round Table radio broadcast, August 12, 1945, Hutchins Papers, Box 369, folder 5.

351. Borgese and McKeon to Hutchins, September 16, 1945, McKeon Papers, Box 26, folder 3.

352. McKeon to Borgese, August 26, 1947, McKeon Papers, Box 26, folder 3.

353. Letter of January 19, 1946, Hutchins Papers, Box 229, folder 11.

354. Letter of November 23, 1947, Hutchins Papers, Box 229, folder 12.

355. Letter of November 26, 1947, Hutchins Papers, Box 229, folder 12.

356. These letters and submissions are filed in Hutchins Papers, Box 229, folder 11 to Box 230, folder 3.

357. *Chicago Tribune*, November 17, 1947, p. 1.

358. "Moscow Radio, September 13, 1948," Hutchins Papers, Box 307, folder 4.

359. Colwell was a New Testament scholar of some note. A graduate of Emory University, he received his PhD from the Divinity School at Chicago in 1930. He served on the faculty of the Divinity School from 1930 to 1951. One of his most remarkable decisions was to veto the appointment of George S. Stigler in 1946 to the faculty of the Department of Economics, on the grounds that Stigler was too empirical. See Ronald Coase, "George J. Stigler," in Edward Shils, ed., *Remembering the University of Chicago: Teachers, Scientists, and Scholars* (Chicago, 1991), p. 470.

360. See the debates in the Minutes of the Committee of the Council of the Senate, June 15, 1945. The faculty representatives on the Committee of the Council grudgingly went along, most likely because the scheme seemed to claim no *more* executive authority for Hutchins himself, but Napier Wilt insisted that "a faculty member with a grievance would want the attention of the Chancellor," which is precisely what happened in the years after 1945.

361. Reubin Frodin, interview by Richard Storr, December 24, 1954, Storr Papers, Box 6, folder 8.

362. Williams to Hutchins, June 24, 1949, Hutchins Administration, Box 67, folder 11.

363. See R. W. Harrison to Glen Lloyd, July 25, 1960 ("because of [the] objection by the faculty, Larry, as you know, has been unwilling to recommend appointment of a President"), Lloyd Papers, Box 24.

364. Swift internal memo, April 15, 1929, Swift Papers, Box 38, folder 11.

365. Swift found himself having to write to Hutchins about the eldest daughter, Franja, who was staying with him at his summer home in Lakeside in Hutchins's ab-

572 * NOTES TO PAGES 312–315

sence that "the situation for her there isn't ideal because of the lack of supervision....
Franja is pretty much of a free-lance and with her energy and spirit, sometimes is
a little unwise. There has been no harm done but I think that you should know the
situation." Swift to Hutchins, July 28, 1939, Swift Papers, Box 49, folder 10.

366. Terry Castle, "Tickle and Flutter: Terry Castle on the Strange Career of
Maude Hutchins," *London Review of Books*, July 3, 2008, pp. 19–22.

367. Mayer, *Hutchins*, pp. 358–60.

368. William T. Hutchinson Diary, entry of October 16, 1934.

369. Benton to Hutchins, March 23, 1956, Benton Papers, Box 100, folder 6.

370. See Hutchins to Swift, August 20, 1946, Bell Papers, Box 2, folder 4. Mortimer Adler urged Hutchins to consider the option of a sabbatical, in a private note
dated September 14, 1946. See Adler to Hutchins, "Saturday afternoon [Septem-
ber 14, 1946]," Adler Papers, Box 28.

371. Minutes of the Board of Trustees, September 12 and 18, 1946.

372. Swift and Bell were able to increase Hutchins's salary from $26,000 in 1946
to $50,000 in the fall of 1947, much of which was likely intended to relieve the
expenses that his failed marriage with Maude was generating. Milton Mayer claims
that Hutchins ran up huge debts trying to pacify Maude and the children. As part of
the uncontested divorce in July 1948, Maude received a cash settlement of $18,000
a year.

373. Adler to Hutchins, September 14, 1946, Adler Papers, Box 28.

374. The original nuclear reactor (Chicago Pile 1), built in an abandoned squash
court under the west stands of the old Stagg Field, was shifted to a safer location at
Red Gate Woods in suburban Palos Park in March 1943. The laboratory was renamed
Argonne National Laboratory on July 1, 1946. In the late 1940s and early 1950s it
moved to its current location in DuPage County.

375. The funds diverted included endowments for the Medical School and for
the Oriental Institute. "1951–52 Budget Operations," August 14, 1952, Swift Papers,
Box 21, folder 16; John I. Kirkpatrick, "The University's Financial Problem," November 18, 1955, p. 5, Swift Papers, Box 77, folder 2. For a complete analysis of the
budget as of May 1948, see "Committee on Budget," May 27, 1948, Bell Papers,
Box 3, folder 3.

376. Included were the inadequacies of the new curriculum, a decline in alumni
children attending the College, a decline in alumni contributions, falling enrollments in the College, and dissatisfaction of the faculty with Hutchins. The protesters
included two lawyers, several businessmen, and a physician who claimed that they
easily could have persuaded a thousand fellow alumni to sign the document. See
Swift to Bell, November 19, 1948, and May 21, 1948, Bell Papers, Box 2, folder 7, and
Box 3, folder 1, which also contains a list of the signatories.

377. Swift to Bell, June 2 and 7, 1950, Swift Papers, Box 90, folder 9.

378. See "Trustees Fund #2," September 26, 1950, Bell Papers, Box 4, folder 1.

379. The files and correspondence are in Bell Papers, Box 3, folder 14. Similarly,
Henry Tenney wrote confidentially to Bell that "to cry for a moment over spilled
milk, I think we have made a mistake in granting top priority for the administration

building. As things have now developed, I think other projects are much more important than that one." Tenney to Bell, May 26, 1947, ibid., Box 4, folder 3.

380. "An Inventory of Fund Raising Resources and Suggested Procedure," December 1, 1950, by Kersting, Brown & Company, Swift Papers, Box 83, folder 13. The research included interviews with fifty-one alumni representatives selected in Chicago; New York; Des Moines and Waterloo, Iowa; and Madison and Milwaukee, Wisconsin; and fifty-six interviews with nonalumni businessmen and professionals as well as members of the board, senior staff, and some foundation leaders.

381. "An Inventory," pp. 13–14.

382. Ibid., p. 13.

383. Ibid., pp. 20, 39.

384. Kirkpatrick, "The University's Financial Problem," November 18, 1955, pp. 4–5.

385. Hutchins "scared the Board to death, in terms of its financial and fiduciary responsibility." "Interview of Christopher Kimball with George H. Watkins," August 25, 1987, p. 16, University of Chicago, Oral History Program.

386. Robert M. Hutchins, "A Farewell Address," January 10, 1951, *University of Chicago Magazine*, February 1951, p. 4.

387. Revealing how out of touch he was with the financial realities that Kimpton and the trustees faced in 1952, Hutchins also claimed that "though one way of fixing a budget—raising money—always appeals to everybody, the other way, which is frequently better for the university—reducing expenses—is often overlooked." Hutchins to Bell, January 15, 1952, Benton Papers, Box 408, folder 2.

388. For the two men, see Riesman, *Thorstein Veblen,* pp. 101–3.

389. Hutchins's famous radio addresses and the University of Chicago Roundtable radio programs that began in February 1931 might be seen as latter-day versions of Harper's correspondence education, adapted to the new media of the 1930s and 1940s and presented with a much more self-consciously intellectual aura.

390. Hutchins was a covert New Deal sympathizer running a university whose board was staunchly Republican and whose former presidents had either been progressive-minded or conservative Republicans, and was thus a poster child of the ideological stresses endured by the University after 1930.

391. David Riesman, who admired Hutchins, once argued that because "in competing with the great endowed universities of the Eastern Seaboard, [Chicago] could not count on loyal generations of alumni who part with their sons and draw their testamentary trusts on the basis of unshakeable tradition," it was forced to "live on high pressure promotion" of itself. Riesman, *Thorstein Veblen,* p. 103. The problem with Riesman's formulation was that, in fact, the University spent much of its time selling its virtues to the big private foundations, and eventually, even that source of revenue proved overtaxed.

392. The personal memoir by Edward Shils about Hutchins, although self-indulgent, captures the aura of excitement that inhabited the campus in the 1930s and early 1940s. See Shils, "Robert Maynard Hutchins," in Shils, ed., *Remembering the University of Chicago*, pp. 185–96.

393. Ralph Tyler, interview by George Dell, March 11, 1978, p. 18, Robert M. Hutchins and Associates, Oral History Interviews, Box 2, folder 13.

394. "Conversations with T.V. Smith," April 12 and 14, 1958, Storr Papers, Box 6, folder 8.

395. Robert Streeter, interview by George Dell, November 1, 1977, Robert M. Hutchins and Associates, Oral History Interviews, Box 2, folder 11.

396. Ruml to Merriam, July 10, 1950, Ruml Papers, Box 3, folder 11; in contrast, with some edginess, Merriam called Hutchins the "Sir Chancellor" who occupied a Chancellery, August 17, 1945, ibid.; "Frodin: conversation, December 24, 1954," Storr Papers, Box 6, folder 8.

397. See Richard McKeon's comments to George Dell, interview, June 3, 1975, Robert M. Hutchins and Associates, Oral History Interviews, Box 2, folder 7.

398. Hutchins to Ward, February 19, 1964, Ward Papers, Box 1, folder 14.

399. See Hutchins's column "What Kind of World?," published on October 26, 1964, Hutchins Papers, Box 352, folder 3.

400. Clark Kerr, *The Uses of the University* (Cambridge, MA, 1963), p. 33; and Howard Gardner, *Leading Minds: An Anatomy of Leadership* (New York, 1995), p. 125.

401. For example, Andrew Hacker and Claudia Dreifus, *Higher Education? How Colleges Are Wasting Our Money and Failing Our Kids—and What We Can Do about It* (New York, 2010). Hacker and Dreifus mention Hutchins twice as a courageous defender of academic freedom and also include him on their list of idealistic and outspoken university leaders, the likes of which we no longer see. See also Charles J. Sykes, *ProfScam: Professors and the Demise of Higher Education* (Washington, DC, 1988). For a more sophisticated critique, also citing Hutchins, see Delbanco, *College. What It Was, Is, and Should Be.*

402. Thomas to Storr, February 20, 1953, Storr Papers, Box 6, folder 11.

Chapter Five

1. Telluride had been founded by Lucien L. Nunn, a wealthy investor in early electric power plants in Utah and Colorado who created the Telluride Association at Cornell in 1911 and who founded Deep Springs College in 1917.

2. See the remarks of Norman Maclean at the memorial service in honor of Lawrence Kimpton, January 12, 1978, *University of Chicago Record*, February 28, 1978, p. 20.

3. Kimpton to Compton, February 6, 1946, Kimpton Papers, Box 4, folder 12.

4. Kimpton wrote of Hutchins in early 1951, "No one else I have known could arouse so much admiration and loyalty, and willingness to support him to the last ditch. This loyalty is partly the result of his remarkable abilities but even more it is engendered by his character. In his writing and speeches he has been largely concerned with spiritual and moral values, and those of us who have seen him in the day-to-day administration of the University of Chicago know that these are not slogans. They are working beliefs by which he tests every problem on which he rests

his solution. That kind of integrity commands something like a crusading zeal from associates." Draft of a statement on Hutchins, May 14, 1951, Hutchins Administration, Box 168, folder 8.

5. Lynn A. Williams Jr. to Kimpton, May 18, 1950, Hutchins Administration, Box 68, folder 1.

6. Letter of September 22, 1950, Kimpton Papers, Box 3.

7. A reminder about titles: from 1945 until 1961, the president's official title was changed to Chancellor. Hence, throughout his regime, Kimpton was addressed as Chancellor. The board of trustees changed the designation back to the conventional title of President in 1961. For Hoffman's tenure and the political maneuvering of the senior staff at the Ford Foundation in the early 1950s, see Francis X. Sutton, "The Ford Foundation: The Early Years," *Daedalus* 116 (1987): 41–91; and more generally Dwight MacDonald, *The Ford Foundation: The Men and the Millions* (New York, 1956).

8. "I talked with him. I urged him that it was a mistake for him to go.... And his reply was that in reviewing the years of his Presidency, it did not seem to him that he had accomplished anything significant in education." See Richard McKeon's comments to George Dell, interview, June 29, 1976, Robert M. Hutchins and Associates, Oral History Interviews, Box 2, folder 8. See also Levi to William H. McNeill, September 17, 1990, p. 2, Levi Papers, Box 46, folder 1.

9. Adler to Hutchins, September 14, 1946, Adler Papers, Box 28. Ashmore, *Unseasonable Truths*, pp. 301–4 provides helpful background on William Benton's role in Hutchins's appointment at Ford.

10. "I returned to Chicago chiefly because of Hutchins." Kimpton to Carl E. Kimpton, December 8, 1950, Kimpton Papers, Box 3.

11. Swift to Lloyd, April 5, 1960, Lloyd Papers, Box 21.

12. Bell to Kimpton, written in longhand and dated "August 1951," Bell Papers, Box 13, folder 2.

13. Kimpton to Carl E. Kimpton, November 9, 1951, Kimpton Papers, Box 3.

14. Letter of November 26, 1951, Kimpton Papers, Box 3.

15. "Interview of Christopher Kimball with George H. Watkins," August 25, 1987, p. 25, University of Chicago, Oral History Program.

16. William H. Warren to F. Champion Ward, April 24, 1992, Ward Papers, Box 1, folder 13.

17. Typical was the protest of the Department of English, which objected to "the disastrous policy of offending high school graduates and high school teachers by implying that the last two years of high school study is practically worthless when compared with the work of the first two years in the 'four-year College.' We doubt the wisdom of alienating teachers who might send students here and students who might come here." The Sub-Committee on English [1953], pp. 2, 7, College Archive, Box 9, folder 2.

18. Kimpton to Carl E. Kimpton, December 1, 1952, Kimpton Papers, Box 3.

19. "Report of the Council Subcommittee on Enrollment," College Archive, Box 4, folder 10.

20. "Public Relations Plan for the University of Chicago" [1954], University Development Campaigns, 1955–58, Box 1.

21. "Report of the Committee on the Bachelor's Degree," Minutes of the Council of the University Senate, April 21, 1953, pp. 268–74; May 7, 1953, pp. 308–37; as well as the documents in Ward Papers, Box 1, folder 11.

22. "Vote 4-year BA; Ward resigns," *Maroon*, May 8, 1953, p. 1.

23. These misunderstandings are evident in the often painful correspondence between the two men from 1953 in Ward Papers, Box 1, folder 5. After leaving Chicago, Ward used his connections with former Chicago colleagues (particularly Clarence Faust, via Philip Coombs) at the Ford Foundation to embark on a successful new career, serving five years (1954–59) in India as a specialist in education to assist the Indian government, and then as vice president for education and research of the Ford Foundation in the 1960s and 1970s.

24. Kimpton to Carl E. Kimpton, May 1, 1953, Kimpton Papers, Box 4.

25. Hutchins to Roger Faherty, July 13, 1953, Benton Papers, Box 408, folder 3.

26. See, for example, Beardsley Ruml, *Memo to a College Trustee: A Report on Financial and Structural Problems of the Liberal College* (New York, 1959), pp. 61, 64–71: "The average faculty member is likely to be quite conservative about educational matters. The status system is a conservative influence."

27. "When I took this big College problem on four years ago, you will recall that the roof blew off. But everything seems to be very quiet and sedate at this point, and I am not anticipating any difficulties." Letter to his father of February 18, 1957, Kimpton Papers, Box 4.

28. See the final debate on the report of the Executive Committee in the Minutes of the Council of the University Senate, May 20, 1958, pp. 127–39; June 3, 1958, pp. 140–59. The vote to adopt was 38 in favor, 4 opposed.

29. Similar skirmishing occurred in the struggle of divisional and some College faculty to curb the authority of the Board of Examinations and end the practice of comprehensive exams, which happened in April 1955. See Boyer, *"Teaching at a University of a Certain Sort,"* pp. 137–55.

30. Streeter to Kimpton, May 7, 1958, College Archive, Box 1, folder 11. For similar anxieties, see the memos of Milton Singer, April 9, 1958, and Howard Stein, April 21, 1958, ibid., Box 27, folder 8.

31. Hutchins to Clarence Ward, June 19, 1953, Ward Papers, Box 1, folder 14.

32. Kimpton to Romer, June 14, 1960, Kimpton Papers, Box 17, folder 10.

33. "Trustee Dinner Speech," January 13, 1954, marked "not for publication," Kimpton Papers, Box 13, folder 36.

34. Duncan to George Watkins, June 2, 1955, Kimpton Administration, Box 100, folder 6.

35. Charles D. O'Connell, interviews by Christopher Kimball, December 8, 1987, pp. 8–9, and December 17, 1987, pp. 3, 41, University of Chicago, Oral History Program.

36. "Remarks to Student Government," January 28, 1952, Swift Papers, Box 21, folder 16.

37. *Maroon*, June 10, 1954, pp. 1–2. In the early 1950s Kimpton deployed the word "queer" to describe students who were, in his mind, strange, eccentric, and antisocial. As far as I can tell, he did not use the word with any deliberate allusion to homosexuality.

38. *Maroon*, April 1, 1955 [April Fools issue, published as *the Chicago Charcoal*], p. 1; and June 10, 1954, p. 1.

39. I told this story in my monograph *"A Noble and Symmetrical Conception of Life": The Arts at Chicago on the Edge of a New Century* (Chicago, 2010). It is a striking fact that the student-run theater programs in the College recruit more students each year than all of the programs in varsity athletics put together. In 2013 more than eight hundred students were involved in student theater and dance programs, almost all of them student organized.

40. See the charming memoir of Herbert J. Gans, "Relativism, Equality, and Popular Culture," in Berger, ed., *Authors of Their Own Lives*, pp. 437–42, 449 n. 5.

41. Netherton, "Some Opinions of Their Education in the College," pp. 64–67, College Archive, Box 101.

42. James E. Newman, "The House System and Student Life," August 1963, p. 12, College Archive.

43. Donald N. Levine, "On Upgrading the 'Quality of Life' in the College," October 1, 1984, p. 4, College Archive.

44. "Planning Conference, March 4–7, 1954," Fifth Session, Kimpton Administration, Box 252, folder 1. Kimpton expressed his preference "for a student body in which there would be 6,000 undergraduates and 4,000 graduates."

45. William C. Bradbury, "Education and Other Aspects of Personal Growth in the College Community: A Report to the College Committee on Policy and Personnel," October 1951, pp. 76, 108–12, College Archive. Of the student culture more generally, Bradbury observed that "Chancellor Hutchins has personified the ideals of the University for many students and, whatever may have been his real attitudes, the image of him that the students saw looked down with utter contempt on physical exercise, dating, aimless camaraderie, even student self-government" (p. 76).

46. As late as the early 1970s the University had a student-faculty ratio of College students compared to the arts and sciences faculty of almost four to one (for the year 1969–70, 527 divisional faculty and 56 College faculty compared to 2,378 undergraduate students), revealing how overtaxed the University's financial situation was. See "Statistical Study of the College," p. 29 and Appendix A, "Faculty Teaching Undergraduates," p. 2, PP Addenda, 1997-060, Box 6.

47. "Undergraduate Fraternities, Spring Quarter 1929," Mason Administration, Box 1, folder 6; "Students at the University of Chicago," 1940–1941, p. 6, College Archive, Box 15, folder 2; James E. Newman to Robert M. Wulff, August 18, 1965, ibid., Box 76. On the change in pledging practices in 1932, see Woodward to Arthur B. Hall, August 2, 1933, Hutchins Administration, Box 91, folder 3. From 1945 to 1951 undergraduates were prohibited from joining fraternities. This ban was lifted in April 1951, but by then the damage had been done. The trustees noted in June 1952 that "the financial wounds of the fraternities are deep and slow in healing."

"Committee on Student Interests Report," p. 8, filed with the Minutes of the Board of Trustees, June 12, 1952.

48. Richard J. McKinlay and James A. Davis, "A Survey of the University of Chicago Class of 1960," May 1961, pp. 38–39, College Archive.

49. Mary Alice Newman, *The Student and the College Community: A Study of Attrition and Persistence in a Highly Selective Liberal Arts College* (Chicago, 1965), pp. 64, 69, 79.

50. Minutes of the Faculty of the College, June 4, 1959, p. 4.

51. Lawrence A. Kimpton, *The State of the University: A Report to the Faculties,* November 11, 1958, p. 7, Kimpton Administration, Box 237, folder 2.

52. Alan Simpson to Edward H. Levi, June 18, 1962, College Archive.

53. *New York Times,* May 21, 1959, p. 33; *Time,* June 1, 1959, p. 51. As damage control, the University published a clunky article for the alumni magazine in which Simpson and Ned Rosenheim assured alumna representative Laura Bergquist (class of 1939) that the University's ideals were still intact. See "The Public Image of the College: A Roundtable Discussion by the Dean, a Faculty Member, and an Alumna," *University of Chicago Magazine,* November 1959, pp. 8–12.

54. Letter to his father, June 15, 1954, Kimpton Papers, Box 4, folder 2.

55. "Revised Budget, 1950–51," Minutes of the Board of Trustees, February 1951.

56. "Chancellor's Docket," March 16, 1953, Kimpton Administration, Box 250, folder 3.

57. Roger L. Geiger, *Research and Relevant Knowledge: American Research Universities since World War II* (New York, 1993), pp. 40–47, 243–52; William G. Bowen, *The Economics of the Major Private Universities* (Berkeley, 1968), pp. 34–56.

58. Bowen, *The Economics of the Major Private Universities,* p. 31.

59. "Planning Conference, March 4–7, 1954," Fifth Session, Kimpton Administration, Box 252, folder 1.

60. Kimpton to Carl Kimpton, March 3, 1954, Kimpton Papers, Box 3. The material from this meeting is filed in Kimpton Administration, Box 252, folder 1.

61. "Effect on Regular Budget of Optimum Enrollment and Projected Expenditures," June 10, 1954, Swift Papers, Box 77, folder 4.

62. Confidential Memo to the Board of Trustees, June 9, 1954, Swift Papers, Box 77, folder 4.

63. See Watkins's account of these early years in his comments to the Lakeside IV Conference, March 15, 1957, Kimpton Administration, Box 253, folder 2.

64. Duncan to Kimpton, March 7, 1956, Kimpton Administration, Box 100, folder 6.

65. "Publicity Schedule for Alumni Campaign," June 25, 1955, Kimpton Administration, Box 100, folder 3.

66. *The 1955–1956 Time-Life Award-Winning Direct Mail Letters of the University of Chicago* (Washington, DC, 1956), p. 1.

67. John J. McDonough and Earle Ludgin, May 23, 1956, Swift Papers, Box 78, folder 4.

68. "Highlights from the 1955 Campaign Analysis," Swift Papers, Box 78, folder 4.

69. Confidential Survey 360, Form 1, 8–9–54, Swift Papers, Box 79, folder 11. The survey of 304 members of the citizens board, and 156 other prominent men and 31 prominent women, was conducted in August and September 1954.

70. "Attitudes of Prominent Citizens towards Problems of Higher Education in the Chicago Area," NORC, Report No. 53, October 22, 1954, marked confidential, Kimpton Administration, Box 185, folder 3.

71. Duncan to Watkins, April 25, 1955, Kimpton Administration, Box 100, folder 1.

72. Kimpton acknowledged the existence of these transfers to faculty leaders in 1952 when he was forced to explain to Carl Kraeling, the director of the Oriental Institute, why a substantial part of the endowment that the OI had possessed as late as 1946 no longer existed. See Kimpton to Kraeling, July 25, 1952, Arnett Papers, Box 1, folder 1.

73. Rockefeller to Kimpton, May 25, 1955, Bell Papers, Box 13, folder 3.

74. Memorandum, May 6, 1955, Swift Papers, Box 79, folder 18.

75. "Trustee Dinner Speech," January 11, 1956, Kimpton Administration, Box 100, folder 1.

76. "Campaign Gifts—Cumulative Summary, June 1, 1954–June 30, 1958," as an attachment to Edward L. Ryerson, "Report of the University of Chicago Campaign," Kimpton Administration, Box 255, folder 1; as well as the additional files in University Development Campaigns, 1955–58, Box 14. This report was drafted by William B. Cannon.

77. Committee on Budget, April 1, 1957, p. 10, Kimpton Administration, Box 253, folder 2; Minutes of the Board of Trustees, April 11, 1957, filed in Swift Papers, Box 79, folder 26. George Watkins later remembered that Kimpton was "mighty upset about the proposal—and I was outraged—for I could see this seriously diverting support from the all-University goals.... Needless to say [the] other deans were furious—for they too had pet projects which they had set aside as campaign objectives to support the all-University campaign concept." "Interview of Christopher Kimball with George H. Watkins," August 25, 1987, p. 70, University of Chicago, Oral History Program.

78. The relevant trends and scholarly literature are nicely summarized in Loss, *Between Citizens and the State*, pp. 123–61; and in Geiger, *Research and Relevant Knowledge*, pp. 3–29, 157–97.

79. In the consolidated budget for 1963–64, total income for education, administration, and instruction was budgeted at $73.9 million. The share billed to government grants was $21.9 million, but the biological sciences and physical sciences divisions alone consumed $16.2 million of these funds.

80. See Quintin Johnstone, "The Federal Urban Renewal Program," *University of Chicago Law Review* 25 (1958–59): 301–54; Ashley A. Foard and Hilbert Fefferman, "Federal Urban Renewal Legislation," *Law and Contemporary Problems* 25 (1960): 635–84; Jennifer S. Light, *The Nature of Cities: Ecological Visions and the American Urban Professions, 1920–1960* (Baltimore, 2009), pp. 134–36, 148–69; Mark I. Gelfand, *A Nation of Cities: The Federal Government and Urban America, 1933–1965* (New York, 1975), pp. 151–98.

81. The history of the urban renewal projects involving Hyde Park in the 1950s and 1960s has generated a substantial literature, scholarly, semischolarly, and popular, much of it containing emotionally charged judgments about the University's plans and motives. See Muriel Beadle, *The Hyde Park–Kenwood Urban Renewal Years* (Chicago, 1964); Peter H. Rossi and Robert A. Dentler, *The Politics of Urban Renewal: The Chicago Findings* (New York, 1961); Arnold R. Hirsch, *Making the Second Ghetto: Race and Housing in Chicago, 1940–1960* (Cambridge, 1983); Rebecca Janowitz, *Culture of Opportunity: Obama's Chicago; The People, Politics, and Ideas of Hyde Park* (Chicago, 2010); Valetta Press, *Hyde Park/Kenwood: A Case Study of Urban Renewal* (Chicago, 1971); Brian J. L. Berry, Sandra J. Parsons, and Rutherford H. Platt, *The Impact of Urban Renewal on Small Business: The Hyde Park–Kenwood Case* (Chicago, 1968); and Julia Abrahamson, *A Neighborhood Finds Itself* (New York, 1959). Jennifer S. Light has recently published a fascinating study of the ways in which urban renewal planning of the 1950s must be situated within wider trends of social ecological theory in Chicago and elsewhere. See her *The Nature of Cities*, esp. pp. 128–71.

82. Tugwell to Colwell, June 14, 1948, Hutchins Administration, Box 166, folder 3.

83. Beadle, *The Hyde Park–Kenwood Urban Renewal Years*, p. 4.

84. Hutchins to his father, September 22, 1937, Box 8, folder 8–3, William J. Hutchins Papers, Berea College Archives. The reference of "Oberlinites" refers to the deep personal connections of both Hutchins and his father to Oberlin College.

85. "The Reminiscences of Julian H. Levi," p. 37, University of Chicago, Oral History Program, 1994, conducted with Daniel Meyer, September 21, 22, and 23, 1992.

86. There was some pressure on Hutchins—from the faculty, community, and board—to do something about the decline of the neighborhood before 1950. These efforts began in earnest in 1944–45, when the University began to take an interest in specific problem properties in the area, either by purchasing and rehabbing them or working with the police to enforce codes. Still, all of this was reactive and uncoordinated. Kimpton later referred to this conundrum when he complained that the University had merely "studied the problem" before 1950, which was in fact worse than ignoring it.

87. John Gunther, *Chicago Revisited* (Chicago, 1967), pp. 70–71.

88. Robert M. Hutchins, "The University and the City," 1941, copy in Adler Papers, Box 27.

89. Draft of "State of the University," June 1, 1952, Kimpton Papers, Box 12, folder 23.

90. See Hutchins to the Board, November 9, 1944, Hutchins Administration, Box 106, folder 9.

91. Rossi and Dentler, *The Politics of Urban Renewal*, pp. 21–22.

92. See Levi to Lloyd, January 3, 1963, Lloyd Papers, Box 25.

93. Sol Tax, "Residential Integration: The Case of Hyde Park in Chicago," paper given to the American Anthropological Association, November 22, 1958, Rachel Goetz Papers, Box 7, folder 1.

94. *Hyde Park Herald*, March 19, 1952, p. 1; *Maroon*, March 28, 1952, p. 1. The *Maroon* reported that another attempted rape had occurred on March 10.

95. "Police Brass Roasted by Indignant Citizens," *Hyde Park Herald*, April 2, 1952, p. 1.

96. "Report of the Citizen's Committee on Law Enforcement, May 19, 1952," Kimpton Papers, Box 12, folder 11.

97. A sympathetic portrait was published by Emil J. Seliga, "Nobody Scares Julian Levi," in *Talmanac Visits a Neighbor: Hyde Park-Kenwood* (1960), in Goetz Papers, Box 7, folder 2.

98. The fourth involved a change in official aesthetic tastes, which Klemek calls "modernist prescriptions for the redesign of cities." See Christopher Klemek, *The Transatlantic Collapse of Urban Renewal: Postwar Urbanism from New York to Berlin* (Chicago, 2011), pp. 48–77, here 77.

99. "The Reminiscences of Julian H. Levi," pp. 24–25. Joel Rast has analyzed the ineffectiveness of Kennelly's administration in the early 1950s. See Joel Rast, "Regime Building, Institution Building: Urban Renewal Policy in Chicago, 1946–1962," *Journal of Urban Affairs* 31 (2009): 173–94; as well as Rast, "Critical Junctures, Long-Term Processes: Urban Redevelopment in Chicago and Milwaukee, 1945–1968," *Social Science History* 33 (2009): 393–426.

100. Daley also had evident political objectives in mind, and for all of the headaches that local civic radicals like Alderman Leon Despres later caused him in meetings of the city council, Daley won widespread electoral support from Hyde Parkers in most of his subsequent reelection campaigns. See Adam Cohen and Elizabeth Taylor, *American Pharaoh: Mayor Richard J. Daley: His Battle for Chicago and the Nation* (Boston, 2000), pp. 209–12.

101. "The Reminiscences of Julian H. Levi," pp. 33–34.

102. A detailed summary of these plans is contained in Julian Levi, *The Neighborhood Program of the University of Chicago* (Chicago, n.d. [1961]). A parallel text is *The Neighborhood Program of the University of Chicago: Statements of Albert C. Svoboda and Julian Levi to the Board of Trustees*, October 12, 1961, College Archive. See also Harvey S. Perloff, *Urban Renewal in a Chicago Neighborhood: An Appraisal of the Hyde Park-Kenwood Renewal Program* (Chicago, 1955).

103. See the *Hyde Park–Kenwood Urban Renewal Project, Community Conservation Board of Chicago* (Chicago, 1961). Many of the new townhomes, apartments, and other structures were plans designed by Webb & Knapp, owned by William Zeckendorf.

104. The politics of this process are well described in Rossi and Dentler, *The Politics of Urban Renewal*, pp. 134–239.

105. "The Reminiscences of Julian H. Levi," p. 65.

106. In a subsequent interview with Daniel Meyer in 1992, Levi reported what had transpired:

LEVI: Monsignor Burke and a number of others concluded that the only way to deal with this problem was to try to suppress black migration into white parishes....

That was the demand that Monsignor Egan and Nick von Hoffman made upon me before the hearings began on the Hyde Park–Kenwood project.

MEYER: What was their demand?

LEVI: "Can you give us assurance that your black relocatees will not move into our white parishes?"

"The Reminiscences of Julian H. Levi," pp. 81–82. For Egan's perspective in this controversy, see Margery Frisbie, *An Alley in Chicago: The Ministry of a City Priest* (Kansas City, MO, 1991), pp. 94–110.

107. This agreement was mediated by Mayor Daley with Arthur Brazier and Julian Levi, and has been the subject of much historical lore. In contrast to Saul Alinsky and John Egan, Levi found Brazier to be a pragmatic deal-maker with whom he could work. See "The Reminiscences of Julian Levi," p. 90, as well as pp. 91–93, 95, 136; and LaDale Winling, "Students and the Second Ghetto: Federal Legislation, Urban Politics, and Campus Planning at the University of Chicago," *Journal of Planning History* 10 (1) (2011): 71–72; John Hall Fish, *Black Power/White Control: The Struggle of the Woodlawn Organization in Chicago* (Princeton, NJ, 1973), pp. 17–73; and Arthur M. Brazier, *Black Self-Determination: The Story of the Woodlawn Organization* (Grand Rapids, MI, 1969), pp.50–58.

108. These figures were provided by Albert C. Svoboda to the board of trustees on October 12, 1961. Svoboda also projected the need for an additional expenditure of $7.6 million for the purchase of threatened properties in the five years after 1961. Edward Levi estimated in 1965 that the University had invested $29 million in the neighborhood renewal projects. See Beadle, *The Hyde Park–Kenwood Urban Renewal Years*, p. 24.

109. Berry, Parsons, and Platt, *The Impact of Urban Renewal on Small Business, pp. 77–81, 155, 170–72;* testimony of John I. Fitzpatrick, 1959, p. 133, Kimpton Administration, Box 102, folder 2. In the central renewal areas designated Hyde Park A and B by the planners, the percentage of white relocatees was higher: 1,032 white families, 84 black families, and 51 Asian American families lost their housing. Ibid.

110. See the critique in Hirsch, *Making the Second Ghetto*, pp. 167–70.

111. "Speech to the Kappa Alpha Psi Fraternity at Mandel Hall," December 27, 1953, Kimpton Papers, Box 12, folder 37.

112. See Hirsch, *Making the Second Ghetto*, pp. 153–54.

113. See Rossi and Dentler, *The Politics of Urban Renewal*, p. 276.

114. This may explain Levi's impatience with those whom he called "little people" in the local community, whose intentions may have been highly idealistic but whose political effectiveness and legal experience in dealing with the city and with the federal government was quite limited. See Levi to Kimpton, September 29, 1954, March 4, 1955, and April 7, 1955, Kimpton Administration, Box 231, folders 1 and 2. See also the comments in Winling, "Students and the Second Ghetto," p. 81 n. 42.

115. By 1959 Kimpton would argue that "faculty who have actually lived in Hyde Park like it, and I seriously doubt that it now constitutes a major factor in the de-

cision of a faculty member to leave the University. But bringing a new and distinguished faculty member to our campus is a different problem." Quoted in Levi, *The
Neighborhood Program,* p. 31.

116. See the excellent study by Margaret Pugh O'Mara, *Cities of Knowledge: Cold
War Science and the Search for the Next Silicon Valley* (Princeton, NJ, 2005), esp.
pp. 58–94.

117. See the comments of Gerald D. Suttles, *The Man-Made City: The Land-Use
Confidence Game in Chicago* (Chicago, 1990), pp. 52–53. University planners believed that most Hyde Park residents would continue to use the Loop as their primary source of shopping and recreation and that they neither expected nor wanted
those relationships to change: "There is no possibility of the creation here of a full
regional type of shopping center. A substantial proportion of the population is now
and has been for many years oriented toward the Loop.... The proposed redevelopment and conservation being undertaken in this area will not change this pattern. If
anything, the orientation towards downtown Chicago will be increased." *South East
Chicago Renewal Project No. 1* (Chicago, n.d. [1954]), p. 73. Similarly, contemporary
public relations materials on the Hyde Park renewal projects stressed the fact that
"private and public transportation bring residents to the central business district
within fifteen minutes." *Hyde Park–Kenwood Urban Renewal Project, Community
Conservation Board of Chicago,* p. 2.

118. Joel Rast, "Creating a Unified Business Elite: The Origins of Chicago Central Area Committee," *Journal of Urban History* 20 (2011): 1–23, who notes that
"the 1958 *Development Plan for the Central Area of Chicago* signaled the triumph
of the corporate-centered, downtown approach to central area development over
the neighborhood approach advanced by such groups as the South Side Planning
Board and the Near West Side Planning Board" (p. 14).

119. Janowitz, *Culture of Opportunity,* pp. 137–38.

120. See Robert J. Sampson, *Great American City: Chicago and the Enduring
Neighborhood Effect* (Chicago, 2012), pp. 390–91.

121. From the very first, Levi was insistent that it should be a goal of the University's efforts to get rid of "slum and blight which attract lower class Whites and
Negroes." Levi to Kimpton, November 3, 1954, marked confidential, Kimpton Administration, Box 231, folder 1. This fundamental assumption in turn may help to
explain Levi's almost paranoid concern with racial balance in local neighborhood
schools and in rental properties, a policy that was extremely controversial at the
time and remains deeply so today. As Winling has rightly noted, "Julian Levi was
particularly sensitive to the impact of racial demographics at local schools, arguing
that significant minority school populations would provoke white disenrollment."
Winling, "Students and the Second Ghetto," p. 84 n. 83.

122. Beadle, *The Hyde Park–Kenwood Urban Renewal Years,* pp. 17–18. Rebecca
Janowitz has (2010) provided a more nuanced and, in my view, fair evaluation of
these processes, arguing that "it is impossible to judge how sincerely white Hyde
Parkers welcomed black neighbors. It is equally impossible to determine how willing either black or white members of the middle class were to live with poorer

people of either race. Regardless, the neighborhood achieved a lasting racial balance and continued to be economically diverse." Janowitz, *Culture of Opportunity*, p. 135.

123. O'Mara, *Cities of Knowledge*, p. 228.

124. "Median Faculty Salaries," April 8, 1959, Kimpton Administration, Box 255, folder 2.

125. "Interview of Christopher Kimball with George H. Watkins," August 25, 1987, p. 109, University of Chicago, Oral History Program.

126. Bundy to Rockefeller, September 2, 1960, Lloyd Papers, Box 6. Bundy's candidacy was especially advocated by trustees William Benton, David Rockefeller, and Charles Percy, in addition to Lloyd himself. On Bundy's tenure at Harvard, see Keller and Keller, *Making Harvard Modern*, pp. 189–91, 211, 214–15.

127. Lloyd to Bundy, December 27, 1965, Lloyd Papers, Box 6.

128. On Beadle at Caltech, see Norman H. Horowitz, "George Wells Beadle, 1903–1989," in *National Academy of Sciences Biographical Memoirs* (Washington, DC, 1990), pp. 38–40.

129. Committee of the Council of the Senate, April 26, 1960, and May 10, 1960; and the draft of a proposed press release by George Poole, dated March 28, 1960, Lloyd Papers, Box 21.

130. See Lloyd to Corson, July 19, 1960, Lloyd Papers, Box 21.

131. For the story behind the gift, see Lowell T. Coggeshall, "The Biological Sciences Division, The University of Chicago, 1949–1962," pp. 49–54, Coggeshall Papers, Box 7, folder 2.

132. Beadle to Wilson, July 18, 1961, Beadle Administration, Box 256, folder 7.

133. Beadle to Lloyd, August 28, 1961.

134. See Muriel Beadle, *Where Has All the Ivy Gone? A Memoir of University Life* (Chicago, 1977), p. 6.

135. The *Hyde Park Herald* endorsed Levi as a possible successor to Kimpton in an editorial on October 5, 1960.

136. Conversation between Edward H. Levi and John W. Boyer, July 12, 1993, Quadrangle Club.

137. Ryerson to Lloyd, undated [late March 1962], Lloyd Papers, Box 25.

138. Minutes of the Board of Trustees, April 12, 1962, p. 53.

139. Comments to W. H. McNeill, Levi Papers, Box 46, folder 3. See also Levi's speech to the Jewish Theological Seminary of America, May 26, 1968, ibid., Box 298, folder 4; and the comments in Levi to Robert Rosenthal, December 16, 1981, ibid., Box 34, folder 5.

140. Appointment recommendation of May 4, 1936, Hutchins Administration, Box 335, folder 12. For Levi's role as a faculty member in the Law School and as dean of the Law School, see the excellent analysis in Dennis J. Hutchinson, "Edward Levi: Legal Scholar, Legal Educator" (presentation at the symposium in honor of Edward H. Levi at the University of Chicago, September 21, 2012).

141. Levi to Hutchins, September 19, 1936, Hutchins Administration, Box 127, folder 13.

142. Levi to Hutchins, June 19, 1939, Hutchins Administration, Box 128, folder 2.

143. Minutes of the Board of Trustees, April 11, 1963, p. 61.

144. Minutes of the Board of Trustees, June 14, 1962, pp. 112–14.

145. See the minutes of the senior staff meeting of May 2, 1962, Coggeshall Papers, Box 7.

146. The six University Professors were Leonard Krieger, Henri Thiel, Albert Wohlstetter, Francois Ayala, Constantine A. Trypanis, and David Atlas.

147. Speech to the National Leadership Conference, October 15, 1966, pp. 8, 11, Beadle Administration, Box 200, folder 2. To give just one example, between 1962 and 1967 the Department of History recruited John Hope Franklin, Ping-ti Ho, Arthur Mann, Richard C. Wade, Leonard Krieger, and William R. Polk, all at the level of full professor, thus completely transforming the intellectual portrait and stature of the department.

148. "Discussion Paper: Special Program in Education," September 1963, Nr. 002221, Ford Foundation Archives.

149. "Termination of the Special Program in Education. Information Paper and Recommended Action," November 1968, Nr. 001356, Ford Foundation Archives.

150. The history of this program is told by Francis X. Sutton, "The Ford Foundation and Columbia: A Paper for the University Seminar on Columbia University, 16 November 1999" (unpublished manuscript). Sutton was a senior official at Ford throughout the period of this program. Robert McCaughey exaggerated only slightly when he characterized these years as a time when the Ford Foundation "established itself as American higher education's underwriter of first resort." Robert A. McCaughey, *International Studies and Academic Enterprise: A Chapter in the Enclosure of American Learning* (New York, 1984), p. 181. Similarly, Waldemar A. Nielsen, *The Big Foundations* (New York, 1972), p. 92 characterizes Heald's view of the foundation as functioning as "a kind of banking partner to higher education."

151. The grant was to be matched on a 3:1 basis.

152. See Leonard K. Olsen to Levi, October 24, 1962, Beadle Administration, Box 256, folder 6. Levi visited F. Champion Ward at the Ford Foundation to enlist his support, and Levi's personal relationship with Ward via Hutchins may have proved of crucial importance. See "Report of the Campaign Planning Committee, May 21, 1965," Lloyd Papers, Box 24. Levi had established a successful track record with Ford during his tenure as dean of the Law School in the 1950s, garnering substantial support for the Law and Behavioral Science Program. See John Henry Schlegel, *American Legal Realism and Empirical Social Science* (Chapel Hill, NC, 1995), pp. 238–44. Francis Sutton also points out that Henry Heald and James W. Armsey, a top Ford official responsible for its higher education programs, had personal connections to the city of Chicago, and this too may have played a role. Heald had served as president of the Illinois Institute of Chicago from 1940 to 1952, and Armsey worked for Heald as his director of public relations.

153. "Report of the Presentation of the Provost to the Board of Trustees of the University of Chicago on February 11, 1965," Lloyd Papers, Box 24.

154. George Beadle, handwritten notes for presentation to the Board of Trustees, March 15, 1965, College Archive.

155. The Ford Profile exists in complete and summary form. The full Ford Profile is a two-volume manuscript on file in the Ford Foundation Archives. Its backup data, including drafts of planning statements on the future of the divisions, schools, and the College generated by Levi and others, are in the Ford Profile files in Beadle Administration, Boxes 272 and 273. In addition, the University produced a detailed executive summary, "Summary of a Profile: The University of Chicago."

156. Clarence H. Faust to Henry T. Heald, August 17, 1965, pp. 2–3, 10–11, 14, Grant File PA65–367, Ford Foundation Archives.

157. George Beadle to Howard R. Dressner, October 9, 1967, Grant File 65–367, Ford Foundation Archives.

158. During the same period endowment income increased from $7 million to only $11.6 million. Edward H. Levi, "The State of the University, November 4, 1969," p. 2, Office of the President, Levi Administration, Records, Box 312, folder 7.

159. Memorandum of October 7, 1965, Beadle Administration, Box 383, folder 1.

160. George Beadle to McGeorge Bundy, September 12, 1966, Grant File 65–367, Ford Foundation Archives.

161. "Summary of a Profile: The University of Chicago," pp. 6, 15.

162. Minutes of the Board of Trustees, October 8, 1964, p. 13.

163. "Memorandum to the President and to the College Faculty," August 25, 1964, Minutes of the College Faculty.

164. Minutes of the Board of Trustees, February 14, 1963, p. 23; October 8, 1964, p. 12.

165. Minutes of the Board of Trustees, March 15, 1965, p. 6.

166. This is clear from Levi's comments to the board in October 1964, in which he noted that one of the great problems facing the University after Kimpton's reforms was that the departments were basically given de facto responsibility for the final two years of the progress of undergraduate students, whereas Levi wanted to ensure that "the College faculty be in charge of the four-year undergraduate program."

167. Remarks at the Conference on the Knowledge Most Worth Having, February 4, 1966, Beadle Administration, Box 200, folder 6.

168. Gerhard Casper, *The Winds of Freedom: Addressing Challenges to the University* (New Haven, CT, 2014), p. 10.

169. Levi to Arnold, December 23, 1968, Levi Papers, Box 12, folder 1.

170. "Interview with Edward Levi, Prof. of Law, U. of Chicago, November 4, 1977," Levi Papers, Box 44, folder 10.

171. Levi to McNeill, September 17, 1990, Levi Papers, Box 46, folder 1.

172. Philipson to Levi, January 17, 1968, and October 7, 1968, Levi Papers, Box 299, folder 11.

173. He wrote to Sydney Hyman in 1989, "I do not think that Hutchins was a failure except in the sense that every noble person probably does not reach the goals that he sets for himself." Letter of October 6, 1989, Levi Papers, Box 23, folder 9. When Hutchins visited campus to speak in 1962, Levi wrote to him, "Your talk was like old times, which I wish would come again." Levi to Hutchins, April 24, 1962, ibid., Box 77, folder 3.

174. Beadle Administration, Box 199, folder 9.

175. Philip G. Altbach, "Harsh Realities: The Professoriate Faces a New Century," in Philip G. Altbach, Robert O. Berdahl, and Patricia J. Gumport, eds., *American Higher Education in the Twenty-First Century,* 2nd ed. (Baltimore, 2005), pp. 287–314, here 294.

176. See Loss, *Between Citizens and the State,* pp. 87, 119–20, 160.

177. See the prescient comments of Roger Geiger, "Research Universities in a New Era: From the 1980s to the 1990s," in Arthur Levine, ed., *Higher Learning in America, 1980–2000* (Baltimore, 1993), pp. 74–77.

178. See Levi's notes to Kimpton for a speech that Kimpton had to give on the fiftieth anniversary of the founding of the Law School, December 19, 1952, Kimpton Administration, Box 159, folder 4.

179. Levi Papers, Box 298, folder 11. See also "The University and the Modern Condition," November 16, 1967, Beadle Administration, Box 200, folder 5.

180. John T. Wilson to Robert Rosenthal, August 12, 1975, Levi Papers, Box 313, folder 7.

181. Beadle's resignation was announced on June 27, 1967, and Levi's appointment was announced on September 14, 1967.

182. Minor disturbances had occurred earlier in the 1960s, including a sit-in in January 1962 on neighborhood housing problems organized by CORE.

183. "Supplementary Statement by Gerhard E. O. Meyer," p. 2, filed with the "Report of the Faculty-Student Committee on Faculty-Student Relationships," April 18, 1967, College Archive.

184. Alan Brinkley, "1968 and the Unraveling of Liberal America," in Carole Fink, Philipp Gassert, and Detlef Junker, eds., *1968: The World Transformed* (Cambridge, 1998), p. 220. The literature on student unrest in the 1960s is massive, but I have found Robert Cohen and Reginald E. Zelnik, eds., *The Free Speech Movement: Reflections on Berkeley in the 1960s* (Berkeley, 2002); Philip G. Altbach, *Student Politics in America: A Historical Analysis* (New York, 1974); and Andrew B. Lewis, *The Shadows of Youth: The Remarkable Journey of the Civil Rights Generation* (New York, 2009) to be especially helpful.

185. Kirkpatrick Sale, *SDS* (New York, 1973), p. 445; Stanley Rothman and S. Robert Lichter, *Roots of Radicalism: Jews, Christians, and the Left,* rev. ed. (New Brunswick, NJ, 1996), p. 36; Irwin Unger, *The Movement: A History of the American New Left, 1959–1972* (New York, 1974), p. 115.

186. The senior faculty of the Committee on Human Development had offered a contrasting recommendation—namely, renewal for a second three-year term. The provost accepted the sociology department's recommendation.

187. Already on January 21 a rump meeting of thirty-three sociology graduate students had voted 18 in favor, 14 against, and 1 abstention to pursue a demand for the rehiring of Marlene Dixon so that her case could be reopened and reconsidered under a new process involving participation by the graduate students and with greater attention to Dixon's teaching. They also voted that "we will implement these demands by any means necessary." Memo of January 21, 1969, copied to the *Maroon.*

188. Letter to Edward H. Levi from "The Negotiating Committee, the Administration Building," January 30, 1969, College Archive. See also "400 Students Occupy Ad Building!," *Maroon*, January 31, 1969, pp. 3–8.

189. The Oaks committee also had four student observers, three of whom subsequently resigned and were replaced.

190. For the details, see "Report on Disciplinary and Appeals Decisions," April 8, 1969, *University of Chicago Record*, May 2, 1969, pp. 22–23.

191. Statement of H. Stanley Bennett, February 8, 1969, College Archive. Similar statements were contained in a public letter of February 5 by Professor O. J. Kleppa, who compared the radical students to students under the Nazis who sought to destroy the German universities.

192. Statement of John Hope Franklin, February 7, 1969, College Archive.

193. Minutes of the College Faculty, February 4, 1969, p. 28.

194. "Statement of a Group of Concerned Faculty Members," February 11, 1969, College Archive. A majority of signatories were members of the social sciences division. Dean of Students Charles D. O'Connell later estimated that about 30 percent of the faculty strongly disapproved of Levi's tough no-amnesty policy toward those students who had been summoned to the disciplinary panels, with a majority of 70 percent supporting the policy. Charles D. O'Connell, interview by John W. Boyer, June 5, 1999. The former group was led by Gilbert White of the Department of Geography, who organized a silent protest by eighty faculty against Levi's disciplinary policies outside the administration building on April 14.

195. The *Maroon* commissioned a survey of student opinion, undertaken by a group of graduate students familiar with survey research techniques. When they interviewed a random sample of 625 students by phone on February 5–8, they found a solid majority against the sit-in but also a majority in favor of greater student rights in academic affairs and in favor of amnesty for the protesters. See *Maroon*, February 10, 1969, p. 4.

196. Paul Schollmeier to Hugo F. Sonnenschein, September 7, 1999, College Archive.

197. Wayne C. Booth, *My Many Selves: The Quest for a Plausible Harmony* (Logan, UT, 2006), pp. 191–93. For a second, very useful memoir, see James W. Vice, "Memoirs: Demonstrations, 1968–1969 1973" (unpublished manuscript, 2004).

198. Booth, *My Many Selves*, p. 194.

199. One of the most significant issues was whether to call in the city police to evict the demonstrators. Both Wayne Booth and James Vice, in their memoirs on the sit-in, report that Levi strongly sided with those opposed to summoning the police, and Vice insists, based on his own knowledge and a communication from Kate Levi, that Levi would have resigned the presidency if such a decision had been taken. But this decision was not popular with faculty hardliners, and Vice further reports, "I was told by [former University Dean of Students Charles] O'Connell that some of Levi's closest faculty friends cooled toward him over this." "Memoirs," pp. 23–25.

200. Memorandum to faculty and students, February 14, 1969, College Archive.

201. Memorandum, February 27, 1967, Beadle Administration, Box 256, folder 13.

202. Levi to Janowitz, May 2, 1968, Beadle Administration, Box 199, folder 3.

203. "The University and Its Budget," *University of Chicago Record*, December 1, 1969, pp. 10–11.

204. Levi, "The State of the University," November 4, 1969, pp. 5, 8.

205. The basic features of the crisis are well described in Geiger, *Research and Relevant Knowledge*, pp. 230–69.

206. Donald Meiklejohn et al., "The College Committee on Residential Policy," June 5, 1961, p. 8, College Archive.

207. Rostow to Levi, December 20, 1965, Blum Papers, Box 16, folder 5.

208. Newman to Wick, May 1, 1963; Wick to Beadle et al., May 2, 1963; Beadle Administration, Box 73, folder 7. See also *Maroon*, April 24, 1963, p. 2.

209. Sheldon to George Beadle et al., May 1, 1963, Beadle Administration, Box 73, folder 7.

210. Wick to Beadle, Levi, and James J. Ritterskamp Jr., July 26, 1965, Blum Papers, Box 15, folder 4.

211. Wick to Beadle et al., February 24, 1964, Beadle Administration, Box 131, folder 11.

212. "Report of the Faculty Advisory Committee on Student Residences and Facilities," pp. 3–4, May 1965, Blum Papers, Box 16, folder 1.

213. Memorandum of transmission, Blum to Levi, June 1, 1965, Blum Papers, Box 16, folder 6.

214. See "The North Quadrangle," *University of Chicago Magazine,* November 1967, pp. 2–9. Barnes's final proposals met with some opposition from the student body, since they increased the number of double rooms substantially and reduced the number of suites.

215. *Maroon*, May 3, 1966, p. 1.

216. See the publicity materials in Beadle Administration, Box 383, folders 1–5.

217. Minutes of the College Council, March 18, 1969, p. 49. This was the public version of a decision to cut the size of the entering class that had, in fact, been made in the president's office and imposed on Booth (so Booth later insisted to me). The decision was discussed in the College's Executive Committee and the College Council, which voted 15–8 to support it.

218. "1972–73 University Budget," *University of Chicago Record*, October 31, 1972, p. 96.

219. "Report of the Advisory Committee on Student Enrollment," *University of Chicago Record*, May 28, 1974, p. 97.

220. For a good survey of the University's economy as a whole in the 1970s, see Kenneth W. Dam, "The University Budget, 1980–81," *University of Chicago Record*, December 31, 1980, pp. 220–21.

221. Earl Cheit suggested in his study of the "academic depression" of the early 1970s that the decline in alumni and other external giving had to do (in part) with negative reactions to the student disturbances, like the 1969 sit-in. Earl F. Cheit, *The New Depression in Higher Education: A Study of Financial Conditions at 41 Colleges and Universities* (New York, 1971), pp. 11, 19.

222. "Memorandum to the Faculty," July 31, 1970, p. 3, PP Addenda, 1997-006, Box 20.

223. See Earl F. Cheit and Theodore E. Lobman, *Foundations and Higher Education: Grant Making from Golden Years through Steady State; A Technical Report for the Ford Foundation and the Carnegie Council on Policy Studies in Higher Education* (Berkeley, 1979), pp. 4–7; and from a broader perspective, the insightful overview by Steven C. Wheatley, "The Partnerships of Foundations and Research Universities," in Helmut K. Anheier and David C. Hammack, eds., *American Foundations: Roles and Contributions* (Washington, DC, 2010), pp. 73–98. Ellen Condliffe Lagemann gives a good portrait of the currents of change in the Carnegie Corporation in the 1970s in *The Politics of Knowledge*, pp. 216–63. Between 1968 and 1978 the value of Carnegie's endowment portfolio (in 1987 dollars) declined by more than half, from $1.1 billion to $465 million.

224. "Ford Foundation: Grants to the University, 1950–1986," College Archive.

225. Earl F. Cheit and Harold Howe II, "The Situation of the Major Research Universities in the United States with Emphasis on the University of Chicago," September 15, 1973, Ford Foundation Archives; Harold Howe II and Earl F. Cheit to Edward H. Levi, November 6, 1973, College Archive.

226. "1971–72 University Budget," *University of Chicago Record*, October 11, 1971, p. 109.

227. "1972–73 University Budget," *University of Chicago Record*, October 31, 1972, p. 96.

228. "Preliminary General Budget, 1972–73, Notes," PP Addenda, 1997-006, Box 20.

229. *University of Chicago Bulletins*, January 7, 1974, pp. 1–2.

230. "Report of the Deans' Budget Committee for 1977–78," *University of Chicago Record*, March 16, 1977, p. 5.

231. *Chicago Tribune*, June 25, 1967, Section 1A, p. 1.

232. Franklin L. Ford, "Our Universities: National and Regional Roles," *Virginia Quarterly Review* 43 (1967): 229.

233. Levi Papers, Box 25, folder 4.

234. Riesman to Levi, January 2, 1981, Levi Papers, Box 34, folder 2.

235. "An Uncertain Future, " in David W. Breneman and Chester E. Finn, Jr., eds., *Public Policy and Private Higher Education* (Washington, DC, 1978), pp. 1–53.

236. Loss, *Between Citizens and the State*, p. 216.

237. Daniel P. Moynihan, "The Politics of Higher Education," *Daedalus* 104 (1975): 140–41.

Chapter Six

1. Jean Allard to Knox C. Hill, July 15, 1975; Roger H. Hildebrand to Knox C. Hill, June 16, 1975, Glen Lloyd Papers, Box 21.

2. See "Search Committee, July 21, 1975," Presidential Search Committee, Records, 1950–77, Box 2.

3. See Stenographic Minutes of the Meeting of November 3, 1975, Presidential Search Committee, Records, 1950–77, Box 2.

4. Minutes of the Council of the Senate, January 11, 1977, pp. 2–4.

5. Minutes of the Council of the Senate, March 15, 1977, pp. 13–14.

6. "Report of the Faculty Committee to Review the Decision with Regard to the Reappointment of Assistant Professor Marlene Dixon," Levi Administration, Box 151, folder 7.

7. "On Achieving Financial Equilibrium at the University of Chicago," July 6, 1979, College Archive.

8. See the reflections of Gerhard Casper about the modernization of the University's budget in the 1980s in his *The Cares of the University: Five-Year Report to the Board of Trustees and the Academic Council of Stanford University* (Stanford, CA, 1997), pp. 39–40.

9. Roger L. Geiger, *Knowledge and Money: Research Universities and the Paradox of the Marketplace* (Stanford, CA, 2004), pp. 34–42; Roger L. Geiger and Donald E. Heller, "Financial Trends in Higher Education: The United States" (working paper, January 2011, Penn State Center for the Study of Higher Education, University Park, PA), pp. 7–9; C. Ronald Kimberling, "Federal Student Aid: A History and Critical Analysis," in John W. Sommer, ed., *The Academy in Crisis: The Political Economy of Higher Education* (New Brunswick, NJ, 1995), pp. 74–75, calls the late 1970s the "era of loans," given that the volume of loans increased from $1.9 billion in 1978 to $7.8 billion in 1982.

10. In 1981–82 Chicago charged $6,000 for undergraduate tuition, whereas tuition at all of its peers was significantly higher: Princeton $7,250; Stanford $7,140; Yale $7,150; Harvard $6,930; Cornell $7,000; and Columbia $6,700. The most important incremental change occurred in February 1986, when tuition for entering first-year students was set at $11,350, significantly more than the increase for continuing students to $10,350.

11. For the national fiscal environment of higher education in the 1980s, particularly the development of the high-tuition / high-need-based-aid model that came fully into play in this decade and that encouraged private universities—relying on federally guaranteed loan funds and grants—to increase tuition levels dramatically over previous decades, see Geiger, *Knowledge and Money,* chap. 2; as well as Charles T. Clotfelter, *Buying the Best: Cost Escalation in Elite Higher Education* (Princeton, NJ, 1996), pp. 7–8, 13, 48, 69; and Ronald G. Ehrenberg, *Tuition Rising: Why College Costs So Much* (Cambridge, MA, 2000), pp. 74–84.

12. Clotfelter, *Buying the Best,* p. 5.

13. The graphs in Clotfelter, *Buying the Best*, pp. 3, 5, are helpful in understanding the scope of these trends.

14. See the comments in Norman M. Bradburn, "The University Budget, 1988–1989: A Report to the University Community," pp. 4–5, January 1989, College Archive.

15. Hanna H. Gray, "The State of the University, February 19, 1986," p. 3, supplement to *Chicago Chronicle*, February 27, 1986.

592 * NOTES TO PAGES 398-402

16. See Bradburn, "The University Budget, 1988–1989."

17. "Halls of Ivy Face Budget Squeeze," *Christian Science Monitor*, February 7, 1992; "Even in the Ivy League Cut Backs Are the Rule," *New York Times*, March 4, 1992; "Recession Takes Its Toll on US Financial Aid," *Chronicle of Higher Education*, June 10, 1992; "Recession Slows Endowment Growth at Colleges," ibid., April 15. 1992.

18. Minutes of the Council of the Senate, November 17, 1992, pp. 9–10.

19. Norman M. Bradburn, "Preliminary Report of the Committee on Enrollment," 1979, College Archive. In the fall quarter of 1939, for example, Chicago enrolled 2,816 undergraduates and 1,569 graduate students in the arts and sciences, and many of the latter were actually students in MA trajectories, not students in doctoral programs. The distribution of academic degrees confirms this trend: from 1931 to 1936 in the social sciences, the University annually awarded 256 BA degrees, 126 MA degrees, and 28 PhD degrees. Of the MAs, 63 percent were awarded by a single department—the Department of Education—and were likely awarded to school teachers or administrators in secondary schools, not individuals intent on scholarly careers. In 1933–34, in the arts and sciences as a whole, the University awarded 736 BAs, 248 MAs, and 145 PhDs. The only university leader who challenged the assumptions of the Bradburn report was the dean of the College at the time, Donald Levine, who pointed out in October 1983 that the University had more undergraduate than graduate students before World War II. Levine's observation, while empirically correct, was ignored. See Minutes of the College Council, October 25, 1983, p. 230.

20. Minutes of the Council of the Senate, January 13, 1981, pp. 4–7.

21. Minutes of the Faculty of the Division of the Social Sciences, November 12, 1979, p. 3.

22. This latter issue was a major preoccupation of a committee chaired by Barry D. Karl in 1982. See "Report of the Committee on the Organization of the College," October 20, 1982, College Archive.

23. Hanna H. Gray to the Divisional Faculties, October 2, 1982, College Archive.

24. "Robert Mc. Adams, "Change and Continuity in Faculty, Student Body, and Research Support: A Decade-Long Perspective," *Chicago Chronicle*, special supplement, May 10, 1984, pp. 2–8.

25. "A Report on the Size and Composition of the University of Chicago," *University of Chicago Record,* April 10, 1986, pp. 7–18. The costs of implementing the report were analyzed in detail by John A. Y. Andrews, "Costs of Undergraduate Enrollment Growth," Office of Financial Planning and Budget, June 1, 1987, College Archive. Andrews found student housing and faculty instructional resources in the social sciences to be the primary pressure points.

26. Minutes of the College Council, February 11, 1986, p. 280; March 4, 1986, p. 288.

27. Minutes of the Council of the Senate, February 18, 1986, p. 106.

28. Minutes of the College Council, October 25, 1966, p. 1.

29. For the collapse of general education after 1970, see Roger L. Geiger, "Demography and Curriculum: The Humanities in American Higher Education from

the 1950s through the 1980s," pp. 65–66; and John Guillory, "Who's Afraid of Marcel Proust? The Failure of General Education in the American University," pp. 38–45, both in David A. Hollinger, ed., *The Humanities and the Dynamic of Inclusion since World War II* (Baltimore, 2006).

30. For the logic of such a common curriculum, see the reports in "Project 1984: Design Issues; Reports of the Task Forces," November 1984, College Archive.

31. Teaching loads for the College faculty ran as high as nine courses a year. See Ginsburg to Simpson, December 3, 1963, College Archive; as well as Jonathan Z. Smith, "Dean's Report to the Faculty of the College," November 25, 1980, ibid. For national trends, see Clotfelter, *Buying the Best*, p. 204; and Massy and Zemsky, "Faculty Discretionary Time."

32. Minutes of the College Faculty, February 4, 1975, p. 205. Ten years later Core chairs like Bert Cohler complained about "a decline in the participation of the faculty in undergraduate instruction, particularly in the common year." Bertram Cohler to George Walsh, March 6, 1986, College Archive.

33. Bernard S. Silberman to the Social Sciences Collegiate Division Governing Committee, May 18, 1979, College Archive.

34. Minutes of the College Council, October 30, 1984, p. 19.

35. Typical responses included the following: "The U of C should concentrate on eradicating the 'bookworm intellectual' reputation which it seems to have earned. The lack of 'social life,' though a misconception, tends to scare prospectives off"; "U of C should be geared more towards undergraduates not graduates"; "The student body seems to be very dry and unstimulating"; "I found the dorms to be dingy, small, run down, and unpleasant to live in"; "The dormitories of the U of C are a depressing place to live"; and "The dorms and some of the buildings looked old and worn and not cared for. The interiors reflected this."

36. For the founding of the University Theater, see John W. Boyer, *"A Noble and Symmetrical Conception of Life": The Arts at Chicago on the Edge of a New Century* (Chicago, 2009), pp. 99–101.

37. "Annual Report of the Standing Committee on Admission and Enrollment," 1983–84, Minutes of the College Council, October 30, 1984, pp. 5–6.

38. In these years the College used a two-part application procedure, the first being the applicant's preliminary notice that she or he intended to apply, the second being the full application with the necessary fee. My comments refer only to Part II data, since this was the component necessary for an admissions decision.

39. In June 1989 the board of trustees considered a north campus plan developed by the architectural firm Hammond Beeby and Babka. It called for the construction of a new neo-Gothic natatorium and gymnasium at Fifty-Fifth Street and Ellis Avenue and the renovation of Bartlett Gymnasium as a Campus Center, as well as the creation of other new public spaces. The estimated cost was $39–$46 million. Given the fiscal situation of the University at the time, the plan was bound to remain in the conceptual stage.

40. "University Weighs Options to Shrink Growing Deficit," *Chicago Journal*, December, 1994; and "Letter to the University Community from President Sonnen-

schein, 15 November 1994," *University of Chicago Chronicle*, November 28, 1994. See also the special report by Mary Ruth Yoe, "Chicago's Long-Term Fiscal Forecast," *University of Chicago Magazine*, June 1994, in which Stone and Furnstahl explained the deficit in great detail.

41. "Undergraduate Net Tuition Compared to Arts & Sciences Faculty Salary Base," in "The Economy of Private Research Universities," 1996, p. 10, College Archive. This report was generated in 1995 but reflected trends that were already apparent by the late 1980s.

42. "Historical Review of the Economy of the University," August 21, 1996, pp. 5, 21, College Archive.

43. For example, the Cambridge Associates' analyses of the University's budgetary situation in 1979 and 1985 contained important comparative data on peer institutions. Comparative information on Chicago's student aid and faculty size was regularly provided to the board of trustees during the Gray administration, particularly in the later 1980s.

44. "Task Forces to Assess Issues of Student Life, Education," *University of Chicago Chronicle*, September 29, 1994.

45. See "Combined Report: Task Force on Undergraduate Education, Task Force on Graduate Education," *University of Chicago Record*, March 14, 1996, esp. p. 3.

46. The letter was previewed and shared with the Council of the Senate earlier in the month. See Minutes of the Council of the Senate, April 16, 1996, pp. 5–7.

47. "Discussion with Historians" in "Faculty Committee for a Year of Reflection," September 11, 1996," College Archive. The third historian was Daniel Meyer.

48. See "Faculty Committee for a Year of Reflection: Report of the Committee to the Council of the Senate," January 1998, College Archive.

49. See Harold Swift's recollections about Burton in "Eighth Session," p. 54, Kimpton Administration, Box 252, folder 1. See also Meyer, "The Chicago Faculty," pp. 449–50.

50. Minutes of the Council of the Senate, November 13, 1990, p. 6.

51. Memo of Bill Brown and Miriam Hansen to John W. Boyer, August, 1996, College Archive.

52. Minutes of the Council of the Senate, March 3, 1998, pp. 2–8.

53. The episode is described in the Minutes of the Council of the Senate, January 26, 1999, pp. 5–8.

54. Ethan Bronner, "Winds of Academic Change Rustle University of Chicago," *New York Times*, December 28, 1998, pp. 1, 24.

55. Stephen H. Balch and Glenn Ricketts, "The University of Chicago's Shrinking Core," *Wall Street Journal*, June 3, 1999, p. A26. The authors' argument that the new changes were part of a longer pattern of "dumbing down and politicization" at Chicago between 1989 and 1999 during which "the proportion of courses on classic authors, major genres and broad periods declined to a mere 25%, while those on literary theory and the race, 'gender' and class trinity rose to 40%" put them squarely in the so-called culture wars disputes that had erupted with such ferocity in the 1980s.

56. Elizabeth Helsinger and Kathleen Neils Conzen to the Editors of the *Wall Street Journal*, June 8, 1999, College Archive; Letter of Scholars for the University of Chicago, c/o the American Council of Trustees and Alumni, to the University Trustees, April 14, 1999, College Archive.

57. Stone to the University faculty, February 16, 1999, College Archive.

58. The monograph generated a range of responses, both harshly negative and warmly positive toward the author and his arguments. One critic insisted, "By moving the College in the direction of a more conventional curriculum, you are moving away from a unique theory of education that is unequaled in this country and into a competitive arena where geography, scenery, sports, social activities, and, maybe, the quality of education drives applicants' decisions." Another concerned alum stated, "You are abandoning the only competitive advantages that the College possesses, while necessarily doing nothing to address its (serious) weaknesses, which are extrinsic and (mostly) beyond your control (i.e., its location and certain annoying and perennial defects in the culture)." Yet a third asserted, "It is not smart merchandising to make your product like everyone else's, especially when the wrapper—in your case, the South Side—can never compete on the level of superficial appearances. You should rather be contemplating differentiating your product by restoring more of Hutchins's rigor to the College." Letters to John W. Boyer, College Archive. Ironically, the book garnered positive reactions from two veterans of the Hutchins era. "A Chicago alumna ... loaned me your three October talks to the College faculty," Champ Ward wrote. "I found them most encouraging, not only in what they say so well about recent and continuing programs, but in what you now foresee as routes to further improvements.... You have renewed my belief that the University of Chicago is an incurably interesting institution." William H. McNeill commented, "The old fire still burns on the Midway, I gather, from your exhortation and reminders.... I wanted to say that I recognize in your words the authentic Chicago voice and concern for the best possible general education, and it stirs me to the core. For that vision of the college was what made me what I am long ago in the 1930s, and it is profoundly cheering to see that it still glows." F. Champion Ward to John W. Boyer, April 5, 1999; William H. McNeill to John W. Boyer, March 6, 1999, College Archive.

59. This is not to say that the senior members of the central administration lacked strong views on the Core. But in the end those views held no more credence or weight than any others.

60. David L. Kirp, "Hurricane Hugo: Following the Stormy Departure of Its President, the University of Chicago Reconsiders His Legacy," *Lingua Franca* 11 (2001): 40–49.

61. The phrase came from an anonymous faculty member's attempt to work through both the advantages and the dangers of the expansion of the College in a broadside memo, entitled "Should the College Be Expanded?," circulated in 1999.

62. "New Aggressiveness at Chicago," *Chronicle of Higher Education*, October 19, 1994, p. 51.

63. See Stone to the Deans, February 16, 1994, College Archive.

64. Roger Geiger has argued that since the 1980s the leading American private universities have been engaged in a process of "privatization" in that they have with often brilliant success found ways to deploy financial resources from the private sector and civil society to enhance their operations, in place of the sources of federal support that were "exhausted" by the later 1970s and early 1980s. See Geiger, "Postmortem for the Current Era: Change in American Higher Education, 1980–2010" (Working Paper No. 3, Penn State Center for the Study of Higher Education, University Park, PA, July 2010), pp. 3–6. While I agree with Geiger's argument, I prefer the term "re-privatization," because I believe that the secular changes occurring after 2000 will force many universities to take much more seriously the service- and teaching-oriented roles that they naturally played before 1945.

65. Geiger, "Postmortem for the Current Era," pp. 4–10.

66. For recent commentaries on the decline of public funding, see the essays in "The Big Picture: Assessing the Future of Higher Education," special issue, *Carnegie Reporter*, Winter 2014.

67. Geiger, "Postmortem for the Current Era," p. 7.

68. Jeffrey S. Slovak, "On Attrition Risk: Some Analyses from the College Quality of Life Survey of Spring, 1995," December 1997, pp. 10–11, College Archive.

69. Minutes of the Council of the Senate, February 23, 1999, p. 10.

70. "Report of the Task Force on the Quality of the Student Experience," *University of Chicago Record*, May 23, 1996, pp. 2–7.

71. See Reeves, Miller, and Russell, *Trends in University Growth*, p. 70.

72. Even so, university leaders realized that the financial advantage still lay with recruiting more undergraduates. Pat Harrison, Kimpton's vice president for academic affairs, estimated that the University recovered about 50 percent of the cost of educating undergraduates from tuition but only 20 percent of the cost of educating graduate students from their tuition. See "Conversation with Pat Harrison," February 10, 1958, Berelson Papers, Box 1, folder 9.

73. Berelson, *Graduate Education in the United States*, pp. 98–101; Patricia J. Gumport, "Graduate Education and Research: Interdependence and Strain," in Altbach, Berdahl, and Gumport, *American Higher Education in the Twenty-First Century*, pp. 437–41; as well as Geiger, *Research and Relevant Knowledge*, pp. 217–29.

74. Gumport, "Graduate Education and Research," p. 440.

75. "Report of the Commission on Graduate Education," *University of Chicago Record*, May 3, 1982, p. 82.

76. In 2004 Chicago had 1,248 students in the humanities and 1,528 in the social sciences, compared with 1,036/975 at Berkeley, 1,063/770 at Columbia, 836/1,391 at Harvard, 558/534 at Stanford, and 651/606 at Yale. "Dwarf Institutions Enrollments," Fall 2004, College Archive.

77. Bradburn report, p. 18.

78. "Report of the Commission on Graduate Education," p. 132.

79. The experience of the history department was probably typical: a report from 1973 predicted that "given the termination of the Ford program, the narrowing of the University's resources, and the expected cuts in Government spending for higher

education, the Department will probably see its aid budget reduced by 50% the year after next." "Appendix C: Student Withdrawals and Financial Aid," in Karl M. Morrison, "Report on the State of the Department of History as of January 27, 1973," Department of History, Records.

80. "Meeting of Social Science Divisional Representatives Re: Baker Commission Report," May 9, 1983, College Archive.

81. Geiger, *Research and Relevant Knowledge*, pp. 227–28.

82. "Report of the Committee on the Undergraduate Program," 1978, p. 2, College Archive.

83. See Barry D. Karl, "Preliminary Report of the Undergraduate Committee," April 2, 1976, p. 4, College Archive. In the six years between 1967–68 and 1972–73 the Department of History had matriculated an average of 63 new doctoral students each year, with an acceptance rate of 60 percent, based on an annual application pool of 422 and an average of positive admissions decisions of 257.

84. John T. Wilson, "Remarks on the College," *University of Chicago Record*, March 17, 1998, p. 40.

85. Minutes of the College Council, October 30, 1984, p. 14.

86. "Departmental Response to the Report of the [Baker] Commission on Graduate Education," November 1, 1982, Department of Anthropology, Records, Box 60, folders 2, 7.

87. "Report of the Commission on Graduate Education," pp. 122, 149, 157.

88. The details are in the Minutes of the Council of the Senate, February 7, 1984, pp. 4–5.

89. Minutes of the Council of the Senate, April 10, 1984, pp. 2–5.

90. Ross B. Emmett, "Sharpening Tools in the Workshop: The Workshop System and the Chicago School's Success," in Robert Van Horn, Philip Mirowski, and Thomas A. Stapleford, eds., *Building Chicago Economics: New Perspectives on the History of America's Most Powerful Economics Program* (Cambridge, 2011) pp. 93–115; Emmett, "Entrenching Disciplinary Competence: The Role of General Education and Graduate Study in Chicago Economics," pp. 134–50.

91. I served as chair of the Council on Advanced Studies for twenty-one years (1986–2009) and observed the transformation of the workshops from simple dissertation-support conventicles to a broader mission of preparing students to give effective job talks, to sharpen conference presentation skills, and to receive feedback on drafts of manuscripts that were to be submitted to scholarly journals.

92. "Report of the Commission on Graduate Education," pp. 89–90.

93. J. Mark Hansen, "Employment Placement for New Doctoral Degree Recipients from the University of Chicago," April 9, 2001, pp. 1, 8, College Archive.

94. I am very grateful to Martina C. Munsters, dean of students in the Division of the Humanities, for providing me with these statistical data.

95. "Report of the Commission on Graduate Education," pp. 115, 117.

96. Humanities yielded 32 percent and social sciences 42 percent in 2006.

97. "University Commits $50 Million over Six Years in Graduate Aid," *University of Chicago Chronicle*, February 15, 2007. The Division of the Humanities had already

begun to move in the direction of fully funded fellowships as early as 2006, paving the way for the new graduate initiative.

98. "Talk with David Riesman," January 31, 1958, Berelson Papers, Box 1, folder 9.

99. Committee on Social Thought to William H. Kruskal, January 21, 1983, College Archive.

100. Hansen, "Employment Placement for New Doctoral Degree Recipients," p. 8.

101. Louis Menand, "How to Make a Ph.D. Matter," *New York Times Magazine*, September 22, 1996, pp. 78–81.

102. Roderick M. Chisholm to Bernard Berelson, May 19, 1958, p. 9, Berelson Papers, Box 1, folder 2.

103. For the early schools, see Storr, *Harper's University*, pp. 134–46, 285–306.

104. Gates, *Chapters in My Life,* pp. 179, 279–80; Ernest E. Irons, *The Story of Rush Medical College* (Chicago, 1953), pp. 32–38.

105. In 1929–30 the Business School awarded only 16 advanced degrees, while the School of Social Service Administration granted 23 MA and PhD degrees, at a time when the arts and sciences departments awarded 526 graduate degrees (the Law School did significantly better, awarding 120 degrees). Between 1919 and 1930 the number of advanced degrees awarded by the arts and sciences departments increased by 72 percent (from 1,711 between 1918 and 1924 to 2,940 between 1925 and 1930), whereas those awarded by the professional schools grew by only 45 percent (324 to 469). Faculty size of these units remained modest: the Law School had, for example, 10 full-time faculty in 1929, SSA had 12, the Divinity School 15, and the School of Business 25, at a time when the total arts and sciences faculty numbered 383. Reeves, Miller, and Russell, *Trends in University Growth*, pp. 11–12, 81, 101, 118.

106. Bradburn report, p. 19. Two of the early schools would not survive: the Graduate School of Education merged with the Department of Education in June 1975, and the Graduate Library School ceased admitting students in January 1989.

107. For the origins of professional education within the American universities, see Andrew Abbott, *The System of the Professions: An Essay on the Division of Expert Labor* (Chicago, 1988), pp. 205–11.

108. *The President's Report: Administration*, p. lxxxiii.

109. For the school's early history, see Frank L. Ellsworth, *Law on the Midway: The Founding of the University of Chicago Law School* (Chicago, 1977); and Bernard D. Meltzer, "The University of Chicago Law School: Ruminations and Reminiscences," *University of Chicago Law Review* 70 (2003): 233–57.

110. Howard W. Mort, "Analysis of Law School Alumni," Kimpton Administration, Box 159, folder 8. Only alumni for whom the alumni office had good addresses were included in this count.

111. Reeves and Russell, *Admission and Retention of University Students*, pp. 264–69.

112. Harry A. Bigelow, "New Law School Curriculum," *University of Chicago Magazine*, March 1937, pp. 5–6, 22; Wilbur G. Katz, "A Four-Year Program for Legal Education," *University of Chicago Law Review* 4 (1937): 527–36. Katz was particu-

larly concerned that as the federal regulatory state expanded under the New Deal, lawyers would be forced to understand accounting and financial economics as a matter of course, and that the Law School had a responsibility to prepare them in these domains.

113. For the history of this course, see Dennis J. Hutchinson, "Elements of the Law," *University of Chicago Law Review* 70 (2003): 141–58.

114. Edward H. Levi, "Report to the Curriculum Committee," undated [most likely March 1941], Law School, Records, Box 8. In 1977 Levi would recall that the new plan "helped to spawn most of the developments in legal education since that date.... It was that new plan which expanded the horizons of the School to include such radical subjects as economics and accounting. But it did not stop there. It included sociology, criminology, and comparative law. It thought legal history was important. It introduced the tutorial system, which when another law school adopted it, was considered invented. It emphasized jurisprudence and ethics.... As with all new plans, it was later modified, but rather more in its structural elements, I think, than in its goals." "Reminiscences," *University of Chicago Law Alumni Journal* 3 (1977): 26.

115. Katz, "A Four-Year Program," p. 530.

116. Harry Kalven, "Law School Training in Research and Exposition: The University of Chicago Program," *Journal of Legal Education* 1 (1948): 107–23.

117. Hutchinson, "Edward Levi: Legal Scholar," p. 6. I am grateful to Dennis Hutchinson for many of the insights contained in the following paragraphs.

118. See R. W. Harrison to Levi, January 14, 1959, Kimpton Administration, Box 159, folder 3.

119. Franklin E. Zimring, "The American Jury Project and the Chicago Law School" (Fulton Lectures 2003); George W. Liebmann, *The Common Law Tradition: A Collective Portrait of Five Legal Scholars* (New Brunswick, NJ, 2006), pp. 79–148; Schlegel, *American Legal Realism and Empirical Social Science*, pp. 238–44. Kurland was hired in 1953 as an associate professor, his salary covered by the Ford fund for the Law and Behavioral Science Program.

120. In 1947 Director was listed on the Law School's budget as an untenured research associate (professor) at a salary of $7,111, eight-ninths of which was paid by the Volker Fund. In August 1948 the Law School changed his title to professor of economics in the Law School. Director was finally approved for tenure in 1953. For the role of the Volker Fund, see now Rob van Horn and Philip Mirowski, "The Rise of the Chicago School of Economics and the Birth of Neoliberalism," in Philip Mirowski and Dieter Plehwe, eds., *The Road from Mont Pèlerin: The Making of the Neoliberal Thought Collective* (Cambridge, MA, 2009), pp. 151–56; and Steven G. Medema, "Wandering the Road from Pluralism to Posner: The Transformation of Law and Economics in the Twentieth Century," in Alain Marciano, *Law and Economics: A Reader* (New York, 2009), pp. 20–25. More generally, see Robin I. Mordfin and Marsha Ferziger Nagorsky, "Chicago and Law and Economics: A History," *University of Chicago Law School Record,* Fall 2011.

121. See Steven G. Medema, "Chicago Price Theory and Chicago Law and Eco-

nomics: A Tale of Two Transitions," in Van Horn et al., *Building Chicago Economics*, pp. 163–74, who does a good job exploring the theoretical differences among Chicago economists relating to law and economics; and Edmund W. Kitch, "The Fire of Truth: A Remembrance of Law and Economics at Chicago, 1932–1970," *Journal of Law and Economics* 26 (1983): 163–234.

122. Robin I. Mordfin, "Workshopping for Success," *University of Chicago Law School Record*, Spring 2014, pp. 46–51.

123. "The Foreign Law Program," Max Rheinstein Papers, Box 48, folder 7.

124. See Edward H. Levi, "The Political, the Professional, the Prudent in Legal Education," *Journal of Legal Education* 11 (1958): 459.

125. In 1955, out of a total alumni population of approximately 3,300, the Law School had 119 alumni in professorial teaching or research positions. See the memo of August 3, 1955, Rheinstein Papers, Box 49, folder 1; as well as Donna Fossum, "Law Professors: A Profile of the Teaching Branch of the Legal Profession," *American Bar Foundation Research Journal* 5 (1980): 508.

126. "Its standards would be those of an educational power house, and not those of an educational cafeteria." Leon C. Marshall, "A University School of Business," in Marshall, ed., *The Collegiate School of Business: Its Status at the Close of the First Quarter of the Twentieth Century* (Chicago, 1928), pp. 190–91.

127. See Thomas W. Goodspeed, "Eli Buell Williams and Hobart W. Williams," in *University of Chicago Biographical Sketches*, vol. 1, pp. 279–87.

128. Roy H. Turner, "A History of the School of Business of the University of Chicago: J. Laurence Laughlin and the Early Years" (Chicago, 1958), p. 57.

129. See Roy H. Turner, "A History of the School of Business of the University of Chicago: Report on Some Aspects of the Period 1920–1940" (Chicago, 1958), pp. 23–28.

130. "A Report on the School of Business at the University of Chicago," January 31, 1957, p. 7, Kimpton Administration, Box 59, folder 3.

131. Quoted in Johan Van Overtveldt, *The Chicago School: How the University of Chicago Assembled the Thinkers Who Revolutionized Economics and Business* (Chicago, 2007), p. 249.

132. Robert A. Gordon and James E. Howell, *Higher Education for Business* (New York, 1959); and Steven L. Schlossman, Michael W. Sedlak, and Harold S. Wechsler, *The "New Look": The Ford Foundation and the Revolution in Business Education, Graduate Management Admission Council* (Los Angeles, 1987). For a good recent survey of Ford's impact, see Rakesh Khurana, *From Higher Aims to Hired Hands: The Social Transformation of American Business Schools and the Unfulfilled Promise of Management as a Profession* (Princeton, NJ, 2007), pp. 233–88.

133. Wallis combined interests in psychology (in which he had majored at the University of Minnesota) with graduate training in mathematical economics and statistics at Chicago and Columbia in the 1930s. While at Chicago he became friends with fellow graduate students Milton Friedman and George Stigler and served with them from 1942 to 1945 in the wartime Statistical Research Group organized as part of the US Office of Scientific Research and Development. Wallis returned to Chicago

in the fall of 1946 as a professor of statistics in the Business School. In 1949 he was instrumental in negotiating the creation of the Committee on Statistics, which was later renamed the Department of Statistics at Chicago in 1957. See Ingram Olkin, "A Conversation with W. Allen Wallis," *Statistical Science* 6 (1991): 121–40; Stephen M. Stigler, "University of Chicago Department of Statistics," in A. Agresti and X.-L. Meng, eds., *Strength in Numbers: The Rising of Academic Statistics Departments in the U.S.* (New York, 2013), pp. 339–51.

134. James H. Lorie, "The School of Business 1957–1966," October 11, 1956. This report was prepared for a conference of the trustees at Lakeside, Michigan.

135. Arnold Harberger, Daniel Boorstin, David Riesman, and Howard Hunt were also members.

136. For the details, see Edward Nik-Khah, "George Stigler, the Graduate School of Business, and the Pillars of the Chicago School," in Van Horn et al., *Building Chicago Economics*, pp. 116–50.

137. Khurana, *From Higher Aims*, p. 274.

138. Marion Fourcade and Rakesh Khurana, "From Social Control to Financial Economics: The Linked Ecologies of Economics and Business in Twentieth-Century America," *Theory and Society* 42 (2013): 136 n. 17, as well as 145–50, 154. By the early 1990s Anne O. Krueger, "Report of the Commission on Graduate Education in Economics," *Journal of Economic Literature* 29 (1991): 1039, reported that "business schools have been a major source of demand for PhD economists within academia." For the professional background, see Marion Fourcade, *Economists and Societies: Discipline and Profession in the United States, Britain, and France, 1890s to 1990s* (Princeton, NJ, 2009).

139. In the 1970s its profile in the behavioral sciences also grew stronger, exemplified by the work of Hillel Einhorn, Robin M. Hogarth, and Joshua Klayman, and the creation of the Center for Decision Research in 1977. See Robin M. Hogarth, ed., *Insights in Decision Making: A Tribute to Hillel J. Einhorn* (Chicago, 1990), p. xiii. In October 1985 the GSB hosted a major national conference on the behavioral foundations of economic theory that, aside from its substantive contributions, signaled the impact that psychology would play in the future intellectual and curricular trajectory of the Business School. See Robin M. Hogarth and Melvin W. Reder, "Prefatory Note," *Journal of Business* 59 (1986): S181–S183.

140. Beadle Administration, Box 67, folder 2.

141. See "A Program for Teachers of Economics, August 1961: Recent Developments in Applied Economics," Beadle Administration, Box 67, folder 2.

142. See Richard N. Rossett to Philip W. K. Sweet, February 8, 1977, Office of the President, Wilson Administration, Records, Box 66, folder 7.

143. *Los Angeles Times*, December 9, 1974, p. 3; *Chicago Tribune*, November 21, 1977, p. E10.

144. *Chicago Daily News*, October 13, 1976, p. 54.

145. "Graduate Ratings," September 1976, Wilson Administration, Box 66, folder 8.

146. *BusinessWeek*, November 28, 1988, pp. 78–79.

147. Francis Fullam, "Initial Analysis of Responses to Open-Ended Questions on MBA Student Survey," February 13, 1989, Merton Miller Papers, Box 80, folder 6.

148. Steven Hoch and Mark Zmjiewski, "Campus and 190 Del Questionnaire Summary," February 13, 1989, Merton Miller Papers, Box 80, folder 6.

149. *New York Times*, November 16, 1958, sec. 3, p. 1.

150. John E. Jeuck, "Curriculum Committee 'Discussion Draft Report'," pp. 14–17, August 28, 1970, College Archive.

151. See "Report of the Council on the Graduate School of Business," enclosed with Irving B. Harris to John T. Wilson, July 21, 1976, Wilson Administration, Box 66, folder 9.

152. "Senior Management Survey (December 1986)." This was based on a survey of 150 executives conducted by Elrick and Lavidge, Inc. A parallel survey of business journalists by Martin E. Janis and Company in the fall of 1986 found that the GSB had a high reputation for academic excellence, but was near the bottom in the ability of its students to combine "theory and practice." See "University of Chicago Graduate School of Business Editorial Audit," November 1986. I am grateful to Harry Davis for providing me with a copy of these documents.

153. "Three Constituencies and Their Key Attributes" (position paper prepared by Gould and Davis, 1987, for presentation to the faculty committee on the deanship). Thanks to Harry Davis for this document as well.

154. For the details, see *Chicago Business*, May 30, 1989, pp. 1–3.

155. A copy of the report, dated May 17, 1989, is filed in the *Merton Miller Papers*, Box 80, folder 6; here pp. 8–9.

156. "Professor French Discusses His Eponymous Report," *Chicago Business*, May 30, 1989, p. 3.

157. "Bringing the Real World to the GSB," *Chicago Booth Magazine*, Winter 2004, p. 24.

158. The organization of the program is described in detail in Jeffrey Anderson and Stacey R. Kole, "Leadership Effectiveness and Development: Building Self-Awareness and Insight Skills," in Scott Snook, Nitin Nohria, and Rakesh Khurana, *The Handbook for Teaching Leadership: Knowing, Doing, and Being* (Thousand Oaks, CA, 2012), pp. 181–96.

159. Harry L. Davis and Robin M. Hogarth, "Rethinking Management Education: A View from Chicago," in *Selected Papers Series, Booth School of Business* (Chicago, 2013), p. 12.

160. *The Dean's Report, 1989, Graduate School of Business* (Chicago, 1989), p. 2.

161. For a balanced view of the controversy, which stirred up much rhetorical dust, see Edward Nik-Khah, "Chicago Neoliberalism and the Genesis of the Milton Friedman Institute (2006–2009)," in Van Horn et al., *Building Chicago Economics*, pp. 368–88. In 1924 Leon Marshall, who by this time was chair of the Department of Economics, and W. H. Spencer, who had succeeded Marshall as dean of the Business School, proposed to President Burton that the two units be united in a new School of Economics and Business Administration. The idea gained some ground for a few years, and a provisional directorate was created to link the two units, but

the scheme eventually collapsed by 1929. See Turner, "A Brief Summary of Certain Elements in the Early History of the Business School of the University of Chicago" (Chicago, 1958), pp. 8–9.

162. In 1971 the school retained 83 percent of its tuition revenue for operating purposes, transferring 17 percent to the central university, but by 1977 the percentage that the GSB was allowed to retain had declined to 57 percent, reflecting the acute financial pressures the central administration found itself facing. The importance of the College and the Business School to the wider economy of the University is apparent in the fact that as of 2014 the College generated 38.2 percent and the Business School 38.3 percent of the University's $378 million in annual net tuition revenue.

163. "By the early 1970s the University stepped back from its overriding concern for community issues. During urban renewal the chancellors and other senior officers of the University spent an extraordinary amount of time and university resources on community issues. With the end of that era, the University reduced its emphasis on community development." Henry S. Webber, "The University of Chicago and Its Neighbors: A Case Study in Community Development," in David C. Perry and Wim Wiewel, eds., *The University as Urban Developer: Case Studies and Analysis* (Armonk, NY, 2005), pp. 73–74. The University did decide to buy the Windermere and Shoreland hotels for slightly less than $2 million to preserve the properties and prevent further deterioration of the housing market in East Hyde Park. See "Neighborhood Committee," report of May 29, 1975, Wilson Administration, Box 104, folder 9. By 1975 Jonathan Kleinbard reported that "the increased level of activities since October 1973, including the purchase of the Windermere and Shoreland Hotels, has allayed the intensity of concerns in East Hyde Park, and people do not appear to be 'running' from the community." Kleinbard to Wilson, May 27, 1975, ibid.

164. "Colleges Open New Doors for the Minority Student," *Chicago Tribune*, February 19, 1989, sec. 2, p. 3.

165. "New Homes on the Horizon," *Hyde Park Herald*, December 29, 1993, pp. 3, 14; "Crossroads for Renewal: How Oakland, N. Kenwood Turn the Corner," *Crain's Chicago Business,* October 7, 1996. For the background, see Mary E. Pattillo, *Black on the Block: The Politics of Race and Class in the City* (Chicago, 2007) pp. 237–40.

166. "Woodlawn Begins New Housing Program," *Hyde Park Herald*, May 4, 1994, p. 3. The Woodlawn Preservation and Investment Corporation, founded in 1987 by Bishop Arthur M. Brazier, played a key role in these developments. For Brazier's later reflections on these events, see his 2008 lecture, "A Community Cannot Develop Itself Unless It's Organized" (LISC Institute for Comprehensive Community Development, October 24, 2011).

167. See, for example, Kleinbard to Paul Petrie, February 26, 1976; December 2, 1976, Wilson Administration, Box 105, folder 2.

168. Kleinbard to John T. Wilson, January 31, 1978, Wilson Administration, Box 105, folder 1.

169. See, for example, Robert McClory, "The Plot to Destroy North Kenwood," *Chicago Reader*, October 14, 1993.

170. "A Proposal to Establish a Center for School Improvement: A Collaboration between the Department of Education, University of Chicago, Department of Research and Evaluation, Chicago Public Schools, and National College of Education," June 14, 1989; and "A Two-Year Proposal to the Chicago Community Trust to Support the Center for School Improvement," October, 1992, provided to the author by Tony Bryk.

171. See Anthony S. Bryk and Penny B. Sebring, "Informing Reform: The Work of the Consortium on Chicago School Research," August, 2000, College Archive; as well as Anthony S. Bryk, Penny B. Sebring, David Kerbow, Sharon Rollow, and John Q. Easton, *Charting Chicago School Reform: Democratic Localism as a Lever for Change* (Boulder, CO, 1998); Penny B. Sebring and Anthony S. Bryk, "School Leadership and the Bottom Line in Chicago" (Consortium on Chicago School Research, February 2000); and Melissa Roderick, John Q. Easton, and Penny B. Sebring, *The Consortium on Chicago School Research: A New Model for the Role of Research in Supporting Urban School Reform* (Chicago, 2009).

172. The center was also interested in larger structural issues involving fostering teacher professionalism and the improvement of operations of local schools as well, with the ultimate goal of having school leaders and teachers create stronger partnerships between home, family, and school and "foster conditions for a more humane social life." "A Proposal to Establish a Center for School Improvement: A Collaboration between the Department of Education, University of Chicago, Department of Research and Evaluation, Chicago Public Schools, and National College of Education," p. 10, College Archive.

173. Bryk and Sebring, "Informing Reform," p. 52.

174. Anthony S. Bryk, Penny B. Sebring, Elaine Allensworth, Stuart Luppescu, and John Q. Easton, *Organizing Schools for Improvement: Lessons from Chicago* (Chicago, 2010).

175. Anthony S. Bryk and Barbara Schneider, "Social Trust: A Moral Resource for School Improvement" (University of Chicago Center for School Improvement, June 1996).

176. See the "Proposal for Center for School Improvement / North Kenwood Charter School, October 6, 1997," p. 28, provided to the author by Tony Bryk. The school started with pupils in pre-kindergarten, kindergarten, and the first and fifth grades, eventually expanding into a K–8 primary school.

177. "Proposal for Center for School Improvement / North Kenwood Charter School, October 6, 1997," p. 3.

178. The staff of the center "decided that in order to move our work in the direction that we hoped it would go, we needed our own school. The kind of literacy instruction that we were training people to do and that we were advocating was running up against all the bureaucratic obstacles that you would expect in a large city system." Marvin Hoffman, "In Pursuit of Hellhounds," interview conducted by the North Dakota Study Group, October 2006, pp. 53–54, College Archive.

179. See Pattillo, *Black on the Block*, pp. 156–58, 174–75.

180. Communication from Anthony S. Bryk to the author, November 11, 2013.

181. The early success of the school is documented in its second five-year renewal application. Marvin Hoffman and Michael T. Johnson, "Charter Renewal Application, 2002–2003," December 16, 2002, pp. 17–26, College Archive. By 2002 the school enrolled 333 students, 75 percent of whom were low income, 38 percent lived in North Kenwood–Oakland, and 100 percent were African American. Ibid., p. 43. Hoffman has since written a candid and moving account of his first years as director of the school, including frank discussions of the latent (and occasionally manifest) racial tensions that were in the background of an operation in which a white director and many white teachers were working in a school filled with African American children. See Lisa Arrastía and Marvin Hoffman, *Starting Up: Critical Lessons from 10 New Schools* (New York, 2012), pp. 12–30.

182. The Donoghue Campus at 707 East Thirty-Seventh Street opened in September 2005, the Woodlawn High School at 6420 South University Avenue in September 2006, and the Woodson Middle School at 4414 South Evans Avenue in September 2008.

183. Unlike traditional teacher training programs, UTEP provided students with hands-on training in the University's charter schools while they were still pursuing course work toward their degrees. The two-year program encompassed the senior year of college, additional postgraduate study, and requisite field training as interns in two Chicago public schools, at the end of which students received an MAT from the Graham School and K–9 or 9–12 certification from the state of Illinois.

184. The UEI began in 2005 as the Urban Education Initiative. See "The University of Chicago: Urban Education Initiative," May 28, 2005, College Archive. The title was changed to Urban Education Institute in June 2008, with a more centralized administrative structure created at that time. In 2004 Bryk left Chicago for a professorship at Stanford. In 2008 he was elected president of the Carnegie Foundation for the Advancement of Teaching.

185. To much consternation in the national education community, the University had abolished its Department of Education in 1997, effective 2001, after a series of negative internal and external evaluations. In the end, the collapse of the department, although painful to those concerned, opened the way for more imaginative approaches to understanding and resolving critical issues in public education policy and practice.

186. Communication from Anthony S. Bryk to the author, November 11, 2013.

187. *Chicago Tribune*, October 16, 2001, p. 5. Police coverage was also extended to North Kenwood–Oakland in 2003. For the background, see Webber, "The University of Chicago and Its Neighbors," pp. 65–79; Webber, "Building Effective City-University Partnerships: Lessons from the Heartland" (Boston Area Research Initiative, Policy Briefs, April 2012); and Henry S. Webber and Mikael Karlström, *Why Community Investment Is Good for Nonprofit Anchor Institutions: Understanding Costs, Benefits, and the Range of Strategic Options* (Chicago, 2009); as well as Pattillo, *Black on the Block*, pp. 286–87.

188. "University of Chicago Works on Its Neighborhood," *New York Times*, October 23, 2012, p. B8.

189. As of 2007 the University owned about 1,900 apartments in Hyde Park, most of them in older, legacy buildings acquired to house graduate students and staff, as well as the Hyde Park Shopping Center. This portfolio gave the University very little leverage in shaping or improving neighborhood amenities. The Fifty-Third Street initiatives therefore represented a significant change in the University's engagement with the commercial real estate sector.

190. For a recent examination of Kerr's work, see now Sheldon Rothblatt, "Clark Kerr: Two Voices," in Rothblatt, ed., *Clark Kerr's World of Higher Education Reaches the 21st Century: Chapters in a Special History* (Dordrecht, 2012), pp. 1–42; and "Clark Kerr's World of Higher Education Reaches the Twenty-First Century: A Symposium on Kerr's Life, Work and Legacy," October 25–26, 2012, New York University, Steinhardt Institute for Higher Education Policy, http://steinhardt.nyu.edu/scmsAdmin/media/users/tln215/NYU_Clark_Kerr_Symposium_-_October_2012.pdf.

191. Zemsky, *Making Reform Work*, pp. 22–56 offers a nuanced summary of many of these literatures from the late 1990s on. Blunter critiques can be found in Benjamin Ginsberg, *The Fall of the Faculty: The Rise of the All-Administrative University and Why It Matters* (New York, 2011); and William Deresiewicz, *Excellent Sheep: The Miseducation of the American Elite and the Way to a Meaningful Life* (New York, 2014), but the genre is large and continually growing.

192. White to Kalven, March 8, 1967, Kalven Papers, Box 28.

193. Stigler's concerns on this point were incorporated in the final version that was presented to the Council of the Senate, in the form of a postscript on p. 5 of the document.

194. See Minutes of the Board of Trustees, June 8, 1967, p. 10. The report was published in early November 1967 in the new *University of Chicago Record*. Glen A. Lloyd, the former chairman of the board of trustees, only received his copy in December 1967. See Kalven to Charles D. O'Connell, December 7, 1967, Kalven Papers, Box 28.

195. Storr used the apt analogy of a medieval artisan whose personal liberty derived from the liberties of the town in which he lived. Storr, *Harper's University,* p. 96.

196. Robert J. Zimmer, address given at a conference on academic freedom at Columbia University, October 21, 2009, http://president.uchicago.edu/page/address-delivered-columbia-university.

197. Roger Kimball, "Tenured Radicals: A Postscript," *New Criterion*, January 1991, arguing that (in Kimball's words) "the priority of Western liberal values" was being systematically undermined by faculty in the universities out of sheer and rank ideological partisanship, is symptomatic of the larger phenomenon. The ways in which the so-called culture wars of the 1980s and 1990s impacted the study of the humanities in major American universities have yet to be fully analyzed. For the critics, see Roger Kimball, *Tenured Radicals: How Politics Has Corrupted Our Higher Education* (New York, 1990); Dinesh D'Souza, *Illiberal Education: The Politics of Race and Sex on Campus* (New York, 1991); and Allan Bloom, *The Closing of the*

American Mind: How Higher Education Has Failed Democracy and Impoverished the Souls of Today's Students (New York, 1987).

198. Richard H. Davis, *South Asia at Chicago: A History* (Chicago, 1985), pp. 18–19.

199. "Area Programs in Education and Research," April 27, 1944, pp. 3, 8, 14, Robert Redfield Papers, Box 60. See also Milton Singer, "Robert Redfield's Development of a Social Anthropology of Civilizations," in John V. Murra, ed., *American Anthropology: The Early Years* (St. Paul, 1976), pp. 191–95.

200. *Annual Report of the Ford Foundation for 1951,* p. 13.

201. Robert Redfield, "A Short Description of the Project," Ford Foundation Cultural Studies Program Records 1951–1961, Box 5, folder 6.

202. Redfield to Hutchins, June 7, 1951, Ford Foundation Cultural Studies Program Records, Box 5, folder 10.

203. Milton Singer, "Robert Redfield, 1897–1958," in Shils, *Remembering the University of Chicago*, p. 420.

204. Davis, *South Asia at Chicago,* p. 38.

205. "Anthropology 342: Summary and Analysis of Spring Quarter 1953," p. 7, Singer Papers, Box 94.

206. "Recommendations for a Joint College–Social Sciences B.A. Program," January 6, 1956, Minutes of the Faculty of the College. In 1963 McNeill would publish his own magnificent world history, *The Rise of the West: A History of the Human Community,* with the University of Chicago Press.

207. *The Order of Assassins: The Struggle of the Early Nizârî Ismâ'îlîs against the Islamic World* (The Hague, 1955).

208. See Marshall G. S. Hodgson, "A Non-Western Civilization Course in a Liberal Education with Special Attention to the Case of Islam," *Journal of General Education* 12 (1959): 39–49.

209. As Edmund Burke III has argued, *The Venture of Islam* is a searching history of Islamic culture and civilization, but it is also a profound exercise in comparative world history, since Hodgson relentlessly sought to understand Islam in the comparative perspective of world history. Marshall G. S. Hodgson, *Rethinking World History: Essays on Europe, Islam, and World History,* ed. Edmund Burke III (Cambridge, 1993), p. 307.

210. "Report on Historical and Cultural Studies," in "Project 1984: Design Issues; Reports of the Task Forces," p. 89.

211. One of the first of these area study committees was the Committee on Southern Asian Studies (COSAS), created in 1955. Ford had awarded Chicago a grant of $5.4 million in 1960 to support the University's new area studies programs for ten years, followed by a second major grant in 1966.

212. Hanna Holborn Gray, *Searching for Utopia: Universities and Their Histories* (Berkeley, 2012), p. 57.

213. David A. Hollinger, introduction to *The Humanities and the Dynamic of Inclusion since World War II*, p. 6. John MacAloon has noted that debates challenging traditional Western cultural canons had a long-standing history in the "Soc 2" Core course, in many ways paralleling the debates engendered by the rise of the non-

European civilizational sequences. See John J. MacAloon, ed., *General Education in the Social Sciences: Centennial Reflections on the College of the University of Chicago* (Chicago, 1992), p. 11.

214. Speech given to the Cleveland Phi Beta Kappa Society, Alumni of Western Reserve University, and Alumni of the University of Chicago on December 5, 1930, pp. 13–14, Hutchins Papers, Box 355, folder 12.

215. Robert M. Hutchins, interview by George Dell, May 29, 1973, Robert M. Hutchins and Associates, Oral History Interviews, Box 1, folder 9.

216. Bradburn report, p. 17.

217. Geiger and Heller, "Financial Trends in Higher Education," p. 16.

218. Casper, *Winds of Freedom*, p. 203.

219. "Report of the Committee on Teaching," *University of Chicago Record*, January 15, 1973, p. 11.

220. Karl J. Weintraub, "In Behalf of the Humanities," in *The University of Chicago: The Freedom to Be Excellent; Three Views* (Chicago, 1974), pp. 19–20.

Bibliography

Archival Sources

UNIVERSITY OF CHICAGO, SPECIAL COLLECTIONS RESEARCH CENTER, JOSEPH REGENSTEIN LIBRARY

Papers

Adler, Mortimer J. Papers.
Arnett, Trevor. Papers.
Bell, Laird. Papers.
Benton, William B. Papers.
Berelson, Bernard L. Study of Graduate Education. Records, 1958–61.
Blum, Walter J. Papers.
Burgess, Ernest Watson. Papers.
Burton, Ernest DeWitt. Papers.
Cate, James L. Papers.
Coggeshall, Lowell T. Papers.
Filbey, Emery T. Papers.
Gates, Frederick Taylor. Papers.
Goetz, Rachael Marshall. Papers.
Goodspeed, Edgar J. Papers.
Goodspeed, Thomas W. Papers.
Harper, Samuel Northrup. Papers.
Harper, William Rainey. Papers.
Hutchins, Robert M. Papers.
Hutchinson, William T. Papers.
Judd, Charles H. Papers.
Kalven, Harry. Papers.
Kimpton, Lawrence A. Papers.
Knight, Frank H. Papers.

Lee, Elon N., and Edson S. Bastin. Papers.
Levi, Edward H. Papers.
Lloyd, Edward H. Papers.
Lloyd, Glen A. Papers.
Maclean, Norman. Papers.
McKeon, Richard P. Papers.
Merriam, Charles E. Papers.
Miller, Merton. Papers.
Nef, John Ulric, Jr. Papers.
Nef, John Ulric, Sr. Papers.
Nitze, William A. Papers.
Ogburn, William F. Papers.
Pierce, Bessie Louise. Papers.
Price, Ira M. Papers.
Redfield, Robert. Papers.
Redfield, Robert. Ford Foundation Cultural Studies Program Records.
Rheinstein, Max. Papers.
Ruml, Beardsley. Papers.
Scott, Arthur P. Papers.
Shorey, Paul. Papers.
Singer, Milton. Papers.
Small, Albion W. Papers.

Storr, Richard J. Papers.
Swift, Harold H. Papers.
Tufts, James Hayden. Papers.
Walker, George C. Scrapbook.

Ward, F. Champion. Papers.
Wirth, Louis. Papers.
Wirth, Mary Bolton. Papers.

Other Sources

American Baptist Education Society. Records, 1887–1902.
American Institute of Sacred Literature. Records, 1880–1943.
Architectural Drawings Collection.
Baptist Theological Union and Baptist Union Theological Seminary. Records, 1865–1944.
Blackfriars. Records.
College Archive.
Department of Anthropology. Records.
Department of Buildings and Grounds. Records.
Department of History. Records.
Department of Mathematics. Records.
Department of Sociology. Interviews.
Development and Alumni Relations. Donor Relations. Records.
Development Campaigns and Anniversaries. Records.
Divinity School. Records.
Division of the Humanities. Records.
Division of the Social Sciences. Records.
The First Annual Report. President Harper, 1892.
Ford Foundation. A Profile of the University of Chicago, 1965–66.
Hutchins, Robert M., and Associates. Oral History Interviews.
Law School. Records.

Minutes of the Board of Trustees.
Minutes of the College Council.
Minutes of the Committee of the Council of the University Senate.
Minutes of the Council of the Senate.
Minutes of the Faculty of the College.
Minutes of the Faculty of the Division of the Humanities.
Minutes of the Faculty of the Division of the Social Sciences.
Minutes of the University Senate.
Office of the President.
 Beadle Administration. Records.
 Harper, Judson, and Burton Administrations. Records.
 Hutchins Administration. Records.
 Kimpton Administration. Records.
 Levi Administration. Records.
 Mason Administration. Records.
 Wilson Administration. Records.
Office of the Vice President Records.
Old University of Chicago. Records, 1856–90.
PP Addenda, 1997-006, 1997-060, 1998-006.
Presidential Search Committee. Records, 1950–77.
University of Chicago Founders' Correspondence, 1886–92.
University of Chicago. Oral History Program.

ADDITIONAL ARCHIVAL COLLECTIONS

Angell, James R. Presidential Records. Manuscripts and Archives. Sterling Memorial Library, Yale University.

First Baptist Church of Hyde Park. Records, Archives of the Hyde Park Union Church, Chicago.

Ford Foundation Records. Rockefeller Archive Center, Pocantico Hills, Sleepy Hollow, NY. Grant File PA65–367.

Hutchins, William J. Papers. Special Collections and Archives. Hutchins Library, Berea College.

Hutchinson, Charles L. Papers, 1854–1924. Special Collections. Newberry Library, Chicago.

Laura Spelman Rockefeller Memorial. Records. Rockefeller Archive Center, Pocantico Hills, Sleepy Hollow, NY.

Payne, William Morton. Papers, 1858–1919. Special Collections. Newberry Library, Chicago

Ryerson, Martin A. Papers. Collections Records. Institutional Archives. The Art Institute of Chicago.

Scott, Walter Dill. Papers. Northwestern University Archives.

Whitney, William D. Papers. Manuscripts and Archives. Sterling Memorial Library, Yale University.

Published Primary Sources

NEWSPAPERS AND JOURNALS

American Bar Foundation Research Journal.

Boston Evening Transcript.

Chicago Booth Magazine.

Chicago Business.

Chicago Journal.

Chicago Maroon.

Chicago Reader.

Chicago Record-Herald.

Chicago Teacher and School-Board Journal.

Chicago Tribune.

Christian Science Monitor.

Christian Times and Witness.

Chronicle of Higher Education.

Crain's Chicago Business.

The Dial: A Semi-Monthly Journal of Literary Criticism, Discussion, and Information.

Educational Review.

Fortune.

Harper's Magazine.

Harvard Monthly.

Hebraica.

The Hebrew Student: A Monthly Journal in the Interests of Old Testament Literature and Interpretation (1882–83).

The Old Testament Student (1883–89).

The Old and New Testament Student (1889–92).

The Biblical World (1893–1920).

Journal of Religion (1920–present).

Herald-Examiner.

Hyde Park Herald.

Journal of Law and Economics.

Journal of Legal Education.

Lingua Franca.

The Living Age.

New York Times.

New York Times Magazine.

North American Review.

Our Day.

The Pulse.

Saturday Evening Post.

School Review.
Scribner's Magazine.
The Standard.
University of Chicago Bulletins.
University of Chicago Chronicle.
University of Chicago Law Alumni
   Journal.
University of Chicago Law Review.

University of Chicago Magazine.
University of Chicago. Official Bulletin.
   Chicago, 1891.
University of Chicago Record.
University of Chicago Weekly.
The Volante.
Wall Street Journal.
The Watchman.

PAMPHLETS, REPORTS, AND PROCEEDINGS

Addresses and Appeals in Behalf of the University of Chicago and the Baptist Theological Seminary. Chicago, 1867.

Annual Register of the University of Chicago, 1916–1919.

Annual Report of the Ford Foundation for 1951. New York, 1951.

Annual Report of the General Education Board, 1923–1924. New York, 1925.

Annual Report of the General Education Board, 1930–1931. New York, 1932.

The Baptist Union Theological Seminary, Morgan Park, Ill.: A Great Opportunity. Morgan Park, IL, 1885.

The Dean's Report, 1989, Graduate School of Business. Chicago, 1989.

First Annual Catalogue of the University of Chicago: Officers and Students for the Academic Year 1859–1860. Chicago, 1860.

The Great Investigation. Chicago, 1949.

Great University Memorials, with a Reference to the Plans for the Development of the University of Chicago. Chicago, 1925.

Morehouse, H. L. "A Seven Years' Survey." In Fifty-Fourth Annual Report of the American Baptist Home Mission Society, Convened in Educational Hall, Asbury Park, NJ, May 27, 28, and 29, 1886. New York, 1886.

The National Baptist Convention and Organization of the American Baptist Education Society Held in the Calvary Baptist Church at Washington, D.C., May 16 and 17, 1888. Washington, DC, 1888.

The President's Report, July, 1892–July 1902: Administration. The Decennial Publications, 1st ser., vol. 1. Chicago, 1903.

The President's Report, July, 1897–July, 1898, with Summaries for 1891–97. Chicago, 1899.

The President's Report, July 1902–July 1904. Chicago, 1905.

The President's Report, July, 1904–July, 1905. Chicago, 1906.

The President's Report, July 1908–July 1909. Chicago, 1910.

The President's Report, Covering the Academic Year July 1, 1919, to June 30, 1920. Chicago, 1921.

The President's Report, Covering the Academic Year July 1, 1922, to June 30, 1923. Chicago, 1924.

The President's Report, Covering the Academic Year July 1, 1923, to June 30, 1924. Chicago, 1925.

The President's Report, Covering the Academic Year July 1, 1924, to June 30, 1925. Chicago, 1926.

The President's Report, Covering the Academic Year July 1, 1926, to June 30, 1927. Chicago, 1928.

The President's Report, Covering the Academic Year July 1, 1929, to June 30, 1930. Chicago, 1931.

The Registrar's Report to the President, 1938–1939; 1941–1942; 1943–1944.

The Regulations of the University of Chicago. Chicago, 1903.

The Responsibility of Greatness: A Statement Presented by the Board of Trustees of the University of Chicago. Chicago, 1955.

Twenty-Seventh Annual Catalogue of the University of Chicago, including the Union College of Law. Chicago, 1886.

The University of Chicago in 1921. Chicago, 1921.

MEMOIRS AND OTHER FACULTY WRITINGS

Adler, Mortimer. "The Chicago School." *Harper's Magazine*, September, 1941, pp. 377–88.

———. *Philosopher at Large: An Intellectual Biography.* New York, 1977.

Benton, William B. *The University of Chicago's Public Relations.* Chicago, 1937.

Boise, James R. *Exercises in Greek Prose Composition, Adapted to the First Book of Xenophon's "Anabasis."* New York, 1867.

———. *First Lessons in Greek, Adapted to the Grammar of Goodwin, and to That of Hadley as Revised by Frederic D. Forest Allen.* Chicago, 1891.

Bolza, Oskar. *Aus meinem Leben.* Munich, 1936.

Booth, Wayne C. *My Many Selves: The Quest for a Plausible Harmony.* Logan, UT, 2006.

Boucher, Chauncey S. "The College of Arts, Literature, and Science." In *The President's Report, Covering the Academic Year July 1, 1927, to June 30, 1928.* Chicago, 1929.

Burton, Ernest D. "Charles L. Hutchinson and the University of Chicago." In *Charles Lawrence Hutchinson, 1854–1924.* Chicago, 1925.

———. *A Critical and Exegetical Commentary on the Epistle to the Galatians.* New York, 1920.

———. *Education in a Democratic World.* Chicago, 1927.

———. *The University of Chicago in 1940.* Chicago, 1925.

Compton, Arthur H. *Atomic Quest: A Personal Narrative.* New York, 1956.

Dewey, John. "Rationality in Education"; "President Hutchins' Proposals to Remake Higher Education"; "The Higher Learning in America." *Social Frontier*, December 1936, pp. 71–73; January 1937, pp. 103–4; March 1937, pp. 167–69.

Douglas, Paul. *In the Fullness of Time: The Memoirs of Paul H. Douglas.* New York, 1972.

Everts, W. W. *The Life of Rev. W. W. Everts, DD.* Philadelphia, 1891.

Faust, Clarence. "How the University of Chicago Is Meeting the Emergency." In

John Dale Russell, ed., *The Colleges in Wartime: New Responsibilities*. Chicago, 1943.

Gates, Frederick Taylor. *Chapters in My Life*. New York, 1977.

Gideonse, Harry D. *Against the Running Tide: Selected Essays on Education and the Free Society*. Edited by Alexander S. Preminger. New York, 1967.

———. *The Higher Learning in a Democracy: A Reply to President Hutchins' Critique of the American University*. New York, 1937.

———. "Integration of the Social Sciences and the Quest for Certainty." *Social Studies* 27 (1936): 363–72.

———. "Quality of Teaching or Content of Education?" In *The Preparation and In-Service Training of College Teachers, Proceedings of the Institute for Administrative Officers of Higher Institutions* 10 (1938): 65–75.

Goodspeed, Edgar J. *As I Remember*. New York, 1953.

———. *The University of Chicago Chapel. A Guide*. Chicago, 1928.

Goodspeed, Thomas W. *The University of Chicago Biographical Sketches*. 2 vols. Chicago, 1922–25.

Harper, Samuel N. *The Russia I Believe In: The Memoirs of Samuel N. Harper, 1902–1941*. Chicago, 1945.

Harper, William Rainey. "The College President." In Robert N. Montgomery, ed., *The William Rainey Harper Memorial Conference, Held in Connection with the Centennial of Muskingum College, New Concord, Ohio, October 21–22, 1937*. Chicago, 1938.

———. *A Critical and Exegetical Commentary on Amos and Hosea*. New York, 1905.

———. "Ideals of Educational Work." In *National Educational Association, Journal of Proceedings and Addresses, Session of the Year 1895*. St. Paul, 1895.

———. "Shall the Theological Curriculum Be Modified, and How?" *American Journal of Theology* 3 (1899): 45–66.

———. "Some Features of an Ideal University." In *Third Annual Meeting of the American Baptist Education Society, Held with the Southern Baptist Convention, Birmingham, Ala., May 8 and 9, 1891*. Chicago, 1891.

———. *The Trend in Higher Education*. Chicago, 1905.

Herrick, Robert. *Chimes*. New York, 1926.

Hutchins, Robert M. *The Higher Learning in America*. New Haven, CT, 1936.

———. *No Friendly Voice*. Chicago, 1936.

———. "The Upper Divisions of the University of Chicago." In William S. Gray, ed., *Recent Trends in American College Education*. Chicago, 1931.

Hutchinson, Dennis J. "Elements at 75." *University of Chicago Law School Record* (Spring 2013): 22–31.

Judson, Harry Pratt. *Caesar's Army: A Study of the Military Art of the Romans in the Last Days of the Republic*. Minneapolis, 1888.

———. *Europe in the Nineteenth Century*. New York, 1900.

———. *The Growth of the American Nation*. New York, 1906.

———. *A History of the Troy Citizens Corps, Troy, N.Y.* Troy, NY, 1884.

Laing, Gordon. "The Graduate School of Arts and Literature." In *The President's Report, Covering the Academic Year July 1, 1923, to June 30, 1924*. Chicago, 1925.

——. "The Graduate School of Arts and Literature." In *The President's Report, Covering the Academic Year July 1, 1927, to June 30, 1928*. Chicago, 1929.

Laughlin, J. Laurence. *Twenty-Five Years of the Department of Political Economy at the University of Chicago*. Chicago, 1916.

Levi, Edward H. *An Introduction to Legal Reasoning*. Chicago, 1961.

——. *Points of View: Talks on Education*. Chicago, 1969.

Levi, Julian. *The Neighborhood Program of the University of Chicago*. Chicago, n.d. [1961].

Lochner, Louis P. *Always the Unexpected: A Book of Reminiscences*. New York, 1956.

Lovett, Robert. *All Our Years: The Autobiography of Robert Morss Lovett*. New York, 1948.

Marshall, Leon C. *The Collegiate School of Business: Its Status at the Close of the First Quarter of the Twentieth Century*. Chicago, 1928.

Meltzer, Bernard D. "The University of Chicago Law School: Ruminations and Reminiscences." *University of Chicago Law Review* 70 (2003): 233–57.

Millis, H. A., et al. *Report of the Faculty-Student Committee on the Distribution of Students' Time, January 1925*. Chicago, 1925.

Mixer, Albert H. *Manual of French Poetry with Historical Introduction, and Biographical Notices of the Principal Authors, for the Use of the School and the Home*. New York, 1874.

Public Statement of H. Stanley Bennett, February 8, 1969. College Archive.

Public Statement of John Hope Franklin, February 7, 1969. College Archive.

Public Statement of a Group of Concerned Faculty Members, February 11, 1969. College Archive.

Public Statement of Professor O. J. Kleppa, February 5, 1969. College Archive.

Rockefeller, John D. *Random Reminiscences of Men and Events*. New York, 1909.

Ruml, Beardsley. *Memo to a College Trustee: A Report on Financial and Structural Problems of the Liberal College*. New York, 1959.

Slosson, Edwin E. "University of Chicago." In *Great American Universities*. New York, 1910.

Small, Albion. "Americans and the World Crisis." *American Journal of Sociology* 23 (1917): 145–73.

——. *The Cameralists: The Pioneers of German Social Polity*. Chicago, 1909.

——. "The Graduate School of Arts and Literature." In *The President's Report, Covering the Academic Year Ending June 30, 1913*. Chicago, 1914.

——. "The Graduate School of Arts and Literature." In *The President's Report, Covering the Academic Year July 1, 1922, to June 30, 1923*. Chicago, 1924.

——. *Origins of Sociology*. Chicago, 1924.

——. "Will Germany War with Us?" *Collier's Weekly*, December 10, 1904.

Vice, James W. "Memoirs: Demonstrations, 1968–1969; 1973." Unpublished manuscript, 2004.

Wayland, Francis. *The Education Demanded by the People of the United States: A Discourse Delivered at Union College, Schenectady, July 25, 1854, on the Occasion of the Fiftieth Anniversary of the Presidency of Eliphalet Nott, DD, LLD*. Boston, 1855.

Secondary Sources

Abbott, Andrew. *Department and Discipline: Chicago Sociology at One Hundred*. Chicago, 1999.

———. "Library Research Infrastructure for Humanistic and Social Scientific Scholarship in the Twentieth Century." In Charles Camic, Neil Gross, and Michèle Lamont, eds., *Social Knowledge in the Making*. Chicago, 2011.

———. "Pragmatic Sociology and the Public Sphere: The Case of Charles Richmond Henderson." *Social Science History* 34 (2010): 337–71.

———. *The System of the Professions: An Essay on the Division of Expert Labor*. Chicago, 1988.

Abrahamson, Julia. *A Neighborhood Finds Itself*. New York, 1959.

Abt, Jeffrey. *American Egyptologist: The Life of James Henry Breasted and the Creation of His Oriental Institute*. Chicago, 2011.

Altbach, Philip G. *Student Politics in America: A Historical Analysis*. New York, 1974.

Altbach, Philip G., Berdahl, Robert O., and Gumport, Patricia J., eds. *American Higher Education in the Twenty-First Century: Social, Political, and Economic Challenges*. 2nd ed. Baltimore, 2005.

Anderson, Earl W. "Salaries in Certain Professions." *Educational Research Bulletin*, January 11, 1933, pp. 1–9.

Anderson, Frederick L. *Galusha Anderson: Preacher and Educator, 1832–1918*. Privately published, 1933.

Anderson, Jeffrey, and Kole, Stacey R. "Leadership Effectiveness and Development: Building Self-Awareness and Insight Skills." In Scott Snook, Nitin Nohria, and Rakesh Khurana, *The Handbook for Teaching Leadership: Knowing, Doing and Being*. Thousand Oaks, CA, 2012.

Andreas, Alfred T. *History of Chicago from the Earliest Period to the Present Time*. 3 vols. Chicago, 1884–86.

Andresen, Julie T. *Linguistics in America, 1769–1924: A Critical History*. London, 1990.

Anheier, Helmut K., and Hammack, David C., eds. *American Foundations: Roles and Contributions*. Washington, DC, 2010.

Archibald, Raymond C. *A Semicentennial History of the American Mathematical Society, 1888–1938*. New York, 1938.

Arnold, Charles H. *God before You and behind You: The Hyde Park Union Church through a Century, 1874–1974*. Chicago, 1974.

Arrastía, Lisa, and Hoffman, Marvin. *Starting Up: Critical Lessons from 10 New Schools*. New York, 2012.

Ash, Mitchell G. "Bachelor of What, Master of Whom? The Humboldt Myth and Historical Transformations of Higher Education in German-Speaking Europe and the US." *European Journal of Education* 41 (2006): 245–67.

————, ed. *German Universities: Past and Future; Crisis or Renewal?* Providence, 1997.

Axtell, James. *The Making of Princeton University: From Woodrow Wilson to the Present.* Princeton, NJ, 2006.

Bachin, Robin F. *Building the South Side: Urban Space and Civic Culture in Chicago, 1890–1919.* Chicago, 2004.

Bailey, Fred Arthur. *William Edward Dodd: The South's Yeoman Scholar.* Charlottesville, VA, 1997.

Bannister, Robert C. *Sociology and Scientism: The American Quest for Objectivity, 1880–1940.* Chapel Hill, NC, 1987.

Barrow, Clyde W. *Universities and the Capitalist State: Corporate Liberalism and the Reconstruction of American Higher Education, 1894–1928.* Madison, WI, 1990.

Beadle, Muriel. *The Hyde Park-Kenwood Urban Renewal Years.* Chicago, 1964.

————. *Where Has All the Ivy Gone? A Memoir of University Life.* Chicago, 1977.

Beasley, James P. "'Extraordinary Understandings' of Composition at the University of Chicago: Frederick Champion Ward, Kenneth Burke, and Henry W. Sams." *College Composition and Communication* 59 (2007): 36–52.

Beck, Kenneth N. "The American Institute of Sacred Literature: A Historical Analysis of an Adult Education Institution." PhD diss., University of Chicago, 1968.

Bell, Daniel. *The Reforming of General Education: The Columbia Experience in Its National Setting.* New ed. New Brunswick, NJ, 2011.

Bender, Thomas. *Intellect and Public Life: Essays on the Social History of Academic Intellectuals in the United States.* Baltimore, 1993.

Bender, Thomas, and Schorske, Carl, eds. *American Academic Culture in Transformation: Fifty Years, Four Disciplines.* Princeton, NJ, 1998.

Berelson, Bernard. *Graduate Education in the United States.* New York, 1960.

Berry, Brian J. L., Parsons, Sandra J., and Platt, Rutherford H. *The Impact of Urban Renewal on Small Business: The Hyde Park-Kenwood Case.* Chicago, 1968.

Biographical Sketches of the Leading Men of Chicago. Chicago, 1868.

Blakey, George T. *Historians on the Homefront: American Propagandists for the Great War.* Lexington, KY, 1970.

Bledstein, Burton J. *The Culture of Professionalism: The Middle Class and the Development of Higher Education in America.* New York, 1976.

Block, Jean F. *The Uses of Gothic: Planning and Building the Campus of the University of Chicago, 1892–1932.* Chicago, 1983.

Bloom, Allan. *The Closing of the American Mind: How Higher Education Has Failed Democracy and Impoverished the Souls of Today's Students.* New York, 1987.

Bowen, William G. *The Economics of Major Private Universities.* Berkeley, 1968.

Boyer, John W., ed. *The Aims of Education.* Chicago, 1997.

——. *"A Noble and Symmetrical Conception of Life": The Arts at Chicago on the Edge of a New Century*. Chicago, 2010.

——. *"Teaching at a University of a Certain Sort": Education at the University of Chicago over the Past Century*. Chicago, 2012.

——. *Three Views of Continuity and Change*. Chicago, 1999.

——. *"A Twentieth-Century Cosmos": The New Plan and the Origins of General Education at the University of Chicago*. Chicago, 2007.

——. *"We Are All Islanders to Begin With": The University of Chicago and the World in the Late Nineteenth and Twentieth Centuries*. Chicago, 2008.

Brand, Edward P. *Illinois Baptists: A History*. Bloomington, IL, 1930.

Brazier, Arthur M. *Black Self-Determination: The Story of the Woodlawn Organization*. Grand Rapids, MI, 1969.

Breasted, Charles. *Pioneer to the Past: The Story of James Henry Breasted, Archaeologist*. New York, 1943.

Breneman, David W., and Finn, Chester E., Jr., eds. *Public Policy and Private Higher Education*. Washington, DC, 1978.

Brereton, Virginia L. "The Public Schools Are Not Enough: The Bible and Private Schools." In David L. Barr and Nicholas Piediscalzi, eds., *The Bible in American Education: From Source Book to Textbook*. Philadelphia, 1982.

——. *Training God's Army: The American Bible School, 1880–1940*. Bloomington, IN, 1990.

Brinkley, Alan. "1968 and the Unraveling of Liberal America." In Carole Fink, Philipp Gassert, and Detlef Junker, eds., *1968: The World Transformed*. Cambridge, 1998.

Brocke, Bernhard vom. "Der deutsch-amerikanische Professorenaustausch: Preussische Wissenschaftspolitik, internationale Wissenschaftsbeziehungen und die Anfänge einer deutschen auswärtigen Kulturpolitik vor dem Ersten Weltkrieg." *Zeitschrift für Kulturaustausch* 31 (1981): 128–82.

Brown, E. Richard. *Rockefeller Medicine Men: Medicine and Capitalism in America*. Berkeley, 1979.

Brubacher, John S., and Rudy, Willis. *Higher Education in Transition: A History of American Colleges and Universities, 1636–1976*. New York, 1976.

Bruendel, Steffen. *Volksgemeinschaft oder Volksstaat: Die "Ideen von 1914" und die Neuordnung Deutschlands im Ersten Weltkrieg*. Berlin, 2003.

Bryk, Anthony S., and Schneider, Barbara. "Social Trust: A Moral Resource for School Improvement." University of Chicago Center for School Improvement, June 1996.

Bryk, Anthony S., and Sebring, Penny B. "School Leadership and the Bottom Line in Chicago." University of Chicago Consortium on Chicago School Research, February 2000.

Bryk, Anthony S., Sebring, Penny B., Allensworth, Elaine, Luppescu, Stuart, and Easton, John Q. *Organizing Schools for Improvement: Lessons from Chicago*. Chicago, 2010.

Bryk, Anthony S., Sebring, Penny B., Kerbow, David, Rollow, Sharon, and

Easton, John Q. *Charting Chicago School Reform: Democratic Localism as a Lever for Change*. Boulder, CO, 1998.

Bucklin, Steven J. "The Wilsonian Legacy in Political Science: Denna F. Fleming, Frederick L. Schuman, and Quincy Wright. PhD diss., University of Iowa, 1993.

Bulmer, Martin. *The Chicago School of Sociology: Institutionalization, Diversity, and the Rise of Sociological Research*. Chicago, 1984.

———. "The Early Institutional Establishment of Social Science Research: The Local Community Research Committee at the University of Chicago, 1923–1930." *Minerva* 18 (1980): 51–110.

Bulmer, Martin, and Bulmer, Joan. "Philanthropy and Social Science in the 1920s: Beardsley Ruml and the Laura Spelman Rockefeller Memorial, 1922–1929." *Minerva* 19 (1981): 347–407.

Burke, Colin B. *American Collegiate Populations. A Test of the Traditional View*. New York, 1982.

Burtchaell, James T. *The Dying of the Light: The Disengagement of Colleges and Universities from Their Christian Churches*. Grand Rapids, MI, 1998.

Calendar of the Martin A. Ryerson Collection of Court and Manorial Documents from the Estate of Sir Nicholas Bacon in the University of Chicago Library. Chicago, 1974.

Callahan, Raymond E. *Education and the Cult of Efficiency: A Study of the Social Forces That Have Shaped the Administration of the Public Schools*. Chicago, 1962.

Carter, Robert L. "The 'Message of the Higher Criticism': The Bible Renaissance and Popular Education in America, 1880–1925." PhD diss., University of North Carolina, 1995.

Casper, Gerhard. *The Cares of the University: Five-Year Report to the Board of Trustees and the Academic Council of Stanford University*. Stanford, CA, 1997.

———. *The Winds of Freedom: Addressing Challenges to the University*. New Haven, CT, 2014.

Castle, Terry. "Tickle and Flutter: Terry Castle on the Strange Career of Maude Hutchins." *London Review of Books*, July 3, 2008.

Chambers, John Whiteclay II. *To Raise an Army: The Draft Comes to Modern America*. New York, 1987.

Chambers, Mortimer. "The 'Most Eminent Living Historian, The One Final Authority': Meyer in America." In William M. Calder and Alexander Demandt, eds., *Eduard Meyer: Leben und Leistung eines Universalhistorikers*. Leiden, 1990.

Cheit, Earl F., and Lobman, Theodore E. *Foundations and Higher Education: Grant Making from Golden Years through Steady State; A Technical Report for the Ford Foundation and the Carnegie Council on Policy Studies in Higher Education*. Berkeley, 1979.

———. *The New Depression in Higher Education: A Study of Financial Conditions at 41 Colleges and Universities*. New York, 1971.

Chernow, Ron. *Titan: The Life of John D. Rockefeller, Sr.* New York 1998.

Chiappetta, Michael. "A Recurrent Problem: The Professional Preparation of College Teachers." *History of Education Journal* 4 (1952): 18–24.

Clotfelter, Charles T. *Buying the Best: Cost Escalation in Elite Higher Education.* Princeton, NJ, 1996.

Cohen, Adam, and Taylor, Elizabeth. *American Pharaoh: Mayor Richard J. Daley; His Battle for Chicago and the Nation.* Boston, 2000.

Cohen, Arthur M. *The Shaping of American Higher Education: Emergence and Growth of the Contemporary System.* San Francisco, 1998.

Cohen, Robert. *When the Old Left Was Young: Student Radicals and America's First Mass Student Movement, 1929–1941.* New York, 1993.

Cohen, Robert, and Zelnik, Reginald E., eds. *The Free Speech Movement: Reflections on Berkeley in the 1960s.* Berkeley, 2002.

Collins, Cherry W. "Schoolmen, Schoolma'ams, and School Boards: The Struggle for Power in Urban School Systems in the Progressive Era." PhD diss., Harvard University, 1976.

Counts, George S. *The Selective Character of American Secondary Education.* Chicago, 1922.

Crandall, Lathan A. *Henry Lyman Morehouse: A Biography.* Philadelphia, 1919.

Crane, Ronald S. "History versus Criticism in the Study of Literature." *English Journal* 24 (1935): 645–67.

Craver, Earlene. "Patronage and the Directions of Research in Economics: The Rockefeller Foundation in Europe, 1924–1938." *Minerva* 24 (1986): 205–22.

Cutlip, Scott M. *Fund Raising in the United States: Its Role in America's Philanthropy.* New Brunswick, NJ, 1965.

Davis, Harry L., and Hogarth, Robin M. "Rethinking Management Education: A View from Chicago." In Selected Papers Series, Booth School of Business. Chicago, 2013.

Davis, Lawrence B. *Immigrants, Baptists, and the Protestant Mind in America.* Urbana, IL, 1973.

Davis, Richard H. *South Asia at Chicago: A History.* Chicago, 1985.

Deegan, Mary Jo. "The Chicago School of Ethnography." In Paul Atkinson et al., *Handbook of Ethnography.* Thousand Oaks, CA, 2001.

Delbanco, Andrew. *College: What It Was, Is, and Should Be.* Princeton, NJ, 2012.

Diggins, John P. *The Bard of Savagery: Thorstein Veblen and Modern Social Theory.* New York, 1978.

———. *The Promise of Pragmatism: Modernism and the Crisis of Knowledge and Authority.* Chicago, 1994.

Dillow, Myron D. *Harvesttime on the Prairie: A History of the Baptists in Illinois, 1796–1996.* Franklin, TN, 1996.

Diner, Steven J. *A City and Its Universities: Public Policy in Chicago, 1892–1919.* Chapel Hill, NC, 1980.

Dorrien, Gary. *The Making of American Liberal Theology: Idealism, Realism, and Modernity, 1900–1950.* Louisville, 2003.

———. *The Making of American Liberal Theology: Imagining Progressive Religion, 1805–1900.* Louisville, 2001.

Douglas, Crerar, ed. *Autobiography of Augustus Hopkins Strong*. Valley Forge, PA, 1981.

Douglass, Paul F. *Teaching for Self Education—As a Life Goal*. New York, 1960.

D'Souza, Dinesh. *Illiberal Education: The Politics of Race and Sex on Campus*. New York, 1991.

Dzuback, Mary Ann. *Robert M. Hutchins: Portrait of an Educator*. Chicago, 1991.

Edwards, Marcia. *Studies in American Graduate Education*. New York, 1944.

Eells, Walter Crosby. *Surveys of American Higher Education*. New York, 1937.

Ehrenberg, Ronald G. *Tuition Rising: Why College Costs So Much*. Cambridge, MA, 2000.

Ehrlich, Thomas. "Dewey versus Hutchins: The Next Round." In Robert Orrill, ed., *Education and Democracy: Reimagining Liberal Learning in America*. New York, 1997.

Ellsworth, Frank L. *Law on the Midway: The Founding of the University of Chicago Law School*. Chicago, 1977.

Elsbach, Kimberley D., and Kramer, Roderick M. "Members' Responses to Organizational Identity Threats: Encountering and Countering the Business Week Rankings." *Administrative Science Quarterly* 41 (1996): 442–76.

Emmett, Ross B. "Entrenching Disciplinary Competence: The Role of General Education and Graduate Study in Chicago Economics." *History of Political Economy* 30 (1998): 134–50.

———. "Sharpening Tools in the Workshop: The Workshop System and the Chicago School's Success." In Robert Van Horn, Philip Mirowski, and Thomas A. Stapleford, eds., *Building Chicago Economics: New Perspectives on the History of America's Most Powerful Economics Program*. Cambridge, 2011.

Evensen, Bruce J. *God's Man for the Gilded Age: D. L. Moody and the Rise of Modern Mass Evangelism*. New York, 2003.

Farge, Arlette. *The Allure of the Archives*. New Haven, CT, 2013.

Finder, Morris. *Educating America: How Ralph W. Tyler Taught America to Teach*. Westport, CT, 2004.

Findlay, James F. *Dwight L. Moody, American Evangelist, 1837–1899*. Chicago, 1969.

Fish, John Hall. *Black Power/White Control: The Struggle of the Woodlawn Organization in Chicago*. Princeton, NJ, 1973.

Fisher, Donald. *Fundamental Development of the Social Sciences: Rockefeller Philanthropy and the United States Social Science Research Council*. Ann Arbor, MI, 1993.

Flanagan, Maureen A. *Charter Reform in Chicago*. Carbondale, IL, 1987.

———. *Seeing with Their Hearts: Chicago Women and the Vision of the Good City, 1871–1933*. Princeton, NJ, 2002.

Flexner, Abraham. *I Remember: The Autobiography of Abraham Flexner*. New York, 1940.

Foard, Ashley A., and Fefferman, Hilbert. "Federal Urban Renewal Legislation." *Law and Contemporary Problems* 25 (1960): 635–84.

Ford, Franklin L. "Our Universities: National and Regional Roles." *Virginia Quarterly Review* 43 (1967): 220–32.

Foster, Laurence. *The Functions of a Graduate School in a Democratic Society*. New York, 1936.

Fourcade, Marion. *Economists and Societies: Discipline and Profession in the United States, Britain and France, 1890s to 1990s*. Princeton, NJ, 2009.

Fourcade, Marion, and Khurana, Rakesh. "From Social Control to Financial Economics: The Linked Ecologies of Economics and Business in Twentieth-Century America." *Theory and Society* 42 (2013): 136–54.

Franklin, John Hope. "*The Birth of a Nation*: Propaganda as History." In *Race and History: Selected Essays, 1938–1988*. Baton Rouge, 1989.

Freeland, Richard M. *Academia's Golden Age: Universities in Massachusetts, 1945–1970*. New York, 1992.

Freeman, Maria. "Study with Open Mind and Heart: William Rainey Harper's Inductive Method of Teaching the Bible." PhD diss., University of Chicago, 2005.

Frisbie, Margery. *An Alley in Chicago: The Ministry of a City Priest*. Kansas City, 1991.

Frumkin, Peter. *Strategic Giving: The Art and Science of Philanthropy*. Chicago, 2006.

Funk, Robert W. "The Watershed of the American Biblical Tradition: The Chicago School, First Phase, 1892–1920." *Journal of Biblical Literature* 95 (1976): 9–14.

Furner, Mary O. *Advocacy and Objectivity: A Crisis in the Professionalization of American Social Science, 1865–1905*. Lexington, KY, 1975.

Furniss, Edgar S. *The Graduate School of Yale: A Brief History*. New Haven, CT, 1965.

Gardner, Howard. *Leading Minds: An Anatomy of Leadership*. New York, 1995.

Gates, Frederick Taylor. *Chapters in My Life*. New York, 1977.

Geiger, Roger L. "The Era of the Multipurpose Colleges in American Higher Education, 1850–1890." In Geiger, ed., *The American College in the Nineteenth Century*. Nashville, 2000.

———. *Knowledge and Money: Research Universities and the Paradox of the Marketplace*. Stanford, CA, 2004.

———. "Postmortem for the Current Era: Change in American Higher Education, 1980–2010." Working Paper No. 3, Penn State Center for the Study of Higher Education, University Park, PA, July 2010.

———. *Research and Relevant Knowledge: American Research Universities since World War II*. New York, 1993.

———. "Research Universities in a New Era: From the 1980s to the 1990s." In Arthur Levine, ed., *Higher Learning in America, 1980–2000*. Baltimore, 1993.

———. *To Advance Knowledge: The Growth of the American Research Universities, 1900–1940*. New York, 1986.

Geitz, Henry, Heideking, Jürgen, and Herbst, Jurgen, eds. *German Influences on Education in the United States to 1917*. Cambridge, 1995.

Gelfand, Mark I. *A Nation of Cities: The Federal Government and Urban America, 1933–1965*. New York, 1975.

George, Timothy, ed. *Mr. Moody and the Evangelical Tradition*. London, 2004.

Germer, Stefan. "Traditions and Trends: Taste Patterns in Chicago Collecting." In Sue Ann Prince, ed., *The Old Guard and the Avant-Garde: Modernism in Chicago, 1910–1940*. Chicago, 1990.

Gerschenkron, Alexander. *Continuity in History and Other Essays*. Cambridge, MA, 1968.

Gilbert, James. *Perfect Cities: Chicago's Utopias of 1893*. Chicago, 1991.

Gilpin, W. Clark. *A Preface to Theology*. Chicago, 1996.

Ginsberg, Benjamin. *The Fall of the Faculty: The Rise of the All-Administrative University and Why It Matters*. New York, 2011.

Goldman, Eric F. "Hermann Eduard von Holst: Plumed Knight of American Historiography." *Mississippi Valley Historical Review* 23 (1936–37): 511–32.

Good, Carter V. *Teaching in College and University: A Survey of the Problems and Literature in Higher Education*. Baltimore, 1929.

Goodspeed, Thomas W. *Ernest DeWitt Burton: A Biographical Sketch*. Chicago, 1926.

———. *A History of the University of Chicago: The First Quarter-Century*. Chicago, 1916.

———. *The Story of the University of Chicago: 1890–1925*. Chicago, 1925.

Gordon, Robert A., and Howell, James E. *Higher Education for Business*. New York, 1959.

Graff, Gerald. *Professing Literature: An Institutional History*. Chicago, 1987.

Gray, Hanna H. *Searching for Utopia: Universities and Their Histories*. Berkeley, 2012.

Gruber, Carol S. *Mars and Minerva: World War I and the Uses of the Higher Learning in America*. Baton Rouge, 1975.

Gumport, Patricia J. "Graduate Education and Research: Interdependence and Strain." In Philip G. Altbach, Robert O. Berdahl, and Patricia J. Gumport, eds., *American Higher Education in the Twenty-First Century: Social, Political, and Economic Challenges*. 2nd ed. Baltimore, 2005.

Gunther, John. *Chicago Revisited*. Chicago, 1967.

Haarlow, William N. *Great Books, Honors Programs, and Hidden Origins: The Virginia Plan and the University of Virginia in the Liberal Arts Movement*. New York, 2003.

Hacker, Andrew, and Dreifus, Claudia. *Higher Education? How Colleges Are Wasting Our Money and Failing Our Kids—and What We Can Do about It*. New York, 2010.

Haggerty, Melvin E. "The Improvement of College Instruction." *School and Society* 27 (1928): 25–36.

Hall, G. Stanley. "How Can Universities Be So Organized as to Stimulate More Work for the Advancement of Science?" *Journal of Proceedings and Addresses of the Eighteenth Annual Conference of the Association of American Universities*, 1917, pp. 25–54.

Harsha, E. Houston. "Illinois: The Broyles Commission." In Walter Gellhorn, ed., *The States and Subversion*. Ithaca, NY, 1952.

Hart, D. G. *The University Gets Religion: Religious Studies in American Higher Education*. Baltimore, 1999.

Haskell, Thomas L., ed. *The Authority of Experts: Studies in History and Theory*. Bloomington, IN, 1984.

——. "Justifying the Rights of Academic Freedom in the Era of 'Power/Knowledge'." In Louis Menand, ed., *The Future of Academic Freedom*. Chicago, 1996.

Heldke, Lisa. "Robert Maynard Hutchins, John Dewey, and the Nature of the Liberal Arts." *The Cresset* 59 (2005): 8–13.

Herbst, Jurgen. "From Moral Philosophy to Sociology: Albion Woodbury Small." *Harvard Educational Review* 29 (1959): 227–44.

——. *The German Historical School in American Scholarship: A Study in the Transfer of Culture*. Ithaca, NY, 1965.

Herrick, Mary J. *The Chicago Schools: A Social and Political History*. Beverly Hills, CA, 1971.

Hewa, Soma. "The Protestant Personality and Higher Education: American Philanthropy beyond the 'Progressive Era'." *International Journal of Politics, Culture and Society* 12 (1998): 135–63.

Hilkey, Judy A. *Character Is Capital: Success Manuals and Manhood in Gilded Age America*. Chapel Hill, NC, 1997.

Hilliard, Celia. *"The Prime Mover": Charles L. Hutchinson and the Making of the Art Institute of Chicago*. Chicago, 2010.

Hirsch, Arnold R. *Making the Second Ghetto: Race and Housing in Chicago, 1940–1960*. Cambridge, 1983.

Hirsch, Edwin F. *Frank Billings, the Architect of Medical Education, an Apostle of Excellence in Clinical Practice, a Leader in Chicago Medicine*. Chicago, 1966.

Hodgson, Marshall. "A Non-Western Civilization Course in a Liberal Education with Special Attention to the Case of Islam." *Journal of General Education* 12 (1959): 39–49.

——. *The Order of Assassins: The Struggle of the Early Nizârî Ismâ'îlîs against the Islamic World*. The Hague, 1955.

——. *Rethinking World History: Essays on Europe, Islam, and World History*. Edited by Edmund Burke III. Cambridge, 1993.

Hoffman, Lars. "William Rainey Harper and the Chicago Fellowship." PhD diss., University of Iowa, 1978.

Hofstadter, Richard. *The Age of Reform: From Bryan to FDR*. New York, 1955.

Hofstadter, Richard, and Hardy, C. DeWitt. *The Development and Scope of Higher Education in the United States*. New York, 1952.

Hofstadter, Richard, and Metzger, Walter P. *The Development of Academic Freedom in the United States*. New York, 1955.

Hofstadter, Richard, and Smith, Wilson, eds. *American Higher Education: A Documentary History*. 2 vols. Chicago, 1961.

Hogan, David J. *Class and Reform: School and Society in Chicago, 1880–1930*. Philadelphia, 1985.

Hogarth, Robin M., ed. *Insights in Decision Making: A Tribute to Hillel J. Einhorn*. Chicago, 1990.

Hogarth, Robin M., and Reder, Melvin W. "Prefatory Note." *Journal of Business* 59 (1986): S181–S183.

Holl, Jack M. *Argonne National Laboratory, 1946–1996*. Urbana, IL, 1997.

Hollinger, David A. *After Cloven Tongues of Fire: Protestant Liberalism in Modern American History*. Princeton, NJ, 2013.

———, ed. *The Humanities and the Dynamic of Inclusion since World War II*. Baltimore, 2006.

———. "Inquiry and Uplift: Late Nineteenth-Century American Academics and the Moral Efficacy of Scientific Practice." In Thomas L. Haskell, ed., *The Authority of Experts: Studies in History and Theory*. Bloomington, IN, 1984.

———. "The Problem of Pragmatism in American History." *Journal of American History* 67 (1980): 88–107.

Horowitz, Helen L. *Campus Life: Undergraduate Cultures from the End of the Eighteenth Century to the Present*. New York, 1987.

———. *Culture and the City: Cultural Philanthropy in Chicago from the 1880s to 1917*. Chicago, 1989.

Horowitz, Norman H. "George Wells Beadle, 1903–1989." In *National Academy of Sciences Biographical Memoirs*. Washington, DC, 1990.

Hughes, Raymond M. *A Study of the Graduate Schools of America*. Oxford, OH, 1925.

Hutchinson, Dennis J. "Elements of the Law." *University of Chicago Law Review* 70 (2003): 141–58.

Hutchison, William R. "Cultural Strain and Protestant Liberalism." *American Historical Review* 76 (1971): 386–411.

Hyman, Sidney. *The Lives of William Benton*. Chicago, 1969.

Irons, Ernest E. *The Story of Rush Medical College*. Chicago, 1953.

Janowitz, Morris, ed. *W. I. Thomas on Social Organization and Social Personality: Selected Papers*. Chicago, 1966.

Janowitz, Rebecca. *Culture of Opportunity: Obama's Chicago; The People, Politics, and Ideas of Hyde Park*. Chicago, 2010.

Jencks, Christopher. "The Next Thirty Years in the Colleges." *Harper's Magazine*, October 1961, pp. 121–28.

Jencks, Christopher, and Riesman, David. *The Academic Revolution*. New York, 1968.

Johannsen, Robert W. *Stephen A. Douglas*. New York, 1973.

Johnstone, Quintin. "The Federal Urban Renewal Program." *University of Chicago Law Review* 25 (1958–59): 301–54.

Jones, Dorothy V. *Harold Swift and the Higher Learning*. Chicago, 1985.

Kalman, Laura. *Legal Realism at Yale, 1927–1960*. Chapel Hill, NC, 1986.

Kalven, Harry. "Law School Training in Research and Exposition: The University of Chicago Program." *Journal of Legal Education* 1 (1948): 107–23.

Kargon, Robert H. *The Rise of Robert Millikan: Portrait of a Life in American Science.* Ithaca, NY, 1982.

Karl, Barry D. *Charles E. Merriam and the Study of Politics.* Chicago, 1974.

Karl, Barry D., and Katz, Stanley N. "Foundations and Ruling Class Elites." *Daedalus* 116 (1987): 1–40.

Kass, Amy A. "Radical Conservatives for Liberal Education." PhD diss., Johns Hopkins University, 1973.

Katz, Friedrich. *The Secret War in Mexico: Europe, the United States, and the Mexican Revolution.* Chicago, 1981.

Katz, Wilbur G. "A Four-Year Program for Legal Education." *University of Chicago Law Review* 4 (1937): 527–36.

Kay, Lily E. *The Molecular Vision of Life: Caltech, the Rockefeller Foundation, and the Rise of the New Biology.* New York, 1993.

Kelley, Brooks Mather. *Yale: A History.* New Haven, CT, 1974.

Kelly, F. J. "The Training of College Teachers." *Journal of Educational Research* 16 (1927): 332–41.

Kennedy, David M. *Over Here: The First World War and American Society.* Oxford, 1980.

Kerr, Clark. *The Uses of the University.* Cambridge, 1963.

Khurana, Rakesh. *From Higher Aims to Higher Hands: The Social Transformation of American Business Schools and the Unfulfilled Promise of Management as a Profession.* Princeton, NJ, 2007.

Kimball, Roger. *Tenured Radicals: How Politics Has Corrupted Our Higher Education.* New York, 1990.

———. "Tenured Radicals: A Postscript." *New Criterion,* January 1991.

Kirp, David L. "Hurricane Hugo: Following the Stormy Departure of Its President, the University of Chicago Reconsiders His Legacy." *Lingua Franca* 11 (2001): 40–49.

Klemek, Christopher. *The Transatlantic Collapse of Urban Renewal: Postwar Urbanism from New York to Berlin.* Chicago, 2011.

Kliebard, Herbert M. *The Struggle for the American Curriculum, 1893–1958.* New York, 1987.

Kloppenberg, James T. "Pragmatism: An Old Name for Some New Ways of Thinking?" *Journal of American History* 83 (1996): 100–138.

Kohler, Robert E. *From Medical Chemistry to Biochemistry: The Making of a Biomedical Discipline.* Cambridge, 1982.

———. "The Management of Science: The Experience of Warren Weaver and the Rockefeller Foundation Programme in Molecular Biology." *Minerva* 14 (1976): 279–306.

———. *Partners in Science: Foundations and Natural Scientists, 1900–1945.* Chicago, 1991.

———. "Science, Foundations, and American Universities in the 1920s." *Osiris*, 2nd ser., 3 (1987): 140–47.

Kronman, Anthony T., ed. *History of the Yale Law School: The Tercentennial Lectures*. New Haven, CT, 2004.

Krueger, Anne O. "Report of the Commission on Graduate Education in Economics." *Journal of Economic Literature* 29 (1991): 1039.

LaCapra, Dominick. "The University in Ruins?" *Critical Inquiry* 25 (1998): 32–55.

Lagemann, Ellen Condliffe. *An Elusive Science: The Troubling History of Education Research*. Chicago, 2000.

———. *The Politics of Knowledge: The Carnegie Corporation, Philanthropy, and Public Policy*. Middletown, CT, 1989.

Learned, William S. *The Quality of the Educational Process in America and in Europe*. New York, 1927.

———. *Realism in American Education*. Cambridge, MA, 1932.

Leslie, William Bruce. *Gentlemen and Scholars: College and Community in the "Age of the University," 1865–1917*. University Park, PA, 1992.

Lester, Robin. *Stagg's University: The Rise, Decline, and Fall of Big-Time Football at Chicago*. Urbana, IL, 1995.

Levine, David O. *The American College and the Culture of Aspiration, 1915–1940*. Ithaca, NY, 1986.

Levine, Donald N. *Powers of the Mind: The Reinvention of Liberal Learning in America*. Chicago, 2006.

Lewis, Andrew B. *The Shadows of Youth: The Remarkable Journey of the Civil Rights Generation*. New York, 2009.

Liebmann, George W. *The Common Law Tradition: A Collective Portrait of Five Legal Scholars*. New Brunswick, NJ, 2006.

Light, Jennifer S. *The Nature of Cities: Ecological Visions and the American Urban Professions, 1920–1960*. Baltimore, 2009.

Lindberg, David L. "The Oriental Educational Commission's Recommendations for Mission Strategy in Higher Education." PhD diss., University of Chicago, 1972.

Lingelbach, Gabriele. "Cultural Borrowing or Autonomous Development: American and German Universities in the Late Nineteenth Century." In Thomas Adam and Ruth Gross, eds., *Traveling between Worlds: German-American Encounters*. College Station, TX, 2006.

———. "The Historical Discipline in the United States: Following the German Model?" In Eckhardt Fuchs and Benedikt Stuchtey, eds., *Across Cultural Borders: Historiography in Global Perspective*. Lanham, MD, 2002.

———. *Klio macht Karriere: Die Institutionalisierung der Geschichtswissenschaft in Frankreich und den USA in der zweiten Hälfte des 19. Jahrhunderts*. Göttingen, 2003.

Livingston, Dorothy Michelson. *The Master of Light: A Biography of Albert A. Michelson*. New York, 1973.

Loss, Christopher P. *Between Citizens and the State: The Politics of American Higher Education in the 20th Century*. Princeton, NJ, 2012.

Mabry, W. Alexander, ed. "Professor William E. Dodd's Diary, 1916–1920." *John P. Branch Historical Papers of Randolph-Macon College*, n.s., 2 (March 1953): 7–86.

MacAloon, John J., ed. *General Education in the Social Sciences: Centennial Reflections on the College of the University of Chicago*. Chicago, 1992.

MacDonald, Dwight. *The Ford Foundation: The Men and the Millions*. New York, 1956.

Maienschein, Jane. "Whitman at Chicago: Establishing a Chicago Style of Biology?" In Ronald Rainger, Keith R. Benson, and Jane Maienschein, eds., *The American Development of Biology*. Philadelphia, 1988.

Marvick, Elizabeth Wirth. "Louis Wirth: A Biographical Memorandum." In Albert J. Reiss Jr., ed., *Louis Wirth: On Cities and Social Life; Selected Papers*. Chicago, 1964.

Massa, Mark S. *Charles Augustus Briggs and the Crisis of Historical Criticism*. Minneapolis, 1990.

May, Henry F. *The End of American Innocence: A Study of the First Years of Our Own Time, 1912–1917*. New York, 1959.

Mayer, Milton. *Robert Maynard Hutchins: A Memoir*. Berkeley, 1993.

McArthur, Benjamin. "A Gamble on Youth: Robert M. Hutchins, the University of Chicago, and the Politics of Presidential Selection." *History of Education Quarterly* 30 (1990): 161–86.

McCarthy, Kathleen D. *Noblesse Oblige: Charity and Cultural Philanthropy in Chicago, 1849 to 1929*. Chicago, 1982.

———. "The Short and Simple Annals of the Poor: Foundation Funding for the Humanities, 1900–1983." *Proceedings of the American Philosophical Society* 129 (1985): 3–8.

McManis, John T. *Ella Flagg Young and a Half Century of the Chicago Public Schools*. Chicago, 1916.

McNeill, William H. *Hutchins' University: A Memoir of the University of Chicago, 1929–1950*. Chicago, 1991.

———. *The Rise of the West: A History of the Human Community*. Chicago, 1963.

Medema, Steven G. "Chicago Price Theory and Chicago Law and Economics: A Tale of Two Transitions." In Robert Van Horn, Philip Mirowski, and Thomas A. Stapleford, eds., *Building Chicago Economics: New Perspectives on the History of America's Most Powerful Economics Program*. Cambridge, 2011.

———. "Wandering the Road from Pluralism to Posner: The Transformation of Law and Economics in the Twentieth Century." In Alain Marciano, ed., *Law and Economics: A Reader*. New York, 2009.

Meier, Christian. *From Athens to Auschwitz: The Uses of History*. Cambridge, MA, 2004.

Menand, Louis. "College: The End of the Golden Age." In Stephen J. Gould and Robert Atwan, eds., *The Best American Essays, 2002*. New York, 2002.

———. *The Marketplace of Ideas: Reform and Resistance in the American University.* New York, 2010.

Merriam, Charles. *The Making of Citizens: A Comparative Study of Methods of Civic Training.* Chicago, 1931.

Meyer, Daniel. "The Chicago Faculty and the University Ideal: 1891–1929." PhD diss., University of Chicago, 1994.

———. *Stephen A. Douglas and the American Union.* Chicago, 1994.

Miller, Donald L. *City of the Century: The Epic of Chicago and the Making of America.* New York, 1996.

Millikan, Robert A. "The New Opportunity in Science." *Science* 50 (1919): 285–97.

Mirowksi, Phillip, and van Horn, Rob. "The Rise of the Chicago School of Economics and the Birth of Neoliberalism." In Phillip Mirowski and Dieter Plehwe, eds., *The Road from Mont Pèlerin: The Making of the Neoliberal Thought Collective.* Cambridge, MA, 2009.

Mordfin, Robin I. "Workshopping for Success." *University of Chicago Law School Record,* Spring 2014, pp. 46–51.

Mordfin, Robin I., and Nagorsky, Marsha Ferziger. "Chicago and Law and Economics: A History." *University of Chicago Law School Record,* Fall 2011, pp. 8–17

Mosher, Frederic J. "William Morton Payne." *Newberry Library Bulletin,* 2nd ser., 7 (October 1951): 193–212.

Moynihan, Daniel P. "The Politics of Higher Education." *Daedalus* 104 (1975): 128–47.

Murchison, Carl. "James Rowland Angell." In Murchison, ed., *A History of Psychology in Autobiography,* vol. 3. Worcester, MA, 1936.

Murphy, Marjorie. "From Artisan to Semi-Professional: White Collar Unionism among Chicago Public School Teachers, 1870–1930." PhD diss., University of California at Davis, 1981.

Nagler, Jörg. "A Mediator between Two Historical Worlds: Hermann Eduard von Holst and the University of Chicago." In Henry Geitz, Jürgen Heideking, and Jurgen Herbst, eds., *German Influences on Education in the United States to 1917.* Cambridge, 1995.

Nasaw, David. *The Chief: The Life of William Randolph Hearst.* Boston, 2000.

Newman, A. H., ed. *A Century of Baptist Achievement.* Philadelphia, 1901.

Niehoff, Richard O. *Floyd W. Reeves, Innovative Educator and Distinguished Practitioner of the Art of Public Administration.* Lanham, MD, 1991.

Nik-Khah, Edward. "George Stigler, the Graduate School of Business, and the Pillars of the Chicago School." In Robert Van Horn, Philip Mirowski, and Thomas A. Stapleford, eds., *Building Chicago Economics: New Perspectives on the History of America's Most Powerful Economics Program.* Cambridge, 2011.

Novick, Peter. *That Noble Dream: The "Objectivity Question" and the American Historical Profession.* Cambridge, 1988.

Olkin, Ingram. "A Conversation with W. Allen Wallis." *Statistical Science* 6 (1991): 121–40.

O'Mara, Margaret Pugh. *Cities of Knowledge: Cold War Science and the Search for the Next Silicon Valley.* Princeton, NJ, 2005.

Osterbrock, Donald E. "Chandra and His Students at Yerkes Observatory." *Journal of Astrophysics and Astronomy* 17 (1996): 233–68.

Osterhammel, Jürgen. "Transnationale Gesellschaftsgeschichte: Erweiterung oder Alternative?" *Geschichte und Gesellschaft* 27 (2001): 464–79.

Overtveldt, Johan van. *The Chicago School: How the University of Chicago Assembled the Thinkers Who Revolutionized Economics and Business.* Chicago, 2007.

Parshall, Karen H. "Eliakim Hastings Moore and the Founding of a Mathematical Community in America, 1892–1902." *Annals of Science* 41 (1984): 313–33.

Parshall, Karen H., and Rowe, David E. *The Emergence of the American Mathematical Research Community, 1876–1900: J. J. Sylvester, Felix Klein, and E. H. Moore.* Providence, 1994.

Pattillo, Mary. *Black on the Block: The Politics of Race and Class in the City.* Chicago, 2007.

Pauly, Philip J. "The Appearance of Academic Biology in Late Nineteenth-Century America." *Journal of the History of Biology* 17 (1984): 369–93.

Pennoyer, John C. "The Harper Report of 1899: Administrative Progressivism and the Chicago Public Schools." PhD diss., University of Denver, 1978.

Perloff, Harvey S. *Urban Renewal in a Chicago Neighborhood: An Appraisal of the Hyde Park-Kenwood Renewal Program.* Chicago, 1955.

Pierson, George W. *Yale College: An Educational History, 1871–1921.* New Haven, CT, 1952.

Potts, David B. *Baptist Colleges in the Development of American Society, 1812–1861.* New York, 1988.

———. *Liberal Education for a Land of Colleges: Yale's Reports of 1828.* New York, 2010.

Press, Valetta. *Hyde Park/Kenwood: A Case Study of Urban Renewal.* Chicago, 1971.

Pugh, Willard J. "A 'Curious Working of Cross Purposes' in the Founding of the University of Chicago." *History of Higher Education Annual* 15 (1995): 93–126.

Purcell, Edward A., Jr. *The Crisis of Democratic Theory: Scientific Naturalism and the Problem of Value.* Lexington, KY, 1973.

Rast, Joel. "Creating a Unified Business Elite: The Origins of Chicago Central Area Committee." *Journal of Urban History* 20 (2011): 1–23.

———. "Critical Junctures, Long-Term Processes: Urban Redevelopment in Chicago and Milwaukee, 1945–1968." *Social Science History* 33 (2009): 393–426.

———. "Regime Building, Institution Building: Urban Renewal Policy in Chicago, 1946–1962." *Journal of Urban Affairs* 31 (2009): 173–94.

Readings, Bill. *The University in Ruins.* Cambridge, MA, 1996.

Reder, Melvin W. "Chicago Economics: Permanence and Change." *Journal of Economic Literature* 20 (1982): 1–9.

Reeves, Floyd W., and Henry, Nelson B. *Class Size and University Costs.* Chicago, 1933.

Reeves, Floyd W., Henry, Nelson B., Kelly, Frederick J., and Klein, Arthur J. *The University Faculty*. Chicago 1933.

Reeves, Floyd W., Kelly, Frederick J., and Works, George A. *The Organization and Administration of the University*. Chicago, 1933.

Reeves, Floyd W., and Miller, Ernest C. *Trends in University Growth*. Chicago, 1933.

Reeves, Floyd W., and Peik, W. E. *Instructional Problems in the University*. Chicago, 1933.

Reeves, Floyd W., and Russell, John Dale. *Admission and Retention of University Students*. Chicago, 1933.

———. *The Alumni of the Colleges*. Chicago, 1933.

———. *Some University Student Problems*. Chicago, 1933.

Reid, Robert L., ed. *Battleground: The Autobiography of Margaret A. Haley*. Urbana, IL, 1982.

———. "The Professionalization of Public School Teachers: The Chicago Experience, 1895–1920." PhD diss., Northwestern University, 1968.

Rhodes, Richard. *The Making of the Atomic Bomb*. New York, 1986.

Riesman, David. *Thorstein Veblen: A Critical Interpretation*. New York, 1953.

Ritchey, Sara M. *Life of the Spirit, Life of the Mind: Rockefeller Memorial Chapel at 75*. Chicago, 2004.

Robertson, Darrel M. *The Chicago Revival, 1876: Society and Revivalism in a Nineteenth-Century City*. Metuchen, NJ, 1989.

Robins, R. H. *A Short History of Linguistics*. Bloomington, IN, 1967.

Roderick, Melissa, Easton, John Q., and Sebring, Penny B. *The Consortium on Chicago School Research: A New Model for the Role of Research in Supporting Urban School Reform*. Chicago, 2009.

Rodgers, Daniel T. *Atlantic Crossings: Social Politics in a Progressive Age*. Cambridge, MA, 1998.

Rose, Kenneth W. "John D. Rockefeller, the American Baptist Education Society, and the Growth of Baptist Higher Education in the Midwest." Unpublished manuscript, 1998.

———. "Why Chicago and Not Cleveland? The Religious Imperative behind John D. Rockefeller's Early Philanthropy, 1855–1900." Unpublished manuscript, 1995.

Rosenthal, Robert, ed. *The Berlin Collection: Being a History and Exhibition of the Books and Manuscripts Purchased in Berlin in 1891 for the University of Chicago by William Rainey Harper with the Support of Nine Citizens of Chicago*. Chicago, 1979.

Ross, Dorothy. *The Origins of American Social Science*. Cambridge, 1991.

Rossi, Peter H., and Dentler, Robert A. *The Politics of Urban Renewal: The Chicago Findings*. New York, 1961.

Rothblatt, Sheldon, ed. *Clark Kerr's World of Higher Education Reaches the 21st Century: Chapters in a Special History*. Dordrecht, 2012.

Rothman, Stanley, and Lichter, S. Robert. *Roots of Radicalism: Jews, Christians, and the Left*. Rev. ed. New Brunswick, NJ, 1996.

Rucker, Darnell. *The Chicago Pragmatists*. Minneapolis, 1969.

Rudolph, Frederick. *The American College and University: A History*. New York, 1962.

———. *Curriculum: A History of the American Undergraduate Course of Study since 1636*. San Francisco, 1977.

———. "Who Paid the Bills? An Inquiry into the Nature of 19th-Century College Finance." *Harvard Educational Review* 31 (1961): 144–57.

Ruegg, Walter, ed. *A History of the University in Europe*. Vol. 3, *Universities in the Nineteenth and Early Twentieth Centuries, 1800–1945*. Cambridge, 2004.

Ryan, Mark B. *A Collegiate Way of Living: Residential Colleges and a Yale Education*. New Haven, CT, 2001.

Ryan, W. Carson. *Studies in Early Graduate Education: The Johns Hopkins, Clark University, the University of Chicago*. New York, 1939.

Sacks, Benjamin J. "Harvard's 'Constructed Utopia' and the Culture of Deception: The Expansion toward the Charles River, 1902–1932." *New England Quarterly* 84 (2011): 287–93.

Sale, Kirkpatrick. *SDS*. New York, 1973.

Sampson, Robert J. *Great American City: Chicago and the Enduring Neighborhood Effect*. Chicago, 2012.

Sams, Henry W. "The Hutchins College after the War." *Journal of General Education* 30 (1978): 59–64.

Sayvetz, Aaron. "The Rational Revolutionary." *Journal of General Education* 30 (1978): 3–9.

Schäfer, Axel R. *American Progressives and German Social Reform, 1875–1920: Social Ethics, Moral Control, and the Regulatory State in a Transatlantic Context*. Stuttgart, 2000.

Schlegel, John Henry. *American Legal Realism and Empirical Social Science*. Chapel Hill, NC, 1995.

Schlereth, Thomas J. "Big Money and High Culture: The Commercial Club and Charles L. Hutchinson." *Great Lakes Review* 3 (1976): 15–27.

Schlossman, Steven L., Sedlak, Michael W., and Wechsler, Harold S. *The "New Look": The Ford Foundation and the Revolution in Business Education*. Graduate Management Admission Council. Los Angeles, 1987.

Schneider, James C. *Should America Go to War? The Debate over Foreign Policy in Chicago, 1939–1941*. Chapel Hill, NC, 1989.

Schrecker Ellen W. *No Ivory Tower: McCarthyism and the Universities*. New York, 1986.

Shavelson, Richard J. *A Brief History of Student Learning Assessment: How We Got Where We Are and a Proposal for Where to Go Next*. Washington, DC, 2007.

Shils, Edward. "Robert Maynard Hutchins." In Shils, ed., *Remembering the University of Chicago: Teachers, Scientists, and Scholars*. Chicago, 1991.

Silverstein, Michael, ed. *Whitney on Language: Selected Writings of William Dwight Whitney*. Cambridge, MA, 1971.

Singer, Milton. "Robert Redfield, 1897–1958." In Edward Shils, ed., *Remembering the University of Chicago: Teachers, Scientists, and Scholars*. Chicago, 1991.

———. "Robert Redfield's Development of a Social Anthropology of Civilizations." In John V. Murra, ed., *American Anthropology: The Early Years*. St. Paul, 1976.

Smith, Alice Kimball. *A Peril and a Hope: The Scientists' Movement in America, 1945–47*. Chicago, 1965.

Smith, Henry Justin. *Chicago: A Portrait*. New York, 1931.

Smith, Joan K. *Ella Flagg Young: Portrait of a Leader*. Ames, IA, 1979.

Smith, John David. *An Old Creed for the New South: Proslavery Ideology and Historiography, 1865–1918*. Athens, GA, 1985.

Smith, Justin A. *A History of the Baptists in the Western States East of the Mississippi*. Philadelphia, 1896.

Smith, Wilson, and Bender, Thomas, eds. *American Higher Education Transformed, 1940–2005: Documenting the National Discourse*. Baltimore, 2008.

Snyder, Thomas D. *120 Years of American Education: A Statistical Portrait*. Washington, DC, 1993.

Stackhouse, Perry J. *Chicago and the Baptists: A Century of Progress*. Chicago, 1933.

Stavish, Mary B. "Leonard Porter Ayres." In *American National Biography*, vol. 1, pp. 800–801.

Stevenson, Louise L. *Scholarly Means to Evangelical Ends: The New Haven Scholars and the Transformation of Higher Learning in America, 1830–1890*. Baltimore, 1986.

Stigler, Stephen M. "University of Chicago Department of Statistics." In A. Agresti and X. L. Meng, eds., *Strength in Numbers: The Rising of Academic Statistics Departments in the U.S.* New York, 2013.

Storr, Richard J. *The Beginnings of Graduate Education in America*. Chicago, 1953.

———. *Harper's University: The Beginnings*. Chicago, 1966.

Strandmann, Hartmut Pogge von. "The Role of British and German Historians in Mobilizing Public Opinion in 1914." In Benedikt Stuchtey and Peter Wende, eds., *British and German Historiography, 1750–1950: Traditions, Perceptions, and Transfers*. Oxford, 2000.

Strassler, Robert B., ed. *The Landmark Thucydides: A Comprehensive Guide to "The Peloponnesian War."* New York, 1998.

Sutton, Francis X. "The Ford Foundation: The Early Years." *Daedalus* 116 (1987): 41–91.

Szöllösi-Janze, Margit. "Science and Social Space: Transformations in the Institutions of 'Wissenschaft' from the Wilhelmine Empire to the Weimar Republic." *Minerva* 43 (2005): 339–60.

Taylor, Marion A. *The Old Testament in the Old Princeton School (1812–1929)*. San Francisco, 1992.

Tewksbury, Donald G. *The Founding of American Colleges and Universities before the Civil War, with Particular Reference to the Religious Influences Bearing upon the College Movement.* New York, 1932.

Thurstone, Louis L. *The Reliability and Validity of Tests: Derivation and Interpretation of Fundamental Formulae Concerned with Reliability and Validity of Tests and Illustrative Problems.* Ann Arbor, MI, 1931.

Tischauser, Leslie V. *The Burden of Ethnicity: The German Question in Chicago, 1914–1941.* New York, 1990.

Towler, Katherine. "The Men behind the Plan." *Exeter Bulletin,* Fall 2006, 24–33, 103.

Towne, Edgar A. "A 'Singleminded' Theologian: George Burman Foster at Chicago." *Foundations* 20 (1977): 36–59, 163–80.

Troncone, Anthony C. "Hamilton Fish, Sr., and the Politics of American Nationalism, 1912–1945." PhD diss., Rutgers University, 1993.

Turner, Roy Steven. "Humboldt in North America? Reflections on the Research University and Its Historians." In Rainer Christoph Schwinges, ed., *Humboldt International: Der Export des deutschen Universitätsmodells im 19. und 20. Jahrhundert.* Basel, 2001.

Unger, Irwin. *The Movement: A History of the American New Left, 1959–1972.* New York, 1974.

Veblen, Thorstein. *The Higher Learning in America: A Memorandum on the Conduct of Universities by Businessmen.* Reprint, New Brunswick, NJ, 1993.

Veith, Ilza, and McLean, Franklin C. *The University of Chicago Clinics and Clinical Departments, 1927–1952: A Brief Outline of the Origins, the Formative Years, and the Present State of Medicine at the University of Chicago.* Chicago, 1952.

Vermeulen, Cornelius W. *For the Greatest Good to the Largest Number: A History of the Medical Center, the University of Chicago, 1927–1977.* Chicago, 1977.

Veysey, Laurence R. *The Emergence of the American University.* Chicago, 1965.

Wacker, Grant. *Augustus H. Strong and the Dilemma of Historical Consciousness.* Macon, GA, 1985.

Wallace, Elizabeth. *The Unending Journey.* Minneapolis, 1952.

Ward, F. Champion. Review of *The Academic Revolution,* by Christopher Jenks and David Riesman. *Ethics* 80 (1969): 74–75.

Ward, Robert D. "The Origin and Activities of the National Security League, 1914–1919." *Mississippi Valley Historical Review* 47 (1960–61): 51–65.

Weart, Spencer R., and Szilard, Gertrud Weiss, eds. *Leo Szilard: His Version of the Facts: Selected Recollections and Correspondence.* Cambridge, MA, 1978.

Weaver, Warren. "Max Mason, October 26, 1877–March 22, 1961." In *National Academy of Sciences Biographical Memoirs.* Washington, DC, 1964.

Webber, Henry S. "The University of Chicago and Its Neighbors: A Case Study in Community Development." In David C. Perry and Wim Wiewel, eds., *The University as Urban Developer: Case Studies and Analysis.* Armonk, NY, 2005.

Webber, Henry S., and Karlstroem, Mikael. *Why Community Investment Is Good for Nonprofit Anchor Institutions: Understanding Costs, Benefits and the Range of Strategic Options.* Chicago, 2009.

Wechsler, Harold S. *The Qualified Student: A History of Selective College Admission in America.* New York, 1977.

Weintraub, Karl J. "In Behalf of the Humanities." In *The University of Chicago: Freedom to Be Excellent; Three Views.* Chicago, 1974.

Wheatley, Steven C. "The Partnerships of Foundations and Research Universities." In Helmut K. Anheier and David C. Hammack, eds., *American Foundations: Roles and Contributions.* Washington, DC, 2010.

White, Woodie T. "The Study of Education at the University of Chicago 1892–1958." PhD diss., University of Chicago, 1977.

Wilde, Arthur H., ed. *Northwestern University: A History, 1855–1905.* New York, 1905.

Wind, James P. *The Bible and the University: The Messianic Vision of William Rainey Harper.* Atlanta, 1987.

Winling, LaDale. "Students and the Second Ghetto: Federal Legislation, Urban Politics, and Campus Planning at the University of Chicago." *Journal of Planning History* 10 (1) (2011): 59–86.

Worcester, Kenton W. *Social Science Research Council, 1923–1998.* New York, 2001.

Wright, Quincy. "International Affairs: International Law and Totalitarian States." *American Political Science Review* 35 (1941): 738–43.

Wrigley, Julia. *Class Politics and Public Schools: Chicago, 1900–1950.* New Brunswick, NJ, 1982.

Yeomans, Henry A. *Abbott Lawrence Lowell, 1856–1943.* Cambridge, MA, 1948.

Young, Warren Cameron. *Commit What You Have Heard: A History of the Northern Baptist Theological Seminary, 1913–1988.* Wheaton, IL, 1988.

Zemsky, Robert. *Checklist for Change: Making American Higher Education a Sustainable Enterprise.* New Brunswick, NJ, 2013.

———. *Making Reform Work: The Case for Transforming American Higher Education.* New Brunswick, NJ, 2009.

Zimring, Franklin F. "The American Jury Project and the Chicago Law School." Fulton Lectures 2003.

Zmarzlik, Hans-Günter. "Hermann Eduard von Holst." In Johannes Vincke, ed., *Freiburger Professoren des 19. und 20. Jahrhunderts.* Freiburg am Breisgau, 1957.

Index

Conservation Community Council, 349

Consortium on Chicago School Research, 453–54, 456

Constitutional and Political History of the United States (Holst), 140

constitution for world government, 307–10

consulting, by faculty, 226

consumption, conspicuous, 23

Contemporary Civilization course (Columbia), Boucher and, 199

continuities between first and second U of C, 58–65

Conzen, Kathleen, 415

Core curriculum, 6, 199, 258, 321, 400–404, 416, 429, 439; and Hutchins College, 240, 253–54, 414; reduction of, 411–14; and student life, 404–5; and study abroad, 426; and world civilization courses, 466–67. *See also* general education curriculum

Cornell, Paul, 8, 30

corporate agent, university as, 460–61

correspondence courses, Harper and, 70, 74, 77–78, 317

corruption, police, 347

Corson, John J., 356

Coser, Lewis, 259

Cosmopolitan Club, 158

Coss, John J., 199

costs, of U of C education, 205, 226. *See also* financial aid, for graduate students; jobs, student part- and full-time

Coulter, John Merle, 131–32, 144, 179–80, 235

Coulter, Merle C., 235, 256

Council of the Senate, 286, 392, 414; and class rankings, 459; and commercial development, 453; and Committee for a Year of Reflection, 411, 414; and Gray, 395, 398, 453; and Greenstone report, 401; and Kalven

report, 459, 462; and scholastic residence, 431; and sit-ins, 372, 374

Council on Advanced Studies in the Humanities and Social Sciences, 431

Council on Teaching, 412

Council on the Graduate School of Business, 445

Counseling Committee, Bell and, 279–80

Counter-Olympics, 263–64

Counts, George, 204, 207

Court Theater, 395

Cowles, H. C., 194

Cox, Garfield V., 442

Craigie, Sir William, 193

Crane, Richard T., 24, 102

Crane, Ronald, 243–44, 252; "History versus Criticism in the University Study of Literature," 244

creation, image of instantaneous, 7

credits: abolished, 232; Hutchins and, 284; under New Plan, 233

Crerar Library, 395

crime, 344, 346–47, 351, 451, 453. *See also* safety, neighborhood

Crime Lab, 457

C Shop, 405

CTA, and U of C advertising, 176

culture, academic, 6, 469; as civic goal, 24; and education, Burton on, 168. *See also* faculty and faculty culture

culture, campus, 6, 16, 100–101, 171–72, 210–14, 251; and professional schools, 437–38. *See also* student life

culture, early Hyde Park, 122

culture, German academic, 135–37, 143

Culver, Helen, 58

Culver, Nathaniel, 24

Cummings Life Science Center, 365

curriculum: Boucher and, 229; and culture, 6; first U of C, 12–18; and Harper, 96; under Hutchins, 203, 251, 253; and Laing report, 189; E. Levi and, 368; Levine and,

Hull House, 107, 125
humanism, vs. science, 243
humanities general survey course, 236;
and World War I, 237
Human Nature in Politics (Wallas), 238
Humboldtian ideal, and university,
133, 142
Hutch Commons, 405
Hutchins, Maude Phelps McVeigh,
311–13
Hutchins, Robert Maynard, 6, 149,
215–320, 385, 458; and academic
freedom, 262–81; and Adler, 241,
250, 458; and Angell, 215–16,
218–20; and atomic bomb, 305–6;
background of, 215–17; and Bronner
story, 416; and budget, 287–300; as
chancellor, 310–20; characterized,
217, 219–21, 312; and constitution
for world government, 307–10;
and deficits, 316–17; and Early
Admission Program, 326–27; and
end of Hutchins College, 329; and
facts vs. ideas, 245–48; and faculty,
221, 295–96; and football, 214; and
graduate programs, 98, 281–87,
431; and Great Books, 241, 243–44,
247, 250, 313, 358; legacy of, 313–21,
369–70, 468–72; and E. Levi, 358,
367–71, 440; marriage of, 311–14;
and New Plan, 231–52; political
views of, 267; "The Proposition Is
Peace," 306–7; and racial covenants,
344–45; and reorganization of the
university, 221–31; reputation of,
274, 319; resignation, 312, 323–24;
and Rockefellers, 184, 296, 299;
and senior faculty, 285, 313, 318, 321;
"University and the City, The," 345;
vision of, 220, 243; "What Good
Are Endowments?," 295; "What Is a
University?," 273; and World War II,
300–310
Hutchins, William J., 215, 218

Hutchins College, 252–61; and alumni,
341; budget of, 313; and conflict
with divisions, 257–61; end of, 328,
354; Kimpton and, 327–28; later
faculty connections to, 412, 417; and
New Plan, 253–54; and student life,
334–35. *See also* Hutchins, Robert
Maynard; hyperintellectualism
Hutchins-Colwell governance, 356
Hutchinson, Benjamin, 106
Hutchinson, Charles L., 4, 24, 51–52,
100–114, 118
Hutchinson, Dennis, 440
Hutchinson, William T., 312
Hutchison, William, 72
Huth, Carl F., 95
Hyde Park; and Cornell, 8, 30; and
faculty residences, 360, 453; Harper
and, 121–22; housing boom, 417;
Hutchins and, 321; and Loop, 352;
religious character of, 121–22; site
for new U of C, 60–61; university
investments in, 343–54. *See also*
Kenwood neighborhood; safety,
neighborhood; South Side; urban
renewal; Woodlawn neighborhood
Hyde Park Baptist Church, 121–22
Hyde Park Coop, 457
Hyde Park Herald, and sectarianism,
33–34
Hyde Park Shopping Center, 453, 457
hyperintellectualism, 326, 328, 331–34,
341, 415

Ickes, Harold, and Hutchins, 296
Ida Noyes Hall, 395
identity, class, 90–91, 180. *See also*
alumni
identity, university: and Bronner story,
417; and first U of C, 34–35; fraternities and, 335–36; and religion, 62,
49–51, 114–15. *See also* faculty and
faculty culture; research; student life
Ilin, 269

university; government support for
graduate programs; social sciences;
teaching and research
Reserve Officers Training Corps
(ROTC), 157, 160, 303
residence halls, 205, 404, 406; and
Baker Commission, 431; Boucher
and, 200; Burton and, 169–71, 208–
9; and enrollment, 380–83, 401; and
Ford Plan, 363, 365; Kimpton and,
336; Klauder design, 209; under
E. Levi, 389; and on-campus requirements, 380; recent construction, 422,
424–25; and residential construction, 457; and World War II, 302,
335. *See also* alumni; south campus
complex, Burton and; student life
resistance to World War I, student, 156,
158–59
Responsibility of Greatness, 7, 340
restricted gifts, Kimpton on, 342
retention, faculty, 166, 178, 223, 338,
353, 359–61, 405
retention, student. *See* dropout rates
"Rethinking Management Education:
A View from Chicago," 449
retirement age: and salary costs, 396;
mandatory, 398. *See also* pension
fund, faculty
reunions, and class identity, 180
Reva and David Logan Center for the
Arts, 457
Reynolds Club, 302
Rheinstein, Max, 304, 441
rhetoric of the West, 28
Riehl, Alois, 136
Riesman, David, 231, 259–60, 388, 435
rights, student, in university governance, 372–73, 376
rigor, academic, 6, 100, 142, 390, 459,
469; and admissions goals, 200; and
Bronner story, 415; and elitism, 370;
at first U of C, 14; and Ford Plan,
363; and foreign study, 192; and Law

School, 441; and New Plan, 239; and
preparation of undergraduates, 196;
and quarter system, 413; and western academic standards, 83
riots, at Democratic National Convention, 373
risk-taking, Harper and, 147
Robertson, David, 154, 174
Rockefeller, David, 355
Rockefeller, John D., 54–55, 64,
126, 149–50, 174, 206, 292; and
Administration Building, 315; and
G. Anderson, 31; and Andrews, 127,
129; and Baptist philanthropy, 36,
118; Burton and, 167; character of as
philanthropist, 37–38; and China,
165; and deficits, 79–80, 108–13,
149, 288, 314, 342; 1888 proposal to,
46; Final Gift (1910), 113, 223, 299–
300; as founder, 7, 48–49, 63, 109–
11, 113, 300; and Gates, 42–56, 119;
and Goodspeed, 38–41; and Harper,
39, 46–49, 52–57, 123, 145–47; and
Harper Memorial Library, 166;
and Hutchins, 296; and Hyde Park
location, 60–61; and Law School,
438–39; and Morgan Park Seminary,
26–27; and Ryerson, 105, 108–13;
total gifts of, 185; and trustees, 109–
14 passim. *See also* endowment
Rockefeller, John D., Jr.: and Baptist
influence on U of C, 119; and fiftieth
anniversary of U of C, 299; and
Kimpton, 342; and Rockefeller
Memorial Chapel, 179; as trustee,
110, 150; and trustees, 110–14
Rockefeller boards, 176, 183–84, 206,
300; Burton and, 167, 174; and
Frank, 187–88; and Hutchins, 289–
90; and overall U of C funding, 291;
total gifts of, 185. *See also* General
Education Board (GEB) grants;
Laura Spelman Rockefeller Memorial; Rockefeller Foundation

suffrage, woman, 151
Summae (Thomas), 242
summer programs, 93, 287, 445, 452
Sumner, W. G., 238
Sunday school, Harper and, 121–22
Sunny, Bernard, 183–84, 262
Supreme Court Review, 441
survey courses. *See* Core curriculum;
  general education curriculum
Sussman, Arthur M., 394
Suzzallo, Henry, 218
Swan, Thomas W., 216
Swett, Leonard, 32
Swift, George, 126
Swift, Harold H.: and academic freedom, 262–64, 266, 270, 272, 274–76,
  279; and Ayres report, 227–28, 232;
  background of, 167; and Burton,
  164, 167, 169, 172–76, 180–81, 194;
  and fund-raising, 173–77, 180–83,
  228, 231, 289, 290–91, 315, 341, 385;
  goals for U of C presidency, 217; and
  Hutchins, 217–19, 227, 231–32, 240,
  262–64, 266, 270, 272, 274–76, 279,
  291, 312–14; and M. Hutchins, 311;
  Judson, 150, 162–63, 167–68, 174;
  and Kimpton, 324, 341; and Mason,
  182–83, 209, 290; and Northwestern
  merger, 288–89; and post–World
  War II finances, 314–15; professorship named for, 360; and research,
  150; and Rosenwald, 209–10; and
  south campus complex, 173, 209–10;
  and Woodward, 173, 209–10, 217,
  262. *See also* trustees
Swift family, and Divinity School, 119
Sykes, Charles, 458
systematic study of U of C, 224–25
Systematic Theology (Strong), 38
Szilard, Leo, 306
Szöllösi-Janze, Margit, 192

Taft, William Howard, 151
Talbot, Marion, 87

Taliaferro, William, 291
Tannhäuser, 143
Taub, Richard P., 404, 411, 424
Tave, Stuart, 470–71
Tawney, R. H., 238
Tax, Sol, 346–47
teachers: demand for, 95; and extension programs, 77; and Harper, 85,
  125–31; and MA degree, 92, 94, 186,
  189; training for, 128–29, 225. *See
  also* College; teaching
teaching: and Catholic influences,
  130–31; collaborative, 180, 188, 229,
  286, 450, 468; as discovery, 64; by
  graduate students, 92, 196, 198, 397,
  401, 433–34, 470; preparation for,
  281–83, 432–33; quality of, 35–36,
  99, 195–96, 198, 448; undergraduate, 84–85, 88, 197–98, 367, 412, 429
teaching and research, 7, 49, 91, 95, 131,
  133, 189, 196, 255, 331, 469; Harper
  and, 98–99; Jencks on, 5–6; Medical Center and, 179–80; in New
  Plan, 236–40, 252; Ryerson and, 105
teaching assistantships, 433–34
teaching loads, 14, 17, 95, 189, 191, 287,
  403, 410
teaching methods, 96, 186, 260. *See
  also* lecture/discussion format;
  seminars
telegraph, 8
tenure, and Hutchins College teaching,
  260
Terry, Benjamin S., 101, 141
testing, 200; expansion of, 257–58;
  intelligence, 207; under New Plan,
  233; psychological, 213, 216. *See also*
  comprehensive exams
Tet Offensive, 373
theater, student, 157, 170, 211, 334, 363,
  395, 405
"Theory of Education, A" (Wilkins),
  194–95
Thomas, Milton H., 320